MODERN
Real Estate Practice IN
PENNSYLVANIA

Tenth Edition

Thomas J. Bellairs

James L. Helsel, Jr.

James L. Goldsmith, Esq.

Jim Skindzier, DREI,
Consulting Editor

Dearborn™
Real Estate Education

This publication is designed to provide accurate and authoritative information in regard to the subject matter covered. It is sold with the understanding that the publisher is not engaged in rendering legal, accounting, or other professional service. If legal advice or other expert assistance is required, the services of a competent professional person should be sought.

President: Roy Lipner
Vice President of Product Development and Publishing: Evan M. Butterfield
Managing Editor: Kate DeVivo
Development Editor: Megan Bacalao Virkler
Director of Production: Daniel Frey
Senior Managing Editor: Jack Kiburz
Creative Director: Lucy Jenkins
Typesetter: Ellen Gurak

Published by Dearborn™ Real Estate Education
30 South Wacker Drive, Ste. 2500
Chicago, IL 60606-7481
(312) 836-4400
www.dearbornRE.com

Printed in the United States of America

06   07   08   10   9   8   7   6   5   4   3   2

Library of Congress Cataloging-in-Publication Data

Bellairs, Thomas J.
    Modern real estate practice in Pennsylvania / Thomas J. Bellairs, James L.
  Helsel, Jr., James L. Goldsmith, Esq. ; Jim Skindzier, DREI, consulting editor—10th ed.
    p. cm.
    Includes index.
    ISBN-13: 978-0-7931-9626-5
    ISBN-10: 0-7931-9626-4
    1. Real property—Pennsylvania.   2. Vendors and purchasers—Pennsylvania.
  3. Real estate business—Law and legislation—Pennsylvania.   I. Helsel, James L.
  II. Goldsmith, James L.   III. Skindzier, Jim.   IV. Title.
  KFP112.B4   2006
  346.74804'37—dc22   2005032717

CONTENTS

ABOUT THE AUTHORS

Thomas J. Bellairs, GRI, GAA, RAA, of Reading, Pennsylvania, is a graduate of Albright College where he majored in Business Economics. He has taught real estate courses at Penn State and Albright College. Mr. Bellairs has been active in the real estate industry since 1976, and has owned Bellairs Real Estate since 1988. He is past president of the Reading-Berks Association of REALTORS®, 1984, and was awarded the Outstanding Realtor of the Year by the Reading-Berks Association of REALTORS® in 2001.

James L. Helsel Jr., CCIM, SIOR, CPM, CRB, GRI, of Camp Hill, Pennsylvania, is a graduate of Lycoming College majoring in Business Administration. He is president of Helsel, Incorporated REALTORS®, specialists in commercial and industrial brokerage, property management, and appraising. He is past president of the Greater Harrisburg (1983) and Pennsylvania (1994) Associations of REALTORS®, and was the National Association of REALTORS® Region 2 vice president presiding over Pennsylvania, New York, and New Jersey in 2001. Jim was awarded the CPM of the Year award by the Delaware Valley Chapter of the Institute of Real Estate Management in 1987, and was awarded the REALTOR® of the Year award by the Pennsylvania Association in 2001. He has served on the National Association of REALTORS® board of directors since 1989. He is currently chairman of the National Association's Real Property Operations Committee overseeing NAR's headquarters building in Chicago as well as their leased space in Washington, D.C. In addition to seminars for his local, state, and national associations, Jim has taught real estate courses for Pennsylvania State University and has been a faculty member of the Pennsylvania REALTORS® Institute since 1980.

James L. Goldsmith, Esquire, is an attorney engaged in the private practice of law in Harrisburg. He is a corporate member of the firm of Caldwell & Kearns which serves as counsel to the Pennsylvania REALTORS®. In cooperation with the Pennsylvania Association of REALTORS®, he has coauthored the *Pennsylvania Real Estate Reporter,* which represents the first and only indexed compilation of Pennsylvania cases devoted to real estate and related issues. He teaches Real Estate Transactions at the Widener University School of Law, Harrisburg campus, and is an instructor for the Graduate REALTORS® Institute. Mr. Goldsmith and his firm are also engaged by insurers to defend insured real estate practitioners and lawyers in lawsuits in which professional negligence is claimed. He has litigated numerous cases at trial and appellate levels of the state and federal court system. He is a graduate of Washington and Jefferson College. He attended Dickinson School of Law and the Temple University School of Law, where he earned his Juris Doctor.

Jim Skindzier, DREI, is president of Career Growth Real Estate Academy, a state-licensed proprietary school. Mr. Skindzier is a graduate of Duquesne University where he earned both a bachelor's and a master's degree in education. He has also completed coursework toward a doctoral degree in adult education at Penn State University. For the past 30 years, Jim has combined his background in education with real estate to become a highly respected, nationally recognized real estate educator. He is active in the Real Estate Educators Association (REEA), having served on the board of directors, and earned the distinction as 2005–2006 president of REEA. Jim was also a founding member and past president of the Pennsylvania Association of Real Estate Educators. As a member of the Volunteer Education Advisory Committee for the past 15 years, Jim has worked with the State Real Estate Commission to develop and implement education programs for licenses throughout the state. He has authored two textbooks and numerous articles, and has conducted many seminars and workshops for real estate professionals.

■ ACKNOWLEDGMENTS

Special recognition is given to **Laurel D. McAdams**, GRI, who served as advisor to the consulting editor. Ms. McAdams has been associated with *Modern Real Estate Practice in Pennsylvania* since its 5th edition. Having served in various roles with each revision, including development writer and consulting editor, she brought invaluable technical expertise and creative insight to this latest edition.

Thanks also go to the members of the **Modern Real Estate Practice in Pennsylvania Editorial Review Board** for their gracious participation in the development of this textbook, and their valuable contributions of time, criticisms, and suggestions:

> John W. Fisher, Schlicher-Kratz Institute and Temple University, Pennsylvania
> Krista A. Csapo, MBA, Director of Educational Expansion, Weichert Realtors
> Mimi Lambert, Director, Institute of Real Estate Studies
> Francis McCarthy, Director, Tri-State Real Estate School

Additional thanks go to reviewers of the previous editions: Robert W. Corl, GRI, CSP; Lawrence J. Dellegrotto, GRI; Norman L. Fehr, Jr.; Harry H. Higgins III; Forrest E. Huffman, PhD; Barry Hoy; Harvey M. Levin; Thomas E. LoDolce, Director, LoDolce Academy of Real Estate; Ruth A. Myers, Allied School of Real Estate, Etters, MAI; Robert M. Rowlands, Esq.; Raymond E. Rysak; CRS, CRB, DREI; Barbara G. Samet, DREI, Owner/Director, Pocono Real Estate Academy; and Ben Simon.

Finally, the authors extend their appreciation to Evan Butterfield, Louise Benzer, Megan Bacalao Virkler, and Dan Frey of Dearborn™ Real Estate Education for their assistance in the production of this 10th edition.

PREFACE

Whether your goal is to gather information for yourself or to become a real estate professional, *Modern Real Estate Practice in Pennsylvania* guides you through each aspect of real estate ownership and each step of a modern real estate transaction. *Modern Real Estate Practice in Pennsylvania* has provided thousands of people with valuable real estate information since its first printing in 1975, and has set the standard for contemporary information in an easy-to-read format, tailored specifically to practices in Pennsylvania.

With this 10th edition, we strive to set a new standard for providing contemporary real estate information in Pennsylvania. The real estate industry is changing more rapidly now than at any time in recent history. This challenges us to provide timely and authoritative information. Although the basic principles of ownership remain the same, little else is static. We meet our challenge by revising this edition to reflect the latest developments in the way real estate professionals provide their services to today's sophisticated consumers. Not the least of the changes we've seen in recent years is the dramatic way technology has altered virtually everything real estate practitioners and consumers do. New laws and regulations are also emerging, due in large part to developments in the real estate industry, heightened consumer concerns, and technological evolutions in transactions.

■ SPECIAL FEATURES

- *Modern Real Estate Practice in Pennsylvania* links you with *Internet Resources*, a list of Web addresses of relevant government and professional Internet sites, essentially bringing a whole world of information to you.
- Each chapter opens with *Learning Objectives* that tell you what concepts and information you should be able to identify, describe, explain, or distinguish after you've finished reading the chapter.
- *Margin notes* direct your attention to important vocabulary, concepts, and memory tips. The margin notes help you move easily through the text and locate issues for review. They also serve as prompts for more efficient and effective study.
- *Pennsylvania icons* identify procedures in Pennsylvania that are especially noteworthy. These may be cases in which Pennsylvania law prescribes very specific procedures or cases in which Pennsylvania law differs from laws enacted elsewhere.
- *Chapter review questions* and additional *review questions in the appendices* provide a study tool not just for exam preparation but also to give readers another learning exercise to enhance understanding of chapter material.
- A user-friendly and easy-to-understand *math review* is located in the back of the book. Even the most math-phobic students can benefit from the review's complete coverage of all the important math concepts that are vital to their professional success.
- The *readable page design* and *conversational tone* provide an easy-to-follow presentation, proving that "textbooks" can be friendly and easy to understand, while still being technically and legally accurate.

■ The *Real Estate Licensing and Registration Act* and accompanying *Rules and Regulations* are included in Appendix C to provide one of the most important references Pennsylvania licensees need to guide them in their daily practice. Provisions in the act and regulations also affect discussions in nearly every chapter of this text.

Modern Real Estate Practice in Pennsylvania, 10th Edition, is divided into two sections. The first section, *Real Estate Fundamentals*, is devoted to the legal concepts of ownership and the laws that govern real estate; the second section, *Real Estate Practice*, discusses real estate brokerage and related activities following the sequence of a real estate transaction. As with other recent editions, the chapter presentation conforms to the curriculum prescribed by the Pennsylvania State Real Estate Commission for Real Estate Fundamentals and Real Estate Practice, the two courses required for licensure as a real estate salesperson in Pennsylvania.

This text is only a tool. It is intended to introduce the reader to a variety of real estate concepts, theories, and specialties in practice. The instructor is encouraged to supplement the text material with classroom discussions and practical examples, and exhibits of forms and other documents commonly used in their marketplace. The reader is encouraged to pursue further study through additional publications and conversations with industry practitioners. Education is a continuous process in which the reader and instructor are active participants.

Dearborn™ Real Estate Education has developed a variety of study materials to aid in the learning process, including the *Study Guide for Modern Real Estate Practice* that contains additional review questions and study problems. To assist instructors, a new comprehensive Instructor's Manual, which follows the 10th edition of *Modern Real Estate Practice in Pennsylvania*, is available. Contact Dearborn™ Real Estate Education for further details about any of these materials.

We like to hear from our readers. You, along with the instructors and real estate professionals who have helped develop this edition, are partners in the real estate education process. Comments about this text or any services the publisher provides are always appreciated, and should be directed to Editorial Assistant, Dearborn™ Real Estate Education, 30 South Wacker Drive, Chicago, IL 60606-1719 or at our Web address, *www.dearbornRE.com*.

1

REAL ESTATE FUNDAMENTALS

The ownership of real estate involves numerous legal concepts. It includes rights that provide for the use, enjoyment, possession, control, and transfer of the real estate. There is a complex body of law that affects every aspect of the ownership, including the government's control of its use, the way people claim and protect their rights and interests in the ownership, and the way ownership is transferred. Laws also affect various aspects of a real estate transaction and the practices of real estate licensees.

Real Estate Fundamentals introduces the language, principles, legal concepts, and laws that govern real estate ownership and its transfer. The concepts covered in this section and the chapters in which they are discussed are

1

REAL PROPERTY AND THE LAW

■ LEARNING OBJECTIVES

When you've finished reading this chapter, you should be able to

■ distinguish among the concepts of land, real estate, and real property;
■ differentiate between real and personal property;
■ explain the test used to identify and classify fixtures and trade fixtures;
■ identify the physical, economic, and social characteristics of land;
■ summarize areas and types of law that affect real estate; and
■ define the key terms.

■ KEY TERMS

air rights	fixture	real property
appurtenance	improvement	severance
bundle of legal rights	land	subsurface rights
chattel	personal property	surface rights
emblement	real estate	trade fixture

■ LAND, REAL ESTATE, AND REAL PROPERTY

We begin the discussion of real property with an explanation of the terms that are commonly used. *Land, real estate,* and *real property* are often used interchangeably, but there are subtle yet important differences in their meanings. By looking at these differences we can also understand exactly what a person owns, what is being sold or transferred to another, and what a new owner is acquiring.

Land

Land is defined as *the earth's surface extending downward to the center of the earth and upward into space, including permanent natural objects such as trees and water.* (See Figure 1.1.)

Land, Real Estate and Real Property

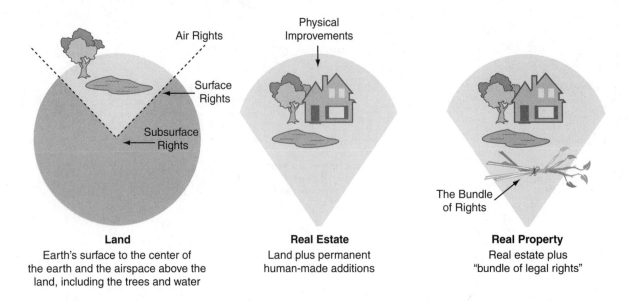

Land
Earth's surface to the center of
the earth and the airspace above the
land, including the trees and water

Real Estate
Land plus permanent
human-made additions

Real Property
Real estate plus
"bundle of legal rights"

The term *land* thus refers to not only the surface of the earth but also includes the underlying soil and things that are naturally attached to the land, such as boulders and plants. Land also includes the minerals and substances below the earth's surface, together with the air above the land into space. These are known respectively as the subsurface and airspace.

Real Estate

Real estate is defined as *land at, above, and below the earth's surface, and all things permanently attached to it, whether natural or artificial.* (See Figure 1.1.)

The term *real estate* is somewhat broader than the term *land;* it includes not only the natural components of the land but also permanent manmade improvements. An **improvement** is any artificial thing attached to land, such as a building or fence, or improvements such as streets, utilities, sewers, and other additions that make it suitable for building.

Real Property

Real property is defined as *the physical land or real estate plus the interests, benefits, and rights that are associated with its ownership.* (See Figure 1.1.)

The general term *property* refers to anything that can be owned. This includes a wide range of things such as stocks, bonds, trademarks, or patents. The common characteristic is that ownership of property provides certain rights, interests, or benefits to the owner.

Real property is *the legal rights of ownership* (the "bundle of rights") *that attach to the physical surface of the land, that which lies above and below it and that which is permanently attached to it.* The term *real property* is broader or more inclusive than either *land* or *real estate* because rights, interests, or benefits are automatically included in the ownership. Real property is often coupled with the term **appurtenance.** Appurtenances are defined as *the rights, privileges,* and *improvements that belong to the land.* This means that appurtances are connected to the real estate and are conveyed when ownership transfers.

IN PRACTICE

When people talk about buying or selling homes, office buildings, land, and the like, they usually call these things *real estate.* For all practical purposes, the term is synonymous with real property as defined here. In everyday usage, real estate includes the legal rights of ownership specified in the definition of real property. Sometimes people use the term *realty* instead.

Subsurface rights.   **Subsurface rights** are *the rights to the natural resources lying below the earth's surface.* The **surface rights** are *the rights to use the surface of the earth.* Although it may be difficult to imagine, the two rights are distinct. An owner may transfer his or her surface rights without transferring the subsurface rights and vice versa.

Because many parts of Pennsylvania are rich in natural resources, multiple owners are likely to have interests in the same parcel of real estate. For example, a landowner may sell the rights to any oil and gas found in the land to an oil company. Later the same landowner may sell the remaining real estate to a purchaser but reserve the rights to all coal that might be found in the land. After these sales, three parties have ownership interests in the same parcel of real estate: (1) the oil company owns all oil and gas rights, (2) the seller owns all coal rights, and (3) the purchaser owns the rights to the remainder of the real estate.

Each of the owners is entitled to use and enjoy their rights without interference from other owners. In the example, the homeowner must be able to fully enjoy his or her rights, but cannot inhibit the owner of the coal from enjoying the mineral rights. Similarly, the coal owner is entitled to extract or mine the coal, but cannot unduly infringe on the rights of the homeowner. To fully understand the surface owner's rights, for example, one must be aware of other owners who may have interests in the real estate.

In Your State   **PA**   A fact of life in coal-rich areas is that mining alters the land. Mining can damage the surface or compromise the underlying support of the surface and result in mine subsidence. Because of the possibility of mine subsidence, Pennsylvania law requires the seller to provide notice to a purchaser about whether a structure on the land is entitled to support from the underlying coal. This is known as the *coal notice.* If the seller cannot certify that the structure is supported, then the seller must inform the purchaser that there is no protection to the structure against subsidence damage from mining operations. Special insurance is available to cover damage due to mine subsidence. This coverage is not included in a typical homeowner's insurance policy. ■

Air rights.   **Air rights** are *the rights to use the open space or vertical plane air above the land.* Ownership of the land includes the right to all air above the property unless the rights have been preempted by law or already sold or leased independently of the land. These rights can be an important part of real estate, particularly in cases where air rights must be purchased to construct large office buildings such as the MetLife Building in New York City and the Merchandise Mart in Chicago. To construct such a building, the developer must purchase not only the air rights but also numerous small portions of the land's surface for the building's foundation supports. These are called *caissons*.

Before air travel was common, a property's air rights were considered to be unlimited, extending upward into the farthest reaches of outer space. Today, however, the courts permit reasonable interference with these rights, such as is necessary for aircraft, as long as the owner's right to use and occupy the land is not unduly lessened. Governments and airport authorities often purchase adjacent air rights to provide approach patterns for air traffic. Pennsylvania law permits local government authorities to obtain aviation easements (air rights) over land surrounding airports to prevent interference with takeoffs and landings.

With the continuing development of solar power, air rights (more specifically, light or solar rights) are being closely examined by the courts. A new tall building that blocks sunlight to a smaller existing building may be held to be interfering with the smaller building's right to sunlight, particularly if systems in the smaller building are solar powered.

■ REAL ESTATE VERSUS PERSONAL PROPERTY

Personal property, sometimes called *personalty*, is considered to be *all property that does not fit the definition of real property*. An important distinction between the two is that personal property is *movable*. Items of personal property, also referred to as **chattels,** include such tangibles as chairs, tables, clothing, and money. (See Figure 1.2.)

In Your State   **PA**   The distinction between real and personal property is important to all real estate transactions, but the distinction is not always obvious. A mobile home, for example, is generally considered to be personal property. In Pennsylvania, new mobile homes are defined as motor vehicles and, as such, are sold by licensed motor vehicle salespersons. Subsequent to the initial purchase, a mobile home may be considered real estate. This will be the case if the

1. mobile home is transferred in conjunction with and as a part of an assignment of a land lease or the transfer of an interest in land on which the mobile home is situated; or
2. mobile home is permanently attached to a foundation, and
3. registration of the mobile home is canceled by the owner with the Pennsylvania Bureau of Motor Vehicles.

If these conditions are met, the mobile home is real estate and may be sold by a real estate licensee. ■

Trees and crops are generally considered in two classes. Trees, perennial bushes, and grasses that do not require annual cultivation are considered real estate.

Real versus Personal Property

Real Estate or Real Property

Land and anything permanently attached to it

Personal Property

Movable items not attached to real estate; items severed from real estate

Fixture

Item of personal property converted to real estate by attaching it to the real estate with the intention that it become permanently a part thereof; may not be removed by tenant

Trade Fixture

Item of personal property attached to real estate that is owned by a tenant and is used in a business; legally removable by tenant

Annual plantings or crops of wheat, corn, vegetables, and fruit, known as **emblements,** are generally considered personal property. As long as an annual crop is growing, it will be transferred as part of the real property (unless other provisions are made in the sales contract). Because a person is entitled to the benefits of his or her labor, the former owner or tenant must be permitted to reenter the land to harvest the crop when it is ready. Perennial crops (like orchards or vineyards) are not personal property and so they convey with the land.

It is possible to change an item of real estate to personal property by **severance.** For example, a growing tree is real estate until the owner cuts it down, literally severing it from the real estate. Similarly, an apple becomes personal property once it is picked from a tree.

It is also possible to change personal property into real property. If a landowner buys cement, stones, and sand, mixes them into concrete, and constructs a sidewalk, the component parts of the concrete, which were originally personal property, are converted into real property as they become a permanent improvement on the land. This process is called *annexation*.

Fixtures

An article that was once personal property but has been affixed to the land or a building in such a way that the law construes it to be a part of the real estate is a **fixture.** Examples are heating plants, elevator equipment in high-rise buildings, radiators, kitchen cabinets, light fixtures, and plumbing fixtures. Almost any item that has been added as a *permanent part* of a building is considered a fixture. The critical factor in determining whether an item is a fixture or personal property is how it stands the tests of law.

Legal tests of a fixture.   Courts apply four basic tests to decide whether an item is a fixture (real property) or personal property:

1. *Intention.* Did the person who installed the item intend for it to remain permanently or for it to be removable?
2. *Method of annexation.* How permanent is the method of attachment? Can the item be removed without causing damage to the surrounding property?
3. *Adaptation to real estate.* What is the character of the item, and is it being used as real property or personal property?
4. *Agreement.* Have the parties agreed to treat an item as though it is real or personal property?

> **Legal Tests of a Fixture**
> 1. Intent
> 2. Method of annexation
> 3. Adaptation to real estate
> 4. Agreement

These tests seem simple and provide fairly straightforward guidance. There are occasions, however, when circumstances are complex and applying the tests can be challenging. When the courts must resolve these issues, sometimes their decisions seem contradictory: Articles that appear to be permanently affixed are judged to be personal property, while items that do not appear to be permanently attached have been ruled as fixtures.

Rather than relying on people's assumptions or court interpretations about what is real estate versus personal property in a real estate transaction, several practical steps can be taken. First, when a property is listed, the owner and the listing salesperson should discuss which items are to be included in the sale. Then, when an agreement of sale is written, the buyer and seller should specify the articles that are to be included in the transaction. This step is especially important if there is any doubt as to whether the items are personal property or fixtures. Articles that might be included in an agreement of sale are television antennas, satellite dishes, built-in appliances, built-in bookcases, wall-to-wall carpeting, wood stoves, chandeliers, ceiling fans, and hot tubs. Landscaping is expected to remain as is.

IN PRACTICE

Real estate licensees need to understand the legal distinction between real estate and personal property so they can properly guide sellers and buyers. A seller, for example, may expect to take the cabinet that he built into the corner of the dining room, but the buyer may expect that the cabinet is included with the house. By taking the steps that are suggested in this chapter, licensees can help avoid misunderstandings between the parties that could result in the collapse of the transaction and expensive lawsuits.

Trade fixtures.   *An article that is attached to a rented space or building for use in conducting a business, but is the personal property of the tenant,* is a **trade fixture.** They are also called *chattel fixtures.* Examples of trade fixtures are bowling alleys, store shelves, bars, and restaurant equipment. Agricultural fixtures such as chicken coops and tool sheds are also included in this definition.

Trade fixtures differ from fixtures generally in these ways:

- Fixtures belong to the owner of the real estate, but trade fixtures are usually owned and installed by a tenant for the tenant's use.
- Fixtures are considered a permanent part of a building, but trade fixtures are removable. Trade fixtures may be affixed to a building so as to appear

FIGURE   1.3

The Bundle of Legal Rights

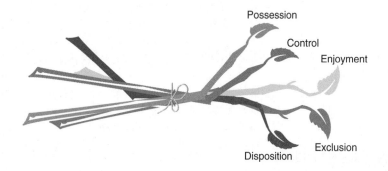

to be fixtures, but the tenant has the right to remove them on or before the last day of the lease. (Otherwise, they become the real property of the landlord by accession.) The rented space must be restored to its original condition, except for reasonable wear and tear.

Legally, fixtures are real property so they are included in any sale or mortgage. Trade fixtures, however, are considered personal property and are not included in the sale or mortgage of real estate except by special agreement.

■ OWNERSHIP OF REAL PROPERTY

Real property ownership is often described as a **bundle of legal rights.** In other words, a purchaser of real estate is actually buying the rights of ownership held by the seller. These rights include the

- right of possession;
- right to control the property within the framework of the law;
- right of enjoyment (to use the property in any legal manner);
- right of exclusion (to keep others from using the property); and
- right of disposition (to sell, will, or otherwise dispose of the property). (See Figure 1.3.)

The concept of a bundle of rights comes from old English law. When the populace could not commonly read or write, a seller transferred property by giving the purchaser a bundle of bound sticks from a tree on the property. This process was referred to as a *livery of seisin* (seizin). The purchaser, who accepted the bundle of sticks, then owned the tree from which the sticks came and the land to which the tree was attached. The individual sticks became symbolic of the rights associated with ownership. Because the rights of ownership (like the sticks) can be separated and individually transferred, several parties (as was mentioned earlier) may have ownership rights in the same parcel of real estate. The various rights in real estate will be discussed in detail later in the text.

■ CHARACTERISTICS OF REAL ESTATE

Real estate possesses seven basic characteristics that define its nature and affect its use. These characteristics fall into two general categories: economic and physical.

Economic Characteristics

The economic characteristics of real estate affect its value as an investment.

Scarcity.   Although we usually do not think of land as a rare commodity, the total supply of land is in fact fixed. Even though a considerable amount of land remains unused or uninhabited, the availability of land in a given location or of a particular quality is limited.

> **Economic Characteristics of Real Estate**
> 1. Scarcity
> 2. Improvements
> 3. Permanence of investment
> 4. Area preference

Improvements.   Improvements such as buildings or utilities affect the usefulness of land and, consequently, its value. Building an improvement on one parcel of land also can affect the value and use of neighboring properties as well as the entire community. For example, improving a parcel of real estate by building a shopping center can change the value of land in a large area.

Permanence of investment.   The capital and labor used to build the improvement represent a large fixed investment. Although even a well-built structure can be razed to make way for a newer building or other use of the land, improvements such as drainage, electricity, water, and sewerage remain because they generally cannot be dismantled or removed economically. The return on such investments tends to be long-term and relatively stable.

Area preferences.   This economic characteristic, sometimes called *situs*, does not refer to a geographical location but rather to people's preferences for a given area. The uniqueness of people's preferences results in different values for similar units. *Area preference is the most important economic characteristic of land.*

Physical Characteristics

Nothing to do with money

> **Physical Characteristics of Real Estate**
> 1. Immobility
> 2. Indestructibility
> 3. Uniqueness

Land also has certain physical characteristics that set it apart from other commodities.

Land is immobile.   Although some of the substances of land are removable and topography of land can be changed, *the geographic location of any given parcel of land can never be changed.* Its location is fixed.

Land is indestructible.   Land can be altered, but it cannot be destroyed. This permanence of land, coupled with the long-term nature of the improvements on it, tends to stabilize investments in land.

The fact that land is indestructible does not, however, change the fact that the improvements depreciate and can become obsolete, thereby reducing values—perhaps dramatically. This gradual depreciation should not be confused with the fact that the economic desirability of a given location can change.

Land is unique. No two parcels of land are ever exactly the same. Although there may be substantial similarity, all parcels differ in some respect. Each has its own geographic location and sun exposure, topography, and even soil conditions. Because of these differences, there is no substitute for an individual parcel. The uniqueness of land is also referred to as *heterogeneity* or *nonhomogeneity*.

Characteristics Affecting Land Use

The physical and economic characteristics of a parcel of real estate affect its desirability for a specific use. Although the real estate could be used in many ways, some are more practical or desirable than others, depending on what is financially feasible, physically possible, and economically productive. The contour and elevation of the land, the prevailing winds, transportation, public improvements, and availability of natural resources (such as water) are factors that affect the use. Hilly, heavily wooded land, for example, would need considerable work before it could be used for industrial purposes, but it could be suitable for residential use. Likewise, flat land located along a major highway network would be undesirable for residential use, but it may be a desirable location for industrial or commercial use.

■ LAWS AFFECTING REAL ESTATE

The unique nature of real estate has given rise to an equally unique set of laws and rights. Virtually every aspect of real estate ownership, even the simplest real estate transaction, involves a body of complex laws. *General property law*, which has been briefly introduced in this chapter, is only one of many areas of law that are important. *Environmental laws, contract law, the law of agency, fair housing laws, tax laws*, and *real estate license laws* affect today's sales transactions. In addition to federal and state laws and regulations, local land-use and zoning laws have a significant bearing on real estate as well.

Real Estate Laws
- General property law
- Environmental laws
- Contract law
- Agency law
- Fair housing laws
- Tax laws
- Zoning and land use laws
- Real estate license law

Obviously, a real estate licensee can't be an expert in all areas of real estate law. However, licensees should know and understand some of the basic principles. Perhaps most important is the ability to recognize issues that should be referred to a competent attorney. All professionals must practice within the limits of their expertise. Providing legal advice or counsel, interpreting laws, preparing documents that transfer the rights in property, or representing a client as an attorney are activities that are beyond the scope of a real estate licensee's authority. *Under no circumstances may a real estate licensee act as an attorney unless he or she is also separately authorized to act as an attorney at law.*

Real estate transactions become more complex as the laws that affect them become more complex. Add an increasingly litigious environment and today's real estate licensees must be diligent about enhancing their competence, exercising care in the way they conduct business, and engaging competent legal counsel when situations arise that are beyond their expertise.

IN PRACTICE

To ensure the smooth transfer of property, real estate licensees aiding in the transaction must be familiar with all applicable laws.

In addition, real estate licensees must conduct themselves in accordance with the state's licensing laws. All 50 states, the District of Columbia, and all Canadian provinces have adopted laws that govern the activities of licensees to ensure that the interests of the public are protected. The license laws of the various states are similar in many respects but differ in some details.

In Your State   **PA**   The Real Estate Licensing and Registration Act and the Rules and Regulations of the State Real Estate Commission govern the activities of licensees in Pennsylvania. These laws require that a person must obtain a license to engage in the real estate business. In most cases, applicants must possess certain educational qualifications and pass written examinations to prove adequate knowledge of the business for which they are seeking licensure. To continue in business, licensees must follow certain prescribed standards of conduct and complete continuing education courses for license renewal. Chapter 13 more fully describes the specific provisions of the Pennsylvania law; a complete copy of the current law is printed in Appendix C.

■ SUMMARY

Although most people think of land as the surface of the earth, land is the earth's surface and also the mineral deposits under the surface and the air above it. The term real estate further expands this definition to include all natural and manmade improvements attached to the land. Real property is the term used to describe real estate plus the bundle of legal rights associated with its ownership.

The different rights to the same parcel of real estate may be owned and controlled by different parties, one owning the surface rights, one owning the air rights, and another owning the subsurface rights.

All property that does not fit the definition of real property is classified as personal property or chattels. When articles of personal property are affixed to land, they may become fixtures and as such are considered a part of the real estate. However, personal property attached to real estate by a tenant for business purposes is classified as a trade, or chattel, fixture and remains personal property.

The special nature of land is apparent in both its economic and its physical characteristics. The economic characteristics consist of scarcity, improvements, permanence of investment, and area preferences. Physically, land is immobile, indestructible, and unique.

Even the simplest real estate transactions reflect a complex body of laws. A purchaser of real estate actually purchases from the seller the legal rights to use the land in certain ways.

Every U.S. state and Canadian province has some type of real estate licensing requirement. Students should become familiar with the licensing law in Pennsylvania.

QUESTIONS

1. Which of the following best defines real estate?
   a. Land and the air above it
   b. Land and all things permanently attached by nature
   c. Land and all things permanently affixed to it
   d. Land and the mineral rights in the land

2. The term *nonhomogeneity* refers to
   a. scarcity.
   b. immobility.
   c. uniqueness.
   d. indestructibility.

3. The bundle of legal rights is included in the definition of
   a. land.
   b. real estate.
   c. real property.
   d. trade fixtures.

4. The bundle of legal rights includes all of the following EXCEPT the right to
   a. possess the property.
   b. enjoy the property within the framework of the law.
   c. sell or otherwise convey the property.
   d. use the property for any purpose, legal or otherwise.

5. All of the following would be considered real estate EXCEPT
   a. fences.
   b. buildings.
   c. growing trees.
   d. farm equipment.

6. Which of the following would NOT be a consideration when determining if an item is real property?
   a. The cost of the item when it was purchased
   b. The method of its attachment to other real property
   c. The intended use of the item by its owner
   d. The manner in which the item is actually used with other real property

7. Which of the following is NOT an economic characteristic of real estate?
   a. Indestructibility
   b. Permanence of investment
   c. Area preference(s)
   d. Scarcity

8. Real property can be converted into personal property through
   a. severance.
   b. accession.
   c. conversion.
   d. inference.

9. M is renting a single-family home under a one-year lease. Two months into the lease she installs an awning over the building's front windows to keep the sun away from some delicate hanging plants. Which of the following is true?
   a. M must remove the awning before the rental period is over.
   b. Because of its nature, the awning is considered personal property.
   c. The awning is considered a fixture.
   d. Because of the nature of the property, the awning is considered a trade fixture.

10. G purchases a parcel of land and sells the rights to minerals located in the ground to an exploration company. After selling the mineral rights, G no longer owns which of the following?
    a. Air rights
    b. Surface rights
    c. Subsurface rights
    d. Air and subsurface rights

ANSWERS

1. C Real estate includes in its definition all things permanently attached to the land either by nature or by man. (p. 4)

2. C Nonhomogeneity is another way of stating one of the physical characteristics of land, the characteristic that recognizes that land is unique. (pp. 10–11)

3. C The definition of real property includes more than the physical nature of either "land" or "real estate." Real property includes interests, rights, and benefits associated with ownership. (p. 4)

4. D The bundle of legal rights recognizes the right of an owner to use the property for a legal purpose. There is no legal right to use property for an illegal purpose. (p. 9)

5. D Farm equipment is an example of personal property. Fences, buildings and growing trees are all included in the definition of real estate. (p. 4)

6. A Tests used to determine whether an article is a fixture include intention, manner of annexation, adaptation to the real estate, and the existence of an agreement. The cost of an article is not a relevant issue. (p. 8)

7. A Indestructibility refers to a physical characteristic of real estate, not an economic characteristic. (p. 10)

8. A It is possible to change an item of real estate to personal property by severance. A growing tree is real estate until the owner cuts it down, at which point the lumber becomes personal property. (p. 7)

9. C Once attached to the real estate, the awning becomes a fixture, and is therefore classified as real estate. The fact that it was attached by a tenant rather than the owner is not relevant. (p. 8)

10. C Rights to the natural resources lying below the earth's surface are classified as subsurface rights, which are distinct from surface or air rights. As such, subsurface rights may be transferred without a transfer of surface rights. (p. 5)

2

LAND-USE CONTROLS AND DEVELOPMENT

■ LEARNING OBJECTIVES

When you've finished reading this chapter, you should be able to

■ explain the concept of police powers;
■ identify various types of public and private controls;
■ summarize key points of the Interstate Land Sales Full Disclosure Act;
■ explain the function and characteristics of building codes and zoning ordinances; and
■ define the key terms.

■ KEY TERMS

buffer zone	deed restriction	restrictive covenants
building codes	enabling acts	subdivision and land development ordinances
building permit	impact fees	
comprehensive plan	nonconforming use	subdivision plat
conditional-use permit	police power	variance
dedication	property report	zoning ordinances

■ LAND-USE CONTROLS

Broad though they may be, the rights of real estate ownership are not absolute. Although an owner is entitled to control the use of the property by virtue of the bundle of rights, there are certain limitations. The use of land is regulated by the government, known as public controls, and by landowners with private restrictions. Federal, state, and local governments also control land by their ownership of property. Consequently, the ownership of a parcel of land is subject to these controls.

■ PUBLIC CONTROLS

The **police power** of the states refers to their inherent authority to adopt regulations necessary to protect the public health, safety, and welfare. The states, in turn, delegate to counties and local municipalities the authority to enact ordinances in keeping with general laws. The largely urban population and the increasing demands placed on our limited natural resources have made it necessary for the government to increase its limitations on the private use of real estate. There are now controls over noise, air, and water pollution, as well as population density.

The use of privately owned real estate is regulated through

- land-use planning,
- zoning ordinances,
- subdivision regulations,
- building codes, and
- environmental protection legislation.

The Comprehensive Plan

Local governments establish development goals through the formulation of a **comprehensive plan**, also referred to as a *master plan*. Municipalities and counties develop plans to ensure that social and economic needs are balanced with environmental and aesthetic concerns. The plan includes the objectives of the municipality for future development and the strategies and timing for implementation. The *Pennsylvania Municipalities Planning Code* contains laws governing the planning process. Municipalities are authorized to establish a comprehensive plan, zoning ordinances, and subdivision regulations to govern land use within their jurisdictions. The comprehensive plan, as provided for in the code, includes the following basic elements:

- *Land use*, including that which may be proposed for residence, industry, business, agriculture, traffic and transit facilities, utilities, community facilities, parks and recreation, floodplains, and areas of special hazards
- *Housing needs* of present and anticipated future residents, which may include rehabilitation in declining neighborhoods and accommodation of new housing in different dwelling types for households in all income levels
- *Movement of people and goods*, which may include highways and public transit, parking facilities, and pedestrian and bikeway systems
- *Community facilities and utilities*, which may include education, libraries, hospitals, recreation, fire and police, water resources, sewerage and waste treatment and disposal, storm drainage, and flood management
- *Energy conservation* to reduce energy consumption and promote utilization of renewable energy sources

The preparation of a comprehensive plan involves surveys, studies and analyses of housing, demographic and economic characteristics, and trends. The natural characteristics of land and the interrelationship of different kinds of land use affect the plan. The planning activities of a municipality are coordinated within the county in which it is located to achieve orderly growth and development. In addition, planning may be coordinated through regional planning commissions comprised of representatives from several counties.

Zoning

Zoning ordinances are local municipal laws that implement the comprehensive plan, and regulate and control the use of land and structures within designated land-use districts. Zoning ordinances cannot be static; they must remain flexible to meet the ever-changing needs of society. Zoning affects such things as

- permitted use of land,
- lot sizes,
- types of structures,
- building heights,
- setbacks (the minimum distance structures may be built from streets or sidewalks),
- density (the ratio of land area to structure area or population), and
- protection of natural resources.

Zoning powers are conferred on municipal governments by state **enabling acts.** There are no nationwide or statewide zoning ordinances. State and federal governments, however, may regulate land use through special legislation, such as scenic easement and coastal management and environmental laws.

Zoning ordinances have traditionally divided land use into residential, commercial, industrial, and agricultural classifications. These land-use areas are further divided into subclasses. For example, residential areas may be subdivided to provide for detached single-family dwellings, semidetached structures containing not more than four dwelling units, walkup apartments, high-rise apartments, and so forth.

Municipalities often incorporate architectural design standards or signage provisions in their ordinances or designate historic preservation districts. The goal of these regulations must be consistent with the purpose of the police powers, not based solely on societal objectives or aesthetics, while not interfering with the private rights of ownership. Municipalities can also use **buffer zones,** such as landscaped parks and playgrounds, to screen residential from nonresidential areas and thus protect the enjoyment of the property owners.

In Your State **PA** The governing body of a municipality is responsible for enacting the comprehensive plan, zoning, and subdivision ordinances in accordance with procedures in the Pennsylvania Municipalities Planning Code. The governing body may appoint a planning commission to be responsible for formulating the recommended plans and ordinances. Public hearings must be held prior to their enactment by the governing body. ■

Adoption of zoning ordinances.   The purpose of zoning ordinances is to promote and protect the public health, safety, and general welfare, while providing for coordinated and practical community development. Zoning ordinances must not violate the rights of individuals and property holders (as provided under the due process provisions of the Fourteenth Amendment to the U.S. Constitution) or the various provisions of the constitution of the state in which the real estate is located. Any land-use legislation that is destructive, unreasonable, arbitrary, or confiscatory is usually considered void. Tests commonly applied in determining the validity of ordinances require that the

- power be exercised in a *reasonable manner*,
- provisions be *clear and specific*,
- ordinances be *nondiscriminatory*,
- ordinances promote *public health, safety, and general welfare* under the police power concept, and
- ordinances *apply to all property* in a *similar* manner.

When land is taken for public use by the government's power of eminent domain, the owner must receive compensation. In general, no land is exempt from government seizure. The rule, however, is that the government cannot seize land without paying for it. This payment is referred to as *just compensation*. Occasionally, a property owner may claim that land-use regulations are so restrictive as to constitute a regulatory taking without compensation. These are cases that typically rise to the courts for interpretation.

When *downzoning* occurs in an area—for instance, when land zoned for residential construction is rezoned for conservation or recreational purposes—the government ordinarily is not responsible for compensating property owners for any resulting loss of value. However, if the courts find that a "taking" has occurred, then the downzoning will be held to be an unconstitutional attempt to use eminent domain without providing fair compensation to the property owner.

Zoning laws are generally enforced through the use of permits. Compliance with zoning can be monitored by requiring that property owners obtain permits before they begin any development. A permit will not be issued unless a proposed development conforms to the permitted zoning, among other land-use requirements. Zoning permits are usually required before building permits can be issued.

Zoning hearing board.   Zoning hearing boards have been established in most communities for the specific purpose of hearing complaints about the effects of zoning ordinances on specific parcels of property. Petitions may be presented to the appeal board for variances or exceptions in the zoning law.

Nonconforming use.   Frequently, a lot or an improvement does not conform to the zoning use because it existed before the enactment or amendment of a zoning ordinance. Consequently, this is a **nonconforming use**, which means that it no longer conforms to current ordinances. The nonconforming use may be allowed to legally continue as long as it complies with the regulations governing nonconformities in the local ordinance or until the improvements are destroyed or torn down or the current use is abandoned. If the nonconforming use is allowed to continue, it is considered to be "grandfathered into the new zoning."

Conditional-use permits.   Each time a plan or zoning ordinance is enacted, the new land-use requirements could inconvenience property owners. One way for an owner to use a property in a manner that does not comply with current zoning is to obtain a **conditional-use permit.** A conditional-use permit authorizes a property to be used for a special purpose. The purpose is defined as an *allowable conditional use* within that zoning district (such as a church in a residential district). This is sometimes known as *special-use zoning*. For each conditional use there are normally certain standards that must be met.

Variances.   A **variance,** as opposed to a conditional-use permit, authorizes a use that is *strictly prohibited* by current zoning laws. A variance provides relief for an owner who can demonstrate that a zoning ordinance deprives him or her reasonable use of the property. To qualify for a variance, the owner must describe the unique circumstances that necessitate a use that is contrary to zoning regulations and prove how the regulations harm and burden the owner. A variance cannot alter the essential character of the locality or be contrary to the intent and the purpose of the zoning code.

> *Conditional-use permits* authorize allowable nonconforming land uses.
>
> *Variances* authorize prohibited land uses to avoid undue hardship.

Variances generally fall into two categories:

■ *Dimensional variances*, which cover physical dimensions such as lot or parcel sizes and setbacks
■ *Use variances*, which cover the specific uses of land

An example of a dimensional variance is one that permits an owner to build closer to the road than the setback allows because the lot slopes too steeply to accommodate a structure within the setback requirements. An example of a use variance is one that permits an owner to construct a multiple-unit dwelling in an area where only single-family detached homes are permitted. Use variances can be more difficult to obtain because of the owner's burden to prove how an ordinance causes harm or hardship.

Property owners can also seek a *change* in the zoning classification of a general area or district, which then changes the permissible use of their specific parcels of land in that area. (The change is applicable to a general area or district, not just an individual parcel.) A change is accomplished by *amending* the district map or a zoning ordinance. The proposed amendment must be brought before a public hearing on the matter and approved by the governing body of the community.

IN PRACTICE

When the character of land use is not controlled, communities can develop in reckless or harmful ways. This can compromise the quality of life in a community and threaten the enjoyment of the property owners' rights. One way communities can enhance the use of land, establish a sound economic base, and revitalize aging neighborhoods is by developing a methodical plan for using their land. In doing so, they protect the general welfare of the community, which is a fundamental use of the police powers.

Subdivision and Land Development Ordinances

To meet the growing demand for a variety of housing and encourage more efficient use of land, municipalities frequently adopt subdivision and land development ordinances as part of their comprehensive plan. **Subdivision and land development ordinances** regulate lot sizes, setbacks, building heights, open spaces, and the like specifically for subdivisions and *Planned Residential*

Developments (PRDs). Area and bulk regulations stimulate efficient land use while also controlling density and overcrowding. Ordinances for *Planned Unit Developments (PUDs)* incorporate residential use with a variety of other land uses within a development.

Before actual subdividing can begin, the developer must submit a subdivision and land development plan for municipal approval. Subdivision ordinances generally include procedures for submitting plans, subdivision plats, and surveys. Engineering studies and environmental impact reports may be required as well. Ordinances also specify fees the municipality may charge and procedures it must follow, including time limits, when reviewing these documents and responding to applications for approval.

The layout of a subdivision is governed by ordinances that typically address issues such as

- location, grading, alignment, surfacing, and widths of streets and walkways;
- location and design of curbs, gutters, streetlights, and water and sewage facilities;
- easements or rights-of-way for drainage and utilities;
- minimum setback lines and lot sizes;
- renewable energy systems and energy-conserving building design; and
- areas to be reserved or dedicated for public use, such as parks or recreation facilities.

In Your State   **PA** The provision of adequate water supplies and environmentally sound sewage disposal are major issues in land development today. Ordinances frequently require that water be supplied by a certificated public utility unless the individual lots within a subdivision can be properly served by private wells. To protect streams, rivers, and underground water supplies from pollution, sewage disposal must comply with the *Pennsylvania Department of Environmental Protection (DEP)* regulations for community and individual sewerage systems. DEP may not permit septic systems where the soil's absorption or drainage capacity, as determined by a *percolation test,* precludes their use. ■

Subdivision plats. The process of laying out a subdivision involves (1) identifying the raw land; (2) analyzing its best use; (3) studying the land with the help of a surveyor to consider natural drainage and land contours; and finally (4) plotting the land into blocks, lots within the blocks, streets, and other improvements and easements in accordance with subdivision ordinances. This last step forms the **subdivision plat,** which is essentially a map of the development. (See Figures 4.2 and 4.4 in Chapter 4.) Close contact between the developer and municipal officials is invaluable during this process.

The completed subdivision plans and plat map are then submitted to the municipality for approval. This is an essential step before a subdivision plat can be filed in the recorder of deeds office in the county where the proposed development is located. A public hearing is normally required as a condition of a *preliminary approval* being granted. The municipality may require the developer to install streets, curbs, gutters, fire hydrants, water mains, and sanitary and storm sewers. Because this is a major financial issue for the developer, the *final approval* of a plat is generally conditioned upon the developer completing these improvements, or providing some form of financial security or bonding to the municipality to ensure they will be completed.

Once all approvals are obtained, the subdivision plat is filed with the recorder of deeds. Land for streets or parks and recreation that are designated for public use are transferred or *dedicated* to the municipality when the subdivision plat is filed. Because the plat will be the basis for future conveyances, the subdivided land, including all lots and streets, must be carefully measured and accurately entered on the document. Subdivision plats are discussed further in Chapter 4, "Legal Descriptions."

In Your State   **PA**   While the developer is responsible for installing streets *within* a subdivision (known as *on-site* improvements), the municipality is responsible for *off-site* improvements. As development increases, the demand for highways, roads, and streets increases as well, often stressing municipal budgets. To help defray the cost, the Pennsylvania Municipalities Planning Code permits the governing body to charge **impact fees** to fund off-site public transportation improvements. ■

Impact fees.   Impact fees are based on the amount of traffic the new project will contribute to the transportation system. A traffic analysis is done to evaluate roadway capacity, deficiencies, cost of needed improvements, and the future impact of a development on the transportation system. The municipality is responsible for improvements to the transportation system to correct deficiencies from past development. The developer is charged a pro-rata share for contributory effect of the project. Impact fees are collected when the new subdivision or development is approved.

Building Codes

Building codes are ordinances that *specify construction standards* that must be met when repairing or erecting buildings. The purpose of these codes is to provide minimum construction standards to protect life, health, property, and the environment for the welfare and safety of the general public and the occupants of buildings. The codes address such things as design, quality of materials, and standards of workmanship that must be followed. Frequently, there are also specialized plumbing, electrical, and fire codes.

In Your State   **PA**   Building codes have generally been local in nature, with each municipality and city exercising its regulatory right to adopt codes specific to construction within those political subdivisions. Construction in some Pennsylvania municipalities, particularly those in rural areas, has been free of any regulatory oversight, as only 1,100 of Pennsylvania's 2,567 municipalities have had any kind of construction code. The lack of construction oversight, and the lack of uniformity where codes have existed, has made the job more difficult for engineers and contractors and has certainly made the rules more confusing for property owners. Safety experts have contended that these conditions also compromise personal safety for both building occupants and fire fighters.

Although not uniformly popular, a statewide Uniform Construction Code (UCC) went into effect in July 2004, as prescribed by the Pennsylvania Construction Code Act that was passed in 1999. The prescribed standards are consistent with those nationally recognized by the Building Officials and Code Administrators International, Inc. (BOCA). In addition to satisfying the purpose of construction codes, the act encourages the use of state-of-the-art construction methods and systems and eliminates existing codes that are obsolete, overly restrictive, or conflicting. ■

Municipalities enforce building codes by issuing building permits and conducting building inspections. A **building permit** is written governmental permission for the construction, substantial repair, or alteration of a structure. Through the permit process, municipal officials are aware of new construction or alterations and can verify compliance with building codes and zoning ordinances by examining the plans and inspecting the work. Once the completed structure has been inspected and found satisfactory, the municipal inspector issues a *certificate of occupancy*. This shows that a building is fit for occupancy and has no building code violations.

If the construction of a building or an alteration violates a deed restriction (discussed later in this chapter), the issuance of a building permit will *not* cure this violation. A building permit is merely evidence of compliance with municipal regulations. Property owners should always check with local officials before beginning repair or renovation projects to determine if building permits are required. Property owners should also be aware that municipalities may charge fees for these permits.

IN PRACTICE

Land planning, zoning, and other land-use restrictions have a significant impact on the use of property and a real estate transaction. A person cannot assume that the owner's current use of a property is legal, especially from a visual inspection, or that a buyer's proposed use or alterations will be permitted. Zoning ordinances should be investigated and specific land-use questions should be addressed with a municipality's code enforcement officer or an attorney.

The State Real Estate Commission's Regulations require the disclosure of the current zoning classification for certain types of properties in an agreement of sale.

Environmental Protection Legislation

In response to growing public concern over the improvement and preservation of our country's natural resources, federal and state governments, as well as some cities and counties, have passed a number of environmental protection laws. For example, wetlands legislation attempts to protect wildlife; pollution control measures intend to protect the quality of air and water; and other environmental regulations govern waste disposal and provide for the cleanup of hazardous substances.

Any of the environmental laws or regulations can ultimately affect builders, developers, and property owners by restricting the way land is used and improvements are constructed. Some of the laws also impose significant financial burden for the removal of environmental hazards. A builder, for example, may be prevented from constructing septic tanks or other effluence-disposal systems in certain areas, particularly where public streams, lakes, and rivers are affected. See Chapter 3 for a detailed discussion of environmental issues in real estate.

■ PRIVATE LAND-USE CONTROLS

Private controls are created by an owner, as opposed to **public** controls, which are exercised by the government.

Not all restrictions on the use of land are imposed by the government. Certain restrictions to *control and maintain the desirable quality and character of a property or subdivision* may be created by private entities, including property owners themselves. These restrictions are separate from, and in addition to, the land-use controls exercised by the government. Private land-use controls may be more restrictive of an owner's use than the local zoning ordinance. The rule is that the more restrictive of the two takes precedence.

Private land-use controls fall into two general categories:

■ **Deed restrictions**—These are provisions placed in a deed by the owner at the time ownership is conveyed to control future use of that property. Examples include a restriction specifying the kind of structure that may be erected on the land, a requirement that the property be used for a specific purpose, or a prohibition of a specific use.

■ **Restrictive covenants**—These are declarations of conditions and restrictions that affect the use of all parcels of land within a specified development or subdivision plat. Restrictive covenants, commonly known as *covenants, conditions, and restrictions (CC&Rs)*, are typically set forth in a separate recorded instrument. The deed to each affected property refers to the plat or declaration of restrictions, thereby imposing these restrictions on that property for the owner first receiving the deed and all future owners as well.

Typical restrictive covenants address the type, height, and size of buildings that may be constructed, as well as land use, architectural style, construction methods, setbacks, and square footage. There also may be restrictions prohibiting livestock or limiting the number of household pets. Often, an architectural control committee (made up of owners within the subdivision) is designated to approve building or landscape designs to ensure they comply with the covenants. Master planned communities of this nature are very popular in many areas.

There is a distinction between restrictions on the right to *sell* and restrictions on the right to *use*. In general, a deed conveying a fee simple estate may not restrict the right of subsequent owners to sell, mortgage, or convey it. Because such restrictions attempt to limit the basic right of the *free alienation (transfer) of property*, the courts consider them against public policy and therefore unenforceable.

Restrictions on *use* are usually considered valid if they are reasonable restraints that benefit all property owners in the subdivision. If, however, the terms of the restrictions are too broad, they are construed as preventing the free transfer of property. If they are "repugnant" to the estate granted, they probably will not be enforceable. If any restrictive covenant or condition is considered ineffective by a court, the estate will then stand free from the invalid covenant or condition.

Restrictions may have *time limitations*. A restriction might state that it is "effective for a period of 25 years from this date." After that time, it becomes inoperative. A time-limited covenant, however, may be extended by majority agreement of the owners.

Enforcement. Private restrictions can be enforced in court. A person who is affected by the failure of a lot owner to comply with restrictions can seek an *injunction*. The court injunction will direct the violator to stop or remove the violation. The court retains the power to punish the violator for failure to obey. If people stand idly by while a violation is being committed, they can *lose the right* to an injunction by their inaction. The court might claim their right was lost through *laches*—that is, the legal principle that a right may be lost through undue delay or failure to assert it.

IN PRACTICE

Covenants, conditions, and restrictions (CC&Rs) in subdivisions and deed restrictions are fairly common. But a potential buyer, who will have to live with these restrictions if he or she purchases the property, may not be aware of their specific details or may not even know that they exist. Licensees should be sure that a buyer is properly informed about any CC&Rs when considering a purchase.

Furthermore, both the Uniform Condominium Act and the Uniform Planned Community Act in Pennsylvania require that buyers of condominium units and parcels within planned developments be given copies of pertinent documents to review. The procedures for these disclosures are discussed in later chapters.

■ DIRECT PUBLIC OWNERSHIP

Over the years the government's general policy has been to encourage private ownership of land. It is necessary, however, for a certain amount of land to be owned by the government for such uses as municipal buildings, state legislative houses, schools, and military stations. Such direct public ownership is a means of land control.

There are other examples of necessary public ownership. Urban renewal efforts, especially government-owned housing, are one way that public ownership serves the public interest. Publicly owned streets and highways serve a necessary function that benefits the entire population. In addition, public land is often used for recreational purposes such as national and state parks and forest preserves, which at the same time help to conserve our natural resources.

At present, the federal government owns approximately 775 million acres of land, nearly one-third of the total area of the United States. At times, the federal government has held title to as much as 80 percent of the nation's total land area.

■ INTERSTATE LAND SALES FULL DISCLOSURE ACT

The federal *Interstate Land Sales Full Disclosure Act* regulates the interstate sale of unimproved lots. This act, which is administered by the Department of Housing and Urban Development (HUD), is designed to prevent fraudulent marketing schemes that may arise when land is sold without being seen by the purchasers. Stories about the "little pieces of paradise" people have purchased that turned out to be worthless swampland or barren desert are the kinds of situations this law intends to prevent.

Specifically, the law requires those engaged in the *interstate sale or leasing of 25 or more lots* to file a statement of record and register the details of the land with HUD. The seller is also required to furnish prospective buyers with a **property report** containing all essential information about the property, such as distance over paved roads to nearby communities, number of homes currently occupied, soil conditions affecting foundations and septic systems, type of title a buyer will receive, and existence of liens. The property report must be given to a prospective purchaser at *least three business days* before any agreement of sale is signed.

Any contract to purchase a lot covered by this act may be revoked at the purchaser's option until *midnight of the seventh day* following the signing of the contract. If a contract is signed for the purchase of a lot covered by the act and a property report is not given to the purchaser, the purchaser may bring an action to revoke the contract within two years.

If the seller misrepresents the property in any sales promotion, a buyer induced by such a promotion is entitled to sue the seller for civil damages. Failure to comply with the law may also subject a seller to criminal penalties of fines and imprisonment.

Additional laws that are specific to sales practices in Pennsylvania are discussed in a later chapter.

■ SUMMARY

The control of land use is exercised in three ways: through public controls, private (or nongovernmental) controls, and direct public ownership.

Through power conferred by state enabling acts, local governments exercise public controls based upon the states' police powers to protect the public health, safety, and welfare. The Pennsylvania Municipalities Planning Code governs the procedures to be followed by communities.

Comprehensive plans set forth the development goals and objectives for the community. Zoning ordinances carrying out the provisions of the plan control the use of land and structures within designated land-use districts. Zoning enforcement problems involve zoning hearing boards, conditional-use permits, variances, and exceptions, as well as nonconforming uses. Subdivision and land development regulations are adopted to maintain control of the development of expanding community areas so that growth will be harmonious with community standards. Increased growth and development frequently necessitate additional capital improvements to provide adequate highways and roads to accommodate increased traffic. Developers may be charged impact fees relating to the increased traffic created by their developments.

Subdividing involves dividing a tract of land into lots and blocks and providing utility easements, as well as laying out street patterns. A subdivision plat is filed with the recorder of deeds once it is approved by the public officials.

In addition to land-use control on the local level, the state and federal governments have occasionally intervened when necessary to preserve natural resources through environmental legislation.

Building codes specify standards for construction, plumbing, sewers, electrical wiring, and equipment.

Private land-use controls are exercised by owners, through deed restrictions and restrictive covenants. These private restrictions may be enforced by obtaining a court injunction to stop a violator. Direct public ownership is a means of land-use control that provides land for such public benefits as parks, highways, schools, and municipal buildings.

Interstate land sales are regulated on the federal level by the Interstate Land Sales Full Disclosure Act. This law requires developers engaged in interstate sales or leasing of 25 or more units to register the details of the land with HUD. At least three business days before any sales contract is signed, such developers must also provide prospective purchasers with a property report containing all essential information about the property. Land sales are also regulated by state law.

QUESTIONS

1. A provision in a subdivision declaration used as a means of forcing the grantee to live up to the terms under which he or she holds title to the land is a
   a. restrictive covenant.
   b. reverter.
   c. laches.
   d. conditional-use clause.

2. A landowner who wants to use the property in a manner that is prohibited by a local zoning ordinance can try to obtain which of the following from the municipality?
   a. Variance
   b. Downzoning
   c. Occupancy permit
   d. Dezoning

3. Public land-use controls include all of the following *EXCEPT*
   a. subdivision regulations.
   b. deed restrictions.
   c. environmental protection laws.
   d. comprehensive plans.

4. The police power allows regulation of all of the following *EXCEPT*
   a. the number of buildings.
   b. the size of the buildings.
   c. building ownership.
   d. building occupancy.

5. The purpose of a building permit is to
   a. override a deed restriction.
   b. maintain municipal control over the volume of the building.
   c. provide evidence of compliance with municipal construction regulations.
   d. show compliance with deed restrictions.

6. The goals of a municipal planning commission include all of the following *EXCEPT*
   a. formulation of policy.
   b. determination of land uses.
   c. conservation of natural resources.
   d. preventing variances from being issued.

7. The grantor of a deed may place effective restrictions on
   a. the right to sell the land.
   b. the use of the land.
   c. who the next purchaser will be.
   d. who may occupy the property.

8. Zoning powers are conferred on municipal governments
   a. by state-enabling acts.
   b. through police powers.
   c. by eminent domain.
   d. through interstate laws.

9. Zoning hearing boards are established to hear complaints about
   a. restrictive covenants.
   b. the effects of a zoning ordinance.
   c. building codes.
   d. the effects of public ownership.

10. A new zoning ordinance is enacted. A building that is permitted to continue in its former use even though that use does not comply with a new zoning ordinance is an example of a(n)
    a. noncomforming use.
    b. variance.
    c. special use.
    d. inverse condemnation.

11. To determine whether a location can be put to future use as a retail store one would examine the
    a. building codes.
    b. list of permitted nonconforming uses.
    c. housing codes.
    d. zoning ordinances.

12. Which of the following would probably *NOT* be included in a list of deed restrictions?
    a. Types of buildings that may be constructed
    b. Allowable ethnic origins of purchasers
    c. Activities that are not to be conducted at the site
    d. Minimum size of buildings to be constructed

13. A restriction in a seller's deed may be enforced by which of the following?
    a. Court injunction
    b. Zoning hearing board
    c. Municipal building commission
    d. State legislature

14. To control and maintain the character and quality of a subdivision a developer may establish which of the following?
    a. Easements
    b. Restrictive covenants
    c. Buffer zones
    d. Building codes

15. A map illustrating the sizes and locations of streets and lots in a subdivision is called a
    a. grid.
    b. survey.
    c. plat.
    d. property report.

16. Soil absorption and drainage are measured by a
    a. land survey.
    b. plat of subdivision.
    c. density test.
    d. percolation test.

17. When a development increases the traffic flow on existing streets and highways, the municipality can fund the cost of transportation improvements that are needed because of this development through
    a. fees for building permits.
    b. fees for variances.
    c. subdivision filing fees.
    d. impact fees.

18. To protect the public from fraudulent interstate land sales, a developer involved in interstate land sales of 25 or more lots must
    a. provide each purchaser with a report of the details of the land, as registered with HUD.
    b. pay the prospective buyers' expenses to see the property involved.
    c. provide preferential financing.
    d. include deed restrictions.

ANSWERS

1. A Restrictive covenants are created by subdividers or developers to affect the use of parcels within a particular subdivision. A purchaser of real estate in that subdivision holds title subject to the recorded covenants, conditions and restrictions. (p. 23)

2. A A variance provides relief for a property owner who can demonstrate that a zoning ordinance deprives him or her of the reasonable use of the property. (p. 19)

3. B Deed restrictions are private restrictions created by an owner of property at the time he or she conveys the ownership. (p. 22)

4. C Police power refers to the inherent authority of the government to adopt regulations necessary to protect the public health, safety and welfare. The government does not regulate ownership of real estate. (p. 16)

5. C Building permits allow municipal officials to verify compliance with building codes and other ordinances that apply to construction, renovation, or repair of buildings. (p. 22)

6. D Municipal planning commissions develop comprehensive plans to ensure that social and economic needs are balanced against environmental and aesthetic concerns. Land use, conservation, and policy issues are within the domain of the planning commission. Zoning issues, including variances, are handled by the municipality's zoning hearing board. (p. 16)

7. B An owner may impose restrictions on the right to use property, but any attempt to restrict the right of free alienation (transfer) or occupancy of the property is considered to be against public policy and therefore unenforceable. (p. 23)

8. A The state confers the authority to local municipalities to adopt zoning ordinances through enabling acts. (p. 17)

9. B Zoning hearing boards are municipal bodies for the specific purpose of hearing about the effects of zoning ordinances on specific parcels of property. (p. 18)

10. A The term "nonconforming use" refers to a use that existed before the enactment or amendment of a zoning ordinance. It indicates that the property use does not conform to the current ordinance. (p. 18)

11. D Zoning ordinances divide land use into residential, commercial, industrial, and agricultural classifications, with further subclasses under each major classification. The permissible use of a particular location would require a review of the municipal zoning ordinances. (p. 17)

12. B Restrictions on the right to sell, mortgage, or convey property based on ethnic origins limit the basic right of free alienation of property and are therefore unenforceable. (p. 23)

13. A When there is a violation of a deed restriction, the party affected by the violation has the right to go to court and seek a court order, or an injunction, that will direct the violator to stop or remove the violation. (p. 24)

14. B Developers often use conditions, covenants, and restrictions (CC & R's) to control and maintain the desirable quality and character of a property or subdivision. (p. 23)

15. C A subdivision plat, which is essentially a map of the development, indicates the size and location of individual lots and streets. The plat serves as the basis for future conveyances. (p. 20)

16. D The purpose of a percolation test is to measure soil absorption or drainage capacity. Percolation tests are often used to determine if the soil being tested will support a septic system. (p. 20)

17. D When development takes place in a municipality, the municipality is responsible for off-site improvements, such as highways, roads and streets. The Pennsylvania Municipalities Planning Code permits the local governing body to charge impact fees to fund off-site public improvements. (p. 21)

18. A The interstate sale of unimproved lots, with land being sold without having been seen by the purchaser, may be subject to the Federal Interstate Land Sales Full Disclosure Act. This law requires registration of the details of the land with HUD and also requires that the purchaser be provided with a detailed property report. (p. 25)

CHAPTER THREE

ENVIRONMENTAL ISSUES IN REAL ESTATE

■ LEARNING OBJECTIVES

When you've finished reading this chapter, you should be able to

- identify the major environmental hazards that impact real estate;
- list appropriate steps to minimize risk and legal liability in real estate transactions;
- identify major environmental laws and their impact on real estate transactions;
- explain duties and responsibilities regarding lead-based paint; and
- define the key terms.

■ KEY TERMS

Comprehensive Environmental Response, Compensation, and Liability Act (CERCLA)

Superfund Amendments and Reauthorization Act (SARA)

■ ENVIRONMENTAL CONCERNS

Changing lifestyles, industries, and technologies have altered our environment over time. We've become a consuming population, taking more from our natural resources and returning greater pollution and waste to the environment in the process. Yet the more scientists learn about health risks, the more demanding people become that their surroundings be free of harmful substances. Today's homebuying decisions are affected as well. A growing number of buyers base their decisions in part on the desire for fresh air, clean water, and enjoyable outdoor recreation.

Heightened awareness of our environment has prompted the government to adopt numerous laws and regulations to preserve vital resources and protect the quality of air, water, and soil. Preservation of the environment must also be balanced with the protection of legitimate commercial uses of real estate. However, as we enhance the quality of life, we also can help to strengthen property values, revitalize land, and create greater opportunities for responsible development. The parties involved in a real estate transaction benefit as well.

Managing Risk

Harmful substances can be found in building products as well as in the ground, water, and air. Consequently, environmental issues have become health issues; these health issues have become real estate issues. The most obvious risk to the purchaser or occupant of a property is personal injury when a toxic or hazardous substance causes a health problem. There are financial risks as well. Identifying, abating or eliminating, and disposing of a hazardous substance can all be expensive. When the cost is greater than the actual market value of the property, the negative effect is even greater. For all of these reasons, prospective purchasers demand protection of their personal and financial interests in their real estate transactions.

Environmental risks impose significant responsibilities on real estate licensees. Virtually every aspect of real estate practice, from appraising, financing, property management, and development to sales and leasing is affected. Today's licensees are involved in a number of discovery and disclosure activities to help consumers make informed decisions and choose appropriate courses of action. Consistent with the notion that "the best offense is a good defense," the best strategy is to attempt to eliminate problems before they arise. Real estate licensees must adopt practices that minimize their legal liability and safeguard the interests of sellers and prospective purchasers. The best way to manage risk for all concerned is to gather and disseminate authoritative information. Several steps are involved in doing this.

> **Steps to Minimize Legal Liability**
> 1. Discovery
> 2. Disclosure
> 3. Documentation

Discovery.   The first step is to discover the presence of environmental hazards. Because real estate licensees usually are more aware of possible hazards, consumers often rely on their knowing what to look for and how to obtain authoritative information about any conditions. Therefore, licensees need to be aware of environmental hazards that are common in their area.

What hazards are you looking for?   Typical hazards, which are discussed later in this chapter, include asbestos, carbon monoxide, mold, lead, radon, and formaldehyde that are found within buildings and toxic substances that pollute the environment. Licensees also need to listen to the individual concerns of their customers and clients. Some people experience acute allergic or life-threatening reactions to some substances that may not cause problems for others.

How do you find the hazards?   Licensees are *not* expected to have the technical expertise to determine whether a hazardous substance is present. However, a number of resources are available. One is the property owner. The owner may have conducted tests for such things as radon, lead, or carbon monoxide. This alerts the licensee to conditions that warrant further investigation. Perhaps the owner has already taken steps to mitigate or eliminate a hazard, which is useful information for future owners and can even be an asset when marketing a property.

Other resources for discovering environmental hazards, which are the most authoritative, are scientific or technical experts. In the case of lead-based paint, radon, and asbestos, the inspectors must be certified. While experts can be called on at any stage in a real estate transaction, most often they are asked to conduct inspections to satisfy a condition in an agreement of sale. Discoveries during these inspections are affecting the outcomes of an increasing number of today's sales transactions. Typical inspections include air-sampling tests for airborne pollutants. Other common inspections include tests to determine the safety of well water or contamination from malfunctioning sewage disposal systems. Although the impartiality of inspectors is suspect if they are also mitigation contractors, they can be valuable resources for scientific information and advice about ways to remedy a condition.

Environmental auditors are usually engaged by developers and purchasers of commercial and industrial properties to prepare a more comprehensive study. An environmental audit includes a history of a property's use plus a wide range of tests to identify detrimental conditions, including the presence or discharge of hazardous substances on the land as well as in any existing buildings.

Disclosure.   The second step is the proper disclosure of information. From a legal point of view, the purpose of discovery is to provide information needed to make accurate disclosures. As will be discussed a number of times in this text, the current trend in law, which is being echoed in the courts, is to advance protections for consumers. This imposes responsibilities on the providers of goods and services to disclose information that consumers need to make prudent purchasing decisions, even when they do not ask for it. This is known as disclosure of *material facts*.

Any physical condition that substantially affects habitability and value must be disclosed to a prospective purchaser or user of a property, even if it could negatively affect a transaction. When a prospective purchaser is aware of problems, he or she can make an informed decision about how to proceed. The prospective buyer may choose to negotiate with the current owner to correct the conditions, avoid the property and its problems entirely, or pursue the purchase of the property with full knowledge of its condition.

In the case of environmental issues, this means disclosing the presence of any hazardous or toxic substance. In fact, there are a number of laws that direct the manner in which real estate licensees, renovators and remodelers, and others must disseminate information and provide disclosures to prospective purchasers. An example discussed later in this chapter is the disclosure procedure for lead-based paint.

Documentation.   The best way to demonstrate that information has been gathered and disseminated is to document the disclosures. One cannot rely on recollections of conversations. Without written documentation there is no proof that proper disclosures have been made. Furthermore, parties can be defenseless without written evidence if a dispute arises. Throughout this text, procedures will be discussed for laying a written trail of the information that has been disclosed during real estate transactions. In addition, the use of certain disclosure forms and precise language that must appear in transaction documents is required to ensure that prospective purchasers are properly informed about material facts.

IN PRACTICE

Environmental issues today can affect the lives of every property owner and the livelihood of anyone associated with a real estate transaction. No one can afford to overlook the importance of these issues. Diligent discovery of environmental problems is essential. In addition to personal injury, concerns are the costs involved to eliminate or mitigate a hazard. Even more burdensome is the responsibility for environmental cleanup imposed by federal and state pollution-control laws. Responsibilities under these laws can fall to not only past and future owners of a contaminated property but also to mortgage lenders who foreclose on the property. Because environmental hazards can significantly affect value, appraisers, too, must be diligent in their discovery.

Treatment and Removal

One of the debates surrounding environmental hazards is whether to treat or to remove the problem. The matter is easily resolved in situations where federal or state law requires the removal of toxic material or where the hazard is so serious that its elimination is the only prudent course of action. A build-up of carbon monoxide from a malfunctioning furnace, for example, can be lethal. The only way to safeguard lives is to eliminate the carbon monoxide by repairing or replacing the heating system.

Other cases are not as clear-cut. Considerations to be weighed include the nature of the structure and the ease with which it can be altered, the effectiveness of a treatment or removal method, the degree of risk for further contamination, and the costs involved. To some people, any cost is worth the price for peace of mind if the presence of a hazard disturbs them.

Radon is often eliminated effectively with ventilation systems. Depending on the structure, the cost relative to the benefit is reasonable and the systems do not typically compromise the use or enjoyment of the property. In the case of asbestos and lead-based paint, often encapsulation rather than removal is preferable. For the most part, asbestos-containing materials are harmless. Injury occurs when the materials deteriorate or are disturbed, thus releasing asbestos particles that can be inhaled. Similarly, harm arises with lead-based paint when people are exposed to lead dust that leaches out of the paint. In both cases, encapsulation will contain the harmful substances without further contaminating the building and is often more affordable. Removal is a more costly and involved process. Experienced and, in many cases, licensed professionals must be employed to do the work, and discarded materials must be disposed of in an approved environmentally safe manner.

Environmental Hazards

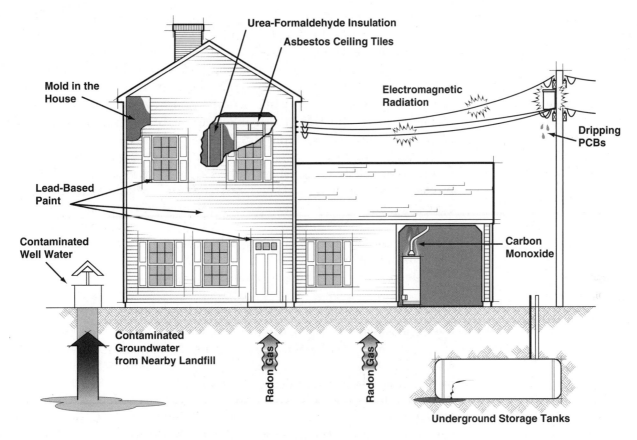

■ ENVIRONMENTAL HAZARDS

We have been surrounded for years by naturally occurring elements in our environment that scientists have only recently determined to be harmful. In addition, changes in construction methods and building systems and even changes in people's immune systems have resulted in the identification of a host of new environmental problems. Additional new problems are emerging. Which ones will become major issues in real estate transactions is anyone's guess. For example, "toxic mold" has recently attracted media attention to homes that became uninhabitable. The following discussion describes a number of environmental hazards that are common concerns in today's real estate transactions and what scientists have learned about their effects. (See Figure 3.1.)

Asbestos

Asbestos is a mineral that has been a popular component in building materials because it is resistant to fire and contains heat effectively. Before 1978, when the Environmental Protection Agency (EPA) restricted the use of asbestos-containing materials, asbestos was used in more than 3,000 types of building materials. It can be found in insulation, floor and ceiling materials, roofing products, vinyl floor tiles, and in the mastic, acoustic ceiling tiles, and wraps used to cover hot water pipes, heating ducts, and heating and hot water units.

Not only are these materials found in residential construction, the EPA estimates that about 20 percent of the nation's commercial and public buildings contain asbestos as well.

The EPA's determination that asbestos was a health hazard set the stage for numerous laws and regulations. Today, asbestos laws affect public school buildings, the rights of employees, indoor air quality, and public, commercial, and apartment buildings with over ten units. The purpose of the laws is to minimize the release of asbestos fibers while handling and processing during construction and removal. Information is available from the EPA at (202) 554-1401 or on its Web site. (See the Internet Resources.)

Carbon Monoxide

Carbon monoxide (CO) is a colorless, odorless gas that occurs as a natural by-product of combustion. Furnaces, space heaters, or other fuel-burning appliances, such as wood stoves and fireplaces, all produce CO. When they function properly and are adequately ventilated, the appliances do not cause a problem. However, malfunctioning or improperly ventilated equipment can emit large amounts of CO, which is a significant health hazard. The fact that CO is so difficult to detect compounds its effect.

CO is quickly absorbed by the body and inhibits the transport of oxygen. People can mistake dizziness, headaches, irritability, and nausea for symptoms of the flu, when in fact they may have symptoms of carbon monoxide poisoning. As concentrations of CO increase, more serious problems occur. More than 200 deaths each year in the United States are attributed to carbon monoxide poisoning. Property owners can protect themselves by annually servicing their heating systems, including chimneys, and installing CO detectors. A variety of detectors is available; some sound an alarm much like smoke detectors when they sense unacceptable levels of CO.

Indoor Mold

Indoor mold is commonplace, thriving in the damp or dark recesses of our buildings. While patches of green, blue, or black discoloration can readily be seen on walls, floors, and ceilings, mold may also be growing in air ducts, wall crevices, or attic or basement areas where it cannot be seen. Some researchers suggest that the increasing prevalence of mold can be attributed to today's building materials, such as plasterboard and plywood, which are more prone to promote the growth of mold when wet. Mold also thrives in today's more efficient heating and air-conditioning systems and better-insulated buildings.

Until recently, mold has been little more than a nuisance for homeowners. Today, people are more wary because of reported allergic reactions and illness, especially respiratory problems, attributed to mold. As molds propagate, some produce mycotoxins (such as the stachybotrys associated with black mold) that can be toxic to humans. While scientists acknowledge that severe contamination can be a problem, they have not yet formulated public health standards to indicate the levels at which mycotoxins become harmful.

The lack of public health standards coupled with the increasing prevalence of molds leaves purchasers, sellers, and real estate licensees in a quandary as to the best way to manage real or perceived health risks. In addition, the environment that fosters the growth of molds can also cause considerable structural damage, a factor that also affects financing and insurability of a property. Several states are contemplating legislation to address indoor air quality in office buildings and to add molds to the list of items required in mandatory property disclosures. Licensees should be vigilant observers of conditions in properties and monitor legal developments.

Lead-Based Paint and Other Lead Hazards

Lead was used as a pigment and drying agent in alkyd oil-based paint. Lead-based paint may be found on any interior or exterior surface, but it is particularly common on doors, window frames, and other woodwork. The federal government estimates that lead is present in about 75 percent of all the private housing built before 1978 or in as many as 57 million homes, ranging from low-income apartments to million-dollar mansions.

Elevated levels of lead in the body can cause serious damage to the brain, kidneys, nervous system, and red blood cells. Lead poisoning occurs when a person is exposed to a large amount of lead that the body is not capable of eliminating. The degree of harm relates to the amount of exposure and the age at which a person is exposed. As many as one in six children today may have dangerously high levels of lead in their bloodstream.

Ingestion of lead dust occurs from the hands by a crawling infant or inhalation by any occupant of a structure. Lead can also be ingested from indoor water supplies because of lead pipes and lead solder used in old plumbing systems. In fact, lead particles can be found in many places. Soil and groundwater may be contaminated by everything from lead plumbing in leaking landfills to discarded skeet and bullets from an old shooting range. High levels of lead have been found in the soil near waste-to-energy incinerators.

> Lead-based paint disclosure requirements apply to the sale and lease of residential structures built before 1978.

The use of lead-based paint in residential structures was banned in 1978. Real estate licensees involved in the sale, management, financing, or appraisal of properties constructed before 1978 face potential liability for any personal injury that an occupant may suffer. Numerous legislative efforts affect licensees, sellers, and landlords. *No federal law requires homeowners to test for the presence of lead-based paint.* However, *known* lead-based paint hazards must be disclosed. (See Figure 3.2.) In addition, federal law requires the distribution of a lead-hazard information pamphlet before a renovator or remodeler starts renovation.

In 1996, the EPA and the Department of Housing and Urban Development (HUD) issued final regulations requiring the disclosure of the presence of any known lead-based paint hazards to potential buyers or renters. The purpose is to ensure that people are aware of the presence of any lead-based paint and are told about its risks and ways to avoid exposure. The Residential Lead-Based Paint Hazard Reduction Act includes the following requirements:

■ Persons selling or leasing residential housing constructed before 1978 must disclose the presence of known lead-based paint and provide purchasers or lessees with any relevant records or reports.

- A lead-based paint disclosure statement must be attached to or included in all agreements of sale and leases involving residential properties built before 1978.
- A lead hazard pamphlet must be distributed to all buyers and tenants.
- Purchasers must be given ten days in which to conduct risk assessments or inspections for lead-based paint or lead-based paint hazards. Purchasers are not bound by any real estate contract until the ten-day period has expired.
- The regulations specifically require that real estate licensees ensure that all parties comply with the law.

In addition to obligations imposed on sellers and landlords, renovators and remodelers, electricians, plumbers, painters, carpenters and others who receive compensation for work if they disturb more than two square feet of painted surfaces have obligations under the Pre-Renovation Education (PRE) Rule. This rule requires, among other things, the distribution of an EPA-approved lead information pamphlet.

Radon Gas

Radon is a radioactive gas produced by the natural decay of other radioactive substances. Although it can occur anywhere, some areas are known to have abnormally high amounts of radon. If it dissipates into the atmosphere, the radon is not likely to cause harm. However, when it infiltrates buildings and is trapped in high concentrations (usually in basements with inadequate ventilation) it can cause health problems. Opinions differ as to minimum safe levels. But growing evidence suggests that radon may be the most underestimated cause of lung cancer, particularly for children, individuals who smoke, and people who spend considerable time indoors.

Because radon is odorless and tasteless, it is impossible to detect without testing. Tests must be done carefully to ensure that the results are accurate. Radon levels vary, depending on the amount of fresh air that circulates through a house, the weather conditions, and the time of year. Because so many factors affect the presence of radon, two houses next door to each other may have very different radon levels. Because the risk of radon increases as it builds up in an enclosed space, testing vacant land for radon is not an accurate indicator of the risk once a building is constructed on the site. While relatively reliable home radon-detection kits are available, professionals can perform more accurate testing. The pamphlet "A Citizen's Guide to Radon" is available from the EPA or the Pennsylvania Department of Environmental Protection (DEP).

Urea-Formaldehyde

Urea-formaldehyde was first used in building materials, particularly insulation, in the 1970s. Gases leach from the urea-formaldehyde foam insulation (UFFI) and become trapped in the interior of a building. In 1982, the Consumer Product Safety Commission banned the use of UFFI. The ban was reduced to a warning after courts determined that there was insufficient evidence to support a ban. Urea-formaldehyde is known to cause cancer in animals, though the evidence of its effect on humans is inconclusive at this time.

Formaldehyde is a common environmental allergen, causing respiratory problems and eye and skin irritations in some people. Although not commonly

F I G U R E   3.2

Lead-Based Paint Disclosure

LEAD-BASED PAINT OR LEAD-BASED PAINT HAZARD ADDENDUM

It is a condition of this contract that, until midnight of _____ , Buyer shall have the right to obtain a risk assessment or inspection of the Property for the presence of lead-based paint and/or lead-based paint hazards* at Buyer's expense. This contingency will terminate at that time unless Buyer or Buyer's agent delivers to the Seller or Seller's agent a written inspection and/or risk assessment report listing the specific existing deficiencies and corrections needed, if any. If any corrections are necessary, Seller shall have the option of (i) completing them, (ii) providing for their completion, or (iii) refusing to complete them. If Seller elects not to complete or provide for completion of the corrections, then Buyer shall have the option of (iv) accepting the Property in its present condition, or (v) terminating this contract, in which case all earnest monies shall be refunded to Buyer. Buyer may waive the right to obtain a risk assessment or inspection of the Property for the presence of lead-based paint and/or lead based paint hazards at any time without cause.

*Intact lead-based paint that is in good condition is not necessarily a hazard. See EPA pamphlet "Protect Your Family From Lead in Your Home" for more information.

Disclosure of Information on Lead-Based Paint and Lead-Based Paint Hazards

Lead Warning Statement
Every Buyer of any interest in residential real property on which a residential dwelling was built prior to 1978 is notified that such property may present exposure to lead from lead-based paint that may place young children at risk of developing lead poisoning. Lead poisoning in young children may produce permanent neurological damage, including learning disabilities, reduced intelligence quotient, behavioral problems, and impaired memory. Lead poisoning also poses a particular risk to pregnant women. The Seller of any interest in residential real property is required to provide the Buyer with any information on lead-based paint hazards from risk assessments or inspections in the Seller's possession and notify the Buyer of any known lead-based paint hazards. A risk assessment or inspection for possible lead-based paint hazards is recommended prior to purchase.

Seller's Disclosure (initial)
_____(a)Presence of lead-based paint and/or lead-based paint hazards (check one below):

    ❏Known lead-based paint and/or lead-based paint hazards are present in the housing (explain).

    _____

    _____

    ❏Seller has no knowledge of lead-based paint and/or lead-based paint hazards in the housing.
_____(b)Records and reports available to the Seller (check one below):

    ❏Seller has provided the Buyer with all available records and reports pertaining to lead-based paint and/or lead-based paint hazards in the housing (list documents below).

    _____

    _____

    ❏Seller has no reports or records pertaining to lead-based paint and/or lead-based paint hazards in the housing.

Buyer's Acknowledgment (initial)
_____(c)Buyer has received copies of all information listed above.
_____(d)Buyer has received the pamphlet *Protect Your Family from Lead in Your Home.*
_____(e)Buyer has (check one below):

    ❏Received a 10-day opportunity (or mutually agreed upon period) to conduct a risk assessment or inspection for the presence of lead-based paint and/or lead-based paint hazards; or

    ❏Waived the opportunity to conduct a risk assessment or inspection for the presence of lead-based paint and/or lead-based paint hazards.

Agent's Acknowledgment (initial)
_____(f)Agent has informed the Seller of the Seller's obligations under 42 U.S.C. 4582(d) and is aware of his/her responsibility to ensure compliance.

Certification of Accuracy
The following parties have reviewed the information above and certify, to the best of their knowledge, that the information provided by the signatory is true and accurate.
Buyer: _____ (SEAL)Date _____
Buyer: _____ (SEAL)Date _____
Agent: _____Date _____
Seller: _____ (SEAL)Date _____
Seller: _____ (SEAL)Date _____
Agent: _____ Date _____

found in insulation today, formaldehyde is prevalent in a number of building products (pressed wood and medium-density fiberboard) and fixtures. Consumers are becoming increasingly wary of the presence of formaldehyde, especially if they are sensitive to it.

Tests can be conducted to determine the level of formaldehyde gas in a house. Again, however, care should be exercised to ensure that the results of the tests are accurate and that the source of the gases is properly identified.

Electromagnetic Fields

Electromagnetic fields (EMFs) are generated by the movement of electrical currents. The use of any electrical appliance creates a small field of electromagnetic radiation: Clock radios, televisions, and computers all produce EMFs. High-tension power lines are a major concern. The EMFs produced by these high-voltage lines, as well as by secondary distribution lines and transformers, are suspected to cause cancer, hormonal changes, and behavioral abnormalities. There is considerable controversy and much conflicting evidence about whether EMFs pose a health hazard. Buyers who are aware of the controversy, however, may be unwilling to purchase property near power lines or transformers. As research into EMFs continues, real estate licensees should stay informed about current findings.

Soil and Groundwater Contamination

Groundwater is the water that exists under the earth's surface within the crevices in geological formations. Groundwater forms the *water table*, the natural level at which the ground is saturated. This may be very near the surface or several hundred feet underground. Surface water can also be absorbed into the groundwater.

Any contamination of underground water can threaten the supply of pure, clean water for private wells or public water systems. If groundwater is not protected, the earth's natural filtering systems may be inadequate to ensure a supply of pure water. Contamination can come from a variety of sources. Run-off from waste disposal sites, abandoned coalmines, underground storage tanks, septic systems, dry wells, and storm drains, as well as the illegal disposal of hazardous materials and the regular use of insecticides and herbicides are all possible sources. Because water flows from one place to another, contamination also can spread far from its original source.

Leaking underground storage tanks (USTs) are a major problem, contaminating not only groundwater but also polluting the soil. Approximately three to five million USTs in the United States may contain hazardous substances. USTs can be found where any number of kinds of commercial and industrial establishments has existed. Also they can be found on residential properties. Substances stored in these tanks are often corrosive or unstable and over time cause the tanks to leak, necessitating major environmental cleanup.

Improper disposal of waste also can contaminate soil and groundwater. Waste disposal sites are necessary because of the vast quantities of garbage and waste materials that we cast off each day. Special hazardous waste disposal sites are also needed to contain radioactive waste, toxic chemicals, and by-products from medical and scientific processes. Unless landfills and other waste-disposal sites are properly constructed and maintained, the environment can be further contaminated by toxic substances that escape into the soil, groundwater, and even the air.

The Resource Conservation and Recovery Act (RCRA) and the Hazardous and Solid Waste Amendments focus on minimizing waste and providing for the safe treatment, storage, and disposal of solid and hazardous wastes and the management of landfills and underground storage tanks. Detailed information about these laws can be obtained from the EPA.

■ ENVIRONMENTAL PROTECTION LAWS

In Your State   **PA** Major federal and state legislation has been adopted in the past two decades to deal with a number of the environmental problems that have been discussed in this chapter. Although the EPA was created at the federal level to oversee such problems, several other federal agencies' areas of responsibility generally overlap. In Pennsylvania, the Department of Environmental Protection oversees our state's laws. As more is learned about our environment and ways to control pollution, new laws emerge and old laws are amended. It is important for licensees to keep abreast of the latest developments. ■

Comprehensive Environmental Response, Compensation, and Liability Act

The **Comprehensive Environmental Response, Compensation, and Liability Act (CERCLA)** was created in 1980. It established a fund of $9 billion, called the *Superfund,* to clean up uncontrolled hazardous waste sites and to respond to spills. It created a process for identifying potential responsible parties and ordering them to take responsibility for the cleanup action. CERCLA is administered by the EPA.

CERCLA is the single most important environmental law affecting real estate transactions because of the broad liability it creates. A landowner is liable under CERCLA when a release or a threat of release of a hazardous substance has occurred on his or her property. Regardless of whether the contamination is the result of the landowner's actions or those of others, the owner can be held responsible for the cleanup. This liability includes the cleanup not only of the landowner's property but also of any neighboring property that has been contaminated. A landowner who did not cause the contamination can seek reimbursement for the cleanup cost from previous landowners, any other responsible party, or the Superfund. However, if other parties are not available, the present landowner (who did not cause the problem) could be solely responsible for the costs.

Once the EPA determines that hazardous material has been released into the environment, it is authorized to begin remedial action. First, it attempts to identify the potentially responsible parties (PRPs). PRPs are defined to include present owners and operators of a landsite, past owners and operators, the parties who generated the hazardous substance, and the persons who arranged for the disposal of the hazardous substance at the site. If the PRPs agree to cooperate in the cleanup, they must then agree on the division of cost. If the

PRPs do not voluntarily undertake the cleanup, the EPA may hire its own contractors to do the work. The EPA then bills the PRPs for the cost. If the PRPs refuse to pay, the EPA can seek damages in court for up to three times the actual cost of the cleanup.

Fundamentally, the liability provision means that all owners and transporters of hazardous waste are liable for the resulting cleanup cost without regard to fault. Therefore, the EPA need not prove wrongdoing to complete the cleanup or obtain recovery costs.

Superfund Amendments and Reauthorization Act

The **Superfund Amendments and Reauthorization Act (SARA)** was passed in 1986 to reauthorize the Superfund that was established by CERCLA. This law contains stronger cleanup standards for contaminated sites and five times the funding of the original Superfund.

SARA also sought to clarify the obligation of mortgage lenders. Because the liability for cleanup extends to the present and all previous owners of a contaminated site, mortgage lenders were very concerned about their liability. A lender unwillingly or unknowingly could be either the present owner or one of the previous owners of a contaminated property through foreclosure proceedings. The amendments clarified the lenders' financial liability for cleanup.

The amendments also created a concept called *innocent landowner immunity.* It recognized that in certain cases a landowner in the chain of ownership was completely innocent of all wrongdoing and therefore should not be held liable. The innocent landowner immunity clause established criteria by which to judge whether a person or business could be exempt from liability. Immunity depends on whether the pollution was caused by a third party, the landowner acquired the property after the pollution occurred, the landowner had actual or constructive knowledge of the damage, the landowner made a reasonable search when purchasing the property to determine that there was no damage, and the landowner took reasonable precautions while exercising the owner-ship rights.

Water Acts

Several federal laws affect the environmental quality of the nation's water. The Clean Water Act (CWA) intends to restore and maintain the chemical, physical, and biological integrity of the nation's water supply. Under this law, the discharge of oil and hazardous substances into the water is governed. The Rivers and Harbors Act was passed in 1899, but is still used to require permits for building a wharf, pier, or other structure in any water outside established harbor lines. The Coastal Zone Management Act, which is primarily imple-mented by the states, addresses coastal environmental problems.

Clean Air Act

The Clean Air Act regulates air pollution. It sets air quality standards to protect human health and safety and our environment and identifies approx-imately 190 different substances that are regulated. In 1993, the EPA issued final regulations that significantly affect property owners and businesses. These apply to appliances used for residential or commercial air-conditioning, cold storage, and refrigeration, and the refrigeration chemicals that are used in these appliances.

Sewage Facilities Act   In Your State   **PA** The state's Department of Environmental Protection passed the Pennsylvania Sewage Facilities Act in 1994. Section 7 of the law gives notice to prospective buyers that if a property is not serviced by a public sewage system and no community sewage system is available, a permit for an individual system must be obtained. As discussed in a later chapter, the act also provides certain notices to buyers that, if applicable, must be included in an agreement of sale. ■

■ SUMMARY

Because people want to be protected from potentially hazardous substances, health issues are becoming increasingly important in real estate. Building products as well as the land, water, and air can contain harmful substances.

Not only must real estate licensees be aware of the environmental hazards that are common in their area, but they must also adopt practices in their transactions to manage risk. In addition to the risk of personal injury to the purchaser or occupant of a property, there is the financial burden for identifying, abating or eliminating, and disposing of a toxic or hazardous substance. Risk can be managed with a diligent plan to discover and disclose hazards and document findings. Resources such as professional inspectors are available to conduct tests for hazardous substances and provide environmental assessments.

Hazardous substances can be abated or removed. In some cases, environmental cleanup laws require removal. In other cases, decisions about how to remedy a hazardous condition depend on the nature of the structure and the ease with which it can be altered, the effectiveness of a method to deal with the hazard, and the costs to correct a hazardous condition. The risk of causing further contamination by removing a substance must also be considered.

Asbestos, carbon monoxide, lead, radon, formaldehyde, electromagnetic fields, and toxic substances that pollute groundwater and soil are all environmental concerns that can arise in real estate transactions.

Numerous federal and state laws have been passed to address current environmental concerns. The Comprehensive Environmental Response, Compensation, and Liability Act (CERCLA) and the Superfund Amendments and Reauthorization Act (SARA) provide broad liability for the cleanup of hazardous waste.

QUESTIONS

1. Under the federal Lead-Based Paint Hazard Reduction Act, which of the following statements is true?
   a. All residential housing built prior to 1978 must be tested for the presence of lead-based paint before being listed for sale or rent.
   b. A disclosure statement must be attached to all sales contracts and leases involving properties built prior to 1978.
   c. A lead hazard pamphlet must be distributed to all prospective buyers, but not to tenants.
   d. Purchasers of housing built before 1978 must be given five days to test the property for the presence of lead-based paint.

2. What do UFFI, lead-based paint, and asbestos have in common?
   a. They all pose a risk to humans because they may emit harmful gases.
   b. They were all banned in 1978.
   c. All three were used in insulating materials.
   d. They were all used in residential housing built in the 1970s.

3. The law that contains the broadest liabilities for environmental cleanup is the
   a. CERCLA.
   b. Resource Conservation and Recovery Act.
   c. Clean Air Act.
   d. Occupational Hazard Administration Act.

4. Which of the following people do not have liability under the environmental law?
   a. Real estate licensees selling property
   b. Mortgage lenders
   c. Real estate educators
   d. Appraisers

5. When attempting to discover environmental hazards in real estate transactions, licensees can do several things to minimize their professional liability. Which of the following is NOT advisable?
   a. Using licensed environmental inspectors
   b. Using environmental inspectors
   c. Conducting their own environmental inspections
   d. Encouraging buyers to have professional inspections conducted

6. The Residential Lead-Based Paint Hazard Reduction Act requires
   a. the seller or the seller's agent to distribute a federal lead hazard pamphlet.
   b. the seller to remove any known lead paint.
   c. the buyer to purchase the property after inspections are performed.
   d. a lead warning statement to be included in a listing agreement.

7. The most common sources of lead poisoning in a home are
   a. auto emissions.
   b. paint and plumbing.
   c. flooring and insulation.
   d. refrigeration equipment.

8. Which of the following is true regarding asbestos?
   a. All asbestos-containing materials must be removed in all commercial buildings.
   b. Asbestos causes a health problem only when ingested.
   c. The level of asbestos in a building is affected by weather conditions.
   d. The removal of asbestos can further contaminate a building.

9. One of the most common sources of carbon monoxide in a house is/are
   a. malfunctioning air conditioners.
   b. crumbling insulation.
   c. leaking heating fuel tanks.
   d. malfunctioning furnaces.

10. Which of the following is true about radon?
    a. It can be reduced in a building with proper ventilation.
    b. It is commonly found in building materials.
    c. It is easy to detect because of its odor.
    d. It is commonly found around landfills.

ANSWERS

1. **B** The Federal Lead-Based Paint Hazard Reduction Act requires owners and landlords of "target housing" (built before January 1, 1978) to disclose what they know about lead-based paint or lead-based paint hazards to prospective buyers or renters in any sales contract or lease. The law does not require testing or removal of the lead-based paint or hazard. (p. 37)

2. **D** All three products were commonly used in residential properties for different purposes prior to the mid-1970s. As potential health risks associated with these products became known, their use was curtailed or eliminated. (pp. 37–38)

3. **A** The Comprehensive Environmental Response, Compensation, and Liability Act (CERCLA) was created in 1980 to address hazardous waste sites and provide a process for identifying parties responsible for clean-up actions. (p. 41)

4. **C** Parties involved in some way in the transaction process, including brokers, mortgage lenders. and appraisers, all have potential liability under current environmental laws. (p. 42)

5. **C** Real estate licensees are not environmental experts and may incur legal liability if they conduct environmental inspections beyond the scope of their professional practice as a real estate licensee. (pp. 32–33)

6. **A** The Residential Lead-Based Paint Hazard Reduction Act imposes duties on sellers and landlords. Sellers and landlords (and their agents) have a duty to provide prospective buyers or tenants with a lead hazard information pamphlet before a contract is entered into. (pp. 37–38)

7. **B** Although lead can be encountered from a number of sources, the most common sources in residential properties are lead-based paint surfaces and older plumbing fixtures such as lead pipes and solder. (p. 37)

8. **D** Asbestos causes health problems when materials deteriorate or are disturbed, thus releasing asbestos particles that can be inhaled. For this reason, encapsulation may be more preferable than removal in some cases. (p. 34)

9. **D** Fuel-burning appliances, such as furnaces, produce carbon monoxide as a natural by-product of combustion. When those appliances malfunction, carbon monoxide can reach dangerous levels and become a significant health hazard. (p. 36)

10. **A** Radon is an odorless, tasteless radioactive gas that is produced by the natural decay of other radioactive substances. When radon infiltrates buildings and is trapped in high concentrations, it can cause health problems. Radon levels can be reduced with proper ventilation. (p. 38)

CHAPTER FOUR

LEGAL DESCRIPTIONS

◼ LEARNING OBJECTIVES

When you've finished reading this chapter, you should be able to

- identify the three methods of describing land;
- define key terms used in constructing legal descriptions using the three methods;
- explain the use of surveys and the information available in recorded plans; and
- define the key terms.

◼ KEY TERMS

air lot	lot and block	principal meridian
base line	metes and bounds	rectangular survey system
benchmark	monument	
datum	plat map	section
legal description	point of beginning	township

◼ DESCRIBING LAND

In everyday life we typically refer to real estate by its street address, such as "1234 Main Street." While that information is usually enough for the average person to find the designated house, it is not precise enough to be used on legal documents affecting the ownership of land. Furthermore, addresses can change as streets are renamed. Agreements of sale and mortgages, for example, require a much more specific description of property.

Courts have stated that a description must be *legally sufficient.* A description meets this standard if a competent surveyor can locate the parcel using the description. In this context, *locate* means that the surveyor can define the exact boundaries of the property. The street address would not tell anyone precisely how large the parcel of land is or where it begins and ends. The identity of land is expressed by a **legal description,** that is, a precise, legally acceptable way of identifying a parcel of land so that its location may be known with certainty. A legal description may be followed by the words "commonly known as" and the street address on documents such as agreements of sale.

IN PRACTICE

Typically, ownership of a parcel of property is transferred many times. The legal description in the documents for each transfer must be identical to the one used in prior transfers. An incorrectly worded legal description may result in a conveyance of more or less land than the parties intended or may create title problems at a later date. Legal descriptions must be copied with extreme care to avoid discrepancies, errors, and future legal problems.

■ METHODS OF DESCRIBING REAL ESTATE

The methods used to describe real estate are metes and bounds, lot and block (recorded plat), and rectangular (government) survey. Although each method can be used independently, the methods may be combined in some situations.

In Your State   **PA**   In Pennsylvania, the methods used are metes and bounds, which is the oldest type of legal description, and lots and blocks. However, all three methods of describing land are discussed here to familiarize readers with systems used throughout the country. ■

Metes and Bounds

A **metes-and-bounds** description relies on the physical features of a property to determine the boundaries and measurements of the parcel of land. The description starts at a designated place on the parcel called the **point of beginning** (POB). From there, it proceeds around the boundaries by referring to linear measurements and directions. A metes-and-bounds description always ends at the POB so that the parcel being described is completely enclosed.

Metes-and-bounds descriptions locate property boundaries by referencing the *direction* and *distance* of the property lines.

Monuments are fixed objects used to locate the point of beginning, the end of boundary segments, or the location of intersecting boundaries. Natural objects such as stones, large trees, lakes, streams, and intersections of major streets or highways, as well as manmade markers placed by surveyors, are commonly used as monuments. Measurements often include the words "more or less" because the location of the monuments is more important than the distance stated in the wording. The actual distance between monuments takes precedence over any linear measurements in the description.

An example of a metes-and-bounds description of a parcel of land (pictured in Figure 4.1) follows.

> ALL THAT CERTAIN *piece or parcel of land situate in Wayne Township, Clinton County, Pennsylvania, bounded and described in accordance with a survey made by H. Richard Ohl, Registered Surveyor, dated November 9, 1984, as follows:*
>
> BEGINNING *at an iron pin on the Easterly line of Pennsylvania Route 18013, which iron pin is on the Boundary line between the parcel to be conveyed and land of the United States of America (United States Army Reserve Center of Lock Haven); thence along the land of the said United States of America, North*

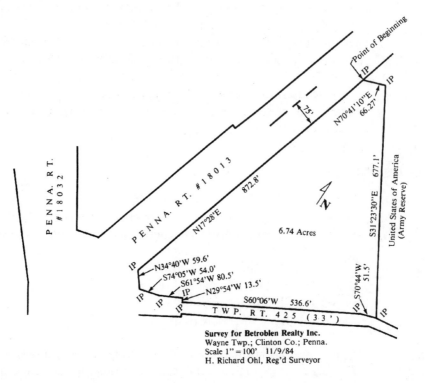

Survey for Betroblen Realty Inc.
Wayne Twp.; Clinton Co.; Penna.
Scale 1" = 100'   11/9/84
H. Richard Ohl, Reg'd Surveyor

70 degrees 41 minutes 10 seconds East a distance of sixty-six and 27/100 (66.27) feet to an iron pin; thence continuing along the same, South 31 degrees 23 minutes 30 seconds East a distance of six hundred seventy-seven and 1/10 (677.1) feet to an iron pin on the Northerly line of Township Route 425, thence along the Northerly line of said Township Route 425, the following five (5) courses and distances: (1) South 70 degrees 44 minutes West a distance of fifty-one and 5/10 (51.5) feet to an iron pin, (2) South 60 degrees 06 minutes West a distance of five hundred thirty-six and 6/10 (536.6) feet to an iron pin, (3) North 29 degrees 54 minutes West a distance of thirteen and 5/10 (13.5) feet to an iron pin, (4) South 61 degrees 54 minutes West a distance of eighty and 5/10 (80.5) feet to an iron pin; (5) South 74 degrees 05 minutes West a distance of 54.00 feet to an iron pin; thence along Pennsylvania Route 18013 North 34 degrees 40 minutes West a distance of fifty-nine and 6/10 (59.6) feet to an iron pin; thence continuing along Pennsylvania Route 18013 North 17 degrees 28 minutes East a distance of eight hundred seventy-two and 8/10 (872.8) feet to an iron pin, the place of beginning, containing an area of 6.74 acres.

BEING a portion of Tract No. 12 of the premises granted and conveyed to the Grantors herein by Deed of Betroblen Realty, Inc., dated January 6, 1986, and recorded in Clinton County Deed Book 295, Page 191.

The description must close by returning to the POB.

Metes-and-bounds descriptions can be very complex and should be handled with extreme care. Descriptions can be difficult to understand when they contain compass directions of boundaries and concave or convex boundary lines. Natural deterioration or destruction of monuments also can make boundaries difficult to identify. Computer programs are available that convert the data of the compass directions and dimensions to a drawing that verifies that the description closes to the POB. Professional surveyors should be consulted for definitive interpretation of any legal description.

Lot and Block

The **lot-and-block** description (or recorded plat system) uses lot and block numbers referred to in a **plat map** filed in the recorder of deeds office in the county where the land is located.

In Your State

PA The lot-and-block system starts with a *subdivision plat* prepared by a licensed surveyor or an engineer. First, a large parcel of land is surveyed and a metes-and-bounds description is developed. Once this large parcel is surveyed, it is broken into smaller parcels. As a result, a lot-and-block description always refers to a prior metes-and-bounds description. The lot-and-block system is used, at least in part, in all states. Some states have passed plat acts that specify the smallest parcel that may be sold without a subdivision plat map being prepared, approved, and recorded. The Pennsylvania Municipalities Planning Code defines a subdivision as two or more lots, tracts, or parcels, unless it is for agricultural purposes. ∎

The description of a lot in a recorded subdivision will include the

■ lot and block number of the lot,
■ name of the subdivision plan, and
■ county and state in which the subdivision is located.

A subdivision plat map, as illustrated in Figure 4.2, shows the division of land into blocks and lots. Streets or access roads for public use are also indicated. The blocks and lots are assigned numbers or letters. Lot sizes and street details must comply with all local ordinances and be indicated precisely. When properly signed and approved, the subdivision plat map is recorded. Then, the legal description of a lot in a recorded subdivision plat consists of the lot and block number, the name or number of the subdivision plat, and the name of the municipality, county, and state where the subdivision is located. For example:

> *Lots 2, 3 and 4 in Block 5 of L. Robinson's Subdivision of the property beginning at a point on the North side of Main Road, 175 feet east from the corner formed by the intersection of the south side of Main Road and the east side of State Route 54; thence . . .*

Rectangular (Government) Survey System

The **rectangular survey system,** sometimes called the *government survey method,* was established in 1785 to provide a standard method of describing all land conveyed to or acquired by the federal government. This included the extensive area of the Northwest Territory, which began in what is the present-day state of Ohio.

The rectangular survey system is based on sets of two intersecting lines: principal meridians and base lines. The **principal meridians** are north and south lines and the **base lines** are east and west lines. Both are exactly located by reference to degrees of longitude and latitude. Each principal meridian has a name or number and crosses a base line. Each principal meridian and its corresponding base line are used to survey a definite area of land within prescribed boundary lines.

F I G U R E   **4.2**

Subdivision Plat Map

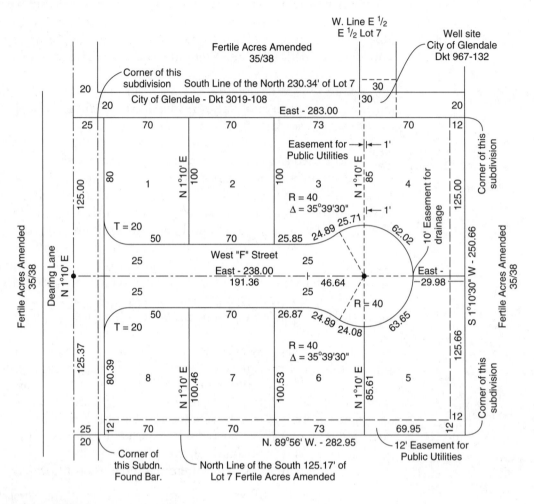

The directions of township lines and range lines may be easily remembered by thinking of the words this way:

Township lines
Range lines

Land parallel to meridians and base lines is divided into ranges and townships, respectively, forming imaginary squares, known as **townships**. Townships are further divided into **sections,** then into fractions of sections. Each township contains 36 sections; each section is one mile square or 640 acres. These descriptions frequently combine with metes-and-bounds or lot-and-block descriptions to define smaller or irregularly shaped parcels of land. Again, remember that Pennsylvania does not describe land using the rectangular survey system.

■ PREPARATION AND USE OF A SURVEY

Legal descriptions should not be created, altered, or combined without adequate information from a surveyor or title attorney. In Pennsylvania, a land surveyor is a licensed professional who is an expert in measurement and boundary issues. Typically, a surveyor must satisfy education and experience requirements, and pass a comprehensive licensing examination.

A licensed surveyor is trained to locate a given parcel of land and to determine its legal description. The surveyor first makes measurements in the field using an instrument called a transit. Then the surveyor prepares a *survey*, which sets forth the legal description of the property, and a *survey sketch*, which shows the location and dimensions of the parcel. A survey that also shows the location, size, and shape of buildings located on the lot is referred to as a *spot survey*. (See Figure 4.3.)

Although surveys are not legally required to transfer title to real estate, surveys are used in a variety of situations. They are required when a portion of a tract of land is conveyed. Lenders require surveys to identify with certainty the real estate to be used as security for a mortgage loan. Surveys are used to determine

FIGURE   4.3

Spot Survey

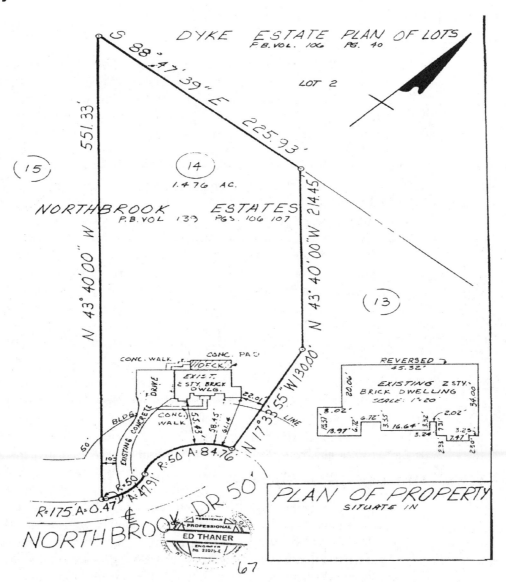

the legal description of the land on which a particular building is located; they indicate the location where a new building is to be constructed; and they indicate the location of roads and highways. Surveys also are used to determine if there are any encroachments, that is, whether an improvement extends or intrudes beyond a building line or property line.

IN PRACTICE

A survey that a seller may have is an excellent source of information for buyers when deciding to purchase a property. A survey is a far more authoritative way for them and real estate licensees to identify property dimensions and boundaries than relying on visual inspection or oral representation. The importance of referring to a professionally prepared survey cannot be overemphasized. Furthermore, a survey can provide information that a buyer needs for determining whether the property will satisfy his or her intended use. If the construction of a particular kind of building or other improvement cannot be accommodated or the parking or open area is insufficient to meet zoning requirements, the buyer could be injured financially. This also creates potential liability for the licensee.

■ MEASURING ELEVATIONS

Just as surface rights must be identified, surveyed, and described, so must rights to the property above the earth's surface. Recall from Chapter 1 that land includes the space above the ground. In the same way land may be measured and divided into parcels, the air itself may be divided. An owner may subdivide the air above the land into **air lots.** Air lots are composed of airspace within specific boundaries located over a parcel of land.

This type of description is found in titles to tall buildings located on air rights, generally over railroad tracks. Similarly, a subdivision plat for a condominium includes a description for each condominium unit referenced by elevation above the city datum. Pennsylvania's condominium property acts require that a registered land surveyor prepare a plat showing the elevations of floors and ceilings on a vertical plane and the boundaries of a condominium unit with reference to an official datum (discussed later in this chapter). Typically, a separate plat will be prepared for each floor in the condominium building.

The following is an example of the legal description of a condominium apartment unit that includes a fractional share of the common elements of the building and land:

THAT certain Unit in the property known, named and identified in the Declaration Plan referred to below as King's Arms Condominium, situate in the Village of Westover, Hampden Township, Cumberland County, Pennsylvania, which has been submitted to the provisions of the Unit Property Act of Pennsylvania, Act of July 3, 1963, P.L. 196 (68 P.S. §700.101 et seq.), by recording in the Office of the Recorder of Deeds of Cumberland County, Pennsylvania, of a Declaration dated May 20, 1975, recorded in Miscellaneous Book 215, Page 836, and a Declaration Plan dated May 21, 1975, recorded in the Office of the Recorder of Deeds of Cumberland County in Plan Book 26, Page 70 and a Code of Regulations, being Exhibit "B" of said Declaration, described as follows:

BEING and designated on the Declaration Plan as Unit A3, detached garage, said garage designated on the Declaration Plan as Unit A3G, together with an undivided interest appurtenant to the Unit in all Common Elements (as defined in the Declaration) of 5.26%.

THE Unit is municipally known and numbered as Three King's Arms, Village of Westover, Mechanicsburg, Pennsylvania.

BEING the same premises which Pennsboro Homes, Inc., by Deed dated August 1, 1975, recorded in the Office of the Recorder of Deeds of Cumberland County in Deed Book E, Volume 26, Page 359, granted and conveyed unto Thomas D. Smith, Seller herein.

Subsurface rights can be legally described in the same manner as air rights. However, they are measured *below* the datum rather than above it. Subsurface descriptions are used not only for coal mining, petroleum drilling, and utility line location but also for multistory condominiums that have several floors below ground level.

Datum

A **datum** is a *point, line, or surface from which elevations are measured or indicated.* For the purposes of the United States Geological Survey (USGS), datum is defined as the mean sea level at New York Harbor. A surveyor would use a datum in determining the height of a structure or establishing the grade of a street.

Virtually all large cities have established a local official datum that is used in place of the U.S. Geological Survey datum. For instance, the official datum for Chicago is known as the *Chicago City Datum*. It is a horizontal plane that corresponds to the low-water level of Lake Michigan in 1847 (the year in which the datum was established) and is considered to be at zero elevation. Although a surveyor's measurement of elevation based on the USGS datum will differ from one computed according to a local datum, it translates to an elevation based on the USGS.

Benchmarks.   To aid surveyors, permanent reference points called **benchmarks** have been established throughout the United States. These are usually embossed brass markers set in solid concrete or asphalt bases. While used to some degree for surface measurements, the primary purpose of benchmarks is to mark datum. Surveyors rely heavily on benchmarks for accuracy rather than monuments, whose placement is questionable because it is subject to the whims of nature and vandals.

Cities with official local datums also normally have designated local benchmarks that are given official status with permanent identifying numbers. Local benchmarks are more convenient for measurements than basic benchmarks that may be miles away.

■ LAND UNITS AND MEASUREMENTS

It is important to know and understand land units and measurements because they are an integral part of legal descriptions. Some commonly used measurements are listed in Table 4.1.

TABLE 4.1

Units of Land Measurement

Unit	Measurement
Mile	5,280 feet; 1,760 yards; 320 rods
Kilometer	0.62 miles
Acre	43,560 square feet; 160 square rods
Section	1 mile square; 640 acres
	160 acres = a quarter section
Square yard	9 square feet
Square foot	144 square inches
Cubic yard	27 cubic feet

■ SUMMARY

Documents used to convey interests in real estate must contain an accurate description of the land involved. A legal description is a precise method of identifying a parcel of land. The three methods used to legally describe land in the United States are metes and bounds, lot and block, and rectangular (government) survey systems. Pennsylvania, however, does not use the rectangular survey system. A property's description should always be the same as the one used in previous documents.

A metes-and-bounds description uses direction and distance measurements to establish precise boundaries for a parcel. Monuments are fixed objects used to establish boundaries. The actual location of monuments takes precedence over the written linear measurement in a document. The metes-and-bounds description must completely enclose the parcel of land; that is, the boundary line must end at the point at which it started.

Lot-and-block descriptions are based on a subdivision plat that shows the division of land into blocks and lots and also shows the streets within the subdivision that are to be dedicated for public use. Once the plat is recorded in the county where the land is located, the legal description of a property can be identified by referring to a subdivision plat, the lot and block, and the municipality, county, and state where the subdivision is located.

The rectangular survey system is based on principal meridians and base lines and uses further divisions to finally describe the identified parcel. This system is not used in Pennsylvania.

A survey, prepared by a licensed surveyor, is the usual method for certifying the legal description of a parcel of land. A survey that also shows the location, size, and shape of the buildings located on a lot is known as a spot survey.

Vertical elevations, either above-surface or below-surface, are measured from datum. Elevation can be further referenced by benchmarks.

QUESTIONS

1. A *monument* is used in which of the following types of legal descriptions?
   a. Lot-and-block
   b. Metes-and-bounds
   c. Rectangular survey
   d. Street address

2. The least acceptable method for identifying real property is
   a. rectangular survey.
   b. metes and bounds.
   c. street address.
   d. lot and block.

3. An *acre* contains
   a. 160 square feet.
   b. 43,560 square feet.
   c. 640 square feet.
   d. 360 degrees.

4. A datum is
   a. used in the description of an air lot.
   b. measured in New York only.
   c. a calendar method of measurement.
   d. all of the above.

5. In describing real estate, a system that uses feet, degrees, and monuments is
   a. rectangular survey.
   b. metes and bounds.
   c. government survey.
   d. lot and block.

6. A woman purchased 4.5 acres of land for which she paid $78,400. An adjoining owner wants to purchase a strip of her land measuring 150 feet by 100 feet. What should this strip cost the adjoining owner if the woman sells it for the same price she originally paid for it?
   a. $3,000
   b. $6,000
   c. $7,800
   d. $9,400

7. A property contained ten acres. How many 50-foot by 100-foot lots could be subdivided from the property if 26,000 square feet were dedicated for roads?
   a. 80
   b. 81
   c. 82
   d. 83

8. At $800 per acre, a lot that is 264 feet wide and 660 feet long would cost
   a. $1,320.
   b. $1,584.
   c. $3,200.
   d. $4,356.

9. A map that shows the location, size, and shape of buildings located on a lot is called a/an
   a. survey sketch.
   b. legal description.
   c. plat map.
   d. spot survey.

Answer questions 10 through 13 according to the information given on the plat of Mountainside Manor in Figure 4.4.

10. Which of the following statements is true?
    a. Lot 9, Block A is larger than Lot 12 in the same block.
    b. The plat for the lots on the southerly side of Wolf Road between Goodrich Boulevard and Carney Street is found on Sheet 3.
    c. Lot 8, Block A has the longest road frontage.
    d. Lot 11, Block B has more frontage than Lot 2, Block A.

11. Which of the following lots has the most frontage on Jasmine Lane?
    a. Lot 10, Block B
    b. Lot 11, Block B
    c. Lot 1, Block A
    d. Lot 2, Block A

12. "Beginning at the intersection of the east line of Goodrich Boulevard and the south line of Jasmine Lane and running south along the east line of Goodrich Boulevard a distance of 230 feet; thence east parallel to the north line of Wolf Road a distance of 195 feet; thence northeasterly on a course N 22 degrees E a distance of 135 feet; and thence northwesterly along the south line of Jasmine Lane to the point of beginning." Which lots are described here?
    a. Lots 13, 14, and 15, Block A
    b. Lots 9, 10, and 11, Block B
    c. Lots 1, 2, 3, and 15, Block A
    d. Lots 7, 8, and 9, Block A

13. On the plat, how many lots have easements?
    a. One
    b. Two
    c. Three
    d. Four

FIGURE 4.4

Plat of Mountainside Manor Subdivision

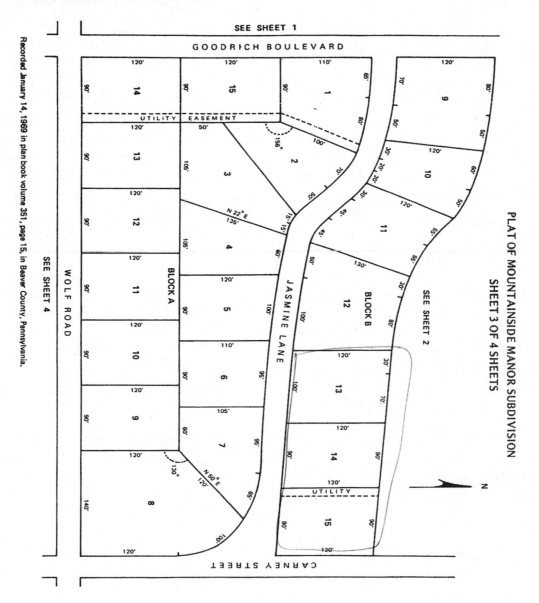

ANSWERS

1. B The term "monument" refers to a fixed, unchanging reference point used to locate the point of beginning (POB) for a specific parcel of real estate. A monument is critical for creating an accurate metes-and-bounds legal description. (p. 47)

2. C A street address is not precise or unique to a particular parcel, nor does it permit a surveyor to define the exact boundaries of the property. (p. 46)

3. B An acre is an area of land containing 43,560 square feet. A parcel measuring 208.71 feet by 208.71 feet would be a one-acre parcel. (p. 54)

4. A The term datum refers to a point, line, or surface from which elevations are measured. It is used for determining the height of buildings or the location of property lines in multistory condominium structures. (p. 53)

5. B Metes-and-bounds legal descriptions utilize references to direction (degree readings) and distance (feet) to establish property lines for a parcel of real estate. A monument is a fixed reference point used to locate the point on the property line known as the point of beginning (POB). (p. 47)

6. B 4.5 acres consists of 196,020 square feet. (4.5 × 43,560). If 196,020 square feet cost $78,400, each square foot cost 40 cents. ($78,400 ÷ 196,020). The adjoining owner wishes to purchase 15,000 sq. ft. (150 × 100). 15,000 sq. ft. at 40 cents per square foot would cost $6,000 (15,000 × 0.40). (p. 54)

7. B Ten acres consists of 435,600 square feet. (43,560 × 10). If 26,000 square feet are reserved for roads, 409,600 square feet are available for subdividing (435,600 − 26,000). Each lot consists of 5,000 square feet (50 × 100). 409,600 square feet divided by 5,000 square feet equals 81.92. Therefore, 81 lots can be created from the parcel. (p. 54)

8. C A lot measuring 264 ft. by 660 ft. is 174,240 sq. ft. If 43,560 sq. ft. equals one acre, 174,240 sq. ft. equals four acres (174,200 ÷ 43,560). At $800 per acre, four acres would cost $3,200 (800 × 4). (p. 54)

9. D A spot survey shows not only the location and dimensions of the parcel of land, but also the location, size and shape of buildings located on the lot. (p. 51)

10. C Road frontage or front footage refers to the lineal measurement that a parcel has facing a public road or street. Block A, lot 8 has the longest road frontage. (p. 57)

11. C Lot 10, Block B has 70 feet frontage; Lot 11, block B has 120 feet frontage; Lot 1, Block A has 145 feet frontage and Lot 2, Block A has 120 feet frontage. Therefore Lot 1, Block A has the most frontage. (p. 57)

12. C The most important point is to locate the key (the direction of North) on the map. From that reference, the east line of Goodrich Boulevard can be located, as well as the south line of Jasmine Lane. Once that point is determined, simply following the appropriate compass directions indicates that Lots 1, 2, 3, and 15 of Block A are covered by the direction. (p. 57)

13. D Easements are shown by dotted lines on the map. Parcels 1, 15 and 14 in Block A and Lot 15 in Block B are shown to have easements. (p. 57)

5

INTERESTS IN REAL ESTATE

■ LEARNING OBJECTIVES

When you've finished reading this chapter, you should be able to

■ summarize the powers and rights of government and their impact on privately owned real estate;
■ describe key features of various freehold and leasehold estates in land;
■ identify common encumbrances and their impact on the ownership and transfer of real estate;
■ distinguish between legal concepts relating to water rights; and
■ define the key terms.

■ KEY TERMS

allodial system	easement in gross	leasehold estate
appurtenant easement	eminent domain	license
condemnation	encroachment	lien
doctrine of prior appropriation	encumbrance	life estate
	escheat	littoral rights
easement	estate in land	party wall
easement by condemnation	fee simple	police power
	fee simple defeasible	remainder interest
easement by necessity	fee simple determinable	reversionary interest
easement by prescription	freehold estate	riparian rights
		taxation

■ HISTORICAL BACKGROUND

Our country's real property law evolved from old English common law. Historically, the monarch held title to all land under what was known as the feudal system. The monarch had the power to grant rights and interests in land to others, but the interests were not absolute ownership rights. The receiver of the rights was a tenant, in this context meaning that the person had rights to possess the property. The tenant's possessory rights were inferior and, therefore, limited by the superior ownership rights of the monarch. By the 17th century, the feudal system evolved into the **allodial system,** which recognizes the free and full ownership of land by private individuals. This system is the basis of real property law in the United States.

The Bill of Rights of the U.S. Constitution firmly establishes the right to private ownership of land. But as has been previously discussed, the enjoyment of the entire bundle of rights associated with the ownership of real property is not absolute. That is, a landowner's power to control his or her property is subject to other interests. A number of parties may hold rights and interests in one parcel of land. Furthermore, as discussed in Chapter 2, ownership rights are limited by public and, possibly, private restrictions.

Real estate licensees must understand the various rights and interests that may exist in order to understand how they impact ownership and the transfer of ownership rights. Sellers can transfer only those rights and interests they own, and buyers can acquire only those that the seller has to convey. This chapter is devoted to a discussion of ownership interests to provide an understanding of how these can affect even the simplest real estate transactions.

■ GOVERNMENT POWERS

Individual ownership rights are subject to certain powers, or rights, held by federal, state, and local governments. These limitations on real estate owner-ship are imposed for the general welfare of the community and, therefore, supersede the rights or interests of the individual. Government powers include police power, eminent domain, taxation, and escheat.

Police Power

As discussed in Chapter 2, every state has the power to enact legislation to preserve order, protect the public health and safety, and promote the general welfare of its citizens. That authority is the state's **police power.** The authority is passed on to municipalities and counties through legislation called *enabling acts.*

Of course, what is "in the public interest" varies widely from area to area. Generally, however, a police power is used to enact environmental protection laws, zoning ordinances, and building codes. Regulations that govern the use, occupancy, size, location, construction, and rents of real estate, the kinds of activities discussed in Chapter 2, also fall within the police powers.

To remember government powers, remember **PETE:**

Police Power
Eminent Domain
Taxation
Escheat

Police powers may be used to achieve a community's needs or goals. A city that deems growth to be desirable, for instance, may exercise its police powers to encourage the purchase and improvement of land. On the other hand, an area that wishes to retain its current character may enact laws that discourage development and population growth.

Like the rights of ownership, the government powers are not absolute. Laws must be uniform and nondiscriminatory; that is, they may not operate to the advantage or disadvantage of any one particular owner or owners.

Eminent Domain

Eminent domain is the right of the government to acquire privately owned real estate for public use. **Condemnation** is the process by which the government exercises this right, by either judicial or administrative proceedings. The proposed use must be for the public good, just compensation must be paid to the owner, and the rights of the property owner must be protected by due process of law. Public use has been defined by the courts very broadly to include public facilities as well as private property that poses a threat to public health and safety, and must be closed or destroyed. That broad interpretation has also been used to justify the taking of private property for economic benefit to the community. A number of lawsuits in recent years, some of which have risen to the U.S. Supreme Court, have raised fundamental constitutional questions about government condemnation actions infringing on individuals' private property rights.

Eminent domain refers to the *right* held by the government.

Condemnation refers to the *process* of exercising that right.

IN PRACTICE

The U.S. Supreme Court in a recent controversial decision appears to be of the broad-mind interpretation of the constitution in concurring that New London, Connecticut acted within its right in taking private property for a redevelopment plan that would be anchored by private business. This decision spawned a groundswell of advocacy for private property rights over the government taking property from one person and then giving it to another person. A number of states are now considering legislation that would more narrowly define rights of eminent domain, which the Supreme Court's decision said they are permitted to do, and very possibly such legislation will be forthcoming in Pennsylvania soon.

Generally, the state delegates its power of eminent domain to local government, quasi-public bodies, and publicly held companies responsible for various facets of public service. For instance, a public housing authority might take privately owned land to build low-income housing; the state's redevelopment authority could use the power of eminent domain to make way for urban renewal. If there were no other feasible way to do so, a railway, utility company, or state highway department might acquire farmland to extend a railroad track, bring electricity to a remote new development, or build a highway. Again, all are allowable as long as the purpose contributes to the public good.

Ideally, the public agency and the owner of the property in question directly negotiate the terms and conditions of a sale, and the government purchases the property for a price considered by the owner to be fair. In some cases, the owner may simply dedicate the property to the government as a site for a school, park, library, or other beneficial public use. Sometimes, however, the owner's consent to sell or transfer the property cannot be obtained. In those cases, the government can initiate condemnation proceedings to acquire the property. Condemnations are presumed to be proper unless the owner objects. Objections are likely when the owner feels the taking is improper or the amount of the compensation is unjust. The owner has the right to file suit for the court to decide these matters.

Taxation

Taxation is a charge on real estate to raise funds to meet the public needs of a government. Real estate taxes are discussed in detail in Chapter 8.

Escheat

Although escheat is not actually a limitation on ownership, it is an avenue by which the state may acquire privately owned real or personal property. State laws provide for ownership to transfer, or **escheat,** to the state when an owner dies leaving no heirs (as defined by the law) and no will that directs how the property is to be distributed. Escheat is intended to prevent property from being ownerless. Although this does not occur in Pennsylvania, real property in some states escheats to the county where the land is located rather than to the state.

■ ESTATES IN LAND

> An estate in land must
> ■ allow possession (now or in the future) and
> ■ be measurable by duration.

An **estate in land** defines the degree, quantity, nature, and extent of an owner's interest in real property. Many types of estates exist. However, not all *interests* in real estate are estates. To be an estate in land, an interest must allow possession (either now or in the future) and must be measurable by duration. Lesser interests such as easements (discussed later in the chapter), which allow use but not possession, are not estates. The various estates in real estate are illustrated in Figure 5.1.

Historically, estates in land have been classified as freehold estates and leasehold estates. According to English common law, freehold estates were real estate, while leasehold (less-than-freehold) estates were merely contracts and thus personal property. Both then and now, the two types of estates are distinguished primarily by their duration and the manner in which they are created.

Freehold estates are ownership interests that last for an *indeterminable length of time,* such as for a lifetime or forever. "Indeterminable" means that, for obvious reasons, the duration of a lifetime or forever can't be defined more precisely by a date. Freehold estates include fee simple (also called an indefeasible fee), defeasible fee, and life estates. The first two of these estates continues for an indefinite period and may be passed along to the owner's heirs. A life estate is based on the lifetime of a person and terminates when that individual dies. Freehold estates are created by deed, by will, or by operation of law.

Leasehold estates are less than ownership interests and last for a *fixed period of time.* This means that they can be measured in calendar time. Types of leasehold estates include estates for years, estates from period to period, estates at will, and estates at sufferance. Leasehold estates are created by contractual agreement. Leasehold estates are discussed in detail in Chapter 6.

Fee Simple Estate

An estate in **fee simple** or fee simple absolute is the *highest quality of interest in real estate recognized by law.* A fee simple estate is absolute ownership. That is, the owner is entitled to all rights to the property. It is limited only by public and private restrictions, such as zoning laws and restrictive covenants. Because

Estates in Real Estate

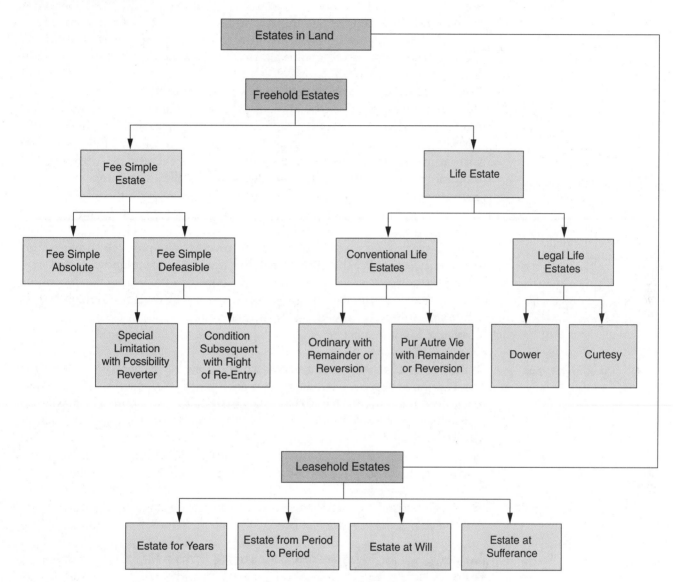

the estate is of unlimited duration, it is said to run forever. Upon the death of its owner it passes to the owner's heirs or as provided by will. A fee simple estate is also referred to as an *estate of inheritance* or simply as *fee ownership*.

Fee simple defeasible.   A **fee simple defeasible** (or *defeasible fee*) estate is a qualified estate. That is, it is subject to the occurrence or nonoccurrence of a specified event. There are two types of defeasible estates: those subject to a condition subsequent and those qualified by a special limitation.

A fee simple estate may be qualified by a *condition subsequent*. This means that some action or activity is specified that the new owner must *not* perform. The former owner retains a *right of reentry* so that if the condition is broken, the former owner can retake possession of the property *through legal action.* Conditions in a deed are different from restrictions or covenants because of the grantor's right to reclaim ownership, a right that does not exist under private restrictions. For example, a grant of land "on the condition that" there is no consumption of alcohol on the premises gives the former owner (or heirs or successors) the right to reacquire full ownership if alcohol is consumed there.

A fee simple estate may be qualified by a *special limitation.* In this case, the estate ends *automatically* upon the current owner's failure to comply with the limitation. The former owner retains a *possibility of reverter.* If the limitation is violated, the former owner (or heir or successor) reacquires full ownership, with no need to reenter the land or go to court. A fee simple with a special limitation is also called a **fee simple determinable.** The language used to distinguish a special limitation—the words "so long as," "while," or "during"—is the key to the creation of this estate. For example, a special limitation when land is granted by an owner to her church "so long as the land is used only for religious purposes" provides that title will revert to the previous owner (or her heirs or successors) if the church uses the land for a nonreligious purpose.

The right of entry and possibility of reverter may never take effect. If they do, it will only be some time in the future. Therefore, both of these rights are considered *future interests.*

IN PRACTICE   The typical real estate owner rarely thinks about the significance of the principles that distinguish one freehold estate from another. It's easy to assume that a sales transaction will involve a fee simple estate because this is the most common one, but that's not always the case. Considerable time and effort can be expended bringing parties together in an agreement of sale, only to later discover that conditions, limitations, or restrictions in the estate that the seller is delivering don't suit the buyer's needs. Because these are significant legal issues with potentially serious consequences, real estate licensees should be alert to the kind of estate the seller owns and if the estate is less than fee simple, should recommend seeking legal counsel for guidance about how to proceed.

Life Estate

A **life estate** is a freehold estate that is limited in *duration to the life of the owner or to the life of some other designated person or persons.* Unlike other freehold estates, a life estate is not inheritable. It passes to future owners according to the provisions of the life estate.

Conventional life estate. A *conventional life estate* is created by the intentional act of the owner. It may be established either by deed at the time the ownership is transferred during the owner's life or by a provision of the owner's will after his or her death. The estate is conveyed to an individual known as the *life tenant.* The life tenant has full enjoyment of the ownership until the death of the person against whose life the estate is measured. At this point, the life tenant's rights cease and the ownership passes as a fee simple estate to another designated individual or returns to the previous owner or heirs.

FIGURE   5.2

Conventional Life Estate

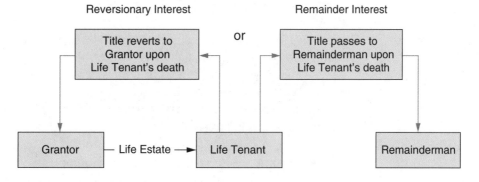

The term *tenant* connotes possession.

A *life tenant* possesses certain ownership rights, as opposed to the tenant in a lease, whose rights extend only to the possession of the property.

A life tenant's rights are less complete than the rights associated with a fee simple estate. A life tenant can enjoy both possession and the ordinary use and profits arising from ownership, just as if the individual were a fee owner, and may sell, mortgage, or lease the property. But because the ownership terminates upon the death of the person against whose life the estate is measured, the life tenant can only sell, lease, or mortgage the interest that lasts for that lifetime. Furthermore, the life tenant may not injure the property, such as destroying a building or allowing it to deteriorate. In legal terms this injury is known as *waste*. Those who will eventually own the property could seek an injunction against the life tenant or sue for damages.

The duration of a life estate can be measured either by the duration of the life tenant's life or the lifetime of another person. For example, A, who has a fee simple estate in Blackacre, may convey a life estate to P as life tenant for P's lifetime. Upon P's death, the life estate terminates. Or A may convey a life estate to P as life tenant for the duration of D's life. Upon D's death, P's life estate terminates. This is known as an *estate pur autre vie*, "for the lifetime of another." If P should die while D is still alive, P's heirs may inherit the life estate. However, when D dies the heirs' estate ends.

Remainder and reversion.   When a life estate terminates, it is replaced by a fee simple estate. As demonstrated in Figure 5.2, the owner of the fee estate may be designated in one of two ways:

1. **Remainder interest**—The fee simple owner who created the life estate may name a *remainderman* as the person to whom the property will pass when the life estate ends. In the example, A conveys Blackacre to P for P's lifetime and designates R to be the remainderman. While P is still alive, R owns a remainder interest, which is a nonpossessory estate. This is a *future interest* in the fee simple estate. When P dies, R becomes the fee simple owner.

2. **Reversionary interest**—The fee simple owner who created the life estate may choose *not* to name a remainderman, but rather retain a future interest and recapture the fee simple estate when the life estate ends. The ownership is said to *revert* to the original owner. In this case, A conveys

Blackacre to *P* for *P's* lifetime. On *P's* death, ownership reverts to *A*. *A* has retained a reversionary interest (nonpossessory estate). If *A* dies before *P*, *A's* heirs (or other individuals specified in *A's* will) will assume ownership when *P* dies.

IN PRACTICE   Conventional life estates may be useful for specific estate-planning purposes. But it is unknown how commonly this strategy is used or how often life estates will arise in a real estate transaction. Because a life tenant's rights are less than those of a fee simple owner, real estate licensees should, again, be alert to the kind of estate the seller owns and if the estate is less than fee simple, should recommend seeking legal counsel for guidance about how to proceed.

Legal life estate.   A *legal life estate (or statutory life estate)* is not created voluntarily by an owner. Rather, it is a form of life estate established by state law. The Pennsylvania Probate, Estates, and Fiduciaries Code (which has been adopted consistent with the Uniform Probate Code) creates a legal life estate for the surviving spouse of a deceased owner. The surviving spouse is permitted 33 percent of the value of the deceased spouse's estate at the time of death. According to the law, the surviving spouse has the option of taking the specified percentage of the estate in lieu of the amount that is directed by the deceased's will. If the spouse dies intestate (without a will), then the statute directs the percentage distribution of assets to the surviving spouse and other specified heirs.

The "marital life estate" arises from the common law concept of *dower* and *curtesy*. This was intended to provide the nonowning spouse a means of support after the death of the owning spouse. (Dower is the life estate that a wife has in the real estate of her deceased husband. Curtesy is a similar interest that the husband has in his deceased wife's ownership.) Common law gave the nonowning spouse the right to a one-half or one-third interest in the real estate for the rest of his or her life, even if the owning spouse willed the estate to others.

In Your State   **PA**   Because a legal life estate provides a future interest in ownership, the possibility exists that a nonowning spouse might attempt to claim an interest, even where there may not be one. Consequently, the nonowning spouse (along with the owning spouse) has been required to sign real estate documents to release any potential common law interest in the property being transferred. Most states, including Pennsylvania, have abolished the common law concepts of dower and curtesy. Although the signature of the nonowning spouse is no longer a legal requirement, some lending institutions or title companies may still hold to the long-standing practice of requiring both signatures in real estate documents. ■

■ ENCUMBRANCES

An **encumbrance** is a claim, charge, or liability that attaches to and is binding on real estate. Simply put, it is a right or interest held by someone other than the fee owner of the property that affects title to real estate. An encumbrance may lessen the value or obstruct the use of the property, but it does not necessarily prevent a transfer of title.

Encumbrances may be divided into two general classifications:

■ *Liens* (usually monetary charges)
■ *Encumbrances* (restrictions, easements, and encroachments that affect the physical condition of the property)

Liens

A **lien** is *a charge against property that provides security for a debt or obligation of the property owner.* If the obligation is not repaid, the lienholder is entitled to collect proceeds from a court-ordered or forced sale of the debtor's property to satisfy the debt. Real estate taxes, mortgages and trust deeds, judgments, and mechanics' liens all represent possible liens against an owner's real estate. Liens are discussed in detail in Chapter 8.

Restrictions

As discussed in Chapter 2, deed restrictions as well as restrictive covenants are private agreements that affect the use of land. They may be imposed by an owner of real estate and included in the seller's deed to the buyer. More commonly, restrictive covenants are imposed by a developer or subdivider to maintain specific standards in a subdivision. Such restrictive covenants are filed in public record when the original subdivision plan is filed and are referenced in the seller's deed to the buyer.

Easements

An **easement** is *the right to use the land of another party for a particular purpose.* An easement may exist in any portion of the real estate, including the airspace above or a right-of-way across the land.

Easements fall into two general categories:

■ *Appurtenant*—An **appurtenant easement** is annexed to the ownership of one parcel of land to permit the owner of this land to use an adjacent parcel of land. Two adjacent parcels of land, owned by two different parties, are involved.
■ *Gross*—An **easement in gross** is an individual interest in or limited right to use someone else's land. This easement benefits a person or entity rather than the land, as is the case with an appurtenant easement.

Typically, appurtenant easements exist when the ability to use or enjoy a property would be diminished without an easement over an adjoining property. Figures 5.3 and 5.4 demonstrate how appurtenant easements provide the owner of one lot access to the neighboring lot. Note that the parcel over which the easement runs is known as the *servient tenement* (meaning that it serves the other property); the neighboring parcel that benefits is known as the *dominant tenement.*

An appurtenant easement is part of and travels with the ownership of the dominant tenement. If the dominant tenement is conveyed to another party, the easement transfers with the title. This type of easement is said to *run with the land.* It is an encumbrance on property and will transfer with the deed of the dominant tenement forever unless the holder of the dominant tenement somehow releases that right. An appurtenant easement is an encumbrance that affects the ownership of the servient tenement.

FIGURE 5.3

Easement: Servient Tenement

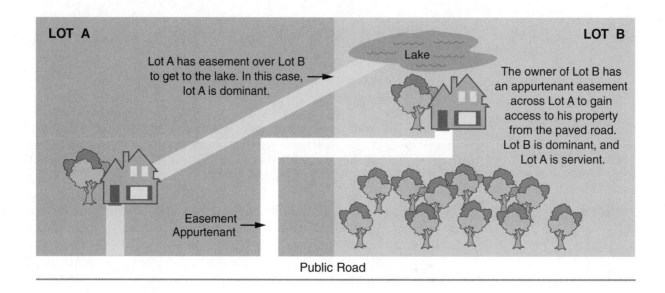

LOT A

Lot A has easement over Lot B to get to the lake. In this case, lot A is dominant.

Lake

LOT B

The owner of Lot B has an appurtenant easement across Lot A to gain access to his property from the paved road. Lot B is dominant, and Lot A is servient.

Easement Appurtenant

Public Road

FIGURE 5.4

Easement: Dominant Tenement

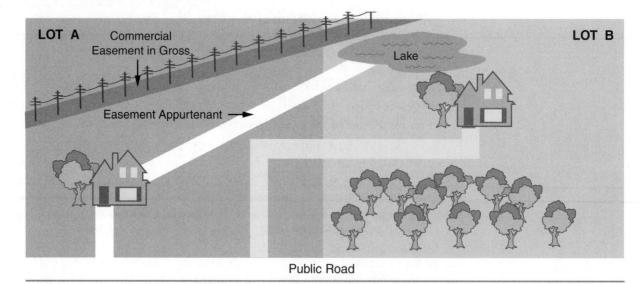

LOT A

Commercial Easement in Gross

Lake

LOT B

Easement Appurtenant

Public Road

The owner of Lot A has an appurtenant easement across Lot B to gain access to the lake. Lot A is dominant and Lot B is servient. The utility company has commercial easement in gross across both parcels of land for its power lines.

Easements in gross, on the other hand, exist to provide entities, such as utility companies, sewage authorities, railroads, and other means of transport, a necessary right of way through people's real estate. Easements in gross may also be granted by a landowner to another person for a specific purpose, such as permitting a friend to cross the property. Commercial easements may be assigned, conveyed, and inherited. However, personal easements in gross terminate on the death of the easement owner. An easement in gross should not be confused with a personal right of license, which will be discussed later in this chapter.

Creating an easement. An easement is commonly created by a written agreement between the parties that establishes the easement right. An easement also may be created by the grantor when a deed is conveyed, with the grantor either reserving an easement over the sold land or granting the new owner an easement over the grantor's remaining land. An easement may be created by longtime usage, as in an easement by prescription; by necessity; and by implication, that is, the parties' actions imply that they intend to create an easement. The creation of an easement involves two separate parties, one of whom is the owner of the land over which the easement runs. The owner of a parcel of property cannot have an easement over his or her own land.

An **easement by necessity** is created by a court order based on the principle that owners have the right to enter and exit their land; that is, they should not be landlocked. The easement is a necessity, not merely for convenience or to validate a shortcut. An easement by necessity commonly arises when an owner sells part of his or her land that has no access to a street or public way except over the seller's remaining land. This easement is an appurtenant easement with a common grantor, that is, the person who grants the ownership of the land is also the grantor of the easement. The party responsible for landlocking the parcel would be required by a court to provide access to that parcel of land.

In Your State

PA An **easement by prescription**, or *prescriptive easement,* is created when the person claiming the easement has made use of another's land for a time period defined by state law, which is 21 years in Pennsylvania. The claimant's use must have been continuous, exclusive, and without the owner's approval. The use must be visible, open, and notorious, that is, the owner must have been able to learn of it. The claimant is entitled to assert a right to use the property and cannot claim ownership. Prescriptive easements cannot usually be acquired on public land. An easement by prescription is awarded if the claimant meets all of the requirements and provides sufficient proof in court. ■

Remember the conditions to claim a prescriptive easement by the acronym **CANOE:**

Continuous
Adverse
Notorious
Open
Exclusive

The concept of *tacking* provides that successive periods of continuous occupation by different parties may be combined (tacked) to reach the required total number of years necessary to establish a claim for a prescriptive easement. To tack one person's possession onto that of another, the parties must have been successors in interest, such as an ancestor and his or her heir, a landlord and a tenant, or a seller and buyer.

An **easement by condemnation** is created under the government's right of eminent domain. This easement is acquired for a public purpose. As with any other condemnation proceeding, the owner of the affected property must be properly compensated for the easement.

Easements also may be created when the improvements on the land straddle property boundaries. A **party wall** can be an exterior wall of a building that sits on the boundary line between two lots, or it can be a commonly shared partition between two properties. Each lot owner owns the half of the wall on his or her lot, and each has an appurtenant easement in the other half of the wall. Typically, a written party wall agreement is used to create the easement rights and provide for shared expenses for building and maintaining the wall. Similarly, a *common* or *party driveway* straddles property boundaries and creates easement rights for the use of the driveway. These rights are usually addressed by written agreement.

Terminating an easement.   Easements may be ended

- when the purpose for which the easement was created no longer exists;
- when the owner of either the dominant or the servient tenement becomes the owner of both and the properties are merged under one legal description (also known as *termination by merger*);
- by release of the right of easement to the owner of the servient tenement;
- by abandonment of the easement (the intention of the parties is the determining factor);
- by nonuse of a prescriptive easement;
- by adverse possession by the owner of the servient tenement;
- by destruction of the servient tenement (for instance, the demolition of a party wall);
- by lawsuit (an action to quiet title) against someone claiming an easement; or
- by excessive use, as when a residential use is converted to commercial purposes.

Note that an easement may not automatically terminate for these reasons. Certain legal steps may be required.

IN PRACTICE

Easements are common encumbrances, especially for public utilities. A landowner cannot interfere with the rights of an easement holder. However, easements can hinder the owner's use of the property. For example, a landowner would be prevented from building a structure where it would block access to a sewer easement. A landowner should be familiar with any easements, preferably before rather than after, he or she purchases a property or makes plans for using it.

License

A **license** is a *personal privilege* to enter the land of another for a specific purpose. A license differs from an easement in that it can be terminated or canceled by the licensor (the person who granted the license). If a right to use another's property is given orally or informally, it generally is considered to be a license rather than a personal easement in gross. A license ends on the death of either party or the sale of the land by the licensor. Examples of a license include permission to park in a neighbor's driveway and the privileges that a ticket to a theater or a sporting event conveys.

Encroachments

An **encroachment** occurs when all or part of an improvement (such as a building, fence, or driveway) *illegally extends beyond the land of its owner or beyond the legal building lines.* The wrongful invasion by a person who has no lawful right to another's property is also known as a *trespass.* Encroachments can occur below the surface and in the airspace (such as overhanging tree limbs) as well as on the land. Encroachments usually occur as the result of poor planning or carelessness, rather than as purposeful illegal acts.

An encroachment usually is disclosed by either a physical inspection of the property or a spot survey. A spot survey shows the location of all improvements located on a property and whether they extend over the lot or building lines. As a rule, a spot survey is more accurate and reliable than a simple physical inspection. If a building encroaches on adjoining land, the neighbor may be able to either recover damages or secure removal of the portion of the building that encroaches. Encroachments that exceed the state's prescriptive period, however, may give rise to easements by prescription.

IN PRACTICE

Because an undisclosed encroachment could make a title unmarketable, an encroachment should be noted in a listing agreement and the agreement of sale. Unless a spot survey is available when the title is being examined, the title evidence customarily provided for settlement of the transaction does not uncover an encroachment.

■ WATER RIGHTS

Waterfront property has always been desirable, whether for agricultural, recreational, or other purposes. Each state has strict laws that govern the ownership and use of water as well as the adjacent land. The laws are also closely linked to climatic, topographical, and environmental conditions. Where water is plentiful, for instance, many states rely on the simple parameters set by the common-law doctrines of riparian and littoral rights. Where water is scarce, a state may control all but limited domestic use of water according to the doctrine of prior appropriation.

Riparian Rights

Riparian refers to **r**ivers, streams, and similar waterways.

Littoral refers to lakes, oceans, and similar commercially navigable waterways.

Riparian rights are common-law rights granted to owners of land along the course of a river, stream, or similar body of water. These owners have the unrestricted right to use the water. The only limitation is that the owner cannot interrupt or alter the flow of the water or contaminate it in any way. In addition, an owner of land that borders a nonnavigable waterway (that is, a body of water unsuitable for commercial boat traffic) owns the land under the water to the exact center of the waterway. Land adjoining navigable rivers, on the other hand, is usually owned to the water's edge, with the state holding title to the submerged land. (See Figure 5.5.) Navigable waters are considered public highways on which the public has an easement or right to travel, even if the navigable waterway flows through privately owned land. The laws governing and defining riparian rights differ from state to state.

Riparian Rights

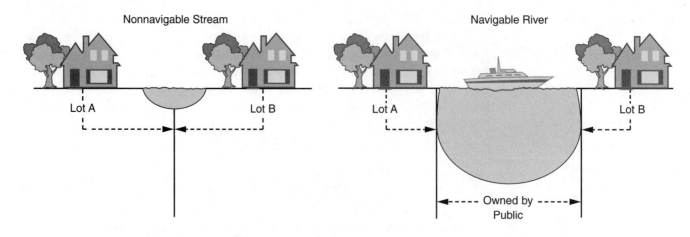

Nonnavigable Stream | Navigable River

Lot A | Lot B | Lot A | Lot B

Owned by
Public

Littoral Rights

Closely related to riparian rights are the **littoral rights** of owners whose land borders commercially navigable lakes, seas, and oceans. Owners with littoral rights enjoy unrestricted use of available waters but own the land adjacent to the water only up to the mean (average) high-water mark. (See Figure 5.6.) All land below this point is owned by the government.

Riparian and littoral rights are appurtenant (attached) to the land and cannot be retained when the property is sold. The right to use the water belongs to whoever owns the bordering land, and the former owner cannot retain that right after the land is sold.

The amount of land an individual owns may be affected by the natural action of the water. An owner is entitled to all land created through *accretion*—increases in the land resulting from the deposit of soil by the water's action. These deposits are *alluvion* or *alluvium*. On the other hand, an owner may lose land through erosion. This is the gradual and imperceptible wearing away of the land by natural forces, such as wind, rain, and flowing water. Fortunately, erosion usually takes hundreds or even thousands of years to have any noticeable effect on a person's property. This contrasts with *avulsion*, which is the sudden removal of soil by an act of nature.

A riparian owner generally does not lose title to land lost by avulsion. Boundary lines stay the same, no matter how much soil is lost. In contrast, a riparian owner loses title to any land washed away by erosion.

Doctrine of Prior Appropriation

In states where water is scarce, the ownership and use of water are often determined by the **doctrine of prior appropriation.** Under this doctrine, the state, rather than the adjacent landowner, controls the right to use any water, with the exception of limited domestic use. Ownership of the land bordering bodies of water in prior appropriation states is generally determined in the same way as riparian and littoral ownership.

Littoral Rights

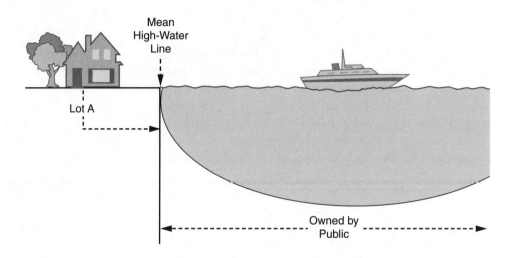

To secure water rights in prior appropriation states, a landowner must demonstrate to a state agency that he or she plans a *beneficial* use for the water, such as crop irrigation. If the state's requirements are met, the landowner receives a permit to use a specified amount of water for the limited purpose of the beneficial use. Although statutes governing prior appropriation vary from state to state, the priority of the water right is usually determined by the oldest recorded permit date.

Once granted, water rights attach to the land of the permit holder. The permit holder may sell such a water right to another party. Issuance of a water permit does not grant access to the water source. All access rights-of-way over the land of another (easements) must be obtained from the property owner.

■ SUMMARY

An individual's ownership rights are subject to the powers held by government. These powers include the police powers, by which states can enact legislation such as environmental protection laws and zoning ordinances. The government may also acquire privately owned land for public use through the power of eminent domain. Real estate taxes are imposed to raise government funds. Ownership of the property may revert, or escheat, to the state when an owner dies with no will and no heirs.

An estate in land refers to the degree, quantity, nature, and extent of interest a person holds. Freehold estates are estates of indeterminate length. Less-than-freehold estates are called leasehold estates. Freehold estates are further divided into estates of inheritance and life estates. Estates of inheritance include fee simple and defeasible fee estates. There are two types of life estates:

conventional life estates, which are created by acts of the parties; and legal life estates, which are created by law.

Encumbrances against real estate may be in the form of liens, restrictions, easements, licenses, and encroachments.

An easement is the right acquired by one person to use another's real estate. Easements are interests in real estate, but are not estates in land. The two categories of easements are appurtenant easements and easements in gross. Appurtenant easements involve two adjacent and separately owned tracts. The tract benefited is known as the dominant tenement; the tract that is subject to (or burdened by) the easement is called the servient tenement. An easement in gross is an individual right, such as that granted to utility companies to maintain poles, wires, and pipelines.

Easements may be created by agreement, grant, or reservation in a deed, longtime usage (a prescriptive easement), necessity, implication, condemnation, or party-wall agreement. They can be terminated when the purpose of the easement no longer exists, by merger of both interests with an express intention to extinguish the easement, by release, or by an intention to abandon the easement.

A license is permission to enter another's property for a specific purpose. A license is usually created orally, is of a temporary nature, and can be revoked.

An encroachment is an unauthorized use of another's real estate.

Ownership of land encompasses not only the land itself but also the right to use the water on or adjacent to it. The common-law doctrine of riparian rights gives the owner of land adjacent to a nonnavigable stream ownership of the land to the stream's midpoint. Littoral rights are held by owners of land bordering commercially navigable lakes and oceans and include rights to the water and ownership of the land up to the mean high-water mark. In states where water is scarce, the doctrine of prior appropriation often decides water use. Under prior appropriation, water belongs to the state and allocates to users who have obtained permits.

QUESTIONS

1. The right of a governmental body to take ownership of real estate for public benefit is called
   a. escheat.
   b. eminent domain.
   c. condemnation.
   d. police power.

2. A purchaser of real estate learned that the ownership rights will continue forever and that no other person claims to be the owner or has any ownership control over the property. This person owns a
   a. fee simple interest.
   b. life estate.
   c. determinable fee estate.
   d. fee simple on condition.

3. *J* owned the fee simple title to a vacant lot adjacent to a hospital and was persuaded to make a gift of the lot. She wanted to have some control over its use, so her attorney prepared her deed to convey ownership of the lot to the hospital "so long as it is used for hospital purposes." After completion of the gift, the hospital will own a
   a. fee simple absolute estate.
   b. license.
   c. fee simple determinable.
   d. leasehold estate.

4. After *D* had purchased his house and moved in, he discovered that his neighbor regularly used his driveway to reach a garage located on the neighbor's property. *D's* attorney explained that ownership of the neighbor's real estate includes an easement over the driveway. *D's* property is called
   a. the dominant tenement.
   b. defeasible estate.
   c. a leasehold.
   d. the servient tenement.

5. A *license* is an example of a(n)
   a. appurtenant easement.
   b. encroachment.
   c. temporary use right.
   d. restriction.

6. Which of the following is classified as a life estate?
   a. An estate *pur autre vie*
   b. An estate held by lease
   c. An estate without condition
   d. A fee simple estate

7. If the owner of real estate does not take action against a trespasser before the statutory period has passed, the trespasser may acquire a(n)
   a. easement by necessity.
   b. license.
   c. easement by implication of law.
   d. prescriptive easement.

8. Many states determine water use by allocating water to users who hold recorded beneficial use permits. This type of water use privilege is called
   a. riparian rights.
   b. littoral rights.
   c. the doctrine of prior appropriation.
   d. the doctrine of highest and best use.

9. All of the following are powers of the government *EXCEPT*
   a. condemnation.
   b. police power.
   c. eminent domain.
   d. taxation.

10. Property deeded to a school "for educational purposes only" convey a
    a. fee simple absolute.
    b. fee simple on condition precedent.
    c. leasehold interest.
    d. fee simple on condition subsequent.

11. *T* has the legal right to pass over the land owned by his neighbor. This is
    a. an estate in land.
    b. an easement.
    c. police power.
    d. an encroachment.

12. A father conveys ownership of his residence to his daughter but reserves for himself a life estate in the residence. The interest the daughter owns during her father's lifetime is
    a. pur autre vie.
    b. a remainder.
    c. a reversion.
    d. a leasehold.

13. K has fenced his property. The fence extends one foot over his lot line onto the property of a neighbor, M. The fence is an example of a(n)
    a. license.
    b. encroachment.
    c. easement by necessity.
    d. easement by prescription.

14. K has permission from X to hike on X's property during the summer. K has
    a. an easement by necessity.
    b. an easement by condemnation.
    c. riparian rights.
    d. a license.

15. Encumbrances on real estate
    a. include easements, encroachments, and licenses.
    b. make it possible to sell the encumbered property.
    c. must all be removed before the title can be transferred.
    d. are of no monetary value to those who own them.

16. A tenant in an apartment holds a(n)
    a. easement.
    b. license.
    c. freehold interest.
    d. leasehold interest.

17. The acquisition of land through deposit of soil or sand washed up by water is called
    a. accretion.
    b. avulsion.
    c. erosion.
    d. condemnation.

ANSWERS

1. B Under our system of property law, the government retains the right to take ownership of privately owned real estate if the taking is for the public good and the owner receives just compensation. The right or power of the government is eminent domain; the method or process is condemnation. (p. 61)

2. A The highest quality of interest in real estate is fee simple ownership. The owner is entitled to all rights of ownership, limited only by public or private restrictions. The owner's rights last for an unlimited duration. (p. 62)

3. C One ownership interest that is subject to a special limitation, such as a limitation on use for a specific purpose, is a fee simple determinable estate. The key phrase is "so long as…" If the new owner fails to comply with the limitation, the former owner reacquires full ownership. (p. 64)

4. D In an easement appurtenant, the parcel over which the easement runs is known as the servient tenement—meaning that it serves the other property. Owner *D*'s property is subject to the easement, which benefits the neighbor, who is the dominant tenement. (p. 67)

5. C A personal privilege or right to use land of another for a specific purpose is known as a license. It does not create an interest in the land for the license holder but provides a temporary right of use. (p. 70)

6. A While the duration of a life estate can be measured by the duration of the life tenant's life, it may also be measured against the life of someone other than the life tenant. Such an estate is known as an "estate *pur autre vie*," meaning "for the lifetime of another." (p. 65)

7. D If a party uses real estate that he or she does not own, does so without the owner's consent, and continues to do so for the period of time established by state law, that party may be able to successfully claim an easement by prescription. (p. 69)

8. C In states that subscribe to the doctrine of prior appropriation, the right to use water is controlled by the state. To secure water rights in these states, a landowner must secure a permit to use a specified amount of water for a beneficial use. (p. 73)

9. A Condemnation is the process by which the government acquires ownership of private property. Condemnation is not a right, but rather the method by which the government exercises its right of eminent domain. (p. 61)

10. D Property conveyed "for educational purposes only" or some other condition creates a fee simple estate qualified by a "condition subsequent." If the condition is broken, the former owner can initiate legal action to reclaim ownership. (pp. 63–64)

11. B A legal right to cross over the land of a neighbor would be classified as an easement. Typically it would be an easement in gross, which benefits a person rather than the land. (p. 67)

12. B The father has conveyed a future interest to his daughter, known as a remainder interest. During his life, the father owns the life estate and is the life tenant. Upon his death, ownership passes to the daughter as the remainderman. (p. 65)

13. B If all, or part, of an improvement, such as a fence, extends beyond the property line, the fence becomes an encroachment on the property of the neighbor. (p. 71)

14. D Permission to enter upon or use property of another for a specific purpose creates a personal privilege or license, which may be unilaterally revoked by the licensor. (p. 70)

15. A Any right or interest held by someone other than the fee owner that affects title to real estate is an encumbrance. Easements, encroachments, and licenses are examples of encumbrances. (pp. 66–67)

16. D A tenant occupying an apartment under a lease acquires a leasehold interest in the property. A leasehold is less than an ownership or freehold interest. (p. 62)

17. A The natural action of water can increase or diminish the amount of land owned. The increase, and hence the acquisition of land, by the water's action is accretion. The actual deposits of soil are known as alluvion or alluvium. Erosion diminishes the amount of land owned. (p. 73)

6

LANDLORD AND TENANT INTERESTS

■ LEARNING OBJECTIVES

When you've finished reading this chapter, you should be able to

■ identify the four types of leasehold estates;
■ recognize the various types of leases and describe requirements for validity;
■ explain how leases may be discharged and rights of the parties in eviction proceedings;
■ explain the impact of civil rights laws on landlord-tenant relationships; and
■ define the key terms.

■ KEY TERMS

actual eviction

assignment

confession of judgment
    clause

constructive eviction

estate (tenancy) at
    sufferance

estate (tenancy) at will

estate (tenancy) for
    years

estate (tenancy) from
    period to period

gross lease

ground lease

holdover tenancy

lease

lessor

lessee

month-to-month tenancy

net lease

percentage lease

periodic tenancy

security deposit

sublease

suit for possession

warranty of habitability

■ LEASEHOLD ESTATES

Estates in land identify the nature and extent of an interest in real property. Freehold estates, which are *ownership* estates, were discussed in Chapter 5. Leasehold (less-than-freehold) estates are *possessory* estates. The person who has a leasehold estate—the tenant—has the exclusive right to possess and occupy a property. The owner of the real estate—the landlord—retains all other rights of ownership. The tenant's right of possession is personal property.

Although written contracts are not necessary to create leasehold estates, they are commonly used and even required in certain situations. A lease agreement serves two purposes: It conveys the possessory interest in the real estate, and it specifies the rent and other rights and obligations of the tenant and the landlord.

Just as there are several types of freehold estates, as was discussed in Chapter 5, there are different kinds of leasehold estates.

■ ESTATE (TENANCY) FOR YEARS

An **estate (tenancy) for years** is a leasehold estate that continues for a *definite period of time*. That period may be years, months, weeks, or even days. An estate for years always has a specific starting and ending date. When the estate expires, the tenant is required to vacate the premises and surrender possession to the owner.

Estate for years = any definite period; specific termination date.

No notice is required to terminate an estate for years. This is because a specific expiration date was determined when the estate was created. When that date comes, the tenant's rights are extinguished. If both parties agree, the estate for years may be terminated prior to the expiration date. Otherwise, neither party may terminate without showing that the contract has been breached. Any extension of the tenancy requires the negotiation of a new contract, unless the original agreement provides for conversion to a periodic tenancy.

As is characteristic of all leaseholds, an estate for years gives the tenant the right to occupy and use the property according to the terms and conditions in the lease agreement. It must be remembered that a tenant has the right to use the premises for the entire period of the estate. That right is unaffected by the landowner's death or the sale of the property, unless a lease agreement specifies otherwise.

Periodic Estate (Tenancy)

A **periodic tenancy,** sometimes called an **estate (tenancy) from period to period** or from *year to year*, is created when landlord and tenant enter into an agreement for an *indefinite time*. That is, the estate does not contain a specific expiration date. Such a tenancy is created initially to run for a definite term—for instance, month to month, week to week, or year to year—but continues indefinitely until proper notice of termination is given.

Periodic estate = indefinite term; automatically renewing; no specific termination date.

A periodic tenancy is characterized by *continuity,* that is, it automatically renews itself under the original terms of the agreement for similar succeeding periods until one of the parties gives notice to terminate. Rent is payable at definite intervals. In effect, the payment and acceptance of rent extends the lease for another period. A **month-to-month tenancy,** for example, is created when a tenant takes possession with no definite termination date and pays rent on a monthly basis. Periodic tenancies are commonly used in residential leases.

An estate from period to period can be created when a tenant with an estate for years remains in possession, or holds over, after the lease term expires. If no new lease agreement has been made, a **holdover tenancy** is created. The landlord may evict the tenant or treat the holdover tenant as one who holds a periodic tenancy. The landlord's acceptance of rent usually is considered conclusive proof of the landlord's acquiescence to the periodic tenancy. The courts customarily rule that a tenant who holds over can do so for a term equal to the term of the original lease, provided the period is for one year or less. For example, a tenant with a lease for six months would be entitled to a new six-month tenancy. However, if the original lease was for five years, the holdover tenancy could not exceed one year. Some leases stipulate that in the absence of a renewal agreement, a tenant who holds over does so as a month-to-month tenant.

In Your State

PA   To terminate a periodic estate, either the landlord or the tenant must give proper notice. The form and timing of the notice are usually stated in the written lease agreement. The Pennsylvania Landlord/Tenant Act also specifies the time period that is required for notice in a variety of circumstances. Normally, one week's notice is required to terminate an estate from week to week; one month's notice is required to terminate an estate from month to month; and three months' notice is required to terminate an estate from year to year. ■

Estate (Tenancy) at Will

Estate at will = indefinite term; possession with landlord's consent.

An **estate (tenancy) at will** gives the tenant the right to possess property *with the landlord's consent for an unspecified or uncertain term*. An estate at will is a tenancy of indefinite duration. It continues until it is terminated by either party giving proper notice. No definite initial period is specified, as is the case in a periodic tenancy. An estate at will automatically terminates by the death of either the landlord or the tenant. It may be created by express agreement or by operation of law. During a tenancy at will, the tenant has all the rights and obligations of a lessor-lessee relationship, including payment of rent at regular intervals.

As a practical matter, tenancy at will is rarely created by written agreement. This tenancy is viewed unfavorably by the courts and is usually interpreted as a periodic tenancy, with the period being defined by the interval of rental payments.

Estate (Tenancy) at Sufferance

Estate at sufferance = tenant's previously lawful possession continued without landlord's consent.

An **estate (tenancy) at sufferance** arises when a tenant who lawfully possessed real property continues in possession of the premises *without the landlord's consent* after the rights expire. This estate can arise when a tenant for years fails to surrender possession at the expiration of the lease. A tenancy at sufferance also can occur after a foreclosure sale when a borrower, without consent of the purchaser, continues in possession of the property.

■ LEASE AGREEMENTS

A **lease** is a contract between an owner of real estate, the landlord or the **lessor,** and a tenant, the **lessee.** In effect the lease agreement is a combination of a conveyance of an interest in the real estate and a contract to pay rent and assume other obligations. The lessor grants the lessee the right to occupy the real estate and use it for certain stated purposes. In return, the landlord receives payment for the use of the premises and retains a reversionary right to retake possession after the lease term has expired. The lessor's interest is called a *leased fee estate plus reversionary right.*

In Your State

PA   No special wording is required to establish the landlord-tenant relationship. The lease may be written, oral, or implied, depending on the circumstances. The statute of frauds in Pennsylvania, which requires contracts conveying interests in real estate be written to be enforceable (to force a party to perform), applies to leases for more than three years' duration. In other words, a lease for more than three years must be in writing. An oral lease for three years or less is usually enforceable. However, a written agreement may be used for any period of time. ■

IN PRACTICE

While the statute of frauds in Pennsylvania requires that leases for more than three years be in writing to enforce performance on the contract, the State Real Estate Commission's Rules and Regulations require licensees to use written contracts. References to oral leases are relevant when no licensee is involved in the transaction. As a practical matter, written leases, as long as they are sufficiently detailed, provide concrete evidence of the terms and conditions to which the parties have agreed and thus help avoid misunderstandings and controversies.

In accordance with contract law, the requirements for a valid lease are essentially the same as for any other contract (discussed in detail in Chapter 11). There must be an offer and acceptance supported by valid consideration. (Rent is the normal consideration given for the right to occupy the leased premises.) The parties must have legal capacity to contract, meaning they are of legal age and have sufficient mental capacity to understand the consequences of their actions, and the objective of the contract must be legal, which means that the contract must contemplate a legal purpose. (An example of a typical residential lease is shown in Figure 6.2 at the end of this chapter.)

Possession of Premises

The lessor, as the owner of the real estate, is usually bound by the implied *covenant of quiet enjoyment.* This covenant is a presumed promise by the lessor that the lessee may take possession of the leased premises. The landlord further guarantees not to interfere in the tenant's legal possession or use of the property or permit any other party to interfere.

In Your State

PA   In Pennsylvania, the landlord must give the tenant *actual* occupancy, or possession, of the leased premises. If the premises are occupied by a holdover tenant or adverse claimant at the beginning of the new lease period, the landlord must take whatever action is necessary (including bearing any expenses involved) to recover actual possession in order to deliver possession to the lessee. ■

Use of Premises

A lessor may restrict a lessee's use of the premises through provisions in the lease. Use restrictions are particularly common in leases for retail and commercial space. For instance, a lease may state that the leased premises are to be used "only for a real estate brokerage office and for no other purpose." In the absence of such limitations, a lessee may use the premises for any lawful purpose.

Term of Lease

The term of a lease is the period of the leasehold estate. The term should be stated precisely, including the beginning and ending date together with a statement of the total period of the lease. For instance, a lease might run for a term of 30 years beginning June 1, 2005, and ending May 31, 2035, or for a term of three years beginning September 1, 2005, and ending August 31, 2008.

In Your State   **PA**   Perpetual leases for an inordinate amount of time or an indefinite term usually are ruled as invalid. However, if the language in the lease and the surrounding circumstances clearly indicate that the parties intend such a term, the lease will be binding on the parties. Some states prohibit leases that run for 100 years or more. In Pennsylvania, the law requires payment of transfer taxes on leases that run for more than a total of 30 years. ■

Security Deposits

Most leases require the tenant to provide the landlord with some form of **security deposit.** If the tenant defaults on rent payments or damages the premises, the lessor may keep all or part of the deposit as compensation for the loss. The specific nature of the loss the landlord is entitled to recover from the security deposit has been subject to various interpretations. Some assert that the intent of the security deposit is to compensate the landlord for damage to the premises, not damage (loss) from defaulted rent. To avoid controversy, the purpose of the security deposit and the recovery the landlord may claim from the security deposit should be clearly stated in the lease agreement.

Other safeguards for nonpayment of rent may be used. The landlord may require the tenant to make an advance rental payment or have a third person guarantee payment, or the landlord may contract for a lien on the tenant's property.

IN PRACTICE

A lease should specify whether a payment is a security deposit or an advance rental payment. If it is a security deposit, the tenant is usually not entitled to apply it to the final month's rent. If it is an advance rental, the landlord must treat it as income for tax purposes.

In Your State   **PA**   **Pennsylvania law.** Landlords are limited in the amount of security deposit they may require residential tenants to pay. For the first year of tenancy, the maximum amount of the security deposit cannot exceed a sum equivalent to two months' rent. At the beginning of the second year of tenancy, the amount drops to a sum equivalent to one month's rent. This means that the landlord must return to the tenant any amount that exceeds the monthly rent being charged in the second year. During the second through fifth years of a lease, the landlord may increase the amount of security deposit, following the same monthly equivalency formula, to keep pace with increasing rents. However, after a lease has run for five years, the landlord cannot increase the amount of security deposit. ■

Landlords are required to hold security deposits in an escrow account in a federally regulated or state-regulated banking or savings institution. The landlord must notify the tenant of the name and address of the institution and the amount of deposit being held on his or her account. The law also states that if the amount of the security deposit exceeds $100, the landlord must deposit the funds in an interest-bearing account commencing on the second anniversary of the lease. Interest earned on the deposit must be paid to the tenant each year on the anniversary of the lease. However, the landlord may retain 1 percent of the annual interest earned to defray administrative expenses.

The landlord must return the tenant's security deposit, including any interest owed, within 30 days of the termination of the tenancy. The tenant must provide a forwarding address, in writing, to the landlord or agent so as not to forfeit a security deposit that might otherwise be returned. If the landlord withholds money for damages, the claim must be substantiated with an itemized list describing the nature and cost of the damages. The difference between the funds being held (including unpaid interest) and the damages is then returned to the tenant. A landlord who fails to settle the security account within the 30-day period forfeits all rights to the security deposit. Furthermore, the landlord is liable for double the amount of the security deposit.

IN PRACTICE

Licensed real estate brokers acting on behalf of a landlord may collect rents and hold security deposits for their clients. In addition to landlord-tenant law, licensees must be familiar with the requirements of license law that address the responsible care and management of these funds. Provisions include the maintenance of rental management accounts, into which rents are deposited, and the administration of escrow accounts, in which security deposits as well as "hand money" in sales transactions are held. Both of these accounts must be separate from the broker's general business accounts.

Bond in lieu of escrowing.   Pennsylvania law permits a landlord to purchase a guarantee, or surety, bond to guarantee the return of a security deposit to the tenant. The landlord may exercise this option in lieu of escrowing a security deposit in a financial institution. The landlord must return the amount of the bond (including any interest) less the cost of any necessary repairs to the tenant at the end of the lease term.

Improvements

Neither the landlord nor the tenant is required to make improvements to the leased property. However, the parties may elect to do so. The tenant may, with the landlord's permission or in accordance with the lease, improve the property to enhance the utility or enjoyment of the property. Unless the parties agree otherwise, the alterations (fixtures) become the landlord's property. Customarily, the tenant is permitted to remove trade fixtures before the lease expires as long as the tenant restores the premises to their previous condition.

Accessibility.   Residential landlords must permit people with disabilities, at their own expense, to make reasonable modifications to the property that may be necessary for their enjoyment of the premises. However, a landlord can require, if it is reasonable to do so, that the interior of the premises be restored to its previous condition if the modifications would make the property undesirable to the general population. Both the federal Fair Housing Act and the Pennsylvania Human Relations Act describe the scope of these rights and the procedures that must be followed. These laws as well as the Americans with Disabilities Act also describe accessibility and usability for commercial properties. These laws are discussed in detail in Chapter 17.

Maintenance of Premises

In Your State

PA   Many states, including Pennsylvania, require a residential lessor to maintain dwelling units in a habitable condition. Landlords must make any necessary repairs to the common areas (hallways, stairs, elevators, etc.) and maintain safety features, such as fire sprinklers and smoke alarms. The tenant does not have to repair the property but must return the premises at the end of the lease in the same condition they were received, with allowances for ordinary wear and tear. ■

Destruction of Premises

In land leases involving agricultural land, the courts have held that when the improvements are damaged or destroyed, even if it is not the tenant's fault, the tenant is obligated to pay rent through the end of the term. This ruling has been extended in most states to include ground leases for land on which the tenant has constructed a building. In many instances, it also includes leases that give possession of an entire building to the tenant. In this case, the tenant leases the land on which that building is located, as well as the structure itself.

A tenant who leases only a part of the building (such as office or commercial space or a residential apartment), however, is not required to continue paying rent after the leased premises are destroyed. In some states, if the property is destroyed as a result of the landlord's negligence, the tenant can even recover damages from the landlord.

Assignment and Subleasing

A tenant who transfers all of the leasehold interests *assigns* the lease. On the other hand, a tenant who transfers *less than all* of the leasehold interests, *subleases* the premises to a new tenant. (See Figure 6.1.) Assignment and subleasing are permitted whenever the lease does not prohibit these actions.

> An assignment transfers all leasehold interests, whereas a sublease transfers less than all leasehold interests.

In most cases, the sublease or assignment of a lease does not relieve the original lessee of the obligation to pay rent. The landlord may, however, agree to waive the former tenant's liability. Most leases prohibit the lessee from assigning or subletting without the lessor's consent. This permits the landlord to retain control over the occupancy of the leased premises. As a rule, the lessor must not unreasonably withhold consent. The sublessor's (original lessee's) interest in the real estate is known as a *sandwich lease*.

Confession of Judgment

To help the landlord collect delinquent rent, a **confession of judgment clause** may be included in a lease. In this clause, the tenant authorizes an attorney of record to appear in court in the tenant's name and confess judgment in

Assignment versus Sublease

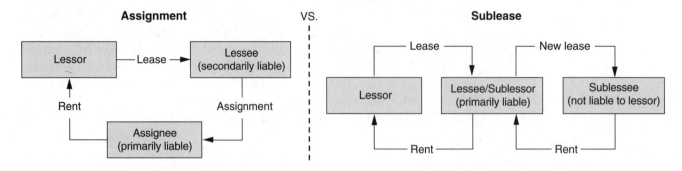

favor of the landlord. This means the tenant agrees that a judgment for the amount of delinquent rent, court costs, and attorney's fees can be entered against the tenant. Because of concerns that tenants may not understand the legal action they authorize, confession of judgment clauses are not permitted in residential leases in many states.

In Your State   **PA**   In Pennsylvania, tenants in certain situations must be given an *explanation of rights* informing them of the consequence of confession of judgment when they sign a lease that contains this clause. ■

Recording a Lease

Possession of leased premises is considered constructive notice to the world of the tenant's leasehold interests. Anyone who inspects the property receives actual notice. For these reasons, recording a lease is usually considered unnecessary. Unless a lease specifically states that recording is prohibited, however, leases can be recorded in the county where the property is located. Furthermore, leases of three years or longer often are recorded as a matter of course. In fact, some states require that long-term leases be recorded, especially when the lessees intend to mortgage the leasehold interest.

In Your State   **PA**   In Pennsylvania, only a memorandum of lease is filed. A memorandum of lease gives notice of the interest but does not disclose the terms of the lease to the public. Only the names of the parties and a description of the property are included. ■

Options

A lease may contain a clause that grants the lessee the *option* or privilege of *renewing* or extending the lease. However, the lessee must give notice before a specific date of the intention to exercise the option. Some leases grant the lessee the *option to purchase* the leased premises. This option normally gives the tenant the right to purchase the property at a predetermined price within a certain time period, possibly the term of the lease. Although it is not required, the owner may give the tenant credit toward the purchase price for some of the rent paid during the lease. The lease agreement is a primary contract over the option to purchase. Options are discussed further in Chapter 19.

An option is not to be confused with a *lease purchase*. In a lease purchase, the tenant simultaneously enters two contracts: an agreement to purchase and a lease. The tenant agrees to purchase the property but has a lease until the terms in the purchase agreement can be fully satisfied. Perhaps the tenant cannot obtain favorable financing or clear title, or the tax consequences of a current purchase would be unfavorable. In the meantime, the tenant has use of the property. Often, part of the periodic rent is applied toward the purchase price until it is reduced to an amount for which the tenant can obtain financing or purchase the property outright. Unlike a lease with an option to purchase, a lease purchase agreement is the primary contract over the lease.

IN PRACTICE

Throughout the discussion about lease contracts, there are repeated references to the fact that the terms of the lease are controlled largely by the specific details in the written contract. A landlord and tenant must be sure that the language, especially when preprinted forms are used, accurately reflects their intentions. The parties to any contract are advised to have their attorneys review the contract before signing it. Real estate licensees are cautioned not to give legal advice or draft language for legal documents.

■ TYPES OF LEASES

The manner in which rent is determined indicates the type of lease that is in force. (See Table 6.1.)

Gross Lease

In a **gross lease,** the tenant pays a *fixed rental*, and the landlord pays all taxes, insurance, mortgage payments, repairs, utilities, and the like associated with the property (usually called *property charges* or *operating expenses*). This is typically the type of rental structure used in residential leasing.

Net Lease

In a **net lease,** the tenant pays *all or some of the operating expenses* in addition to the rent. The rent paid is "net" to the landlord. A *triple net* is the label given to leases where the tenant pays all operating and other expenses, such as taxes, insurance premiums, assessments, maintenance costs, and other

TABLE   6.1

Types of Leases

Type of Lease	Lessee	Lessor
Gross lease (residential)	Pays basic rent	Pays property charges (taxes, repair costs, insurance, and the like)
Net lease (commercial/industrial)	Pays basic rent plus all or most property charges	May pay some property charges
Percentage lease (commercial/industrial)	Pays basic rent plus percent of gross sales (may pay property costs)	May pay some or all property charges

charges related to the premises. Rather than relying on broad interpretations given to the term net lease, it is essential to specify exactly which property expenses will be the tenant's responsibility. Leases for entire commercial or industrial buildings and the land on which they are located, ground leases, and long-term leases are usually net leases.

Percentage Lease

Either a gross lease or a net lease may be a **percentage lease.** The rent is based on a *percentage of the gross or net income* received by the tenant doing business on the leased property. This type of lease, which is usually used for retail businesses, gives both the landlord and tenant a share in locational advantages of the leased premises.

Under the typical percentage lease, the lessee pays a fixed minimum rent and a percentage of the tenant's gross business income (usually gross sales). The terms of the contract will specify the way the percentage is calculated. The percentage charged is negotiable and varies depending on the nature of the business, the location of the property, and general economic conditions. A tenant's bargaining power is determined by the volume of business the tenant does.

MATH CONCEPTS

% ÷
X +

CALCULATING PERCENTAGE LEASE RENTS

Percentage leases usually call for a minimum monthly rent plus a percentage of gross sales income over a stated annual amount. For example, a lease might require minimum rent of $1,300 per month plus 5 percent of the business's sales over $160,000. On an annual sales volume of $250,000, the annual rent would be calculated as follows:

$1,300 per month × 12 months = $15,600

$250,000 − $160,000 = $90,000

$90,000 × 0.05 (5%) = $4,500

$15,600 base rent + $4,500 percentage rent = $20,100 total rent

---

Other Lease Types

Variable leases.   Several types of leases allow for increases in the fixed rental charge during the lease period. One of the more common is the *graduated lease*, which provides for increases in rent at set future dates in specified amounts. Another is the *index lease*, which allows rent to be increased or decreased periodically based on changes in the consumer price index or some other index agreed to by the landlord and tenant.

Ground leases.   When a landowner leases unimproved land to a tenant who agrees to erect a building on it, the lease is usually referred to as a **ground lease.** Ground leases usually involve separate ownership of the land and building. These leases must be for a long enough term to make the transaction desirable to the tenant investing in the building. They often run for terms of 50 up to 99 years. Ground leases are generally net leases: The lessee pays rent on the ground as well as real estate taxes, insurance premiums, and upkeep and repair costs. Although ground leases are considered personal property, certain states' laws give leaseholders some of the rights and obligations of real property owners.

Oil and gas leases.   A special lease agreement is negotiated for a company to explore for oil or natural gas. Usually, the landowner receives a cash payment for executing the lease. If no well is drilled within the period stated in the lease, the lease expires. However, most agreements permit the company to continue its rights for another year by paying another flat rental fee. Such rentals may be paid annually until a well is produced. If oil or gas is found, the landowner usually receives a percentage of its value as a royalty. As long as oil or gas is obtained in significant quantities, the lease will continue indefinitely.

■ DISCHARGE OF LEASES

As with any contract, a lease is discharged when the contract terminates. Termination can occur when all parties have fully performed their obligations under the agreement or by operation of law, as in a bankruptcy or condemnation proceeding. In addition, the landlord and tenant can mutually agree to terminate the lease. For instance, the tenant may offer to surrender the leasehold interest and if the landlord accepts, the lease is terminated. However, a tenant who simply abandons the property does not terminate the lease and remains liable for the obligations stated in the lease, including rent. The lease agreement usually indicates whether the landlord must try to re-rent the space. If the landlord sues for unpaid rent, however, most states require the landlord to attempt to mitigate damages by re-renting the premises.

A lease does not terminate if the parties die; the heirs of the deceased are bound by the terms of existing leases. There are two exceptions to this general rule. A lease from the owner of a life estate (discussed in Chapter 5) ends with the death of the person against whose life the estate is measured. Similarly, a tenancy at will terminates with the death of either the landlord or tenant.

If leased real estate is sold or otherwise conveyed, the new owner takes the property subject to the rights of existing tenants. A lease agreement may, however, contain language that permits the new landlord to terminate their leases. This language, commonly known as a *sale clause*, enables the new owner to take possession of the premises and/or negotiate his or her own terms and conditions in new leases. The sale clause generally requires that the tenant be given some period of notice before the existing lease terminates.

IN PRACTICE   Both federal and state laws have been enacted to provide for termination of leases without penalty for military personnel in certain situations. Pennsylvania's military affairs law, which was amended by Act 57 of 2004, is uniform with recent amendments to federal legislation and provides for state National Guard personnel as well. As the law currently stands, a member of the armed services or Pennsylvania National Guard on full-time duty, or a civil service technician with a National Guard unit may terminate a lease provided he or she has received permanent change of station orders, temporary duty orders for a period longer than three months, an honorable discharge or release from active duty or employment, or orders for base military housing, which results in forfeiture of Basic Allowance for Housing (BHA) pay.

Breach of Lease

When a tenant breaches or violates any lease provision, the landlord may sue the tenant to obtain a judgment for past-due rent, damages to the premises, or other defaults. Likewise, when a landlord breaches any lease provision, the tenant is entitled to certain remedies.

In Your State

PA   **Suit for possession—actual eviction.** When a tenant breaches a lease or improperly retains possession of the premises, the landlord may regain possession through a **suit for possession.** This process is known as **actual eviction.** Pennsylvania law requires that the landlord serve notice to the tenant at an appropriate interval before commencing the suit. This time period could be 15 days to three months, depending on the circumstances. Once the tenant has been served notice, the landlord files a complaint; then the district justice issues a summons for the tenant to appear and answer the complaint. If the complaint is proven, the district justice enters a judgment against the tenant, ordering the tenant to deliver the property to the landlord. The judgment also may include monetary damages for the unjust detention of the premises, delinquent and unpaid rent, and other costs permitted by law or the terms of the written lease, including reasonable attorney fees. ■

When the court orders delivery of the property to the landlord, the tenant must peaceably remove himself or herself and all belongings. Otherwise, the landlord can have the judgment enforced by a constable who will *forcibly* remove the tenant and his or her possessions. Until a judgment is issued, the landlord must be careful *not* to harass the tenant in any manner such as locking the tenant out of the property, impounding the tenant's possessions, or making the property uninhabitable by disconnecting services (such as electricity and natural gas).

Tenants' remedies—constructive eviction. If a landlord breaches the terms of a lease, the tenant may sue and recover damages against the landlord. If a landlord's action or omission causes the premises to become uninhabitable for the purpose intended in the lease, the tenant has the right to abandon the property. This action, which also terminates the lease, is called **constructive eviction.**

To exercise the right of constructive eviction, the tenant must prove that the premises are uninhabitable because of the landlord's conscious neglect and the tenant must actually leave the property while uninhabitable conditions exist. For instance, if the landlord fails to repair a defective heating system and the lack of heat makes the property uninhabitable, the tenant may abandon the property. The lease, however, may describe reasonable remedies or events that are beyond the landlord's control that affect the tenant's right to constructively evict.

In Your State   **PA**   **Warranty of habitability.**   Pennsylvania courts recognize a doctrine known as **warranty of habitability** in residential leases. The theory of this warranty is that the lessor who leases residential premises warrants that the premises shall be fit for habitation. If the tenant proves that the premises are not fit for habitation, the court can order a reduction or cessation of rental payment. ■

Pro-Tenant Legislation

For the most part, leases have been drawn up to benefit the landlord. However, recent tenants' rights movements and increased consumer awareness have caused many states to adopt some variation of the *Uniform Residential Landlord and Tenant Act*. This model law takes a more balanced view of lease agreements, addressing the need for both landlord and tenant (not just the tenant) to fulfill certain obligations. The act addresses such issues as the

- landlord's right to enter the property;
- use and maintenance of the premises;
- tenant's protection against retaliation by the landlord for complaints;
- disclosure of the property owners' (or manager's) names and addresses to the tenants; and
- remedies for both the landlord and the tenant if the lease agreement is breached.

In addition, several other laws have been adopted to protect tenants. The *Tenants' Eviction Procedures Act* is a federal law that was passed in 1976 to standardize eviction procedures for people living in multiunit residential buildings that are owned or subsidized by HUD and buildings that have government-insured mortgages. The law requires the landlord to have a valid reason for evicting the tenant and to give the tenant proper notice of eviction. While this act does not supersede state laws, it does provide recourse for tenants in states where no laws exist.

In Your State   **PA**   In Pennsylvania, the *Landlord and Tenant Act of 1951* contains remedies for landlords if a lease is in default and rules of civil procedures for district justices in these cases. The Pennsylvania *Consumer Protection Law*, which prohibits unfair practices in the conduct of commerce, also provides remedies for tenants of residential property. ■

■ CIVIL RIGHTS LAWS

In Your State   **PA**   The fair housing laws affect landlords and tenants just as they do sellers and purchasers. All persons must have access to housing of their choice under the *Pennsylvania Human Relations Act* without any differentiation in the terms and conditions because of their race, color, religion, national origin, sex, age (40 years old or older), handicap, use of guide or support animals due to a handicap or disability, or familial status. Additional protected classes (such as sexual orientation) may be defined in local fair housing laws. ■

Withholding an apartment that is for rent, segregating certain persons in separate sections of an apartment complex or parts of a building, and charging different amounts for rent or security deposits when serving people in the protected classes are examples of violations of the laws. Advertising practices also are addressed, making language in an ad such as "No Children Allowed" a violation. Fair housing laws are discussed in detail in Chapter 17.

Landlords must be aware of how changes in the federal *Fair Housing Amendments Act of 1988*, followed by changes to the *Pennsylvania Human Relations Act*, significantly alter past practices, particularly when dealing with people with disabilities and families with children. Several issues relating to people with disabilities were discussed earlier in this chapter. To protect families with children, the laws require the criteria applied to adult tenants also be applied to families with children. An apartment that is suitable for two people, for instance, must be available to any two people—two adults or one adult and one child. A landlord cannot charge a different amount of rent or security deposit because one of the tenants is a child. While landlords have historically argued that children are noisy or destructive, the fact is that many adults are noisy and destructive as well.

■ SUMMARY

Leasehold estates are possessory rather than ownership estates. A leasehold estate that runs for a specific length of time creates a tenancy for years; one that runs for an indefinite period creates a periodic tenancy (year-to-year, month-to-month). An estate at will runs as long as the landlord permits, and an estate at sufferance is possession without the consent of the landlord. A leasehold estate is generally classified as personal property.

A lease agreement is a combination of a conveyance creating a leasehold interest in the property and a contract outlining the rights and obligations of the landlord and the tenant. The requirements of a valid lease include offer and acceptance, consideration, capacity to contract, and legal objective. In addition, the Pennsylvania statute of frauds requires that any lease of more than three years must be in writing to be enforceable. However, Pennsylvania real estate licensees are required to use written agreements. Leases also generally include clauses relating to rights and obligations of the landlord and tenant such as the use of the premises, subletting, judgments, maintenance of the premises, and termination of the lease period.

There are several basic types of leases, including net leases, gross leases, and percentage leases. These leases are classified according to the method used in determining the rental rate.

Leases may be terminated by the expiration of the lease period, the mutual agreement of the parties, or a breach of the lease by either landlord or tenant. In most cases, neither the death of the tenant nor the landlord's sale of the rental property terminates the lease.

Upon a tenant's default on the lease, a landlord may sue for a money judgment or for actual eviction in a case where a tenant has improperly retained possession of the premises. If the premises have become uninhabitable due to the landlord's negligence, the tenant may have the right of constructive eviction, that is, the right to abandon the premises and refuse to pay rent until the premises is repaired.

In Pennsylvania, the fair housing laws protect tenants from discrimination based on race, color, religion, national origin, sex, age (40 years or older), handicap or disability, use of guide or support animals because of a handicap or disability, or familial status.

A note to the reader: In addition to the lease information provided in this chapter, Chapter 23 introduces the reader to the activities of leasing, management, marketing, and maintenance of rental property. These activities are commonly associated with property management, an activity for which a real estate license is required in many circumstances in Pennsylvania.

F I G U R E   **6.2**

Example of a Residential Lease

RESIDENTIAL LEASE   **LR**

This form recommended and approved for, but not restricted to use by, the members of the Pennsylvania Association of REALTORS® (PAR).

LANDLORD'S BUSINESS RELATIONSHIP WITH PA LICENSED BROKER

BROKER (Company) _____ PHONE _____

AGENT _____ FAX _____

ADDRESS _____

Designated Agent(s) for Landlord, if applicable: _____

OR

Broker is NOT the Agent for Landlord and is a/an: ☐ AGENT FOR TENANT ☐ TRANSACTION LICENSEE

TENANT'S BUSINESS RELATIONSHIP WITH PA LICENSED BROKER

BROKER (Company) _____ PHONE _____

AGENT _____ FAX _____

ADDRESS _____

Designated Agent(s) for Tenant, if applicable: _____

OR

Broker is NOT the Agent for Tenant and is a/an: ☐ AGENT FOR LANDLORD ☐ SUBAGENT FOR LANDLORD ☐ TRANSACTION LICENSEE

When the same broker is Broker for Landlord and Broker for Tenant, Broker is a Dual Agent. All of Broker's licensees are also Dual Agents UNLESS there are separate Designated Agents for Landlord and Tenant. If the same Licensee is designated for Landlord and Tenant, the Licensee is a Dual Agent. Broker(s) may perform services to assist unrepresented parties in complying with the terms of this Lease.

PARTIES

1. This LEASE, dated_____is between
   LANDLORD(S) _____
   _____ called "Landlord," and
   TENANT(S)_____
   _____ called "Tenant,"
   for the Property located at _____
   _____ called "Property"
   Each Tenant is individually responsible for all obligations of this Lease, including rent, late fees, damages and other costs.
2. **CO-SIGNERS**
   Co-signers: _____
   _____
   Each Co-signer is individually responsible for all obligations of this Lease, including rent, late fees, damages and other costs.
   Co-signers do not have the right to occupy the Property as a Tenant without the Landlord's prior written permission.
3. **LANDLORD CONTACT INFORMATION**

   Rental Payments: **Maintenance Requests:**
   Payable to: _____ Contact: _____
   Address: _____ Address: _____
   _____ _____
   Phone:_____Fax:_____ Phone:_____Fax:_____

RENTAL TERM

4. **START AND END DATES OF LEASE** (also called "Term")
   (A) **Start Date:** _____, at _____ a.m./p.m.
   (B) **End Date:** _____, at _____ a.m./p.m.
5. **RENEWAL TERM (check one)**
   ☐ This Lease will AUTOMATICALLY RENEW for a term of _____(also called the "Renewal Term") at the End Date of this Lease or at the end of any Renewal Term unless:
       1. Tenant gives Landlord at least _____ days written notice before End Date or before the end of any Renewal Term, **OR**
       2. Landlord gives Tenant at least _____ days written notice before End Date or before the end of any Renewal Term.
   ☐ This Lease will TERMINATE on the End Date unless extended in writing.

RENT AND DEPOSIT

6. **RENT**
   (A) Rent is due in advance, without demand, on or before the _____ day of each month.
   (B) The total Rent due each month is: ....$ _____
   (C) The total amount of Rent due during the Term is: ....$ _____
   (D) If Rent is more than _____ days late, Tenant pays a Late Charge of: ....$ _____
   (E) All other payments due from Tenant to Landlord, including Late Charges or utility charges, are considered to be Additional Rent. Failure to pay this Additional Rent is a breach of the Lease in the same way as failing to pay the regular Rent.
   (F) Tenant agrees that all payments will be applied against outstanding Additional Rent that is due before they will be applied against the current Rent due.
   (G) Tenant will pay a fee of $ _____ for any payment that is returned by any financial institution for any reason. Any Late Charges will continue to apply until a valid payment is received.
   (H) Landlord will accept the following methods of payment: ☐ Cash ☐ Money Order ☐ Personal Check
       ☐ Credit Cards ☐ Other:_____ ☐ Other: _____

7. **PAYMENT SCHEDULE**

		Due Date	Paid	Due
(A)	Security Deposit, held in escrow by: _____	_____	$ _____	$ _____
	Held at (financial institution): _____			
(B)	First month's rent: _____	_____	$ _____	$ _____
(C)	Other: _____	_____	$ _____	$ _____
(D)	Other: _____	_____	$ _____	$ _____
	Total Rent and security deposit received to date: ....$ _____			
	Total amount due .... $ _____			

Tenant Initials:_____   LR Page 1 of 4   Landlord Initials:_____

Pennsylvania Association of REALTORS®
The Voice for Real Estate® in Pennsylvania

F I G U R E   6.2

Example of a Residential Lease (continued)

51 **8. RETURN OF SECURITY DEPOSITS (see Information Regarding Security Deposits on back)**
52   (A) When Tenant moves from the Property, Tenant will return all keys and give Landlord written notice of Tenant's new mail-
53   ing address where Landlord can return the Security Deposit.
54   (B) Within 30 days after Tenant moves from the Property, Landlord will give Tenant a written list of any damage to the
55   Property that Landlord claims Tenant is responsible for.
56   (C) Landlord may deduct repair costs and any unpaid rents from Tenant's Security Deposit. Any remaining Security Deposit
57   will be returned to Tenant within 30 days after Tenant moves from the Property.

CARE AND USE OF PROPERTY

58 **9. USE OF PROPERTY AND AUTHORIZED OCCUPANTS**
59   (A) Tenant will use Property as a residence ONLY.
60   (B) Not more than _____ people will live on Property. List all other occupants who are not listed as Tenants in
61   paragraph 1: _____
62   _____

63 **10. POSSESSION**
64   (A) Tenant may move in (take possession of the Property) on the Start Date of this Lease.
65   (B) If Tenant cannot move in within _____ days after Start Date because the previous tenant is still there or because of
66   property damage, Tenant's exclusive rights are to:
67   1. Change the starting date of the Lease to the day when Property is available. Tenant will not owe rent until Property
68   is available; OR
69   2. End the Lease and have all money already paid as rent or security deposit returned, with no further liability on the
70   part of Landlord or Tenant.

71 **11. LANDLORD'S RIGHT TO ENTER**
72   (A) Tenant agrees that Landlord or Landlord's representatives may enter the Property at reasonable hours to inspect, repair,
73   or show the Property. Tenant does not have to allow possible tenants to enter unless they are with the Landlord or
74   Landlord's representative, or they have written permission from the Landlord.
75   (B) When possible, Landlord will give Tenant_____ hours notice of the date, time, and reason for the visit.
76   (C) In emergencies, Landlord may enter Property without notice. If Tenant is not present, Landlord will tell Tenant who was
77   there and why within 24 hours of the visit.
78   (D) Landlord may put up For Sale or For Rent signs on or near Property.

79 **12. CONDITION OF PROPERTY AT MOVE IN**
80   Tenant has inspected the Property and agrees to accept the Property "as-is," except for the following: _____
81   _____
82   _____

83 **13. APPLIANCES INCLUDED**
84   ☐ Stove   ☐ Refrigerator   ☐ Dishwasher   ☐ Washer   ☐ Dryer   ☐ Garbage Disposal   ☐ Microwave
85   ☐ Air Conditioning _____   ☐Other_____   ☐Other_____
86   Landlord is responsible for repairs to appliances listed above unless otherwise stated here: _____
87   _____

88 **14. UTILITIES AND SERVICES**
89   Landlord and Tenant agree to pay for the charges for utilities and services provided for the Property as marked below. If a serv-
90   ice is not marked as being paid by the Landlord, it is the responsibility of Tenant to pay for that service. Landlord is not respon-
91   sible for loss of service if interrupted by circumstances beyond the Landlord's control.

Landlord pays	Tenant pays		Landlord pays	Tenant pays	
☐	☐	Cooking Gas	☐	☐	Air Conditioning
☐	☐	Electricity	☐	☐	Cable Television
☐	☐	Heat	☐	☐	Condominium Fee
☐	☐	Hot Water	☐	☐	Parking Fee
☐	☐	Cold Water	☐	☐	Maintenance of Common Areas
☐	☐	Trash Removal	☐	☐	Pest/Rodent Control
☐	☐	Sewage Fees	☐	☐	Snow/Ice Removal
☐	☐	Sewer Maintenance	☐	☐	Telephone Service
☐	☐	Lawn and Shrubbery Care	☐	☐	_____
☐	☐	Heater Maintenance Contract	☐	☐	_____

104   Comments: _____
105

106 **15. TENANT'S CARE OF PROPERTY**
107   (A) Tenant will:
108   1. Keep the Property clean and safe.
109   2. Dispose of all trash, garbage and any other waste materials as required by Landlord and the law.
110   3. Use care when using any of the electrical, plumbing, heating, ventilation or other facilities or appliances on the
111   Property, including any elevators.
112   4. Tell Landlord immediately of any repairs needed and of any potentially harmful health or environmental conditions.
113   5. Obey all laws.
114   (B) Tenant will not:
115   1. Keep any flammable, hazardous and/or explosive materials on the Property.
116   2. Destroy, damage or deface any part of the Property or common areas.
117   3. Disturb the peace and quiet of other tenants or neighbors.
118   4. Make changes to the property, such as painting or remodeling, without the written permission of Landlord. Tenant
119   agrees that any changes or improvements made will belong to the Landlord.
120   5. Perform any maintenance or repairs on the Property unless otherwise stated in the Rules and Regulations, if any.
121   (C) Tenant is solely responsible to pay the costs for repairing any damage that is the fault of Tenant or Tenant's family or
122   guests.

123 **Tenant Initials:_____**   LR Page 2 of 4   **Landlord Initials:_____**

FIGURE 6.2

Example of a Residential Lease (continued)

124 **16. SUBLEASING AND TRANSFER**
125   (A) Landlord may transfer this Lease to another landlord. Tenant agrees that this Lease remains the same with the new
126   landlord.
127   (B) Tenant may not transfer this Lease or sublease (rent to another person) the Property or any part of the Property without
128   Landlord's written permission.
129 **17. PETS**
130   Tenant will not keep or allow any pets on any part of the Property, unless checked below.
131   ☐ Tenant may keep pets with Landlord's written permission according to the terms of the attached Rules and Regulations.
132 **18. RULES AND REGULATIONS**
133   (A) Rules and Regulations for use of the Property and common areas are attached.   ☐ Yes   ☐ No
134   (B) Any violation of the Rules and Regulations is a breach of this Lease.
135   (C) Landlord may change the Rules and Regulations if the change benefits the Tenant or improves the health, safety, or wel-
136   fare of others. Landlord agrees to provide all changes to Tenant in writing.
137   (D) Tenant is responsible for Tenant's family and guests obeying the Rules and Regulations and all laws.
138 **19. SMOKE DETECTORS AND FIRE PROTECTION SYSTEMS**
139   (A) Landlord has installed smoke detectors in the Property. Tenant will maintain and regularly test smoke detectors to be sure
140   they are in working order, and will replace smoke detector batteries as needed.
141   (B) Tenant will immediately notify Landlord or Landlord's agent of any broken or malfunctioning smoke detectors.
142   (C) Failure to properly maintain smoke detectors, replace smoke detector batteries or notify Landlord or Landlord's agent of
143   any broken or malfunctioning smoke detectors is a breach of this Lease.
144   (D) Landlord may provide additional fire protection systems for the benefit of Tenant. Responsibility for maintaining these
145   systems is stated in the Rules and Regulations, if any.
146   (E) Tenant will pay for damage to the Property if Tenant fails to maintain smoke detectors or other fire protection systems.
147 **20. LEAD-BASED PAINT HAZARD DISCLOSURES FOR PROPERTY BUILT BEFORE 1978**
148   ☐ Property was built in or after 1978. This paragraph does not apply.
149   ☐ Property was built before 1978. Landlord and Tenant must provide information in this paragraph.
150   **(A) Landlord does not know of any lead-based paint or lead-based paint hazards on the Property unless stated below:**
151   _____ Landlord knows that there is lead-based paint, or that there are lead-based paint hazards on the Property. Landlord
152   must explain what Landlord knows about the lead-based paint and hazards, including how Landlord learned that it
153   is there, where it is, and the condition of painted walls, trim and other surfaces. Landlord must give Tenant any
154   other information Landlord has about the lead-based paint and lead-based paint hazards.
155   **(B) Landlord has no reports or records about lead-based paint or lead-based paint hazards on the Property unless stat-**
156   **ed below:**
157   _____ Landlord has given Tenant all available records and reports about lead-based paint or lead-based paint hazards on
158   the Property. List records and reports: _____
159   _____
160   (C) Tenant initial all that are true:
161   _____ Tenant has received the pamphlet *Protect Your Family From Lead in Your Home*.
162   _____ Tenant has read the information given by Landlord in paragraph 20 (A) and (B) above.
163   _____ Tenant has received all records and reports that Landlord listed in paragraph 20 (B) above.
164   (D) Landlord and Tenant certify, by signing this Lease, that the information given is true to the best of their knowledge.
165 **21. DESTRUCTION OF PROPERTY**
166   (A) Tenant will notify Landlord or Landlord's agent immediately if the Property is severely damaged or destroyed by fire or
167   by any other cause. Tenant will immediately notify Landlord or Landlord's agent of any condition in the Property that
168   could severely damage or destroy the Property.
169   (B) If the Property is severely damaged or destroyed for any reason:
170   1. Tenant may continue to live on the livable part of the Property and pay a reduced rent as agreed to by Tenant and
171   Landlord until the damages are repaired, OR
172   2. If the law does not allow Tenant to live on the Property, this Lease is ended.
173   (C) If Lease is ended, Landlord will return any unused security deposit or advanced rent to Tenant.
174   (D) If Tenant, Tenant's family, or Tenant's guests cause damage by fire or by other means, this Lease will remain in effect and
175   Tenant will continue to pay rent, even if Tenant cannot occupy the Property.
176 **22. INSURANCE AND RELEASE**
177   (A) Tenant understands that Landlord's insurance does not cover Tenant, Tenant's property, or Tenant's guests. Tenant is
178   advised to obtain property and liability insurance to protect Tenant, Tenant's property and Tenant's guests who may be
179   injured while on the Property.
180   ☐ **IF CHECKED,** Tenant must have insurance policies providing at least $_____ property insurance
181   and $ _____ liability insurance to protect Tenant, Tenant's property and Tenant's guests who may
182   be injured while on the Property. Tenant must maintain this insurance through the entire Term and any Renewal Term.
183   Tenant will provide proof of insurance upon request.
184   (B) Landlord is not legally responsible for any injury or damage to Tenant or Tenant's guests that occurs on the Property.
185   (C) Tenant is responsible for any loss to Landlord caused by Tenant, Tenant's family or Tenant's guests, including attorney's fees.

<u>**ENDING LEASE**</u>

186 **23. LANDLORD REMEDIES IF TENANT BREACHES LEASE**
187   (A) If Tenant breaches Lease for any reason, Landlord's remedies may include any or all of the following:
188   1. Taking possession of the Property by going to court to evict Tenant. Tenant agrees to pay Landlord's legal fees and
189   reasonable costs, including the cost for Landlord or Landlord's agent to attend court hearings.
190   2. Filing a lawsuit against Tenant for rents, damages and unpaid charges, and for rents and charges for the rest of the
191   Lease term. If Landlord wins (gets a money judgment against Tenant), Landlord may use the court process to gar-
192   nish Tenant's wages and take Tenant's personal goods, furniture, motor vehicles and money in banks.
193   3. Keeping Tenant's Security Deposit to be applied against unpaid rent or damages, or both.
194   (B) If Tenant breaches Lease for any reason, Landlord can begin eviction proceedings without written notice.
195   **TENANT WAIVES OR GIVES UP TENANT'S RIGHT TO A NOTICE TO MOVE OUT UNLESS A DIFFERENT**
196   **NOTICE PERIOD IS STATED HERE:** _____
197   _____

198 **Tenant Initials:_____**   LR Page 3 of 4   **Landlord Initials:_____**

F I G U R E   6.1

Example of a Residential Lease (continued)

199 **24. TENANT ENDING LEASE EARLY**
200   Tenant may end this Lease and move out of the Property before the End Date of the Lease or any Renewal Term only with writ-
201   ten permission of Landlord, and only if:
202   (A)   Tenant gives Landlord at least _____ days written notice, AND
203   (B)   Tenant pays Landlord a Termination Fee of _____, AND
204   (C)   Tenant continues to pay all rent until the End Date of the Lease, or any Renewal Term, or until a new tenant is approved
205   by Landlord and a new lease takes effect, whichever happens first.
206 **25. ABANDONMENT**
207   (A)   If Tenant abandons Property while Rent is due and unpaid, Landlord has the right to take possession of the Property
208   immediately and to rent the Property to another tenant.
209   (B)   Any of Tenant's personal property or possessions remaining on the Property after Tenant moves out will be considered
210   to be abandoned property. Landlord will have the right to remove and dispose of any abandoned property in any man-
211   ner determined by Landlord. Tenant will pay for the cost of removal and disposal of abandoned property.
212 **26. SALE OF PROPERTY**
213   (A)   If Property is sold, Landlord will give Tenant in writing:
214   1.   Notice that the Security Deposit has been given to the new landlord, who will be responsible for it.
215   2.   The name, address and phone number of the new landlord and where rent is to be paid, if known.
216   (B)   Tenant agrees that Landlord may transfer Tenant's Security Deposit and advanced rent to the new landlord.
217   (C)   Landlord's responsibilities to Tenant under this Lease end after the Property has been sold and the Lease transferred to a
218   new landlord.
219   (D)   If Landlord sells the Property during the Lease or any Renewal Term, Landlord has the right to terminate this Lease if
220   Landlord gives at least _____ days written notice to Tenant. Tenant is not entitled to any payment of damages.
221 **27. IF GOVERNMENT TAKES PROPERTY**
222   (A)   The government or other public authority can take private property for public use. The taking is called condemnation.
223   (B)   If any part of the Property is taken by the government, Landlord will reduce Tenant's rent proportionately. If all the
224   Property is taken or is no longer usable, this Lease will end and Tenant will move out. Landlord will return to Tenant any
225   unused Security Deposit or advanced rent.
226   (C)   No money paid to Landlord for the condemnation of the Property will belong to Tenant.

ADDITIONAL TERMS

227 **28. TENANT HAS FEWER RIGHTS THAN MORTGAGE LENDER**   Landlord may have a mortgage on the Property.   The
228   rights of the mortgage lender come before the rights of the Tenant. (Example: If Landlord fails to make mortgage payments,
229   the mortgage lender could take the Property and end this Lease.)
230   **TENANT MAY BE WAIVING OR GIVING UP TENANT'S RIGHTS. TENANT UNDERSTANDS THAT IF THERE**
231   **IS A FORECLOSURE, THE NEW OWNER WILL HAVE THE RIGHT TO END THIS LEASE.**
232 **29. CAPTIONS**   The headings in this Lease are meant only to make it easier to find the paragraphs.
233 **30. ENTIRE AGREEMENT**   This Lease is the entire agreement between Landlord and Tenant. No spoken or written agree-
234   ments made before are a part of this Lease unless they are included in this Lease in writing. No waivers or modifications of
235   this Lease during the Term of this Lease are valid unless in writing signed by both Landlord and Tenant.

236 **NOTICE BEFORE SIGNING: If Tenant has legal questions, Tenant is advised to consult an attorney.**

237 **If Landlord or Tenant are represented by a licensed real estate broker, Tenant and/or Landlord acknowledge receipt of the**
238 **Consumer Notice as adopted by the State Real Estate Commission at 49 Pa. Code §35.336 and/or §35.337.**

239 **By signing below, Landlord and Tenant acknowledge that they have read and understand the notices and explanatory infor-**
240 **mation set forth in this Lease.**

241 **WITNESS** _____ **TENANT** _____ **DATE** _____

242 **WITNESS** _____ **TENANT** _____ **DATE** _____

243 **WITNESS** _____ **TENANT** _____ **DATE** _____

244 **WITNESS** _____ **CO-SIGNER** _____ **DATE** _____

245 **WITNESS** _____ **CO-SIGNER** _____ **DATE** _____

246 **WITNESS** _____ **CO-SIGNER** _____ **DATE** _____

247 **WITNESS** _____ **LANDLORD** _____ **DATE** _____

248 **WITNESS** _____ **LANDLORD** _____ **DATE** _____

249 **Brokers'/Licensees' Certifications**   By signing here, Brokers and Licensees involved in this transaction certify that: (1) The informa-
250 tion given is true to the best of their knowledge; AND (2) They have told Landlord of Landlord's responsibilities under the Residential
251 Lead-Based Paint Hazard Reduction Act (42 U.S.C. §4852d), described in the Lead Hazard Disclosure Requirements (see Lead-Based
252 Paint Hazards Notice). Brokers and Licensees must make sure that Landlord gives Tenant the information required by the Act.

253 **BROKER FOR LANDLORD (Company Name)** _____
254   **ACCEPTED BY** _____ **DATE** _____

255 **BROKER FOR TENANT (Company Name)** _____
256   **ACCEPTED BY** _____ **DATE** _____

257   **LANDLORD TRANSFERS LEASE TO A NEW LANDLORD**

258 As part of payment received by Landlord, _____ (current Landlord) now transfers to
259 _____ (new landlord) his heirs and estate, this Lease and the right to receive the rents and other benefits.

260 **WITNESS** _____ **LANDLORD** _____ **DATE** _____
261 **WITNESS** _____ **LANDLORD** _____ **DATE** _____

Example of a Residential Lease (continued)

NOTICES AND INFORMATION

PENNSYLVANIA PLAIN LANGUAGE CONSUMER CONTRACT ACT

The Office of Attorney General has not pre-approved any special conditions or additional terms added by any parties. Any special conditions or additional terms must comply with the Pennsylvania Plain Language Consumer Contract Act.

INFORMATION REGARDING SECURITY DEPOSITS

Taking Security Deposits
During the first year of a Lease, a Landlord may not require a security deposit of more than two months' rent. After the first year of a Lease, this amount cannot exceed one month's rent, and any security deposit of more than one month's rent must be returned to the Tenant. If rent is increased during the first five years a Tenant is in a Property, Landlord may require that the amount of the security deposit be increased as well. After five years, the security deposit cannot be increased even if the rent goes up.

Holding Security Deposits
If a Security Deposit is more than $100, the Landlord must keep the Security Deposit in a special bank account called an escrow account. Landlord is required to tell Tenant the name and address of the bank where the escrow account is located, as well as the amount of the deposit in the escrow account. After the second year of a lease the Security Deposit must be in an escrow account that earns interest. Interest that is earned on Security Deposits belongs to the Tenant, but each year Landlord has the right to keep some or all of that interest up to an amount equal to 1% of the Security Deposit to cover certain administrative expenses. [For example, if a Security Deposit of $500 is held in an escrow account that earns $10 of interest in a year, Landlord has the option to retain up to 1% of the Security Deposit amount ($5) out of that interest.] If the interest earned is less than 1% of the Security Deposit amount, Landlord may keep all the interest, but Landlord can **never** take any money out of the original Security Deposit for administrative expenses. After the second year of a lease, any interest belonging to Tenant must be returned to Tenant once a year on the anniversary of the first day of the original lease term.

Returning Security Deposits
When a lease is ended, Landlord has 30 days to give Tenant a written list of any damage to the Property that Landlord claims Tenant is responsible for. If the cost to repair this damage is less than the amount of the Security Deposit being held, Landlord must return the amount of the deposit not being held back to fix those damages when the list is provided, along with any additional interest that has not yet been paid to Tenant. If damages are more than the amount of the Security Deposit plus interest, Landlord may keep the entire Security Deposit. *Landlord may not keep any of the Security Deposit to cover damages if a list of damages is not given to Tenant within that 30 day period.* If Landlord doesn't return Tenant's Security Deposit within 30 days of the end of the Lease, Tenant may sue and Landlord may be required to pay Tenant up to twice the amount of the portion of the Security Deposit that should have been returned. It is the responsibility of Tenant to give Landlord his/her new address after the Lease is ended. *If Tenant does not provide a new address to Landlord, Landlord is not liable for damages for failing to return Security Deposit monies within 30 days.*

LEAD-BASED PAINT HAZARDS

Lead Hazards Disclosure Requirements
The Residential Lead-Based Paint Hazard Reduction Act says that any Landlord of property built before 1978 must give the Tenant an EPA pamphlet titled *Protect Your Family From Lead in Your Home*. The Landlord also must tell the Tenant and the Broker for Landlord what the Landlord knows about lead-based paint and lead-based paint hazards that are in or on the property being rented. Landlord must tell the Tenant how the Landlord knows that lead-based paint and lead-based paint hazards are on the property, where the lead-based paint and lead-based paint hazards are, and the condition of the painted surfaces. Any Landlord of a pre-1978 structure must also give the Tenant any records and reports that the Landlord has or can get about lead-based paint or lead-based paint hazards in or around the property being rented, the common areas, or other dwellings in multi-family housing. It is also required that the EPA pamphlet be given to tenants before the Landlord starts any major renovations on a pre-1978 structure. The Act does not apply to housing built in 1978 or later.

Lead Warning Statement
Housing built before 1978 may contain lead-based paint. Lead from paint, paint chips, and dust can pose health hazards if not taken care of properly. Lead exposure is especially harmful to young children and pregnant women. Before renting pre-1978 housing, Landlords must disclose the presence of known lead-based paint and lead-based paint hazards in the dwelling. Tenants must also receive a federally approved pamphlet on lead poisoning prevention.

INFORMATION REGARDING MEDIATION

Mediation is a way of resolving problems. A mediator may help the disputing parties reach an agreeable solution without having to involve the courts. Landlord and Tenant may agree to take any disputes arising from this Lease to a mediation program offered by the local association of REALTORS® or to another mediator. Landlord and Tenant can agree to mediation as part of this Lease (by signing a mediation form to attach to this Lease), or they can sign an agreement to mediate after a dispute arises.

INFORMATION REGARDING TENANTS' RIGHTS

Landlord cannot increase rents, decrease services, or threaten to go to court to evict Tenant because Tenant: (1) complains to a government agency or to Landlord about a building or housing code violation; (2) organizes or joins a Tenant's organization; or (3) uses Tenant's legal rights in a lawful manner.

INFORMATION REGARDING MOLD AND INDOOR AIR QUALITY

Indoor mold contamination and the inhalation of bioaerosols (bacteria, mold spores, pollen, and viruses) have been associated with allergic responses including upper respiratory congestion, cough, mucous membrane irritation, fever, chills, muscle ache or other transient inflammation or allergy. Claims have been made that exposure to mold contamination and bioaerosols has led to serious infection, immunosuppression and illnesses of neuro or systemic toxicity. Sampling of indoor air quality and other methods exist to determine the presence and scope of any indoor contamination. Because individuals may be affected differently, or not affected at all, by mold contamination, the surest approach to determine the presence of contamination is to engage the services of a qualified professional to undertake an assessment and/or sampling. Assessments and samplings for the presence of mold contamination can be performed by qualified industrial hygienists, engineers, laboratories and home inspection companies that offer these services. Information pertaining to indoor air quality is available through the United States Environmental Protection Agency and may be obtained by contacting IAQ INFO, P.O. Box 37133, Washington, D.C. 20013-7133, 1-800-438-4318. Tenants should immediately notify Landlord if there is any condition in the Property that may lead to the growth of mold or if the Tenant believes that mold growth is present in the Property.

QUESTIONS

1. Which of the following transactions would best be described as involving a ground lease?
   a. A landowner agrees to let a tenant drill for oil on a property for 75 years.
   b. With the landowner's permission, a tenant builds and owns a shopping center on vacant land leased from the landowner.
   c. A landlord charges a commercial tenant separate amounts of rent for the land and the trade fixtures.
   d. A tenant pays a base amount for the property, plus a percentage of business-generated income.

2. A *percentage lease* is a lease that provides for a
   a. rental of a percentage of the value of a building.
   b. definite periodic rent not exceeding a stated percentage.
   c. definite monthly rent plus a percentage of the tenant's gross receipts in excess of a certain amount.
   d. graduated amount due monthly and not exceeding a stated percentage.

3. If several tenants move out of a rented store building because the building has collapsed,
   a. it would be an actual eviction.
   b. the tenants would be liable for the rent until the expiration of their leases.
   c. the landlord would have to provide substitute space.
   d. it would be a constructive eviction.

4. R's written five-year lease with monthly rental payments expired last month, but R has remained in possession and the landlord has accepted his most recent rent payment without comment. At this point
   a. R is a holdover tenant.
   b. R's lease has been renewed for another five years.
   c. R's lease has been renewed for another month.
   d. R is a tenant at sufferance.

5. A lease for more than three years must be in writing because
   a. either party may forget the terms.
   b. the tenant must sign the agreement to pay rent.
   c. the statute of frauds requires it.
   d. it is the customary procedure to protect the tenant.

6. A tenant who transfers his or her entire rights for the remaining term of the lease to a third party is
   a. a sublessor.
   b. assigning the lease.
   c. automatically relieved of any further obligation under it.
   d. giving the third party a sandwich lease.

7. A tenant's lease has expired. The tenant has neither vacated nor negotiated a renewal lease, and the landlord has declared that she does not want the tenant to remain in the building. The tenant holds a(n)
   a. estate for years.
   b. periodic estate.
   c. estate at will.
   d. estate at sufferance.

8. F has a lease that will expire in two weeks. At that time he will move into larger quarters on the other side of town. To terminate the agreement,
   a. in two weeks F must give his landlord prior notice.
   b. the landlord must give F prior notice.
   c. nothing needs to be done—the agreement will terminate automatically.
   d. The agreement will terminate only after both parties renegotiate the original agreement.

9. When a tenant holds possession of a landlord's property without a current lease agreement and without the landlord's approval,
   a. the tenant is maintaining a gross lease.
   b. the landlord can file suit for possession.
   c. the tenant has no obligation to pay rent.
   d. the landlord may be subject to a constructive eviction.

10. Under the negotiated terms of a residential lease, the landlord is required to maintain the water heater. If a tenant is unable to get hot water because of a faulty water heater that the landlord has failed to repair after repeated notification, all of the following remedies would be available to the tenant *EXCEPT*
    a. suing the landlord for damages.
    b. suing the landlord for breach of the covenant of seisin.
    c. abandoning the premises under constructive eviction.
    d. terminating the lease agreement.

11. The leasehold interest that automatically renews itself at each expiration is the
    a. tenancy for years.
    b. tenancy from period to period.
    c. tenancy at will.
    d. tenancy at sufferance.

12. *K* has leased space in her shopping center to *B* for *B's* dress store. However, *B's* business fails and *B* sublets the space to *D*. Then *D* fails to make rental payments when they are due. The lease has been breached. Therefore
    a. *K* would have recourse against *B* only.
    b. *K* would have recourse against *D* only.
    c. *K* would have recourse against both *B* and *D*.
    d. *D* would have recourse against *B*.

13. Which of the following best describes a *net lease*?
    a. An agreement in which the tenant pays a fixed rent and the landlord pays all taxes, insurance, and so forth on the property
    b. A lease in which the tenant pays rent in addition to some or all operating expenses
    c. A lease in which the tenant pays the landlord a percentage of the monthly income derived from the property
    d. An agreement granting an individual a leasehold interest in fishing rights for shoreline properties

14. A lease calls for a minimum rent of $1,200 per month plus 4 percent of the annual gross business over $150,000. If the total rent paid at the end of one year was $19,200, how much business did the tenant do during the year?
    a. $159,800
    b. $25,200
    c. $270,000
    d. $169,200

15. Which of the following would automatically terminate a residential lease?
    a. Total destruction of the property
    b. Sale of the property
    c. Failure of the tenant to pay rent
    d. Death of the tenant

ANSWERS

1. B In a ground lease, the landowner leases unimproved land to a tenant who agrees to construct a building, which the tenant then owns. A ground lease is generally a long-term net lease, which provides certain tax advantages to the lessee. (p. 88)

2. C A common form of lease used in retail businesses is one that requires the tenant to pay rent based on a percentage of the gross or net income generated by the business. This is known as a percentage lease. (p. 88)

3. D If the property becomes uninhabitable for the purpose intended in the lease, a tenant has the right to abandon the property. This action terminates the lease and is known as constructive eviction. (p. 90)

4. A When a tenant remains in possession, or holds over, after the lease term expires, a holdover tenancy is created. The landlord's acceptance of rent indicates consent to a periodic tenancy. A tenancy at sufferance would be created if the tenant remained in possession without the consent of the landlord. (p. 81)

5. C In Pennsylvania, the statute of frauds requiring contracts conveying interests in real estate to be in writing in order to be enforceable applies to leases for more than three years' duration. (p. 82)

6. B A tenant who transfers all of his rights to a third party for the remainder of the lease term assigns his lease. An assignment does not automatically relieve the original lessee of his obligations under the lease. (p. 85)

7. D An estate at sufferance is created when a tenant who lawfully possessed property remains in possession without the consent of the landlord after the lease expires. (p. 81)

8. C F will vacate the leased property at the expiration of the lease term. The lease is discharged and the contractual relationship terminates at that time. Neither the landlord nor tenant is required to take any further action. (p. 89)

9. B When a tenant remains in possession without a current lease and without the consent of the landlord, the tenant is a tenant at sufferance. The landlord may regain possession through a suit for possession. (p. 89)

10. B If the landlord breaches the terms of the lease, the tenant may sue and recover damages. The tenant may also have the right to abandon the property and have the lease terminated under the theory of constructive eviction. The covenant of seisin refers to deeds, not leases. (p. 90)

11. B The key feature of a tenancy from period to period is that it automatically renews itself under the original terms until one of the parties gives notice to terminate. This tenancy may run for an indefinite duration. (p. 80)

12. A The original lessee B remains primarily liable for payment of rent to the original lessor K. The original lessor has recourse against B only; K has no contractual relationship with D. (p. 85)

13. B Under the terms of a net lease, the tenant pays all or some of the operating expenses in addition to the rent. Operating expenses include such items as taxes, insurance premiums, maintenance costs, and assessments. (p. 87)

14. C The base rent paid for one year would be $14,400 ($1,200 × 12). If the total paid was $19,200, it means that $4,800 (($19,200 − $14,400) was the portion attributed to the terms of the net lease. If $4,800 equals 4 percent of the gross business over $150,000, then $120,000 (4,800 ÷ 4%) equals the amount over $150,000. The total volume therefore is $270,000 ($150,000 + $120,000). (p. 87)

15. A A tenant who leases part of the building, such as a residential apartment, is released from the lease when the premises are totally destroyed. (p. 83 in 9e) Sale of the property or death of the tenant does not terminate the lease. (p. 89)

CHAPTER SEVEN

FORMS OF REAL ESTATE OWNERSHIP

■ LEARNING OBJECTIVES

When you've finished reading this chapter, you should be able to

- ■ recognize the various ways title to real estate can be held and the characteristics of each form of ownership;
- ■ explain the differences between joint tenancy, tenancy in common, tenancy by the entireties, and community property;
- ■ identify forms of ownership used by business organizations;
- ■ distinguish between condominium and cooperative forms of ownership; and
- ■ define the key terms.

■ KEY TERMS

common elements

community property

condominium

cooperative

corporation

general partnership

joint tenancy

limited liability company
  (LLC)

limited partnership

partnership

Pennsylvania Uniform
  Condominium Act

right of survivorship

separate property

severalty

syndication

tenancy by the entirety

tenancy in common

time-share

title

trust

■ LEGAL FORMS OF OWNERSHIP

Chapter 5 describes many different interests that a person can have in land. Understanding this makes it possible to identify exactly what sellers have to convey and, therefore, what buyers are acquiring. The next step is to look at the various forms of legal ownership, that is, the ways title to ownership can be held.

The term **title** refers to *the right to* or *ownership of* real property. Title represents the owner's bundle of rights to the real estate. If a person owns real property, the person is said to hold title to it. "Title" is simply a way of referring to ownership of property.

In Your State

PA   Each of the ways ownership can be held has distinguishing characteristics, depending on whether one individual holds title or several individuals concurrently hold title. Title can be held in severalty, which is by one person, or concurrently by two or more people as tenants in common or as joint tenants. In Pennsylvania, married couples may own property as tenants by the entireties. In addition, corporations and partnerships can hold title, and title can be held in trust. The characteristics of each form of ownership are important because they not only identify who holds title, but they also determine how the owner or owners can exercise their rights in the title. ■

In a real estate transaction, these distinctions are important because they determine who is entitled to make decisions about the property involved in the transaction. This is especially significant when two or more parties hold title concurrently. Also, purchasers have to think about the form of ownership that best suits their needs when they take title. As a practical matter, real estate licensees must understand the fundamental principles of the various forms of ownership. However, interpretations of the legal significance of the forms of ownership should be referred to an attorney at law.

■ OWNERSHIP IN SEVERALTY

When real estate is owned by one party, that party is said to own the property in **severalty.** The party holding title may be one natural person or one recognized legal entity. The term "severalty" comes from the fact that the sole owner is severed or cut off from other owners. A severalty owner has sole rights to the ownership and sole discretion over its transfer.

■ CO-OWNERSHIP

Forms of Co-ownership
- Tenancy in common
- Joint tenancy
- Tenancy by the entireties
- Community property

When title to one parcel of real estate is held by two or more persons or entities, these parties are called co-owners, or concurrent owners. Concurrent ownership means that one title is held by two or more owners at the same time, with each sharing the rights of ownership, possession, and so forth. The forms of co-ownership that are commonly recognized include tenancy in common, joint tenancy, tenancy by the entirety, community property, and partnership property. The unique legal characteristics of each do not affect the owners' physical use or occupation of the property. The differences are most apparent when one of the owners dies or wishes to convey his or her interest in the property.

Tenancy in Common

One way for two or more people to hold title is as tenants in common. In a **tenancy in common,** each tenant holds an *undivided fractional interest* in the property. A tenant in common may hold, say, a one-half or one-third interest in the title. The physical property, however, is not divided into a specific half

Tenancy in Common

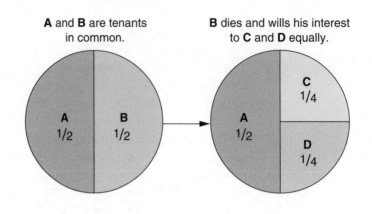

A and **B** are tenants in common.

B dies and wills his interest to **C** and **D** equally.

or third. The co-owners have *unity of possession*. That is, they are entitled to possession of the whole property. It is the ownership interest, not the property, which is divided.

When a tenancy in common is created, the document may state the fractional interest held by each co-owner. Tenants A and B could each have one-half interest, or the interest could be unequal with A having one third and B having two-thirds interest. If no fractions are stated, the tenants are presumed to hold equal interests. For instance, if two people hold title, each has an undivided one-half interest. Likewise, if five people hold title, each would own an undivided one-fifth interest.

Each tenant in common holds his or her ownership interest in severalty. Each co-owner can sell, convey, mortgage, or transfer his or her interest without the consent of the other co-owners. However, no individual tenant may transfer ownership of the entire property. When one co-owner dies, that tenant's undivided interest passes to a devisee (person named in a will) or to the tenant's heirs as defined by state law. The interest of a deceased tenant in common does not pass to another tenant in common unless the surviving co-owner is an heir, devisee, or purchaser. (See Figure 7.1.)

In Your State   **PA**   When two or more new owners acquire title to a parcel of real estate and the deed does not stipulate the tenancy, they acquire title, by operation or rule of law, as tenants in common. But if the conveyance is made to a husband and wife with no further explanation, in Pennsylvania a tenancy by the entirety is created (to be discussed later in this chapter). ■

Joint Tenancy

Two or more people can hold title as joint tenants. The distinguishing feature of **joint tenancy** is *unity of ownership*. This means that title is held as though all owners collectively constitute one unit (as opposed to the multiple units that exist in a tenancy in common.) To form this unity of ownership, there must be

1. *unity of possession*—all joint tenants hold an undivided right to possession;
2. *unity of interest*—all joint tenants hold equal ownership interests;

Remember the four unities in a joint tenancy by the acronym **PITT:**

Possession
Interest
Time
Title

3. *unity of time*—all joint tenants acquire their interest at the same time; and
4. *unity of title*—all joint tenants acquire their interest by the same document.

A joint tenancy can be created only by an intentional act of conveying a deed or giving the property by will, which forms the unity of ownership. Also, the parties must be explicitly identified as joint tenants. A joint tenancy cannot be implied or created by operation of law. The four unities are present when

■ title is acquired by one document or deed;
■ the deed is executed and delivered at one time;
■ the deed conveys equal interests to all of the parties; and
■ the parties hold undivided possession of the property as joint tenants.

Joint tenants A, B, and C, for example, control the ownership, transfer the title, and incur indebtedness associated with the property as a unit. A joint tenant is free to convey his or her *interest* in the title of the jointly held property, but doing so destroys the original unities of time and title. If A conveys her interest to D, D cannot become a joint tenant. Instead, D owns an undivided fractional interest as a tenant in common with B and C, who continue as joint tenants. The tenant in common may be presumed to have a one-third interest unless otherwise stated. (See Figure 7.2.)

Death of one of the joint tenants does not destroy the unit. The surviving joint tenant(s) acquire(s) the interest of the deceased tenant. This occurs by **right of survivorship,** which is another distinguishing characteristic of joint tenancy. The unit is still preserved; only the number of owners who make up the unit is reduced. The joint tenancy continues until only one owner remains. This owner then holds title in severalty and has all of the rights associated with sole ownership. (See Figure 7.3.)

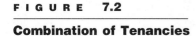 **PA** In a joint tenancy with right of survivorship, the disposition of the deceased tenant's ownership is governed by the joint tenancy rather than by

F I G U R E   7.2

Combination of Tenancies

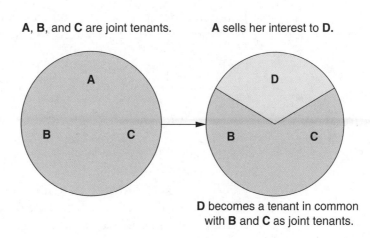

A, B, and C are joint tenants.   A sells her interest to D.

D becomes a tenant in common with **B** and **C** as joint tenants.

F I G U R E   7.3

Joint Tenancy with Right of Survivorship

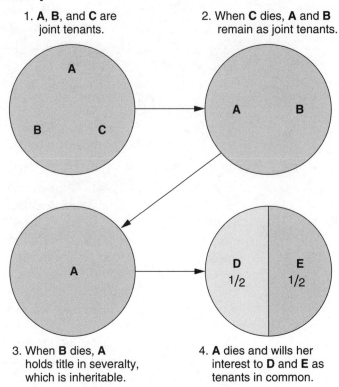

1. **A, B,** and **C** are joint tenants.

2. When **C** dies, **A** and **B** remain as joint tenants.

3. When **B** dies, **A** holds title in severalty, which is inheritable.

4. **A** dies and wills her interest to **D** and **E** as tenants in common.

the person's will or the state's inheritance laws. (Although a dangerous substitute, joint tenancy is sometimes known as "the poor man's will.") Pennsylvania law requires that right of survivorship be clearly stated for survivorship to occur. For example, the document would say, "A and B as Joint Tenants with Right of Survivorship and not as Tenants in Common." Otherwise, the co-ownership would operate as a tenancy in common even though the parties are called joint tenants. In this case, the distinction between a joint tenancy and a tenancy in common is more technical than actual.

Joint tenancies may be terminated by operation of law, such as in bankruptcy or foreclosure sale proceedings. In addition, in states where a mortgage on real property is held to be a conveyance of land, a joint tenant who mortgages his or her property without the other tenants joining in the mortgage will also destroy the joint tenancy.

Termination of Co-Ownership by Partition Suit

Concurrent tenants who wish to terminate their co-ownership may file a suit in court to partition the property. Partition is a legal way to dissolve the relationship when the parties do not voluntarily agree to its termination. If the court determines that the land cannot be physically divided into separate parcels without destroying its value, the court will order the real estate sold. The proceeds of the sale will then be divided among the co-owners according to their fractional interests.

Tenancy by the Entirety

In Your State

PA A **tenancy by the entirety** is a special form of joint tenancy between husband and wife that is recognized in Pennsylvania. Each spouse has an equal, undivided interest in the property. The term *entirety* comes from the early common law view that a married couple is one legal person and, therefore, is an indivisible unit. Like a joint tenancy, a tenancy by the entirety must be created by deed or will. However, the words "tenancy by the entirety" do not need to be expressly stated. Unless another form of co-ownership is specified, a tenancy by the entirety is automatically created, by virtue of a legally formed marriage, when the owners take title as husband and wife. ■

As with joint tenancy, the husband and wife who are tenants by the entirety control the ownership, transfer the title, and incur indebtedness against the property as a unit. One party cannot encumber or convey a one-half interest, and generally, they have no right to partition or divide. Because tenants by the entirety have rights of survivorship, the surviving spouse automatically becomes the severalty or sole owner when the other spouse dies. Married couples often take title as tenants by the entirety so that the surviving spouse can enjoy the benefits of ownership without the delay of probate proceedings.

> Tenancy by the entirety may be terminated by **J's DAD:**
>
> **J**udgment sale
> **D**eath
> **A**greement
> **D**ivorce

In addition to the death of one spouse, a tenancy by the entirety may be terminated by

- agreement between both parties (through the execution of a new deed);
- divorce (which leaves the parties as tenants in common); and
- court-ordered sale of the property to satisfy a judgment against the husband and wife as joint debtors. (The tenancy is dissolved so that the property can be sold to pay the judgment.)

IN PRACTICE

A combination of interests can exist in one parcel of real estate. For example, when *M* and *M's* spouse hold title to an undivided one-half as joint tenants and *S* and *S's* spouse hold title to the other undivided one-half as joint tenants, the relationship among the owners of the two half interests is that of tenants in common.

Community Property Rights

Community property laws are based on the idea that a husband and wife, rather than merging into one entity, are equal partners in the marriage. Any property acquired during a marriage is considered obtained by mutual effort. Community property laws vary widely throughout the country and some states, like Pennsylvania, do not recognize community property.

Property falls into two general categories. **Separate property** is real or personal property owned solely by either spouse before the marriage. It also includes property acquired by gift or inheritance during the marriage as well as any property purchased with separate funds after the marriage. Any income earned from a person's separate property generally remains part of the separate property. Separate property can be mortgaged or conveyed by the owning spouse without the signature of the nonowning spouse.

Community property, on the other hand, consists of all other real and personal property acquired by either spouse during the marriage. Any conveyance or encumbrance of community property requires the signatures of both spouses.

Trust Ownership

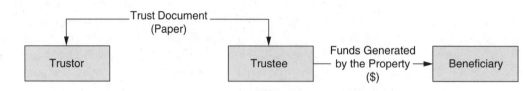

When one spouse dies, the survivor automatically owns one-half of the community property. The other half is distributed according to the deceased's will. If the spouse dies without a will, the other half is inherited by the surviving spouse or by the deceased's other heirs, depending upon state law.

IN PRACTICE

The form of title ownership, whether real estate or personal property such as stocks, bonds, or checking accounts, should always be discussed with an attorney. One form may be more advantageous than another depending on individual circumstances. There are significant legal implications involving estate planning and the protection of assets from creditors or divorce actions that should be considered, but these are matters about which only an attorney should advise.

Trusts

A **trust** is a device by which a person transfers ownership of property to someone else to hold or manage for the benefit of a third person. The original owner of the property and the person who creates the trust is the *trustor* (known as a *settlor* in Pennsylvania). The person who benefits from the trust is the *beneficiary*. The party who holds the legal title and is entrusted with the responsibility of carrying out the trustor's instructions regarding the purpose of the trust is the *trustee*. The trustee is a *fiduciary*, who acts in confidence or trust and has a special legal relationship with the beneficiary. The trustee's power and authority are limited by the terms of the trust agreement. Title to real property is transferred to the trustee by a will or a deed in trust. (See Figure 7.4.)

Trusts can be created for a variety of purposes. Perhaps a grandfather wishes to ensure the college education of his granddaughter. He can do this by transferring an investment property he owns to his grandchild's mother. He then instructs the child's mother to use its income to pay for the grandchild's college tuition. Trusts also could be created to prevent an heir from using bequeathed property unwisely, to provide funds for a specific anticipated need when that need arises, to preserve anonymity of a real estate purchaser, to enable a group to invest in property that individually they could not afford, or to give a settlor (trustor) tax benefits. The legal and tax implications of setting up a trust are complex and vary widely from state to state, so attorneys and tax experts should always be consulted.

Depending on the type of trust and its purpose, the settlor (trustor), trustee, and beneficiary can all be either natural persons or legal entities, such as corporations. *Trust companies* are corporations set up for the specific purpose of being trustees.

Real estate can be owned under living or testamentary trusts and land trusts. It can also be held by investors in a *real estate investment trust (REIT)*.

Living and Testamentary Trusts

Property owners may provide for their own financial care and/or that of their families by establishing a trust. This trust may be created by agreement during a property owner's lifetime (a living trust) or established by will after his or her death (a testamentary trust).

The person who creates the trust conveys real or personal property to a trustee (usually a corporate trustee), with the understanding that the trustee will perform certain duties. These duties may include the care and investment of the trust assets to produce an income. After paying the trust's operating expenses and trustee's fees, the income is paid to or used for the benefit of the beneficiary. The trust may continue for the beneficiary's lifetime, or the assets may be distributed when the beneficiary reaches a certain age or when other conditions of the trust agreement are met.

Land Trusts

A few states, including Pennsylvania, permit the creation of land trusts, in which real estate is the only asset. As in all trusts, the legal title to the property is conveyed to a trustee, and the beneficial interest belongs to the beneficiary. In the case of land trusts, however, the beneficiary is usually also the trustor. While the beneficial interest is personal property, the beneficiary retains management and control of the real property and has the right of possession and the right to any income or proceeds from its sale.

One of the distinguishing characteristics of a land trust is that the *public records do not usually name the beneficiary*. A land trust may be used for secrecy when assembling separate parcels. There are other benefits as well. A beneficial interest can be transferred by assignment, making the formalities of a deed unnecessary. The property can be pledged as security for a loan without having a mortgage recorded. Real property is subject to the laws of the state in which it is located. But because the beneficiary's interest is personal, it will pass at the beneficiary's death under the laws of the state in which the beneficiary resided. If the deceased owned property in several states, additional probate costs and inheritance taxes can thus be avoided.

Usually only individuals create land trusts, but corporations as well as individuals can be beneficiaries. A land trust generally continues for a definite term, such as 20 years. If the beneficiary does not extend the trust term when it expires, the trustee is usually obligated to sell the real estate and distribute the net proceeds to the beneficiary.

IN PRACTICE

Licensees should exercise caution in using the term "trust deed." It can be used to mean a deed *in* trust (which relates to the creation of a living, testamentary, or land trust) or a deed *of* trust (which is a financing document similar to a mortgage). Deed of trust is discussed in Chapter 12. Because these documents are not interchangeable, using an imprecise term can cause serious misunderstandings.

■ OWNERSHIP OF REAL ESTATE BY BUSINESS ORGANIZATIONS

A business organization is a legal entity that exists independently of its members. Ownership by a business organization makes it possible for a number of people to hold an interest in the same parcel of real estate. Investors may be organized to finance a real estate project in various ways. Some provide for the real estate to be owned by the entity; others provide for direct ownership by the investors. These are not simply real estate transactions, but ones that may be significantly affected by tax and securities laws as well. Professional legal, tax, and securities advisors play critical roles as business entities are formed for the purchase or sale of real estate. They can also advise in the proper way to solicit participation or investment in these ventures.

Partnerships

A **partnership** is *an association of two or more people who carry on a business as co-owners and share in the business's profits and losses.* There are general and limited partnerships. In a **general partnership,** all partners participate to some extent in the operation and management of the business and share full personal liability for business losses and obligations. A **limited partnership,** on the other hand, consists of one or more general partners as well as limited, or silent, partners. The general partner or partners run the business. The limited partners are not legally permitted to participate in the business, and each partner's liability for losses is limited to only the amount of his or her investment. Limited partnerships enable investors with small amounts of capital to share in large real estate projects at minimum personal risk.

In Your State

PA Under common law, a partnership is not a legal entity and technically cannot own real estate. Individual partners must hold title as tenants in common or joint tenants. However, in states that have adopted the *Uniform Partnership Act*, including Pennsylvania, a partnership is recognized as a legal entity and can hold title in the partnership's name. Similarly, under the *Uniform Limited Partnership Act*, a limited partnership is recognized as a legal entity that can hold title to property in the limited partnership's name. Profits and losses are passed through the partnership to each partner, whose individual tax situation determines the tax consequences. ■

General partnerships are dissolved and must be reorganized if one partner dies, withdraws, or goes bankrupt, unless a partnership agreement makes provisions for these events. In a limited partnership, however, the partnership agreement may provide for the continuation of the organization following the death or withdrawal of one of the partners.

Corporations

A **corporation** is *a legal entity* (a nonnatural person) created under the laws of the state from which the corporation receives its charter. The entity is operated by its *board of directors* and exists in perpetuity until it is formally dissolved. Unlike a partnership, the corporation's existence is not affected by the death of one of the officers or directors.

The corporate charter sets forth the powers of the corporation, including its right to purchase and sell real estate (based on a resolution by the board of directors). Some charters permit the corporation to purchase real estate for any purpose; others limit purchases to those needed to fulfill corporate purposes. As a legal entity, the corporation holds title to real estate in *severalty*. As sole owner, the corporation controls all ownership decisions and incurs any liability. Individual shareholders participate by investing in corporate stock, which is *personal property*. They do not hold title to the real estate, and their liability is usually limited to the amount of their investment.

One of the disadvantages of corporations, especially when income-producing property is involved, is double taxation. As a legal entity, a corporation must pay tax on its profits. Dividends from the remaining corporate profits are then distributed to the shareholders and are taxed again as part of the shareholders' individual incomes.

An alternative form of organization is known as an *S corporation*. An S corporation is a legal corporate entity, a form of ownership for small business corporations that provides all the benefits of a corporation, but avoids double taxation. Corporate profits are not taxed; only the dividends distributed to shareholders are taxed as part of their individual incomes. This favorable tax treatment can be lost and the entity will be redefined as some other form of business organization, however, if the IRS determines that the S corporation failed to comply with strict requirements regulating its structure, membership, and operation.

Limited Liability Companies

A **limited liability company (LLC)** is a hybrid organization that combines the most attractive features of a partnership and a corporation. It is a business entity organized under the *Limited Liability Company Act*. The owners are characterized as members rather than partners or shareholders. The members enjoy the limited liability offered by a corporation and the tax advantages of a partnership. In addition, the LLC offers flexible management structures without the complicated requirements of S corporations or the restrictions of limited partnerships. For Pennsylvania taxes, however, an LLC is treated as a corporation but may be considered an S corporation if it meets the requirements for this type of an organization.

Syndications

Generally speaking, **syndication** is the process of *two or more people or firms joined together to make and operate a real estate investment*. A syndicate may be formed to acquire, develop, manage, market, or operate real estate. The syndicate is not in itself a legal entity. Instead, it organizes as co-ownership (tenancy in common, joint tenancy), a partnership (general or limited), a trust, or a corporation.

A *joint venture* is a form of partnership in which two or more people or firms join to engage in a *single business project*. Joint ventures are not intended to establish permanent relationships beyond the project that brought them together.

Condominium Ownership

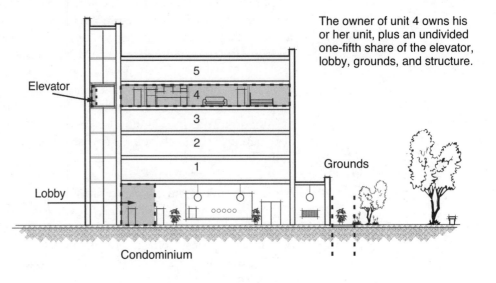

The owner of unit 4 owns his or her unit, plus an undivided one-fifth share of the elevator, lobby, grounds, and structure.

Elevator

Grounds

Lobby

Condominium

■ CONDOMINIUMS, COOPERATIVES, AND TIME-SHARES

A growing urban population, diverse lifestyles, changing family structures, and heightened mobility have created a demand for new forms of real estate ownership. Although some of the population's housing needs can be satisfied with rental units, the traditional rental system doesn't satisfy the urge to "own a part of the land" or provide the tax advantages associated with real estate ownership. This has led to the creation of condominiums, cooperatives, and time-share arrangements to serve the changing needs of today's residential, commercial, and industrial markets.

Condominium Ownership

A condominium is a form of real estate ownership that has a unique legal structure constituted under the condominium laws. These laws are often called horizontal property acts because ownership consists of a specific horizontal layer of airspace, as opposed to traditional vertical ownership (from the center of the earth to the sky). Ownership in a **condominium** consists of *a fee simple estate* to the individual condominium unit and a specified share of the undivided interest in the common areas in the condominium development. (See Figure 7.5.)

The common areas, known as the **common elements,** are the real estate that exists beyond the individual units. The physical property categorized as common elements varies with the design of the condominium project. Typically, they include items such as land, courtyards, lobbies, exterior structures, hallways, elevators, stairways, and the roof, as well as any recreational facilities such as swimming pools, tennis courts, and golf courses. The individual unit owners own these common elements together as tenants in common. However, state law usually provides that unit owners do not have the same right of partition that other tenants in common have.

The distinguishing feature of a condominium is its form of ownership rather than the physical development or architectural style of the property. In fact, the form of ownership cannot be discerned from the physical appearance of the real estate. Although many people associate condominium ownership with high-rise apartment buildings, other residential uses, ranging from single freestanding units and townhouses to low-rise apartments, can be condominiums. Townhouses, especially, must be scrutinized to determine whether they are condominium units or separately owned lots and buildings. Commercial uses, such as office buildings and multiuse properties comprised of offices and retail shops as well as residential units, can also be condominiums. Parking spaces in parking garages may also be condominiums.

> In Your State

PA Creation of a condominium. Condominium ownership is constituted under the *Uniform Condominium Act,* which has been enacted throughout the country, including in Pennsylvania. Under its provisions, a condominium is created and established when the owner of an existing building or the developer of unimproved property executes and records a *declaration of condominium.* The declaration includes

- a legal description of the condominium units and the common elements (including *limited* common elements—those that serve only one particular unit);
- the condominium's bylaws, governing the operation of the owners' association;
- a survey of the property;
- an architect's drawings and surveyor's legal descriptions, illustrating both the vertical and horizontal boundaries of each unit; and
- any restrictive covenants controlling the rights of ownership. ■

Owning a condominium. Once the property is established as a condominium, each unit becomes a separate parcel of real estate that is owned in fee simple like any other real estate. Title may be held by one or more people in any type of ownership or tenancy recognized by state law. Like any other parcel of real estate, a condominium unit may be mortgaged and sold or transferred to whomever the owner chooses, unless the condominium association provides for a first right of refusal. In this case, the owner is required to offer the unit at the same price to the other owners in the condominium or the association before accepting an outside offer to purchase.

Real estate taxes are assessed and collected on each unit as an individual property. Default in the payment of taxes or a mortgage loan by one unit owner may result in a foreclosure sale of that owner's unit, but it does not affect the ownership of the other unit owners.

Operation and administration. The condominium property generally is administered by an association of unit owners, according to the bylaws in the declaration. The association may be governed by a board of directors or another official entity, and it may manage the property on its own or hire a professional property manager.

The association must enforce the restrictive covenants and any rules it adopts regarding the operation and use of the property. The association is responsible for the maintenance, repair, cleaning, and sanitation of the common elements. The association must also maintain fire and extended-coverage insurance as well as liability insurance for these portions of the property.

The expense of maintaining and operating the condominium development is paid by the unit owners in the form of maintenance fees and assessments imposed and collected by the owners' association. The recurring maintenance fees may be due monthly, quarterly, semiannually, or annually, depending on provisions in the bylaws. The size of an individual owner's fee is generally determined by the size of his or her unit. For instance, the owner of a three-bedroom unit pays a larger share of the total expense than the owner of a one-bedroom unit pays. If the fees are not paid, the association may file a lien against the unit owner's property and seek a court-ordered judgment to force its sale to collect the outstanding debt.

Assessments are special payments required of unit owners for a major repair or capital improvement that is not covered by the recurring maintenance fees. These may be items like a new roof and elevators or new recreational facilities. Assessments are like maintenance fees: owners of larger units pay proportionately higher assessments than owners of smaller units, and unpaid assessments can become liens on the unit owner's property.

In Your State   **PA** Changes in the Uniform Condominium Act in Pennsylvania were signed into law November 30, 2004, and took effect January 30, 2005. For the most part, these amendments affect the governance by a board of directors and its management and operation of a condominium, including the manner in which maintenance fees and special assessments may be secured. Although these amendments have little bearing on the actual transfer of condominium ownership, they are worthy of study by prospective purchasers to ensure that they are familiar with routines of governance in a condominium. ■

In Your State   **PA** **Condominium conversions.** When an existing rental property is converted to condominium ownership, Pennsylvania law requires that the owner of the property take certain steps to protect existing tenants. The conversion from rental to ownership may be appealing to some tenants, but for tenants who are not interested in purchasing, the prospect of being dislocated could be very unsettling. The law requires that property owners comply with a variety of procedures to ensure that tenants are properly informed about the pending conversion and given ample opportunity to either purchase their units or continue as tenants for a period of time. The law is also explicit about the way leases and rental rates can be administered during a conversion. ■

In Your State   **PA** **Condominium sales.** Pennsylvania's Uniform Condominium Act requires that prospective purchasers be furnished with a variety of information to ensure that they are properly informed about the operation of the condominium association, including the fees that unit owners must pay, and the covenants and restrictions that will affect their ownership.

Prospective purchasers in a new condominium or condominium conversion must be given a *public offering statement* at least 15 days before a sales contract is signed. The document must detail 22 separate categories of information, including such items as bylaws, rules and regulations, projected operating budgets for the building, liens or encumbrances on the property, and so forth. A purchaser who is not provided the statement within the prescribed time period may cancel the contract without penalty within 15 days after receiving the material. In addition, the prospective buyer may recover an amount equal to 5 percent of the unit's sale price, up to a maximum of $2,000 or actual damages, whichever is greater. ■

Prospective purchasers of newly *converted* units must also be given a two-year warranty (which takes effect the day the units are conveyed) against structural defects in both the building's units and the common elements. In addition, purchasers must be furnished with a report prepared by an independent architect or engineer that describes the age and condition of all structural components, and mechanical and electrical systems.

Each succeeding purchaser (not the first purchaser) of a condominium unit must be given copies of the condominium declaration, bylaws and rules and regulations of the association, and a *resale certificate*. The certificate, which is prepared by the owners' association, contains pertinent financial information such as maintenance fees, possible assessments, capital expenditures, and insurance coverage. (The association may charge the seller for the expense of preparing this information.) The unit owner must furnish the resale certificate along with the condominium documents for the prospective purchaser's review prior to the closing. Buyers who receive this information after they've signed an agreement of sale have the right to void the agreement within five days after receiving the information, if they so choose.

Cooperative Ownership

In a **cooperative**, a corporation holds title to the land and the entire building. The corporation then offers *shares of stock* to prospective tenants. The price the corporation sets for each apartment becomes the price of the stock. The purchaser becomes a shareholder in the corporation by virtue of stock ownership and receives a *proprietary* (owner's) *lease* to the apartment for the life of the corporation. Because stock is personal property, the cooperative tenant-owners do not own real estate, as is the case in a condominium. Instead, they own an interest in a corporation that has only one asset: the real estate.

Operation and management.   The operation and management of a cooperative are determined by the corporation's bylaws. Through their control of the corporation, the shareholders of a cooperative control the property and its operation. They elect officers and directors who are responsible for operating the corporation and its real estate assets. The services of a professional property manager may be engaged to assist them.

Ownership in the cooperative is accompanied by the individual shareholder's commitment to abide by the corporation's bylaws that govern the tenant's use of the property (similar to the matters addressed in the restrictive covenants in a condominium) and the transfer of the shares in the corporation. The bylaws may require that the board of directors approve any prospective shareholders. In some cooperatives, a tenant-owner must sell the stock back to the corporation at the original purchase price so that the corporation will realize any profits when the shares are resold.

The corporation incurs costs to operate and maintain both the common property and the individual apartments. These costs include real estate taxes and any mortgage payments that the corporation may have. The corporation also budgets for such expenses as insurance, utilities, repairs and maintenance, janitorial and other services, replacement of equipment, and reserves for capital expenditures. Funds for the budget are assessed to the individual shareholders, generally in the form of monthly fees similar to those charged by a condominium association.

Unlike a condominium association, which can impose a lien on the unit owned by a person who defaults on maintenance payments, the burden for default in a cooperative falls on the remaining shareholders. Consequently, each shareholder is affected by the financial ability of the others. For this reason, approval of prospective tenant-owners by the board of directors frequently includes financial evaluation. If the corporation is unable to make mortgage and tax payments because of shareholder defaults, the property might be sold by court order in a foreclosure suit. This would destroy the interests of all tenant-shareholders, including those who have paid their assessments. (Nonpayment in a condominium would result in foreclosure against only the property of the defaulting owner.)

Cooperative ownership, despite its risks, has become more desirable in recent years for several reasons. Lending institutions view the shares of stock, although personal property, as acceptable collateral for financing, which was not always the case. The availability of financing expands the transferability of shares beyond wealthy cash buyers. As a tenant-owner, rather than a tenant who pays rent to a landlord, the shareholder has some control over the property. Tenants in cooperatives also enjoy certain income tax advantages from the payment of property taxes. Finally, owners also enjoy freedom from maintenance.

Time-Share Interests

A **time-share** permits multiple purchasers to buy interests in real estate (usually in a resort area), with each purchaser having the right to use the property for a certain period of time. A *time-share estate* is a real property interest in a condominium. A *time-share use* is a contract right to use the real estate owned by the developer.

A time-share *estate* is a fee simple interest. The purchaser owns the use of the property only for the period that is purchased—for instance, the 17th complete week, Sunday through Saturday, of each calendar year. The owner is assessed a maintenance fee, based on the ratio of the ownership period to the total number of ownership periods in the property. Because time-share estates are real property interests, theoretically they never end. However, the physical life of the improvements is limited and unless they are maintained in good condition, the value of the estate can diminish over time.

Time-share *use*, on the other hand, is a right conveyed by contract (personal property) to occupy and use the facilities for a certain number of years. At the end of that time, the rights terminate. In effect, the developer has sold only a right of occupancy and use to the owner, not a fee simple estate.

Typically, time-share properties are used 50 weeks each year; the remaining 2 weeks are reserved for maintenance. The time period a purchaser acquires may be stated in various ways. Some time-share programs specify a particular week or month of the year during which the owner can use the property. Others provide a rotation system so the owner can use the property at different times each year. Still other programs specify a length of time (for instance, seven days) that can be scheduled by reservation (similar to a hotel). To provide variety and convenience, some developments also offer a swapping privilege so that a time-share owner can use a similar right in another property.

Campground membership is similar to a time-share *use*. The owner purchases the right to use the developer's facilities, which usually consist of an open area with minimal improvements (such as camper/trailer hookups and restrooms). Normally, a campground membership does not specify a particular time period; the use of the property is limited only by availability and weather.

IN PRACTICE

Laws governing the development and sale of time-shares and campground memberships are generally complex and vary substantially from state to state. Time-share properties may be subject to subdivision regulations, and the sale may be subject to federal securities laws. The *Pennsylvania Real Estate Licensing and Registration Act,* which can be found in Appendix C, requires licensure for a time-share salesperson and a campground membership salesperson.

■ SUMMARY

Sole ownership, or ownership in severalty, means that title is held by one person or legal entity. Under co-ownership, title can be held concurrently by more than one person in several ways.

In a tenancy in common, each party holds an undivided fractional interest in severalty. Individual owners may sell their interests. Upon death, a tenant in common's interest passes to the tenant's heirs or according to a will. There are no special requirements to create this interest. When two or more parties hold title to real estate, they hold title as tenants in common unless another intention is expressed.

In joint tenancy, title is held by two or more owners as though all owners collectively constitute one unit. The four unities of possession, interest, time, and title must be present. To establish a joint tenancy with right of survivorship, the intentions of the parties must be stated clearly.

Tenancy by the entirety resembles a joint tenancy but can only exist between husband and wife. It gives the surviving spouse sole ownership upon the death of the other owner. During their lives, both must sign the deed for any title to pass to a purchaser. Community property rights exist only in certain states and pertain only to property owned by husband and wife.

Real estate ownership may also be held in trust. To create a trust, the settlor (trustor) conveys title to the property to a trustee, who owns and manages the property. Other trusts include living trusts, testamentary trusts, and land trusts.

Various types of business organizations may own real estate. A corporation is a legal entity and can hold title to real estate in severalty. An S corporation, as long as it meets all the strict requirements, can avoid the double taxation that applies to other corporations. Although a partnership is technically not a legal entity, the *Uniform Partnership Act* and the *Uniform Limited Partnership Act* adopted in Pennsylvania recognize a partnership as an entity and permit it to own property in the partnership's name. A limited liability company is a hybrid organization that combines the most attractive features of a partnership and a corporation. A syndicate is an association of two or more people or firms organized to make an investment in real estate. Many syndicates are joint ventures and are organized for only a single project. A syndicate may be organized as a co-ownership, trust, corporation, or partnership.

In condominium ownership, an occupant/owner holds a fee simple estate to the unit plus a share of the common elements. Each owner receives an individual property tax bill and may mortgage the unit as desired. Expenses for operating the common elements are collected by an owners' association through periodic assessments. The *Pennsylvania Uniform Condominium Act* is the Pennsylvania law governing condominiums.

In cooperative ownership, title to real estate is held by a corporation. Shareholders in the corporation have proprietary, long-term leases entitling them to occupy their apartments. The corporation is responsible for paying taxes, mortgage interest and principal, and all operating expenses. Shareholders are responsible for supporting these expenditures through periodic assessments.

A time-share enables multiple purchasers to own an estate or use an interest in real estate, with the right to use it for a part of each year.

QUESTIONS

1. The four unities of possession, interest, time, and title are associated with
   a. tenancy by the entirety.
   b. severalty ownership.
   c. tenants in common.
   d. joint tenancy.

2. A parcel of real estate was purchased by *K* and *Z*. The deed they received from the seller at the closing conveyed the property "to *K* and *Z*" without further explanation. Therefore, *K* and *Z* most likely took title as
   a. joint tenants.
   b. tenants in common.
   c. tenants by the entirety.
   d. community property owners.

3. *M*, *B*, and *F* are joint tenants with rights of survivorship in a tract of land. *F* conveys her interest to *V*. Which of the following statements is true?
   a. *M* and *B* are joint tenants.
   b. *M*, *B*, and *V* are joint tenants.
   c. *M*, *B*, and *V* are tenants in common.
   d. *V* now has severalty ownership of the land.

4. In Pennsylvania, a conveyance made "to Arnold and Julia Haber, Husband and Wife," without further elaboration, creates a
   a. joint tenancy.
   b. tenancy in common.
   c. tenancy by the entirety.
   d. partnership.

5. Individual ownership of a single unit and concurrent ownership of the common areas best describes
   a. a cooperative.
   b. a condominium.
   c. a time-share.
   d. membership camping.

6. *E*, *J*, and *Q* were concurrent owners of a parcel of real estate. *J* died, and his interest passed according to his will to become part of his estate. *J* was a
   a. joint tenant.
   b. tenant in common.
   c. tenant by the entirety.
   d. severalty owner.

7. Paul conveys a vineyard in trust to Ruth, with the instruction that any income derived from the vineyard is to be used for Tanya's medical care. Which of the following statements most accurately describes the relationship of these parties?
   a. Paul is the trustee, Ruth is the trustor, and Tanya is the beneficiary.
   b. Paul is the trustor, Ruth is the trustee, and Tanya is the beneficiary.
   c. Paul is the beneficiary, Ruth is the trustor, and Tanya is the trustee.
   d. Paul is the trustor, Ruth is the beneficiary, and Tanya is the trustee.

8. A condominium is created when
   a. the construction of the improvements is completed.
   b. the owner files a declaration in the public record.
   c. the condominium owners' association is established.
   d. all of the unit owners file their documents in the public record.

9. Ownership that allows possession for a specific time each year is a
   a. cooperative.
   b. condominium.
   c. time-share.
   d. trust.

10. Which of the following forms of ownership may be created by operation of law?
    a. Joint tenancy
    b. Tenancy by the entirety
    c. Joint tenancy with right of survivorship
    d. Tenancy in common

11. A corporation may own real estate in all of the following manners *EXCEPT* in
    a. trust.
    b. severalty.
    c. partnership.
    d. joint tenancy.

12. All of the following are forms of concurrent ownership *EXCEPT*
    a. tenancy by the entirety.
    b. community property.
    c. tenancy in common.
    d. severalty.

13. The right of survivorship is associated with
    a. severalty ownership.
    b. community property.
    c. tenancy in common.
    d. joint tenancy.

14. All of the following involve a freehold interest *EXCEPT* a
    a. condominium.
    b. time-share use.
    c. tenancy by the entirety.
    d. tenancy in common.

15. If a property is held by two or more owners as tenants in common, the interest of a deceased cotenant will pass to the
    a. surviving owner or owners.
    b. heirs of the deceased.
    c. state by the law of escheat.
    d. trust under which the property was owned.

16. Sandra lives in the elegant Howell Tower. Sandra's possessory interest is evidenced by a proprietary lease. What does Sandra own?
    a. Condominium unit
    b. Cooperative unit
    c. Time-share
    d. Leasehold

17. A proprietary lease is characteristic of the ownership of a
    a. condominium unit.
    b. cooperative unit.
    c. time-share estate.
    d. membership camping interest.

18. A trust created by will after a property owner's death is called a
    a. real estate endowment trust.
    b. testamentary trust.
    c. real estate investment trust.
    d. beneficiary trust.

19. *T* owns a fee simple interest in Unit 9 and 5 percent of the common elements. *T* owns a
    a. campground membership.
    b. time-share estate.
    c. cooperative unit.
    d. condominium unit.

20. An owner or developer of a newly built condominium building must provide each prospective unit purchaser with all of the following *EXCEPT* a
    a. public offering statement.
    b. two-year warranty against structural defects.
    c. resale certificate.
    d. property report.

ANSWERS

1. D   The distinguishing feature of joint tenancy is unity of ownership. In order to form the unity of ownership four key elements must be present—possession, interest, time, and title (PITT). The owners hold title as though they were one unit. (p. 105)

2. B   If the deed of conveyance does not stipulate the tenancy being created, Pennsylvania law recognizes the concurrent owners as tenants in common. (p. 104)

3. A   While a joint tenant is free to convey his or her interest in the property, doing so destroys the joint tenancy between M, B, and F. While M and B remain as joint tenants with regard to their two-thirds ownership interest, V becomes a tenant in common with regard to his one-third interest. (p. 105)

4. C   When property is conveyed to grantees or devisees who are clearly identified as husband and wife, Pennsylvania law recognizes the estate created to be a tenancy by the entirety. (p. 107)

5. B   Real estate ownership that involves holding title to an individual unit and a specified share of the undivided interest in the common elements is a condominium. (p. 112)

6. B   If a concurrent owner has the right to dispose of his or her interest under the terms of a will or the interest passes to his or her heirs, the concurrent owner is a tenant in common. J's interest is that of tenant in common. (p. 104)

7. B   The trustor (Paul) is the party creating the trust. Title to the vineyard is held by the trustee (Ruth) for the benefit of the beneficiary of the trust (Tanya). (p. 108)

8. B   A condominium is created and established when the owner of an existing building or developer of unimproved property executes and records a declaration of condominium in public records. (p. 113)

9. C   When a party owns a time-share estate, the party owns the right to use the property for the period of time specified, possibly a specific week (or weeks) of each calendar year. (p. 116)

10. D   "Operation of law" refers to creation by a legal mechanism, such as a statutory law or legal proceeding such as probate, marriage, and so on. While a tenancy in common may be created by operation of law, a joint tenancy can only be created by deed or by will. (p. 105)

11. D   A corporation is a recognized legal entity that can hold title to real estate. It may be a sole owner (severalty); it may own real estate in trust (as a trustee); or the corporation may hold title with others as a partner in a partnership. A corporation is not a joint tenant. (p. 111)

12. D   Concurrent ownership exists when two or more parties hold title to real estate. Ownership in severalty exists when a sole or singular owner holds title to the real estate and has complete discretion over its transfer. (p. 103)

13. D   The "right of survivorship" refers to a key characteristic of joint tenancy. When a joint tenant dies, that party's interest belongs to the remaining (surviving) joint tenants. A joint tenant's interest does not pass to the heirs of the deceased joint tenant, nor may the joint tenant will the interest to a devisee. (p. 106)

14. B   Freehold interests are ownership interests. A time-share use interest refers to the contract right to use real estate owned by a developer for a specified time. It differs from a time-share estate, which does create an ownership interest in property. (p. 117)

15. B   In a tenancy in common, each cotenant holds interest in severalty. When the cotenant dies, the undivided interest passes to heirs of the cotenant or is passed to a devisee under the terms of a will. (p. 104)

16. B Sandra lives in a cooperative. She has a possessory interest as evidenced by a proprietary lease. A corporation holds title to the land and building, with tenants owning shares of stock (personal property) in the corporation. The tenant-shareholder occupies a unit under the terms of a proprietary (owner's) lease. (p. 115)

17. B A proprietary (owner's) lease is found in a cooperative. It creates the right for the cooperative tenant/shareholder to occupy a unit in the building. (p. 115)

18. B Trusts may be created by agreement during a property owner's lifetime (a living trust) or established by the terms of a will (a testamentary trust). (p. 109)

19. D *T* has condominium ownership. Ownership of a fee simple interest in an individual unit and a specified share of the undivided interest in "common areas" is condominium ownership. (p. 112)

20. C A resale certificate prepared by the owner's association and containing pertinent financial information must be provided to second and subsequent owners. First purchasers of newly constructed units must be provided with a public offering statement, property report, and a two-year warranty against structural defects. (p. 115)

CHAPTER EIGHT

REAL ESTATE TAXES AND LIENS

■ LEARNING OBJECTIVES

When you've finished reading this chapter, you should be able to

- classify various liens by type (voluntary, involuntary, specific, general);
- explain how liens affect title and how priority of liens is determined;
- describe how real estate taxes are applied and become tax liens;
- identify nontax liens that may be charged against real estate;
- explain how judgments are enforced, and
- define the key terms.

■ KEY TERMS

, Value of property

ad valorem tax
assessment
attachment
equalization factor
general lien
involuntary lien
judgment

lien
lis pendens
mechanic's lien
mill
mortgage lien
real estate tax

special assessment
specific lien
subordination
  agreement
tax sale
voluntary lien

■ LIENS

An encumbrance, as discussed in Chapter 5, is a right or interest that someone other than the fee owner has in a property. One kind of an encumbrance is a lien. A **lien** is a charge or claim against a property that is made to enforce the payment of a debt of the property owner. All liens are viewed as encumbrances, but not all encumbrances are liens. The distinction between the two is that liens are financial or monetary in nature, while other encumbrances may be physical in nature, such as easements and encroachments.

Types of Liens

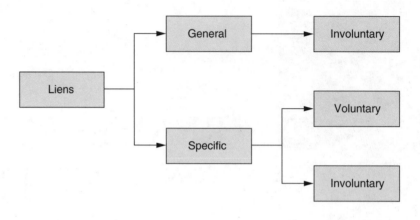

All liens are encumbrances, but not all encumbrances are liens.

A lien represents only an *interest in* the ownership; it does not constitute ownership in the property. The lienholder's interest gives him or her the right to force the sale of the property if necessary to collect a debt. Generally, a lienholder must institute a legal action to force the sale or acquire title. The debt is then paid out of the sale's proceeds.

Liens can be classified in several ways. (See Figure 8.1.) One way liens are classified is by how they are created. A **voluntary lien** is created intentionally by a debtor's action. When someone borrows money, the lender generally requires some form of security. *Security,* also referred to as *collateral,* is something of value the borrower promises to give the lender if the borrower fails to repay the debt. When the security is real estate, the borrower gives the lender the right to file a lien on the property. An **involuntary lien,** on the other hand, is not a matter of choice for the property owner; it is created by law. Examples include a real estate tax lien and a court-ordered judgment that requires payment of an obligation.

Liens are also classified according to the type of property involved. **General liens** usually affect all property, both real and personal, of a debtor. These liens include judgments, estate and inheritance taxes, debts of a deceased person, corporation franchise taxes, and Internal Revenue Service taxes. There is a difference, however, between a lien on real property and a lien on personal property. A lien on real property attaches when it is filed. In contrast, a lien on personal property does not attach until the personal property is seized. **Specific liens** are secured by a specific parcel of real estate and affect only that particular property. Specific liens on real estate include mechanics' liens, mortgage liens, taxes, and liens for special assessments and utilities.

Effects of Liens on Title

The existence of a lien does not necessarily prevent the property owner from conveying title to someone else. However, the lien might reduce the property's value or make the property less desirable because few people are willing to take on the risk of an encumbered property. The lien attaches to the property, not the property owner, so a new owner could lose the property if the creditor takes legal action to enforce payment of the lien. Once properly established, a lien *runs with the land* and binds all successive owners until the lien is cleared. A purchaser, for example, would take title along with the existing liens unless the sales documents provided for the seller to satisfy the debts and deliver title without the liens. Although sales transactions customarily require that liens be satisfied, the important point is that liens are not automatically extinguished simply because a property is sold or title transfers. Future transfers could also be jeopardized if the debt is not satisfied.

Priority of liens.   *Priority of liens* refers to the order in which claims against the property will be satisfied (that is, paid off). In general, the rule for priority of liens is "first come, first served." Liens take priority from the *date of recording* in public records of the county where the property is located.

> **Priority of Liens**
>
> Generally, the rule is *the first in time is first in line*. There are some notable exceptions, however.

There are notable exceptions to this rule, however. For instance, real estate taxes and special assessments generally take priority over all other liens, regardless of the order in which the liens are recorded. This means that if the property goes through a court sale to satisfy unpaid debts or obligations, outstanding real estate taxes and special assessments will be paid from the proceeds *first*. The remainder of the proceeds will be used to pay other outstanding liens in the order of their priority. Mechanics' liens take priority as provided by state law but never take priority over tax and special assessment liens.

Subordination agreements are written agreements between lienholders to change the priority of their liens. Under a subordination agreement, the holder of a superior or prior lien agrees to permit a junior lienholder's interest to move ahead of his or her lien. Decisions to enter into this agreement are typically driven by the nature of the first and junior liens and the amount of the financial interests that are at stake. Recording of liens is discussed further in Chapter 10.

■ REAL ESTATE TAXES

As discussed in Chapter 5, the ownership of real estate is subject to certain government powers. One of these is the right of state and local governments to levy **real estate tax** to pay for their operations. Because the location of real estate is permanently fixed, the government can levy taxes with a high degree of certainty that they will be collected. Real estate tax liens usually have priority over other previously recorded liens. This position is especially desirable if the lien must be enforced by a court-ordered sale.

There are two types of real estate taxes: general real estate taxes (also called *ad valorem taxes*) and special assessments or improvement taxes. Both are levied against specific parcels of property and automatically become liens on those properties.

General Tax (Ad Valorem Tax)

The general real estate tax, or **ad valorem tax,** is made up of the taxes levied on real estate by various government bodies and municipalities. These taxes are known as *ad valorem* (Latin for "according to value") *taxes* because the amount is based on the *value of the property being taxed*. General real estate taxes are levied for the general operation of the government body or agency authorized to levy the tax. These taxing bodies include

- counties, cities, boroughs, and townships;
- school districts or boards;
- drainage, water, and sanitary districts; and
- municipal authorities operating parks, forest preserves, and recreational districts.

Historically, real estate taxes have been the principal source of revenue for local government in Pennsylvania. Real estate taxes are one of those certainties in life that property owners cannot escape. Rising costs of government coupled with increasing costs to operate and maintain real estate, however, have raised debate over the fairness of real estate taxes. Homeowners argue that the ownership of a basic necessity does not connote affluence or wealth. Furthermore, real estate tax bills are not tied to the owner's income or ability to pay. This is especially problematic for people living on fixed incomes. Property owners also often argue that they are paying for services, such as public schools, they do not personally use.

In Your State

PA The Pennsylvania legislature has attempted to alleviate the dependence on real estate tax by permitting local government bodies to collect sales or income tax in lieu of real estate tax. However, few taxing bodies have embraced these alternatives. Recently, legislators made another attempt at tax reform when they passed Act 72 in 2004, the slot-machine gambling legislation. This would funnel money generated from the newly legalized gambling to local school districts. They, in turn, would reduce property tax bills to homeowners. The Act also requires school districts to increase local income taxes and to place on ballot for voter approval certain proposed property tax increases. As of this writing, the slot machine legislation and provisions of Act 72 are subjects of debate and may possibly be amended. The public dialogue continues in search of workable solutions for property tax reform. ■

In Your State

PA **Exemptions from general taxes.** Certain real estate is exempt from taxation in most states. Exemptions in Pennsylvania are authorized by the state's constitution, by statute (the General County Assessment Law), and other assessment laws that apply to specific classes of counties. The general theory is that property used for certain public purposes is tax exempt. Common exemptions are granted for property owned by

- city, state, and federal governments;
- municipal authorities;
- educational institutions;
- hospitals;
- religious institutions; and
- public charities.

As simple as this sounds, the laws are fairly complex, giving rise to considerable case law in Pennsylvania that interprets the circumstances in which tax-exempt status can be granted. Even though a property is owned by a tax-exempt organization, the controlling factor is whether the property is used for public, charitable, or not-for-profit purposes. For instance, the building a church owns and uses for religious activities is exempt; the parking lot adjacent to the church's building is not exempt because the purpose of the lot is for parking cars, not religious activities.

State laws also allow special exemptions to reduce real estate tax bills for certain property owners or land users. For instance, senior citizens are granted reductions or limited increases in assessed values on their homes, known as Homestead Exemptions. These exemptions are especially important for long-time residents in neighborhoods where significant increases in property values would otherwise make the taxes unaffordable. Other temporary reductions in real estate taxes are frequently used to attract industries, stimulate economic growth and development, or encourage rehabilitation of property. ■

Assessment.   An assessment, or *assessed value*, is the official value of real estate that is used for tax purposes. Real estate is valued, or assessed, for tax purposes by county assessors, evaluators, or appraisers. Assessments are normally a percentage of the property's fair market value. Depending on the type of property and the taxing jurisdiction within which it is located, one value may be assigned to the total property or separate values may be assigned to the land and the building.

In Your State   **PA**   Each of Pennsylvania's 67 counties has an official responsible for determining the taxable value of all real estate within that county. Individual municipalities and school districts use the county-developed assessed values when determining tax rates. In other words, the county establishes the assessed value; the taxing jurisdiction establishes the tax rate. ■

A property owner who feels that the county made an error in determining the assessed value of the property may appeal the assessment. The assessed value is the subject of an appeal, not the amount of the tax bill. Taxing bodies also may appeal the assessment. Property owners generally claim that the assessment is too high; taxing bodies typically assert that it is too low. Appeals are first heard by a county assessment appeals board. Appellants who are not satisfied with the board's decision can ultimately take an appeal to court.

Equalization.   In some jurisdictions, when it is necessary to correct general inequalities in statewide tax assessments, an **equalization factor** is used to achieve uniformity. This factor may be applied to raise or lower assessments in a particular county. The assessed value of each property in the area is multiplied by the equalization factor; the tax rate is then applied to the equalized assessment. For instance, if the assessments in one county are determined to be 20 percent lower than the average assessments throughout the rest of the state, the underassessment can be corrected by applying an equalization factor of 120 percent to each assessment in that county. A parcel of real estate assessed at $98,000, for example, would be taxed on an equalized value of $117,600 ($98,000 × 1.20 = $117,600).

Five Variable Used to Compute Real Estate Taxes
1. Market value
2. Tax ratio
3. Assessed value
4. Tax rate
5. Tax amount

Tax rates. The process of determining a real estate tax rate begins with the *adoption of a budget* by each taxing body. Each budget covers the financial requirements of the taxing body for the coming fiscal year. The fiscal year may be the January to December calendar year or some other 12-month period designated by statute. The budget includes an estimate of all expenditures for the year and an estimate of all income expected from fees, revenue sharing, and other sources. The difference between income and expenses is the amount that must be raised from real estate taxes.

The next step is *appropriation.* This is the way a taxing body authorizes the expenditure of funds and the acquisition of funding. Appropriation generally involves the adoption of an ordinance or passage of a law that states the specific terms of the proposed taxation and authorizes the tax levy. The levy is the taxing body's formal action that imposes the general real estate tax on the property owners.

The *tax rate* for each individual taxing body is computed separately. To arrive at a tax rate, the total monies needed for the coming fiscal year are divided by the total assessments of all real estate located within the taxing body's jurisdiction. For example, the budget indicates that $300,000 must be raised from real estate tax, and the assessment roll (assessor's record) of all taxable real estate within the taxing body's district is $10,000,000. The tax rate is computed thus:

$$\$300,000 \div \$10,000,000 = 0.03 \ or \ 3\%$$

The tax rate may be expressed in a number of different ways. In many areas it is expressed in mills. A **mill** is *1/1,000 of a dollar, or $0.001.*

The tax rate computed in the foregoing example could be expressed as 30 mills (.030) or $3 per $100 of assessed value or $30 per $1,000 of assessed value.

Tax bills. A property owner's *tax bill* is computed by applying the tax rate to the assessed valuation of the property. For example, on a property assessed for tax purposes at $90,000 in a taxing district with a tax rate of 30 mills, the tax bill would be $2,700 ($90,000 × 0.03 = $2,700).

In Your State

PA The property owner may receive one tax bill that incorporates all real estate taxes levied by the various taxing bodies or separate bills from the individual taxing bodies. When taxing bodies operate on different budget or fiscal years, there could be separate tax bills at various times throughout the year. If a property is mortgaged, tax bills are often sent to the mortgage holder rather than the property owner, and the bills are paid from escrow or impound accounts established for this purpose. Pennsylvania law requires counties and municipal governments to adopt budgets and set tax rates on a January-to-December calendar year. Most school districts in Pennsylvania, however, are required to prepare budgets and set tax rates on a fiscal year that begins July 1. Due dates for paying taxes are also set by law. ■

IN PRACTICE

All parties involved in a real estate transaction need complete and accurate information about the real estate taxes. This includes verifying the amount of the county, school, and municipal taxes levied against a property, when each tax is due, and the payment schedule. This information is important for computing the taxes that will be owed when the sales transaction is completed (at closing or settlement) as well as for calculating the buyer's yearly ownership costs.

Enforcement of tax liens.   Real estate taxes must be valid to be enforceable. This means they must be levied properly, be used for a legal purpose, and be applied equitably (that is, fairly) to all property. Real estate taxes that have been delinquent for the period of time specified by state law can be collected through a tax foreclosure or a **tax sale.**

Individual counties may set up tax claim bureaus. Under this system, the names of real estate owners who have not paid their taxes after one year are turned over to the tax claim bureau. Their properties may be sold after the second week in September of the following year. Once the property is sold, the owner usually does *not* have the right to redeem the interest, that is, buy back the real estate by settling all back taxes and other costs. In counties that do not have tax claim bureaus, the county treasurer holds tax sales and a redemption period is granted. Separate laws govern tax sales in the cities of Pittsburgh and Scranton. Be sure to consult local authorities about the procedures used in specific areas.

Special Assessments (Improvement Taxes)

Special assessments, the second category of real estate taxes, are special taxes levied to fund public improvements that benefit the property. Property owners in the area of the improvements are required to pay for them because their properties benefit directly from the improvements. The installation of paved streets, curbs, gutters, sidewalks, storm sewers, and street lighting increases the values of the affected properties. The owners, in effect, reimburse the levying authority for that increase. However, the improvements rarely result in dollar-for-dollar increases in value.

Property owners may recommend improvements by petitioning the government to install them, or a legislative authority such as the city council or board of commissioners may initiate the action. Public hearings are held, for which the owners of the affected properties are given notice. After the preliminary legal steps have been taken, the government body adopts an *ordinance* that states the nature of the improvement, its cost, and a description of the area to be assessed.

Typically, each property in the improvement district will be charged a prorated share of the total amount of the assessment. The share is determined either on a fractional basis (four houses may equally share the cost of one streetlight) or on a cost-per-front-foot basis (wider lots incur a greater cost than narrower lots for street paving and curb and sidewalk installation).

In most states, an assessment becomes a *lien* following the confirmation of the assessment roll (the approval of the improvements to be made). In Pennsylvania, if the assessment is determined by the front footage method, it becomes a lien from the date the lien is filed. If the assessment is determined by the benefit method, it becomes a lien from the date the taxing authority determines an assessment of benefits.

Special assessments plus interest are usually due and payable in equal annual installments over five to ten years. The first installment, including one year's interest on the entire assessment, is generally due during the year following confirmation. Subsequent installments plus one year's interest on the unpaid balance are billed in the following years. Property owners usually have the right to prepay any or all installments and thereby stop the interest charges.

IN PRACTICE Although real property taxes are deductible for income-tax purposes, only the annual interest charged in connection with special assessments is deductible, not the assessments themselves. When an agreement of sale is negotiated, any pending or existing special assessments should be disclosed and the person who is responsible for payment should be identified.

■ OTHER LIENS ON REAL PROPERTY

In addition to general real estate tax and special assessment liens, the following types of liens may be charged against real property.

Mortgage Lien

A **mortgage lien** is a specific, voluntary lien *on real estate given to a lender by the borrower as security for a mortgage loan*. It becomes a lien on real property when the lender records the mortgage in the recorder of deeds office in the county where the property is located. Mortgage lenders generally require a first lien, referred to as a *first mortgage lien*. This means that, aside from real estate taxes, no other major liens against the property would take priority over the mortgage lien. Subsequent liens are referred to as *junior liens*. A second mortgage, for example, would be junior to a first mortgage lien. Mortgages will be discussed in greater detail in a later chapter.

Mechanic's Lien

A **mechanic's lien** is a specific, involuntary lien that *gives security to those who perform labor or furnish material to improve real property*. The right to file a mechanic's lien is based on the enhancement of value theory; that is, the labor performed and materials furnished have enhanced the value of the real estate. Contractors, subcontractors, architects, equipment lessors, surveyors, laborers, and others have the right to file a lien.

To be entitled to a mechanic's lien, the person who did the work or furnished materials must have a contract with the owner or owner's authorized representative. The lien intends to cover situations in which the owner has not fully paid for the work or when the general contractor has been paid but has failed to pay the subcontractors who actually furnish the labor or materials.

In Your State **PA** Under the Pennsylvania Mechanic's Lien Law, a contractor or subcontractor can file a claim with the court of common pleas in the county in which the property is located. This must be done within four months after the work is completed. (Entitlement to a lien is subject to certain exceptions and compliance with procedures for serving notice on the property owner.) If the claim is successful, the mechanic's lien takes priority as of the date on which the first "visible construction" begins when an improvement is erected or constructed or as of the date the claim is filed when an existing improvement is altered or repaired. A claimant must take steps to enforce the lien within two years of the date the claim is filed. Enforcement is a court action to foreclose the lien through the sale of the real estate. Proceeds from the sale are then used to pay the lien. ■

Title can be protected from mechanics' liens in several ways:

- A *waiver of liens* can be included in the construction contract to protect the title from liens being filed by the general contractor. This waiver, however, does not protect against liens filed by subcontractors.
- A *stipulation against liens* can be filed in the prothonotary's office to protect the title from subcontractors' liens. Because the general contractor is liable to subcontractors for payment, a stipulation against liens serves notice that subcontractors cannot file liens, but rather they must seek recovery from the general contractor.
- A *release of liens* can be signed by everyone who has furnished material or labor after work is completed. Essentially, this is a notice that all the signatories release their lien rights, which presumably they would not do if they have not been paid. A release of liens is not foolproof because it does not show that all persons who have the right to a lien have signed the release.
- A *notice of nonresponsibility* can be posted on the property and recorded in public record by the property owner. This may be used only when a third party, such as a tenant, orders improvements; it is the property owner's notice that he or she will not be responsible for any charges.

Mechanic's lien insurance, which accompanies a title insurance policy, may be purchased. The insurance provides payment of a mechanic's lien that surfaces after the title is searched and the policy is issued. However, *mechanic's lien* insurance does not protect against a lien being filed. Because a mechanic's lien can be filed within four months after the work has been completed, a lien would not be discovered during the search of title records before the expiration of that time. This can cause problems when a recently constructed, altered, or repaired property is sold. The purchaser's mortgage lender would expect to be the senior lien, but an outstanding mechanic's lien would have priority. The lender may require evidence that no work has recently been done or, if it has, require that a release of liens be signed. Because of the failings in a release, lenders commonly require mechanic's lien insurance to protect their lien position.

Judgments

A **judgment** is a *decree issued by a court.* When the decree establishes the amount a debtor owes and provides for money to be awarded, it is referred to as a *money judgment.*

A judgment becomes a general, involuntary lien on *both real and personal property* owned by the debtor. A judgment is not the same as a mortgage because no specific parcel of real estate was given as security at the time the debt was created. A lien usually covers only property located within the county in which the judgment is issued. As a result, notices of the lien must be filed in any county to which a creditor wishes to extend the lien coverage. Judgments against real estate take priority as of the date they are filed in the prothonotary's office; judgments against personal property become a lien when the creditor orders the sheriff to levy the property and the property is actually seized.

In Your State   **PA** Judgments may be obtained as a result of a court suit. Amicable judgments, on the other hand, result from *confessions of judgment*. These are clauses that are often included in notes, bonds, and leases. They authorize an attorney to confer a judgment against the borrower or lessee for nonpayment of the debt. In Pennsylvania, when a person signs a document that contains a confession of judgment clause, he or she must also be given an explanation of rights. This document explains the rights that are waived when a party agrees to a confession of judgment. The signed explanation of rights must be recorded along with the judgment. ■

To enforce a judgment, the creditor must obtain a *writ of execution* from the court. The writ directs the sheriff to seize and sell as much of the debtor's property as is necessary to pay both the debt and the expenses of the sale. When real property is sold to satisfy the debt, the debtor should demand a legal document known as a *satisfaction of judgment* (or *satisfaction piece*). This is filed with the prothonotary so that the record is cleared of the judgment.

Lis pendens.   There is often a considerable delay between the time a lawsuit is filed and the time final judgment is rendered. When any suit is filed that affects title to real estate, a special notice, known as a **lis pendens** (Latin for "litigation pending") is recorded. A lis pendens is not itself a lien, but rather a *notice of a possible future lien*. Recording a lis pendens notifies all interested parties, such as prospective purchasers and lenders, that there is a potential claim against the property. It also establishes a priority for the later lien; the lien is backdated to the recording date of the lis pendens.

Attachments.   To prevent a debtor from conveying title to previously unsecured real estate (realty that is not mortgaged or is similarly unencumbered) while a court suit is being decided, a creditor may seek a writ of **attachment.** By this writ, the court retains custody of the property until the suit concludes. The creditor must first post a surety bond with the court or deposit sufficient money to cover any possible loss or damage to the debtor while the court has custody of the property.

Commercial Real Estate Broker Lien

A *commercial real estate broker lien* is a specific, involuntary lien filed against a property involved in a commercial real estate transaction. The *Commercial Real Estate Broker Lien Act* enables licensed real estate brokers (not their associate brokers or salespeople) to file a lien for payment of services rendered. *This law applies only to commercial real estate transactions.* It does not include real estate zoned for one to four residential units or real estate zoned for agricultural purposes.

In general, a broker who represents the owner of the property under a listing agreement, has provided real estate services, and whose listed property is subject to an agreement of sale may file a lien prior to settlement. A broker who represents a buyer may file a lien no later than 90 days after the buyer takes title to the property. A lien can also be filed against a leased property no later than 90 days after the procurement of a lease. In order to file a lien, a broker must follow detailed procedures as stated in the law, including requirements to notify the owner prior to filing. The lien takes priority as of the date of filing and will be paid in the order filed, except for mortgages and mechanics' liens. The broker must initiate formal proceedings to collect the debt within two years of recording.

Domestic Support Lien

In Your State

PA *Domestic support liens* are involuntary liens that may be filed on all real estate owned by a person who has overdue child support obligations. These liens are authorized by Pennsylvania's *Domestic Relations Code* as amended in 1997. Known as the "Deadbeat Parent Law," the amendments provide that overdue child support obligations existing as of January 1, 1998, constitute a lien on real property owned by the obligor within the judicial district where the overdue support is owed. Lien priority is determined by the date that each support payment (which makes up the lien) becomes overdue. Only the portion of a support lien that predates a creditor's judgment or mortgage will have priority over the creditor's lien. When a property encumbered by a domestic support lien is sold, a statement must be obtained from the domestic relations section of court in the county where the property is located to verify the current status of any lien. ■

Other General and Specific Liens

Real estate taxes are not the only tax liens that can encumber a property. Other kinds of tax liens also can be filed. These are *general, involuntary* liens and include the following:

- *Internal Revenue Service (IRS)*—An IRS lien results from a person's failure to pay any portion of federal taxes, such as income and withholding taxes. All real and personal property held by the delinquent taxpayer is encumbered by an IRS lien.
- *Federal estate taxes and state inheritance taxes* (as well as the debts of deceased persons)—These liens encumber a deceased person's real and personal property. Normally, these obligations are paid or cleared in probate court proceedings.
- *Corporate franchise tax*—State governments generally levy a corporation franchise tax on corporations as a condition of allowing them to do business in the state. All real and personal property owned by the corporation is encumbered by this lien.

In addition to the specific liens that have been discussed, several others include the following:

- *Municipal utility liens*—Municipalities generally have the right to file a *specific, involuntary* lien on the property of an owner who refuses to pay bills for water or other municipal utility services. (Utilities like electricity and natural gas are generally provided by private service contracts and are not lienable.)

■ *Surety bail bond lien*—A real estate owner charged with a crime for which he or she must face trial may post bail in the form of real estate rather than cash. The execution and recording of such a bail bond creates a *specific, voluntary* lien against the owner's real estate. If the accused fails to appear in court, the lien may be enforced by the sheriff or other court officer.

■ SUMMARY

Liens are claims of creditors or tax officials against the real and personal property of a debtor. A lien is a type of encumbrance. Liens are either general, covering all real and personal property of a debtor/owner, or specific, covering only identified property. They are also either voluntary (arising from an action of the debtor) or involuntary—created by statute.

With the exception of real estate tax liens and mechanics' liens, the priority of liens generally is determined by the order in which they are filed in the prothonotary's office of the county in which the debtor's property is located.

Real estate taxes are levied annually by local taxing authorities and are generally given priority over other liens. Payments are required before stated dates, after which penalties accrue. An owner may lose title to the property for nonpayment of taxes, because such tax-delinquent property can be sold at a tax sale. Some states allow a time period during which a defaulted owner can redeem the real estate from a tax sale.

Special assessments are levied to allocate the cost of improvements such as new sidewalks, curbs, or paving to the real estate that benefit from them. Assessments are usually payable annually over a five-year or ten-year period, together with interest due on the balance of the assessment.

Mortgage liens are voluntary, specific liens given to lenders to secure payment for mortgage loans.

Mechanics' liens protect general contractors, subcontractors, and material suppliers whose work enhances the value of real estate.

A judgment is a court decree obtained by a creditor, usually for a money award from a debtor. The lien of a judgment can be enforced by issuance of a writ of execution and sale by the sheriff to pay the judgment amount and costs.

Attachment is a means of preventing a defendant from conveying real estate before completion of a suit in which a judgment is sought. Lis pendens is a recorded notice of a lawsuit that is awaiting trial in court and that may result in a judgment that will affect title to a parcel of real estate.

Commercial real estate broker liens are specific, involuntary liens that a broker who meets the statutory requirements may file for payment of services rendered. Domestic support liens are involuntary liens that are filed against real property for overdue child support obligations.

Internal Revenue Service tax liens are general liens against the property of a person who has failed to pay IRS taxes. Federal estate taxes and state inheritance taxes are general liens against a deceased owner's property. Corporation franchise tax liens are general liens against a corporation's assets.

Liens for water charges or other municipal utilities and surety bail bond liens are specific liens.

QUESTIONS

1. Which of the following best refers to the type of lien that affects all real and personal property of a debtor?
   a. Specific lien
   b. Voluntary lien
   c. Involuntary lien
   d. General lien

2. *Priority of liens* refers to the
   a. order in which a debtor assumes responsibility for payment of obligations.
   b. order in which liens will be paid if property is sold by court order to satisfy a debt.
   c. dates liens are filed for record; the lien with the earliest recording date will always take priority over other liens.
   d. fact that specific liens have greater priority than general liens.

3. A lien on real estate made to secure payment for specific municipal improvements made to a parcel of real estate is a(n)
   a. mechanic's lien.
   b. special assessment.
   c. ad valorem tax.
   d. utility lien.

4. Which of the following is classified as a general lien?
   a. Mechanic's lien
   b. Surety bail bond lien
   c. Judgment
   d. General real estate taxes

5. In disbursing funds from a foreclosure sale, the highest priority would usually be given to
   a. a mortgage dated last year.
   b. real estate taxes due.
   c. a mechanic's lien for work started before the mortgage was made.
   d. a judgment rendered the day before foreclosure.

6. A specific parcel of real estate has a market value of $80,000 and is assessed for tax purposes at 25 percent of market value. The tax rate for the county in which the property is located is 30 mills. The tax bill will be
   a. $500.
   b. $550.
   c. $600.
   d. $700.

7. The cost of public services is distributed among real estate owners through
   a. personal property tax.
   b. sales tax.
   c. real property tax.
   d. special assessment.

8. A mechanic's lien claim arises when a general contractor has performed work or provided material to improve a parcel of real estate on the owner's order and the work has not been paid for. Such a contractor has a right to
   a. remove his or her work.
   b. record a notice of the lien.
   c. record a notice of the lien and file a court suit within the time required by state law.
   d. have personal property of the owner sold to satisfy the lien.

9. What is the annual real estate tax on a property valued at $135,000 and assessed for tax purposes at $47,250 with an equalization factor of 125 percent, when the tax rate is 25 mills?
   a. $1,418
   b. $1,477
   c. $945
   d. $1,181

10. Which of the following is a voluntary, specific lien?
    a. IRS tax lien
    b. Mechanic's lien
    c. Mortgage lien
    d. Seller's lien

11. A seller sold a buyer a parcel of real estate. Title has passed, but to date the buyer has not paid the purchase price in full, as originally agreed on. To force payment, the seller should seek a(n)
    a. attachment.
    b. mechanic's lien.
    c. lis pendens.
    d. judgment.

12. In two weeks, a general contractor will file a suit against a homeowner for nonpayment. The contractor just learned that the homeowner has listed the property for sale with a real estate broker. In this situation, to protect the contractor's interest, the contractor's attorney will use a(n)
    a. seller's lien.
    b. buyer's lien.
    c. assessment.
    d. lis pendens.

13. Special assessment liens
    a. are general liens.
    b. are paid on a monthly basis.
    c. take priority over mechanics' liens.
    d. cannot be prepaid in full without penalty.

14. Which of the following is a lien on real estate?
    a. An easement running with the land
    b. An unpaid mortgage loan
    c. An encroachment
    d. A license

15. Both a mortgage lien and a judgment lien
    a. must be entered by the court.
    b. involve a debt.
    c. are general liens.
    d. are involuntary liens.

16. A mechanic's lien would be available to all of the following EXCEPT
    a. a supplier who provided materials used in construction.
    b. a subcontractor employed by a general contractor.
    c. a surveyor who prepared a survey of a subdivision.
    d. a broker employed by a builder to market homes in a new subdivision.

17. Taxes levied for the operation of the government are called
    a. assessment taxes.
    b. ad valorem taxes.
    c. special assessments.
    d. improvement taxes.

18. All of the following would probably be exempt from real estate taxes EXCEPT a(n)
    a. medical research facility.
    b. public golf course.
    c. community church.
    d. apartment building.

ANSWERS

1. **D** The terms voluntary or involuntary refer to the manner in which a lien is created, not what property the lien affects. Specific liens affect only one particular property. A general lien affects all property, real and personal, owned by a debtor. (p. 124)

2. **B** Priority refers to the order in which claims against the property will be satisfied. While the general rule is "first in time is first in line," there are exceptions. For example, a real estate tax lien would take priority over a previously recorded lien for an unpaid debt. (p. 125)

3. **B** Municipal improvements that benefit particular parcels of property are funded by special assessments levied against those properties. (p. 129)

4. **C** A judgment is a decree issued by a court that becomes a general, involuntary lien on both real and personal property owned by the debtor. (p. 132)

5. **B** If a property is sold at a foreclosure proceeding, outstanding real estate taxes and special assessments will be paid first. Tax liens take priority over other liens. (p. 125)

6. **C** Market value ($80,000) times the tax ratio (25%) equals the assessed value ($20,000). A tax rate of 30 mills is expressed as 0.030. Therefore, $20,000 × 0.030 equals a tax bill of $600. (p. 128)

7. **C** Municipalities and other taxing bodies fund the cost of public services by levying taxes on real property. These are commonly known as ad valorem taxes because the amount is based on the value of the property being taxed. (p. 125)

8. **C** In Pennsylvania, a contractor can record a notice of the lien and enforce the lien by court action (a foreclosure) to collect the debt from the sale of the real estate. (p. 131)

9. **B** Equalization factors are applied to achieve uniformity by raising or lowering assessments. The assessed value of the property is multiplied by the equalization factor, then the tax rate is applied to the equalized assessment. A

property assessed at $47,250 with an equalization factor of 125 percent would be taxed at a value of $59,062.50 ($47,250 × 125%). With a tax rate of 25 mills (0.025) the tax would be $1,477 ($59,062.50.× 0.025). (p. 127)

10. **C** A mortgage lien is voluntarily given by a borrower to a lender. It creates a specific lien against the property pledged as security for the debt. (p. 130)

11. **D** The seller of the real estate can sue the purchaser in court. If the suit is successful the court issues a decree establishing the amount the debtor owes and provides for money to be awarded. This decree is known as a money judgment. (p. 131)

12. **D** The general contractor would protect his interest or claim by recording a notice of lis pendens (litigation pending). This serves as notice of a possible future lien against the property. (p. 132)

13. **C** Special assessments are tax liens affecting a particular property. They take priority over other types of liens, including mechanics' liens. (p. 129)

14. **B** All liens are encumbrances but not all encumbrances are liens. Easements and encroachments are encumbrances, not liens. Liens are financial claims to enforce payment of a debt. An unpaid mortgage loan creates a specific, voluntary lien against the property. (p. 123)

15. **B** A mortgage lien is a specific voluntary lien. A judgment is a general involuntary lien that results from a court decree. Both involve a debt incurred by the property owner. (p. 124)

16. **D** 16. A mechanic's lien right is based upon the enhancement of value theory and may be awarded to those who perform labor or furnish material to improve real property. A broker employed to market homes is not entitled to a mechanic's lien. (p. 130)

17. B   General real estate taxes are levied and assessed according to the value of the property subject to taxation. Ad valorem is the Latin term for according to value. (pp. 125–26)

18. D   In Pennsylvania, the general theory is that property used for certain public purposes is tax exempt. Apartment buildings owned by private individuals or entities are generally not exempt from real estate taxes. (p. 126)

9

TRANSFER OF TITLE

■ LEARNING OBJECTIVES

When you've finished reading this chapter, you should be able to

- ■ list and explain the basic requirements for a valid deed;
- ■ describe the types of deeds commonly used to transfer real estate;
- ■ explain how property ownership can be transferred through voluntary alienation;
- ■ summarize key points regarding transfer of a deceased person's property; and
- ■ define the key terms.

■ KEY TERMS

acknowledgment	grantor	special warranty deed
adverse possession	habendum clause	testate
bargain and sale deed	heir	testator
deed	intestate	title
deed in trust	involuntary alienation	transfer tax
devise	judicial deed	trustee's deed
general warranty deed	power of attorney	voluntary alienation
grantee	probate	will
granting clause	quitclaim deed	

■ TITLE

The term **title** has two functions. In Chapter 7, title was explained as the right to or ownership of the real property; it represents the owner's bundle of rights. Title also serves as *evidence* of that ownership. A person who holds title would, if challenged in court, be able to recover or retain ownership or possession of a parcel of real estate. Title is not an actual printed document but rather a way of referring to ownership.

F I G U R E   9.1

Requirements for a Valid Deed

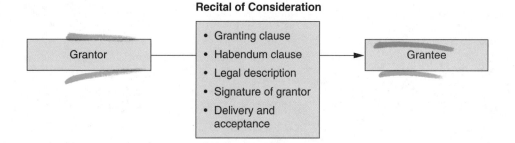

Recital of Consideration

| Grantor | → | • Granting clause
• Habendum clause
• Legal description
• Signature of grantor
• Delivery and acceptance | → | Grantee |

Real estate ownership may be transferred in several ways: it may be transferred *voluntarily* by the owner; or it may be transferred *involuntarily* by operation of law. The ownership may be transferred while the owner is living or by will or descent after the owner dies. In any event, it is the title that is transferred as a symbol of ownership. That transfer must meet certain basic requirements prescribed by state law to effect a valid conveyance.

■ VOLUNTARY ALIENATION

> A *grantor* conveys title by deed.
>
> A *grantee* receives title by deed.
>
> A *deed* is a written instrument used to transfer title to real estate.

Voluntary alienation is the legal term for the voluntary transfer of title. The owner may voluntarily transfer title by either selling or making a gift of the property. To transfer during one's lifetime, the owner must use some form of deed of conveyance.

A **deed** is a *written instrument by which an owner of real estate intentionally conveys the owner's right, title, or interest in a parcel of real estate to another.* The statute of frauds requires all deeds to be in writing. The owner who transfers title is referred to as the **grantor.** The person who is acquiring title is called the **grantee.** A deed is executed (that is, signed) only by the grantor.

Elements of a Deed

In Your State

PA Although the formal requirements vary from state to state, a deed must contain certain elements to be valid. (See Figure 9.1.) In Pennsylvania, these include

- a *grantor* who has the legal capacity to execute (sign) the deed;
- a *date*;
- a *grantee* named with reasonable certainty to be identified;
- a recital of *consideration*;
- a *granting clause* (words of conveyance);
- a *habendum clause* (to define ownership taken by the grantee); *Legal descriptor meter & bounds*
- an accurate *legal description* of the property conveyed;
- the *signature of the grantor,* sometimes with a seal or witness; and
- the *delivery* of the deed and acceptance by the grantee to pass title. ■

A deed also may include a description of any *limitations* on the conveyance of a full fee simple estate, a recital of any *exceptions* and *reservations* affecting the title ("subject to" clause), and an *acknowledgment.*

Grantor. A grantor must be of lawful age, generally at least 18 years old. As is the case with most documents, a deed executed by a *minor* (one who has not reached majority or lawful age) is generally *voidable*. A minor can disaffirm, or repudiate, the conveyance of real estate during minor age and within a reasonable period after reaching majority.

A grantor also must be of sound mind. Generally any grantor who can understand the action will be viewed as mentally capable of executing a valid deed. A deed executed by someone who is mentally impaired at the time will be *voidable* but not void. If, however, the grantor has been judged legally incompetent, the deed will be void. Real estate owned by one who is legally incompetent can be conveyed only with the court's approval.

The grantor's name must be spelled correctly and consistently throughout the deed. If the grantor's name has changed since the title was acquired, such as when a person marries, both names should be shown as, for example, "Mary Smith, formerly Mary Jones."

Grantee. A deed must name a grantee and do so in such a way that the person or persons who are acquiring the ownership can be readily identified. This means using proper legal names and indicating the relationship or form of ownership the multiple owners intend to hold. A sole owner, for example, would be identified as "Mary J. Smith, single," or "Mary J. Smith, married."

Multiple owners would be identified by their names and the tenancy they intend (refer to the discussion in Chapter 7). A deed naming a wholly fictitious person, a company that does not legally exist, or a society or club that is not properly incorporated is considered void.

Consideration. A deed must contain a clause acknowledging that the grantor has received consideration. Consideration can be anything the parties consider sufficiently valuable to be given in exchange for the ownership. Generally, consideration is stated in dollars. When a deed conveys real estate as a gift to a relative, "love and affection" may be adequate consideration. However, it is customary in most states to recite at least a *nominal* consideration, such as "$10 and other good and valuable consideration," along with love and affection.

Granting clause (words of conveyance). A deed must contain a **granting clause** that states the grantor's intention to convey the property. Depending on the type of deed and the obligations agreed to by the grantor, the wording would be similar to one of the following:

- "I, BKG, convey and warrant ..."
- "I, BKG, grant ..."
- "I, BKG, grant, bargain, and sell ..."
- "I, BKG, remise, release, and quitclaim ..."

A deed that conveys the grantor's entire fee simple interest usually contains wording such as "to Jacqueline Smith and to her heirs and assigns forever." If the grantor is conveying less than his or her complete interest, such as a life estate, the wording must indicate this limitation: for example, "to Jacqueline Smith for the duration of her natural life."

If more than one grantee is involved, the granting clause shall specify their rights in the property. The clause might state, for example, that the grantees will take title as joint tenants or tenants in common. The wording is especially important where specific wording is necessary to create a joint tenancy.

Habendum clause.   When it is necessary to define or explain the ownership to be enjoyed by the grantee, a **habendum clause** follows the granting clause. The habendum clause begins with the words "to have and to hold." Its provisions must agree with those stated in the granting clause. For example, if the grantor conveys a time-share interest or an interest less than fee simple absolute, the habendum clause would specify the owner's rights as well as how those rights are limited (a specific time frame or certain prohibited activities, for instance).

In Your State   **PA**   **Legal description of real estate.**   A valid deed must contain an accurate description of the real estate conveyed. Land is considered adequately described if a competent surveyor can locate the property using the description. In Pennsylvania, a metes-and-bounds and/or a lot-and-block description would be used. ■

Exceptions and reservations ("subject to" clauses).   A deed should specifically note any encumbrances, reservations, or limitations that affect the title being conveyed. This might include such things as restrictions and easements that run with the land. In addition to existing encumbrances, a grantor may reserve some right in the land (such as an easement) for his or her own use. As discussed in Chapter 2, a grantor may also place certain restrictions on a grantee's use of the property. For example, a developer may restrict the number of houses that may be built on a one-acre lot in a subdivision. Such private restrictions must be stated in the deed or contained in a previously recorded document (such as the subdivider's master deed) that is expressly referred to in the deed. Many of these deed restrictions have time limits and often include renewal clauses.

Signature of grantor.   To be valid, a deed must be signed or executed by *all grantors* named in the deed and in some states their signatures must be witnessed. A grantor who is unable to write is permitted to sign by *mark*. With this type of signature, usually two persons other than the notary public taking the acknowledgment must witness the grantor's making of the mark and then sign as witnesses. In Pennsylvania, unlike some other states, it is not necessary for a seal or the word *seal* to be written or printed after the grantor's signature. The use of a corporate seal by corporations, however, is always required.

In Your State   **PA**   A grantor's nonowning spouse may be required to sign a deed to waive any marital rights. This requirement varies according to state law and the manner in which title is held by the grantor(s). In lieu of a nonowning spouse's signature, the owning spouse may be required to sign an affidavit that no domestic litigation is pending. The Pennsylvania law that governs property distribution in the event of a divorce provides for "equitable distribution" of assets. An affidavit of no pending domestic litigation intends to ensure that the title would not be clouded by claims in a property settlement. ■

Most states, including Pennsylvania, permit an attorney-in-fact to sign for a grantor. An *attorney-in-fact* is the person designated by a power of attorney to act on behalf of the principal, who in the case of a deed is the grantor. A **power of attorney** is the specific written authority to execute legal instruments or perform other designated acts for another person. The power of attorney must be recorded in the county where the property is located before the deed is executed. Because a power of attorney terminates on the death of the principal, evidence must be submitted that the principal was alive when the attorney-in-fact signed the deed.

In Your State **PA** Act 39 of 1999 amended the law governing powers of attorney in Pennsylvania. An attorney-in-fact is defined as the principal's *agent* and as such is obligated to exercise the powers with certain due care on the principal's behalf. The document must state precisely what the principal intends to empower the agent to do. The scope of authority may be very broad or limited, depending on the principal's directives. Powers of attorney executed after April 12, 2000, must include a notice to the principal as prescribed in the law and an agent's acknowledgement that demonstrate the terms under which the powers are granted and the agent agrees to perform. Only a *durable* power of attorney confers authority for the agent to act notwithstanding the principal's disability or incapacity. ■

Acknowledgment. An **acknowledgment** is a formal declaration that a person who is signing a written document does so *voluntarily* and that the person's *signature is genuine*. This declaration is made before a *notary public* or authorized public officer, such as a judge, district justice, or recorder of deeds. An acknowledgment usually states that the person signing the deed or other document is known to the officer or has produced sufficient identification to prevent a forgery.

In Your State **PA** Although an acknowledgment is not essential to the *validity* of a deed, a deed that is not acknowledged is not a completely satisfactory instrument. In Pennsylvania, an unacknowledged deed is not eligible for recording. An unrecorded deed is valid between the grantor and the grantee, but it may not be a valid conveyance (to secure good title) against claims by subsequent innocent purchasers. Therefore, the grantee should require acknowledgment of the grantor's signature to help ensure good title. ■

Transfer of Title

Requires both *delivery* and *acceptance* of the deed.

Delivery and acceptance. Ownership is not considered "transferred" until the deed is actually *delivered* to and *accepted* by the grantee. The grantor may deliver the deed to the grantee either personally or through a third party. The third party, commonly known as an escrow agent, will deliver the deed to the grantee as soon as certain requirements have been satisfied. *Title is said to* *"pass" when a valid deed is delivered and accepted.* The effective date that title transfers is the date the deed itself is delivered. Generally, this must occur during the lifetime of the grantor. When a deed is delivered in escrow, the date of delivery generally "relates back" to the date that it was deposited with the escrow agent.

Execution of Corporate Deeds

The laws governing a corporate conveyance of real estate are complex and vary widely, especially for religious and not-for-profit corporations. Because the legal requirements must be followed explicitly, it is advisable to consult an attorney for all corporate conveyances. The basic rules that apply are the following:

■ A corporation can convey real estate only by authority granted in its *bylaws* or on a proper resolution passed by its *board of directors.* If all or a substantial portion of a corporation's real estate is being conveyed, a resolution authorizing the sale must be secured from the *stockholders.*
■ Deeds to real estate can be signed *only by an authorized officer.*
■ The corporate *seal* must be affixed to the conveyance.

Types of Deeds

The deed can take several forms, depending on the extent of the grantor's pledges to the grantee. Regardless of any guarantees the deed offers, however, the grantee will want additional assurance that the grantor indeed has the rights being represented in the deed. To obtain this protection, grantees request evidence of title, discussed in Chapter 11. The most common deed forms are the

■ general warranty deed,
■ special warranty deed,
■ bargain and sale deed,
■ quitclaim deed,
■ deed in trust,
■ trustee's deed, and
■ deed executed pursuant to a court order.

General warranty deed.   A **general warranty deed** provides a grantee with the greatest estate or greatest protection of any deed. It is called a general warranty deed because the grantor is legally bound by certain covenants or warranties. The warranties are express or implied by the use of certain words specified in state statutes. The basic warranties are as follows:

■ *Covenant of seisin*—The grantor warrants that he or she is the owner of the property and has the right to convey its title. (Seisin simply means "possession.") The grantee may recover damages up to the full purchase price if this covenant is broken.
■ *Covenant against encumbrances*—The grantor warrants that the property is free from any liens or encumbrances, except those specifically referenced in the deed. Encumbrances generally include mortgages, mechanics' liens, and easements. If this covenant is breached, the grantee may sue for expenses to remove the encumbrance(s).

- *Covenant of quiet enjoyment*—The grantor guarantees that the grantee's title will be good against third parties who might bring court actions to establish superior title to the property. If the grantee's title is found to be inferior, the grantor is liable for damages.
- *Covenant of further assurance*—The grantor promises to obtain and deliver any instrument needed to make the title good. For instance, if the grantor's spouse has failed to sign away spousal rights, the grantor must deliver a quitclaim deed executed by the spouse to clear the title.
- *Covenant of warranty forever*—The grantor guarantees to compensate the grantee for the loss sustained if the title fails any time in the future.

These covenants in a general warranty deed are not limited to matters that occurred during the time the grantor owned the property; they extend back to its origins. In other words, the grantor is obligated to defend the title against all claims, including those arising during the time all former owners held that title.

Special warranty deed. A special warranty deed contains two basic warranties: That the grantor received title and that the property was not encumbered *during the time the grantor held title*, except as noted in the deed.

In effect, the grantor defends the title against himself or herself. The granting clause generally contains the words "grantor remises, releases, alienates, and conveys." Because grantors are not warranting against acts of predecessors in title (the former owners), they often prefer to convey by a special warranty rather than a general warranty deed. Of course, the grantor may include additional warranties, but these must be specifically stated in the deed. Fiduciaries (such as trustees, executors, and corporations), who have no authority to warrant against acts of prior owners, and grantors, who acquired title at a tax sale, often convey title by special warranty deeds. When a special warranty deed is used, the grantee's purchase of title insurance is considered to provide adequate protection in lieu of a general warranty deed.

Bargain and sale deed. A bargain and sale deed contains no express warranties against encumbrances. It does, however, *imply* that the grantor holds title to the property. The words in the granting clause are usually "grant and release" or "grant, bargain, and sell." Because the warranty is not specifically stated, the grantee has little legal recourse if title defects later appear. In some areas this deed is used in foreclosures and tax sales. The grantee should purchase title insurance for protection.

A standard bargain and sale deed may be enhanced with covenants or warranties to create protections that are roughly equivalent to those in other forms of deeds. A grantor may include a covenant against encumbrances and convey a *bargain and sale deed with covenant against the grantor's acts*. This is similar to a special warranty deed. Warranties used in a general warranty deed may be inserted in a bargain and sale deed to give the grantee similar protection.

Quitclaim deed. A quitclaim deed provides *no covenant or warranties* and therefore, the *least protection* to the grantee of any of the deed forms. The

---

General Warranty Deed

Five Covenants:

1. Covenant of seizing
2. Covenant against encumbrances
3. Covenant of quiet enjoyment
4. Covenant of further assurance
5. Covenant of warranty forever

Special Warranty Deed

Two Warranties:

1. Warranty that grantor received title
2. Warranty that property was not encumbered by grantor

Bargain and Sale Deed

No Express Warranties:

- Implication that grantor holds title and possession

grantor of a quitclaim deed only "remises, releases, and quitclaims" his or her interest in the property to the grantee. This means that a quitclaim deed conveys only the interest, if any, the grantor has when the deed is delivered. If the grantor has no interest, the grantee acquires nothing and, furthermore, has no right of claim against the grantor. A quitclaim deed can convey title just as effectively as a warranty deed if the grantor has good title when the deed is delivered, but it does not provide any of the guarantees in a warranty deed.

A quitclaim deed is typically used to convey *less than a fee simple estate* because it conveys only the grantor's right or interest (such as an easement) or to cure *a title defect,* called a "cloud on the title." For instance, if the name of the grantee is misspelled on a warranty deed, a quitclaim deed with the correct spelling may be executed to the grantee to perfect the title. A quitclaim deed may also be used when a grantor allegedly inherits property but is not certain that the decedent's title was valid. A warranty deed in this instance would obligate the grantor to warranties he or she may not want to assume, while a quitclaim deed would convey only whatever interest the grantor has.

Deed in trust. A deed in trust is the means by which a *trustor* conveys real estate to a *trustee* for the benefit of a *beneficiary.* The real estate is held by the trustee to fulfill the purpose of the trust, as was discussed in Chapter 7.

Trustee's deed. A deed executed by a trustee is a **trustee's deed.** It is used when a trustee conveys real estate held in the trust to anyone *other than the trustor.* The trustee's deed must state that the trustee is executing the instrument in accordance with the powers and authority granted by the trust instrument.

Deeds executed pursuant to court order. This classification, also known as **judicial deed,** covers such deed forms as executors' or administrators' deeds, masters' deeds, sheriffs' deeds, and many others. These statutory deed forms are used to convey title to property that is transferred by court order or by will. The forms of these deeds must conform to the laws of the state where the property is located.

One common characteristic of such instruments is that the *full consideration* is usually stated in the deed. This is done because the deed is executed pursuant to a court order and, because the court has authorized the sale of the property for a given amount of consideration, this amount must be exactly stated in the document.

IN PRACTICE

People transfer ownership for a number of reasons, the sale of a property being only one of them. An agreement of sale typically specifies the form of deed the grantor will execute to convey title at settlement. Because of the legal significance of a deed, real estate licensees should not advise parties as to which type of deed should be used nor should they prepare the deed. Only an attorney should give this advice and actually prepare the deed.

Realty Transfer Tax

Most states' laws require that conveyances of real estate be taxed, commonly referred to as a **transfer tax.** The tax is usually payable when the deed is recorded. The amount of tax paid is noted on the deed, often by affixing stamps the taxpayer purchases (hence the term "transfer stamps" that is sometimes used).

In Your State

PA In Pennsylvania, a state transfer tax, currently 1 percent, is imposed on the full consideration paid for the real estate. In addition, state law also permits local taxing districts (city, borough, township, and school district) to impose a transfer tax. Local transfer taxes are generally 1 percent of the consideration, though municipalities with a "Home Rule Charter Government" are permitted to charge more. For instance, their transfer taxes may be 1.5 or 1.75 percent, or more. Although the real estate transaction itself (not the buyer or seller) is taxed, state and local transfer taxes are paid by the seller and/or the buyer according to the terms stated in the agreement of sale. ■

Certain deeds that normally are *exempt* from the transfer tax include:

- transfers between parent and child or between siblings;
- deeds not made in connection with a sale, such as changing joint tenants;
- conveyances to, from, or between governmental bodies;
- deeds between charitable, religious, or educational institutions;
- deeds securing debts or deeds releasing property as security for a debt;
- partitions;
- tax deeds;
- deeds pursuant to mergers of corporations; and
- deeds from subsidiary to parent corporations for cancellations of stock.

Transfer of property by ground lease is accomplished by lease assignment. As discussed in a previous chapter, transfer taxes are charged on leases in excess of 30 years.

IN PRACTICE

In the certainty of the death-and-taxes scheme of life is also the certainty that real estate will transfer, which makes taxes on transfers an attractive source of government revenue. Although exempt transfers have remained untouched, taxable transfers are often seen as lucrative targets for additional revenue. Increases in transfer taxes have also been part of the discussion as legislators attempt to reform the general platform of taxation in Pennsylvania. The real estate industry has long held the position that the transfer of real estate should not be the convenient "golden goose" for revenue, that transfer taxes thwart attempts to foster ownership and development. Legislators, on the other hand, often see transfer taxes as benign ways to capture revenue, simply becoming a cost of the transaction without the regressive impact of some other taxes, such as real estate taxes. As the tax-reform dialogue continues in Harrisburg, increases in state transfer taxes remain on the table for consideration as well.

■ INVOLUNTARY ALIENATION

Title to property can be transferred by **involuntary alienation,** that is, without the owner's consent. (See Figure 9.2.) Involuntary transfers are usually carried out by operation of law, such as by condemnation or foreclosure sales to satisfy

FIGURE   9.2

Involuntary Alienation

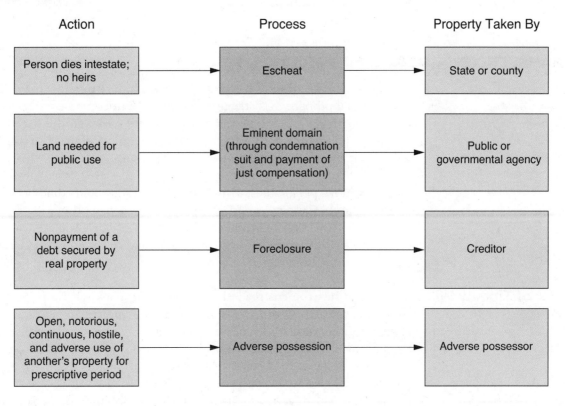

Action	Process	Property Taken By
Person dies intestate; no heirs	Escheat	State or county
Land needed for public use	Eminent domain (through condemnation suit and payment of just compensation)	Public or governmental agency
Nonpayment of a debt secured by real property	Foreclosure	Creditor
Open, notorious, continuous, hostile, and adverse use of another's property for prescriptive period	Adverse possession	Adverse possessor

debts. When a person dies intestate and leaves no heirs, the title to the estate passes to the state by the state's power of escheat. As discussed in Chapter 5, ownership can also be transferred involuntarily by natural forces.

Adverse Possession

Adverse possession is another means of involuntary transfer. An individual who makes a claim to a property, takes possession of it and, most important, uses it may take title away from an owner who fails to use or inspect the property for a period of years. The law recognizes that the use of land is an important function of its ownership. Usually, the possession by the claimant must be all of the following:

- *Open* (that is, obvious to anyone who looks)
- *Notorious* (that is, known by others)
- *Continuous* and uninterrupted
- *Hostile* (that is, without the true owner's consent)
- *Adverse* to the true owner's possession

In Your State   **PA**   Uninterrupted possession must endure for the statutory period of time, which in Pennsylvania is 21 years. Through the principle of *tacking* (discussed in Chapter 5), successive periods of adverse possession by different adverse possessors can be combined so that a person who is not in possession for the entire statutory time may establish a claim. ■

The adverse possessor can secure undisputed title by filing an action in court to quiet title. In many cases, an adverse user's rights may supersede those of a fee owner. A claimant who does not receive title might acquire an easement by prescription.

■ TRANSFER OF A DECEASED PERSON'S PROPERTY

A person who dies **testate** has prepared a will indicating how the person's real and personal property is distributed after death. In contrast, a person who dies **intestate** does not have a will, and the property passes to the decedent's heirs according to the *statute of descent and distribution*. In effect, the state makes a will for an intestate decedent.

Legally, when a person dies, ownership of real estate immediately passes either to the heirs by descent or to the persons named in the will. Before these individuals can take full title and possession of the property, however, the estate must go through a judicial process called *probate* and all claims against the estate must be satisfied.

Transfer of Title by Will   A **will** is an instrument made by the owner to convey title to property after the owner's death. A will is a testamentary instrument, which means it takes effect only after death. This differs from a deed, which *must* be delivered during the lifetime of the grantor and which conveys a present interest in property. While the **testator** or devisor (the person who makes the will) is alive, any property included in the will still can be conveyed by the owner. The parties named in a will have no rights or interests as long as the person who made the will is living; they acquire interest or title only after the owner's death.

Only property owned by the testator at the time of death may be transferred by will. The gift of *real property* by will is known as a **devise;** the person who receives the property is a *devisee*. Legally, an **heir** is one who receives property by the law of descent, but the term is often used to include devisees as well.

For title to pass to devisees, state law requires the will to be filed with the court on the death of the testator and *probated*. **Probate** is a legal procedure that confirms the validity of a will and accounts for the decedent's assets.

When a will does not provide the minimum statutory inheritance for a surviving spouse, the person has the option of informing the court that he or she will take the minimum statutory share rather than a lesser share provided in the will. This is called *renouncing* (or *taking against*) *the will* and is a right reserved only for a surviving spouse.

Legal requirements for making a will.   A will must be executed and prepared according to the laws of the state in which the real estate is located. Only a valid and probated will can effectively convey title to real estate.

In Your State   **PA**   A testator must have legal capacity to make a will. There are no rigid tests to determine the capacity to make a will. Pennsylvania law states that a person must be of *legal age* (18) and *sound mind*. To demonstrate sound mind, the testator must have sufficient mental capacity to understand the nature and extent of the property owned. A testator must understand the identity of his or her natural heirs and that the property will go to those persons named in the will. The drawing of a will must be a voluntary act, free of any undue influence by other people. ■

Pennsylvania law requires that a will be signed by the testator. The signature does not have to be witnessed or acknowledged; however, steps will have to be taken when the will is probated to prove the document's validity when these signatures are absent. If the testator is unable to sign the will, the person may make a mark (usually an "x") on the document, with the name subscribed. This mark must have two witnesses' signatures to be valid. A handwritten will, or *holographic will*, and a *nuncupative will*, one that is given orally and put into writing by a witness, are also permitted in Pennsylvania.

The testator may alter the will any time before his or her death. Any modification, amendment, or addition to a previously executed will is set forth in a separate document called a *codicil*.

Transfer of Title by Descent

In Your State

PA When a person dies intestate (without a will), title to his or her property passes to the decedent's heirs according to Pennsylvania's law of descent and distribution. The primary heirs of the deceased are the spouse and close blood relatives (such as children, parents, brothers, sisters, grandparents, aunts, uncles, and, in some cases, first cousins). The specific rights of the heirs and their shares of the estate are defined by the law and depend on which parties survive the decedent and the closeness of their relationship. Legally adopted children are considered heirs of the adopting parents but not heirs of the adopting parents' ancestors. In Pennsylvania, illegitimate children may inherit from both the father and the mother as long as parentage has been legally established. ■

Probate Proceedings

Probate is the formal judicial process that

- proves or confirms the validity of a will,
- determines the precise assets of the deceased person, and
- identifies the person(s) to whom the assets are to pass.

The purpose of probate is to see that the assets are distributed correctly. All assets must be accounted for, and the decedent's debts and taxes on the estate must be satisfied before any distribution. Assets distributed through probate are those which do not otherwise distribute themselves. For instance, property held in joint tenancy or tenancy by the entirety is distributed according to the title. Probate proceedings take place in the county in which the decedent resided. If the decedent owned real estate in another county, probate would occur in that county as well.

When a person dies *testate*, probate is necessary to prove the validity of the will before the assets can be distributed. The person who has possession of the will and any codicils (normally the individual designated in the will as the *executor* or *executrix*) presents the document for filing with the Register of Wills in the county in which the testator last resided. The will must meet the statutory requirements for its form and execution. A will is assumed to be valid unless it is challenged. The court rules on a challenge and in instances where more than one will exist determines which will prevail. Once the will is upheld, the assets can be distributed according to its provisions.

When a person dies *intestate*, the court determines who inherits the assets by reviewing proof from the decedent's relatives of their entitlement under the statute of descent and distribution. To initiate probate proceedings, the court will appoint an *administrator* (in lieu of an executor, who would have been named in a will) to oversee the administration and distribution of the estate.

The administrator, executor, or executrix is responsible for assembling an inventory of the estate's assets and having them appraised. The estate's representative is also responsible for ensuring that all the decedent's debts are satisfied and that federal estate taxes and state inheritance taxes are paid. Once all obligations have been satisfied, the representative distributes the remaining assets of the estate according to the will or the state's law.

IN PRACTICE

A broker entering into a listing agreement with the executor or administrator of an estate in probate should be aware that the amount of compensation must be approved by the court. Compensation is payable only from the proceeds of the sale and if the court deems the amount to be wasteful and, therefore, unreasonable, the court could reduce it. The broker cannot be paid unless the court approves the sale.

■ SUMMARY

Title to real estate is the right to and evidence of ownership of the land. It may be transferred by voluntary alienation, involuntary alienation, will, and descent.

The voluntary transfer is made by a deed, executed (signed) by the owner as grantor to the grantee. The form and execution of a deed must comply with the statutory requirements of the state in which the land is located.

Among the most common of these requirements are a grantor with legal capacity to contract, a readily identifiable grantee, a granting clause, a legal description of the property, a recital of consideration, exceptions and reservations on the title, and the signature of the grantor. In addition, the deed should be acknowledged to provide evidence that the signature is genuine and to allow recording of the deed. Title to the property passes when the grantor delivers a deed and it is accepted by the grantee. Deeds are subject to transfer taxes when they are recorded.

The obligation of the grantor is determined by the form of the deed. The words of conveyance in the granting clause are important in determining the form of deed.

A general warranty deed provides the greatest protection of any deed by binding the grantor to certain covenants or warranties. A special warranty deed warrants that the grantor received title and that the grantor did not encumber the estate except as stated in the deed. A bargain and sale deed carries with it no warranties but implies that the grantor holds title to the property. A quitclaim deed carries with it no warranties whatsoever and conveys only the interest, if any, that the grantor possesses in the property.

Property may be involuntarily transferred, that is, without the owner's permission. This can occur by a court action, such as a foreclosure or judgment sale, a tax sale, condemnation, adverse possession, or escheat. Land also may be transferred by the natural forces of water and wind, which either increase property by accretion or decrease it through erosion or avulsion.

The property of an owner who makes a valid will (a person who dies testate) passes to the devisees through the probating of the will. The title of an owner who dies without a will (intestate) passes according to the law of descent and distribution. Probate is the judicial process by which assets are properly accounted for and distributed after the debts of the decedent are paid.

QUESTIONS

1. The basic requirements for a valid conveyance are governed by
   a. state law.
   b. local custom.
   c. national law.
   d. law of descent.

2. It is essential that every deed be signed by the
   a. grantor.
   b. grantee.
   c. grantor and grantee.
   d. devisee.

3. *H*, age 15, recently inherited many parcels of real estate from his late father and has decided to sell one of them to pay inheritance taxes. If *H* enters into a deed conveying his interest in the property to a purchaser, such a conveyance would be
   a. valid.
   b. void.
   c. invalid.
   d. voidable.

4. An instrument authorizing one person to act for another is called a(n)
   a. power of attorney.
   b. release deed.
   c. quitclaim deed.
   d. acknowledgment.

5. The grantee receives greatest protection with what type of deed?
   a. Quitclaim
   b. General warranty
   c. Bargain and sale
   d. Executor's

6. Determination of the type of deed used in conveying title can be made by examining the
   a. grantor's name.
   b. grantee's name.
   c. granting clause.
   d. acknowledgment.

7. Which of the following best describes the covenant of quiet enjoyment?
   a. The grantor promises to obtain and deliver any instrument needed to make the title good.
   b. The grantor warrants that no mortgages, mechanics' liens, or easements affect title to the property being conveyed.
   c. The grantor warrants that he or she is the owner and has the right to convey title to it.
   d. The grantor assures that the title will be good against the title claims of third parties.

8. Which of the following deeds would be most likely to recite the full, actual consideration paid for the property?
   a. Gift deed
   b. Trustee's deed
   c. Deed in trust
   d. Deed executed pursuant to court order

9. Which of the following deeds merely implies but does not specifically warrant that the grantor holds good title to the property?
   a. Special warranty deed
   b. Bargain and sale deed
   c. Quitclaim deed
   d. Trustee's deed

10. Title to property transfers at the moment a deed is
    a. signed.
    b. acknowledged.
    c. delivered and accepted.
    d. recorded.

11. Consideration in a deed refers to
    a. gentle handling of the document.
    b. something of value given by each party.
    c. the habendum clause.
    d. the payment of transfer taxes.

12. A declaration before a notary or other official providing evidence that a signature is genuine is an
    a. affidavit.
    b. acknowledgment.
    c. affirmation.
    d. estoppel.

13. *R* executes a deed to *P* as grantee, has it acknowledged, and receives payment from the buyer. *R* holds the deed, however, and arranges to meet *P* the next morning at the courthouse to deliver the deed to her. In this situation at this time
    a. *P* owns the property because she has paid for it.
    b. title to the property will not officially pass until *P* has been given the deed the next morning.
    c. title to the property will not pass until *P* has received the deed and recorded it the next morning.
    d. *P* will own the property when she has signed the deed the next morning.

14. Title to real estate may be transferred during a person's lifetime by
    a. devise.
    b. descent.
    c. involuntary alienation.
    d. escheat.

15. *F* bought acreage in a distant county, never went to see it, and did not use the ground. *H* moved his mobile home onto the land, had a water well drilled, and lived there for 22 years. *H* may become the owner of the land if he has complied with the state law regarding
    a. requirements for a valid conveyance.
    b. adverse possession.
    c. avulsion.
    d. voluntary alienation.

16. Which of the following is *NOT* a way in which title to real estate may be transferred by involuntary alienation?
    a. Eminent domain
    b. Escheat
    c. Erosion
    d. Deed

17. A house is selling for $89,500. The buyer pays $50,000 cash and gives the seller a mortgage for the balance. The amount of state transfer tax that must be paid on this transaction is
    a. $895.
    b. $3,950.
    c. $8,950.
    d. $500.

18. A person who has died leaving a valid will is called
    a. a devisee.
    b. a testator.
    c. an escrow agent.
    d. intestate.

19. Title to real estate can be transferred at death by a
    a. warranty deed.
    b. special warranty deed.
    c. trustee's deed.
    d. will.

20. An owner of real estate was declared legally incompetent and was committed to a state mental institution. While institutionalized, the owner wrote and executed a will. The owner later died and was survived by a spouse and three children. The real estate will pass
    a. to the owner's spouse.
    b. to the heirs mentioned in the owner's will.
    c. according to the state law of descent.
    d. to the state.

ANSWERS

1. A Conveyance of title to real estate is governed by the laws of the state in which the property is located, regardless of whether title transfers by voluntary or involuntary alienation, will, or descent. (p. 141)

2. A Only a grantor executes (signs) the deed. Title passes when the deed is delivered and accepted by the grantee. (p. 141)

3. D A deed executed by a minor is voidable, not void. The minor can disaffirm the conveyance until he or she reaches majority age and for a reasonable time thereafter. (p. 142)

4. A Most states, including Pennsylvania, permit documents to be signed by an attorney-in-fact, the person designated by a power of attorney to act on behalf of the principal. The term power of attorney refers to the specific written authorization to act in that capacity. (p. 144)

5. B A general warranty deed binds the grantor to covenants or warranties that provide a grantee with the greatest protection of any type of deed. (p. 145)

6. C The granting clause states the grantor's intention to convey the property. By examining the wording in this clause, it is possible to determine the type of deed being used to convey title. (p. 142)

7. D Of the five covenants in a general warranty deed, the covenant of quiet enjoyment establishes that the grantee's claim to title will be defended against third parties who bring court action in an attempt to establish superior title to the property. (p. 146)

8. D Deeds executed pursuant to court order recite the full, actual consideration paid for the property. When a court authorizes the sale of a property for a specific amount of consideration, this amount must be exactly stated in the document. (p. 147)

9. B A bargain and sale deed contains no expressed warranties against encumbrances. It does, however, imply that the grantor holds title to the property. (p. 146)

10. C Title to real estate is transferred when the deed is delivered and accepted by the grantee. The grantor's signature, in and of itself, does not transfer title. (p. 144)

11. B Consideration is something of value exchanged between the parties. Generally it is a stated dollar amount but other forms of consideration are acceptable, such as "love and affection." (p. 142)

12. B A formal declaration made before a notary public or authorized public officer that verifies that the person is voluntarily signing a document and that the person's signature is genuine is an acknowledgement. (p. 144)

13. B Although R executed the deed, had the signature acknowledged, and received consideration, title will not pass until the deed is delivered and accepted by the grantee the next morning. (pp. 144–45)

14. C Devise, descent, and escheat all refer to transfer of title subsequent to the death of the titleholder. Involuntary alienation occurs by operation of law, as in a foreclosure or condemnation action. (p. 149)

15. B The law recognizes the use of land is an important function of ownership. An individual who takes possession and uses the property for the period of time prescribed by state law may be able to take title away from an owner who fails to use or inspect the property. This is known as adverse possession. (p. 149)

16. D Eminent domain, escheat, and erosion are involuntary transfers. A deed is an intentional, voluntary transfer of title by the grantor. (p. 141)

17. A The amount of state transfer tax is currently 1 percent of the consideration. The tax paid would be $895 ($89,500 × 0.01).

18. B   From a legal perspective, a person dies either testate (with a will) or intestate (without a will.) The person who dies leaving a will is known as the testator. (p. 150)

19. D   A warranty deed, special warranty deed, and trustee's deed transfer an owner's interest during the lifetime of the grantor. A will is an instrument made by the owner to convey title after the owner's death. (p. 150)

20. C   An individual declared legally incompetent does not have capacity to execute legal documents. Therefore, the will would be considered void and title to the real estate would pass according to the state's laws of descent and distribution. (p. 151)

10

TITLE RECORDS

■ LEARNING OBJECTIVES

When you've finished reading this chapter, you should be able to

- explain the rationale for recording documents affecting title to real estate;
- distinguish between actual notice and constructive notice;
- describe the steps involved in searching a title;
- describe key elements of a title insurance policy; and
- define the key terms.

■ KEY TERMS

abstract of title	constructive notice	security agreement
actual notice	financing statement	subrogation
attorney's opinion of title	marketable title	suit to quiet title
certificate of title	priority	title insurance
chain of title	recorder of deeds	title search
	recording	

■ PUBLIC RECORDS

In Your State

PA Public records contain detailed information about each parcel of real estate. These records are crucial in establishing ownership, giving notice of encumbrances, and establishing priority of liens. They protect the interests of real estate owners, taxing bodies, creditors, and the general public. The real estate recording system includes written documents that affect title such as deeds and mortgages. Public records regarding taxes, judgments, probate, and marriage also may offer important information about title to a particular property. In Pennsylvania, the county **recorder of deeds** maintains most of the public records that affect title to real property. The county treasurer and clerks of courts and other county and municipal offices maintain important records as well. ■

Because the records are open to the public, anyone can review the records of any documents, claims, or other interests that affect a particular property. An examination of these records is especially important for anyone taking title to a property. A prospective purchaser, for example, can examine the kind and condition of the title before taking ownership. A review of the public records will verify whether the seller possesses title to the property he or she is representing to own and will help identify any liens or other encumbrances that might exist. A purchaser can then ascertain that he or she will receive good title and that any debts secured by liens will be properly accounted for at the settlement.

Recording

> Written documents affecting land must be recorded in the county where the land is located.

Recording is the act of placing documents in public record. The specific rules for recording documents are a matter of state law. Although the details may vary, all recording acts essentially provide that any written document that affects any estate, right, title, or interest in land *must be recorded in the county where the land is located* to serve as public notice. That way, anyone interested in the title to a parcel of real estate can discover the various interests of all parties. From a practical point of view, the recording acts give legal priority to those interests that are recorded first. Recall from the discussion of liens in Chapter 8 that the general recording principle is "first come, first served."

In Your State

PA   To be eligible for recording in Pennsylvania, a document must be in writing and properly executed (signed). Persons unable to place their signatures on a document may sign by mark in a manner that complies with statutory requirements. The document also must be acknowledged before a notary public. Public record offices may have specific rules about the size of documents and the color and quality of paper they are printed on. Electronic recording (using computers or fax transmittal, for instance) is permitted in a growing number of locations. ■

Notice

Anyone who has an interest in a parcel of real estate can take certain steps, called *giving notice*, to ensure that the interest is known to anyone who inquires. There are two basic types of notice: constructive notice and actual notice.

Constructive notice is the legal presumption that information is available and can be obtained by an individual through diligent inquiry. Properly recording documents in the public record serves as constructive notice to the world of an individual's rights or interest. So does taking physical possession of a property. Because the information or evidence is readily available, a prospective purchaser or mortgage lender is responsible for discovering the interest.

For instance, A purchases a property and takes possession, but does not record the deed. At a later date, B purchases the same property from the original owner, though fails to inspect the property, and promptly records her deed. Even though the first deed was not recorded, A's rights are superior to B's because A served constructive notice by taking possession of the property. Obviously, B should have inspected the property.

In contrast, **actual notice** means that not only is the information available but someone has been given the information and actually knows it. An individual who has searched the public records and inspected the property has actual notice. Actual notice is also known as *direct knowledge*. If an individual can be proved to have actual knowledge of information, he or she cannot use a lack of constructive notice (such as an unrecorded deed) to justify a claim.

Priority

Priority refers to the order of rights in time. Many complicated situations can affect the priority of rights—who recorded first; which party was in possession first; who had actual or constructive notice. The way the courts will rule in any situation depends, of course, on the specific facts of the case. These are strictly legal questions that should be referred to the parties' attorneys.

Unrecorded Documents

Deeds and mortgages that are not recorded cannot serve constructive notice. Although these documents are not necessarily void, they *may not be effective on future owners*, according to Pennsylvania law, unless they have been *recorded*.

Certain types of liens are not recorded. Real estate taxes and special assessments are liens on specific parcels of real estate and are not usually recorded until some time after the taxes or assessments are past due. Inheritance taxes and franchise taxes are statutory liens. They are placed against all real estate owned by a decedent at the time of death or by a corporation at the time the franchise tax became a lien. Like real estate taxes, they are not recorded.

Notice of these liens must be gained from sources other than the recorder's office. Evidence of the payment of real estate taxes, special assessments, municipal utilities and other taxes can be gathered from paid tax receipts and letters from municipalities. Notice of unpaid child support can be obtained from the Domestic Relations section of Orphan's Court. Often considerable time must be spent gathering information about these "off the record" liens.

Chain of Title

Chain of title is the record of a property's ownership over a period of time. Beginning with the earliest or original owner, title may pass to many individuals. Each owner is linked to the next so that a "chain" is formed. An unbroken chain of title can be traced through linking conveyances from the present owner back to the earliest recorded owner. In some counties of Pennsylvania, for example, recorded deeds can be traced to the 1770s.

If ownership cannot be traced through an unbroken chain, it is said that there is a *gap* in the chain. In these cases, the cloud on the title makes it necessary to establish ownership by a court action called a **suit to quiet title**. A suit might be required, for instance, when a grantor acquired title under one name and conveyed it under a different name. Or there may be a forged deed in the chain, after which no subsequent grantee acquired legal title. All possible claimants to the ownership are allowed to present evidence during a court proceeding; then the court's judgment is filed. Often, the simple procedure of obtaining any relevant quitclaim deeds is used to establish ownership.

Title Search and Abstract of Title

A **title search** is an examination of all public records to determine whether any defects exist in the chain of title. The records of conveyances of ownership are examined, beginning with the present owner. Then the title is traced back to its origin or 40 years to 60 years, depending on local custom or the requirements of a title insurer. Some states (though not Pennsylvania) have adopted the Marketable Title Act, which extinguishes certain interests and cures certain defects arising before the *root of the title*—the conveyance that establishes the source of the chain of title.

A title search is normally performed by an *abstractor.* This is the person who examines the public records in the recorder of deeds and prothonotary's offices as well as other government offices. In addition to searching deed conveyances, the abstractor looks for wills, judicial proceedings, and other encumbrances—such as taxes, assessments, and other liens—that may be in effect.

Following the search, the abstractor prepares an **abstract of title,** which is a summary report of the various events and proceedings that affected the title throughout its history. The report begins with the original grant (or root), then provides a chronological list of recorded instruments. All recorded liens and encumbrances are included, along with their current status. A list of all the public records examined is also provided as evidence of the scope of the search. An abstract of title is a condensed history of those items that can be found in public records. It does not reveal such items as encroachments or forgeries or any interests or conveyances that have not been recorded.

> An abstract of title will not reveal items such as liens, encroachments, or any other interests that have not been recorded.

A completed abstract of title is then submitted to an attorney for review. The attorney examines the abstract, looking at each section from the origin of the title to the present, and evaluates all facts and material. Following the examination, the attorney prepares a written report about the condition of the ownership. This report is called an **attorney's opinion of title.**

Marketable Title

Under the terms of the typical real estate agreement of sale, the seller is required to deliver **marketable title** to the buyer at the closing. To be marketable, a title must

- disclose no serious defects and not depend on doubtful questions of law or fact to prove its validity;
- not expose a purchaser to the hazard of litigation or threaten the quiet enjoyment of the property; and
- convince a reasonably well-informed and prudent person, acting on business principles and with knowledge of the facts and their legal significance, that he or she could sell or mortgage the property at a later time.

Although a title that does not meet these requirements still could be transferred, it contains *certain defects that may limit or restrict its ownership.* A buyer cannot be forced to accept a conveyance that is materially different from the one bargained for in the sales contract. However, questions of marketable title must be raised by a buyer (or the buyer's attorney) *before acceptance of the deed.* Once a buyer has accepted a deed with unmarketable title, the only available legal recourse is to sue the seller under any covenants of warranty contained in the deed.

IN PRACTICE

Normally a title search is not ordered until major contingencies in the agreement of sale have been cleared, such as mortgage contingency. Before providing money for a loan, a lender generally requires a title search to ascertain the condition of the title and assure that there are no liens superior to the one the lender will file.

■ PROOF OF OWNERSHIP

In Your State

PA Proof of ownership is evidence that title is, in fact, marketable. A deed by itself is not considered sufficient evidence of ownership. Even though a warranty deed conveys the grantor's interest, it contains no proof of the condition of the grantor's title at the time of the conveyance. The grantee needs some assurance that he or she is actually acquiring ownership and that the title is marketable. Customarily, in Pennsylvania, a certificate of title or title insurance is used as proof of ownership. ■

Certificate of Title

A **certificate of title** is a statement of opinion of the title's status as of the date it is issued. *A certificate is not a guarantee of ownership.* Rather, it certifies the condition of the title based on the title search. The certificate, which is prepared by a title company or an attorney, is an opinion of the validity of the grantor's title and of the existence of liens and encumbrances.

Although a certificate of title can be used as evidence of ownership, it is not perfect. Unrecorded liens or rights of parties in possession cannot be discovered by a search of public records. Nor can hidden defects, such as transfers involving forged documents, incorrect marital information, incompetent parties, minors, or fraud be detected. A certificate offers no defense against these defects because they are unknown. The person who prepares the certificate is liable only for negligence in preparing the certificate and only to the extent of his or her personal assets.

Title Insurance

Title insurance protects the insured from an event that occurred before the policy was issued rather than against future events.

Title insurance is a contract under which the policyholder is protected from losses arising from defects in the title. A title insurance company determines whether the title is insurable, based on a review of the public records. If so, a policy is issued. Unlike other insurance policies that insure against future losses, title insurance protects the insured from an event that occurred before the policy was issued. *Title insurance is considered to be the best defense of title.* The title insurance company will defend any lawsuit based on an insurable defect and pay claims if the title proves to be defective.

After examining the public records, the title insurance company usually issues what may be called a *preliminary report of title* or a *commitment* to issue a title policy. This describes the policy that will be issued and includes

- the name of the insured party;
- the legal description of the real estate;
- the estate or interest covered;
- the conditions and stipulations under which the policy is issued; and
- a schedule of all exceptions, including encumbrances and defects found in the public records and any known unrecorded defects.

T A B L E   10.1

Owner's Title Insurance Policy

Standard Coverage	Extended Coverage	Not Covered by Either Policy
1. Defects found in public records 2. Forged documents 3. Incompetent grantors 4. Incorrect marital statements 5. Improperly delivered deeds	Standard coverage plus defects discoverable through: 1. Property inspection including unrecorded rights of persons in possession 2. Examination of survey 3. Unrecorded liens not known of by policyholder	1. Defects and liens listed in policy 2. Defects known to buyer 3. Changes in land use brought about by zoning ordinances

The premium for the policy is paid once, at closing. (See Chapter 22 for information about title insurance rates.) The maximum loss for which the company may be liable cannot exceed the face amount of the policy (unless the amount of coverage has been extended with an inflation rider). When a title company makes a payment to settle a claim covered by a policy, the company generally acquires the right to any remedy or damages available to the insured. This right is called **subrogation.**

Coverage.   Exactly which defects the title company will defend depends on the type of policy. (See Table 10.1.) A *standard coverage policy* normally insures the title as it is known from the public records. In addition, the standard policy insures against such hidden defects as forged documents, conveyances by incompetent grantors, incorrect marital statements, and improperly delivered deeds.

Extended coverage, as provided by an American Land Title Association policy, includes the protections of a standard policy plus additional protections. An extended policy protects against defects that may be discovered by inspection of the property, such as rights or parties in possession, examination of a survey, and certain unrecorded liens. None of these defects are defended by a certificate of title.

Title insurance, however, will not protect against all defects. A title company will not insure a bad title or offer protection against defects that clearly appear in a title search. The policy generally names certain uninsurable losses, called *exclusions*. These include zoning ordinances, restrictive covenants, easements, certain water rights, and current taxes and special assessments.

Types of policies.   The different types of policies depend on who is named as the insured. An *owner's policy* is issued for the benefit of the owner and his or her heirs or devisees. A *lender's policy* is issued for the benefit of the mortgagee. In this case, the amount of the coverage is commensurate with the amount of the mortgage loan. As the loan balance is reduced, the coverage decreases. Because only the lender's interest is insured, it is advisable for the owner to obtain a policy as well.

A lessee's interest can be insured with a *leasehold* policy. *Certificate of sale* policies are available to insure the title to property purchased in a court sale.

Although title insurance is not required to transfer title, mortgage lenders normally require title insurance policies when transfers involve mortgage loans. Buyers should be aware that their interests also should be insured along with the lenders'. Because title defects can be costly, buyers should consider purchasing title insurance even when they do not finance their purchases and title insurance is not required. Title insurance is more commonly used as proof of ownership than a certificate of title.

■ UNIFORM COMMERCIAL CODE

The *Uniform Commercial Code (UCC)* is a commercial law statute that has been adopted to some extent in all 50 states. The UCC is concerned with personal property transactions; it does not apply to real estate. The UCC governs the documents when personal property is used as security for a loan.

For a lender to create a security interest in personal property, including personal property that will become fixtures, the code requires the borrower to sign a **security agreement**. The agreement must contain a complete description of the items against which the lien applies. A short notice of this agreement, called a **financing statement** or UCC-1, must be filed with the recorder of deeds. It identifies any real estate involved when personal property is made part of the real estate. Once the financing agreement is recorded, subsequent purchasers and lenders are put on notice of the security interest in personal property and fixtures. Many lenders require that a security agreement be signed and a financing statement be filed when the real estate pledged as collateral includes chattels or readily removable fixtures. If the borrower defaults, the creditor can repossess the chattels and remove them from the property.

■ SUMMARY

Public records give legal, public, and constructive notice to the world of parties' interests in real estate. These records are needed to establish ownership, give notice of encumbrances and liens, and establish the priority of rights to property. These records are especially important when property is transferred.

Possession of real estate is generally interpreted as constructive notice of the rights of the person in possession. Actual notice is knowledge acquired directly and personally.

Unrecorded documents and certain types of liens that are not recorded do not serve constructive notice, but they still affect title.

Chain of title is the record of a property's ownership over time. A gap in the chain results when ownership cannot be traced through an unbroken chain. A suit to quiet title is required in this case. A title search, performed by an abstractor, is an examination of public records to determine whether there are any defects in the chain of title, including any liens, encumbrances, or other rights that might exist.

A marketable title is one that does not have any serious defects and, therefore, does not expose a purchaser to litigation or threaten quiet enjoyment. Because a title that is not marketable can still be transferred, purchasers seek proof of ownership to ensure they are obtaining marketable title. A deed conveys a grantor's interest but is not evidence of the kind or condition of the title.

Two kinds of proof of ownership are commonly used in Pennsylvania: certificate of title, which is an attorney's opinion of the validity of title; and title insurance, which is an insurance policy issued that protects the insured against events that occurred before the policy was issued.

Under the *Uniform Commercial Code (UCC)*, security interests in chattels must be recorded using a security agreement and financing statement. The recording of a financing statement gives notice to purchasers and lenders of the security interests in chattels and fixtures on a specific parcel of real estate.

QUESTIONS

1. Public records may be inspected by
   a. anyone.
   b. attorneys and abstractors only.
   c. attorneys, abstractors, and real estate licensees only.
   d. anyone who obtains a court order under the Freedom of Information Act.

2. Which of the following statements *BEST* explains why instruments affecting real estate are recorded?
   a. Recording gives constructive notice to the world of the rights and interests in a particular parcel of real estate.
   b. The law requires that such instruments be recorded.
   c. The instruments must be recorded to comply with the terms of the statute of frauds.
   d. Recording proves the execution of the instrument.

3. A purchaser checked the public records and learned that the seller was the grantee in the last recorded deed and that no mortgage was on record against the property. Thus, the purchaser may assume which of the following?
   a. All taxes are paid and no judgments are outstanding.
   b. The seller has good title.
   c. The seller did not mortgage the property.
   d. No one else is occupying the property.

4. The date and time a document was recorded establish which of the following?
   a. Priority of rights
   b. Chain of title
   c. Subrogation
   d. Marketable title

5. *P* bought *L*'s house, received a deed, and moved into the residence but neglected to record the document. One week later *L* died, and his heirs in another city, unaware that the property had been sold, conveyed title to *M*, who recorded the deed. Who owns the property?
   a. *P*
   b. *M*
   c. *L*'s heirs
   d. Both *P* and *M*

6. If a property has encumbrances, it
   a. cannot be sold.
   b. can be sold only if title insurance is provided.
   c. cannot have a deed recorded without a survey.
   d. can be sold if a buyer agrees to take it subject to the encumbrances.

7. *Chain of title* refers to
   a. a summary or history of all instruments and legal proceedings affecting a specific parcel of land.
   b. a series of links measuring 7.92 inches each.
   c. an instrument or document that protects the insured parties (subject to specific exceptions) against defects in the examination of the record and hidden risks such as forgeries, undisclosed heirs, errors in the public records, and so forth.
   d. the succession of conveyances from some starting point whereby the present owner derives title.

8. Evidence of the kind of estate and all liens against a parcel of real estate can usually be proven by
   a. a recorded deed.
   b. a court suit for specific performance.
   c. one of the forms of proof of ownership.
   d. a foreclosure suit.

9. The person who prepares an abstract of title for a parcel of real estate
   a. writes a brief history of the title after inspecting the county records for documents affecting the title.
   b. insures the condition of the title.
   c. inspects the property.
   d. issues a certificate of title.

10. *S* is frantic because she cannot find her deed and now wants to sell the property. She
    a. may need to file a suit to quiet title.
    b. will have to buy title insurance.
    c. does not need the original deed in order to sell if it was recorded.
    d. should execute a replacement deed to herself.

11. When a title insurance policy is being issued, the public records are searched and the title company's record of title is continued to date. When the title examination is completed, the title company notifies the parties in writing of the condition of the title. This notification is referred to as a(n)
    a. chain of title.
    b. report of title or commitment for title insurance.
    c. certificate of title.
    d. abstract.

12. When a claim is settled by a title insurance company, the company acquires all rights and claims of the insured against any other person who is responsible for the loss. This is called
    a. escrow.
    b. abstract of title.
    c. subordination.
    d. subrogation.

13. A title insurance policy with standard coverage generally covers all of the following EXCEPT
    a. forged documents.
    b. incorrect marital statements.
    c. rights of parties in possession.
    d. incompetent grantors.

14. The document(s) referred to as title evidence include
    a. title insurance.
    b. warranty deeds.
    c. security agreements.
    d. abstract of title.

15. To give notice of a security interest in personal property items, a lienholder must record which of the following?
    a. Security agreement
    b. Financing statement
    c. Chattel agreement
    d. Quitclaim deed

ANSWERS

1. A By entering documents in public record, the information becomes available to anyone who may be interested in researching the title to a parcel of real estate. Access to public records in unlimited. (p. 159)

2. A Properly recording documents in public record serves as constructive notice to the world of a party's right, claim, or interest in real estate. The information is available to and can be obtained by anyone through diligent inquiry. (p. 159)

3. C Recording a mortgage serves constructive notice of the claim to the property by the mortgage holder. Because there was no mortgage in the public record, the purchaser may assume that the seller did not mortgage the property. (p. 159)

4. A Priority refers to the order of rights in time. The date and time a document is recorded establishes the priority of the right or interest. (p. 160)

5. A By taking physical, actual possession of the property, P has given constructive notice of his or her interest. Even though P did not record the deed, his or her interest would be superior to that of future purchaser M. (p. 159)

6. D An encumbrance is a right, claim, or interest held by someone other than the landowner. The fact that title is encumbered does not prevent title from being transferred, but the new owner's title would be subject to those existing encumbrances. (p. 159)

7. D The term chain of title refers to the record of a property's ownership over a period of time. Each owner is linked to the next, and then to the next and so on, so that a "chain" is formed. (p. 160)

8. C Proof of ownership is evidence that title to the property is marketable. The grantor's interest in the property, as well as proof of the condition of the grantor's interest at the time of conveyance, can be ascertained by a certificate of title or title insurance. Both are used as proof of ownership. (p. 162)

9. A An abstractor examines public records in the recorder of deeds and other government offices. Following the search, the abstractor prepares a summary report of events and proceedings throughout the title's history. This report is an abstract of title. (p. 161)

10. C If the deed had been recorded when S took title, her interest is a matter of public record. She does not need the original document in order to transfer title to a purchaser. (p. 159)

11. B After examining public records, the title insurance company issues what may be called a preliminary report of title or a commitment to issue a title policy. (p. 162)

12. D Subrogation is used by title insurance companies to acquire from the insured party rights to initiate legal action to recover any claims that have been paid to the insured. (p. 163)

13. C A standard coverage title insurance policy normally insures the title as it is known from public records. This coverage does not include rights of parties in possession, but it does include such defects as forged documents, conveyances by incompetent grantors, incorrect marital statements, and improperly delivered deeds. (p. 163)

14. A Title evidence establishes proof of ownership. In Pennsylvania, a certificate of title or title insurance is used as proof of ownership. (p. 162)

15. B For a lender to create a security interest in personal property, the UCC requires the borrower to sign a security agreement. A short notice of this agreement, called a financing statement or UCC-1, must be filed with the recorder of deeds. (p. 164)

11

PRINCIPLES OF REAL ESTATE CONTRACTS

■ LEARNING OBJECTIVES

When you've finished reading this chapter, you should be able to

■ list the essential elements that are necessary to form a valid contract;
■ distinguish among express and implied, bilateral and unilateral, and executed and executory contracts;
■ explain the differences among valid, void, voidable, and unenforceable contracts;
■ identify the methods by which contracts may be discharged; and
■ define the key terms.

■ KEY TERMS

acceptance	executory contract	time is of the essence
assignment	express contract	unenforceable
bilateral contract	implied contract	unilateral contract
breach of contract	novation	valid
consideration	offer	void
contract	statute of frauds	voidable
counteroffer	suit for specific	
executed contract	performance	

■ CONTRACT LAW

The real estate business is driven by contracts. Virtually every aspect of a transaction and nearly everything a real estate licensee does involves a contract. Although the purpose and specific terms and conditions vary, all contracts have one thing in common: They are governed by a general body of law known as *contract law*. A **contract** is a voluntary agreement or promise between legally competent parties to perform or refrain from performing some legal act, which is supported by legal consideration. Contract law sets forth certain basic rules or principles for forming a contract between the parties.

Depending on the situation and the nature or language of the agreement, a contract may be categorized in several ways.

Express and Implied Contracts

> **Express** contracts are created by words.
>
> **Implied** contracts are created by actions or conduct.

A contract may be express or implied depending on how it is created. An **express contract** exists when the parties state the terms and show their intentions in *words*. An express contract may be either oral or written. The majority of real estate contracts are express contracts, reduced to writing. Under the statute of frauds, contracts for conveyances of real estate must be in writing to be enforceable (to force performance) in court. In contrast, an **implied contract** is an agreement that is demonstrated by the *acts and conduct* of the parties. The restaurant patron who orders a meal has an implied obligation to pay for the food.

Bilateral and Unilateral Contracts

> **Bilateral and Unilateral**
>
> "Bi" means "two"—a bilateral contract has two promises being exchanged.
>
> "Uni" means "one"—a unilateral contract is based on only one party promising to perform.

Contracts also may be classified as either bilateral or unilateral. In a **bilateral contract,** both parties promise to do something; one promise is given in exchange for another. "I will do this, *and* you will do that." "Okay." A real estate sales contract is a bilateral contract because the seller promises to sell a parcel of real estate and deliver title to the buyer, who promises to pay a certain sum of money for the property.

A **unilateral contract,** on the other hand, is a one-sided agreement. One party makes a promise to induce a second party to do something. The second party is not legally obligated to act. However, if the second party does comply, the first party is obligated to keep the promise. "I will do this *if* you will do that." For example, a law enforcement agency might offer a monetary payment to anyone who can aid in the capture of a criminal. The reward is paid only if someone does aid in the capture. An option to purchase real estate is another example of a unilateral contract.

Executed and Executory Contracts

> An **executory contract**—one or both parties still have an act to perform.
>
> An **executed contract**—all parties have completely fulfilled their obligations.

A contract may be classified as either executed or executory, depending on whether the obligation is completely performed. An **executed contract** is one in which all parties have fulfilled their promises and thus the contract has been performed. This usage is not to be confused with the verb, *execute*, which means the contract is *signed*. An **executory contract** exists when one or both parties still have some act to perform. An agreement of sale is an executory contract from the time it is signed until closing: Ownership has not yet changed hands, and the seller has not received the full sales price. At closing, these obligations are satisfied and the contract is fully *executed*.

Validity of Contracts

A contract can be described as valid, void, voidable, or unenforceable, depending on the circumstances.

A contract is **valid** when it meets all the essential requirements of a contract that make it legally sufficient to be enforceable in court.

A contract may be

- **valid**—meets all the essential elements that make it legally sufficient to be enforceable
- **void**—has no legal force or effect and is, therefore, not binding on the parties
- **voidable**—appears valid but may be rescinded or disaffirmed
- **unenforceable**—valid between the parties but the court cannot force the parties to perform

A contract is **void** when it has no legal force or effect because it lacks some or all of the essential requirements to be recognized as a contract. For instance, an agreement to perform an illegal act would be void because one of the essential requirements for a valid contract is that it be for a legal purpose. A void contract essentially has no legal existence.

A **voidable** contract is one that appears on the surface to be valid but may be rescinded or disaffirmed by one or both parties based on some legal principle. A voidable contract is considered by the courts to be valid if the party who has the option to disaffirm the agreement does not do so within a period of time prescribed by law. For instance, a contract with a minor (under the age of 18 in Pennsylvania) is usually voidable. This is because minors are generally permitted to disaffirm or negate a real estate contract at any time while underage and for a certain period of time after reaching majority age. By the same token, a minor may affirm a contract entered into while underage, in effect validating the contract after the fact. The contract is voidable only by the minor, not by a person of majority age who enters into the contract with the minor. The absence of other essential requirements also may cause a contract to be voidable.

A contract that is **unenforceable** also seems on the surface to be valid; however, neither party can sue the other to force performance. Because the *statute of frauds* requires contracts for the conveyance of real estate to be in writing, oral real estate contracts are generally unenforceable. This means that if either party does not comply with the contract, the defaulting party could not be taken to court and forced to perform. There is, however, a distinction between a suit to force performance and a suit for damages, which is permissible in an oral agreement. The defaulting party could be sued for damages the other party suffered because of the default. Oral contracts are said to be "valid as between the parties," because once the agreement is fully performed, neither has reason to initiate a lawsuit to force performance.

■ ESSENTIALS OF A VALID CONTRACT

Essentially, a contract is an enforceable promise that someone may be compelled by a court to keep. However, a contract should be dated and must meet certain minimum requirements to be considered legally valid. According to contract law, the following are essential requirements for a valid contract.

Offer and Acceptance

There must be an offer by one party that is accepted by the other. The person who makes the offer is the *offeror*. The person who accepts the offer is the *offeree*. This requirement is also called *mutual assent*. It means that there must be a "meeting of the minds." That is, there must be complete agreement between the parties about the purpose and terms of the contract. Courts look to the *objective intent of the parties* to determine whether they intended to enter into a binding agreement. In cases where the statute of frauds applies, the offer and acceptance must be in writing. The wording of the contract must express all the agreed-on terms and must be clearly understood by the parties.

Essentials of a Contract
- Offer and acceptance
- Consideration
- Competent parties
- Reality of consent
- Legal purpose

An **offer** is a promise made by one party, requesting something in exchange for that promise. The offer is made with the intention that the offeror will be bound to the terms if the offer is accepted. The terms of the offer must be definite and specific, and the offer must be communicated to the offeree.

An **acceptance** is the promise by the offeree to be bound to the exact terms proposed by the offeror. The acceptance must be communicated to the offeror. Proposing any deviation from the terms of the offer constitutes a rejection of the original offer and becomes a new offer. This is known as a **counteroffer,** which must be communicated to the original offering party and accepted for a contract to exist.

Besides being terminated by a counteroffer, an offer may be terminated by the offeree's outright rejection of it. Alternatively, an offeree may fail to accept the offer before it expires. The offeror may revoke the offer at any time before receiving the acceptance. This revocation must be communicated to the offeree by the offeror, either directly or through the parties' agents. The offer is also revoked if the offeree learns of the revocation and observes the offeror acting in a manner that indicates that the offer no longer exists.

Consideration

The contract must be based on consideration. **Consideration** is something of legal value offered by one party and accepted by another as an inducement to act or to refrain from some act. There must be a definite statement of consideration in a contract to evidence that something of value was given in exchange for the promise made.

Consideration must be that which is "good or valuable" between the parties. The courts do not inquire into the adequacy or kind of consideration. Adequate consideration ranges from a promise of "love and affection" to a substantial sum of money. However, consideration does not have to be money. Anything that has been bargained for and exchanged is legally sufficient to satisfy the requirement for consideration. The only requirements are that the parties agree and that no undue influence or fraud has occurred.

Legally Competent Parties

All parties to the contract must have *legal capacity* or *contractual ability*. That is, they must be of legal age and have sufficient mental capacity to understand the nature or consequences of their actions in the contract. As in most states, persons in Pennsylvania who are age 18 or older have contractual capacity. A contract entered into by a person who has a mental illness is usually voidable during the episode of illness and for a reasonable period after the person recovers. On the other hand, a contract made by a person who has been judged insane is void; it may be voidable once the individual is judged capable to contract. Mental capacity is not the same as medical sanity.

Legality of Object

A contract must be for a *legal purpose*. This means that parties cannot mutually agree to acts that are contrary to law. A contract that contemplates a purpose that is illegal or against public policy is void, even if it has all the other elements (competent parties, consideration, and offer and acceptance). Any provision in a contract that violates criminal or civil law will result in all or part of the contract being void and, therefore, unenforceable.

Reality of Consent

A contract that has all of the essentials that have been discussed may still be either void or voidable. This is because of the doctrine of *reality of consent*. A contract must be entered into as the free and voluntary act of each party. Each party must be able to make a prudent and knowledgeable decision about the subject matter of the contract. A mistake, misrepresentation, fraud, undue influence, or duress would deprive a person of that ability. If any of these circumstances is present, the contract is voidable by the injured party. If the other party were to sue for breach, the injured party could use a lack of reality of consent as a defense. If unlawful force was used or the fraudulent act was so deceptive that a party was induced to enter into a contract that he or she had no intention of being binding, the contract could be void.

Statute of Frauds

Oral contracts can be just as valid as written contracts as long as the basic requirements for a contract exist. In certain circumstances, however, a contract must be in writing to be enforceable. The **statute of frauds** requires that contracts for the sale of real estate be in writing and signed by the seller to be enforceable in a court of law. This statute also applies to certain lease agreements, as was described in Chapter 6. The *parol evidence* rule states that a written contract takes precedence over oral agreements or promises.

In Your State

PA   The Pennsylvania State Real Estate Commission's Rules and Regulations require that a real estate broker representing a party to a transaction must ensure that all contracts are in writing. As stated in previous chapters, this means that real estate licensees must use written rather than oral agreements. As a practical matter, the printed word, as long as it is sufficiently complete and specific, gives all parties written evidence of their rights and responsibilities under the contract and minimizes the likelihood of controversies. ■

■ DISCHARGE OF CONTRACTS

A contract is *discharged* when the agreement is terminated. Obviously, the most desirable case is when a contract terminates because it has been completely performed, with all of the obligations the parties agreed to being fulfilled. A contract can also terminate when it is breached or broken. This means that one of the parties defaults, leaving the other party to seek remedies for the broken contract.

Performance of a Contract

Each party has certain rights and duties to fulfill. It's important to know exactly when these acts must be performed so that it's clear precisely when the contract is discharged. Many contracts call for a specific time by which the agreed-upon acts must be completely performed. In addition, many contracts provide that **time is of the essence.** This means that the contract must be performed within the time limit specified. A party who fails to perform on time is liable for breach of contract.

When a contract does not specify a date for performance, the acts it requires should be performed within a reasonable time. The interpretation of what constitutes a reasonable time depends on the situation. Generally, unless the parties agree otherwise, if the act can be done immediately, it should be performed immediately. Courts have sometimes declared contracts to be invalid because they did not contain a time or date for performance.

IN PRACTICE

Agreements of sale in Pennsylvania commonly provide for a number of events (such as structural inspections, environmental assessments, and commitments for financing) that must occur by certain dates stated in the contract. When dates are specified as "time is of the essence," a contract could be breached if the parties fail to meet their obligations by those dates. Real estate licensees should be aware of the legal significance of performance dates and the precise manner in which the contract states that the parties must satisfy their obligations. Licensees should also use care in recommending time frames so that performance dates are practical to achieve.

Assignment and Novation

After a contractual relationship has been formed, one party may want to withdraw from the contract without jeopardizing the performance of an agreement. This may be accomplished through either assignment or novation.

Assignment is a transfer of rights and/or duties under a contract. Normally, rights may be assigned to a third party (called the *assignee*) unless the contract forbids it. Contractual obligations may also be assigned (or delegated), but the original party remains primarily liable unless specifically released. A party might elect to assign obligations in lieu of defaulting or performing on a contract that is no longer in the party's best interest. Many contracts include a clause that either permits or forbids assignment.

A contract may also be performed by novation. **Novation** is the substitution of a new contract in place of the original one. The new agreement may be between the same parties, or a new party may be substituted for either (this is *novation of the parties*). The parties' intent must be to discharge the old obligation. For instance, when a real estate purchaser assumes the seller's existing mortgage loan, the lender may choose to release the seller and substitute the buyer as the party primarily liable for the mortgage debt.

Breach of Contract

A contract may be terminated if it is breached by one of the parties. A **breach of contract** is a violation of any of the terms or conditions without legal excuse. For instance, a seller who fails to deliver title to the buyer under the conditions stated in the agreement breaches the contract. The breaching or defaulting party assumes certain burdens, and the nondefaulting party has certain remedies. Normally, the contract states the rights and remedies that are available to the nondefaulting party.

If the seller breaches a real estate agreement of sale, the buyer may sue for *specific performance* unless the contract specifically states otherwise. In a **suit for specific performance,** the buyer asks the court to force the seller to go through with the sale and convey the property as previously agreed. Or the buyer may choose to sue for damages, in which case the seller is asked to pay for any costs and hardships suffered by the buyer as a result of the seller's breach.

If the buyer defaults, the seller can sue for damages or the purchase price. A suit for the purchase price is essentially a suit for specific performance: The seller tenders the deed and asks that the buyer be compelled to pay the agreed price.

The contract may limit the remedies available to the parties, however. A *liquidated damages* clause permits the seller to keep the earnest money deposit and any other payments received from the buyer as the seller's sole remedy. The clause may limit the buyer's remedy to a return of the earnest money and other payments should the seller default.

Statute of limitations.   State law limits the time within which parties to a contract may bring legal suit to enforce their rights. In Pennsylvania, the *statute of limitations* is four years from the date the contract is breached. Any rights that are not enforced within the applicable time period are lost.

Other reasons for termination.   Contracts may also be discharged or terminated when any of the following occurs:

- *Partial performance* of the terms, along with a written acceptance by the other party. For instance, if the parties agree that performance is "close enough" to complete, they can agree that the contract is discharged even if some minor elements remain unperformed.
- *Substantial performance*, in which one party has substantially performed on the contract but does not complete all the details exactly as the contract requires. (Such performance may be enough to force payment, with certain adjustments for any damages suffered by the other party.)
- *Impossibility of performance*, in which an act required by the contract cannot be legally accomplished.
- *Mutual agreement* of the parties to cancel, which returns the parties to their position prior to the contract, so any monies that have been exchanged must be returned.
- *Operation of law*, such as a minor voiding a contract or as a result of fraud, the expiration of the statute of limitations, or the alteration of a contract without the written consent of all parties involved.

◼ USE OF CONTRACTS IN THE REAL ESTATE BUSINESS

The increasing complexity of real estate transactions and the contracts and documents that have become the routine in those transactions have created fertile ground for problems, both for the consumer and the real estate licensee. Consumers need guidance in navigating the intricacies of today's transactions. At the same time, real estate licensees are challenged to help consumers without overstepping the professional limits of their licenses into the unauthorized practice of law. The potential for harm is enormous if consumers get inappropriate or inadequate advice and the person providing that counsel is not licensed to engage in the practice of law.

In Your State   **PA** Pennsylvania law prohibits providing legal advice unless properly licensed to do so. The consequences of the unauthorized practice of law are far reaching. Engaging in this activity is a criminal offense, punishable by up to one-year imprisonment and a $2,500 fine. Also, the State Real Estate Commission can take disciplinary action against licensees who provide legal advice, resulting in a fine, or the suspension or revocation of a license. Finally, a party who is injured by the advice can file a lawsuit, which can result in an award of monetary damages against the individual who provided that advice. A lawyer is an essential professional in today's transactions, a benefit for both the consumer and the real estate licensee. ■

In every transaction, there is at least one legal contract, and often there are several. The preparation of legal documents is considered a practice of law, but real estate licensees must be able to prepare contracts during the normal course of the transactions. Many states address this dilemma by establishing specific guidelines about the circumstances and manner in which real estate licensees are permitted to prepare contracts. This may be directed by statute or by court decision, or there may be agreements between lawyer and real estate associations for the preparation of contracts. Licensees must still use great care in completing these forms because they, just like attorneys, are liable for any injury resulting from errors in the documents.

The types of written agreements most commonly used by real estate licensees are

■ listing agreements,
■ buyer agency agreements,
■ agreements of sale,
■ options,
■ land contracts or contracts for deed,
■ leases, and
■ escrow agreements.

Preprinted Forms   In Your State   **PA** Because many real estate transactions are very similar in nature, preprinted forms are available for most kinds of contracts. In Pennsylvania, licensees are permitted to fill in the blanks on certain preprinted documents such as agreements of sale and leases as long as they do not charge a separate fee for completing the forms. A number of preprinted forms prepared by REALTOR® associations and/or bar associations are available, both in hard copy and on computer disk. ■

The use of printed forms raises three issues:

■ What to write in the blanks
■ What printed words should be ruled out (by drawing lines through them) because they don't apply to the particular transaction
■ What additional clauses or agreements (called riders or addenda) should be included

Often, preprinted forms provide a number of alternate provisions, which must be either checked for use or ruled out depending upon the parties' desires. All changes and additions to preprinted forms are usually initialed and dated in the margin when the contract is executed. Similarly, riders or addenda must also be signed and dated.

IN PRACTICE

It is essential that all parties to a contract understand exactly what they are agreeing to, especially when the contract contains complicated legal language. The parties should be encouraged to have contracts and other legal documents examined by their attorneys *before they are signed* to ensure that their respective interests are protected and their intentions are properly stated. Poorly drafted documents can be subject to various interpretations and lead to litigation. As a general rule, the farther one strays from preprinted language that has passed prior legal scrutiny, the greater the risk. When preprinted forms do not adequately address the desires of the parties and the circumstances of a specific transaction, an attorney should draft a suitable contract.

Plain Language

In Your State

PA Many consumers (or anyone who does not have legal training) have difficulty understanding the words commonly used in legal documents. The *Plain Language Consumer Contract Act* in Pennsylvania intends to protect consumers from making contracts they do not understand by promoting the use of plain language. Agreements that must be written in plain language include contracts in which a consumer ■

- ■ borrows money;
- ■ buys, leases, or rents personal property or real property; and
- ■ engages services for cash or on credit for personal, family, or household purposes.

Agreements that are not covered by this law include deeds, mortgages, certificates of title and title insurance contracts, documents used by state or federal financial institutions, contracts to buy securities, insurance policies, and commercial leases.

The guidelines for plain language include the use of short words, sentences, and paragraphs, and the use of active verbs. Contracts should not contain technical legal terms (other than those that are commonly understood), Latin or foreign words, double negatives, and exceptions to exceptions. Definitions for words should use commonly understood language. There are also guidelines for the type size, spacing, headings, and page layout.

Any creditor, lessor, or seller who does not comply with the tests of readability (as defined by the law) is liable to the consumer for any loss caused by the violation, statutory damages of up to $100, court costs, and attorney fees. Anyone drafting consumer contracts should refer to the law for the specific guidelines. Contracts may be submitted to the attorney general for approval before being used, to avoid problems that could arise in the future.

Electronic Transactions

Traditionally, contracts have been typewritten documents, personally signed with pen and blue ink by the parties. When facsimile machines became popular, federal and state laws responded with guidance permitting signatures by fax (as opposed to original signatures) as sufficient evidence of the parties' agreement to a contract. Now, technology has opened another venue as consumers contract for goods and services in the electronic marketplace. While the basic principles of contract law haven't changed, the application of those laws in the global environment of electronic commerce (known as "e-commerce") certainly has changed.

The Internet and e-mail communications are important contemporary aids for negotiating contracts and transmitting documents, and can make fully automated transactions possible. But human interaction in cyberspace also involves a degree of anonymity and a lack of control over transmissions and even the actions of people on behalf of others that don't exist in pretechnology commerce. Furthermore, there are no geographic or governmental boundaries. State consumer protection laws, which also address rights in contracts, have customarily governed commerce within a state's boundaries, with federal law doing likewise for commerce that crosses state lines. Although there is often some amount of uniformity in these laws, the seamless marketplace also means that regulatory jurisdiction is less clear. Lawmakers are being challenged to rethink the entire platform of commerce and the way products and services are marketed, contracted, and taxed in cyberspace.

| In Your State | **PA**   The federal *Uniform Electronic Transaction Act* and corresponding state laws, Pennsylvania's being the *Electronic Transaction Act* enacted in January 2000, have been adopted to facilitate e-commerce and also protect the rights of consumers in electronic transactions. The electronic transaction laws intend to ensure the validity and enforcement of electronic signatures, records, and writings. Essentially, the laws give legal effect to agreements bargained for electronically, as long as they meet all other provisions of contract law. Obviously, the electronic mechanics are different from those anticipated when contract law originated, and necessitate regulatory directives to translate the basic principles of contract law into electronic application. As more is learned about electronic transactions, new rules and procedures will emerge. In addition, it's unknown at the moment how dramatically electronic commerce may alter the customary course of real estate transactions. Real estate licensees are well-advised to seek knowledgeable legal counsel as they tread down this path of commerce. ■

■ SUMMARY

A contract is a legally enforceable promise or set of promises that must be performed. The law provides a remedy in the case of a breach of those promises.

Contracts may be classified according to whether the parties' intentions are express or merely implied by their actions. They may also be classified as bilateral (when both parties have obligated themselves to act) or unilateral (when one party is obligated to perform only if the other party acts). In addition, contracts may be classified according to their legal enforceability as valid, void, voidable, or unenforceable.

The essentials of a valid contract are (1) offer and acceptance, (2) consideration, (3) legally competent parties, (4) legality of object, and (5) reality of consent. The contract should be in writing and signed by all parties to be enforceable in court.

Many contracts specify a time for performance. In any case, all contracts must be performed within a reasonable time. An executed contract is one that has been fully performed. An executory contract is one in which some act remains to be performed.

In many types of contracts, either of the parties may transfer his or her rights and obligations under the agreement by assignment of the contract or novation (substitution of a new contract).

Contracts usually provide that the seller has the right to declare a sale canceled if the buyer defaults. In general, if either party suffers a loss because of the other's default, he or she may sue for damages to cover the loss. If the buyer defaults, the seller can sue for the purchase price; if the seller defaults, the buyer can sue for specific performance.

Contracts frequently used in the real estate business include listings, agreements of sale, options, installment contracts (contracts for deed), leases, and escrow agreements. Licensees are not authorized to practice law; however, they are permitted to prepare contracts in certain circumstances. The use of preprinted forms has become common practice.

Consumer contracts must comply with the Plain Language Act in Pennsylvania. With advances in technology, new laws have recently been adopted to govern electronic commerce.

QUESTIONS

1. A legally enforceable agreement under which two parties agree to do something for each other is known as a(n)
   a. escrow agreement.
   b. legal promise.
   c. valid contract.
   d. option agreement.

2. *D* drives into a filling station and tops off her gas tank. Why is *D* obligated to pay for the fuel she has pumped into the tank of her car?
   a. *D* has entered into an express contract.
   b. *D* has entered into an implied agreement.
   c. *D* has a fully executed bilateral contract.
   d. *D* is obligated to pay for the gas under provisions of the statute of frauds.

3. A contract is said to be *bilateral* if
   a. one of the parties is a minor.
   b. the contract has yet to be fully performed.
   c. only one party to the agreement is bound to act.
   d. all parties to the contract are bound to act.

4. During the period of time after a real estate agreement of sale is signed but before title actually passes, the status of the contract is
   a. void.
   b. executory.
   c. unilateral.
   d. implied.

5. A contract for the sale of real estate that does not state the consideration to be paid for the property and is not signed by the parties is considered to be
   a. voidable.
   b. executory.
   c. void.
   d. enforceable.

6. The statute of frauds which requires that a contract must be in writing to be enforceable applies to
   a. all real estate sales agreements.
   b. all real estate contracts of any sort.
   c. all contracts.
   d. bilateral contracts only.

7. The buyer asked the seller to leave the washing machine. The seller said yes, but because the agreement of sale said nothing about the seller's leaving the washing machine, the seller took it with her. The buyer has no right to legal recourse because of the rule of
   a. partial performance.
   b. novation.
   c. undue influence.
   d. parol evidence.

8. A suit for specific performance filed by a purchaser under a real estate contract asks for
   a. money damages.
   b. a new contract.
   c. a deficiency judgment.
   d. the conveyance of the property.

9. If a real estate sales contract states that time is of the essence and the stipulated date of transfer comes and goes without a closing, the contract is
   a. binding for only 30 more days.
   b. novated.
   c. still valid.
   d. breached.

10. In filling out a sales contract, someone crossed out several words and inserted others. To eliminate future controversy about whether the changes were made before or after the contract was signed, the usual procedure is to
    a. write a letter to each party listing the changes.
    b. have each party write a letter to the other approving the changes.
    c. redraw the entire contract.
    d. have both parties initial or sign and date the margin near each change.

11. Under the statute of frauds, contracts for the sale of real estate must be
    a. originated by a real estate broker.
    b. on preprinted forms.
    c. in writing to be enforceable.
    d. accompanied by earnest money deposits.

12. *T* has an executory contract to buy property but would rather let his friend M buy it instead. If the contract allows, M can take over *T's* obligation by the process known as
    a. assignment.
    b. substantial performance.
    c. subordination.
    d. mutual consent.

13. Broker *J* has found a buyer for G's home. The buyer has indicated in writing his willingness to buy the property for $1,000 less than the asking price and has deposited $5,000 earnest money with broker *J*. G is out of town for the weekend, and *J* has been unable to inform him of the signed document. At this point, the buyer has signed a(n)
    a. voidable contract.
    b. offer.
    c. executory agreement.
    d. implied contract.

14. Which of the following is *NOT* one of the essentials of a valid contract?
    a. Offer and acceptance
    b. Earnest money
    c. Legality of object
    d. Consideration

ANSWERS

1. **C** A contract is a voluntary agreement or promise between legally competent parties to do or refrain from doing certain things. A contract is valid if it meets the essential requirements of contract law that make it legally sufficient to be enforceable in court. (p. 170)

2. **B** An implied contract is an agreement that is demonstrated by the actions or conduct of the parties. *D* has an implied obligation to pay for the gas. (p. 170)

3. **D** A bilateral contract is one in which all parties (both sides of the contract) promise to do something. The basis of the contractual relationship is an exchange of promises: "I will do this, and in return you will do that." (p. 170)

4. **B** Although the contractual relationship is created when the agreement of sale is entered into, the obligations under the contract will not be completed until settlement or closing. From the point when the agreement is created up to closing, the contract is classified as an executory contract. (p. 170)

5. **C** A definite statement of consideration must be included in a contract to evidence that something of value was given in exchange for the promises made. If there is no consideration, the contract is void. (p. 172)

6. **A** The statute of frauds requires certain types of contracts to be in writing to be enforceable. By statute, agreements of sale for real estate and certain lease agreements must be written. (p. 173)

7. **D** Written agreements take precedence over oral agreements by the parol evidence rule. Because the written agreement of sale did not include the obligation to leave the washing machine, the seller may take it with her. (p. 173)

8. **D** Specific performance is the legal remedy by which an aggrieved party asks the court to force the other party to perform the obligation or fulfill the promise agreed to in the contract. The buyer is asking the court to require the seller to convey title to the property. (p. 174)

9. **D** "Time is of the essence" means that the contract obligations must be performed within the specific time frames stated in the contract. A party who fails to perform on time is liable for breach of contract. (p. 173)

10. **D** All changes and additions to preprinted forms are usually initialed and dated in the margin in order to eliminate future controversy as to the agreement between the parties and the date the changes or additions were actually made. (p. 177)

11. **C** The statute of frauds requires contracts for the sale of real estate to be in writing in order to be enforceable. There is no requirement that preprinted forms be used, that the contract be originated by a broker, or that an earnest money deposit be provided. (p. 173)

12. **A** Unless the original contract prohibits it, a party to a contract may transfer his or her rights and/or duties under the contract. This is known as an assignment. *T* may transfer or assign his position to *M*. (p. 174)

13. **B** Offer *and acceptance* is essential for a valid contract. *G* has not accepted the terms of the offer made by the buyer. Therefore, the buyer has only signed and made an offer to purchase, but the document has no legal standing as a contract. (p. 172)

14. **B** The requirements of a valid contract include offer and acceptance, consideration, and legality of object. An earnest money deposit is not necessary for a contract to exist. (p. 172)

CHAPTER TWELVE

PRINCIPLES OF REAL ESTATE FINANCING

■ LEARNING OBJECTIVES

When you've finished reading this chapter, you should be able to

- explain the role of the federal reserve and the primary and secondary mortgage market, and their impact on real estate finance;
- identify key provisions in promissory notes and mortgage documents;
- distinguish between methods of repayment commonly used in real estate finance;
- describe remedies when loans default, including rights in foreclosure proceedings; and
- define the key terms.

■ KEY TERMS

acceleration clause	Federal Reserve System (the Fed)	mortgagor
alienation clause	foreclosure	note
amortized loan	Freddie Mac	prepayment penalty
deed in lieu of foreclosure	Ginnie Mae	primary mortgage market
deed of trust	hypothecation	satisfaction
defeasance clause	interest	secondary mortgage market
deficiency judgment	lien theory	straight loan
equitable right of redemption	loan origination fee	title theory
Fannie Mae	mortgage	usury
	mortgagee	

■ THE FLOW OF MONEY

The interaction of a complex network of forces in the economy shapes the supply and demand of money. As economic conditions change, monetary policies are instituted to reshape supply and demand to manage growth or stimulate the economy as needed. This affects the cost of money and ultimately the way people borrow it. Because most real estate transactions require some sort of financing, the nation's monetary policies have a direct bearing on real estate. These policies affect the amount of money available for mortgage loans and the interest rates.

To understand the real estate financing market, it is important to understand the three major components:

■ The Federal Reserve System
■ The primary mortgage market
■ The secondary mortgage market

Under the umbrella of monetary policies set by the Federal Reserve System, the primary mortgage market originates loans that are bought, sold, and traded in the secondary mortgage market. Before turning to a discussion of mortgages and notes, it is important to have a clear understanding of the bigger picture: the market in which those mortgages and notes exist.

Federal Reserve System

The role of the **Federal Reserve System** (also known as "the Fed") is to maintain sound credit conditions, help counteract inflationary and deflationary trends, and create a favorable economic climate. The Federal Reserve System divides the country into 12 federal reserve districts, each served by a federal reserve bank. All nationally chartered banks must join the Federal Reserve and purchase stock in its district reserve banks.

> The **Fed** regulates the flow of money by controlling
> ■ reserve requirements and
> ■ discount rates.

The Federal Reserve regulates the flow of money and interest rates in the marketplace indirectly through its member banks by controlling their reserve requirements and discount rates. The Fed also can regulate the money supply through the *Federal Open Market Committee (FOMC)*, which buys and sells U.S. government securities on the open market. When the FOMC sells securities, it effectively removes money paid from circulation. When it buys them, it infuses its own reserves back into the general supply.

Reserve requirements.   The Federal Reserve requires each member bank to keep a certain amount of its assets on hand as reserve funds. These reserves are unavailable for loans or any other use. Reserve requirements not only protect customer deposits, but also provide a mechanism for manipulating the flow of cash in the marketplace.

By increasing reserve requirements, the Federal Reserve in effect limits the amount of money that member banks can use to make loans. When the amount of money available for lending decreases, interest rates (the amount lenders can charge for the use of their money) rise. By causing interest rates to rise, the government can slow down an overactive economy by limiting the number of loans that would have been directed toward major purchases of goods and services. The opposite is also true: By decreasing reserve requirements, the Fed can encourage more lending. Increased lending causes the amount of money circulating in the marketplace to rise, while simultaneously causing interest rates to drop.

Discount rates.   Federal Reserve member banks are permitted to borrow money from the district reserve banks to expand their lending operations. The interest rate that the district banks charge for the use of this money is called the *discount rate*. This rate is the basis on which the banks determine the rate of interest that they, in turn, will charge their loan customers. Theoretically, when the Federal Reserve discount rate is high, bank interest rates are high. When bank interest rates are high, fewer loans are made and less money circulates in the marketplace. Conversely, a lower discount rate results in lower interest rates, more bank loans, and more money in circulation.

The Primary Mortgage Market

The **primary mortgage market** is where borrowers directly interact with lenders.

The primary mortgage market is made up of lenders who originate the loans. These lenders make money available directly to borrowers. From a borrower's point of view, a loan is a means of financing an expenditure; from a lender's point of view, a loan is an investment. All investors look for profitable returns on their investments. For a lender, a loan must generate enough income to be an attractive investment. Income on the loan is realized from two sources:

1. Finance charges collected at closing, such as loan origination fees and discount points (discussed in Chapter 20)
2. Recurring income, which is the interest collected during the term of the loan

Like any other investor, lenders adopt investment strategies that suit their individual objectives. Some lenders invest in mortgage loans primarily for the recurring income. Others look to the income generated from fees collected when originating loans. Obviously, as these lenders originate more loans, they generate more income. Often, they sell the loans to investors, thereby generating additional funds with which to originate more loans. Some lenders derive income from servicing loans for other lenders or for the investors who have purchased the loans. Sometimes, lenders establish affiliated companies whose sole purpose is to service mortgage loans. The servicing agreement stipulates the fees and the specific responsibilities, but servicing could include activities such as

- collecting payments (including insurance and taxes),
- accounting,
- bookkeeping,
- preparing insurance and tax records,
- processing payments of taxes and insurance, and
- following up on loan payment and delinquency.

Many different types of lenders make up the primary mortgage market. Today, that market has no geographic boundaries with a number of lenders advancing loans by way of the Internet. Because lenders accumulate money from different sources and have a variety of obligations to satisfy with those funds, their strategies for investing in mortgage loans are different. Some lenders originate many individual loans while others invest large sums of money in relatively few loans, typically large residential complexes and commercial or industrial projects. For some, a longer-term investment is preferable to a short-term one. There are also occasions when the lender has an equity position (known as an *equity kicker*) in the real estate. Lenders in the primary mortgage market include:

- *Thrifts*, *savings institutions*, and *commercial banks*—known as *fiduciary lenders* because of their fiduciary obligations to protect depositors' funds, which they then invest in loans
- *Insurance companies*—invest money accumulated from premiums paid by their policyholders
- *Credit unions*—provide mortgage loans as well as consumer and home improvement loans to their member-depositors
- *Pension funds*—invest contributors' funds in mortgage loans primarily through mortgage bankers, mortgage brokers, and life insurance companies
- *Endowment funds*—hospitals, universities, colleges, charitable foundations, and other institutions who invest in mortgage loans typically through commercial banks and mortgage bankers
- *Investment group financing*—joint ventures such as syndicates, limited partnerships, and real estate investment trusts who invest in large real estate projects
- *Mortgage banking companies*—originate loans with money from investors, as well as their own, with the intention of later selling the loans and receiving servicing fees; mortgage bankers are *not* mortgage brokers
- *Mortgage brokers*—intermediaries who bring borrowers and lenders together by locating potential borrowers and then submitting preliminary loan applications to lenders for final approval; *mortgage brokers do not lend money nor do they service loans*. They may, however, be affiliated with mortgage banking companies.

In Your State **PA** In Pennsylvania, mortgage bankers and mortgage brokers must be licensed and conduct business in accordance with the Mortgage Bankers and Brokers Act. Current regulations require the completion of six hours of continuing education by one person from each office licensed to engage in mortgage banking and brokering activities. The Department of Banking issues these licenses and governs the licensees' activities, with the State Real Estate Commission also having certain limited authority when these individuals are licensed real estate brokers and salespersons as well. The Department of Banking has also expanded the activities for which licenses are required, and in 2003, began issuing Limited Mortgage Broker licenses. These licenses were created to permit individuals employed by insurance companies and professionally recognized financial planners to engage in refinance activities. As of this writing, legislation requiring licenses for loan originators and loan correspondents is being discussed in Harrisburg. ∎

The Secondary Mortgage Market

As previously mentioned, lenders in the primary mortgage market often seek investors for the loans they originate. The **secondary mortgage market** is where loans are bought and sold only after they have been funded. Lenders often sell loans to avoid interest rate risks and to realize profits on the sales.

This secondary market activity helps lenders raise capital to continue making mortgage loans. Secondary market activity is especially desirable when money is in short supply; it stimulates both the housing construction market and the mortgage market by expanding the types of loans available.

When a loan is sold, the original lender or another loan servicer collects the payments from the borrower and then passes them along to the investor who purchased the loan. The investor is charged a fee for the servicing.

Warehousing agencies purchase a number of mortgage loans and assemble them into packages of loans (called *pools*). Securities that represent shares in these pooled mortgages are then sold to investors. Loans are eligible for sale to the secondary market only when the collateral, borrower, and documentation meet certain requirements to provide a degree of safety for the investors. The following are the major warehousing agencies.

Fannie Mae.   Fannie Mae (formerly the *Federal National Mortgage Association* or *FNMA*) is a quasi-governmental agency. It is organized as a privately owned corporation that issues its own common stock and provides a secondary market for mortgage loans. Fannie Mae deals in conventional as well as FHA and VA loans (discussed in Chapter 20). Fannie Mae buys a block or pool of mortgages from a lender in exchange for *mortgage-backed securities*, which the lender may keep or sell. Fannie Mae guarantees payment of all interest and principal to the holder of the securities.

Government National Mortgage Association.   Unlike Fannie Mae, **Ginnie Mae** (formerly the *Government National Mortgage Association* or *GNMA*) is entirely a government agency. Ginnie Mae is a division of the Department of Housing and Urban Development (HUD), organized as a corporation without capital stock. Ginnie Mae administers special-assistance programs and works with Fannie Mae in secondary market activities.

In times of tight money and high interest rates, Fannie Mae and Ginnie Mae can join forces through their *tandem plan*. The *tandem plan* provides that Fannie Mae can purchase high-risk, low-yield (usually FHA) loans at full market rates, with Ginnie Mae guaranteeing payment and absorbing the difference between the low yield and current market prices.

Ginnie Mae also guarantees investment securities issued by private offerors (such as banks, mortgage companies, and savings and loan associations) and backed by pools of FHA and VA mortgage loans. The Ginnie Mae pass-through certificate is a security interest in a pool of mortgages that provides for a monthly "pass-through" of principal and interest payments directly to the certificate holder. These certificates are guaranteed by Ginnie Mae.

Federal Home Loan Mortgage Corporation.   Freddie Mac (the *Federal Home Loan Mortgage Corporation* or *FHLMC*) provides a secondary market for mortgage loans, primarily conventional loans. Freddie Mac has authority to purchase mortgages, pool them, and sell bonds in the open market with the mortgages as security. However, Freddie Mac does not guarantee payment of Freddie Mac mortgages.

Many lenders use standardized Fannie Mae and Freddie Mac forms and loan procedures. In fact, they are mandatory for lenders who wish to sell mortgages to the agencies in the secondary mortgage market. The standardized documents include loan applications, credit reports, appraisal forms, mortgages, and notes. Because Fannie Mae and Freddie Mac's involvement in the secondary market is so prevalent, many of the paperwork details and loan qualifications that confront borrowers are tied to Fannie Mae and Freddie Mac requirements.

■ MORTGAGE LAW

Mortgage loans are viewed as relatively secure, desirable investments because of the principles under which mortgages are executed. The borrower, or **mortgagor,** pledges the real estate to the lender, or **mortgagee,** as security for the debt. A mortgage is considered a voluntary lien on real estate. That is, the person who borrows money willingly gives the lender certain rights to the property. The lender has both the borrower's personal promise to pay the debt as well as the right to take the property if the borrower fails to meet that obligation.

> **Parties to a Mortgage**
>
> Mortgagor = borrower
>
> Mortgagee = lender

Some states, known as **title theory** states, view a mortgage as a conveyance of legal title to the mortgagee. Legal title is returned to the mortgagor only when the debt is paid in full (or some other obligation is performed). In theory, the mortgagee actually owns the real estate until the debt is paid. In the meantime, the borrower has all the usual rights of ownership, such as possession and use. In effect, because the lender actually holds legal title, the lender has the right to immediate possession of the real estate and rents from the property if the mortgagor defaults.

On the other hand, states in which the mortgage is viewed simply as a lien on the property are called **lien theory** states. The mortgage is nothing more than collateral for the loan. If the mortgagor defaults, the mortgagee must go through a formal foreclosure procedure to obtain legal title. The property is offered for sale, and the funds from the sale are used to pay all or part of the remaining debt. In some states, a defaulting mortgagor may redeem (buy back) the property during a certain period after the sale. A borrower who fails to redeem the property during this time loses the property irrevocably.

In Your State **PA** A number of states, including Pennsylvania, have adopted an *intermediary theory*. This is a hybrid philosophy that is based on the principles of title theory but, like the principles of lien theory, requires that the mortgagee foreclose to obtain legal title. Pennsylvania, historically, has been a title theory state. But as an intermediary theory state, the property owner does not automatically forfeit the real estate on default of the debt. The borrower must first be given a *notice of intention to foreclose* before the lender can file suit and proceed with foreclosure. The notice essentially forewarns the borrower and provides an opportunity to resolve the matter before the lender takes legal action. ■

In reality, the differences in theories are more technical than actual. All borrowers and lenders observe the same general requirements to protect themselves. Real estate loans are formal contracts, consisting of a mortgage document, which gives the property as security for the debt, and a note, which is the evidence of the debt.

Security and Debt

Generally, any interest in real estate that may be sold may be pledged as security for a debt. A basic principle of property law is that no one can convey more than he or she actually owns. This principle also applies to mortgages. The owner of a fee simple estate can mortgage the fee; the owner of a leasehold or subleasehold can mortgage the leasehold interest. The owner of a condominium unit can mortgage the fee interest in the condominium. The owner of a cooperative, even though the interest is personal rather than real property, can pledge the ownership as collateral.

Mortgage Loan Instruments

There are two parts to a mortgage loan: the debt itself and the security for the debt. When a property is to be mortgaged, the owner must execute (sign) two separate instruments:

> **Mortgage Loan Instruments**
>
> The **note,** which is the finance instrument and
>
> The **mortgage,** which is the security instrument

1. The **note,** or financing instrument, is the borrower's personal promise to repay a debt according to agreed-on terms. The note exposes all of the borrower's assets to claims by creditors. The mortgagor executes one or more promissory notes to total the amount of the debt.
2. The **mortgage,** or security instrument, is the document that creates the lien on the property. The mortgage exposes the real estate to claim by the mortgagee and is the document that gives the creditor the right to sue for foreclosure.

Hypothecation is the term used to describe the pledging of property as security for payment of a loan without surrendering possession of the property. A pledge of security—a mortgage—cannot be legally effective unless there is a debt to secure. Both a note and a mortgage are executed to create a secured loan.

Deed of trust.   In some areas of the country, the custom is to use a three-party instrument known as a **deed of trust,** or a trust deed, rather than a mortgage document. In Pennsylvania, however, deeds of trust are rarely used. A trust deed conveys "naked title," that is, title without the right of possession. The deed is given as security for the loan to a third party, called the *trustee.* The trustee holds bare title on behalf of the lender, who is known as the *beneficiary.* The beneficiary is the holder of the note. The conveyance establishes the actions that the trustee may take if the borrower (the *trustor*) defaults on any of the terms. (See Figure 12.1 for a comparison of mortgages and trust deeds.) Foreclosure procedures for default are usually simpler and faster than for mortgage loans.

■ PROVISIONS OF THE NOTE

A promissory note executed by a borrower (known as the maker or payor) generally states the amount of the debt, the time and method of payment, the rate of interest, and all other terms of the actual loan. If the note is used

F I G U R E   12.1

Mortgage versus Deed of Trust

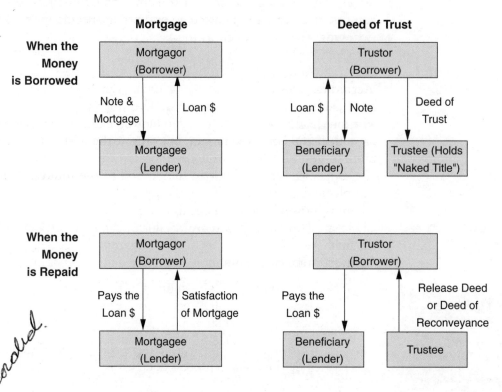

Note is not recorded.

Parties to the Note
Payor = borrower
Payee = lender

with a mortgage, it names the lender (mortgagee) as the payee; if it is used with a trust deed, the note may be made payable to the bearer. The note may also refer to or repeat several of the clauses that appear in the mortgage document. The note, like the mortgage, should be signed by all parties who have an interest in the property. Unlike a mortgage, which is recorded as a lien on the title, the note is not recorded or otherwise filed on public record.

A note is a *negotiable instrument* like a check or bank draft. The individual who holds the note is referred to as the payee. He or she may transfer the right to receive payment to a third party in one of two ways:

1. By signing the instrument over (that is, by assigning it) to the third party
2. By delivering the instrument to the third party

Because a note is a negotiable instrument, a mortgage lender may sell or transfer it to the secondary mortgage market.

Interest

Among the items addressed in a note is the rate of interest. **Interest** is the charge for the use of the money. Interest may be due either at the end or beginning of each payment period. When payments are made at the end of a period, it is known as payment *in arrears*. Payments made at the beginning of each period are known as payment *in advance*. Whether interest is charged in arrears or in advance is specified in the note. This distinction is important if the property is sold before the debt is repaid in full.

Usury.   To protect consumers from unscrupulous lenders, many states have enacted laws limiting the interest rate that may be charged on loans. In some states, the legal maximum rate is a fixed amount. In others, it is a floating interest rate, which is adjusted up or down at specific intervals based on some economic standards, such as the prime lending rate or the rate of return on government bonds.

Regardless of which approach is used, charging interest that exceeds the permissible maximum rate is called **usury.** Lenders are penalized for making usurious loans. In some states, a lender who makes a usurious loan is permitted to collect the borrowed money, but only at the legal rate of interest. In other states, a usurious lender may lose the right to collect any interest or may lose the entire amount of the loan in addition to the interest.

There is, however, a broad exemption from state usury laws. Residential first-mortgage loans made by federally chartered institutions, or by lenders insured or guaranteed by federal agencies, are exempt from state interest limitations. In effect, state usury laws apply to private lenders. Loans made to corporations are generally exempt from usury laws as well.

Loan origination fee.   The processing of a mortgage application is known as *loan origination*. When a mortgage is originated, a **loan origination fee** (or loan fee) is charged to cover the lender's initial cost of generating the loan. These include the costs to process documents related to credit, appraisals, and inspections as well as salaries and other related business expenses. The typical fee is 1 percent of the face amount of the loan, although the fees could range between 1 and 3 percent, depending on the type of loan. Some lenders include an additional charge within the origination fee that could be classified as prepaid interest.

Prepayment

Most mortgage loans are paid in installments over a long period of time. As a result, the total interest paid by the borrower may add up to more than the principal of the loan. That does not come as a surprise to the lender; the total amount of accrued interest is carefully calculated during the origination phase to determine the profitability of each loan. If the borrower repays the loan before the end of the term, the lender collects less than the anticipated interest. For this reason, some mortgage notes contain a *prepayment clause*. This clause requires that the borrower pay a **prepayment penalty** against the unearned portion of the interest for any payments made ahead of schedule.

In Your State   **PA**   Lenders are not permitted to charge prepayment penalties on mortgage loans insured or guaranteed by the federal government. In addition, Pennsylvania law does not permit prepayment penalties on residential mortgage loans when the principal amount is $50,000 or less. Otherwise, lenders can include in the note whatever penalty conditions they choose. The lender may permit a borrower to pay off a certain percentage of the original loan without penalty or may permit the payoff of the entire principal without penalty in certain situations. The lender may also reserve the right to waive a penalty provision.

A waiver could be used to encourage a borrower to pay off a low-yield loan when money is scarce and interest rates rise. ■

Payment Plans

Prior to the 1930s, a **straight loan** (or term loan) was the only type of payment plan. In a straight loan, the periodic payments are allocated only to interest. The entire principal is paid at the end of the loan term. These are short-term loans, with the principal commonly being due in three to five years. When the principal comes due, the borrower must have sufficient cash to repay the principal or must obtain another loan. During the depression of the 1930s, many loans went into foreclosure because borrowers were unable to repay or refinance the debt. Savings and loan associations were instrumental in introducing amortized loans to protect the lenders' investments in mortgage loans.

Amortized loans involve systematic payments of principal along with interest, with the result that loans are gradually paid off over time. Amortized loans are typically long-term loans, the most common terms being 15 and 30 years. At the end of the loan period, the full amount of the principal and all interest due is reduced to a zero balance. The principal is directly reduced (hence the term *direction reduction loan*) or amortized over the life of the loan.

IN PRACTICE

Although the fundamental principles behind amortized loans are still valid, straight or interest-only loans have gained popularity, representing 30 percent (or more) of the mortgage loans written for housing purchases in many areas. Repaying only interest is a lower out-of-pocket expenditure than repaying principal as well, and in turn makes home purchases possible, especially in areas where property values are rapidly appreciating. In some cases, this added buying power has fueled that appreciation and, perhaps, overspending by some buyers as well. While purchasers can buy now, they still have to pay later when the total amount of the loan becomes due. Interest-only loans are further discussed in Chapter 20.

The note specifies the manner in which an amortized loan is repaid. A *fully amortized mortgage loan*, or *level-payment* loan, is the most frequently used plan. The borrower pays a *constant amount*, usually monthly. The lender credits each payment first to the interest due, then to the principal amount of the loan. As a result, while the payment remains the same, the portion applied to interest decreases, and the portion applied to principal increases. This is because less interest is due as the balance of the loan is reduced. A borrower can minimize the amount of interest he or she pays by making additional payments directly to principal and paying off the loan before the end of its term. Of course, lenders are aware of this, too, and may guard against the loss of income with a lock-in clause (to prevent the borrower from deviating from the repayment plan) or a penalty for early payment.

A *straight-line amortized loan* differs from a fully amortized loan. While the outcome is the same (the principal is fully repaid at the end of the term), the borrower pays a different (rather than the same) amount for each installment. A fixed amount is credited to principal; the interest portion of the payment changes as the balance of the principal declines.

MATH CONCEPTS

AMORTIZED PRINCIPAL AND INTEREST PAYMENTS

A lender applies a portion of each amortized payment to interest and the remainder of the payment to principal. The amount that is applied to interest for any one installment payment is calculated by computing the total yearly interest on the unpaid principal balance and then dividing that figure by the number of payments made each year. For example, if the current outstanding loan balance is $70,000, the interest rate is 7.5 percent per annum, and the constant monthly payment is $489.30, the principal and interest on the next payment would be computed as shown:

$70,000.00		$437.50	month's interest
× .075		12)$5,250.00	
$ 5,250.00	annual interest		

$ 489.30	monthly payment	$70,000.00	principal
− 437.50	month's interest	− 51.80	month's principal
$ 51.80	month's principal	$69,948.20	new principal balance

This process is repeated to calculate the new principal balance after each monthly payment.

The constant payment is determined from a mortgage factor chart. (See Table 12.1.) The chart indicates the monthly payment per $1,000 of loan, depending on the term and interest rate. The factor is multiplied by the number of thousands (and fractions thereof) of the loan amount. Computer programs also are available to calculate payments and show how the loan amortizes as each monthly payment is made.

Other amortized payment plans (to be discussed in Chapter 20) come into vogue from time to time as the cost and availability of money fluctuate. While any of the loans that have been discussed are commonly referred to as "mortgages," they actually are loans that are secured by a mortgage.

■ PROVISIONS OF THE MORTGAGE DOCUMENTS

The mortgage document clearly establishes that the property is security for a debt and becomes a voluntary, specific lien when properly recorded. It identifies the lender and the borrower, includes an accurate legal description of the property, and is signed by all parties who have an interest in the real estate. The mortgage document refers to the terms of the note by reference. Common provisions of a mortgage document are discussed next. A Fannie Mae/Freddie Mac uniform instrument is typically used so that the loan can be traded in the secondary mortgage market.

T A B L E   12.1

Mortgage Factor Chart

<table>
<tr><td rowspan="2">How To Use This Chart</td><td rowspan="2">Rate</td><td>Term 10 Years</td><td>Term 15 Years</td><td>Term 20 Years</td><td>Term 25 Years</td><td>Term 30 Years</td></tr>
<tr><td colspan="5"></td></tr>
<tr><td rowspan="55">To use this chart, start by finding the appropriate interest rate. Then follow that row over to the column for the appropriate loan term. This number is the interest rate factor required each month to amortize a $1,000 loan. To calculate the principal and interest (PI) payment, multiply the interest rate factor by the number of 1,000s in the total loan.

For example, if the interest rate is 10 percent for a term of 30 years, the interest rate factor is 8.78. If the total loan is $100,000, the loan contains 100 1,000s. Therefore

100 × 8.78 = $878 PI only

To estimate a mortgage loan amount using the amortization chart, divide the PI payment by the appropriate interest rate factor. Using the same facts as in the first example:

$878 ÷ 8.78 = $100 1,000s, or $100,000</td><td>4</td><td>10.13</td><td>7.40</td><td>6.06</td><td>5.28</td><td>4.78</td></tr>
<tr><td>4⅛</td><td>10.19</td><td>7.46</td><td>6.13</td><td>5.35</td><td>4.85</td></tr>
<tr><td>4¼</td><td>10.25</td><td>7.53</td><td>6.20</td><td>5.42</td><td>4.92</td></tr>
<tr><td>4⅜</td><td>10.31</td><td>7.59</td><td>6.26</td><td>5.49</td><td>5.00</td></tr>
<tr><td>4½</td><td>10.37</td><td>7.65</td><td>6.33</td><td>5.56</td><td>5.07</td></tr>
<tr><td>4⅝</td><td>10.43</td><td>7.72</td><td>6.40</td><td>5.63</td><td>5.15</td></tr>
<tr><td>4¾</td><td>10.49</td><td>7.78</td><td>6.47</td><td>5.71</td><td>5.22</td></tr>
<tr><td>4⅞</td><td>10.55</td><td>7.85</td><td>6.54</td><td>5.78</td><td>5.30</td></tr>
<tr><td>5</td><td>10.61</td><td>7.91</td><td>6.60</td><td>5.85</td><td>5.37</td></tr>
<tr><td>5⅛</td><td>10.67</td><td>7.98</td><td>6.67</td><td>5.92</td><td>5.45</td></tr>
<tr><td>5¼</td><td>10.73</td><td>8.04</td><td>6.74</td><td>6.00</td><td>5.53</td></tr>
<tr><td>5⅜</td><td>10.80</td><td>8.11</td><td>6.81</td><td>6.07</td><td>5.60</td></tr>
<tr><td>5½</td><td>10.86</td><td>8.18</td><td>6.88</td><td>6.15</td><td>5.68</td></tr>
<tr><td>5⅝</td><td>10.92</td><td>8.24</td><td>6.95</td><td>6.22</td><td>5.76</td></tr>
<tr><td>5¾</td><td>10.98</td><td>8.31</td><td>7.03</td><td>6.30</td><td>5.84</td></tr>
<tr><td>5⅞</td><td>11.04</td><td>8.38</td><td>7.10</td><td>6.37</td><td>5.92</td></tr>
<tr><td>6</td><td>11.10</td><td>8.44</td><td>7.16</td><td>6.44</td><td>6.00</td></tr>
<tr><td>6⅛</td><td>11.16</td><td>8.51</td><td>7.24</td><td>6.52</td><td>6.08</td></tr>
<tr><td>6¼</td><td>11.23</td><td>8.57</td><td>7.31</td><td>6.60</td><td>6.16</td></tr>
<tr><td>6⅜</td><td>11.29</td><td>8.64</td><td>7.38</td><td>6.67</td><td>6.24</td></tr>
<tr><td>6½</td><td>11.35</td><td>8.71</td><td>7.46</td><td>6.75</td><td>6.32</td></tr>
<tr><td>6⅝</td><td>11.42</td><td>8.78</td><td>7.53</td><td>6.83</td><td>6.40</td></tr>
<tr><td>6¾</td><td>11.48</td><td>8.85</td><td>7.60</td><td>6.91</td><td>6.49</td></tr>
<tr><td>6⅞</td><td>11.55</td><td>8.92</td><td>7.68</td><td>6.99</td><td>6.57</td></tr>
<tr><td>7</td><td>11.61</td><td>8.98</td><td>7.75</td><td>7.06</td><td>6.65</td></tr>
<tr><td>7⅛</td><td>11.68</td><td>9.06</td><td>7.83</td><td>7.15</td><td>6.74</td></tr>
<tr><td>7¼</td><td>11.74</td><td>9.12</td><td>7.90</td><td>7.22</td><td>6.82</td></tr>
<tr><td>7⅜</td><td>11.81</td><td>9.20</td><td>7.98</td><td>7.31</td><td>6.91</td></tr>
<tr><td>7½</td><td>11.87</td><td>9.27</td><td>8.05</td><td>7.38</td><td>6.99</td></tr>
<tr><td>7⅝</td><td>11.94</td><td>9.34</td><td>8.13</td><td>7.47</td><td>7.08</td></tr>
<tr><td>7¾</td><td>12.00</td><td>9.41</td><td>8.20</td><td>7.55</td><td>7.16</td></tr>
<tr><td>7⅞</td><td>12.07</td><td>9.48</td><td>8.29</td><td>7.64</td><td>7.25</td></tr>
<tr><td>8</td><td>12.14</td><td>9.56</td><td>8.37</td><td>7.72</td><td>7.34</td></tr>
<tr><td>8⅛</td><td>12.20</td><td>9.63</td><td>8.45</td><td>7.81</td><td>7.43</td></tr>
<tr><td>8¼</td><td>12.27</td><td>9.71</td><td>8.53</td><td>7.89</td><td>7.52</td></tr>
<tr><td>8⅜</td><td>12.34</td><td>9.78</td><td>8.60</td><td>7.97</td><td>7.61</td></tr>
<tr><td>8½</td><td>12.40</td><td>9.85</td><td>8.68</td><td>8.06</td><td>7.69</td></tr>
<tr><td>8⅝</td><td>12.47</td><td>9.93</td><td>8.76</td><td>8.14</td><td>7.78</td></tr>
<tr><td>8¾</td><td>12.54</td><td>10.00</td><td>8.84</td><td>8.23</td><td>7.87</td></tr>
<tr><td>8⅞</td><td>12.61</td><td>10.07</td><td>8.92</td><td>8.31</td><td>7.96</td></tr>
<tr><td>9</td><td>12.67</td><td>10.15</td><td>9.00</td><td>8.40</td><td>8.05</td></tr>
<tr><td>9⅛</td><td>12.74</td><td>10.22</td><td>9.08</td><td>8.48</td><td>8.14</td></tr>
<tr><td>9¼</td><td>12.81</td><td>10.30</td><td>9.16</td><td>8.57</td><td>8.23</td></tr>
<tr><td>9⅜</td><td>12.88</td><td>10.37</td><td>9.24</td><td>8.66</td><td>8.32</td></tr>
<tr><td>9½</td><td>12.94</td><td>10.45</td><td>9.33</td><td>8.74</td><td>8.41</td></tr>
<tr><td>9⅝</td><td>13.01</td><td>10.52</td><td>9.41</td><td>8.83</td><td>8.50</td></tr>
<tr><td>9¾</td><td>13.08</td><td>10.60</td><td>9.49</td><td>8.92</td><td>8.60</td></tr>
<tr><td>9⅞</td><td>13.15</td><td>10.67</td><td>9.57</td><td>9.00</td><td>8.69</td></tr>
<tr><td>10</td><td>13.22</td><td>10.75</td><td>9.66</td><td>9.09</td><td>8.78</td></tr>
<tr><td>10⅛</td><td>13.29</td><td>10.83</td><td>9.74</td><td>9.18</td><td>8.87</td></tr>
<tr><td>10¼</td><td>13.36</td><td>10.90</td><td>9.82</td><td>9.27</td><td>8.97</td></tr>
<tr><td>10⅜</td><td>13.43</td><td>10.98</td><td>9.90</td><td>9.36</td><td>9.06</td></tr>
<tr><td>10½</td><td>13.50</td><td>11.06</td><td>9.99</td><td>9.45</td><td>9.15</td></tr>
<tr><td>10⅝</td><td>13.57</td><td>11.14</td><td>10.07</td><td>9.54</td><td>9.25</td></tr>
<tr><td>10¾</td><td>13.64</td><td>11.21</td><td>10.16</td><td>9.63</td><td>9.34</td></tr>
</table>

Duties of the Mortgagor

The borrower is required to fulfill certain obligations. These usually include

- payment of the debt in accordance with the terms of the note;
- payment of all real estate taxes on the property given as security;
- maintenance of adequate insurance to protect the lender if the property is destroyed or damaged by fire, windstorm, or other hazard;
- maintenance of the property in good repair; and
- receipt of lender authorization before making any major alterations to the property.

Failure to meet any of these obligations can result in a borrower's default. The loan documents may, however, provide for a grace period (such as 30 days) during which the borrower can meet the obligation and cure the default. If the borrower does not do so, the lender has the right to foreclose the mortgage and collect on the note.

Provisions for Default

The mortgage typically includes an **acceleration clause** to assist the lender in foreclosure. If a borrower defaults, the lender has the right to accelerate the maturity of the debt. This means the lender may declare the entire debt due and payable immediately. Without the acceleration clause, the lender would have to sue the borrower every time a payment was overdue.

Other clauses in a mortgage enable the lender to take care of the property in the event of the borrower's negligence or default. If the borrower does not pay taxes or insurance premiums or fails to make necessary repairs on the property, the lender may step in and do so. The lender has the power to protect the security (the real estate). Any money advanced by the lender to cure a default may be either added to the unpaid debt or declared immediately due from the borrower.

Assignment of the Mortgage

As mentioned previously, a note may be sold to a third party, such as an investor or another mortgage company. The original mortgagee endorses the note to the third party and executes an *assignment of mortgage*. The assignee becomes the new owner of the debt and security instrument. When the debt is paid in full (or satisfied), the assignee is required to execute the satisfaction (or release) of the security instrument.

Release of the Mortgage Lien

When all loan payments have been made and the note has been paid in full, the borrower will want the public record to show that the debt has been satisfied and that the lender is divested of all rights conveyed under the mortgage. By the provisions of the **defeasance clause** in the typical mortgage document, the mortgagee is required to execute a **satisfaction** of mortgage (also known as a *release* of mortgage) when the note has been fully paid. This document returns to the borrower all interest in the real estate originally conveyed to the lender. Entering this release in the public record shows that the mortgage lien has been removed from the property. If the mortgage has been assigned by a recorded assignment, the release must be executed by the assignee/mortgagee.

Tax and Insurance Reserves

The basic recurring components of a borrower's monthly loan payment may be remembered as **PITI:**

Principal
Interest
Taxes
Insurance

Many lenders require borrowers to provide a reserve fund for future real estate taxes and insurance premiums. This fund is called an *impound, trust,* or *escrow* account. When the mortgage loan is made, the borrower starts the reserve by depositing funds to cover the amount of unpaid real estate taxes. If a new insurance policy has just been purchased, the insurance premium reserve will be started with the deposit of one-twelfth of the annual insurance premium. Thereafter, the borrower's monthly payments will include principal, interest, taxes, and insurance reserves (PITI—Principal, Interest, Taxes, and Insurance), and perhaps other costs, such as flood insurance or homeowners' association dues. RESPA, the federal Real Estate Settlement Procedures Act (discussed in a later chapter), limits the amount of tax and insurance reserves that a lender may require.

Federal flood insurance program. The *National Flood Insurance Reform Act of 1994* imposes certain mandatory obligations on lenders and loan servicers to set aside (escrow) funds for flood insurance on new loans for property in flood-prone areas. However, this act also applies to any loan still outstanding on September 23, 1994. This means that if a lender or servicer discovers that a secured property is in a flood hazard area, it must notify the borrower. The borrower then has 45 days to purchase flood insurance. If the borrower fails to procure the insurance, the lender must purchase the insurance on the borrower's behalf. The cost of the insurance may be charged back to the borrower.

Assignment of Rents

If the property involved includes rental units, the borrower may provide for rents to be assigned to the lender in the event of the borrower's default. The assignment may be included in the mortgage or it may be a separate document. In either case, the assignment should clearly indicate that the borrower intends to assign the rents, not merely pledge them as security for the loan.

Buying Subject to or Assuming a Seller's Mortgage

When a person purchases real estate that is encumbered by an outstanding mortgage, the buyer may take the property in one of two ways. The property may be purchased *subject to* the mortgage, or the buyer may *assume* the mortgage and *agree to pay* the debt. This technical distinction becomes important if the buyer defaults and the mortgage is foreclosed.

When the property is sold *subject to* the mortgage, the buyer is not personally obligated to pay the debt in full. The buyer takes title to the real estate knowing that he or she must make payments on the existing loan. Upon default, the lender forecloses and the property is sold by court order to pay the debt. If the sale does not pay off the entire debt, the purchaser is not liable for the difference. In some circumstances, however, the original seller might continue to be liable.

In contrast, a buyer who purchases the property and *assumes and agrees to pay* the seller's debt becomes personally obligated for the payment of the entire debt. If the mortgage is foreclosed and the court sale does not bring enough money to pay the debt in full, a *deficiency judgment* against the assumer and the original borrower may be obtained for the unpaid balance of the note. If the original borrower has been released by the assumer, only the assumer is liable.

In many cases, a loan may not be assumed without lender approval. The lending institution would require the assumer to meet certain financial qualifications. Once approved, the institution may charge a transfer fee to cover the costs of changing the records. The purchaser customarily pays this fee.

Alienation clause.   The lender may want to prevent a future purchaser of the property from being able to assume that loan, particularly because interest rates fluctuate. For this reason, some lenders include an **alienation clause** (also known as a *resale clause* or *due-on-sale clause*) in the note. An alienation clause provides that when a property is sold, the lender may either declare the balance of the seller's debt due immediately (the buyer must obtain new financing) or permit the buyer to assume the loan at an interest rate acceptable to the lender. Some types of loans prohibit the use of alienation clauses.

Recording Mortgages

The mortgage document must be recorded in the recorder's office of the county in which the real estate is located. Recording gives constructive notice to the world of the borrower's obligations and also establishes the lien's priority, as discussed in previous chapters.

Priority of mortgages and other liens normally is determined by the order in which they were recorded. A mortgage on real estate that has no prior mortgage lien is a *first mortgage*. If the owner later executes another loan for additional funds, the new loan becomes a *second mortgage*, or *junior* lien, when it is recorded. The second lien is subject to the first lien; the first has prior claim to the property pledged as security. Because second loans represent greater risk to the lender, they are usually issued at higher interest rates.

The priority of mortgage liens may be changed by the execution of a *subordination agreement*. This means that the first lender subordinates its lien to that of the second lender. To be valid, a subordination agreement must be signed by both lenders.

IN PRACTICE

As a condition of granting the mortgage loan, lenders may prohibit a prospective mortgagor from borrowing any portion of the down payment. The possibility of a prior claim on the property, that is, a lien by the person or institution who lent the down payment, can threaten the position of the lender who intends to be the first recorded lien.

■ FORECLOSURE

Low interest rates and easy credit policies of recent years have pushed home-ownership to record levels in the United States. In 2002 and 2003, lenders nationwide originated approximately $5.7 trillion in mortgage loans. While a number of federal, state, and private loan programs are available to help people become homeowners, few safety nets exist when homeowners just barely making their mortgage payments hit a "bump in the road." Illness, loss of a steady good-paying job, and mounting personal or credit card debt can quickly lead to default on mortgage payments and foreclosure.

Foreclosure is a legal procedure in which property pledged as security is sold to satisfy the debt. A mortgage lender's rights can be enforced through foreclosure if the borrower defaults on mortgage payments or fails to fulfill any of the other obligations in the mortgage. The foreclosure procedure brings the rights of all parties to a conclusion, with the result that title passes to either the person holding the mortgage document or to a third party who purchases the real estate at a foreclosure sale. The purchaser could be the mortgagee. Property is sold free of the foreclosing mortgage and all junior liens.

In Your State

PA Pennsylvania has the seventh highest rate of mortgage loan foreclosure in the nation, slightly more than 2 percent of mortgage loans. In Allegheny County, for example, the number of properties sold at sheriff sale more than tripled in five years. The Pennsylvania Housing Finance Agency, the Department of Banking, and other groups are currently analyzing reasons for the dramatic increase in foreclosures. Some relief is available to qualifying Pennsylvanians from the Homeowner Emergency Mortgage Assistance Program (HEMAP). This program was created during the early 1980s when record numbers of homes were threatened by job loss in the steel industry. Since 1983, the Pennsylvania Housing Finance Agency has helped thousands of families facing foreclosure with the HEMAP. Program recipients may receive loans to help pay delinquent mortgages and, in some cases, may qualify for continuing monthly-payment assistance for up to 24 months. ■

Methods of Foreclosure

There are three general types of foreclosure proceedings—judicial, nonjudicial, and strict foreclosure. One, two, or all three may be available. The specific provisions and procedures for each vary from state to state.

Judicial foreclosure. Judicial foreclosure allows the property to be sold by court order after the mortgagee has given sufficient public notice. When a borrower defaults, the lender may *accelerate* the due date of all remaining monthly payments. The lender's attorney can then file a suit to foreclose the lien after the borrower has been informed of the lender's intention. After presentation of the facts in court, the property is ordered to be sold. A public sale is advertised and held, and the real estate is sold to the highest bidder. This is the prevalent type of mortgage foreclosure in Pennsylvania.

Nonjudicial foreclosure. Some states allow nonjudicial foreclosure procedures to be used when the security instrument contains a *power of sale clause*. In nonjudicial foreclosure, no court action is required. In states where deed of trust loans are used, the trustee is generally given the power of sale. Some states allow a similar power of sale to be used with a mortgage loan.

To institute a nonjudicial foreclosure, the mortgagee may be required to file a notice of default in the county recorder's office. The default must be recorded within a designated time period to give adequate notice to the public of the intended auction. This official notice is generally accompanied by advertisements published in local newspapers that state the total amount due and the date of the public sale. After selling the property, the trustee or mortgagee may be required to file a copy of a notice of sale or an affidavit of foreclosure.

Strict foreclosure. Although judicial foreclosure is the prevalent practice, it is still possible in some states for a lender to acquire mortgaged property through a strict foreclosure process. First, appropriate notice must be given to the delinquent borrower. Once the proper papers have been prepared and recorded, the court establishes a deadline by which time the balance of the defaulted debt must be paid in full. If the borrower does not pay off the loan by that date, the court simply awards full legal title to the lender. No sale takes place.

The Foreclosure Process in Pennsylvania

The likelihood of a property being for sale in the marketplace that is also a candidate for foreclosure increases when foreclosure rates are high. The term "short sale" is sometimes heard, meaning that the property in the marketplace is at some point in the foreclosure process. The steps in that process have legal ramifications along the way that a real estate licensee should be aware of when handling a marketplace sale in the midst of foreclosure. In Pennsylvania, the foreclosure process begins when

- a borrower fails to make required payments on a mortgage loan;
- an owner fails to pay municipal, property, or school district taxes, or water or sewer bills; or
- any other lienholder pursues its right to collect a debt.

If the foreclosure is caused by *default on a mortgage loan*, the borrower first receives an Act 91 notice. This is notice of payments being in arrears; it also advises the borrower to file an application for the state's HEMAP assistance. Completion and acceptance of that application can provide a 120-day stay of foreclosure. The borrower then receives an Act 6 notice, otherwise known as a notice of intention to foreclose. At this point, the borrower has 30 days to contact the lender and set up a schedule of payments. If the borrower takes no action, the lender or its service company issues a complaint, which is the beginning of a lawsuit to foreclose. The borrower has 30 days to respond to that complaint. If the borrower fails to answer, the lender may obtain a judgment against the borrower, followed by a writ of execution, which permits the property to be sold at sheriff sale.

If the owner *fails to pay taxes or other specific lien charges*, the homeowner receives an Act 1 "demand" letter. This demand gives the owner 15 days' notice to pay the amount owed; it also states that attorney's fees involved during collection can be charged. If the owner fails to make payment, the next step is the owner receives a complaint and has 30 days to file an affidavit of defense. If the owner fails to file a defense, the municipality or its service company may obtain a judgment against the owner, followed by a writ of execution permitting the property to be sold at sheriff sale.

Deed in Lieu of Foreclosure

As an alternative to foreclosure, the lender may accept a **deed in lieu of foreclosure** from the borrower. This is sometimes known as a *friendly foreclosure* because it is carried out by mutual agreement rather than by lawsuit. The major disadvantage of the deed in lieu of foreclosure is that the mortgagee takes the real estate subject to all junior liens. In a foreclosure action, all junior liens are eliminated. A deed in lieu of foreclosure is still considered an adverse element in the borrower's credit history.

Redemption `In Your State`

PA Most states give a defaulting borrower a chance to redeem their property through the **equitable right of redemption.** After default but *before the foreclosure sale*, the borrower (or any other person who has an interest in the real estate, such as another creditor) may pay the lender the amount in default plus costs and the debt will be reinstated. In some cases, the person who redeems may be required to repay the accelerated loan in full. In Pennsylvania, a borrower may cure the default of a residential mortgage loan with an outstanding balance of $50,000 or less by merely bringing the payments up to date. If some person other than the mortgagor redeems the real estate, the borrower becomes responsible to that person for the amount of the redemption. ■

> **Redemption Rights**
>
> **Equitable**—before the foreclosure sale
>
> **Statutory**—after the foreclosure sale

Certain states, though not Pennsylvania, also allow defaulted borrowers a period in which to redeem their real estate *after the sale*. During this period (which may be as long as two years), the borrower has a *statutory right of redemption*. The mortgagor who can raise the necessary funds to redeem the property within the statutory period pays the redemption money to the court. Because the debt was paid from the proceeds of the sale, the borrower can take possession free and clear of the former defaulted loan.

Deed to Purchaser at Sale

If redemption is not made or if state law does not provide for a redemption period, the successful bidder at the sale receives a deed to the real estate. A sheriff or master-in-chancery executes this deed to the purchaser to convey whatever title the borrower had. The deed contains no warranties. Title passes as is, but it is free of the former defaulted debt.

Deficiency Judgment

The foreclosure sale may not produce enough cash to pay the loan balance in full after deducting expenses and accrued unpaid interest. In this case, the mortgagee may be entitled to a *personal judgment* against the borrower for the unpaid balance. Such a judgment is a **deficiency judgment.** It may also be obtained against any endorsers or guarantors of the note and against any owners of the mortgaged property who assumed the debt by written agreement. However, if any money remains from the foreclosure sale after paying the debt and any other liens (such as a second mortgage or mechanic's lien), expenses, and interest, these proceeds are paid to the mortgagor.

■ SUMMARY

The availability of money for mortgage loans and the interest rates are affected to a large degree by the Federal Reserve Board's discount rate and reserve requirements. The primary mortgage market consists of lenders that originate the loans such as thrift and savings institutions, commercial banks, life insurance companies, credit unions, pension funds, endowment funds, investment group financing, and mortgage banking companies. Mortgage brokers are instrumental in bringing borrowers and lenders together, but they are not lenders themselves.

The secondary market is generally comprised of the investors that ultimately purchase and hold the loans as investments. Fannie Mae, Ginnie Mae, and Freddie Mac take an active role in creating a secondary market by regularly purchasing mortgage loans from originators and retaining or warehousing them until investment purchasers are available.

Mortgage loans provide the principal sources of financing for real estate. Mortgage loans involve a borrower, called the mortgagor, and a lender, called the mortgagee.

Some states recognize the lender as the owner of mortgaged property; these are known as title theory states. Others recognize the borrower as the owner of mortgaged property and are known as lien theory states. Intermediary theory states, such as Pennsylvania, recognize modified versions of these theories.

After a lending institution has received, investigated, and approved a loan application, it issues a commitment to make the mortgage loan. The borrower is required to execute a note, agreeing to repay the debt, and a mortgage, placing a lien on the real estate to secure the note. This is recorded in the public record to give notice to the world of the lender's interest.

The note for the amount of the loan usually provides for amortization of the loan. The note also sets the rate of interest at which the loan is made and that the mortgagor must pay as a charge for borrowing the money. If a state has usury laws for mortgages, lenders are not permitted to charge more than the maximum interest rate allowed by law.

The mortgage document secures the debt and sets forth the obligations of the borrower and the rights of the lender. Payment in full of the note by its terms entitles the borrower to a satisfaction, or release, which is recorded to clear the lien from the public records. Default by the borrower may result in acceleration of payments, a foreclosure sale, and loss of title.

Note: Chapter 20 is a companion to the discussions in this chapter.

QUESTIONS

1. Which of the following is *NOT* a participant in the secondary market?
   a. FNMA
   b. GNMA
   c. the Fed
   d. FHLMC

2. The person who obtains a real estate loan by executing a note and a mortgage is called the
   a. mortgagor.
   b. beneficiary.
   c. mortgagee
   d. vendor.

3. The borrower under a deed of trust is known as the
   a. trustor.
   b. trustee.
   c. beneficiary
   d. vendee.

4. Which of the following is true about a second mortgage?
   a. It has priority over a first mortgage.
   b. It cannot be used as a security instrument.
   c. It is not negotiable.
   d. It is usually issued at a higher rate of interest than a first mortgage.

5. Laws that limit the amount of interest that can be charged to the borrower are
   a. established by the Federal Reserve.
   b. usury laws.
   c. established by the country's monetary policy.
   d. illegal in Pennsylvania.

6. After the foreclosure sale, a borrower who has defaulted on the loan may seek to pay off the debt plus any accrued interest and costs under the right of
   a. equitable redemption.
   b. defeasance.
   c. usury.
   d. statutory redemption.

7. The clause in a note that gives the lender the right to have all future installments become due upon default is the
   a. escalation clause.
   b. defeasance clause.
   c. alienation clause.
   d. acceleration clause.

8. What document is recorded by the mortgagee to show that the mortgage debt is completely repaid?
   a. A satisfaction
   b. A defeasance certificate
   c. A deed of trust
   d. A mortgage estoppel

9. Which of the following *BEST* describes the secondary market?
   a. Lenders who deal exclusively in second mortgages
   b. Where loans are bought and sold after they have been originated
   c. The major lender of residential mortgage loans
   d. The major lender of government-sponsored loans

10. With a fully amortized mortgage loan
    a. interest may be charged in arrears, meaning at the end of each period for which interest is due.
    b. the interest portion of each payment remains the same throughout the entire term of the loan.
    c. interest only is paid each period.
    d. a portion of principal will still be owed at the end of the term of the loan.

11. Freddie Mac
    a. buys mortgages that are guaranteed by the full faith and credit of the federal government.
    b. buys and pools blocks of primarily conventional mortgages, selling bonds with such mortgages as security.
    c. can tandem with GNMA to provide special assistance in times of tight money.
    d. buys and sells only VA and FHA mortgages.

12. In theory, when the Federal Reserve Board raises its discount rate, all of the following will happen *EXCEPT*
    a. interest rates will rise.
    b. interest rates will fall.
    c. mortgage money will become scarce.
    d. less money will circulate in the marketplace.

13. A borrower obtains a $76,000 mortgage loan at 7½ percent interest. If the monthly payments of $531.24 are credited first on interest and then on principal, what will the balance of the principal be after the borrower makes the first payment?
    a. $75,468.76
    b. $75,525
    c. $75,943.76
    d. $70,300

ANSWERS

1. C The Federal Reserve System (the Fed) regulates the flow of money and interest rates in the marketplace by establishing reserve requirements and discount rates. It does not purchase loans in the secondary market. (p. 184)

2. A When a borrower pledges real estate to a lender as security for a debt, the borrower "gives" a mortgage to the lender. The borrower is the mortgagor; the lender is the mortgagee. (p. 188)

3. A In financing arrangements in which a deed of trust rather than a mortgage is used, the borrower transfers title to the property to a trustee, who then holds title for the lender as the beneficiary. The borrower is the trustor. (p. 190)

4. D A second mortgage creates a junior lien, which is subject to the first lien. Because it represents a greater risk to the lender, second mortgage loans are usually issued at higher interest rates. (p. 197)

5. B Many states, including Pennsylvania, have enacted laws limiting the interest rate that may be charged on most consumer loans. These are known as usury laws. (p. 191)

6. D Certain states, though not Pennsylvania, allow defaulted borrowers a period of time during which to redeem their real estate after the foreclosure sale. This period is known as a statutory redemption period. (p. 200)

7. D When a borrower is delinquent in making payments or breaches other conditions of the mortgage, the lender may declare the entire debt due and payable immediately. This right is provided in the acceleration clause. (p. 195)

8. A When a mortgage is recorded, this creates a lien on the title. To release the lien, the mortgage holder (mortgagee) must record a satisfaction or release of liens. (p. 195)

9. B Primary mortgage lenders conduct business directly with consumers/borrowers. The lenders, in turn, package and sell the mortgage loans to secondary-market investors. (p. 185)

10. A A fully amortized mortgage loan requires fixed payments at regular intervals, usually monthly. Interest is paid in arrears and is calculated on the principal owed for that period. The amount attributed to principal and interest changes with each payment, with the entire debt and all interest having been paid in full at the end of the loan term. (p. 192)

11. B The Federal National Mortgage Corporation (Freddie Mac) was created to provide a secondary market for conventional loans. Freddie Mac pools the loans and sells bonds to investors with the mortgage loans as security. (p. 187)

12. B If the Federal Reserve Board (Fed) raises the discount rate, less money is available to circulate in the marketplace. Less money means that interest rates will go up rather than down. (p. 185)

13. C At a 7½ percent interest rate, a $76,000 loan would result in $5,700 interest per year ($76,000 × 7.5 % or 0.075). Interest for one month would equal $475 ($5,700 divided by 12). If the principal and interest payment was $531.24, the amount attributed to principal is $56.24 ($531.24 – $475). After that payment the remaining principal balance would be $75,943.76. (p. 193)

CHAPTER THIRTEEN

PENNSYLVANIA REAL ESTATE LICENSING LAW

■ LEARNING OBJECTIVES

When you've finished reading this chapter, you should be able to

- define activities that require licensure and the parties who are exempt from the license law;
- list the different licenses and the requirements for obtaining them;
- identify major ethical duties of licensees, and conduct specifically prohibited by law or regulation;
- summarize disciplinary procedures and remedies available for violations of the law or rules, including civil and criminal penalties, and
- define the key terms.

■ KEY TERMS

associate broker

broker

broker of record

builder-owner
   salesperson

business name

campground
   membership

campground
   membership
   salesperson

cemetery associate
   broker

cemetery broker

cemetery salesperson

Real Estate Licensing
   and Registration Act

Real Estate Recovery
   Fund

rental listing referral
   agent

rules and regulations

salesperson

State Real Estate
   Commission

time-share salesperson

■ PENNSYLVANIA REAL ESTATE LICENSING AND REGISTRATION ACT

All 50 states, the District of Columbia, and all Canadian provinces license and regulate the activities of real estate brokers and salespersons. Uniform policies and standards for administering and enforcing state license laws are promoted by an organization of state license law officials known as *ARELLO* (the *Association of Real Estate License Law Officials*). While the laws share a common purpose, the details vary.

Real estate license laws have been enacted to protect the public by ensuring a standard of competence and professionalism in the real estate industry. The laws achieve this goal by

- establishing basic requirements for obtaining a real estate license and, in many cases, requiring continuing education to keep a license;
- defining activities for which a license is required;
- describing acceptable standards of conduct and practice for licensees; and
- enforcing those standards through a disciplinary system.

The purpose of these laws is not merely to regulate the real estate industry. Their main objective is to protect the rights of purchasers, sellers, tenants, and landlords from unscrupulous or sloppy practices. The laws are not intended to prevent licensees from conducting business successfully, to restrain trade, or to interfere in legitimate transactions. Laws cannot create an ethical or moral marketplace. However, by establishing minimum levels of competency and limits of permitted behavior, laws can make the marketplace safer and more honest.

Pennsylvania's first real estate license law was adopted May 1, 1929, and was amended numerous times to reflect changes in the industry. On February 19, 1980, the current law, known as the **Real Estate Licensing and Registration Act (RELRA),** or the Act, was adopted. The RELRA is a statutory law, meaning that it was created by legislation enacted by the state legislature, and signed into law by the governor. The State Real Estate Commission does not have the authority to amend or modify the Act; that can be done only by the state legislature.

State Real Estate Commission

Section 202 of the RELRA establishes the **State Real Estate Commission** to administer the Act and supervise the activities of licensees in Pennsylvania. Section 404 of the RELRA authorizes the Commission to promulgate **rules and regulations** that implement and further define the statutory law. Rules and regulations of the State Real Estate Commission are enumerated in Chapter 35, Title 49 (Professional and Vocational Standards of the Department of State) of the Pennsylvania Code. The rules and regulations provide procedures for administering the law and set operating guidelines for licensees. *The rules and regulations have the same force and effect as the law.* Both the law and the rules are enforced through fines and the denial, suspension, or revocation of licenses. Civil and criminal actions can be brought against violators in serious cases.

The State Real Estate Commission functions under the Bureau of Professional and Occupational Affairs within the Pennsylvania Department of State. The Commission is comprised of 11 members that include:

- the commissioner of the Bureau of Professional and Occupational Affairs,
- the director of the Bureau of Consumer Protection or a designee,
- three members who represent the public at large (known as public members),
- five members licensed as real estate brokers, and
- one member licensed as a broker or cemetery broker (representing the cemetery business).

The five commissioners licensed as brokers shall have been engaged in the real estate business for at least ten years. The commissioner representing the cemetery business shall have been licensed as a real estate broker or cemetery broker for at least five years and shall have been engaged in selling cemetery lots for at least ten years prior to appointment. All of the commissioners are appointed by the governor and confirmed by the senate for five-year staggered terms. The Commission elects a chairman from its members.

The Commission conducts regularly scheduled business meetings that, under the state "sunshine laws," are open to the public. Normally, these meetings are held in Harrisburg. In addition, the Commission conducts formal and informal hearings relating to complaints filed against licensees. The Commission is also required to hold *public meetings* to solicit suggestions, comments, and objections about real estate practices from members of the public. These meetings are held each year in Philadelphia, Harrisburg, and Pittsburgh; frequently, public meetings are also held elsewhere in the state. Commissioners are compensated on per diem as stipulated in the Act. Staff is employed by the Bureau of Professional and Occupational Affairs to support the Commission's activities.

The major provisions of the Act and the Commission's regulations discussed in this text are those in effect as of the publication date. Readers must be aware that the Act and the regulations can be amended at any time. References to appropriate sections in the Act and regulations are provided throughout this chapter. A complete text of the Act and rules and regulations appears in Appendix C. Information about licensing procedures, real estate activities, and current laws and regulations may be obtained from the State Real Estate Commission at P.O. Box 2649, Harrisburg, PA 17105-2649, at (717) 783-3658, or on the commission's Web site. (See the Internet Resources.)

IN PRACTICE

Pay careful attention to the licensed activities that are described in this chapter. It's important that people have the appropriate license before engaging in any activity for which a license is required. Otherwise, they are in violation of the law and can be subject to disciplinary action by the Commission. Unlicensed activity is one of the most frequent violations of the Act.

■ LICENSED ACTIVITIES

The RELRA defines activities relating to real estate for which licensure is required and the procedures for obtaining those licenses. *Real estate* is defined as *any interest or estate in land, whether corporeal, incorporeal, freehold or non-freehold, situated in this Commonwealth or elsewhere, including leasehold interests, time-share and similarly designated interests.* The sale of mobile homes is deemed to be a transfer of a real estate interest if *the sale is accompanied by the assignment of a lease or sale of the land on which the mobile home is situated.*

> Appraisal activities are regulated by the State Board of Certified Appraisers, not the State Real Estate Commission.

There are currently ten separate licenses that may be issued by the Department of State. Licenses shall be granted to persons who bear a good reputation for honesty, trustworthiness, integrity, and competence. In addition to meeting requirements for specific licenses, all applicants must submit to the Commission the appropriate fees and details of a conviction, plea of guilty or nolo contendere to a felony or misdemeanor, and any sentence imposed.

In addition, as of October 1, 2003, the Real Estate Commission requires each applicant to attach a criminal record check completed by the Pennsylvania State Police to their application for licensure. The criminal record check must be dated within 90 days of submission of the license application.

Broker

As stated in Sections 201 of the RELRA and 35.201 of the Regulations, a **broker** is an individual or entity (corporation, partnership, or association) who, for another and for a fee, commission, or other valuable consideration, performs one or more of the following acts:

- Negotiates with or aids a person in locating or obtaining for purchase, lease, or acquisition any interest in real estate
- Negotiates the listing, sale, purchase, exchange, lease, time-share, financing, or option for real estate
- Manages real estate
- Represents himself or herself to be a real estate consultant, counselor, agent, or house finder
- Undertakes to promote the sale, exchange, purchase, or rental of real estate (does not apply to an individual or entity whose main business is advertising, promotion, or public relations)
- Undertakes to perform a comparative market analysis
- Attempts to perform any of these acts

Licensure requirements (Sections 511, 512, and 513 of the RELRA and 35.221, 35.222, and 35.271 of the Regulations).   An applicant for a broker license must

> Note that candidates for licensure are not required to be either U.S. citizens or residents of Pennsylvania in order to be issued a license.

- be at least 21 years of age.
- be a high school graduate or equivalent.
- have completed 240 hours (16 credits) of real estate instruction as prescribed by the Commission within ten years of the date of passing both portions of the licensing examination; instruction required for the salesperson license does not qualify for broker licensure.

- have been engaged as a licensed real estate salesperson for at least three years or have experience and/or education that the Commission considers equivalent. (The Commission uses a "point system" as a guide for evaluating the experience of an applicant.)
- pass both portions of a written examination within three years of the date of the license application. (Examinations consist of two portions: the national exam, which is general real estate information relating to the licensed practice, and the state exam, which covers the Act and the Commission's regulations.)
- submit a written application including the name and address under which the applicant will do business and recommendations attesting to the applicant's reputation for honesty, trustworthiness, integrity, and competence.

Broker of record.   The **broker of record** is defined in the regulations as the individual broker who is responsible for the real estate transactions of a partnership, association, or corporation licensed as a broker. This individual assumes all responsibility for the business conducted by the firm. There is only one individual recognized as the broker of record, regardless of the number of offices the firm operates.

Because the broker in a sole proprietorship or broker of record of a licensed entity is crucial to the operation of the business, the Commission has adopted regulations providing for procedures to be followed in the event of the death or incapacity of the individual in this position. Within 15 days of death or incapacity of that person, an authorized party must notify the Commission and appoint another qualified person to serve as the broker or broker of record.

Associate Broker

An **associate broker** is an individual broker who is *employed by another broker*. Associate brokers may perform all of the activities of licensed brokers, though they may *not* employ other licensees or engage in the real estate business in their own name or from their own place of business. Licensing requirements are the same as for a broker. A broker who wishes to be employed by another broker is issued an associate broker license. An individual who wants to manage a branch office for a licensed broker must have an associate broker license.

Salesperson

Sections 201 of the RELRA and 35.201 of the Regulations define a **salesperson** as an individual who is employed by a licensed broker to do one or more of the following:

- Sell or offer to sell real estate, or list real estate for sale
- Buy or offer to buy real estate
- Negotiate the purchase, sale, or exchange of real estate
- Negotiate a loan on real estate
- Lease or rent real estate or offer to lease or rent real estate
- Collect, offer, or attempt to collect rent for the use of real estate
- *Assist* a broker in managing property
- Perform a comparative market analysis

The activities for which a salesperson is licensed are performed under the supervision and responsibility ultimately of the employing broker. "Employment" is defined in the Act to include independent contractors. This means that, regardless of whether salespersons are employees or independent contractors for income-tax purposes, they are still accountable to the broker under the license law and are considered employees of the broker.

The Commission has determined that any activities that involve the public or are customary in selling real estate must be performed by licensees. These activities include *showing properties, preparing and presenting offers, preparing listing information, soliciting listings, hosting open houses for the public, and disseminating any real estate information to the public.* Unlicensed people (including unlicensed personal assistants) may not perform activities for which a license is required, including telemarketing. They may, however, host open houses that are *not* conducted for the public (such as open house tours for other licensees) and communicate, but not interpret or explain, property information to the licensees.

A salesperson must be at least 18 years of age, complete 60 hours of real estate as prescribed by the Commission, and pass both portions of the examinations prior to being issued a license (Section 521 and 522 of the RELRA and Sections 35.223 and 35.272 of the Regulations).

Supervised property management activities (Section 35.287 of the Regulations). The assistance rendered by a salesperson in property management activities is directly supervised and controlled by the employing broker. The salesperson is not permitted to independently negotiate the terms of a lease or execute a lease on behalf of the lessor.

Cemetery Broker

Sections 201 of the RELRA and 35.201 of the Regulations define a **cemetery broker** as an individual or entity who engages in the business in the capacity of a broker, exclusively within the limited field of business that applies to cemetery lots, plots, and mausoleum spaces or openings. The cemetery broker is responsible for the business activities and maintenance of an office in the same manner as a licensed broker. Sections 531, 532, and 533 of the RELRA and 35.224 and 35.273 of the Regulations describe the requirements and procedures for licensure. The cemetery broker must obtain 60 hours of instruction as approved by the Commission, be engaged for three years (or equivalent) as a salesperson or cemetery salesperson (as determined by the Commission), and pass a written examination prior to licensure.

Cemetery Associate Broker

Section 35.201 of the Regulations defines a **cemetery associate broker** as an individual cemetery broker who is employed by another cemetery broker or broker. This individual has the same relationship with the employing broker as an associate broker.

Cemetery Salesperson

Sections 201 of the RELRA and 35.201 of the Regulations define a **cemetery salesperson** as an individual who is employed by a broker or cemetery broker for the exclusive purpose of engaging in the specialized field of cemetery lot sales, as described for the cemetery broker. The cemetery salesperson must be at least 18 years of age and submit a sworn affidavit from the employing broker or cemetery broker attesting to the applicant's good reputation and that the broker will actively supervise and train the applicant. There is no education or examination requirement for licensure. (See Sections 541 and 542 of the RELRA and Section 35.225 of the Regulations.)

Builder-Owner Salesperson

While builders are not licensed in Pennsylvania, certain individuals employed by builders of single and/or multifamily dwellings must be licensed. Sections 201 of the RELRA and 35.201 of the Regulations define a **builder-owner salesperson** as an individual who is a *full-time employee* of a builder-owner of single-family and multifamily dwellings and who performs one or more of the following activities:

- Lists for sale, sells, or offers for sale real estate of the builder-owner
- Negotiates the sale or exchange of real estate of the builder-owner
- Leases or rents real estate of the builder-owner
- Collects or offers or attempts to collect rent for the real estate of the builder-owner

The applicant must be at least 18 years of age, be employed by the builder-owner (who is not licensed), and complete a written examination prior to licensure. There is no education requirement. (See Sections 551 and 552 of the RELRA and 35.226 and 35.274 of the Regulations.)

Rental Listing Referral Agent

Sections 201 of the RELRA and 35.201 of the Regulations define a **rental listing referral agent** as an individual or entity who owns or manages a business that collects rental information for the purpose of referring prospective tenants to rental units. This licensee does not lease or show property but rather sells lists of available rentals. Section 35.289 describes requirements for compiling the list of rentals and verifying their availability for a prospective tenant.

The applicant must satisfy licensing requirements that are essentially the same as for a salesperson licensee; however, the rental listing referral agent is not affiliated with a broker. A rental listing referral agent is responsible for maintaining an office under the same requirements as a broker and cemetery broker. (See Sections 561 of the RELRA and 35.227 and 35.275 of the Regulations.)

Campground Membership Salesperson

Sections 201 of the RELRA and 35.201 of the Regulations define a **campground membership salesperson** as an individual who, either as an employee or independent contractor, sells campground memberships under the supervision of a broker. **Campground memberships** are interests (other than in fee simple or by lease) that give the purchaser the right to use a unit of real property for the purpose of locating a recreational vehicle, trailer, tent, tent trailer, pickup camper, or other similar device on a periodic basis. This right is conveyed by a membership contract.

The applicant must be at least 18 years of age, complete 15 hours of instruction in specific topics, and complete not less than 30 days of on-site training at a campground membership facility prior to licensure. (See Sections 581 and

582 of the RELRA.) The broker is responsible for further training and supervising the licensee. Licensed salespersons, brokers, and time-share salespersons do not need a separate license to sell campground memberships.

Time-Share Salesperson

Sections 201 of the RELRA and 35.201 of the Regulations define a **time-share salesperson** as an individual who, either as an employee or independent contractor, sells time-shares under the supervision of a broker. *Time-share* is the right, however evidenced or documented, to use or occupy one or more units on a periodic basis according to an arrangement allocating use and occupancy rights of that unit or units between other similar users.

A time-share salesperson must be at least 18 years of age, complete 30 hours of instruction in specific topics, and complete not less than 30 days of on-site training at a time-share facility prior to licensure. (See Sections 591 and 592 of the RELRA.) The broker is responsible for further training and supervising the licensee. Licensed salespersons and brokers do not need a separate license to sell time-shares.

Unlicensed Activity

Maximum Penalty for Engaging in Unlicensed Activity

First offense—fine of up to $500 and/or imprisonment, not to exceed three months

Second or subsequent offenses—fine of $2,000 to $5,000 and/or imprisonment for one to two years

Section 301 of the RELRA states that it is unlawful for any unlicensed individual or entity to be engaged in activity for which licensure is required. It is also unlawful for an unlicensed person to advertise or in other ways represent that he or she is engaged in activity for which licensure is required. A current license must be issued at the time a service is offered as well as at the time the service is rendered. Because unlicensed persons are not entitled to compensation, they are prohibited from entering into a civil suit to recover payment.

Any person who engages in activity for which licensure is required or employs an individual or entity that does not possess a current license is subject to *criminal penalties* according to Section 303 of the RELRA. This includes situations in which a license has been suspended or revoked. The first conviction for unlicensed activity is a summary offense and involves payment of a fine not to exceed $500 and/or imprisonment not to exceed three months. A second or subsequent offense is a felony of the third degree and involves payment of a fine between $2,000 to $5,000 and/or imprisonment for one to two years.

Exclusions

While penalties for unlicensed activity are intended to ensure that individuals engaging in real estate activities are properly licensed to do so, the Act and the Commission's rules also recognize that there are certain individuals and entities that can be appropriately excluded from licensure. Sections 304 of the RELRA and 35.202 of the Regulations establish the following exclusions from requirements for licensure:

■   Owners of real estate performing activities associated with the ownership, lease, or sale of their own property. To prevent this exclusion from being used to circumvent licensure, the exclusion does not extend to more than five partners in a partnership or officers of a corporation or to other employees.

- Employees of a public utility acting in the ordinary course of the utility-related business under provisions of Title 66 of the Pennsylvania Consolidated Statutes, with respect to negotiating the purchase, sale, or lease of property.
- Officers or employees of a partnership or corporation whose principal business involves the discovery, extraction, distribution, or transmission of energy or mineral resources. This exclusion applies to the purchase, sale, or lease of real estate during the conduct of this business.
- An attorney-in-fact who renders services under a properly executed and recorded power of attorney from the owner or lessor of real estate. The power of attorney cannot be used to circumvent licensure. The Commission has determined that granting a power of attorney to an unlicensed person to manage property circumvents the intent of the Act.
- An attorney-at-law who receives a fee from a client for rendering services within the scope of the attorney-client relationship and does not represent himself as a broker.
- A trustee in bankruptcy, administrator, executor, trustee, or guardian who is acting under the authority of a court order, will, or trust instrument.
- The elected officer or director of any banking institution, savings institution, savings bank, credit union, or trust company operating under federal or state laws involving only the property owned by these institutions.
- An officer or employee of a cemetery company who, as incidental to principal duties, shows cemetery lots without compensation.
- A cemetery company or cemetery owned by a bona fide church, religious congregation, or fraternal organization. (This applies to the requirement for registration.)
- An auctioneer, licensed under the Auctioneers' License Act, while performing duties at a bona fide auction.
- Any person employed by an owner of real estate for the purpose of managing or maintaining multifamily residential property. This person is not authorized to enter into leases on behalf of the owner, negotiate terms or conditions of leases, or hold money belonging to tenants other than on behalf of the owner. As long as the owner retains authority to make all such decisions, the employees may show apartments and provide information about rental rates, building rules and regulations, and leasing qualifications.
- The elected officer, director, or employee of any banking institution, savings institution, savings bank, credit union, or trust company operating under federal or state laws, when acting on behalf of the institution in performing appraisals or other evaluations of real estate in connection with a loan transaction.

■ LICENSING PROCEDURES

The Department of State issues licenses and registration certificates to individuals who meet the requirements established by the Act. The State Real Estate Commission approves proprietary real estate schools, sets fees subject to review under applicable Pennsylvania law, and prescribes the subject matter for written examinations required for licensure. The Department of State contracts with an independent testing agency to oversee the administration of licensing examinations.

The Commission prescribes the form for license applications and is authorized to investigate the accuracy of the information submitted. Inaccurate or untruthful information could result in denial of an application or disciplinary action against any license the individual currently possesses.

The license period for all real estate licenses currently begins June 1 and ends the last day of May in each even-numbered year (a two-year license period). When a license is first issued, it expires on the last day of May of the current license period. A license is considered *active* once the license is issued and remains properly renewed.

License Renewal

Prior to the end of each license period, the Commission establishes procedures for submitting documentation and fees to renew a license. The Bureau of Professional and Occupational Affairs is moving forward with online procedures to make the renewal of all licenses more efficient. For license renewals beginning in 2006, renewal notices will not be mailed to licensees. Instead, licensees will be notified approximately 90 days prior to the license expiration date that it is time to renew. This notice will provide instructions and a unique renewal code required for completing the renewal online.

For licensees who choose not to renew electronically, renewal applications will be available for download on the Commission's Web site, and can be completed and mailed to the Commission. A licensee who does not have Internet access will be required to submit a request for application by mail or e-mail. A fax option will also be available.

Continuing education.   Licensed brokers and salespersons are required to satisfy a 14-hour continuing education requirement during each two-year period in order to renew the license. The purpose of continuing education is to maintain and increase competency to engage in licensed activities, keep licensees abreast of changes in laws, regulations, practices, and procedures that affect the business, and better ensure that the public is protected from incompetent licensees. The continuing education requirement applies only to brokers and salespersons.

The Commission's regulations as amended from time to time state the type of course work and topics that are acceptable for continuing education. The Commission is responsible for approving courses, materials, locations, and instructors for continuing education. The commission also has the authority to waive all or part of the requirement for a salesperson or broker who demonstrates that he or she is unable to complete the requirement due to illness, emergency, or hardship. (See Section 404a of the RELRA and Subchapter H of the rules and regulations for more details about continuing education procedures.)

Changes to the Commission's rules and regulations that were adopted in 2004 significantly affect both licensees and providers of continuing education courses. Distance education, defined as real estate instruction delivered in an independent or instructor-led format during which the student and the instruction are separated by distance and sometimes time, is now reality in Pennsylvania. Licensees will be able to satisfy continuing education requirements either by participating in traditional instructor-led classroom instruction or by engaging in some form of distance learning. Distance education providers and the course offerings must be approved and are regulated by the Commission.

Continuing education providers are required to electronically transfer their continuing education rosters to the Commission; providers are no longer required to provide paper transcripts to licensees at the completion of course work. Licensees who desire written transcripts may request a copy from the education provider, but it is not necessary for the licensee to send paper transcripts to the Commission for license renewal.

Inactive Licenses

A license becomes *inactive* when an individual voluntarily relinquishes a license, sometimes referred to as putting a license in "escrow," or when an individual fails to properly renew a license. When a license is inactive, the person is prohibited from performing the activities for which the license was issued. A license may be *reactivated* by submitting the proper forms and required fees within five years of the date the license became inactive. Brokers and salespersons must obtain 14 hours of continuing education before they can reactivate a license. An individual who does not reactivate a license within five years must retake the appropriate examination in order to be issued a license.

Out-of-State Licenses and License Reciprocity

An individual who holds a license issued by another jurisdiction and wants to engage in real estate in Pennsylvania may do so by satisfying certain requirements prescribed by the Commission rules and regulations. Because real estate practices today are more global in nature, state laws are being amended around the country to streamline licensing procedures among states. (ARELLO's goal is to eventually achieve universal licensure.) In Pennsylvania, Act 58 of 2003, which was signed into law December 30, 2003, authorized the Commission to enter into reciprocal licensing agreements with other states. A list of states with which those agreements exist can be found on the Commission's Web site.

The following terms apply to each agreement the Commission enters into with another licensing jurisdiction:

- Each state would recognize the education, experience, and examination requirements that applicants must satisfy for licenses issued in the "home" state as satisfying the requirements for licenses in the reciprocal state.
- Applicants would be required to consent to service of process in the state where they would be receiving licensure by reciprocity.

- Applicants would be required to verify that they have received, read, and agree to comply with all laws of the state where they would be receiving licensure.
- Applicants other than brokers or cemetery brokers must provide certification from the employing broker that the broker is currently licensed and will actively and personally supervise the applicant.
- Each state would not require additional continuing education in order to renew a reciprocal license. (The continuing education required in the "home" state would be sufficient.)
- The applicant's "home" state would furnish a certificate of licensure or record of good standing to the state in which the applicant is seeking a license by reciprocity.

The intent of reciprocity agreements is to allow licensees from one state to engage in licensed activities in other states. Reciprocal licenses are not intended to replace or circumvent a state's licensing requirements when the principal place of business is located in that state. If a licensee changes his or her principal place of business to the state where the reciprocal license is held, the licensee would be required to obtain the standard license from that state and may be required to pass an examination or satisfy other requirements prescribed for that license.

■ OPERATION OF REAL ESTATE BUSINESS

Section 601 of the RELRA requires each resident licensed broker, cemetery broker, and rental listing referral agent to maintain a fixed office, the address of which shall be included in all applicable licenses. The current licenses of these individuals or entities and each of the licensees employed by them shall be *prominently displayed in the office*. The Regulations (Section 35.242) require that the office be devoted to the transaction of real estate business and be arranged to permit business to be conducted in privacy. If the office is located in a private residence, the entrance to the office shall be separate from the entrance to the residence.

Business name. The **business name** is the name under which a broker, cemetery broker, or rental listing referral agent license is issued (an individual or a business entity). The business name becomes the name under which business is conducted. The name designated on the license must be displayed *prominently and in a permanent fashion outside all offices*. Any time the name of the business is represented, it must appear *exactly* as it appears on the license.

Branch Offices

If a broker or cemetery broker intends to maintain more than one place of business, the licensee must obtain an additional license for each office location. A branch office license, including its address, must be obtained before any office is opened. This license is issued in the same name under which the broker or cemetery broker is licensed to conduct business at the main office.

A branch office shall meet the same requirements as the main office. The broker or broker of record is responsible for the activities of all licensees in each office. Branch offices may not be operated in a manner that permits a licensee to carry on business for the person's sole benefit. If the broker delegates the duties of supervising and directing an office (as manager), the person assuming these duties must be an *associate broker*. The broker, however, is still ultimately responsible for the activities in a branch office.

In addition to the branch office license, the broker must maintain a list of licensees employed by or affiliated with the broker at the branch office out of which each licensee works. The current license of the broker and all licensees employed by or affiliated with the broker must be maintained at the main office.

Because of technology, it is increasingly more common for licensees to perform duties incidental to their real estate business at home. However, a *home office* is simply a workspace and *cannot* in any way be represented as a branch office. The Real Estate Commission recommends that brokers establish policies and procedures to ensure that licensees comply with the Act and the Commission's Regulations when working at home.

Change of Address; Change of Employment

Section 603 of the RELRA states that no associate broker or other underlying licensee (associate cemetery broker, salesperson, time-share salesperson, campground membership salesperson, or cemetery salesperson) shall be employed by any broker other than the broker designated on the license. Section 604 prohibits any licensee from receiving compensation from anyone other than the employing broker. A broker is not permitted to pay a commission or any valuable consideration to anyone who is not his licensed employee or another licensed real estate broker (as in cooperating transactions) for any activities specified in the Act.

If a broker's office is removed from the location designated in the license, all licensees working at that location shall make application to the commission designating the new location of the office. This application must be filed *before the removal or within ten days thereafter*. A current license will be issued at the new location (as long as it is an approved office) for the unexpired license period.

When a licensee changes employment from one broker to another, the licensee shall notify the commission *no later than ten days after the intended date of change*, return the current license, and pay the required fee. When the new broker acknowledges the employment, a new license will be issued. A copy of the change of employment notification serves as the temporary license until the new license is received. The applicant is responsible for notifying the commission if the new license is not received within 30 days.

■ DISCIPLINARY ACTIONS

The Real Estate Commission is empowered by RELRA to enforce the Act and its rules and regulations. When a complaint alleging a violation of the Act and/or the Regulations is received, the Bureau of Professional and Occupational Affairs conducts an investigation to determine if a violation has occurred. The Commission is authorized to suspend or revoke a license or

The State Real Estate Commission has the authority to

- Suspend a license
- Revoke a license
- Levy fines, not exceeding $1,000

registration certificate and/or levy fines up to $1,000. Generally, the nature and severity of the violation(s) are considered. Before the Commission can take any disciplinary action, the accused party must be given an opportunity to have a hearing. Section 701 of the RELRA states the manner in which a hearing before the commission shall be conducted.

Section 702 of the RELRA limits the disciplinary action that may be taken against an employing broker when disciplinary action is taken against a licensee employed by that broker. If it appears from evidence at a hearing that the employing broker had *actual knowledge of a violation* or permitted a *course of dealing that violates the law,* the Commission may suspend or revoke the employing broker's license or levy a fine. A "course of dealing" constitutes *prima facie evidence* of knowledge on the part of the employer. If these conditions do not exist, the Commission may find that the broker failed to properly supervise the licensee and take a lesser disciplinary action.

Act 48 of 1993 authorizes the Bureau of Professional and Occupational Affairs to adopt a schedule of civil penalties that may be imposed by investigators and inspectors for lesser violations of the RELRA and Regulations. When these violations are discovered during the routine inspection of a real estate office or proprietary school or during the investigation of a complaint, a citation can be issued and the licensee can admit fault and pay the predetermined penalty. This procedure is intended to free the Real Estate Commission's resources to concentrate on more serious offenses. Of course, a licensee can refuse to accept the citation and pursue the rights of due process previously described.

Prohibited Acts

Section 604 of the RELRA lists specifically prohibited acts. Common violations include misrepresentation, mishandling escrow funds, inappropriately paying commissions, and misleading advertising. Licensees who engage in a prohibited act may be fined or have their licenses suspended or revoked. For easy reference, a summary of the prohibited acts follows:

- Making any substantial misrepresentation
- Making any false promise to influence, persuade, or induce a person into a contract when the licensee could not or did not intend to keep the promise
- Pursuing a continued and flagrant course of misrepresentation or making false promises through any licensee or any medium of advertising
- Using misleading or untruthful advertising; using any trade name or insignia of a real estate association of which the licensee is not a member
- Failing to comply with all of the escrow requirements
- Failing to preserve records relating to any real estate transaction for three years following consummation of the transaction
- Acting for more than one party in a transaction without the knowledge of and consent in writing from all parties
- Placing a "for sale" or "for rent" sign on or advertising any property without the written consent of the owner
- Failing to voluntarily furnish a copy of any contract to all signatories at the time of execution

- Failing to specify a definite termination date that is not subject to prior notice in any listing agreement
- Inducing any party to a contract to break that contract for the purpose of substituting a new one, when the substitution is motivated by personal gain of the licensee
- Accepting a commission or other valuable consideration from any person except the licensed broker who is the employer
- Paying of a commission by a broker to anyone other than the broker's licensed employee or another broker
- Failing to disclose in writing to the owner the licensee's interest in purchasing or acquiring an interest in a property listed with the licensee's office
- Being convicted in court of, or pleading guilty or nolo contendere to, forgery, embezzlement, obtaining money under false pretenses, bribery, larceny, extortion, conspiracy to defraud, or any felony
- Violating any rule or Regulation of the Commission
- Failing to provide a disclosure required by this Act or any other federal or state law imposing a disclosure obligation on licensees in connection with real estate transactions
- In the case of a broker, failing to exercise adequate supervision over the activities of the employed licensees
- Failing to provide information requested by the Commission as the result of a formal or informal complaint
- Soliciting or selling real estate by offering free lots, conducting lotteries or contests, or offering prizes for the purpose of influencing a purchase by deceptive conduct
- Paying or accepting, giving or charging an undisclosed commission, rebate, or compensation on expenditures for a principal
- Performing any act that demonstrates bad faith, dishonesty, untrustworthiness, or incompetency
- Performing any act for which an appropriate license is required if such license is not currently in effect
- Violating any provision of the *Pennsylvania Human Relations Act*, such as accepting a listing with the understanding that illegal discrimination is to be practiced, giving false information for the purpose of discriminating, making a distinction in location of housing or dates of availability for the purpose of discriminating
- Violating the Pennsylvania statutes relating to burial grounds (if a cemetery company registrant)
- Violating Sections 606 and 608 of the RELRA
- Failing as a broker, campground membership salesperson, or time-share salesperson to comply with the requirements for handling deposits or other monies

Posting Suspension Notices

Section 35.291 of the Regulations states that a broker or cemetery broker whose license is suspended shall return the license to the Commission and prominently post a Commission-approved notice of the suspension at the public entrance of the main office and any branch offices. Failure to post the notice is grounds for further disciplinary action.

Relicensure after revocation (Sections 501 of the RELRA and 35.251 of the Regulations). A revocation of a license lasts for at least five years from the date revocation begins. After the five-year period, the individual may petition the Commission for relicensure. If the Commission authorizes relicensure, the individual shall comply with prevailing, current licensing requirements before the license is issued.

Civil Penalties

Section 305 of the RELRA provides that, in addition to other remedies or criminal penalties permitted, the Commission may levy a civil penalty of up to $1,000 against any current licensee who violates the Act or any person who practices real estate without being properly licensed.

Reporting Crimes and Disciplinary Actions

Section 35.290 of the Regulations states that a licensee shall notify the Commission of a conviction or pleading of guilty or nolo contendere to a felony or misdemeanor. The report must be made within 30 days of the verdict or plea. If a licensing authority in another jurisdiction takes disciplinary action, the licensee must notify the Commission in Pennsylvania within 30 days of that action.

■ REAL ESTATE RECOVERY FUND

The **Real Estate Recovery Fund** was established to provide a means for aggrieved persons to collect judgments awarded in civil court. These judgments must result from civil suits against real estate licensees for fraud, deceit, or misrepresentations in a real estate transaction. Judgments involving the sale of a campground or a campground membership salesperson cannot be recovered from this fund. The aggrieved party must first exhaust all other avenues to collect the judgment before applying to the fund.

Maximum Amount Payable from Recovery Fund
$20,000 per claim
$100,000 per licensee

To collect from the fund, the aggrieved person must show that he or she is not a spouse or personal representative of the spouse of the licensee; that a final judgment was awarded; that all reasonable remedies have been exhausted to collect the judgment; and that the application is being made within one year after the termination of the proceedings (including appeals). The maximum amount that may be paid from the fund for any one claim is $20,000 and $100,000 per licensee. If $100,000 is insufficient to settle the claims against a licensee, the $100,000 shall be distributed according to the same ratio as the respective claims. If the balance in the Real Estate Recovery Fund is insufficient to satisfy any claim or portion thereof, the Commission shall satisfy unpaid claims plus accumulated interest at the rate of 6 percent per year once the fund is reestablished.

Monies for the fund are collected from licensees. When the fund was originally established in 1980, each licensee paid $10 into the fund when the licenses were renewed. Subsequently, any person to whom a license is issued and who has not previously contributed to the fund pays $10. According to Section 802 of the RELRA, the Commission may assess an additional fee (not to exceed $10 per licensee) if the fund drops to $300,000 or less to bring the fund's balance up to $500,000. The fees are paid into the state treasury and are allocated exclusively for the purposes of the fund. The money shall be invested, and interest and dividends shall accrue to the fund.

The license of the person involved in a claim is automatically suspended as of the date a payment is made from the fund. The license cannot be reinstated until the licensee repays the amount of the claim plus interest at 10 percent per year. The Commission can also take action in an attempt to recover monies paid out of the fund.

■ REAL ESTATE DOCUMENTS

The Act and the Regulations prescribe mandatory language that must appear in certain written documents licensees use. The purpose is to ensure that consumers are properly informed about their rights in a transaction and that certain procedures are properly disclosed. Except for the *Consumer Notice*, the Commission does not require the use of any specific form for the document. The legal references are as follows:

- Section 608a of the RELRA and Sections 35.331 and 35.332 of the Regulations prescribe information that must appear in any written agreement between a broker and a principal, or between a broker and consumer, describing services to be rendered and fees to be paid.
- Section 608b of the RELRA and Section 35.333 of the Regulations prescribe mandatory provisions that must appear in an agreement of sale or sales contract and, if the agreement is conditioned on the ability of the buyer to obtain a mortgage, language that must be included in mortgage contingencies.
- Section 608c of the RELRA prescribes the disclosure statement that must appear in a comparative market analysis.
- Section 608d of the RELRA provides for disclosures that must appear in an agreement of sale used by cemetery brokers.
- Section 35.284 of the Regulations provides for preagreement disclosures that must be presented to a buyer and seller at an initial interview.
- Section 35.334 of the Regulations provides for estimates of cost and return that must be prepared by the licensee before buyers and sellers execute an agreement of sale.
- Section 35.336 of the Regulations provides a specific format and language that must appear in the *Consumer Notice*, which describes all the types of business relationships between licensees and consumers that are permitted in real estate sales transactions. Section 35.337 provides the notice to be used in the lease of residential or commercial property; Section 35.338 does likewise for time-share estates.

Because of the importance of the specific requirements, they will be discussed in detail when the contracts and documents are presented in later chapters.

Other Disclosures

The document requirements that have been referenced so far are ones that affect the most common real estate transactions. However, consumers in all transactions are entitled to proper disclosures. The RELRA and the Regulations provide for disclosures that are applicable to the following specialized services or types of real estate.

Rental listing referral services.   Section 35.335 of the Regulations provides language that must be included in a rental listing referral agreement. The agreement must include in bold print the following statement: *"We are a referral service only. We are not acting as real estate salespersons or brokers. We do not guarantee that the purchaser will find a satisfactory rental unit through our service. Our only purpose is to furnish the purchaser with lists of available rental units."*

Time-share and campground membership contracts.   Section 609 of the RELRA gives purchasers of time-share and campground memberships the right to cancel a purchase. The cancellation right exists until midnight of the fifth day following the date on which the purchaser executed the contract. The provisions of this section of the Act apply to time-share and campground memberships located in Pennsylvania as well as outside the state if the purchase contract *was executed by the purchaser in Pennsylvania.*

The right-to-cancel notice shall be printed conspicuously in boldface type immediately above the signature of the purchaser and must be separately initialed. The right of cancellation shall not be waivable by any purchaser nor can the purchaser be held liable for any damages resulting from exercising this right. The statement required by Section 609 of the RELRA is as follows:

> *"You, the purchaser, may cancel this purchase at any time prior to midnight of the fifth day following the date of this transaction. If you desire to cancel, you are required to notify the seller, in writing, at [address]. Such notice shall be given by certified return receipt mail or by any other bona fide means of delivery which provides you with a receipt. Such notice shall be effective upon being postmarked by the U.S. Postal Service or upon deposit of notice with any bona fide means of delivery which provides you with a receipt."*

Within ten days after receipt of a notice of cancellation, all payments made under the contract shall be refunded to the purchaser and an acknowledgment that the contract is void shall be sent to the purchaser. Any promotional prizes, gifts, and premiums issued to the purchaser by the seller shall remain the property of the purchaser.

Document Procedures

Section 35.281 of the Regulations requires that a licensee who acts in a representative capacity in a real estate transaction shall ensure that all sale or lease contracts, commitments, and agreements regarding the transaction are *in writing.* All parties to a contract must receive a copy of executed agreements, and the broker is responsible for maintaining copies of records pertaining to any transaction for at least *three years following consummation* of the transaction. The broker also is required to produce the records for examination by the Commission upon written request.

■ RELATIONSHIPS BETWEEN LICENSEES AND CONSUMERS

The Act permits licensees to form several different kinds of working relationships with consumers. Most often, the licensee will have an agency relationship with the consumer. An agency relationship is defined as "a relationship whereby the broker or licensees in the employ of the broker act as fiduciaries for a consumer of real estate services by the express authority of the consumer of real estate services." The following definitions explain the permissible roles for a licensee in a real estate transaction:

- *Consumer*—A person who is the recipient of any real estate service.
- *Principal*—A consumer of real estate services who has entered into an agency relationship with a broker.
- *Seller agent*—Any licensee who has entered into an agency relationship with a seller of real estate.
- *Subagent*—A broker, not in the employ of the listing broker, who is engaged to act for or cooperate with the listing broker in selling property as an agent of the seller. A subagent is deemed to have an agency relationship with the seller.
- *Listing broker*—A broker engaged as a seller's agent, dual agent, or transaction licensee to market the property of a seller/landlord.
- *Dual agent*—A licensee who acts as an agent for the buyer and seller or lessee and landlord in the same transaction.
- *Designated agent*—One or more licensees designated by the employing broker with the consent of the principal to act exclusively as agent(s) on behalf of the principal to the exclusion of all other licensees within the broker's employ.
- *Transaction licensee*—A licensed broker or salesperson who provides communication or document preparation services or performs acts described under the definition of "broker" or "salesperson" for which a license is required, without being an agent or advocate of the consumer.

The broker ultimately determines the role or roles that the licensees employed by that broker are permitted to assume. Section 35.336 of the Regulations requires licensees to provide a disclosure summary, entitled "Consumer Notice," to all consumers at the first contact where a substantive discussion about real estate occurs. The purpose of the notice is to advise consumers of all business relationships permitted by the Act. By describing the various relationships, the notice helps consumers make informed decisions when engaging the services of a licensee.

General Duties of Licensees

A licensee has certain duties or obligations to the parties with whom he or she works in a transaction, regardless of whether or not the licensee is acting within the scope of an agency relationship. Section 606.1 of the RELRA and Section 35.292 of the Regulations state that a licensee owes the following duties to all consumers:

- reasonable professional skill and care;
- honest dealings in good faith;

- presentation, in a timely manner, of all written offers, notices, and communications to and from the parties to a transaction, except when otherwise waived;
- compliance with the Real Estate Seller Disclosure Act;
- an accounting, in a timely manner, for all money and property received from or on behalf of any consumer to a transaction;
- proper information at the initial interview;
- timely disclosure of any conflicts of interest;
- guidance regarding the use of expert advice for matters that are beyond the licensee's expertise (including the use of attorneys for legal advice);
- information about the status of the transaction;
- information regarding tasks that must be completed to satisfy an agreement or condition for settlement, regarding document preparation, and regarding compliance with laws pertaining to real estate transactions;
- timely presentation of all offers and counteroffers, unless otherwise directed in writing; and
- disclosure of any financial interest (including a referral fee or commission) in a service, such as financial title, transfer and preparation services, insurance, construction, repair or inspection, at the time a service is recommended or the licensee learns that the service will be used.

Agent Duties

In addition to the duties generally required of a licensee, the RELRA prescribes specific duties that are required when a licensee is an agent. The Act also describes duties of a transaction licensee, a relationship in which the licensee is not acting as an agent or advocate of the principal. Agency relationships will be discussed in Chapter 16. The legal references are as follows:

- Section 606b of the RELRA—Duties of seller's agent
- Section 606c of the RELRA—Duties of buyer's agent
- Section 606d of the RELRA—Duties of dual agent
- Section 606e of the RELRA—Duties of designated agent
- Section 606f of the RELRA—Duties of transaction licensee

■ ESCROW REQUIREMENTS

Section 604(5) of the RELRA and Sections 35.32135.328 of the Regulations set forth detailed requirements for handling escrow funds. Brokers are responsible for depositing funds they receive that belong to others (for example, hand money and security deposits) into an escrow account in a federally insured or state-insured bank or depository *pending consummation or termination of the transaction*.

The escrow account must be used exclusively for escrow purposes. The broker may not *commingle* these monies with the broker's business or personal funds; nor may the broker misappropriate money that should be held in escrow with the broker's business or personal funds. However, the broker is permitted to deposit personal money into the escrow account to cover service charges assessed by the banking institution on the account.

If escrow money is expected to be held for more than six months, the broker is encouraged to deposit the funds into an interest-bearing account. The interest follows the principal amount of the escrow funds, unless the parties state otherwise in the agreement.

The broker's duty to escrow *cannot be waived or altered* by agreement between the parties to the transaction.

The account is established in the name of the broker as it appears on the license, with the broker being designated as trustee of the account. The broker may give written authority to an employee to make deposits and authority to a licensed employee to make withdrawals. However, the broker remains responsible for seeing that the requirements of the regulations are met. Records must be maintained, including the name of the party from whom the money is received; the name of the party to whom the money belongs; and the dates the money is received, deposited, and withdrawn. These records are subject to inspection by the Commission.

Responsibility for Deposits

If a sales deposit is tendered by a buyer to the *listing broker* rather than the selling broker, the listing broker shall assume the escrow duty. If the sales deposit is tendered by a buyer to the selling broker, the *selling broker* assumes responsibility.

In co-brokerage transactions, however, it may be the intention of the listing broker to escrow the sales deposit, but the money is tendered to the selling broker. In this case, there must be written notice to the buyer that the selling broker intends to deliver the deposit to the listing broker. The listing broker then assumes the responsibility for the funds. The buyer must acknowledge in writing, prior to signing an agreement of sale, the name of the listing broker; that the selling broker is receiving these funds on behalf of the listing broker; and that the listing broker is to be designated as payee if the buyer's deposit is in the form of a check.

Deadlines for Deposits

A broker is responsible for depositing the funds in escrow *by the end of the next business day following receipt*. In the case of multiple office firms, the deadline applies to receipt by the office out of which the account is administered. If the money has been tendered in the form of a check when an offer to purchase or lease is made, the broker may, with *written permission* from both the buyer and the seller, refrain from depositing the money pending *acceptance* of the offer. In this case, the broker must deposit the funds within *one business day following acceptance of the offer.*

Withdrawal of Funds

A broker must retain all funds in the escrow account until the transaction is consummated or terminated. Consummation is simple to identify if, in the case of an agreement of sale, the sale proceeds through to settlement and the seller delivers title. However, there are situations in which, following the signing of an agreement of sale, a dispute arises between the parties and the sale does not proceed to closing. The broker must retain the escrow money until the dispute is resolved and the parties agree as to whom the deposit money belongs. If resolution of the dispute appears remote without legal action, the broker may, following 30 days' notice to the parties, petition the county court to interplead the rival claimants. The broker may not appropriate any part of the earnest money as compensation as the broker's commission.

Rental Management Account

Rents that a broker receives as a property manager for a lessor shall be deposited into a rental management account. This account is separate from the broker's escrow account (in which security deposits are held) and the general business accounts.

■ GENERAL ETHICAL RESPONSIBILITIES

Subchapter E in the Regulations, "Standards of Conduct and Practice," lists a number of responsibilities for licensees. Many of the requirements relate to issues that are raised in Section 604 of the RELRA, which addresses prohibited practices. In addition to items that have already been discussed relating to escrow deposits and real estate documents, a number of other very important issues are discussed in Subchapter E.

Misleading Advice, Assurances, and Representations

Section 35.282 of the Regulations states that licensees may not give assurances or advice concerning any aspect of a real estate transaction that they know is *incorrect, inaccurate, or improbable*. This includes information it is reasonable to believe that a licensee *should* know. Licensees may not knowingly be a party to a *material false or inaccurate representation* in a written document regarding a real estate transaction when acting in a representative capacity.

Conflict of Interest

Section 35.283 of the Regulations states that licensees must *disclose any ownership interest* they have in a property involved in a real estate transaction in which they are participating. It also says that a broker who manages rental property *may not accept commission, rebate, or profit on expenditures made for the lessor* without the owner's *written consent*. The Regulations intend to ensure that licensees protect the interests of the people they are supposed to be serving and not use their position for personal profit.

The Regulations also require that if a licensee *represents more than one party* in a transaction (dual agency), all parties must give *written consent* to the multiple representation. This consent intends to ensure that the parties are aware that conflicts can arise when the licensee is attempting to represent two opposite parties in the same transaction.

Disclosure of Real Estate Affiliations

Because the franchise, network, or other parent real estate company with which a broker is affiliated is not part of the license name, Section 35.285 of the Regulations requires that the Commission be notified of this affiliation.

Duties When Selling or Leasing Own Real Estate

Once licensed, brokers and salespersons must comply with all requirements of the Act and Section 35.288 of the Regulations when selling or leasing their own property. They must disclose their license status to a prospective buyer or tenant before the person enters into an agreement with the licensee.

Licensees also must disclose that they are licensed when advertising their own properties for sale or rent.

■ ADVERTISING AND SOLICITATION

A licensee may not advertise, solicit prospective buyers or tenants, or place a "for sale" or "for rent" sign on a property without the *written consent of the owner*. A rental listing referral agent may not publish information about a rental property if the lessor or property manager expressly states that the property is not to be included in the inventory list prepared by the rental listing referral agent.

Business Name

When advertising a property for sale or rent, the broker's business name as it appears on the license must appear in the ad; "blind ads" (advertisements by a broker without including the broker's business name) are prohibited. Advertising by a broker's licensees must include the business name of the employing broker. The business name of the broker and the broker's phone number must appear in the same size type or prominence as that of the employee if that employee's name and phone number(s) appear. If a licensee uses a nickname, that name must be filed with the Real Estate Commission.

Internet Advertising and Web Pages

The Commission has developed policy to guide advertising procedures on the Internet. The policy applies to *licensed firms* and *licensees* advertising or marketing on an Internet site and using Internet electronic communication, including e-mail, e-mail discussion groups, Web sites, and bulletin boards. Information that must appear includes

- the firm's name as registered on the license. (If the Internet activity is a licensee's, the firm's name must appear along with the licensee's name.)
- the city and state/province where the firm's (and licensee's) office is located. (Although not required, stating the country is strongly recommended.)
- the regulatory jurisdiction(s) in which the firm holds a broker license. (If the Internet activity is a licensee's, the jurisdiction(s) where the licensee holds a broker or salesperson license must be included. Also, although not required, stating the license number(s) is strongly recommended.)

When marketing or advertising on the Internet, this information must appear on *each page* of the site. For electronic communication, the information is to be included on the *first or last page* of the communication.

Advertisement of Lotteries, Contests, Prizes, Certificates, Lots, and Gifts

According to Section 604 of the RELRA and 35.306 of the Regulations, advertisements for the solicitation or sale of real estate that employ lotteries or contests or that offer prizes, certificates, gifts, or free lots shall contain

- a description of each prize, certificate, gift, or lot offered;
- the prerequisites for receiving the awards;
- the limitation on the number of awards;
- the fair market value (*not* suggested retail value) of each award; and
- the odds of winning or receiving the award.

If the awards are offered through the mail, the licensee shall maintain records that contain the number of awards that were made and the names and addresses of both the individuals who receive and who do not receive them. The Commission requires that disclosures be made if there is a possibility that a particular award is not available and prohibits advertising an award that is not available for distribution. The description of an award cannot be misleading, and a statement of value and odds shall be printed in a clear and conspicuous manner. If the prizewinner must pay any fees, such as dealer preparation, shipping, handling, or insurance, these must be disclosed.

Advertising Sales Volume, Market Position, and Number of Offices

According to Section 35.307 of the Regulations, advertising by a broker about "sales volume" or "production" shall refer only to closed transactions. These are listings or sales that have gone to settlement or when a fully executed deed has been delivered. An advertisement by a broker about production or position in the "market" shall identify the municipality that the market comprises. An advertisement about the number of offices that the broker operates shall refer only to offices that have been issued branch office licenses.

Harassment

According to Section 35.302 of the Regulations, a licensee, whether acting on behalf of a prospective buyer or not, must not solicit the sale or other disposition of real estate with such frequency as to amount to clear harassment of the owner of the property. This includes personal contact or the use of telephone, mail, or other advertising.

Panic Selling

In Section 35.303 of the Regulations, panic selling is defined as frequent efforts to sell residential real estate in a particular neighborhood due to fear of declining real estate values when that fear is not based on facts relating to the intrinsic value of the real estate. (Federal law describes this conduct as *blockbusting*.) The Commission regards an attempt by a licensee to bring about panic selling in order to gain profit as an act of bad faith under Section 604 of the RELRA. Proof of systematic solicitation of sales listings may be considered sufficient, but not conclusive, evidence of an attempt to bring about panic selling.

■ PROMOTIONAL LAND SALES

Section 605 of the RELRA requires that any person who proposes to engage in real estate transactions of a promotional nature in Pennsylvania, regardless of whether the property is located within or outside Pennsylvania, shall first register with the Commission. The Act specifies the information that must be submitted for the Commission to grant approval before the property can be promoted. "Promotional real estate" is an interest in property that is part of a promotional plan that offers real estate through advertising by mail, newspaper, or periodical, or by radio, television, telephone, or other electronic means. Promotional real estate does not involve fewer than 50 lots or shares or land areas of less than 25 acres. The registration is not required if the promotional property is already registered with the Department of Housing and Urban Development under the Interstate Land Sales Full Disclosure Act.

■ SUMMARY

Real estate licenses are granted to qualified individuals, corporations, and partnerships under the provisions of the Real Estate Licensing and Registration Act. The Act is administered by the State Real Estate Commission. The Commission has the authority to promulgate the rules and regulations, which elaborate on the license law and provide additional legal guidance for Pennsylvania licensees. The purpose of the RELRA and the Regulations is to protect the public interest.

A real estate licensee is required to perform for others, and for a fee, such activities as brokerage, property management, leasing, and exchanging. Licenses are issued to brokers, salespersons, builder-owner salespersons, cemetery brokers and cemetery salespersons, rental listing referral agents, time-share salespersons, and campground membership salespersons.

Certain individuals are exempt from licensure requirements, such as owners, attorneys-in-fact, attorneys-at-law (within the scope of the attorney-client relationship), officers and directors of banking institutions (when dealing with institution-owned real estate), trustees, executors, auctioneers, and officers and employees of banking institutions when appraising real estate on behalf of the institution.

Licenses are issued by the Department of State to individuals who meet the requirements for licensure. The licenses are renewed every two years, and such renewal includes the payment of appropriate fees. Brokers and salespersons must also satisfy a 14-hour continuing education requirement for license renewal.

The Act regulates such matters as the general operation of a real estate business, real estate documents, earnest money deposits, advertising, and ethical considerations. There are procedures for the Commission to investigate the activities and take disciplinary actions against licensees. The law establishes the Real Estate Recovery Fund, from which aggrieved persons may collect unpaid judgments resulting from a civil court suit for damages due to fraud, misrepresentation, or deceit.

QUESTIONS

1. A broker may pay a commission to a(n)
   a. developer.
   b. licensed salesperson who works for another broker.
   c. attorney.
   d. licensed salesperson employed by the broker.

2. If a licensed salesperson violates a provision of the license law without the consent or knowledge of the supervising broker
   a. the salesperson may have his or her license revoked.
   b. only the broker may lose his or her license.
   c. both the salesperson and the broker may lose their licenses.
   d. the broker will be fined for the salesperson's violation.

3. All of the following are true regarding the requirements for a broker's office *EXCEPT*
   a. the broker's license must be prominently displayed.
   b. the office must be equipped with a telephone.
   c. the licenses of the salesperson must be prominently displayed.
   d. the business name must be prominently displayed on the outside of the place of business.

4. A broker must keep records of all real estate transactions.
   a. for at least one year following the closing date.
   b. for at least three years following the listing date.
   c. for at least three years following the date of consummation or termination.
   d. indefinitely.

5. The Real Estate Commission may take disciplinary action against a licensee for all of the following *EXCEPT* violating the
   a. Real Estate Licensing and Registration Act.
   b. rules and regulations.
   c. Pennsylvania Human Relations Act.
   d. blue-sky laws.

6. When advertising a property for sale, the broker must include which of the following in the advertisement?
   a. Listing price
   b. Legal description of property
   c. Broker's address
   d. Broker's business name

7. Which of the following is true regarding the Real Estate Recovery Fund?
   a. The maximum amount that may be paid the aggrieved person is $30,000.
   b. The licensee's license is automatically revoked.
   c. The aggrieved person may sue the licensee for further damages if the amount paid is insufficient.
   d. The licensee's license is suspended until he or she repays the full amount recovered out of the fund, plus interest.

8. Which of the following is *NOT* cause for disciplinary action against a licensee?
   a. Accepting a listing with the understanding that illegal discrimination will be exercised in the sale of the property.
   b. Failure to provide the client with a copy of the listing contract at the time it is signed.
   c. Placing a "for sale" sign on a property without written permission of the owner.
   d. Payment of a commission by a licensed broker to another licensed broker.

9. A licensed salesperson may do which of the following?
   a. Leave the employment of one broker and become associated with another broker without reporting the change to the Commission.
   b. Place an advertisement using only the salesperson's name and phone number
   c. Sell the salesperson's own property without telling a buyer that she is licensed
   d. Sell condominiums

10. Licensure is required for which of the following activities?
    a. Owners selling their own properties
    b. Trustees selling trust properties
    c. Bank employees appraising property for the banking institution
    d. Selling campground memberships

11. A broker of record
    a. is employed by another broker.
    b. is the licensee responsible for the activities in a real estate corporation.
    c. is a broker who is permitted to sell dwellings only for the builder-owner.
    d. oversees the activities of a cemetery broker.

12. Which of the following is true regarding the laws for escrow accounts?
    a. Rents the broker collects must be deposited in the broker's escrow account.
    b. The salesperson must deposit escrow funds as soon as they are received.
    c. Escrow funds must be deposited in an interest-bearing account.
    d. The buyer and seller can agree in writing that the escrow money will not be deposited until the agreement of sale is accepted.

13. All of the following must satisfy an education requirement prior to licensure EXCEPT
    a. cemetery salespersons.
    b. campground membership salespersons.
    c. time-share salespersons.
    d. rental listing referral agents.

14. All of the following must take a license examination EXCEPT
    a. brokers.
    b. salespersons.
    c. builder-owner salespersons.
    d. time-share salespersons.

ANSWERS

1. D   A licensed real estate broker is prohibited from paying a commission or any valuable consideration to anyone other than the individuals licensed with the broker or another broker. (p. 219)

2. A   Section 702 of the RELRA limits the disciplinary action that may be taken against an employing broker when a licensee is disciplined. If the broker had no knowledge and did not consent, the salesperson's license may be revoked without action against the broker. (p. 218)

3. B   Section 601 of the RELRA establishes requirements for the office of a licensed broker. There is no stated requirement that the office be equipped with a telephone. (p. 216)

4. C   Records of real estate transactions must be retained for three years following the consummation or termination of the transaction. (p. 222)

5. D   Violation of the Blue Sky Laws would result in prosecution by federal and state authorities, but not the State Real Estate Commission (SREC). The SREC has jurisdiction over violations of the RELRA and its rules and regulations, which includes Sec. 604 (22) of the rules for violations of the Pennsylvania Human Relations Act. (pp. 218–19)

6. D   Commission rules and regulations require the broker's business name to be included exactly as it appears on the license. Blind ads are expressly prohibited. (p. 227)

7. D   Chapter 8 of the RELRA addresses the Real Estate Recovery Fund, including the fact a license is suspended until the amount paid from the fund is restored in full plus interest at the rate of 10 percent per year. (p. 221)

8. D   A broker is permitted to pay a commission to another licensed broker. Prohibitions in Sec. 604 of the Commission rules and regulations include failing to provide a consumer with a copy of contracts at the time of execution, erecting "for sale" or "for rent" signs without written consent, and accepting listings with the understanding that illegal discrimination will be practiced. (pp. 218–19)

9. D   A licensed salesperson is authorized to handle the sale of condominium interests on behalf of the employing broker. (p. 209)

10. D   Campground membership sales require licensing as a campground membership salesperson. (p. 203) Section 304 of the RELRA provides exclusions to the law. (pp. 212–13)

11. B   Broker of record refers to the individual broker who is responsible for the licensed real estate activities of a partnership, association, or corporation licensed as broker. (p. 209)

12. D   The Commission rules and regulations provide that a broker negotiating an agreement of sale may, with the written consent of both the buyer and seller, refrain from depositing hand money into the escrow account until the agreement is signed by both parties. (p. 225)

13. A   A cemetery salesperson is employed by a broker or cemetery broker for the exclusive purpose of the cemetery lot sales. No education or examination is required for this license. (p. 210)

14. D   The RELRA requires candidates for broker, salesperson and builder-owner salesperson licenses to pass written exams to qualify for licensure. Time-share salespersons do not have an examination requirement. (p. 212)

REAL ESTATE PRACTICE

Real estate transactions are complex business dealings, beginning with the introduction of a property in the marketplace and progressing to the settlement or closing of the transaction. Because of the complex nature of these transactions, consumers rely on the expertise of real estate licensees to assist them. Real estate licensees provide a variety of services to buyers, sellers, property owners, and tenants. As licensees provide these services, certain procedures and ethical behavior must be followed to protect the interests of consumers.

Real Estate Practice introduces the various facets of the real estate business and the techniques, procedures, and ethics involved in a real estate transaction. The concepts in this section and the chapters in which they are discussed are:

CHAPTER FOURTEEN

THE REAL ESTATE BUSINESS

■ LEARNING OBJECTIVES

When you've finished reading this chapter, you should be able to

- ■ identify the various careers available in real estate;
- ■ explain the operation of supply and demand in the real estate market;
- ■ distinguish the economic, political, and social factors that influence supply and demand;
- ■ describe the issues involved in making a home ownership decision; and
- ■ define the key terms.

■ KEY TERMS

capital gain	equity	replacement cost
coinsurance clause	liability coverage	supply
demand		

■ THE SCOPE OF THE REAL ESTATE BUSINESS

Hundreds of billions of dollars circulate in our economy each year because of real estate. Property is bought and sold, rents are paid and collected, and billions of dollars in loans are made to support the purchase and development of real estate. Today's buyers and sellers, landlords and tenants, investors and developers depend on many professionals to help orchestrate their transactions. This also means that millions of people depend on some aspect of the real estate business for their livelihood.

Despite the size and complexity of the real estate business, many people think of it as being made up of only brokers and salespeople. Actually, the services of many highly trained individuals are required, especially as the technical aspects of real estate grow more complex. People trained in areas of specialization such as appraisal, property management, financing, subdivision and development, home inspection, counseling, and education provide valuable expertise. Attorneys, banks, trust companies, abstract and title insurance companies, architects, surveyors, accountants, and government agencies also depend on real estate specialists.

The real estate business offers many opportunities for people to pursue their individual interests. Some people become generalists; that is, they develop expertise in several areas of real estate practice. Others are specialists, becoming highly skilled in a selected area of practice. The following discussion introduces a variety of activities that can be considered for a real estate career.

In Your State

PA Brokerage. Brokerage is the business of bringing people together in a real estate transaction. These people may be interested in purchasing, selling, leasing, or renting housing, commercial, or industrial real estate, or other types of properties. Some real estate practitioners broker several types of property, and others specialize in selected kinds of property. The Real Estate Licensing and Registration Act and the State Real Estate Commission's Rules and Regulations govern the way licensees provide these services in Pennsylvania. The licensing law sets forth a hierarchy within a real estate firm, with the broker or broker of record being at the top. This person determines the firm's services, sets policies and compensation arrangements, and hires licensed associate brokers and salespeople to provide these services on behalf of the broker. Brokerage is discussed in Chapter 15. ■

In Your State

PA Appraisal. Appraisal is the process of estimating a *property's value*. Although all real estate licensees must have some understanding of the valuation process, professional appraisers are trained specifically in the detailed methodology of valuing properties and developing appraisal reports. Their professional opinions of value, known as *appraisals*, are commonly used when property is financed, sold by court order, or condemned. Appraisals also are used when property is partitioned, tax assessments are appealed, and property is valued for an estate. Appraisers may be independent business owners or may be employed by the government, lending institutions, or trust companies. In Pennsylvania, appraisers must be certified by the State Board of Certified Appraisers to engage in this activity. Appraising is discussed in Chapter 21. ■

Property management. A property manager is a person hired to maintain and manage property on behalf of its owner. The property manager's basic responsibility is to protect the value of the owner's investment while maximizing the owner's return on that investment. In that role, the property manager might be responsible for soliciting tenants, collecting rents, altering or constructing new space for tenants, ordering repairs, and overseeing the general maintenance of the property. The scope of a property manager's responsibility varies according to the terms of the individual employment contract, known as a *management agreement*. Property management is discussed in Chapter 23.

Financing.   Financing is the business of providing the funds necessary to complete real estate transactions. Most transactions are financed by means of a mortgage loan secured by the property. Individuals involved in financing real estate may work for commercial banks, savings and loan associations, mortgage banking, and mortgage brokerage companies. A growing number of real estate brokerage companies affiliate with mortgage lenders to provide consumers with "one-stop-shopping" real estate services.

Subdivision and development.   Subdivision is the splitting of a large property into smaller parcels. Development involves the construction of improvements on the land. While subdivision and development are normally related, particularly in housing, they are independent processes that can occur separately. People may specialize in one or both activities. Subdivision and development are discussed in Chapter 2.

In Your State

PA **Home inspection.**   Home inspection is a profession that allows practitioners to combine their interest in real estate with their professional skill and training in the construction trades or engineering. Professional home inspectors conduct a thorough visual survey of a property's structure, systems, and site conditions, and prepare an analytical report that is valuable to both purchasers and homeowners. Increasingly wary consumers are relying on the inspector's report to help them make purchase decisions. Frequently, an agreement of sale is contingent upon the inspector's report. The qualifications and practices of home inspectors who provide this service to satisfy contingencies in residential transactions are governed by legislation in Pennsylvania that became effective December 20, 2001, and was amended by Act 51 of 2004. ■

Counseling.   Counseling is a highly specialized profession in which counselors furnish independent real estate advice to help clients make informed investment decisions. Real estate investment decisions are highly individual, and the financial and tax consequences can be very complex. Professional real estate counselors must have a high degree of real estate expertise. Some counselors today may also have international expertise as well. In Pennsylvania, real estate counselors or consultants must be licensed real estate brokers.

Education.   Education is the provision of real estate information to both practitioners and consumers. Colleges, universities, and proprietary real estate schools conduct courses that are required for licensure and continuing education. Along with trade associations and professional designation groups, they provide a broad range of courses and seminars for professional development. Many of these institutions, as well as real estate companies, conduct programs designed specifically to help consumers understand today's real estate transactions.

Other areas.   Many other people are also part of the real estate business. These include people who are affiliated with mortgage banking firms, people who negotiate mortgage loans for banks and savings and loan associations, people in property management and real estate departments of corporations, and officials and employees of such government agencies as zoning boards and property assessment offices.

■ TYPES OF REAL PROPERTY

Just as there are areas of specialization within the real estate industry, there are different types of property in which to specialize. Real estate can generally be classified as

- *residential*—all property used for housing, from acreage to small city lots, both single-family and multifamily, in urban, suburban, and rural areas;
- *commercial*—business property, including office space, shopping centers, storefronts, theaters, hotels, and parking facilities;
- *industrial*—warehouses, factories, land in industrial districts, and power plants;
- *agricultural*—farms, timberland, pastureland, ranches, and orchards;
- *special-purpose*—churches, schools, cemeteries, and government-held lands; or
- *recreational*—vacation property such as time-shares and campground membership.

In theory, a single real estate firm or individual licensee could provide all the professional services related to all classes of property (unless restricted by licensing laws). As a practical matter, however, this is rarely feasible. Each type of property, as well as professional activity, requires considerable expertise. Most real estate firms specialize to some degree, especially in urban areas. Some companies are highly specialized, performing only appraisal services or property management, or specializing in market niches such as vacation properties or condominiums.

IN PRACTICE

Before engaging in any real estate activity, consider the licenses or certifications that may be required. Use Chapter 13 and Appendix C to identify the education and experience that is required and the procedures for obtaining real estate licenses. Appraisal activities, as well as mortgage banking and brokering activities, are governed by separate laws, copies of which can be obtained from the State Board of Certified Appraisers and the Department of Banking, respectively, in Harrisburg.

■ PROFESSIONAL ORGANIZATIONS

The real estate business has many trade associations. The largest is the *National Association of REALTORS*® (NAR). NAR is composed of state, regional, and local associations. Active members of these affiliated state associations and local boards are known as REALTORS®. Not all real estate licensees are REALTORS®. REALTOR® is a registered trademark of the National Association of REALTORS®. Some local associations or boards offer a separate category of membership, called REALTOR® Associate, to salespeople affiliated with a REALTOR®.

The mission of NAR is to promote programs and services that enhance the ability of its members to conduct business successfully and ethically and to promote the preservation of the right to own, transfer, and use real property.

Its members subscribe to a Code of Ethics. NAR sponsors specialized institutes that offer professional designations. To obtain these designations, people must satisfy certain education and experience requirements in specialized fields of practice. Designations can be obtained by counselors in real estate; specialists in farm and land; specialists in commercial, industrial, office, or international property; property managers; real estate securities; residential brokers; and sales specialists.

The *National Association of Real Estate Brokers (NAREB)*, whose members are known as Realtists, also adheres to a code of ethics. NAREB arose out of the early days of the civil rights movement as an association of racial minority real estate brokers in response to the conditions and abuses that eventually gave rise to fair housing laws. Today, NAREB remains dedicated to equal housing opportunity.

Other professional associations include the Appraisal Institute, the American Society of Appraisers (ASA), the National Association of Independent Fee Appraisers (NAIFA), and the Real Estate Educators Association (REEA). The growth in buyer brokerage led to the formation of organizations such as the Real Estate Buyer's Agent Council, now associated with NAR, and the National Association of Exclusive Buyers' Agents. Other organizations include the Building Owners and Managers Association (BOMA), the Institute of Real Estate Management (IREM), the Commercial Investment Real Estate Institute (CIREI), and the American Society of Real Estate Counselors (ASREC). Home inspectors may be members of the American Society of Home Inspectors (ASHI) or the National Association of Home Inspectors (NAHI).

■ THE REAL ESTATE MARKET

A *market* is a place where goods can be bought and sold. It also may be a vast, complex, worldwide economic system for moving goods and services around the globe. The function of a market is to provide a setting in which supply and demand can establish market value, making it advantageous for buyers and sellers to trade.

To understand the real estate business, it's important to understand the real estate market. The goods in the real estate market are the properties. How readily can buyers and sellers trade properties? What is the value of the properties they are trading? Commonly the terms "buyer's market" and "seller's market" are used to describe the prevailing conditions in the marketplace. What do these terms mean to the industry and the individual buyers and sellers? To answer these questions, look at how the forces of supply and demand interact.

■ SUPPLY AND DEMAND

The forces of **supply** and **demand** in the market influence the price of goods and services. Essentially, when supply increases and demand remains stable,

When supply increases and demand remains stable, prices go down.

When demand increases and supply remains stable, prices go up.

prices will go down. When demand increases and supply remains stable, prices will go up. Greater supply means producers need to attract more buyers, so they lower prices. Greater demand means producers can raise their prices because more buyers compete with one another for the product.

Following this theory, a buyer's market is characterized by a relatively large number of properties available for sale, while a seller's market is characterized by fewer properties. This theory also says that in a buyer's market, the buyers would not be paying as high a price as the seller could command in a seller's market.

Two characteristics of real estate govern the way the market reacts to the pressures of supply and demand: *uniqueness* and *immobility*. Uniqueness means that, no matter how identical they may appear, no two parcels of real estate are ever exactly alike; each occupies its own unique geographic location. Immobility refers to the fact that property cannot be relocated to satisfy demand where supply is low. Nor can buyers always relocate to areas with greater supply. For these reasons, real estate markets have tended to be fairly local in nature. Each geographic area has different types of real estate and different conditions that drive prices.

Uniqueness and *immobility* are the two characteristics of land that have the most impact on market value.

Because of real estate's uniqueness and immobility, the market generally adjusts slowly to the forces of supply and demand. Though a home offered for sale can be withdrawn in response to low demand and high supply, it is much more likely that oversupply will result in lower prices. When supply is low, on the other hand, a high demand may not be met immediately because development and construction are lengthy processes.

Even when supply and demand can be forecast with some accuracy, natural disasters such as hurricanes and earthquakes can disrupt market trends. Similarly, sudden changes in financial markets or local events such as plant relocations or environmental factors can dramatically disrupt a seemingly stable market. Communities face formidable challenges to meet the unanticipated demand of dislocated families and businesses whose properties are damaged or destroyed.

Historically, geographic market areas have been very local. Today's technological advances, however, have widened the marketplace. With electronic commerce, forces of supply and demand can reach far across the country and even around the globe. Goods and services can be offered and traded virtually everywhere. For real estate companies, this means learning to conduct business in the electronic marketplace. In fact, this is what today's consumers expect real estate firms to do.

Factors Affecting Supply

Factors that tend to affect the supply side of the real estate market's supply and demand balance include the labor force, construction and material costs, and government controls and fiscal policies.

Factors Affecting the Supply of Real Estate
■ Labor force ■ Construction materials ■ Government controls ■ Government fiscal policies

Labor force and construction costs. A shortage of skilled labor or building materials or an increase in the cost of materials or labor can decrease the amount of new construction. High transfer costs (such as taxes) and construction permit fees can also discourage development. Increased construction costs may be passed along to buyers and tenants in the form of higher prices and increased rents. Because there is a limit to how much more consumers are willing to pay, this can further slow the market. To offset this effect, cheaper materials and more efficient means of construction may be used.

Government controls and fiscal policies. The government's financial policies can have a substantial impact on the real estate market. As the Federal Reserve increases interest rates for the money it lends to commercial banks, the banks in turn charge higher rates to borrowers. These rates play a significant role in people's ability to buy homes. Taxation takes money out of circulation. Conversely, government spending programs, ranging from welfare to farm subsidies, put money into circulation. As the amount of money in circulation fluctuates, so, too, does people's ability to spend.

Because real estate taxes are a primary source of revenue for local government, taxation policies can have either positive or negative effects. High taxes may deter investors or discourage homebuyers from considering a certain community. On the other hand, tax incentives can attract new businesses and industries. And, of course, along with these enterprises come increased employment and expanded residential real estate markets.

Virtually any government action has some effect on the real estate market. For instance, federal environmental regulations may increase or decrease the supply and value of land in a local market. Local land-use policies, building codes, and zoning ordinances can either encourage or discourage development. Careful planning and policies that foster responsible economic growth and development can increase supply and ultimately affect the value of land.

Factors Affecting Demand

Factors that tend to affect the demand side of the real estate market's supply and demand balance include population, demographics, and employment and wage levels.

Population. Shelter is a basic human need, so the demand for housing grows with the population. Conversely, demand declines as population declines. Although the nation's population continues to rise, growth is not uniform throughout the country. The effect is that demand for real estate increases faster in some parts of the country than in others. In some areas, population has declined or growth has ceased altogether. This may be due to economic changes (such as plant closings), social concerns (such as the quality of schools or a desire for more open space), or population changes (such as population shifts from colder to warmer climates). The result can be a drop in demand for real estate in one area, matched by an increased demand elsewhere.

Demographics. While the population of a community is important, the *composition* of that population is a major factor in driving demand for various types of housing in certain price ranges in a community. *Demographics* is the description or composition of the population. Family size, the ratio of adults to children, the ages of children, the number of retirees, household income, lifestyle, and the number of single-parent and "empty-nester" households are all demographic factors that contribute to the amount and type of housing needed. The growing number of people moving into retirement communities or senior care facilities and the increasing number of households that are made up of several generations within the family are demographic factors that significantly impact today's housing market.

Employment and wage levels. The real estate market is closely tied to the job market. When job opportunities are scarce, wage levels are low, or workers feel insecure about their continued employment, demand for real estate usually drops. On the other hand, favorable employment conditions generally increase the demand for housing. There are issues to consider beyond the effect of businesses moving into or out of an area and the expansion or downsizing of their operations. The wage scales that accompany these jobs affect demand for higher or lower priced properties, depending on ability to pay.

The general economic climate in the area also affects demand. The level of confidence people have in the economy affects their decisions about whether to spend or save, buy or rent, invest in the community, or go elsewhere. All of these decisions ultimately affect the demand for real estate.

> **Factors Affecting Demand for Real Estate**
> - Population
> - Demographics
> - Employment and wage levels

■ THE HOUSING MARKET

The housing market is shaped by the personal motivations of buyers as well as the economic forces of supply and demand. People buy homes for psychological as well as financial reasons. To many, home ownership represents financial stability and an investment that can appreciate in value. Home ownership also offers benefits that may be less tangible but are no less valuable, such as pride, security, and a sense of belonging to the community. A basic necessity in a roof overhead becomes not only an ownership asset but also an opportunity to become a stakeholder in the community.

Types of Housing

As society evolves, the needs of homebuyers become more specialized. A variety of housing types, in addition to single-family homes, is available to meet these needs. Some housing types are innovative uses of real estate and often incorporate a variety of ownership concepts. As you read the following paragraphs, notice how the different forms of housing respond to the demands of a diverse marketplace.

Apartment complexes are groups of apartment buildings with any number of units in each building. The buildings may be lowrise or highrise, and on-site amenities may include such facilities as parking, clubhouses, swimming pools, and even golf courses.

The *condominium* is a popular form of ownership, particularly for people who want the security of owning real estate without the care and maintenance that a house demands. The governing body of a condominium association oversees the management and maintenance of building exteriors and common facilities and collects periodic fees from the unit owners to cover these expenses. Office buildings and shopping centers may also be established as condominiums, allowing businesses to build equity in the space they occupy while avoiding unpredictable rent increases. Condominiums are discussed in detail in Chapter 7.

A *cooperative* also has units that share common walls and facilities within a larger building. The owners, however, do not actually own the units. Instead, a corporation holds title to the real estate itself. The unit owners actually purchase shares of stock in the corporation, not the individual units, and receive proprietary leases that entitle them to occupy particular units. Like condominium unit owners, cooperative unit owners pay their share of the building's expenses. Cooperatives are discussed in detail in Chapter 7.

Planned residential developments (PRDs) merge a variety of residential housing types within one development. *Planned unit developments* (PUDs) merge such diverse land uses as housing, recreation, and commercial units in one self-contained development. PRDs and PUDs are zoned under special ordinances. These ordinances permit high-density use of the land and maximize the use of open space by reducing lot sizes and street areas. Owners do not have direct ownership interest in the common areas. A community association is formed to maintain these areas with fees collected from the owners.

Converted-use properties are factories, office buildings, hotels, schools, churches, and other structures that have been converted to other uses. Renovation of such properties is often more aesthetically and economically appealing than demolishing a perfectly sound structure to build something new. An abandoned warehouse may be transformed into luxury loft housing units, a closed hotel may reopen as an apartment building, or an old factory may be recycled into a profitable shopping mall.

Retirement communities, many of them in temperate climates, are often structured as PUDs. They may provide shopping, recreational opportunities, and healthcare facilities, in addition to residential units. Security and convenience are major advantages that retirement communities offer for older residents. Providing facilities and services to meet the physical, recreational, and social needs of older persons is one of several requirements in the fair housing laws for a development to restrict families with children from occupancy.

High-rise developments often combine office space, stores, theaters, and apartment units in a single vertical community. These mixed-used buildings are self-contained developments, often including laundry facilities, restaurants, food stores, valet shops, beauty parlors, barbershops, swimming pools, and other attractive and convenient features.

Mobile homes were once considered useful only as temporary residences or for travel. Now, however, they are more often permanent, principal residences or stationary vacation homes. Relatively low cost, coupled with increased living space in the newer double-wide and triple-wide models, has made mobile homes more attractive. Increased sales have resulted in growing numbers of "housing parks" in some communities. These parks offer complete residential environments with permanent community facilities as well as semipermanent foundations and hookups for gas, water, and electricity.

Modular homes (also referred to as prefabricated homes) are also gaining popularity as the price of newly constructed homes rises. Each room is preassembled at a factory, transported to the building site, and then placed on a foundation. Later, workers finish the structure and connect plumbing and wiring. Entire developments can be built at a fraction of the time and cost of conventional types of construction.

Through *time-shares*, multiple purchasers share ownership of a single property, usually a vacation home. Each owner is entitled to use the property for a certain period of time each year, usually a specific week. In addition to the purchase price, each owner pays a maintenance fee. Due to high initial marketing costs and the uncertain resale market, time-share resale prices can be significantly lower than their original purchase prices.

■ HOUSING AFFORDABILITY

While the desire and motivation to own a home may be great, the affordability of that housing plays a major role in people's ability to convert their aspirations of ownership into reality. Social and economic conditions can make the affordability hurdle more challenging to overcome and for some segments of the population, simply insurmountable. During periods of high inflation, housing prices can rise rapidly. These increases tend to outpace increases in people's income. During periods of recession, housing prices rise more slowly (if they increase at all), but the general economic climate and employment conditions can prevent people from taking advantage of more affordable housing prices. The people who are most vulnerable during these economic cycles are low-income to moderate-income purchasers.

The challenge for people who want to enter the housing market is accumulating enough money for a down payment and closing costs to obtain a conventional mortgage loan. First-time buyers can be helped over this hurdle with loan programs that offer lower closing costs, or deferred interest or principal payments. Real estate and related industry groups, along with Congress, state legislatures, and local government bodies, have been instrumental in developing a variety of programs to assist first-time homebuyers and increase the availability of suitable and affordable housing for all segments of the population. The results of these initiatives can be seen in recent increases in the number of people who have become homeowners.

As advantageous and achievable as home ownership can be, not everyone should own a home. Home ownership involves substantial commitment and responsibility. For some people, the flexibility of renting is more suitable. People whose work requires frequent moves or whose financial position is uncertain particularly benefit from renting. People who rely on income-producing assets may prefer to rent rather than invest capital assets in a home. Renting also provides more leisure time by freeing tenants from the responsibilities of management and maintenance.

The decision to purchase rather than rent must be weighed carefully. Prevailing loan terms, expenses of ownership, and investment and tax implications should be considered in light of each individual's financial circumstances.

Mortgage Loans

Liberalized mortgage loan terms and payment plans offer many people the option of purchasing a home. Low-down-payment loans, those in which the loan-to-value ratio (the amount of the loan in relation to the value of the property) is 95 percent or higher, enable people who do not have the customary 20-percent down payment to purchase a property. The Federal Housing Administration (FHA), the Department of Veterans Affairs (commonly called the VA), the Pennsylvania Housing Finance Agency, and local community reinvestment programs sponsor many of these mortgage programs.

The tradeoff, however, is that a smaller down payment means that the loan amount is higher. The borrower must be able to afford the monthly payments on a larger loan. In addition, the annual interest rate is typically higher than on loans with lower loan-to-value ratios. This increases the monthly payment as well. Depending on an individual's income-tax situation, a buyer may find that the mortgage interest deduction is sufficient to offset the added expense and, therefore, makes the loan more affordable. Borrowers are also aided with today's adjustable-rate mortgage loans that offer lower initial interest rates.

The length of a loan also affects housing affordability. For some borrowers, a 15-year loan term is desirable. If the borrower can afford the higher payments to pay off the loan faster, he or she can own the home free-and-clear in a shorter period of time. For others, stretching out payments over a 30-year (or even a 40-year) loan term fits better into the monthly budget because the payments are lower.

In addition to the down payment, funds for closing costs and prepaid items can be problematic for buyers. But there are ways to cope with this situation as well. Some loan programs offer lower closing costs, particularly for first-time homebuyers. Or the seller might agree to assist with some of the costs to get the house sold.

Buyer's Ability to Pay

The cost of acquiring a property is only one consideration for a buyer. Home ownership involves many expenses, including utilities (such as electricity, natural gas, and water), trash removal, sewer charges, and maintenance and repairs. Owners also must pay real estate taxes and buy property insurance, as well as repay the mortgage loan with interest.

To determine whether a prospective buyer can afford a certain purchase, most lenders have traditionally used a "rule of thumb" formula: The monthly cost of buying and maintaining a home (mortgage payment of principal and interest plus tax and insurance) should not exceed 28 percent of gross (pretax) monthly income. This payment plus the payments on all recurring debts should not exceed 36 percent of monthly income. Many lenders today have more generous guidelines, depending on the type of loan and incentives associated with various loan programs as well as the borrower's earnings, number of debts, credit history, number of dependents, and assorted other factors.

Investment Considerations

Purchasing a home offers several financial advantages. First, if the property's value increases, a sale could bring more money than the owner paid—a long-term gain. Of course, the amount a property's value will increase is affected by the specific nature of the property and its location, the value of surrounding properties, the general economic climate, and interaction of supply and demand when the property is sold. Second, as the total mortgage debt is reduced through monthly payments, the owner's actual financial ownership in the property increases. This increasing ownership interest, called **equity,** represents the paid-off share of the property held free of any mortgage. Some people view this as forced savings because as they repay the loan, they are gaining an asset. Equity builds even further as the property value rises. The third financial advantage concerns income tax deductions available to homeowners.

Tax Benefits

To encourage home ownership, the federal government allows homeowners certain income tax advantages. Homeowners may deduct from their adjusted gross income some or all of the mortgage interest, as well as real estate taxes and certain other expenses. They may even eliminate tax on the profit received from selling the home. Depending on a person's individual circumstances, tax considerations may be an important part of any decision to purchase a home.

Beginning in 1997, several federal tax reforms were enacted that significantly changed the importance of tax considerations for most home sellers. For instance, while the amount of a homeowner's **capital gain** on the sale of a residence was once an important tax consideration, the federal government now excludes $500,000 from capital gains tax for profits on the sale of a principal residence by married taxpayers who file jointly. Taxpayers who file singly are entitled to a $250,000 exclusion. The exemption may be used repeatedly (regardless of a person's age as was previously the case), as long as the homeowners have occupied the property as their primary residence for at least two of the past five years.

For most homeowners, the net result of the 1997 law is that they will never pay capital gains tax on the sale of their homes. Of course, sellers of higher-priced homes, or those who have accumulated profits over time that exceed $500,000, will face federal capital gains tax. Individual state tax laws may or may not reflect the federal reforms. In addition, a law passed in 1998 reduces the required holding period for a long-term capital gain for noncorporate taxpayers from 18 months to 12 months. Even if the sale is subject to federal tax, the tax rate on capital gains is lower than the tax rate on ordinary income.

Another federal reform will benefit the real estate market by making it easier for people to obtain down payments. First-time homebuyers may make penalty-free withdrawals from their tax-deferred individual retirement funds (IRAs) for down payments on their homes. The limit on such withdrawals is $10,000. In short, the present trend is to reform and simplify federal taxes that affect home ownership.

Tax deductions.   Homeowners may deduct from their gross income

- mortgage interest payments on first and second homes that meet the definition of "qualified residence interest,"
- ad valorem real estate taxes (but not interest paid on overdue taxes),
- certain loan origination fees,
- discount points (whether paid by buyer or seller), and
- loan prepayment penalties.

Qualified residence interest is limited as follows: All debt secured by a principal and second home and used to buy, construct, or substantially improve those residences, called acquisition indebtedness, can equal no more than $1 million. Home equity loans secured by the property for amounts not exceeding the owner's equity in the property may not be more than $100,000.

IN PRACTICE

The circumstances of all investors and taxpayers are not the same. For instance, a taxpayer who does not itemize deductions may not have the same tax advantages as a taxpayer who does. Also, the tax benefits for homeowners can change as tax law changes. Buyers and sellers should be referred to the Internal Revenue Service, a certified public accountant, or other tax specialist for specific information. A real estate licensee should not attempt to give tax advice.

■ INSURANCE

Although real estate and insurance are separate businesses, there is a logical connection between the two. Once people invest in real estate, they insure the real estate to protect their investment. Mortgage lenders, to lessen their own risk of loss, usually require insurance to protect the property that is pledged as collateral for the loan. While individual policies can be purchased to insure against destruction of property by fire or windstorm, injury to others and theft of personal property, most owners buy packaged homeowner's insurance policies to cover all these risks.

Homeowner's Insurance

The most common homeowner's insurance policy is called a *basic form*. It provides property coverage against

- fire or lightning,
- glass breakage,
- windstorm or hail,
- explosion,
- riot or civil commotion,

- damage from aircraft,
- damage from vehicles,
- damage from smoke,
- vandalism and malicious mischief,
- theft, and
- loss of property removed from the premises when endangered by fire or other perils.

A *broad form* policy, in addition to the coverage listed above, covers

- falling objects;
- weight of ice, snow, or sleet;
- collapse of the building or any part of it;
- bursting, cracking, burning, or bulging of a steam or hot water heating system or appliances used to heat water;
- accidental discharge, leakage, or overflow of water or steam from within a plumbing, heating, or air conditioning system;
- freezing of plumbing, heating and air conditioning systems, and domestic appliances; and
- injury to electrical appliances, devices, fixtures, and wiring from short circuits or other accidentally generated currents.

Further insurance is available from policies that cover almost all possible perils. Special apartment and condominium policies generally provide fire and wind-storm, theft, and public **liability coverage** for injuries or losses sustained within the unit. However, they do not usually cover losses or damages to the structure. The basic structure is insured by either the landlord or the condominium owners' association.

Most homeowner's insurance policies contain a **coinsurance clause.** This provision usually requires that the owner maintain insurance equal to at least 80 percent of the replacement cost of the dwelling (not including the price of the land). An owner who has this type of a policy may make a claim for the full cost of the repair or replacement of the damaged property without deduction for depreciation.

If the homeowner carries less than 80 percent of the full **replacement cost,** however, the claim will be handled in one of two ways. Either the loss will be settled for the actual cash value (replacement cost less depreciation) or it will be prorated by dividing the percentage of replacement cost actually covered by the policy by the minimum coverage requirement (usually 80 percent).

Financial Pressures on Insurers. Property loss after 9/11 and several devastating hurricane seasons coupled with litigation that has forced payment of claims for a variety of other losses have increased the financial pressures on casualty insurers. The effect is that today's homeowner policies are not only more expensive (particularly in some geographic areas), but also the terms of replacement recovery are often more stringent than in the past. Insurers are also more closely scrutinizing property conditions (particularly those related to moisture or water) to determine insurability as well as the amount of premiums.

In recent years, builders have been using a synthetic stucco finish on the exterior of some residential structures. Exterior insulating finishing system (EIFS) is a highly effective moisture barrier, but one that also tends to seal in moisture. Improper installation can trap water in the structure's walls, with the result being massive wood rot. Frequently, the effects of rot cannot be detected until the damage is extensive and sometimes irreparable. The use of EIFS has resulted in not only class-action lawsuits being filed by distressed homeowners against builders and developers, but also some insurance companies refuse to issue policies for houses with EIFS exteriors.

Water damage inside a house (from any number of sources) frequently leads to the growth of mold. It's possible that the mold may not even be detected by visual inspection. Although relatively few types of mold have been determined to be health hazards, insurance companies have been involved in litigation over responsibility for repairing homes with mold problems. As a result, insurance companies have adopted guidelines about the insurability of properties with water or mold-related problems.

Guidelines for insurability vary from company to company, and often vary in different parts of the country. A common trend today is for casualty insurers to use a Comprehensive Loss Underwriting Experience (CLUE) report or similar scoring device to determine insurability of both the property and the property owner. Existing property conditions and the insurance-claim history on that particular property as well as the individual owner's claim history, creditworthiness, and other financial conditions all factor into the decision to issue a policy and the premium that will be charged.

Federal Flood Insurance Program

The National Flood Insurance Act helps owners of property in flood-prone areas by subsidizing flood insurance and by taking land-use and control measures to improve future management for floodplain areas. The *Federal Emergency Management Agency (FEMA)* administers the flood program. The Army Corps of Engineers maintains flood plain maps that identify specific flood-prone areas throughout the country. Owners in flood-prone areas must obtain flood insurance to finance property with federally related mortgage loans. If they do not obtain the insurance (either because they don't want it or don't qualify because their communities have not properly entered the program), they are not eligible for financial assistance.

In designated areas, flood insurance is required on all types of building—residential, commercial, industrial, and agricultural—for either the value of the property or the amount of the mortgage loan, subject to the maximum limits available. Policies are written annually and can be purchased from any licensed property insurance broker, the National Flood Insurance Program, or the designated servicing companies in each state. However, if a borrower can produce a survey showing that the lowest part of the building is located above the 100-year flood mark, the borrower may be exempted from the flood insurance requirement, even if the property is in a flood-prone area.

Mine Subsidence Insurance

In Your State

PA Damage or loss of a property due to mine subsidence is not covered by homeowner's insurance policies. However, property owners can obtain insurance for mine subsidence through the Mines Subsidence Insurance Fund administered by the Department of Environmental Protection in Pennsylvania. The recoverable loss under these policies is limited to damage to the structure; damage to the surrounding site is not covered. The Bureau of Mines is a good resource for information about mine subsidence. Although the Bureau does not warrant or guarantee against subsidence, it can provide information about the location of mines and help property owners evaluate the likelihood of subsidence. ∎

■ SUMMARY

Although brokerage is the most widely recognized activity of the real estate business, many other services are also provided by the industry, such as appraisal, property management, property development, counseling, home inspection, property financing, and education. Most real estate firms specialize in only one or two of these areas.

Real property can be classified according to its general use as residential, commercial, industrial, agricultural, special purpose, or recreational. Although many brokers deal with more than one type of real property, they tend to specialize to some degree.

A market is a place where goods and services can be bought and sold and price levels are established. The ideal market allows for a continual balancing of the forces of supply and demand. Because of its unique characteristics, real estate is relatively slow to adjust to the forces of supply and demand.

The balance of supply and demand in the real estate market is affected by many factors, including changes in population numbers and demographics, wage and employment levels, construction costs and availability of labor, and government monetary policy and controls.

The housing market includes apartment complexes, condominiums, cooperatives, planned unit developments and planned residential developments, retirement communities, high-rise developments, converted-use properties, modular homes, mobile homes, and time-shares in addition to single-family homes.

Prospective buyers should be aware of both the advantages and disadvantages of home ownership. Although a homeowner gains financial security and pride of ownership, the costs of ownership (both the initial price and the continuing expenses) must be considered.

One of the income tax benefits available to homeowners is the ability to deduct mortgage interest payments (within certain limitations) and property taxes on their federal income tax returns. In addition, changes in the income tax exemptions in the Taxpayer Relief Act of 1997 mean that most homeowners will never need to pay capital gains taxes on the sale of properties in which they reside.

To protect their investment in real estate, most homeowners purchase insurance. A standard homeowner's insurance policy covers fire, theft, and liability and can be extended to cover many other risks. Another type of insurance, which covers personal property only, is available to people who live in apartments and condominiums.

Many homeowner's policies contain a coinsurance clause that requires the policyholder to maintain insurance in an amount equal to 80 percent of the replacement cost of the home. If this percentage is not met, the policyholder may not be reimbursed for the full repair costs if a loss occurs.

In addition to homeowner's insurance, the federal government requires flood insurance for properties located in flood-prone areas when federally related mortgage loans are involved. The Coal Mines Subsidence Insurance Fund in Pennsylvania provides insurance to cover damage or loss of a building due to mine subsidence.

QUESTIONS

1. Commercial real estate includes all of the following *EXCEPT*
   a. an office building for sale.
   b. apartments for rent.
   c. a retail space for lease.
   d. fast-food restaurants.

2. In general, when the supply of a certain commodity increases
   a. prices tend to rise.
   b. prices tend to drop.
   c. demand tends to rise.
   d. demand tends to drop.

3. All of the following factors tend to affect supply *EXCEPT*
   a. the labor force.
   b. construction costs.
   c. government controls.
   d. employment and wage level.

4. Which of the following best expresses the concept of equity?
   a. Current Market Value—Capital Gain
   b. Current Market Value—Property Debt
   c. Current Market Value—Cost of Land
   d. Replace Cost—Depreciation

5. The real cost of owning a home includes certain costs or expenses that many people tend to overlook. Which of the following is *NOT* a cost or expense of owning a home?
   a. Interest paid on borrowed capital
   b. Homeowner's insurance
   c. Maintenance and repairs
   d. Taxes on personal property

6. When a person buys a house using a mortgage loan, the difference between the amount owed on the property and what it is worth represents the homeowner's
   a. tax basis.
   b. equity.
   c. replacement cost.
   d. capital gain.

7. A building that is remodeled into residential units and is no longer used for the purpose for which it was originally built is a(n)
   a. converted-use property.
   b. example of urban homesteading.
   c. planned unit development.
   d. modular home.

8. The two characteristics that have the most impact on the market value of land are
   a. uniqueness and immobility.
   b. rental market and sales market.
   c. demographics and construction costs.
   d. residential and commercial.

9. Carol and her husband bought their house in 1968 (when they were 21) for $25,000. Today, the neighborhood has become very fashionable, and they sell the house for $450,000. How much of the gain is taxable on the couple's joint return this year?
   a. $25,000
   b. All
   c. None
   d. $637,000

10. For which of the following risks would a homeowner have to purchase a special policy in addition to a typical basic or broad form homeowner's insurance policy?
    a. The cost of medical expenses for a person injured in the policyholder's home
    b. Theft
    c. Vandalism
    d. Flood damage

11. What is the capital gains tax exclusion available to homeowners who file their income tax singly?
    a. $125,000
    b. $250,000
    c. $225,000
    d. $500,000

12. One result of the 1997 tax law is that *MOST* homeowners
    a. will pay capital gains tax at an 8 percent lower rate on their home sales.
    b. may use a one-time $500,000 exclusion if they file their taxes jointly.
    c. will never pay capital gains tax on the sale of their homes.
    d. will be taxed at a lower rate as they get older.

ANSWERS

1. B   Commercial real estate refers to business property such as office space, shopping centers, storefronts, theaters, hotels, and parking facilities. An apartment building is an example of residential multifamily property. (p. 238)

2. B   When the supply of a commodity increases, producers need to attract buyers so they lower prices. (p. 239)

3. D   The nature of the labor force, construction costs, and government controls affect supply. Employment and wage levels have an impact on the demand side of the supply and demand scale. (p. 241)

4. B   The term equity represents the owner's actual financial ownership in property. Equity is determined by subtracting debts owed against the property from the current market value of the property. (p. 246)

5. D   Expenses included in the cost of home ownership include interest on the mortgage debt, homeowner's insurance, maintenance, and property repairs. Taxes on personal property (not real estate) are not a cost of home ownership. (p. 245)

6. B   The difference between the amount owed on the property and the current market value of the property represents the equity in the property. (p. 246)

7. A   Factories, office buildings, hotels, schools, churches, and other structures that have been converted to residential use are classified as converted-use properties. (p. 243)

8. A   Market value of land is influenced most by the economic characteristic of uniqueness and the physical characteristic of immobility. Uniqueness refers to the fact that no two parcels of real estate are ever exactly alike; immobility refers to the fact that real estate cannot be relocated to satisfy demand where supply is low. (p. 240)

9. C   The federal government excludes up to $500,000 from capital gains tax on the sale of a principal residence by married taxpayers filing joint tax returns. Therefore, Carol and her husband would owe no tax on the gain. (p. 246)

10. D   Owners in flood-prone designated areas are required to have flood insurance. A typical basic or broad form homeowner's policy does not cover damage from floods. (p. 249)

11. B   A taxpayer filing singly is entitled to up to a $250,000 exclusion from capital gains tax liability. (p. 246)

12. C   The net impact of the reforms to federal capital gains tax law that occurred in 1997 is that most homeowners will not have to pay capital gains tax on the sale of their home. (p. 246)

CHAPTER FIFTEEN

REAL ESTATE BROKERAGE

■ LEARNING OBJECTIVES

When you've finished reading this chapter, you should be able to

- identify the role of technology, personnel, and license law in the operation of a real estate business;
- describe antitrust violations common in the real estate industry and the penalties involved with each;
- explain how a broker's compensation is usually determined;
- distinguish employees from independent contractors and explain why the distinction is important; and
- define the key terms.

■ KEY TERMS

antitrust laws	independent contractor	procuring cause
brokerage	personal assistant	ready, willing, and able buyer
commission	price-fixing	
employee		

■ INTRODUCTION TO BROKERAGE

Generally, real estate is an industry driven by small businesses. Most brokerage firms are not giant national companies. Even those that are members of large franchises are still small businesses at heart, and run locally to serve what is essentially a local market. Like any small business, there are challenges and advantages. To be successful, a licensee needs to know not only his or her product (real estate) but also how businesses are run.

Every business owner faces manpower as well as financial decisions. What jobs need to be done, and what kinds of skills are needed to do them? How many people should be hired? Who is the firm's competition and how can the company succeed when 5, 10, 20, or more brokerage companies are all competing for the same business? The answers to these questions are not easy ones, but a successful licensee must think of himself or herself as a businessperson, not just as a salesperson.

As defined in Chapter 14, **brokerage** is the business of bringing parties together for the purpose of purchasing, selling, leasing, or exchanging property. The way brokerage firms do this is governed to a large degree by the state's license law. As discussed in Chapter 13, the law governs such procedures as the brokers' authority and responsibility for the activities of the licensees, the requirements for establishing offices, advertising and escrow account procedures, and the preparation and handling of documents. (Refer to the RELRA and rules and regulations in Appendix C.)

Today's real estate company uses many tools to compete in the marketplace and to enhance the services it provides. Some companies are independently owned and may also be affiliated with national franchises or referral companies; other companies are nationally owned but operated by local brokers. Many companies are affiliated with multiple-listing services (MLSs) to expand the marketing of their listings. By investigating a number of brokerage operations in an area, prospective licensees can learn how companies do business and what benefits are derived from their various affiliations.

The real estate industry has become an information and service business, more so than a land and building business. Today's consumers crave information and a high level of professional service, and as their lives become more hectic, they look for expedient ways to do business. Instant and convenient ways to communicate and access information, all of which are possible because of technology, are essential to their way of life. This means that today's real estate licensees must learn to serve consumers by providing more meaningful and relevant information, producing more comprehensive and professional documents, and relying more on electronic communication than has been customary in the past.

Technology

The provincial way of providing real estate services has given way to a more global approach. Technology has expanded the geographic area licensees serve with regional MLSs. National, and even global, exchange of property information is also possible. Because of computers, information about mortgage loans, demographics, neighborhoods and school districts, cost-of-living comparisons, job-growth and economic conditions, and cultural opportunities—just about any information buyers and sellers need—is readily available. Real estate licensees are a resource to not only provide but also interpret information. Interpretation will become increasingly important because of the volume of information consumers can access themselves on the Internet.

A wide range of technology is available to help a real estate licensee do his or her job more efficiently and effectively. Computers are a necessary ingredient in any modern real estate brokerage operation. Community and mortgage information is accessible on the Internet via the major Internet service providers. Multiple listing and homefinder services are available to real estate professionals through their professional associations. Numerous software packages have been designed specifically for real estate professionals. Some of these programs help real estate brokers and salespersons with such office management tasks as billing, accounting, and timekeeping. Other software assists with marketing and advertising and the design and production of flyers, business cards, pamphlets, and other promotional materials.

Real estate Web sites, home pages, and computer networks help licensees keep in touch, and some cable and satellite television channels are dedicated solely to real estate programming for both consumers and licensees. In some states, including Pennsylvania, continuing education requirements can be met through the use of specially designed continuing education software and the delivery of courses via the Internet. "Distance education," as this is known, is becoming commonplace.

Real estate brokers and salespersons can carry laptop computers with portable modems that link them to their offices, the Web, an MLS, or a mortgage company from virtually anywhere. Portable fax machines, personal digital assistants (PDAs), and cellular telephones keep licensees in touch with their offices, customers, and clients virtually 24 hours a day. Voice-mail systems can track caller response to advertisements and give callers information about specific properties when the broker or salesperson is unavailable. Yard signs are available that prompt passing drivers to tune in to broadcast details about a property on an AM radio band.

All this technology is a great boon to practitioners, but licensees must make wise decisions when selecting high-tech tools. Cost versus benefits, as well as the licensee's technological proficiency, must be weighed. The ultimate decision, however, is based on what the licensee needs to be competitive in today's marketplace.

IN PRACTICE

Home listings are readily available to the general public on Internet Web sites such as *www.homegain.com, www.homes.com,* and *www.cyberhomes.com.* By accessing these sites, potential buyers can preview photographs of properties and search for listings by price range, number of rooms, amenities, neighborhood, or school district. Licensees today report that an increasing number of buyers are previewing properties on the Internet often before they contact a professional for assistance. Recent research indicates that over 70 percent of today's home purchasers begin their search process by first accessing information on the Internet. Not only does the Internet expedite the search process for buyers, but it also helps licensees spend more productive time with their customers and clients.

Personnel

Today's brokerage company hires a variety of personnel. In addition to licensed salespeople, more firms are hiring support staff. These people, who are not licensed, perform clerical and administrative tasks for the company and the salespeople. Their work frees the licensees to devote more time to sales activities and less time to paperwork. Salespeople may also hire their own unlicensed personal assistants.

Real estate assistants.   One member of the support staff that has assumed a prominent role in some brokerage firms is the **personal assistant.** Personal assistants may be licensed or unlicensed. A licensed associate broker or salesperson may employ an *unlicensed* personal assistant to perform activities that do not require licensure. These activities may include erecting "For Sale" signs, maintaining lock-boxes on listed properties, and performing clerical and administrative tasks for the licensee. An unlicensed personal assistant does not have a direct working relationship with a consumer. For example, an unlicensed assistant is not permitted to hold open houses for the public or do telemarketing. The relationship between the associate broker or salesperson and the unlicensed assistant is an employer-employee relationship. The licensee must adhere to all applicable employment and tax laws and may directly compensate the unlicensed assistant.

Licensed personal assistants are employed by the broker. They also are directly compensated by the broker rather than by the associate broker or salesperson they assist. This arrangement requires a three-way agreement with the employing broker, the associate broker or salesperson who is served by the assistant, and the licensed personal assistant. The agreement specifies the responsibilities of all parties, including the activities the assistant is to perform. Because the assistant is licensed (as opposed to unlicensed), the person's activities are not as limited. The employer-broker must adhere to all applicable employment and tax laws and is ultimately responsible under the licensing laws for the licensed assistant's conduct.

■ BROKER-SALESPERSON RELATIONSHIP

Although brokerage firms vary widely in size, few brokers today perform their duties without the assistance of salespersons. Consequently, much of the business's success hinges on the broker-salesperson relationship.

A salesperson is licensed to perform real estate activities on behalf of a licensed broker. The broker is responsible for the actions of all licensees affiliated with the broker. In turn, all of a salesperson's activities must be performed in the name of that broker. The salesperson acts as an extension of the employing broker in providing services to the public. A salesperson is permitted to engage in only those activities assigned by the broker and is permitted to receive compensation for those real estate activities only from the employing broker. As an agent of the broker, the salesperson has no authority to make contracts with or receive compensation from any other party, be it another broker, the buyer, the seller or a referral organization.

Independent Contractor versus Employee

The broker can hire the salesperson as an employee or as an independent contractor. An **employee** is a person who works under the supervision and control of another. On the other hand, an **independent contractor** is a person who is retained to perform a certain act but who is not subject to the control and direction of another. The critical distinction, which is established by the income tax laws, is the degree of control an employer can exercise over a person's activities. The employer cannot control how an independent contractor performs the activities for which he or she is hired.

In Your State **PA** A broker can *require* an employee to follow rules governing such matters as working hours, office routine, attendance at office meetings, and dress codes. As an employer, a broker is required to withhold income, Social Security, and Medicare taxes from wages paid to employees. In Pennsylvania, the broker is also required to withhold state income tax and pay unemployment and workers' compensation. In addition, employees might receive benefits such as health insurance and profit sharing. ∎

A broker's relationship with an independent contractor is quite different. As an independent contractor, a salesperson operates with more autonomy than an employee does. The broker is permitted to control *what* the independent contractor does, but *not how* it is done (as long as all laws are adhered to). The broker cannot require the independent contractor to keep specific office hours or attend sales meetings. Independent contractors are responsible for paying their own income, Social Security, and Medicare taxes. They cannot receive anything from the broker that could be construed as an employee benefit, such as health insurance.

To establish that a salesperson is an independent contractor, the federal tax laws require that

- a person must be properly licensed,
- gross income must be based on production rather than on the number of hours worked, and
- work must be done pursuant to a written agreement in which the independent contractor status is clearly stated.

Because the IRS scrutinizes claims of independent contractor status, it is essential to meet at least these three requirements, otherwise known as the *safe harbor test*. In addition, the employer must also appropriately supervise the person as an independent contractor and not as an employee. In the event of an IRS audit, a written agreement will carry little weight if the actions of the parties contradict the provisions of the contract. The agreement between a broker and a salesperson should also define their respective obligations and responsibilities.

Independent contractor agreement. A written agreement is an essential requirement of the safe harbor test. A broker should have a standardized agreement drafted and scrutinized by an attorney to ensure its compliance with federal law. (See Figure 15.1 for a sample independent contractor agreement.) As a practical matter, a written agreement is simply good business, spelling out the specific terms of the relationship and, thus, minimizing controversies between the broker and the salesperson. Because of the legal and tax implications for the independent contractor as well, the broker isn't the only one who needs professional advice. The independent contractor should

F I G U R E   15.1

Sample Independent Contractor Agreement

BROKER / SALESPERSON   **150**
INDEPENDENT CONTRACTOR AGREEMENT
This form recommended and approved for, but not restricted to use by, the members of the Pennsylvania Association of REALTORS® (PAR).

This Agreement is entered into this (date) _____ between _____
hereinafter referred to as "Broker," and _____, hereinafter referred to as "Salesperson."

Whereas, Broker is engaged in business as a Real Estate Broker and is duly licensed to engage in the activities of a "Broker" as defined by the Pennsylvania Licensing and Registration Act, Act of February 19, 1980, P.L. 15, No. 9, as amended, and

Whereas, Broker maintains one or more offices properly equipped with furnishings, listing books and other equipment necessary and incidental to the proper operation of said business, and staffed with clerical employees, and is thereby suitable to serving the public as a real estate broker; and

Whereas, Salesperson is duly licensed by the Commonwealth of Pennsylvania as a real estate "salesperson" or "associate broker" as defined by the Pennsylvania Licensing and Registration Act, and whereas it is deemed to be to the mutual advantage of Broker and Salesperson to enter this contract upon the terms and conditions hereinafter set forth.

NOW THEREFORE, for and in consideration of the mutual covenants and promises herein contained, the undersigned hereby enter into the following articles of agreement:

1. *Independent Contractor.*
The relationship of Salesperson to Broker is that of an independent contractor. In performing the activities of a real estate "salesperson" as defined by the Real Estate Licensing and Registration Act (hereinafter referred to as "Act"), salesperson shall be free to devote such portion of his/her time, energy, efforts and skill, as he/she deems appropriate. In keeping with the independent contractor status, Salesperson shall be responsible for completing any training required by the Act or other laws of the Commonwealth of Pennsylvania; Salesperson shall work on a commission basis and receive no salary, fringe benefits, medical benefits, pension benefits, or profit sharing; no state, local, unemployment, Social Security or business privilege taxes (where applicable) shall be withheld from Salesperson. Salesperson shall pay all professional licensing fees, errors and omissions insurance premiums (except as otherwise provided herein), multi-listing fees and/or computer access fees. **Salesperson shall not be treated as an employee with respect to the services performed hereunder for federal or state tax purposes or for purposes under the Workers' Compensation Act.**

2. *Sales Effort.*
Salesperson agrees to act as an independent real estate salesperson and shall faithfully, loyally and legally engage his/her efforts to sell, trade, lease or rent any and all real estate listed with Broker, to solicit additional listings, customers and clients for Broker, and to otherwise promote the business of serving the public in real estate transactions to the end that each of the parties hereto may derive the greatest profit possible.

3. *Office Facilities.*
Broker shall from time to time designate the office with which the Salesperson shall be associated. That office shall be provided with such furnishings and equipment as deemed necessary at the discretion of Broker for the proper operation of a real estate office. Broker shall make available to the Salesperson all current listings of the office, and agrees, upon request, to assist the Salesperson in his/her work by advice, instruction, and cooperation, to the extent deemed appropriate by Broker. Salesperson shall pay for long distance telephone charges and for such other forms, equipment, supplies as shall be set forth in Broker's written office policies.

4. *Automobile.*
Salesperson shall furnish his/her own automobile and pay all related expenses and Broker shall have no responsibility relating to Salesperson's automobile or transportation. Salesperson agrees to carry liability insurance upon his/her automobile with minimum liability limits of $300,000 for each person and $500,000 for each accident and with property damage liability limits of $50,000. Salesperson agrees to furnish Broker with a certificate certifying compliance with this requirement to be deposited with Broker on or before the effective date and each renewal date of this Agreement, or at other times as Broker may reasonably request.

5. *Commissions.*
Salesperson shall be entitled to a share of the commissions earned and received by Broker in accordance with Broker's Salesperson Commission Schedule in effect on the date of the act entitling Salesperson to a commission (e.g., obtaining listing, placing property under agreement of sale, etc.) or as otherwise agreed by the parties in writing as to a particular transaction. Broker may alter its Salesperson Commission Schedule from time to time without prior notification. Revisions to the schedule shall be immediately applicable to all future transactions. The division of commissions between Broker and Salesperson shall follow deduction of all expenses according to the Salesperson Commission Schedule. In no case shall Broker be liable to Salesperson for any commissions not collected. All commissions derived from a transaction shall be deposited with the Broker as required by the Act and/or Rules and Regulations of the Real Estate Commission and subsequently paid according to the Salesperson Commission Schedule. This distribution shall take place as soon as practicable after collection and receipt of such commissions. It is understood and agreed that the Salesperson's only remuneration for the services being rendered under this Agreement is the Salesperson's share of the commissions paid by the parties to real estate transactions.

6. *Client Fees.*
In no event shall Salesperson charge less than the commission or fee established by the Broker without the prior written consent of Broker. If Broker shall have entered into a special contract or agreement pertaining to any particular transaction, Broker shall advise Salesperson of such special arrangement. All commissions and fees from a particular transaction shall be payable to the Broker. Salesperson shall not be personally liable to Broker for any commissions not received by Broker from parties to a transaction unless such nonpayment is the result of collusion, intentional or reckless conduct. Broker shall have the exclusive right to determine whether to commence litigation to collect a commission or fee, or to settle any claim for the same.

7. *Ethic and Trade Associations.*
Salesperson and Broker shall conduct business and regulate working schedules so as to maintain and to increase the good will, business, profits, and reputation of Broker and Salesperson and each agrees to conform to and abide by all laws, rules and regulations, and code of ethics that are binding on, or applicable to, real estate brokers and salespersons. Salesperson and Broker shall be governed by the Code of Ethics of the National Association of REALTORS®, the Act, Rules and Regulations of the Real Estate Commission, as the same may be from time to time amended or supplemented, the constitution and by-laws of the local realty board (or such other board or association as may be agreed upon), and the rules and regulations of any multiple listing service with which Broker may now or in the future be affiliated. Broker and Salesperson shall retain membership in good standing with the National Association of REALTORS®, the Pennsylvania Association of REALTORS®, and the local realty board or association designated by Broker or as may be agreed upon by the parties. Whenever Broker is a member of any real estate organization which requires membership of Salesperson in said organization, then Salesperson agrees that he/she shall become a member and pay fees or dues required by such membership. Broker and Salesperson agree to be bound by the rules and regulations of such organizations pertaining to ethics and standards of conduct and procedure. Salesperson acknowledges possession of a current copy of the Pennsylvania Real Estate Licensing and Registration Act, the Rules and Regulations of the Pennsylvania Real Estate Commission, and the Code of Ethics of the National Association of REALTORS® and agrees to be apprised of the provisions thereof so that Salesperson will conduct all activities in a manner consistent with such laws and ethics.

8. *Real Estate License and Dues.*
Salesperson shall pay the cost of any real estate license required by the provisions of any law or regulation of the Commonwealth of Pennsylvania. Salesperson shall further ensure that the requirements for licensure as a real estate salesperson by the Commonwealth of Pennsylvania are satisfied in every respect, including the timely satisfaction of mandatory continuing educational requirements. Salesperson shall pay all dues for membership in the associations set forth in the preceding paragraph of this Agreement in a timely fashion and shall pay all taxes as may be levied upon income or productivity by the federal government, the Internal Revenue Service, the Commonwealth of Pennsylvania, or any local municipality or school district or other such taxing authority including but not limited to income taxes, occupation and occupation privilege taxes, per capita taxes, mercantile or business privilege taxes.

9. *Authority to Contract.*
Salesperson shall have no authority to bind, obligate or commit Broker by any promise or representation, unless specifically authorized by Broker in writing; provided, however, that Salesperson shall and is hereby authorized to execute listing agreements, buyer agency contracts, lease management contracts, as well as all addenda and agreements appurtenant thereto for and on behalf of Broker where not in conflict with Broker's agency practices and provided that the commission involved in such transaction is not less than that determined for such transaction or service by Broker. Prior to entering into any such contract or agreement, Salesperson shall determine the agency and management practices of Broker.

10. *Errors and Omissions Insurance.*
Salesperson shall cooperate fully with Broker in obtaining errors and omissions coverage in an amount, and with deductible, as shall from time to time be determined by Broker. Said insurance shall protect Salesperson against liability which may arise in connection with the conduct of Salesperson as an active real estate licensee. Said policy or policies shall contain an endorsement naming Broker and any subsidiaries of Broker as an additional insured and shall not be subject to cancellation except on a minimum of ten (10) days prior written notice to Broker. A certificate of said insurance shall be deposited with Broker on or before the effective date and each renewal date of this Agreement. The cost of said insurance shall be paid pursuant to the written policy of Broker, or, in the absence thereof, such cost shall be borne by Broker and Salesperson in the same proportion as they would normally share in the commission resulting from a listing and sale of a property as is set forth in the Salesperson Commission Schedule.

FIGURE 15.1

Sample Independent Contractor Agreement (continued)

11. *Listings, Contracts, Correspondence, Records and Forms.*
Salesperson agrees that any and all listings of property, agency agreements, and all actions taken in connection with the real estate business, shall be in the name of Broker. Listings and agency contracts shall be filed with Broker within twenty-four (24) hours after receipt by Salesperson. All listings and agency contracts shall be and remain the exclusive property of Broker. All correspondence received, copies of correspondence written, plats, listing information, memoranda, files, photographs, reports, legal opinions, accounting information, and any and all other instruments, documents or information of any nature whatsoever concerning transactions handled by Broker or Salesperson, or jointly, are and shall remain the property of Broker provided that Salesperson is entitled to a copy of such instruments and information upon reasonable request concerning any transaction in which he/she is personally involved. The parties hereto shall mutually approve and agree upon all correspondence from the office of Broker pertaining to transactions handled by Salesperson, and shall further agree on the forms to be used and the contents of all contracts and other forms before they are presented to clients and customers for signature.

12. *Deposits.*
All deposits received by Salesperson in the course of a real estate transaction of any nature shall be immediately transferred to Broker for deposit pursuant to the Act, the Rules and Regulations of the Real Estate Commission and the agreement of the parties to the transaction; provided, however, that any deposit to be maintained by another broker of record pursuant to the Act, Rules and Regulations of the Real Estate Commission and agreement of the parties to a transaction shall be immediately transferred to such broker with the appropriate notice to the person making such deposit and to Broker.

13. *Indemnification.*
Salesperson shall indemnify and hold Broker harmless from any and all claims, costs, liabilities, and judgments, including attorney's fees, arising from the intentional or reckless acts of Salesperson, or acts outside the scope of Salesperson's authority. When litigation or a dispute arises concerning a transaction in which Salesperson was involved, the parties hereto shall mutually cooperate with each other. In disputes or litigation where there is a claim to the effect that Salesperson has acted intentionally or recklessly or outside the scope of Salesperson's authority, Salesperson shall bear the costs, expenses and liabilities including judgments and awards arising from the dispute or litigation. In disputes or litigation where there is a claim to the effect that Salesperson has acted negligently, Salesperson shall share the costs, expenses and liabilities including judgments and awards arising from the dispute or litigation. Such sharing shall be in the same proportion as the division of commission was, or would have been, from the subject transaction. The sharing of costs, expenses, and liabilities shall be without prejudice to Broker's rights of indemnification unless there has been a resolution of the indemnification issue between the parties hereto. Broker shall select counsel to represent Broker's and Salesperson's interests in litigation with costs borne by the parties in proportion as set forth above pertaining to the sharing of costs.

14. *Termination.*
This Agreement, and the relationship created hereby, may be terminated by either party hereto, with or without cause, at any time upon written notice. Upon termination, all negotiations commenced by Salesperson during the term of this Agreement shall be handled through Broker and with such assistance and cooperation by Salesperson as is reasonable under the circumstances for the protection of the interests of the parties to the real estate transactions involved. Salesperson, upon termination, shall furnish Broker with a bona fide list of all prospects, leads, and probable transactions developed by Salesperson as well as all correspondence and documents described in Paragraph 11 above, which are deemed to be the property of Broker. Salesperson further agrees that upon termination, or in anticipation thereof, he/she will not furnish to any person, firm, company or corporation engaged in the real estate business any information as to Broker's clients, customers, properties, prices, terms of negotiations nor Broker's policies or relationships with clients and customers nor any other information concerning Broker and/or his/her business. Salesperson shall not, after termination of this Agreement, or in contemplation thereof, remove from the files or from the office of Broker any materials, data, publications, correspondence, files or information that is property of Broker. Salesperson shall be entitled to copies of certain instruments pertaining to transactions in which Salesperson has a bona fide interest or pertaining to earnings of Salesperson.

15. *Commissions upon Termination.*
Upon termination, Salesperson's share of commissions on any transactions where a sales contract exists but the transaction has not closed, shall, after the closing of such transaction, be paid to Salesperson in accord with the Salesperson Commission Schedule in effect at the time of termination. There shall be deducted from such share, however, a servicing charge of $ _____ or _____ % of the amount of the listing and/or sales commission, whichever is higher. No commission other than for those properties on which an agreement has been signed and accepted in writing by the buyer and seller on or before termination shall be deemed earned by Salesperson, unless otherwise agreed in writing. Likewise, no commission resulting from the listing for rent, or the rental of property shall be paid to Salesperson following termination with the exception of commissions arising from leases fully executed prior to termination and to the extent that lease payments are received prior to termination. Salesperson shall not, however, share in the commissions payable in the future and based upon the lease options or lease payments not yet due and payable.

16. *Termination Procedure.*
Upon termination by either party, Salesperson shall immediately:
   a) submit a letter of termination with a complete accounting of commissions, listings and buyer clients;
   b) return all supplies, client/customer prospect lists, keys and documents considered property of Broker pursuant to the provisions of this Agreement;
   c) meet with Broker for purposes of attempting to mutually agree upon a final accounting of commissions due and payable;
   d) cooperate in the notification of the Real Estate Commission regarding the termination of the relationship of Broker and Salesperson.

17. *Arbitration of Disputes.*
Disagreements or disputes between Salesperson and Broker, or between Salesperson and a real estate licensee associated with or contracted to Broker, and which arise out of, or in connection with, the real estate business, and which cannot be adjusted by and between the parties involved, shall be submitted for arbitration in accordance with Article XIV of the Code of Ethics of the National Association of REALTORS®. By this Agreement said arbitration shall be mandatory and Broker and Salesperson agree to provide a written agreement to the local association of REALTORS® as may be required by said association as a condition precedent to arbitration. Broker and Salesperson agree to be bound by the decision of the arbitration panel of the local association or the Pennsylvania Association of REALTORS® which has entertained the dispute or disagreement. The conduct of the arbitration shall be governed by the *Code of Ethics and Arbitration Manual* most recently published by the National Association of REALTORS® prior to Arbitration, as amended by the local association hearing the dispute.

18. *Amendments.*
This Agreement may be amended only by the parties hereto, in writing.

19. *Governing Law.*
This Agreement shall be governed by and interpreted pursuant to the laws of the Commonwealth of Pennsylvania.

20. *Successors in Interest.*
This Agreement shall inure to the benefit and be binding upon the successors in interest of Broker. This Agreement, however, is based on the personal services of Salesperson and Salesperson shall not delegate or assign any of Salesperson's rights or duties hereunder without the prior written consent of Broker.

21. *Policy Manual.*
Any office policy or rules and procedures manual now existing or hereafter adopted or amended shall be binding on the parties.

22. *Entire Agreement.*
This Agreement constitutes the entire agreement between the Broker and Salesperson, and there are no agreements or understandings not expressed herein.

IN WITNESS WHEREOF, this Agreement has been executed on the date first above written.

Witness (or attest):

_____   By _____
                                                Broker

Witness:

_____   By _____
                                                Salesperson

Broker should ensure that written office policies describing Salesperson's financial obligations with respect to office supplies, telephone, etc., and a Salesperson Commission Schedule are provided to Salesperson.

get advice about setting up income and expense records and filing appropriate tax returns.

IN PRACTICE

Pennsylvania's real estate license law treats the salesperson as an employee of the broker, regardless of whether the salesperson is considered an employee or an independent contractor for income tax purposes. In the hierarchy of a real estate firm, the broker is accountable for the salesperson's licensed activities and, therefore, can control *what* that individual does to ensure that the conduct complies with the law. Note that this is the "what" in the independent contractor discussion, so the salesperson's status for income tax purposes is immaterial in the context of license law.

A personal assistant is most commonly considered an employee for tax purposes, simply by the very nature of the way the individual's activities are directed, regardless of whether she or he is employed by the broker, associate broker, or salesperson. Obviously, if the personal assistant is licensed, that person is treated as an employee of the broker under license law.

Broker's Compensation

The broker's compensation is normally specified in a listing, buyer agency, or management agreement. Compensation may be a **commission** computed as a *percentage of the amount of consideration in a transaction* (for example, sales price), a *flat fee*, a *fee for service*, or an *hourly rate*. According to the state's license law, compensation must be determined as a result of negotiations. Attempting, however subtly, to impose uniform rates or fees is also a clear violation of state and federal antitrust laws (discussed later in this chapter). A broker may, however, independently determine a compensation structure for that broker's firm. The important point is that the broker and the consumer must agree on compensation arrangements before any services are rendered.

Compensation arrangements between consumers and brokers are beginning to take many forms. As consumers become more aware of the brokerage business and as new service providers enter the industry, the "traditional" business model of broker compensation is undergoing significant change. Traditionally, a seller employed a broker and agreed to pay a percentage of the selling price as the broker's fee. The listing broker often shared the compensation with a selling or cooperating broker. Today, the buyer may directly compensate the buyer's broker, while the seller compensates only the listing broker. It's also possible that the compensation is based on some factor other than a percentage of the selling price.

Some companies charge hourly fees for the services they provide, much like other professions do. Others provide a "cafeteria style" menu of services, with an accompanying schedule of fees for each service. The consumer selects and pays for only those services he or she wishes to use. Still other companies charge a flat fee or discounted commission, depending on the extent of the services provided. In any case, the point is that the needs of today's consumers vary widely. Hence, many brokers are tailoring their services (and accompanying fees) to suit different needs in the marketplace.

Compensation is earned when the work for which the broker was hired to perform has been accomplished. Most sales commissions are *payable* when the sale is consummated by delivery of the seller's deed. However, the commission is generally considered to be *earned* when a ready, willing, and able buyer signs an offer to purchase that is then accepted and executed by the seller, and copies of the agreement of sale have been delivered to all parties.

> To be a *procuring cause*, the broker must have started an unbroken chain of events that ultimately resulted in a sale.

To be entitled to compensation, the broker must be properly licensed, must have been employed to render the service under a valid contract, and must have performed according to the terms of the contract. That broker then compensates the salesperson who represented him or her in the transaction. To be considered the **procuring cause** of a sale, the broker must have taken action to start or to cause a chain of events that resulted in the sale. The specific actions that cause the chain of events are unique in each transaction. The important point is that merely being involved in a transaction, such as showing the property, is different from being the procuring cause. One of the most frequent sources of controversy between licensees involves disputes over which one is the procuring cause.

> A *ready, willing, and able buyer* is one who is prepared to buy on the seller's terms and ready to complete the transaction.

When a seller employs a broker and the seller accepts an offer from a ready, willing, and able buyer, the seller is technically liable for the broker's compensation. A **ready, willing, and able buyer** is one who is *prepared to buy on the seller's terms and ready to take positive steps toward consummating the transaction.* Courts may prevent the broker from receiving compensation if the broker knew the buyer was unable to perform. If the transaction is not consummated, the broker may still be entitled to compensation if the seller

- has a change of mind and refuses to sell;
- has a spouse who refuses to sign the deed;
- has a title with uncorrected defects;
- commits fraud with respect to the transaction;
- is unable to deliver possession within a reasonable time;
- insists on terms not in the listing (for example, the right to restrict the use of the property); or
- has a mutual agreement with the buyer to cancel the transaction.

In other words, a listing broker is *generally due the agreed amount of compensation if a sale is not consummated because of the principal's default.*

When a buyer employs a broker as the buyer's representative to provide services related to the purchase of property, the broker is entitled to the agreed-upon compensation if he or she performs according to the terms of the contract. The buyer could be liable for the compensation even if he or she decided not to purchase the property or purchased a property directly from a "for sale by owner" or through another broker, depending on the terms of the buyer agency contract. Buyer agency contracts are discussed in detail in Chapter 16.

In Your State **PA** According to Pennsylvania license law, it is illegal for a broker to share fees with anyone other than the salesperson licensed with the broker or another licensed broker. Fees, commission, or other compensation cannot be paid to unlicensed persons for services for which real estate licensure is required. Compensation is construed to include personal property (a new television or other premiums, such as vacations and the like) as well as money. This is not to be confused with referral fees paid between brokers for business. Such fees are legal as long as the individuals are licensed brokers. ■

Salesperson's Compensation

The salesperson's compensation is determined by a mutual agreement between the broker and the salesperson. Their agreement should be clearly spelled out in the written contract. The broker may pay a salary (which is becoming more popular in some areas) or pay a share of the commissions from transactions originated by a salesperson. Many companies have graduated commission programs. In these cases, the salespeople earn larger shares of the gross commissions they generate for the company as their production increases. In some companies, a salesperson may draw from an account against earned shares of commissions. In addition, today's brokerage companies often require salespeople to pay sales or administrative expenses, such as promotion, advertising, or clerical fees.

Some firms have adopted a 100 percent commission plan. Salespeople in these companies pay a monthly service charge to the broker to cover the costs of office space, telephones, and supervision. In return, the salespeople receive 100 percent of the commissions from the sales they negotiate. In these situations, the salesperson is typically responsible for advertising, marketing, and other promotional expenses.

Regardless of how the salesperson's compensation is structured, only the employing broker can pay it. In cooperating transactions, the cooperating broker pays a portion of the compensation to the employing broker who then pays the salesperson. (See the Math Concept, Sharing Commissions, which follows.)

MATH CONCEPTS

SHARING COMMISSIONS

A commission might be shared by many people: the listing broker, the listing salesperson, the selling broker, and the selling salesperson. Drawing a diagram can help you determine which person is entitled to receive what amount of the total commission.

Salesperson E, while working for broker H, took a listing on a $73,000 house at a 6 percent commission rate. Salesperson T, while working for broker M, found the buyer for the property. If the property sold for the listed price, the listing broker and the seller broker shared the commission equally, and the selling broker kept 45 percent of what he received, how much did salesperson T receive? (If the broker retained 45 percent of the total commission that he received, his salesperson would receive the balance: 100% − 45% = 55%.)

■ ANTITRUST LAWS

Antitrust Violations
- Price fixing
- Group boycotting
- Allocation of customers
- Allocation of markets
- Tie-in agreements

The real estate industry is subject to federal and state **antitrust laws**. At the federal level, the Sherman Antitrust Law provides specific penalties for a number of illegal business activities. These laws prohibit monopolies as well as any contracts, combinations, and conspiracies that unreasonably restrain trade—that is, acts that interfere with the free flow of goods and services in a competitive marketplace. The most common antitrust violations are price-fixing, group boycotting, allocation of customers or markets, and tie-in agreements.

Price-Fixing

Price-fixing is the practice of setting prices for products or services rather than letting competition in the open market establish those prices. In real estate, price-fixing occurs when competing brokers agree to set uniform sales commissions, fees, or management rates. *Price fixing is illegal.* Brokers must *independently* determine commission rates or fees for *only* their own firms. These decisions must be based on a broker's business judgment and revenue requirements without input from other brokers. Discussions of rates among licensees from different firms could be construed as a price-fixing activity and should be scrupulously avoided.

Multiple-listing organizations, REALTOR® associations, and other professional organizations are not permitted to set fees or commission splits. Nor can they deny membership to a broker based on the broker's compensation schedule. Either practice could lead the public to believe that the industry sanctions not only the unethical practice of withholding cooperation from certain brokers but also condones the illegal practice of restricting open-market competition.

Both brokers and salespeople must avoid conduct that could be perceived as price-fixing as well as the actual practice. For instance, hinting to a prospective client that there is a "going rate" of commission or "normal" fee simply implies that rates are, in fact, standardized. A licensee must make it clear that a stated rate or fee is only what his or her firm charges for services.

Group Boycotting

Group boycotting occurs when two or more businesses conspire against other businesses or agree to withhold their patronage to reduce competition. Group boycotting is also illegal under the antitrust laws. Examples include several brokers conspiring to avoid cooperating with brokers who charge less commission or who practice a different kind of agency representation than they do. A boycott could also arise if a professional organization or a multiple-listing service takes actions or adopts policies that preclude members whose business does not fit with the "mainstream" practices of the organization's members from enjoying the same benefits of affiliation as all other members.

Allocation of Customers or Markets

Allocating customers or markets involves an agreement between brokers to divide their markets and refrain from competing for each other's business. Allocations may be made on a geographic basis, with brokers agreeing to specific territories within which they will operate exclusively. The division may also occur by price range or category of housing. These agreements conspire to eliminate competition.

Tie-in Agreements

Tie-in agreements (also known as tying agreements) are arrangements in which a party agrees to sell one product only on the condition that the buyer also purchases a different or tied product. Frequently, the tied product is less desirable or unique than the other product. These agreements restrain competition because the buyer has to relinquish his or her choice of the tied product to gain access to the tying product. An example is requiring a party to use the broker's services to purchase a new property as a condition of a listing agreement.

Penalties

The penalties for antitrust violations are severe. Violations of the Sherman Antitrust Act are felony offenses punishable by a maximum $100,000 fine and/or imprisonment up to three years for individuals; fines for corporations are higher. In a civil suit a person who has suffered a loss because of the antitrust activities may recover triple the value of the actual damages plus attorney's fees and costs.

IN PRACTICE

Business practices in the real estate industry rise on the Department of Justice's radar screen for scrutiny from time to time. Commission rate practices have traditionally been examined most closely, with percentage rate "norms" or "customs" being targeted for their anticompetitive effect. With some residential brokerage companies today offering menus of services from which consumers can choose (and charging fees for only those selected) and offering discounted packages of services, the price and service options for the consumer have certainly expanded. More competitive options are also available from Internet service providers. But these innovations have also caught the attention of the Department of Justice and the Federal Trade Commission, though not for the reasons one might think. Concerns arise not because more options are available, but from concerns that "traditional" full service brokers may be attempting to restrict the very competition these options create. State real estate regulators, professional associations and multiple-listing services are being challenged to "think outside the box" of full service practices to ensure that their regulations and member service policies don't restrict competition or violate antitrust laws. The Justice Department recently filed legal actions against several industry organizations, but as of this writing, the outcomes are unknown.

■ SUMMARY

Real estate brokerage is the act of bringing people together who wish to buy, sell, exchange, or lease real estate and charging a fee or commission for the service.

Real estate assistants and technology are changing the way that brokerage offices are managed and operated.

The broker's compensation in a real estate sale may take the form of a commission, a flat fee, or an hourly rate. The broker is entitled to compensation when the broker performs according to the terms of the contract he or she entered into with the buyer or seller.

A broker may hire a salesperson to assist in this work. The salesperson works on the broker's behalf as either an employee or an independent contractor. The salesperson's compensation is determined by agreement with the employing broker.

Federal and state antitrust laws prohibit brokers from conspiring to fix prices, engaging in boycotts, allocating customers or markets, or establishing tie-in agreements.

QUESTIONS

1. Which of the following statements best explains the meaning of this sentence: "To recover a commission for brokerage services, a broker must be employed by the seller"?
   a. The broker must work in a real estate office.
   b. The seller must have made an express or implied agreement to pay a commission to the broker for selling the property.
   c. The broker must have asked the seller the price of the property and then found a ready, willing, and able buyer.
   d. The broker must have a salesperson employed in the office.

2. A licensee who is paid in a lump sum and who is personally responsible for paying his or her own taxes is probably a(n)
   a. transactional broker.
   b. buyer's agent.
   c. independent contractor.
   d. employee.

3. M is a licensed real estate salesperson. M's written contract with broker G specifies that M is not an employee. In the last year, just less than half of M's income from real estate transactions came from sales commissions. The remainder was based on an hourly wage paid by G. Using these facts, it is likely that the IRS would classify M as which of the following for federal income tax purposes?
   a. Self-employed
   b. Employee
   c. Independent contractor
   d. Part-time real estate salesperson

4. When acting as an employee rather than an independent contractor, a salesperson is obligated to
   a. list properties in his or her own name.
   b. assume responsibilities assigned by the broker.
   c. accept a commission from another broker.
   d. advertise property on his or her own behalf.

5. A real estate broker learns that her neighbor wishes to sell his house. The broker knows the property well and is able to persuade a buyer to make an offer for the property. The broker then asks the neighbor if the broker can present an offer from the prospective buyer, and the neighbor agrees. At this point, which of the following statements is true?
   a. The neighbor is not obligated to pay the broker a commission.
   b. The buyer is obligated to pay the broker for locating the property.
   c. The neighbor is obligated to pay the broker a commission.
   d. The broker may not be considered the procuring cause without a written contract.

6. A broker would have the right to dictate which of the following to an independent contractor?
   a. Number of hours the person would have to work
   b. Work schedule the person would have to follow
   c. Minimum acceptable dress code for the office
   d. Compensation the person would receive

7. Licensed brokers Fred and Rick were found guilty of conspiring with each other to allocate real estate brokerage markets. Lucy suffered a $90,000 loss because of their activities. If Lucy brings a civil suit against Fred and Rick, what can she expect to recover?
   a. Nothing, a civil suit cannot be brought for damages resulting from antitrust activities
   b. Only $90,000—the amount of actual damages Lucy suffered
   c. Actual damages plus attorney's fees and costs
   d. $270,000 plus attorney's fees and costs

8. Jim and Ruth are both salespersons who work for NMN Realty. One afternoon, they agree to divide their town into a northern region and a southern region. Jim will handle listings in the northern region, and Ruth will handle listings in the southern region. Which of the following statements is true regarding this agreement?
   a. The agreement between Jim and Ruth does not violate antitrust laws.
   b. The agreement between Jim and Ruth constitutes illegal price fixing.
   c. Jim and Ruth have violated the Sherman Antitrust Act and are liable for triple damages.
   d. Jim and Ruth are guilty of group boycotting with regard to other salespersons in their office.

9. A real estate broker will lose the right to compensation in a real estate transaction if he or she
   a. does not advertise the property.
   b. is not licensed when employed.
   c. does not personally market and sell the listing.
   d. accepts a commission from another licensee.

10. After a particularly challenging transaction finally closes, the client gives the listing salesperson, Louise, a check for $500 "for all your extra work." Which of the following statements is accurate?
    a. While such compensation is irregular, it is appropriate for Louise to accept the check.
    b. Louise may receive compensation only from her broker.
    c. Louise should accept the check and deposit it immediately in a special escrow account.
    d. Louise's broker is entitled to 80 percent of the check.

11. A broker has established the following office policy: "All listings taken by any salesperson associated with this real estate brokerage must include compensation based on a 7 percent commission. No lower compensation rate is acceptable." If the broker attempts to impose this uniform commission requirement, which of the following statements is true?
    a. A homeowner may sue the broker for violating the antitrust law's prohibition against price fixing.
    b. The salespersons associated with the brokerage will not be bound by the requirement and may negotiate any commission rate they choose.
    c. The broker must present the uniform commission policy to the local professional association for approval.
    d. The broker may, as a matter of office policy, legally set the minimum commission rate acceptable for the firm.

12. GHI Realty has adopted a 100 percent commission plan. The monthly desk rent required of sales associates is $900, payable on the last day of the month. In August, a sales associate closed an $89,500 sale with a 6 percent commission and a $125,000 sale with a 5.5 percent commission. The salesperson's additional expenses for the month were $1,265. How much of her total monthly income did the salesperson keep?
    a. $10,080c. $11,345
    b. $10,980d. $12,245

13. Diana, a salesperson, took a listing on a house that sold for $129,985. The commission rate was 8 percent. Carol, a salesperson employed by another broker, found the buyer. Diana's broker received 60 percent of the commission on the sale; Carol's broker received 40 percent. If Diana's broker kept 30 percent and paid Diana the remainder, how much did she earn on the sale?
    a. $1,247.86c. $4,367.50
    b. $2,911.66d. $6,239.28

14. A real estate broker who engages salespeople as independent contractors must
    a. withhold income tax from all commissions earned by them.
    b. require them to participate in office insurance plans offered to other salespeople hired as employees.
    c. withhold Social Security from all commissions earned by them.
    d. refrain from controlling how the salesperson conducts his or her business activities.

15. While in the employ of a real estate broker, a salesperson has the authority to
    a. independently negotiate fees for the services they provide.
    b. assume responsibilities assigned by the broker.
    c. accept a commission from another broker.
    d. advertise the property on his or her own behalf.

ANSWERS

1. B The obligation to pay, or entitlement to receive, compensation is a contractual issue. In order for a broker to receive compensation from a seller, they must have an express or implied agreement regarding compensation. (p. 262)

2. C An independent contractor is responsible for paying his or her own income, Social Security, and Medicare taxes. The earnings are not subject to withholding by the employing broker. (p. 258)

3. B The fact M received income based on an hourly wage paid by G demonstrates that M does not meet one of the basic requirements under federal law to be considered an independent contractor. Notwithstanding the contract, M would be classified as an employee. (p. 258)

4. B The primary distinction between an employee and an independent contractor is the extent of control exercised by the employing broker. An employee would be responsible for performing tasks assigned by the broker. (p. 258)

5. A The broker and consumer must agree on compensation arrangements before any services are rendered. Because there was no such discussion, the neighbor is not obligated to pay the broker anything for the service rendered. (p. 261)

6. D The employing broker establishes compensation policies for the firm. An independent contractor and employing broker agree to terms of compensation in a written agreement. The broker does not dictate work schedule, number of hours worked or specific dress code. (p. 258)

7. D In a civil suit alleging a violation of antitrust laws, a person who has suffered a loss because of the activities may recover triple the value of the actual damages plus attorney fees and costs. Lucy could recover $270,000 ($90,000 × 3). (p. 265)

8. A Because Jim and Ruth are both employed by NMN Realty, there is no violation of antitrust laws. Allocating customers or markets involves an agreement between competing

brokerage companies to refrain from competing for each other's business. (p. 264)

9. B For a broker to be entitled to compensation, the broker must be properly licensed, be employed under a valid contract, and perform under the terms of that agreement. An unlicensed party is not entitled to compensation. (p. 262)

10. B As a licensed salesperson, the only party Louise can receive compensation from is her employing broker. Acceptance of any fee, compensation, or other valuable consideration by a salesperson or from anyone other than the employing broker violates the licensing law. (p. 263)

11. D The broker establishes compensation policies for the firm, which the salespersons employed by that broker must then follow. An antitrust violation occurs when two or more competing brokers conspire to fix prices or establish uniform policies. (p. 264)

12. A Commissions earned by the salesperson during the month total $12,245 ($89,500 × 6% or $5,370 plus $125,000 × 5.5% or $6,875). If expenses for the month total $2,165 ($900 desk rent plus $1,265 other expenses), the salesperson kept $10,080 ($12,245 – $2,165). (p. 263)

13. C Total commission earned on the transaction was $10,393.80 ($129,985 × 8%). Diana's broker received 60 percent of the total commission or $6,239.28 ($10,393.80 × 60%). Diana received 70 percent of the amount paid to the broker of $4,367.50 ($6,239.28 × 70%). (p. 263)

14. D The key distinction between a licensed salesperson who is an employee and one who is an independent contractor is the extent of the control exercised by the broker over the salesperson's activities. (p. 258)

15. B A licensed salesperson employed by a broker assumes responsibilities assigned by the broker. The salesperson has no authority to independently negotiate fees, advertise solely in his or her own name or receive compensation from anyone other than the employing broker. (p. 257)

16

AGENCY IN REAL ESTATE

■ LEARNING OBJECTIVES

When you've finished reading this chapter, you should be able to

- identify the various types of agency relationships common in real estate practice and the characteristics of each;
- describe the fiduciary duties involved in an agency relationship;
- explain the process by which agency is created and terminated and the role of disclosure in agency relationships;
- distinguish the duties owed by a licensee to a consumer in the relationships permitted by Pennsylvania license law; and
- define the key terms.

■ KEY TERMS

agency	designated agent	listing broker
agency relationship	dual agency	principal
agency coupled with an interest	express agency	seller's agent
	fiduciary duties	single agency
agent	general agent	special agent
buyer's agent	implied agency	subagency
client	initial interview	subagent
consumer	law of agency	transaction licensee
Consumer Notice		

■ INTRODUCTION TO REAL ESTATE AGENCY

The relationship between a real estate licensee and the parties involved in a real estate transaction is not a simple one. In addition to the parties' assumptions and expectations, the licensee is subject to a wide range of legal and ethical requirements designed to protect the seller, the buyer, and the transaction itself. **Agency** is the word used to describe that special relationship between a real estate licensee and the person he or she represents. Agency is governed by two kinds of law: *common law* (the rules of a society established by tradition and court decisions) and *statutory law* (the laws, rules, and regulations enacted by legislatures and other governing bodies).

History of Agency

The basic framework of the law that governs the licensee's legal responsibilities to the people he or she represents is known as the *common-law law of agency*. The fundamental principles of agency law have remained largely unchanged for hundreds of years. However, practices under the law, particularly in residential real estate transactions, have changed dramatically in recent years. As states enact legislation governing broker-client relationships, brokers face a number of decisions. They must decide whether their firms will represent the seller, the buyer, or both (if permitted by state law) in a transaction. They also must decide how they will cooperate with other brokers, depending on which party each broker represents. In short, the brokerage business is undergoing many changes as brokers strive to enhance their services for buyers and sellers.

Even as laws change, however, the underlying principles that govern the agency relationship remain intact. The principal-agent relationship evolved from the master-servant relationship under English common law. In that relationship, the servant owed absolute loyalty to the master. This loyalty replaced the servant's personal interests as well as any loyalty the servant might owe to others. In a modern-day agency relationship, the agent owes the principal similar loyalty. Just as masters used the services of servants to accomplish what they could not or did not want to do for themselves, principals use the services of agents. The agent is regarded as an expert on whom the principal can rely for specialized professional advice.

■ LAW OF AGENCY

The **law of agency** defines the rights and duties of the principal and the agent. It applies in a variety of business relationships. In real estate transactions, contract law and real estate licensing law—in addition to the law of agency—interpret the relationship between licensees and their clients. Although the law of agency is a common-law concept, it may be (and increasingly is) redefined or replaced by states' statutory laws.

Definitions

> An *agent* is a person authorized to act on behalf of another.
> A *principal* is the one who authorizes an agent to act on his or her behalf.

Both real estate brokers and salespeople have commonly been called "agents." Legally, however, the term **agent** refers to a strictly defined relationship under the law of agency. Real estate licensees are agents only when they are properly authorized to act in this capacity. The law of agency gives specific definitions to the following terms.

■ *Agent*—the person who is authorized and consents to act on behalf of and represent the interest of another. In real estate, a firm's broker is the agent, and he or she shares this responsibility with the licensees who work for the firm.

- *Subagent*—the agent of an agent. If permitted by the original agency agreement, an agent may delegate some authority or responsibility to another party, the subagent. The subagent, because of this extension of the agent's authority, is also an agent of the principal.
- *Principal*—the individual who hires the agent and delegates the responsibility of representing the principal's interests. In real estate, the principal could be the buyer, the seller, the landlord, or the tenant.
- *Agency*—the fiduciary relationship between the principal and the agent.
- *Fiduciary*—the relationship in which the agent is placed in the position of trust and confidence to the principal.
- *Client*—the principal whom the agent represents.
- *Customer*—the third party for whom some level of service is provided, though without representation.

In Your State **PA** In Pennsylvania, agency practices in real estate are defined by the real estate licensing law. Section 201 of the law specifically defines agency relationship, buyer agent, designated agent, dual agent, principal, seller agent, subagent, and transaction licensee. These definitions are intended to clarify the working relationships permitted between licensees and consumers. A **consumer** (a person who is the recipient of any real estate service) may engage a broker to provide services under a variety of working relationships, not all of which cast the broker as an agent or rise to the level of an agency relationship. It is imperative that both the licensee and the consumer clearly understand the scope of the duties and obligations involved in the relationship they create. ■

IN PRACTICE

The practice of agency in real estate will most likely continue to be refined to meet the changing needs of consumers. The fundamentals of agency discussed in this text are consistent with Pennsylvania law that prevails as of this writing. Licensees must monitor legislative and regulatory developments to ensure that their practices are consistent with current laws, rules, and policies.

Fundamentals of Agency

Under the law of agency, an agency relationship is created when one person—the *principal*—delegates to another person—the *agent*—the right to act on his or her behalf in business transactions with third parties. The principles that govern the relationship are:

- The relationship must be consensual. This means the principal delegates authority; the agent consents to act.
- The parties must mutually agree to form the relationship. The agent may reject an agency that he or she is incapable of performing.
- A fiduciary relationship is formed. This means the agent has certain obligations to the principal, including the duty of loyalty (similar to the loyalty the servant owes to the master). The principal regards the agent as an expert on whom the principal can rely to represent his or her best interests.

An agent may be a general agent or special agent, depending on the scope of authority given by the principal. A **general agent** represents the principal in a broad range of matters and may bind the principal to any contracts within the scope of the agent's authority. This type of agency can be created by a general power of attorney. Typically, a broker does not have this scope of authority as an agent in real estate transactions.

A **special agent** represents the principal in one specific act with detailed instructions from the principal. A special agent, however, is not authorized to bind the principal to any contract. The principals must bind themselves to the terms of contracts. *A real estate broker is usually a special agent.*

By definition in the real estate licensing law, an **agency relationship** is one whereby the broker, or licensees in the employ of the broker, acts in a fiduciary capacity for a consumer of real estate services, with the express authority of the consumer. The salesperson is essentially the broker's representative, providing agency services to whomever the broker represents. If the seller is the principal, this means that the broker is the seller's agent; if the buyer is the principal, this means that the broker is the buyer's agent. The salesperson does not become the agent of a buyer or seller independent of directives from the broker.

An agent works *for* the client by working *with* customers.

Client versus customer service. There is a distinction between the level of service an agent provides a client and the level of service a licensee provides a customer. An agent has fiduciary obligations to the *client* and is permitted to offer advice and counsel as a guide for future action or conduct. The act of giving advice implies that the agent has expert professional or technical knowledge the client can rely on (although the agent does not provide legal advice unless separately licensed to do so). In contrast, a *customer* is provided factual information and is entitled to fair and honest dealings as a consumer but does not receive advice and counsel. The agent works *for* the principal and *with* the customer. Essentially, the agent is the principal's advocate, supporting and defending the principal's interests, not the customer's.

Fiduciary Responsibilities

The cornerstone of the law of agency is the *fiduciary responsibilities* an agent assumes on behalf of a principal. These duties are not simply moral or ethical, they are the law—*the law of agency.* Furthermore, the state licensing law imposes statutory requirements on licensees acting as agents, obligating them to perform in ways that protect their clients' interests in real estate transactions. The **fiduciary duties** an agent owes the principal are *care, obedience, accounting, loyalty* (including confidentiality), and *disclosure.* Table 16.1 illustrates how a real estate licensee meets these fiduciary obligations when selling real estate to a buyer who is a client (with representation) as compared to a buyer who is a customer (without representation).

Remember the *five* common-law fiduciary duties by the acronym **COALD:**
■ Care
■ Obedience
■ Accounting
■ Loyalty
■ Disclosure

Care. The agent must exercise a reasonable degree of care while transacting business entrusted to the agent by the principal. The principal expects the agent's skill and expertise in real estate matters to be superior to that of the average person. The most fundamental way in which the broker exercises care is to use that skill and knowledge on the principal's behalf. To do this, the agent should know all facts pertinent to the principal's affairs that will impact the transaction.

T A B L E 16.1

Customer-Level versus Client-Level Service to a Buyer

Customer-Level Service as Subagent	*Client-Level Service as Buyer's Broker*
RESPONSIBILITIES	
Be honest with buyer, but responsible to seller, including duty of skill and care to promote and safeguard seller's best interests.	Be fair with seller, but responsible to buyer, including duty of skill and care to promote and safeguard buyer's best interests.
EARNEST MONEY DEPOSIT	
Collect amount sufficient to protect seller.	Suggest minimum amount, perhaps a promissory note; put money in interest-bearing account; suggest that forfeiture of earnest money may be sole remedy if buyer defaults.
SELLER FINANCING	
Can discuss, but should not encourage, financing terms and contract provisions unfavorable to seller, such as (1) no due-on-sale clause, (2) no deficiency judgment (nonrecourse), (3) unsecured note. If a corporate buyer, suggest seller require personal guaranty.	Suggest terms in best interests of buyer, such as low down payment, deferred interest, long maturity dates, no due-on-sale clause, long grace period, nonrecourse.
DISCLOSURE	
Disclose to seller pertinent facts (which might not be able to disclose if a buyer's broker), such as (1) buyer's willingness to offer higher price or better terms, (2) buyer's urgency to buy, (3) buyer's plans to resell at profit or resubdivide to increase value, (4) buyer is sister of broker.	Disclose to buyer pertinent facts (which might not be able to disclose if subagent of seller), such as (1) seller near bankruptcy or foreclosure, (2) property overpriced, (3) other properties available at better buys, (4) negative features such as poor traffic flow, (5) construction of chemical plant down the street that may affect property value.
NONDISCLOSURE	
Refrain from disclosing to buyer facts that may compromise seller's position (e.g., seller's pending divorce) unless under legal duty to disclose (e.g., zoning violation).	Refrain from disclosing to seller such facts regarding buyer's position as buyer has options on three adjoining parcels. No duty to disclose name of buyer or that broker is loaning buyer money to make down payment.
PROPERTY CONDITION	
Suggest use of "as is" clause, if appropriate to protect seller (still must specify hidden defects).	Require that seller sign property condition statement and confirm representations of condition; require soil and termite inspections, if appropriate; look for negative features and use them to negotiate better price and terms.
DOCUMENTS	
Give buyer a copy of important documents, such as mortgage to be assumed, declaration of restrictions, title report, condominium bylaws, house rules.	Research and explain significant portions of important documents affecting transaction, such as prepayment penalties, subordination, right of first refusal; refer buyer to expert advisers when appropriate.
NEGOTIATION	
Use negotiating strategy and bargaining talents in seller's best interests.	Use negotiating strategy and bargaining talents in buyer's best interests.

Source: *Agency Relationships in Real Estate*, 2nd Edition, by John Reilly. © 1994 Dearborn Financial Publishing®. Used with permission.

TABLE   16.1

Customer-Level versus Client-Level Service to a Buyer (continued)

Customer-Level Service as Subagent	*Client-Level Service as Buyer's Broker*
SHOWING	
Show buyer properties in which broker's commission is protected, such as in-house or MLS-listed properties. Pick best times to show properties. Emphasize attributes and amenities.	Search for best properties for buyer to inspect, widening marketplace to "for sale by owner" properties, lender-owned (REO) properties, probate sales, unlisted properties. View properties at different times to find negative features, such as evening noise, afternoon sun, traffic congestion.
PROPERTY GOALS	
Find buyer the type of property buyer seeks; more concerned with *sale* of seller's property that fits buyer's stated objectives.	Counsel buyer as to developing accurate objectives; may find that buyer who wants apartment building might be better with duplex at half the price or that buyer looking for vacant lot would benefit more from investment in improved property.
OFFERS	
Can help prepare and transmit buyer's offer on behalf of seller; must reveal to seller that buyer has prepared two offers, in case first offer not accepted.	Help buyer prepare strongest offer; can suggest buyer prepare two offers and have broker submit lower offer first without revealing fact of second offer.
POSSESSION DATES	
Consider best date for seller in terms of moving out, notice to existing tenants, impact on insurance, risk of loss provision.	Consider best date for buyer in terms of moving in, storage, favorable risk of loss provision if fire destroys property before closing.
DEFAULT	
Discuss remedies upon default by either party. Point out to seller any attempt by buyer to limit liability (nonrecourse on deposit money is sole liquidated damages).	Suggest seller's remedy be limited to retention of deposit money; consider having seller pay buyer's expenses and cancellation charges if seller defaults.
BIDDING	
Can bid for own account against buyer customer but must disclose this to buyer and seller.	Cannot bid for own account against buyer client.
EFFICIENCY	
Don't expend much time and effort, as in an open listing, because in competition with the listing broker, seller, and other brokers to sell buyer a property before someone else does.	Work with exclusive listing, realizing that broker's role is to assist buyer in locating and acquiring best property, not to sell buyer a particular property.
APPRAISAL	
Unless asked, no duty to disclose low appraisal or fact that broker sold similar unit yesterday for $10,000 less.	Suggest independent appraisal be used to negotiate lower price offer; review seller's comparables from buyer's perspective.
BONUS	
Cannot agree to accept bonus from buyer for obtaining reduction in listed price.	Can receive incentive fee for negotiating reduction in listed price.
TERMINATION	
Easier to terminate subagency relationship (as when broker decides to bid on property).	Legal and ethical implications of agency relationship and certain duties may continue even after clearly documented termination.

If the agent represents the seller, care and skill include helping the seller arrive at an appropriate and realistic listing price, discovering and disclosing facts that affect the seller, and properly presenting the contracts that the seller signs. It also means making reasonable efforts to market the property, such as advertising and holding open houses, and helping the seller evaluate the terms and conditions of offers to purchase.

An agent who represents the buyer is expected to help the buyer locate suitable property and evaluate property values, neighborhood and property conditions, financing alternatives, and offers and counteroffers, all with the buyer's interest in mind.

An agent who fails to make a reasonable effort to properly represent the interests of the principal could be found negligent in court. The agent is liable to the principal for any loss resulting from negligence or carelessness.

Obedience.   The fiduciary relationship obligates the agent to act in good faith at all times, obeying the principal's instructions in accordance with the contract. That obedience, however, is not absolute. The agent may not obey instructions that are unlawful or unethical. The agent, for instance, may not follow instructions that violate the fair housing laws or conceal a defect in the property. Because illegal acts do not serve the principal's best interests, obeying such instructions violates the agent's duty of loyalty. On the other hand, an agent who exceeds the authority assigned in the contract will be liable for any losses that the principal suffers as a result.

Accounting.   The agent must be able to report the status of all funds received from or on behalf of the principal. Brokers are required to deposit and account for escrow funds in the manner prescribed in Pennsylvania's licensing law. Commingling these monies with personal or general business funds is strictly prohibited. Brokers are also required to give copies of all documents to all parties affected by them and keep records of these documents for at least three years.

Loyalty.   The duty of loyalty requires that the agent place the principal's interest above those of all others, including the agent's own self-interest. The agent must be particularly sensitive to any possible conflicts of interest. *Confidentiality* about the personal affairs of the principal is a key element of loyalty (similar to the relationship between a client and an attorney). An agent may not, for example, disclose the principal's financial position.

When the principal is the seller, the agent may not reveal such things as the principal's willingness to accept less than the listing price or his or her anxiousness to sell unless the principal has authorized the disclosure. The agent, however, must disclose material facts about the property. If the principal is the buyer, the agent may not disclose, for instance, that the buyer will pay more than the offered price if necessary, that the buyer is under a tight moving schedule, or any other fact that might harm the principal's bargaining position.

An agent's duty of confidentiality exists not only during the term of the agency relationship but also extends beyond the expiration of that relationship. This means that personal information gained during the course of the relationship with the client may not be disclosed at a later date, even to a subsequent agent. The confidences shared during the agency relationship remain confidential.

An agent may not act out of self-interest. This means that the negotiation of sales agreements must be conducted without regard to how much compensation the agent will receive from the transaction. In addition, a licensee must disclose any personal interest he or she has in purchasing a listed property and must inform a purchaser of any personal interest the licensee has in the property being offered for sale.

Disclosure. The agent has a duty to inform the principal of all facts or information that could affect the principal's position in a transaction. This duty includes the disclosure of pertinent information or material facts that the agent *knows* or *should have known*. A material fact is any information that is relevant to making an informed decision.

The agent is obligated to discover facts that a reasonable person would feel are important in choosing a course of action, regardless of whether they are favorable or unfavorable to the principal's position. The agent may be held liable for damages for failing to disclose such information. For example, an agent for the seller has the duty to disclose:

- all offers;
- the identity of the prospective purchasers, including any relationship the agent has to them (such as when the licensee or a relative is the purchaser);
- the purchaser's ability to complete the sale or offer a higher price;
- any interest the agent has in the buyer (such as the broker's agreement to manage the property after it is purchased); and
- the buyer's intention to resell the property for a profit.

However, a seller's agent is required to disclose to prospective buyers all information about known material defects in the property. While this might seem like a violation of the agent's duty of total allegiance to the seller, this requirement falls under the real estate professional's broader duty to deal honestly with the public, and is in the principal's long-term best interest as well.

An agent for the buyer must disclose deficiencies of a property as well as provisions in a sales contract and financing terms that do not suit the buyer's interests. The agent would suggest the lowest price that the buyer should pay based on comparable values, regardless of the listing price. The agent also would disclose such information as how long the property has been listed or why the seller is selling, which would affect the buyer's ability to negotiate the lowest purchase price. If the agent represents the seller, of course, disclosing any of this information would violate the agent's fiduciary duty to the seller.

Creation of Agency

Agents are employed for their expertise. However, providing services does not in itself create an agency relationship. As previously mentioned, agency exists by mutual consent between the principal and the agent, with the principal authorizing the agent to perform certain acts (subject to the principal's control) and the agent consenting to undertake these duties on behalf of the principal.

Express agency. The principal and agent may enter into a contract, or an *express agreement*, in which the parties formally express their intention to establish an agency relationship and state its terms and conditions. This agreement may be either oral or written. An agency relationship between a seller and a broker is generally created by a written employment contract, commonly referred to as a *listing agreement*. This contract authorizes the broker to find a ready, willing, and able buyer or tenant for the owner's property. An **express agency** relationship between a buyer and a broker is created by a *buyer agency agreement*. Similar to a listing agreement, it stipulates the activities and responsibilities the buyer expects from the broker in finding a suitable property for purchase or rent.

In Your State **PA** In Pennsylvania, all exclusive listing agreements and other contracts of employment must be in writing. Furthermore, the real estate commission's regulations prohibit a licensee from marketing or advertising the sale or lease of real estate or otherwise soliciting prospective buyers without the written authority of the seller or owner (or the owner's agent). ∎

Implied agency. A written contract is not necessary to create an agency relationship. An agency may also be created by *implied agreement*. This occurs when the actions of the parties indicate that they have mutually consented to an agency. A person acts on behalf of another as agent; the other person, as principal, delegates the authority to act. The parties may not have consciously planned to create an agency relationship—nonetheless, it can result *unintentionally, inadvertently,* or *accidentally* by their actions.

Even though licensees are required to disclose their agency status, it is often difficult for customers to understand the complexities of the law of agency. A buyer can easily assume that when he or she contacts a salesperson to show the buyer property, the salesperson becomes his or her agent, even though the salesperson may be *legally* representing the seller under a listing contract. An **implied agency** with a buyer can result if the words and actions of a salesperson do not dispel this assumption. Otherwise, one agency relationship is created in conflict with another. Dual representation, which will be discussed in detail later in this chapter, may occur even though it was not intended.

Compensation

An exchange of consideration can be bargained for (a contractual relationship), or there may be no consideration (a gratuitous agency). The basis of an agency relationship is authorization and consent, *not* compensation. The fiduciary obligations are exactly the same regardless of whether or not the agent is being compensated. Representation is an agency issue while compensation is a contract issue.

The source of the compensation does not determine who is being represented. An agent does not necessarily represent the person who compensates the agent. Responsibility for compensation is determined by specific arrangements in the listing and buyer agency agreements. Traditionally in residential real estate, the seller compensated the broker as agreed to in the listing contract. With the emergence of buyer agency, alternative arrangements have become more common. For instance, the seller may agree to pay the buyer's agent, or the buyer and seller may share the responsibility for compensating their respective agents.

Termination of Agency

An agency may be terminated at any time (except in the case of an agency coupled with an interest) for any of the following reasons:

- Death or incapacity of either party (notice of death is not necessary)
- Destruction or condemnation of the property
- Expiration of the terms of the agency
- Mutual agreement to terminate the agency
- Breach by one of the parties, such as abandonment by the agent or revocation by the principal (in which case the breaching party may be liable for damages)
- By operation of law, as in a bankruptcy of the principal (which terminates the agency contract and title to the property transfers to a court-appointed receiver)
- Completion, performance, or fulfillment of the purpose for which the agency was created

An **agency coupled with an interest** is an agency relationship in which the agent is given an interest in the subject of the agency, such as the property being sold. An agency coupled with an interest *cannot be revoked by the principal or be terminated upon the principal's death.* For example, a broker might agree to supply the financing for a condominium development in exchange for the exclusive right to sell the completed units. Because this is an agency coupled with an interest, the developer would not be able to revoke the listing agreement after the broker provided the financing.

■ TYPES OF AGENCY RELATIONSHIPS

In Your State   **PA**   The Pennsylvania Real Estate Licensing and Registration Act (RELRA) permits a broker to act as

- the agent of a buyer or tenant (known as a *buyer's agent*);
- the agent of a seller or landlord (known as a *seller's agent*);
- a *dual agent* for the seller/landlord and buyer/tenant in the same transaction; or
- a *transaction licensee*. This means that the broker provides customer-level service for both the buyer/tenant and seller/landlord in the transaction and does *not* represent anyone. ■

While the RELRA permits the broker to engage in any of these relationships, the law does not require a broker to offer all of them. The broker may make business or policy decisions about which of the relationships the broker's

FIGURE 16.1

Single Agency

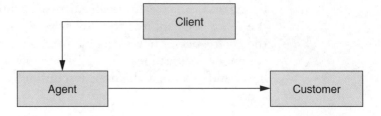

company will offer. This means deciding the parties for whom the company will provide client-level services and those for whom it will provide customer-level services. Because fiduciary obligations cannot be taken lightly, the broker must be sure that the company's agency policies are supported by the company's ability to perform the services.

Regardless of which services the broker's firm offers, the licensees are required to disclose all of the relationships that are permitted by state law so that consumers are aware of their options. This disclosure is provided in the Consumer Notice that is discussed later in this chapter. While licensees have fiduciary responsibilities to their clients, licensees have certain obligations to *all* consumers of their services. These are spelled out in Section 606a of RELRA and can be found in Chapter 13 and Appendix C.

Single Agency

In **single agency,** the agent represents only one party in any single transaction. The agent owes fiduciary duties exclusively to one principal, who may be *either* the buyer or seller (or the landlord or tenant), in the same transaction. The other party receives customer-level services. (See Figure 16.1.)

A single agency broker may choose to *exclusively* represent buyers or sellers. When a company represents buyers exclusively, for example, this means that the sellers of all properties the buyers are shown are that broker's customers. Conversely, when a company represents sellers exclusively, all buyers are customers. Rather than offering exclusive services, a single agency broker may choose to represent both buyers and sellers in *separate* transactions. This must be done carefully, however, to avoid problems that can arise in dual agency, which will be discussed later in this chapter.

Seller as principal. If a seller contracts with a broker to market the property and represent the seller's interests, the broker becomes the **seller's agent.** The seller is the *principal*—the broker's *client*. In single agency, a buyer who contacts the broker to review properties listed with the broker's firm is the broker's *customer*. Though obligated to deal fairly with all parties to a transaction and to comply with all aspects of the license law, the broker is strictly accountable only to the principal—in this case, the seller. The customer (in this case, the buyer) represents himself or herself.

When acting as a seller's agent, licensing law specifically states that a licensee is obligated to make a continuous and good faith effort to find a buyer for the property. The exception is that the seller's agent is not obligated to seek additional offers to purchase the property while the property is subject to an existing agreement of sale.

A listing broker may or may not have a single agency with the seller. According to license law, the **listing broker** may be engaged (in accordance with a written agreement) as a seller's agent, a dual agent, or a transaction licensee to market a property for sale or rent. Although the listing broker may have a single agency, *this is not always the case*. The controlling factor is the nature of the relationship established between the property owner and the broker.

The relationship of a salesperson or an associate broker to an employing broker is also an agency. These licensees are thus agents of the broker and owe the same fiduciary duties as the broker to the principal, who in this case is the seller.

Buyer as principal.   When a buyer contracts with a broker to locate property and represent his or her interests in a transaction, the broker is the **buyer's agent.** The buyer is the *principal*—the broker's *client*. The broker, as agent, is strictly accountable to the buyer. The seller is the *customer*. A buyer agency relationship is established the same way as any other agency relationship: by contract or agreement. This contract also obligates all licensed salespeople affiliated with the broker to represent the buyer. Contrary to popular belief, buyer agency is not a new phenomenon; brokers have been representing buyers in commercial transactions for years. Today, a growing number of homebuyers want to be represented in sales transactions as well.

When acting as a buyer's agent, licensing law specifically states that the licensee must make a continuous and good faith effort to find a property for the buyer. The exception to this is that a buyer's agent is not obligated to seek additional properties for purchase while the buyer is subject to an existing agreement of sale. The law also states that the buyer's agent must disclose to the listing broker that he or she has been engaged to represent the buyer. In the absence of a listing broker, this disclosure shall be made to the seller.

Landlord as principal.   A landlord may employ a broker to market a property for rent to prospective tenants (similar to a listing for sale), or the owner may employ a broker to manage the property under a property management agreement. In either case, the owner is the *principal* and the broker is the agent with fiduciary responsibilities to the property owner, as in any other agency relationship. A written listing agreement or property management agreement sets forth the scope of services to be performed.

Tenant as principal.   A tenant may contract with a broker to locate property suitable for the tenant's specific purposes. In this case, the broker becomes the agent of the tenant (similar to the relationship a broker has with a buyer-client) and the tenant is the principal. The broker has fiduciary obligations to the tenant-client and the landlord/property owner is the broker's customer. It is not uncommon in commercial transactions for brokers to represent tenants in their quest for suitable office or retail space.

Subagency.   A **subagency** is created when one broker appoints other brokers, as subagents, to help perform client-based functions on the principal's behalf. A **subagent** is a broker, not in the employ of the listing broker, who is engaged to act for or cooperate with the listing broker as an agent of the seller. The subagent assumes the same fiduciary obligations to the principal that the agent has. (See Figure 16.2.)

Subagency arises from the theory under common law that the agent of a principal can authorize other agents to act on the principal's behalf. However, license law states that a broker must obtain the *written consent of the principal* to extend subagency. While a broker is permitted to compensate another broker who assists in the marketing and sale or lease of a consumer's property, the payment of compensation alone does not create an agency relationship between the consumer and the other broker.

Multiple-listing services (MLSs) are largely responsible for subagency practices in real estate. These organizations were formed to enable broker-agents to share listings with other MLS brokers, thereby gaining their assistance in locating buyers for the listed properties. A broker's participation in an MLS does not, by itself, create subagency, however. The broker must offer subagency and the seller must authorize it. Today, fewer brokers are offering and fewer principals are authorizing subagency because of the associated liability. In some market areas, the practice of subagency has ceased entirely.

Brokers do commonly cooperate with one another in a sales transaction, but there is a distinction between being a subagent and a cooperating broker. A *cooperating broker*, normally referred to as the selling broker, may be *either* a subagent acting on behalf of the seller *or* a buyer's agent who cooperates with the listing broker to bring a buyer-client and a seller together to effect a sale. In the latter case, the resulting relationship is single agency: The selling broker represents the buyer and the listing broker represents the seller.

The cooperation among brokers who are also competitors is a unique relationship but one that benefits both the industry and the consumer. Even

F I G U R E   16.2

Subagency

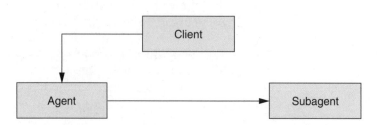

FIGURE   16.3

Dual Agency

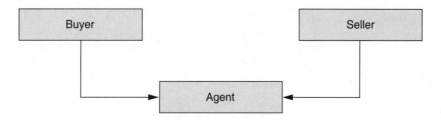

without subagency, the seller/client benefits from the larger pool of potential buyers when brokers cooperate with one another. In fact, a listing broker who refuses to cooperate with a buyer's agent may injure the seller.

Dual Agency

In **dual agency,** the agent—a *dual agent*—represents two principals in the same transaction. (See Figure 16.3.) Dual agency requires equal loyalty to two separate principals at the same time. Because agency originates with the broker, dual agency arises when the broker is the agent of the buyer *and* either the agent or subagent of the seller. The salespeople, as agents of the broker, have fiduciary responsibilities to the same principals as well.

In the strictest terms of the law of agency, the agent must scrupulously fulfill fiduciary obligations to two principals. However, attempting to serve two masters without compromising either principal's interests puts the agent in a virtually impossible position, especially when the parties' interests may not only be separate but even opposite. The confidential information of one principal may be material to the bargaining position of the other. For example, a buyer-client who confides that he or she will pay $5,000 more than the offered price provides information that the agent should communicate to the seller-client.

Both principals ultimately have a common goal—a contract and the satisfactory conclusion of a transaction—and must eventually find common ground for agreement. During the process, the agent is caught in the middle trying to balance fiduciary obligations to both principals. While practical methods of ensuring fairness and equal representation may exist, it should be noted that a dual agent can never fully represent either party's interests. To avoid conflicting agencies or even the appearance of conflict, many agents and principals avoid dual agency entirely.

In Your State

PA **Disclosed dual agency.**   Pennsylvania licensees are not permitted to act for more than one party in a transaction without the knowledge and written consent of all parties being represented. This means that dual agency is permitted only if the buyer and seller are *informed* and *consent* to the broker's representation of both in the same transaction. This is known as *disclosed dual agency*. Merely disclosing that the agent is representing two opposing principals in the same transaction is not sufficient. The disclosure must provide sufficient information so that the parties can make an intelligent determination about whether to authorize dual representation. The Consumer Notice explains the licensee's duties when acting as a dual agent. ∎

Although the possibility of conflict of interest still exists, disclosure intends to minimize the risk for the broker by ensuring that both principals are aware of the effect of dual agency on their respective interests. Presumably, principals are alerted that they may have to assume greater responsibility for protecting their own interests than they otherwise would if they had separate agents. The broker must reconcile how, as agent, he or she will discharge the fiduciary duties on behalf of both principals, particularly providing loyalty and protecting confidential information.

Despite disclosure, debate continues about whether brokers can properly represent both buyers and sellers in the same transaction, particularly when the buyer-principal wants to purchase a property listed by the same broker-agent (known as an in-house sale). Some brokers avoid this situation entirely by representing only buyers *or* sellers as exclusive single agents.

In Your State

PA **Designated agency.** In Pennsylvania, the license law provides an alternative for the dual agency dilemma by permitting the broker (with written consent of the principal) to designate a licensee within the firm to represent the interests of a principal—known as a **designated agent.** The broker is still a dual agent, but separate designated agents, one as the exclusive agent of the seller/landlord and another as the exclusive agent of the buyer/tenant, serve as the legal representatives of the principals. To protect the clients' interests, the law imposes certain duties on the broker and the designated agents. While license law states that licensees employed by a broker bear the same relationship to the consumer as the broker, designated agency is an exception to this rule. In effect, Pennsylvania license law creates a split-agency, which is quite a departure from the common-law doctrines of agency. ∎

Undisclosed dual agency. A broker may not intend to create a dual agency. However, like any other agency, dual agency can occur *unintentionally* or *inadvertently.* Sometimes the cause is carelessness. Other times the salesperson may not fully understand his or her fiduciary responsibilities. Some salespeople lose sight of these responsibilities when their focus is on making the sale. For instance, a salesperson representing the seller might suggest to a buyer that the seller will accept less than the listing price. Or the same salesperson might promise the buyer to persuade the seller to accept an offer that is in the buyer's interest. In these examples, the licensee's conduct can lead the buyer to believe the salesperson is the buyer's advocate.

Any of these actions can create an implied agency with the buyer and violate the duties of loyalty and confidentiality to the principal-seller. Because neither party has been informed of the situation and been given the opportunity to seek separate representation, the interests of both are jeopardized. Not only does undisclosed dual agency violate license law, it also can result in rescission of the agreement of sale, forfeiture of commission, or a lawsuit for damages.

Disclosure   In Your State

PA   State laws throughout the country require licensees to disclose the nature and consequences of the business relationships they may form with consumers. Commonly, these are known as *agency disclosure laws*. Obviously, from the previous discussion, there is considerable information that a person should have before engaging the services of a licensee. In Pennsylvania, the disclosure process begins with the Consumer Notice. The license law requires that licensees give this document to parties before they sign agency contracts or agreements of sale. The purpose is to give a prospective buyer, tenant, seller, or landlord an understanding of the services that are provided to clients and customers. ■

The **Consumer Notice** is a specific form adopted by the Real Estate Commission, which appears in Figure 16.4. This notice is also available in Spanish. (The Commission has adopted different forms for the lease of residential or commercial real estate, and time-share estates.) Note that the consumer must sign and date the form to indicate that it has been received. The major provisions of the Consumer Notice are

- a statement advising the party that a licensee is not representing the consumer unless an agency relationship is selected by signing a written agency agreement;
- general duties a licensee owes all consumers, regardless of the nature of the business relationship;
- descriptions of the business relationships permitted in Pennsylvania: seller agency, buyer agency, dual agency, designated agency, and transaction licensee;
- other information that a consumer should be aware of about real estate transactions; and
- a statement about the Real Estate Recovery Fund.

The Consumer Notice shall be presented to the parties at an initial interview. This is the *first contact between a licensee and a consumer of real estate-related services where a substantive discussion about real estate occurs* (certainly, this should be *before* the licensee provides any services). The law contemplates that this will be the first face-to-face meeting between a licensee and a consumer. However, in practice, telephone conversations or e-mail communications can involve substantive discussions before an in-person meeting. If that occurs, the licensee is required to make the following disclosure to the consumer:

> The initial interview is the first contact where a substantive discussion about real estate occurs.

> *"The real estate law requires that I provide you with a written consumer notice that describes the various business relationship choices that you may have with a real estate licensee. Since we are discussing real estate without you having the benefit of the Consumer Notice, I have the duty to advise you that any information you give me at this time is not considered to be confidential, and any information you give me will not be considered confidential unless and until you and I enter into a business relationship. At our first meeting I will provide you with a written Consumer Notice which explains those business relationships and my corresponding duties to you."*

The Consumer Notice

CONSUMER NOTICE
THIS IS NOT A CONTRACT

CN

Pennsylvania Law requires real estate brokers and salespersons (licensees) to advise consumers who are seeking to sell or purchase residential or commercial real estate or tenants who are seeking to lease residential or commercial real estate where the licensee is working on behalf of the tenant of the business relationships permitted by the Real Estate Licensing and Registration Act. **This notice must be provided to the consumer at the first contact where a substantive discussion about real estate occurs** unless an oral disclosure has been previously provided. If the oral disclosure was provided, this notice must be provided at the first meeting or the first time a property is shown to the consumer by the broker or salesperson.

Before you disclose any information to a licensee, be advised that unless you select an agency relationship the licensee is NOT REPRESENTING YOU. A business relationship of any kind will NOT be presumed but must be established between the consumer and the licensee.

Any licensee who provides you with real estate services owes you the following duties:
*   Exercise reasonable professional skill and care which meets the practice standards required by the Act.
*   Deal honestly and in good faith.
*   Present, in a reasonably practicable period of time, all offers, counteroffers, notices, and communications to and from the parties in writing. The duty to present written offers and counteroffers may be waived if the waiver is in writing.
*   Comply with Real Estate Seller Disclosure Act.
*   Account for escrow and deposit funds.
*   Disclose all conflicts of interest in a reasonably practicable period of time.
*   Provide assistance with document preparation and advise the consumer regarding compliance with laws pertaining to real estate transactions.
*   Advise the consumer to seek expert advice on matters about the transaction that are beyond the licensee's expertise.
*   Keep the consumer informed about the transaction and the tasks to be completed.
*   Disclose financial interest in a service, such as financial, title transfer and preparation services, insurance, construction, repair or inspection, at the time service is recommended or the first time the licensee learns that the service will be used.

A licensee may have the following business relationships with the consumer:

Seller Agency:
Seller agency is a relationship where the licensee, upon entering into a written agreement, works only for a seller/landlord. Seller's agents owe the additional duties of:
*   Loyalty to the seller/landlord by acting in the seller's/landlord's best interest.
*   Confidentiality, except that a licensee has a duty to reveal known material defects about the property.
*   Making a continuous and good faith effort to find a buyer for the property, except while the property is subject to an existing agreement.
*   Disclosure to other parties in the transaction that the licensee has been engaged as a seller's agent.

A seller's agent may compensate other brokers as subagents if the seller/landlord agrees in writing. Subagents have the same duties and obligations as the seller's agent. Seller's agents may also compensate buyer's agents and transaction licensees who do not have the same duties and obligations as seller's agents.

If you enter into a written agreement, the licensees in the real estate company owe you the additional duties identified above under seller agency. The exception is designated agency. See the designated agency section in this notice for more information.

Buyer Agency:
Buyer agency is a relationship where the licensee, upon entering into a written agreement, works only for the buyer/tenant. Buyer's agents owe the additional duties of:
*   Loyalty to the buyer/tenant by acting in the buyer's/tenant's best interest.
*   Confidentiality, except that a licensee is required to disclose known material defects about the property.
*   Making a continuous and good faith effort to find a property for the buyer/tenant, except while the buyer is subject to an existing contract.
*   Disclosure to other parties in the transaction that the licensee has been engaged as a buyer's agent.

A buyer's agent may be paid fees, which may include a percentage of the purchase price, and, even if paid by the seller/landlord, will represent the interests of the buyer/tenant.

If you enter into a written agreement, the licensees in the real estate company owe you the additional duties identified above under buyer agency. The exception is designated agency. See the designated agency section in this notice for more information.

Dual Agency:
Dual agency is a relationship where the licensee acts as the agent for both the seller/landlord and the buyer/tenant in the same transaction with the written consent of all parties. Dual agents owe the additional duties of:
*   Taking no action that is adverse or detrimental to either party's interest in the transaction.
*   Unless otherwise agreed to in writing, making a continuous and good faith effort to find a buyer for the property and a property for the buyer, unless either are subject to an existing contract.
*   Confidentiality, except that a licensee is required to disclose known material defects about the property.

COPIES: GREEN–CONSUMER; WHITE–BROKER 4/02

FIGURE   16.4

The Consumer Notice (continued)

Designated Agency:

In designated agency, the employing broker may, with your consent, designate one or more licensees from the real estate company to represent you. Other licensees in the company may represent another party and shall not be provided with any confidential information. The designated agent(s) shall have the duties as listed above under seller agency and buyer agency.

In designated agency, the employing broker will be a dual agent and have the additional duties of:
- Taking reasonable care to protect any confidential information disclosed to the licensee.
- Taking responsibility to direct and supervise the business activities of the licensees who represent the seller and buyer while taking no action that is adverse or detrimental to either party's interest in the transaction.

The designation may take place at the time that the parties enter into a written agreement, but may occur at a later time. Regardless of when the designation takes place, the employing broker is responsible for ensuring that confidential information is not disclosed.

Transaction Licensee:

A transaction licensee is a broker or salesperson who provides communication or document preparation services or performs other acts for which a license is required **WITHOUT being the agent or advocate** for either the seller/landlord or the buyer/tenant. Upon signing a written agreement or disclosure statement, a transaction licensee has the additional duty of limited confidentiality in that the following information may not be disclosed:
- The seller/landlord will accept a price less than the asking/listing price.
- The buyer/tenant will pay a price greater than the price submitted in a written offer.
- The seller/landlord or buyer/tenant will agree to financing terms other than those offered.

Other information deemed confidential by the consumer shall not be provided to the transaction licensee.

OTHER INFORMATION ABOUT REAL ESTATE TRANSACTIONS

The following are negotiable and shall be addressed in an agreement/disclosure statement with the licensee:
- The duration of the employment, listing agreement or contract.
- The fees or commissions.
- The scope of the activities or practices.
- The broker's cooperation with other brokers, including the sharing of fees.

Any sales agreement must contain the zoning classification of a property except in cases where the property is zoned solely or primarily to permit single family dwellings.

A Real Estate Recovery Fund exists to reimburse any person who has obtained a final civil judgment against a Pennsylvania real estate licensee owing to fraud, misrepresentation, or deceit in a real estate transaction and who has been unable to collect the judgment after exhausting all legal and equitable remedies. For complete details about the Fund, call (717) 783-3658.

ACKNOWLEDGMENT

I acknowledge that I have received this disclosure.

Date: _____

Print (Consumer)	Print (Consumer)
Signed (Consumer)	Signed (Consumer)
Address (optional)	Address (optional)
Phone Number (optional)	Phone Number (optional)

I certify that I have provided this document to the above consumer.

Date: _____

Print   (Licensee)

Signed   (Licensee)

Adopted by the State Real Estate Commission at 49 Pa. Code §35.336.

This disclosure statement intends to make sure a consumer is aware that he or she may be divulging personal information to a licensee who is not, and may not ever become, the consumer's agent. Hopefully, the consumer will be discouraged from sharing confidential information that should not be entrusted to a licensee without the benefit of an agency relationship.

The disclosure process does not end with the Consumer Notice. The broker of the real estate firm must establish procedures for disclosing

- the specific types of services the firm provides;
- the party the licensee represents in a specific transaction;
- company policies regarding dual agency and designated agency; and
- company policies regarding cooperation with other brokers.

IN PRACTICE

Licensees must be familiar with the various business relationships permitted in Pennsylvania and the activities involved when serving clients versus customers so they can properly explain their services to consumers. Equally important is that licensees must also conduct themselves in ways that are consistent with the level of service a consumer engages them to provide.

■ CUSTOMER-LEVEL SERVICE

Customarily, the broker is an agent for someone in a real estate transaction. This means that in addition to providing client-level service, the broker is also providing customer-level service to someone in the transaction. There are times, however, when the licensee doesn't represent anyone in a transaction. This means that the licensee is providing customer-level services to all parties. While considerable discussion has been devoted to the obligations of agents, licensees have equally important duties when servicing customers. The licensee must adhere to the consumer protection laws and the ethical provisions of the licensing law. Licensees also owe certain duties to all consumers as provided in Section 606a of the license law.

Transaction Licensee In Your State

PA In Pennsylvania, a licensee is permitted to act as a **transaction licensee.** In this relationship, a broker or salesperson provides communications, document preparation services, and otherwise assists both parties in a transaction without being an agent or advocate of either party. A transaction licensee is required to advise the consumer that the licensee is not acting as an agent and should not be provided with confidential information. The law does state, however, that a transaction licensee must provide limited confidentiality. This means that a licensee is not permitted to disclose that the seller will accept less than the asking or listed price, that the buyer will pay more than the price submitted in a written offer, or that either the seller or buyer will agree to financing terms other than those offered. While permissible under the law, transaction licensees are not very common. ■

■ SUMMARY

The law of agency governs the principal-agent relationship. The license law in Pennsylvania defines the relationships between consumers and licensees that are permitted. Agents have fiduciary duties to their clients. Licensees owe both clients and customers certain duties as well.

Agency relationships may be expressed either by the words of the parties or written agreements, or implied by their actions. The source of compensation does not determine the party who is being represented.

In single agency, the broker/agent represents one party in a transaction. The agent may seek the participation of subagents to assist the broker in serving the principal. Dual agency occurs when the broker represents two opposite parties in the same transaction. Disclosed dual agency requires that both principals be informed of and give consent to the broker's multiple representations. Licensees must be careful not to create a dual agency when none was intended.

Pennsylvania law requires licensees to provide a Consumer Notice at an initial interview. This is a disclosure notice that informs consumers about permitted relationships and describes the licensees' duties.

Customer-level service is provided to a consumer in a transaction when the licensee is not acting as his or her agent. In addition, a transaction licensee may provide customer-level services to all parties in a transaction.

QUESTIONS

1. A person who has the authority to enter into contracts concerning all business affairs of another is called
   a. a general agent.
   b. a secret agent.
   c. a special agent.
   d. an attorney.

2. The term *fiduciary* refers to
   a. the sale of real property.
   b. principles by which a seller must conduct his or her business affairs.
   c. one who authorizes another to act on his behalf.
   d. the principal-agent relationship.

3. The legal relationship between broker and seller is most frequently a
   a. special agency.
   b. general agency
   c. secret agency.
   d. universal agency.

4. A real estate broker acting as the agent of the seller
   a. is obligated to render faithful service to the seller.
   b. can make a profit, if possible, in addition to the commission.
   c. can agree to a change in price without the seller's approval.
   d. can accept a commission from the buyer without the seller's approval.

5. In a dual agency situation, a broker may be compensated by both the seller and the buyer if
   a. the broker has informed either the buyer or the seller that he or she will receive a commission from both parties.
   b. the buyer and the seller are related by blood or marriage.
   c. both parties give their informed written consent to the dual compensation.
   d. both parties are represented by attorneys.

6. A broker may represent both the seller and the buyer when
   a. the broker holds a state license as a dual agent.
   b. the buyer and the seller are related.
   c. both parties give informed written consent to such a transaction.
   d. both parties have attorneys who authorize the dual representation.

7. In a fiduciary relationship, the agent is primarily responsible to the
   a. customer.c. lender
   b. client.d. lending broker.

8. Under the law of agency, a real estate broker owes all of the following to the principal *EXCEPT*
   a. care.
   b. obedience.
   c. disclosure.
   d. advertising.

9. Which of the following events terminates an agency in a broker-seller relationship?
   a. The broker discovers that the market value of the property is such that he or she will not make an adequate commission.
   b. The owner declares personal bankruptcy.
   c. The owner abandons the property.
   d. The broker appoints other brokers to help sell the property.

10. A licensee is hired by a first-time buyer to help the buyer purchase a home. The buyer confides that being approved for a mortgage loan may be complicated by the fact that the buyer filed for bankruptcy two years ago. A correct statement about the licensee's responsibility regarding this information during the presentation of an offer to purchase a property that is for sale by owner is that the licensee is
    a. required to disclose it under the Fair Credit Registry Act.
    b. required to disclose it because bankruptcies are a matter of public record.
    c. not required to disclose it owing to the client's request for confidentiality.
    d. not required to disclose it because the licensee has no agency relationship with the seller.

11. Broker *D* lists *K*'s residence for $87,000. *K*'s employer has transferred her to another state, and she must sell her house quickly. To expedite the sale, *D* tells a prospective purchaser that *K* will accept at least $5,000 less than the listed price for the property. Based on these facts, all of the following statements are true *EXCEPT*
    a. *D* has violated his agency responsibilities to *K*.
    b. *D* should not have disclosed this information, regardless of its accuracy.
    c. *D* should have disclosed only the lowest price that *K* would accept.
    d. *D* has a special agency relationship with *K*.

12. A buyer who is a client of the broker wants to purchase a house that the broker has listed for sale. Which of the following is true?
    a. If the listing salesperson and selling salesperson are two different people, there is no conflict of interest.
    b. The broker should refer the buyer to another broker to negotiate the sale.
    c. The seller and buyer must be informed and agree to have the broker represent both of them.
    d. The buyer should not have been shown a house listed by the broker representing them.

13. A seller lists a home with a broker for $98,000. Later that week, an acquaintance comes into the broker's office and asks for general information about homes for sale in the $90,000 to $100,000 price range. Based on these facts, which of the following statements is true?
    a. Both the seller and the buyer are the broker's customers.
    b. The seller is the broker's customer; the buyer is the client.
    c. The buyer is the broker's customer; the seller is the broker's client.
    d. If the buyer asks the broker to present an offer to the seller, the broker must ask both parties to sign a disclosed dual agency agreement.

14. A real estate licensee was representing a buyer. At their first meeting, the buyer explained that he planned to operate a dog-grooming business out of any house he bought. The licensee did not check the local zoning ordinances to determine in which parts of town such a business could be conducted. Which fiduciary duty did the licensee violate?
    a. Care
    b. Obedience
    c. Loyalty
    d. Accounting

ANSWERS

1. A A general agent represents the principal in a broad range of business matters and has the power to bind the principal to contracts within the scope of the agent's authority. (p. 272)

2. D The term fiduciary refers to the nature of the relationship created when the agent is placed in the position of trust and confidence when representing the principal. (p. 273)

3. A When a broker is engaged by a seller to represent the seller in the sale of a property, the broker is a special agent. The broker is authorized to represent the seller in one specific act with detailed instructions as specified in a contract. (p. 273)

4. A As an agent of the seller, the broker owes full fiduciary duties to the principal-seller. Faithful service to the seller when acting as the seller's advocate is of utmost importance under the agent's fiduciary duties to the principal-seller. (p. 272)

5. C Representation is an agency issue; compensation is a contract issue. When the broker represents both the buyer and the seller in the same transaction, the dual representation must be fully disclosed and both parties must give their informed consent in writing. The broker may be compensated by both the buyer and seller as stipulated in the agency contracts. (p. 279)

6. C Brokers can provide dual agency only if the buyer and seller are fully informed and consent in writing to the broker's representation of both parties in the same transaction. The parties must be provided sufficient information to make an intelligent determination about whether or not to agree to the dual representation. (p. 284)

7. B In a fiduciary relationship, the primary responsibility of an agent is to protect the interests of the client in a transaction. The agent is morally, ethically and legally responsible to the client if there is a breach of the fiduciary duties owed to the principal. (p. 273)

8. D Fiduciary duties an agent owes the principal include care, obedience, accounting, loyalty (including confidentiality) and disclosure. Advertising is not a fiduciary duty. (p. 273)

9. B An agency relationship may be terminated in a number of ways. One is by operation of law, such as personal bankruptcy of the principal. The relationship between the seller and agent-broker terminates and title to the property transfers to a court-appointed receiver. (p. 279)

10. D The licensee has an agency relationship with the buyer, who is the principal. Fiduciary duties, including confidentiality about the bankruptcy proceeding, are owed to the buyer. The licensee has no agency relationship with the for-sale-by-owner seller. (p. 277)

11. C Broker D owes fiduciary duties to client K, including the obligation to work in K's best interest and be an advocate for her position. Disclosing the lowest price K would accept would be a violation of D's duty to K. (p. 273)

12. C The broker has created an agency relationship with both the buyer and the seller. This dual agency is permitted only after full disclosure and the informed consent by both parties. Informed consent must be in writing in Pennsylvania. (p. 284)

13. C The seller and broker have created an agency relationship, with the seller being the principal or client of the broker. There is no agency relationship with the prospect inquiring about homes for sale, so the buyer-prospect is a customer of the broker. (p. 273)

14. A A licensee who has been provided specific information by a client has a duty to exercise care while transacting business on behalf of that client. This duty would include determining suitability of the property for the client's intended use. (p. 273)

17

ETHICAL PRACTICES AND FAIR HOUSING

■ LEARNING OBJECTIVES

When you've finished reading this chapter, you should be able to

- distinguish between law and ethics;
- identify protected classes under applicable state and federal fair housing laws;
- describe how state and federal fair housing laws are enforced, including penalties and sanctions;
- explain the impact of federal and state fair housing laws on the conduct of licensees, including advertising and marketing practices; and
- define the key terms.

■ KEY TERMS

Americans with Disabilities Act (ADA)	disparate impact	Fair Housing Act
blockbusting	Equal Credit Opportunity Act (ECOA)	Pennsylvania Human Relations Act (PHRA)
Civil Rights Act of 1866		redlining
code of ethics	ethics	steering

■ PROFESSIONAL ETHICS

Professional conduct involves more than just complying with the law. In real estate, the state licensing laws establish those activities that are illegal and therefore prohibited. However, merely complying with the letter of the law may not be enough. Licensees may perform *legally*, yet not *ethically*. **Ethics** involves a set of beliefs that guide a person's actions. Behavior is right, wrong, good, bad, and so forth, as defined by the ethics of various groups or cultures. Business organizations develop a system of moral principles, rules, and standards of conduct to guide behavior that goes beyond merely complying with the law. These systems create standards of professional ethics.

Professional ethics involve moral principles that establish standards for integrity and competence when dealing with the consumers of an industry's services and a code of conduct for relations among professionals within the industry. A fundamental rule of professional ethics is to "above all, do no harm." A course of action may appear to be justified because it is not illegal. However, if it causes harm to the client, the customer, the public, or other licensees, it violates the rule of ethical behavior.

Code of Ethics

One way many organizations address ethics among their members or within their companies is by adopting codes of professional conduct. A **code of ethics** is a written system of standards for that conduct. These codes contain statements that are designed to advise, guide, and regulate job behavior. Lofty statements of positive goals are not especially helpful, however. To be effective, a code of ethics must be specific by dictating rules that either prohibit or demand certain behavior. The code usually includes references to topics such as conflict of interest, compliance with the law, commitment to protecting the public good, and maintaining a high standard of business conduct. By including sanctions for violators, a code of ethics becomes more effective.

The National Association of REALTORS® (NAR), the largest trade association in the country, adopted a Code of Ethics for its members in 1913. REALTORS® are expected to subscribe to this strict code of conduct. NAR has established procedures for professional standards committees to administer compliance at the local, state, and national levels of the organization. Interpretations of the Code are known as Standards of Practice. Although the Code of Ethics is adopted specifically for NAR members, it can be a useful guide of conduct for all real estate licensees. The REALTOR® Code of Ethics and Standards of Practice is reprinted in Appendix D.

Code for Equal Opportunity

The *Code for Equal Opportunity* prescribes standards of conduct to help REALTORS® comply with the letter as well as the spirit of the fair housing laws (to be discussed later in this chapter). The Code provides five basic guides for conduct:

1. In the sale, purchase, exchange, rental, or lease of real property, members have the responsibility to offer equal service to all clients and prospects without regard to race, color, religion, sex, handicap, familial status, or national origin. Activities include
   - entering broker-client relationships to sell or show property equally to members of all races, religious creeds, or ethnic groups; receiving all formal written offers and communicating them to the owner;
   - exerting their best efforts to conclude all transactions; and
   - maintaining equal opportunity employment practices.
2. When performing their agency functions, members have no right or responsibility to volunteer information regarding the race, religious creed, or ethnic composition of any neighborhood.
3. Members shall not engage in any activity that has the purpose of inducing panic selling.
4. Members shall not print, display, or circulate any statement or advertisement with respect to the sale or rental of a dwelling that

indicates any preference, limitations, or discrimination based on race, color, religion, sex, or ethnic background.

5. Members who violate the spirit or any provision of the Code of Equal Opportunity shall be subject to disciplinary action.

The NAR has also entered into a Fair Housing Partnership Agreement with HUD to jointly promote fair housing and address common concerns. The Fair Housing Partnership Agreement is based on the principle that achieving fair housing requires cooperative efforts among all participants in the housing community. HUD and NAR work through the National Homeownership Strategy to broaden the impact of the partnership with other community housing organizations.

■ EQUAL OPPORTUNITY

The purpose of civil rights laws in real estate is to create a marketplace in which all persons of similar financial means have a similar range of choices in the purchase, rental, or financing of real property. The goal is to create an open, unbiased housing market in which everyone has the opportunity to live where he or she chooses. Owners, real estate licensees, apartment management companies, real estate organizations, lending agencies, builders, and developers must all take part in creating this single housing market. Federal, state, and local fair housing or equal opportunity laws affect every phase of a real estate transaction, from listing to closing.

The U.S. Congress and the Supreme Court have created a legal framework that preserves the constitutional rights of all citizens. However, while the passage of laws may establish rules for public conduct, centuries of discriminatory practices and attitudes are not so easily changed. Real estate licensees cannot allow their own prejudices to interfere with the ethical and legal conduct of their business. Similarly, the discriminatory attitudes of property owners or property seekers must not be allowed to affect compliance with the fair housing laws. This is not always easy, and the pressure to avoid offending the person who pays the commission can be intense. However, *failure to comply with fair housing laws is both a civil and criminal violation, and grounds for disciplinary action against a licensee.*

■ FEDERAL LAWS

The federal government's effort to guarantee equal housing opportunities to all U.S. citizens began with the passage of the **Civil Rights Act of 1866.** This law prohibits any type of discrimination based on race, stating that "All citizens of the United States shall have the same right in every state and territory as is enjoyed by white citizens thereof to inherit, purchase, lease, sell, hold, and convey real and personal property."

In 1896, the U.S. Supreme Court established the "separate but equal" doctrine of legalized segregation. A series of court decisions and federal laws in the 20 years between 1948 and 1968 attempted to address the inequities in housing that resulted from the 1896 case. Those efforts, however, tended to address only certain aspects of the housing market (such as federally funded housing programs). As a result, their impact was limited. Not until Title VIII of the Civil Rights Act of 1968 was passed were specific discriminatory practices throughout the real estate industry prohibited.

Fair Housing Act

Title VIII of the Civil Rights Act of 1968 originally prohibited discrimination in housing because of race, color, religion, and national origin. In 1974, the Housing and Community Development Act added sex to the list of protected classes. In 1988, the Fair Housing Amendments Act included handicap and familial status. Today, the law is known as the **Fair Housing Act.** It prohibits discrimination based on *race, color, religion, sex, handicap, familial status, and national origin*, which are known as the *protected classes*.

The Fair Housing Act prohibits discrimination based on

■ Race
■ Color
■ Religion
■ Sex
■ Handicap
■ Familial status
■ National origin

The Department of Housing and Urban Development (HUD) administers the Fair Housing Act, and has promulgated rules and regulations to interpret legal practices further. The regulations define housing as a dwelling, being any building or portion thereof (including a single-family house, condominium, cooperative, or mobile home), designed for occupancy as a residence by one or more families. This also includes vacant land for sale or lease for the location or construction of these structures.

The Fair Housing Act states that, relating to persons in the protected classes, it shall be unlawful to

■ refuse to sell, rent, or negotiate with any person or otherwise make a dwelling unavailable;
■ differentiate in terms, conditions, or services for the purpose of discriminating;
■ practice discrimination through any statement or advertisement that indicates any preference, limitation, or discrimination;
■ represent that a property is not available when in fact it is available for sale or rent;
■ make a profit by inducing owners to sell or rent because of the prospective entry into the neighborhood of persons in the protected classes;
■ alter the terms or conditions for a loan for the purchase, construction, improvement, or repair of a dwelling as a means of discrimination; or
■ deny membership or limit the participation in any real estate organization as a means of discriminating.

In addition to these general provisions of the law, HUD's rules and regulations define specific procedures that affect practices in the real estate industry, mortgage lending, and advertising.

Familial status. *Familial status* refers to the presence of one or more individuals who have not reached the age of 18 and who live with either a parent or guardian. The term also includes a woman who is pregnant. In effect, this means that the Fair Housing Act's protections extend to families with children. Unless a property qualifies as housing for older persons, all properties must be made available to families with children under the same terms and conditions as to anyone else. It is illegal to advertise properties as being for adults only or to indicate a preference for a certain number of children. The number of persons permitted to reside in a property (the occupancy standards) must be based on such objective factors as sanitation or safety. Landlords cannot restrict the number of occupants with the intent of eliminating families with children.

> The definitions of *handicap* under the Fair Housing Act and *disability* under the Americans with Disabilities Act are the same. "Disability" is the socially preferred of the two terms.

Handicap or disability.   *Handicap* is defined in the law as a physical or mental impairment that substantially limits one or more of a person's major life activities. The term also includes having a history of, or being regarded as having, such a condition. It does *not* include the current illegal use of or addiction to a controlled substance. However, a person in an addiction recovery program may qualify under the definition. Persons who have the HIV virus (AIDS), with or without evidence of disease, are protected by the fair housing laws.

It is unlawful to discriminate against prospective buyers or tenants based on a handicap. Landlords must make reasonable accommodations to existing policies, practices, or services to permit persons with disabilities to have equal enjoyment of the premises. For instance, it would be reasonable for a landlord to permit support animals (such as guide dogs) in a normally "no-pet" building or to provide a designated handicapped parking space in a generally unreserved lot.

People with disabilities must be permitted, at their own expense, to make reasonable modifications to the premises that may be necessary for their full enjoyment. However, the law recognizes that some reasonable modifications might make a rental property undesirable to the general population. In such a case, the landlord is allowed to require that the tenant restore the interior of the property to its previous condition when the lease period ends.

The law does not prohibit restricting occupancy exclusively to persons with a handicap in dwellings that are designed specifically for their accommodation.

New construction of certain multifamily properties built with federal funds must meet accessibility requirements for public and common-use portions of the buildings and adaptive and accessible design standards for the interior of dwelling units.

Exemptions to the Fair Housing Act   `In Your State`

PA   The federal Fair Housing Act provides for certain exemptions. It is important for licensees to know in what situations they apply. There are *no* exceptions involving race *or* in transactions involving a real estate licensee. In addition, *most of the exemptions in the federal law do not apply under Pennsylvania law* (which is discussed later in this chapter). The federal exemptions—with Pennsylvania exceptions—include the following:

■ The sale or rental of a single-family home is exempt when the home is owned by an individual who does not own more than three such homes at one time (and who does not sell more than one every two years) and when a real estate licensee and discriminatory advertising is not used in the transaction. *This exemption does not apply under Pennsylvania law.*

■ The rental of rooms or units is exempt in an owner-occupied one- to four-family dwelling. *Pennsylvania law only recognizes an exemption in the rental of an owner-occupied two-unit dwelling; an owner-occupied rooming house with a common entrance and shared bathroom facility; or (in the case of sex) the rental of housing accommodations in a single-sex dormitory.*

■ Dwelling units owned by religious organizations and not operated for commercial purposes may be restricted to people of the same religion if membership in the organization is not restricted based on race, color, or national origin.

■ A private club that is not open to the public may restrict the rental or occupancy of lodgings that it owns to its members as long as the lodgings are not operated commercially. The private club may not discriminate in its requirements for membership. ■

The Fair Housing Act does not require that housing be made available to individuals whose tenancy would constitute a direct threat to the health or safety of other individuals or that would result in substantial physical damage to the property of others. Individuals who have been convicted of the illegal manufacture or distribution of a controlled substance are not protected under this law.

Housing for older persons.   While the Fair Housing Act protects families with children, certain properties can be restricted to occupancy by elderly persons. Housing intended solely for persons age 62 or older or housing occupied by at least one person 55 years of age or older per unit (where 80 percent of the units are occupied by at least one person 55 or older) is exempt from the familial status protection.

Jones v. Mayer.   In 1968, the Supreme Court heard the case of *Jones v. Alfred H. Mayer Company*, 392 U.S. 409 (1968). In its decision, the Court upheld the Civil Rights Act of 1866. This decision is important because although the federal law exempts individual homeowners and certain groups, the 1866 law *prohibits all racial discrimination without exception*. A person who is discriminated against may recover damages under the 1866 law. *Where race is involved, no exceptions apply.*

Supreme Court interpretation.   A U.S. Supreme Court decision in 1987 expanded the definition of race beyond the 19th century usage when the Civil Rights Act of 1866 was passed. In deciding two cases, the court included ancestry or ethnic characteristics—meaning that one possesses certain physical, cultural, or linguistic characteristics commonly shared by a national origin group—to define race. These rulings are significant because discrimination based on race, as it is now defined to refer to more than nonwhite persons, affords due process for a greater number of complainants under the provisions of the Civil Rights Act of 1866.

Equal Housing Opportunity Poster

The Fair Housing Act instituted the use of an equal housing opportunity poster. This poster, obtainable from HUD and illustrated in Figure 17.1, features the equal housing opportunity logo (shown in Figure 17.2) and an equal housing statement pledging adherence to the Fair Housing Act and

F I G U R E   17.1

Equal Housing Opportunity Poster

U.S. Department of Housing and Urban Development

EQUAL HOUSING
OPPORTUNITY

We Do Business in Accordance With the Federal Fair Housing Law

(The Fair Housing Amendments Act of 1988)

It is Illegal to Discriminate Against Any Person Because of Race, Color, Religion, Sex, Handicap, Familial Status, or National Origin

---

- In the sale or rental of housing or residential lots

- In advertising the sale or rental of housing

- In the financing of housing

- In the provision of real estate brokerage services

- In the appraisal of housing

- Blockbusting is also illegal

Anyone who feels he or she has been discriminated against may file a complaint of housing discrimination:
   1-800-669-9777 (Toll Free)
   1-800-927-9275 (TDD)

**U.S. Department of Housing and Urban Development
Assistant Secretary for Fair Housing and Equal Opportunity
Washington, D.C. 20410**

Previous editions are obsolete

form HUD-928.1A (2/2003)

F I G U R E   17.2

Equal Housing Opportunity Logo

EQUAL HOUSING
OPPORTUNITY

support of affirmative marketing and advertising programs. When HUD investigates a broker for discriminatory practices, the broker's failure to prominently display the poster in the place of business (in accordance with HUD's regulations) may be considered prima facie evidence of discrimination.

Equal Credit Opportunity Act

The federal **Equal Credit Opportunity Act (ECOA)** prohibits discrimination based on race, color, religion, national origin, sex, marital status, or age (if the applicant has reached the age of contractual capacity) in the granting of credit. Note the dissimilarity in the protected classes between the Fair Housing Act and the ECOA. The ECOA bars discrimination based on *marital status* and *age*. It also prevents lenders from discriminating against recipients of public assistance programs such as food stamps and Social Security. As in the Fair Housing Act, ECOA requires that credit applications be considered only based on income, net worth, job stability, and credit rating.

Americans with Disabilities Act

> The Americans with Disabilities Act requires *reasonable accommodations* in employment and access to goods, services, and public buildings.

The **Americans with Disabilities Act (ADA)** intends to enable people with disabilities to become part of the economic and social mainstream of society by opening doors both literally and physically. Although ADA is not a housing or credit law, it still has a significant effect on the real estate industry. ADA is important to licensees because it addresses the rights of people with disabilities in employment and public accommodations. Real estate brokers are often employers, and real estate brokerage offices are public places.

Employment practices.   Title I of the ADA prohibits discrimination against qualified job applicants and employees who have a disability. It requires employers with 15 or more employees to adopt nondiscriminatory employment procedures. (The Pennsylvania Human Relations Act is broader by requiring employers in Pennsylvania with *four or more employees* to adopt nondiscriminatory practices.) The law does not expect preferential treatment or preference for people with disabilities. Instead, the law prevents employers from basing hiring and employment decisions on assumptions about the effects of a disability.

Recruitment, job application procedures, hiring, firing, advancement, compensation, training, and other privileges of employment cannot be discriminatory. Employers must provide any *reasonable accommodations* that a person with a disability needs to perform the essential functions of a job. Reasonable accommodations include making the work site accessible, restructuring a job, providing part-time or flexible work schedules, and modifying equipment that is used on the job.

In Your State **PA** **Public accommodations.**   Title III of the ADA provides that no person with a disability shall be discriminated against in the full and equal enjoyment of goods, facilities, privileges, or accommodations. Public accommodations include establishments such as lodging facilities, eating establishments, entertainment and amusement facilities, museums and libraries, and retail and consumer services. The Pennsylvania Human Relations Act includes *commercial property* (any building or vacant land used for the purpose of operating a business, an office, or a manufacturing facility). ∎

These properties must be free of architectural and communication barriers or other accommodations must be provided if this is not feasible. *The Americans with Disabilities Act Accessibility Guidelines (ADAAG)* for buildings and facilities contain detailed specifications for such items as parking, passenger loading zones, curb ramps, stairs, elevators, doors, drinking fountains and water coolers, alarms and detectable warnings, toilet facilities, signage, and telephones.

Eliminating all architectural barriers in existing commercial buildings is a massive undertaking and often impractical. Many of these buildings are difficult to retrofit not only because of their existing design but also because of the enormous expense that could be involved. The ADA provides reasonable approaches for bringing existing buildings into compliance. Barriers must be removed to maximize accessibility if it is *readily achievable* to do so. That is, it can be done with little difficulty or expense. If a barrier cannot be removed, the law provides alternatives, known as *reasonable accommodations*, to provide accessibility.

Accessibility standards for new construction of commercial properties are more strict than for existing facilities. Newly constructed properties must be *readily accessible and usable* as defined in ADAAG to the extent that it is structurally practical. Incorporating accessibility features in new construction is estimated to be less than 1 percent of the overall construction cost. ADAAG contains general design standards for both the building and the site.

ADA in the real estate business.   The broker's office and places where the firm conducts public functions, such as seminars, meetings, conferences, or classes, must be accessible, or reasonable accommodations must be provided. Brokers also should be prepared to accommodate a person with a physical disability at an open house if the property or model home is not accessible. Architectural barriers are not the only obstacles. Communication barriers for people with visual and hearing disabilities must also be considered. Brokers should be prepared to provide text telephones, interpreters, signers, or large print materials to help people access the broker's services and engage in real estate transactions. Finally, brokers need to scrutinize their employment practices to be sure that anyone (including licensees) protected under the law is properly served.

Providers of real estate services must be aware of how *communication* and *architectural* barriers can impact their ability to serve consumers with disabilities.

IN PRACTICE

Real estate licensees need a general knowledge of ADA. It not only affects a broker's workplace and employment policies but also salespeople's daily activities when working with buyers and sellers. Licensees who are building managers must ensure that the properties are accessible to protect the buildings' owners as well as themselves from liability. Appraisers who fail to identify and account for a property's noncompliance may be liable as well. Unless a licensee is a qualified ADA expert, it is best to engage the services of an attorney, architect, or consultant who specializes in ADA.

■ PENNSYLVANIA HUMAN RELATIONS ACT

The **Pennsylvania Human Relations Act (PHRA)** is the state law that prohibits certain discriminatory practices in housing and employment. While the PHRA is deemed to be "substantially equivalent" to the federal Fair Housing Act (an administrative issue), the state law is more restrictive in some respects. In addition to the protected classes and prohibited acts provided in federal law, the Pennsylvania law recognizes *age* (being a person 40 years of age or older) as a protected class. Also, the PHRA defines "handicap" more specifically:

> Pennsylvania law prohibits discrimination in *both* housing and commercial properties.

> *handicap or disability, use of guide animal because of blindness or deafness, use of support animal because of a physical handicap, a handler or trainer of a support or guide animal, or because of the handicap or disability of a person with whom an individual has a relationship or association.*

Housing accommodations and commercial property. A major difference between the state and federal law is that the Pennsylvania law applies to housing accommodations and *commercial property*. The discussions earlier in this chapter about unlawful practices are applicable to more than dwellings. Prospective purchasers or tenants of commercial property in Pennsylvania are afforded the same protections as those seeking housing.

Exemptions

Exemptions defined in the federal Fair Housing Act have limited application in Pennsylvania. The federal exemptions apply only to federally assisted privately owned housing and government housing located in the state. In the previous discussion relating to exemptions, pay particular attention to the explanations regarding Pennsylvania law.

Pennsylvania Real Estate Licensing and Registration Act

Violating any provision of the Pennsylvania Human Relations Act is also a violation of the licensing law. Section 604 of the Real Estate Licensing and Registration Act *specifically prohibits*

- accepting listings that illegally discriminate against certain persons or groups in the sale or rental of property;
- giving false information for the purpose of discrimination; and
- making distinctions, for discriminatory purposes, in the location of housing or dates of availability.

The State Real Estate Commission can take disciplinary action against a licensee, in addition to any action taken by the Human Relations Commission.

Official Notice and Poster

The Pennsylvania Human Relations Commission prepares and distributes fair housing and fair lending posters that any individual subject to the Pennsylvania Human Relations Act must prominently display in the place of business. Failure to do so can be considered evidence of discrimination. All real estate licensees are required to furnish an Official Notice (Figure 17.3) to a person contemplating listing a property for sale. The purpose of the notice is to inform the property owner of both the owner's and the licensee's obligations under the fair housing laws. The notice contains practices that are considered discriminatory under the Pennsylvania Human Relations Act and a summary of the Civil Rights Act of 1866, applicable federal laws, and related parts of the Pennsylvania Real Estate Licensing and Registration Act.

■ FAIR HOUSING PRACTICES

For the civil rights laws to accomplish their goal of eliminating discrimination, licensees must apply them in their daily practice. The following discussion examines some of the legal and ethical issues that confront real estate licensees.

Blockbusting and Panic Selling

Blockbusting is the unlawful act of inducing, or attempting to induce, people to sell or rent their homes by claiming that the entry or prospective entry of a protected class of people into the neighborhood will have some sort of negative impact on property values. Blockbusting was a common practice during the 1950s and 1960s, as unscrupulous real estate licensees and speculators profited by fueling "white flight" from city neighborhoods. Any action (including uninvited solicitation for business) that conveys the message, however subtle, that property should be sold or rented because a neighborhood is "undergoing change" is considered blockbusting. It is illegal to assert that the presence of certain persons will cause property values to decline, crime or antisocial behavior to increase, and the quality of schools to suffer.

A critical element in blockbusting, according to HUD's regulations, is the profit motive. A property owner may be intimidated into selling his or her property at a depressed price to the blockbuster, who in turn sells the property to another person at a higher price. Another term for this activity is *panic selling*, as it is referred to in the Pennsylvania law. To avoid accusations of blockbusting or panic selling, real estate licensees should use good judgment when choosing locations and methods for marketing their services and soliciting listings.

Steering

Steering is the channeling of home-seekers to or away from particular neighborhoods. The effect of steering is to limit people's options, which is contrary to the spirit of an open housing market, as well as a violation of the fair housing laws.

Steering attempts to either preserve the character of a neighborhood or intentionally change its character. Many cases of steering are subtle, motivated by assumptions or perceptions about a home-seeker's desires or preferences, based on some stereotype. Assumptions are not only dangerous; they are often *wrong*. The licensee cannot *assume* that a prospective home-seeker expects to be

FIGURE   17.3

Official Notice

The Commonwealth of Pennsylvania
HUMAN RELATIONS COMMISSION

OFFICIAL NOTICE

**Responsibilities of Owners of Real Property
under
the PENNSYLVANIA HUMAN RELATIONS ACT of
October 27, 1955, P.L. 744, as amended**

The Pennsylvania Legislature has made it illegal: To refuse to sell, lease, finance or otherwise deny or withhold residential or commercial property located in the Commonwealth of Pennsylvania because of any person's ...

Race, Color, Sex, Religious Creed, Ancestry, National Origin, Disability, Age or Familial Status

or

To refuse to lease, or discriminate in the terms of selling or leasing, or in furnishing facilities, services or privileges in connection with the ownership, occupancy or use of any residential or commercial property because of any person's ...

Race, Color, Sex, Religious Creed, Ancestry, National Origin, Disability, Age, Familial Status, Use of a Guide or Support Animal Because of the Blindness, Deafness or Physical Disability of the User or Because the User is a Handler or Trainer of Support or Guide Animals

or

F I G U R E   17.3

Official Notice (continued)

Construct, operate, offer for sale, lease or rent or otherwise make available housing or commercial property which is not accessible. The term **"accessible"** means being in compliance with the applicable standards as provided under the **Fair Housing Act, the Americans with Disabilities Act of 1990 and the Universal Accessibility Act.**

IT IS ALSO UNLAWFUL FOR:

Any person to retaliate against an individual because the individual has filed a complaint with the Commission, or has otherwise participated in any Commission proceeding, or for any person to aid or abet any unlawful discriminatory practice under the Human Relations Act.

OR, BECAUSE OF:

The disability of an individual with whom the person is known to have a relationship or association.

OTHER APPLICABLE LAWS EXPLAINED:

1. The **CIVIL RIGHTS ACT OF 1866** provides that all citizens of the United States shall have the same right in every state and territory thereof to inherit, purchase, lease, sell, hold and convey real and personal property, and prohibits all racial and ethnic discrimination without exception in the sale or rental of property.

2. **TITLE VIII** of the **FEDERAL CIVIL RIGHTS ACT OF 1968** prohibits discrimination in housing based on **race, color, sex, religion, national origin, familial status, disability or intimidation.**

3. **COURT AWARDS:** Under either of the above laws, federal courts may award successful plaintiffs actual and punitive damages, attorney's fees and injunctive relief.

4. **TITLE IX** of the **CIVIL RIGHTS ACT OF 1969** provides criminal penalties for the willful or attempted injury, intimidation or interference with any person because of his/her **race, color, sex, religion, national origin, familial status or disability** who is selling, purchasing, renting, financing or occupying any dwelling or contracting or negotiating for the sale, purchase, rental, financing or occupation of any dwelling or applying for or participating in any service, organization or facility relating to the business of selling or renting dwellings.

5. **REAL ESTATE BROKERS LICENSE ACT OF MAY 1, 1929, P.L. 1216,** as amended, makes it unlawful for a real estate broker or salesperson to accept a listing with an understanding that illegal discrimination in the sale or rental of property is to be practiced.

6. **LOCAL ORDINANCES** prohibiting discrimination in housing may exist in your locality, and should be consulted for any additional protection these ordinances may provide.

F I G U R E   **17.3**

Official Notice (continued)

7. **AMERICANS WITH DISABILITIES ACT OF 1990** prohibits discrimination because of a disability in employment, public service and public accommodation (which includes commercial property).

8. **UNIVERSAL ACCESSIBILITY ACT (PA ACT 166)** requires accessibility for persons with disabilities in certain new and rehabilitated residential and commercial property.

TO OWNERS OF REAL PROPERTY WITHIN THE COMMONWEALTH:

- **YOU ARE LEGALLY RESPONSIBLE** for your own actions and the actions of any agent acting on your behalf. Under the Pennsylvania Human Relations Act and other state and federal legislation which prohibit discrimination in housing, you bear the responsibility for seeing that discriminatory acts do not occur.

- **PROTECT YOURSELF** by providing your agent with verbal and written instructions that in all transactions relating to your property -- including all services provided in connection with the transactions -- you wish to comply with all civil rights ordinances including, but not limited to: **The Pennsylvania Human Relations Act, The Civil Rights Act of 1866, Title VIII of the Civil Rights Act of 1968, the Americans with Disabilities Act of 1990 and the Universal Accessibility Act (PA Act 166).**

- **UNDER THE PENNSYLVANIA HUMAN RELATIONS ACT, NEITHER YOU NOR YOUR BROKER/SALESPERSON OR AGENT MAY ...**

1. Steer or otherwise direct a property seeker's attention to a particular neighborhood based on the race, color, religion, national origin, ancestry, sex, disability, age, familial status or use of a guide or support animal because of the blindness, deafness or physical disability of the user, or because the user is a handler or trainer of support or guide animals, of either the property seekers or persons already residing in that neighborhood.

2. Volunteer information to or invite questions from property seekers concerning the race, color, religion, national origin, ancestry, sex, disability, age, familial status or use of a guide or support animal because of the blindness, deafness or physical disability of the user or because the user is a handler or trainer of support or guide animals of persons already residing in a neighborhood.

3. Answer questions from or initiate a discussion with persons who are selling, renting or otherwise making housing or commercial property available concerning the race, color, religion, national origin, ancestry, sex, disability, age, familial status or use of a guide or support animal because

F I G U R E   17.3

Official Notice (continued)

of the blindness, deafness or physical disability of the user or because the user is a handler or trainer of support or guide animals of prospective buyers, applicants or others seeking housing.

4. Engage in certain practices which attempt to induce the sale, or discourage the purchase or lease of housing accommodations or commercial property by making direct or indirect reference to the present or future composition of the neighborhood in which the facility is located with respect to race, color, religion, sex, ancestry, national origin, disability, age, familial status or guide or support animal dependency.

5. Engage in any course of action which could be construed as reluctant or delayed service having the effect of withholding or making unavailable housing accommodations or commercial property to persons because of their race, color, religion, national origin, ancestry, sex, disability, age, familial status or use of a guide or support animal.

• **RULES AND REGULATIONS OF THE PENNSYLVANIA HUMAN RELATIONS COMMISSION** (16 Pennsylvania Code 43.14) require that all licensed brokers or salespersons with whom you list your property for sale or rent **shall provide you with a copy of this notice** in order that you may be made aware of the laws you are required to obey.

The Commission provides equal opportunity in employment and service to the public.

For further information, write, phone or visit:

Pennsylvania Human Relations Commission
Headquarters Office
Pennsylvania Place
301 Chestnut Street, Suite 300
Harrisburg, PA 17101-2702

Telephone: (717) 783-8274 (VOICE)
(717) 787-4087 (TT)

visit us at www.phrc.state.pa.us

To file a complaint contact the regional office nearest you:

Pittsburgh	**Harrisburg**	**Philadelphia**
11th Floor State Office Building	Riverfront Office Center	711 State Office Building
300 Liberty Avenue	1101-1125 South Front Street 5th Floor	Broad and Spring Garden Streets
Pittsburgh, PA 15222-1210	Harrisburg, PA 17104-2515	Philadelphia, PA 19130-4088
(412) 565-5395 (VOICE)	(717) 787-9784 (VOICE)	(215) 560-2496 (VOICE)
(412) 565-5711 (TT)	(717) 787-7279 (TT)	(215) 560-3599 (TT)

directed to certain neighborhoods or properties. A salesperson's role is to objectively identify the home-seeker's specific property requirements and recommend suitable properties based on the individual's needs and financial ability. The prospective home-seeker selects the neighborhoods or specific properties to view. Steering is illegal.

Intent and Effect

If the owner or real estate licensee *purposely* sets different sale or rental prices or sets different requirements for down payments or security deposits to "chill the interest" of certain individuals, the *intention* to discriminate is obvious. Intent is also obvious if policies are established to segregate families with children in certain parts of a housing complex. However, even without intent, policies and procedures can have a discriminatory *effect*.

In the ordinary course of doing business, policies and procedures are adopted for a variety of purposes. If they affect people in the protected classes differently from other people, however, then the policies or procedures are discriminatory. This effect is known as **disparate impact.** When the outcome or *result* of any action is unequal treatment of people in the protected classes, regardless of the motivation, discrimination has occurred. This is known as the "*effects test*," which is the criterion used by compliance agencies to determine if an individual has been discriminated against.

Advertising

No advertisement of property for sale or rent may include language that indicates a preference or limitation. No exception to this rule exists, regardless of how subtle the choice of words. Words that even *appear* to be discriminatory are not permitted. HUD's regulations and the Pennsylvania Human Relations Commission's real estate advertising guidelines provide examples of language and practices considered discriminatory, including

- the use of words such as *adult building, Jewish home, restricted, private, integrated, traditional;*
- references to a property's location that could imply discriminatory preference or limitation, such as its proximity to landmarks associated with a nationality or religion (a parish, synagogue, club, etc.), or a school attended exclusively by one sex;
- pictorial representations of human models as residents or customers that depict one segment of the population while not including others; and
- the selective use of media (newspapers, radio, or television stations), whether by language or geography, to promote property or real estate services that target one population to the exclusion of others—unless the advertisement also appears in general-circulation media as well.

The accepted rule: *Always describe property; never describe people.* Consult HUD's regulations and the Pennsylvania guidelines for a full list of words that are acceptable and not acceptable for advertising purposes.

Appraising

People who prepare appraisals or any statements of valuation, whether they are formal or informal, oral or written (including a comparative market analysis), may consider any factors that affect value. However, factors such as race, color, religion, national origin, sex, handicap, or familial status may *not* be considered.

Redlining

The practice of refusing to make mortgage loans or issue insurance policies in specific areas for reasons other than the economic qualifications of the applicants is known as **redlining.** Redlining refers to literally drawing a line around particular areas. Lenders or insurance companies make policy decisions that no property in certain areas (frequently based on racial grounds) is qualified collateral or insurable, no matter who the prospective borrower or owner is or the individual's personal qualifications. This practice is often a major contributor to the deterioration of older or transitional neighborhoods.

The federal Fair Housing Act prohibits discrimination in mortgage lending and covers not only the actions of primary lenders but also activities in the secondary mortgage market. A lending institution, however, can refuse a loan solely on *sound* economic grounds. In an effort to counteract redlining, the federal government passed the *Home Mortgage Disclosure Act.* This requires all institutional mortgage lenders with assets in excess of $10 million and one or more offices in a given geographic area to make annual reports. The reports must detail all mortgage loans the institution has made or purchased, broken down by census tract. This law enables the government to detect patterns that might constitute redlining.

■ ENFORCEMENT OF THE FAIR HOUSING ACT

The federal Fair Housing Act is administered by the Office of Fair Housing and Equal Opportunity (OFHEO) under the direction of the secretary of HUD. Any aggrieved person who believes illegal discrimination has occurred may file a complaint with HUD within one year of the alleged act. HUD may also initiate its own complaint. Complaints may be reported to the Office of Fair Housing and Equal Opportunity, Department of Housing and Urban Development, Washington, DC 20410, or to the Office of Fair Housing and Equal Opportunity, in care of the nearest HUD regional office. Online forms are also available on HUD's Web site. (See the Internet Resources.)

Upon receiving a complaint, HUD initiates an investigation. Within 100 days of the filing of the complaint, HUD determines either that reasonable cause exists to bring a charge of illegal discrimination or dismisses the complaint. During this investigation period, HUD can attempt to resolve the dispute informally through conciliation. *Conciliation* is the resolution of a complaint by obtaining assurance that the person against whom the complaint was filed (the respondent) will remedy any violation that may have occurred. The respondent further agrees to take steps to eliminate or prevent discriminatory practices in the future. If necessary, these agreements can be enforced through civil action.

The aggrieved person has the right to seek relief through administrative proceedings. These proceedings are hearings held by an administrative law judge (ALJ), either during the investigation period or after a charge has been decided. The ALJ has the authority to award actual damages to the aggrieved person or persons and, if it serves the public interest, also to impose monetary penalties. The penalties range from up to $10,000 for the first offense to

$25,000 for a second violation within five years and $50,000 for further violations within seven years. The ALJ also has the authority to issue an injunction to order the offender to either do something (such as rent the apartment to the complaining party) or refrain from doing something.

The parties may elect civil (judicial) action in federal court at any time within two years of the discriminatory act. For cases heard in federal court, unlimited punitive damages can be awarded in addition to actual damages. The court can also issue injunctions. Real estate licensees' errors and omissions insurance normally does not pay on violations of the fair housing laws.

Whenever the Attorney General has reasonable cause to believe that any person or group is engaged in a pattern or practice of resistance to the full enjoyment of any of the rights granted by the federal fair housing laws, the Attorney General may commence a civil action in any federal district court. Civil penalties may result in an amount not to exceed $50,000 for a first violation and an amount not to exceed $100,000 for second and subsequent violations.

Complaints brought under the Civil Rights Act of 1866 are taken directly to a federal court. The only time limit for action would be the state's statute of limitation for torts, that is, injuries done by one individual to another.

State and Local Enforcement

In Your State

PA When a state or municipality has a fair housing law that has been ruled *substantially equivalent* to the federal law, all complaints in the state filed with HUD are referred to and handled by the local enforcement agency responsible for those laws. To be considered substantially equivalent, the local law and its related regulations must contain prohibitions comparable to those in the federal law. In addition, the state or locality must show that its local enforcement agency is taking sufficient affirmative action in processing and investigating complaints and in finding remedies for discriminatory practices. The PHRA as well as some local acts are substantially equivalent, and complaints would be referred by HUD to the Pennsylvania Human Relations Commission or, if the complaint falls within the jurisdiction of a local human relations commission, to that local body. ■

IN PRACTICE

Some cities and municipalities in Pennsylvania have ordinances that deal with discriminatory housing practices and often include additional protected classes. Real estate licensees should be familiar with provisions of any local as well as state and federal laws.

Threats or Acts of Violence

In Your State

PA The federal Fair Housing Act protects the rights of those who seek the benefits of the open housing law. It also protects property owners, brokers, and salespeople who aid or encourage the enjoyment of open housing rights. Threats, coercion, and intimidation are punishable by criminal action. In such cases, the victim should report the incident immediately to the local police and to the nearest office of the Federal Bureau of Investigation. A victim in Pennsylvania is also protected under the *Ethnic Intimidation and Vandalism Act.* This law also prohibits retaliation against those who file complaints alleging discrimination, fair housing activists, and real estate licensees who are attempting to conduct business in compliance with the fair housing laws. The Interagency Task Force on Civil Tension investigates incidents relating to the Ethnic Intimidation and Vandalism Act. ■

■ IMPLICATIONS FOR BROKERS AND SALESPEOPLE

The real estate industry is largely responsible for creating and maintaining an open housing market. Brokers and salespeople are a community's real estate experts. Along with the privilege of profiting from real estate transactions comes social and legal responsibility to ensure protection of everyone's civil rights. The reputation of the industry cannot afford *any* appearance that its licensees are not committed to the principles of fair housing. Licensees and the industry must be publicly conspicuous in their equal opportunity efforts. Establishing relationships with community and fair housing groups to discuss common concerns and develop solutions to problems is a constructive activity.

Fair housing *is* the law, and the consequences for anyone who violates the law are serious. In addition to the financial penalties, a real estate licensee's livelihood is endangered if his or her license is suspended or revoked. That the offense was unintentional is no defense. Beyond the law, fair housing is *good business*. It ensures the greatest number of properties available for sale and rent and the largest possible pool of potential purchasers and tenants.

Proactive Practices

After a discrimination complaint is filed is not the time to think about fair housing. Anyone who even *suspects* that illegal discrimination has occurred may file a complaint. The complainant does not have to prove guilty knowledge or specific intent. The job of the enforcement agency is to investigate and uncover the facts of the case to determine if there are grounds for the complaint. For a licensee, the investigation process can be time consuming and expensive, even if a complaint turns out to be unfounded. Avoiding a complaint in the first place is prudent; developing defensible practices is essential.

One of the best ways to ensure compliance with the laws is with policies and procedures that ensure the same standard of service, that is, "equal treatment," for everyone based on a person's property requirements, financial ability, and experience in the marketplace. A good test is to answer the question, "Are we doing this for everyone?" If an act is not consistently performed or if an act affects some people differently than others, it could be discriminatory. Licensees also must be careful not to fall victim to clients or customers who expect or attempt to discriminate.

In Your State   **PA**   The Pennsylvania Human Relations Commission and the Pennsylvania Association of REALTORS® have jointly authored the Fair Housing Guidelines. This is a useful resource for developing nondiscriminatory policies and procedures. Included are recommendations for

■ a *standardized inventory* of properties available for sale or rent to ensure that all persons who inquire about availability will be offered a uniform listing of properties;

■ *consistent practices* for qualifying prospective purchasers and tenants, showing properties, following the progress of a transaction, and presenting offers to ensure equal treatment for everyone;

■ *verifiable and measurable* criteria that can be justified as prudent business decisions with which to qualify all tenant applicants equally; and

■ *written documentation* of applications, conversations, showings, and follow-up contacts, which is essential evidence to defend against a complaint. The complexities of a real estate transaction are commonplace to a licensee, but they can be a confusing maze for a client or customer. Actions can be misinterpreted if they are not completely explained. ■

Discrimination may be blatant as in the case of a landlord who says that he or she won't rent to a person of a particular race, for instance. More often, however, people's prejudices surface in more subtle ways. That subtlety is challenging because without knowing the motivations for a person's questions or conduct, the licensee could unwittingly participate in discriminatory activity. A seller who asks a question about a prospective purchaser's nationality, family status, or age, for instance, may be idly curious, hoping that a certain profile buyer will purchase the home. Or, the seller may be seeking information with which to discriminate. In this example, if answering the question results in the seller's refusal of an offer or the pursuit of different terms in negotiations, the effect is discriminatory. A licensee must be aware of how actions could be construed.

Public declarations of a broker's commitment to equal opportunity help licensees, consumers, and the community. Using HUD's equal opportunity logo, posting the Pennsylvania Human Relations Commission fair housing poster, and following HUD's and PHRC's advertising procedures are not only legal requirements but also demonstrate that commitment. In addition, brokers and local associations or boards of REALTORS® may further pledge their commitment as signatories of the Memorandum of Understanding. This is a voluntary agreement between the Pennsylvania Human Relations Commission and the Pennsylvania Association of REALTORS®.

■ SUMMARY

A real estate business is only as good as its reputation. Real estate licensees can maintain good reputations by demonstrating good business ability and adhering to an ethical standard of business practices. Many licensees subscribe to a code of ethics as members of professional real estate organizations. The Code of Ethics of the National Association of REALTORS® is an example. The provisions of this and the Code for Equal Opportunity suggest an excellent set of standards for all licensees to follow.

The federal regulations regarding equal opportunity in housing are principally contained in two laws. The Civil Rights Act of 1866 prohibits all racial discrimination, and the Fair Housing Act (Title VIII of the Civil Rights Act of 1968) prohibits discrimination based on of race, color, religion, sex, handicap, familial status, or national origin in the sale, rental, or financing of residential property. Discriminatory actions include refusing to deal with an individual or a specific group, changing any terms of a real estate or loan transaction, changing the services offered for any individual or group, making statements or advertisements that indicate discriminatory restrictions, or otherwise attempting to make a dwelling unavailable to any person or group because of race, color, religion, sex, handicap, familial status, or national origin.

The Americans with Disabilities Act addresses the rights of people with disabilities in employment and public accommodations. The act provides for nondiscriminatory employment practices and architectural alteration and design for accessibility.

The Pennsylvania Human Relations Act is more restrictive than the federal Fair Housing Act. The Pennsylvania law expands the protected classes and is more widely applicable in Pennsylvania. It covers commercial property as well as housing and does not recognize many of the exemptions that the federal law does.

Complaints under the Fair Housing Act may be reported to and investigated by the Department of Housing and Urban Development (HUD). Such complaints may also be taken directly to a U.S. district court. In states and localities that have enacted fair housing legislation that is substantially equivalent to the federal law, complaints are handled by state and local agencies and state courts. Complaints under the Civil Rights Act of 1866 must be taken to a federal court.

QUESTIONS

1. Which of the following acts is permitted under the federal Fair Housing Act?
   a. Advertising property for sale only to a specific nationality group
   b. Altering the terms of a loan because the borrower is a member of a minority group
   c. Refusing to finance a home for an individual who has a poor credit history
   d. Telling an individual that an apartment has been rented when in fact it has not

2. Complaints relating to the Civil Rights Act of 1866
   a. are taken directly to a federal court.
   b. are no longer reviewed in the courts.
   c. are handled by HUD.
   d. are handled by state enforcement agencies.

3. The Civil Rights Act of 1866 is unique because it
   a. has been broadened to protect age.
   b. adds welfare recipients as a protected class.
   c. contains "choose your neighbor" provisions.
   d. provides no exceptions to racial discrimination.

4. "I hear *they're* moving in. There goes the neighborhood! Better put your house on the market before values drop!" This is an example of what illegal practice?
   a. Steering
   b. Blockbusting
   c. Redlining
   d. Fraudulent advertising

5. The act of channeling home-seekers to a particular area either to maintain or to change the character of a neighborhood is
   a. blockbusting.
   b. redlining.
   c. steering.
   d. permitted under the Fair Housing Act of 1968.

6. A lender's refusal to lend money to potential homeowners attempting to purchase property located in predominantly minority neighborhoods is
   a. redlining.
   b. blockbusting.
   c. steering.
   d. qualifying.

7. Which of the following is *NOT* permitted under the federal Fair Housing Act?
   a. The Harvard Club in New York will rent rooms only to graduates of Harvard who belong to the club.
   b. The owner of a 20-unit apartment building rents to women only.
   c. A Catholic convent refuses to furnish housing for a Jewish home.
   d. An owner refuses to rent the duplex home in which she lives to families with children.

8. Under federal law, families with children may be refused rental or purchase in a building where occupancy is reserved exclusively for those aged at least
   a. 40.
   b. 60.
   c. 62.
   d. 65.

9. Guiding prospective buyers to a particular area because the agent feels they belong there is
   a. blockbusting.
   b. redlining.
   c. steering.
   d. bird-dogging.

10. A minority real estate broker's practice of offering a special discount to minority clients is
    a. satisfactory.
    b. illegal.
    c. legal but ill advised.
    d. not important.

11. Which of the following statements describes the Supreme Court's decision in the case of *Jones v. Alfred H. Mayer Company?*
    a. Racial discrimination is prohibited by any party in the sale or rental of real estate.
    b. Sales by individual residential homeowners are exempted, provided the owners do not use brokers.
    c. Laws against discrimination apply only to federally related transactions.
    d. Persons with disabilities are a protected class.

12. After a broker takes a listing agreement for a residence, the owner specifies that he will not sell his home to any Asian family. Which of the following should the broker do?
    a. Advertise the property exclusively in Asian-language newspapers
    b. Explain to the owner that the instruction violates federal law and that the broker cannot comply with it
    c. Abide by the principal's directions despite the fact that they conflict with the fair housing laws.
    d. Require that the owner sign a separate legal document stating the additional instruction as an amendment to the listing agreement.

13. The fine for a first violation of the federal Fair Housing Act could be as much as
    a. $500.
    b. $1,000.
    c. $5,000.
    d. $10,000.

14. The REALTORS® Code of Ethics suggests a set of standards for all brokers and salespeople to follow who are members of its association. Which of the following provisions is NOT contained in the Code?
    a. A REALTOR® should not engage in the practice of law.
    b. A REALTOR® must protect the public against fraud and unethical practices in the real estate field.
    c. A REALTOR® should not accept compensation from more than one party without the full knowledge of all parties to the transaction.
    d. In the event of a REALTOR®'s dispute with another REALTOR®, the matter should be settled through litigation.

ANSWERS

1. C   If a person is denied a loan because of poor credit history, there is no violation of either the federal Fair Housing Act or the Equal Credit Opportunity Act. (p. 296)

2. A   Complaints brought under the Civil Rights Act of 1866 involving racial discrimination are taken directly to federal court rather than to HUD or state enforcement agencies. (p. 310)

3. D   While the federal Fair Housing Act of 1968 (as amended) provides for exceptions, the Civil Rights Act of 1866 is unique in that there are no exceptions for racial discrimination. Racial discrimination is always illegal. (p. 298)

4. B   Blockbusting is the unlawful act of inducing or attempting to induce people to sell their homes on the basis that the entry, or prospective entry, of members of a protected class will adversely affect property values in the area. Pennsylvania law refers to this activity as panic selling. (p. 303)

5. C   Steering is the act of guiding prospective home-seekers into or away from particular neighborhoods. This conduct limits options, which is contrary to the concept of an open housing market. (p. 303)

6. A   Redlining refers to a refusal to make loans or write insurance policies in a particular area as a result of policy decisions that properties in that area are not suitable collateral or insurable, regardless of the individual's qualifications. (p. 309)

7. B   A 20-unit apartment building would not qualify under the exclusions of the federal Fair Housing Act. The owner of this property may not discriminate against a prospective tenant who is a member of a protected class. Limiting rental based on sex would be illegal. (p. 297)

8. C   Housing intended solely for persons age 62 or older is exempt from protections afforded to families with children and may be restricted to elderly persons. (p. 298)

9. C   Home-seekers, not their agents, decide the areas in which they want to explore houses for sale. An agent who restricts the home-seeker's options is engaging in the illegal activity of steering. (p. 303)

10. B   Differentiating in terms, conditions, or services because a person is a member of a protected class is a violation of the federal Fair Housing Act. A broker who is a member of a minority group who offers special discounts to clients who are also minorities is a violation of the law. (p. 296)

11. A   In the 1968 Supreme Court case of *Jones v. Alfred H. Mayer Company*, the court upheld the Civil Rights Act of 1866 and clearly established that racial discrimination is illegal without exception. (p. 298)

12. B   A broker who accepts a listing with the understanding that illegal discrimination will be practiced is in violation of the federal Fair Housing Act. Both the broker and owner could be prosecuted. The broker must explain that the instruction violates the law and that the broker cannot accept the listing under that condition. (p. 302)

13. D   An administrative law judge (ALJ) may impose monetary penalties for violations of the federal Fair Housing Act. The penalty for a first offense can be a fine of up to $10,000. (p. 309)

14. D   Professional codes of ethics address the way in which members of a professional organization shall conduct business. The NAR Code of Ethics dictates rules that prohibit or demand certain behavior as well as establishes procedures for resolving disputes among members. REALTORS® agree to arbitrate rather than litigate disputes. (Article 17 of the NAR Code.)

CHAPTER EIGHTEEN

LISTING AGREEMENTS AND BUYER REPRESENTATION CONTRACTS

■ LEARNING OBJECTIVES

When you've finished reading this chapter, you should be able to

- identify and distinguish between the different types of listing and buyer representation agreements;
- describe the ways listing contracts and buyer representation agreements can be terminated;
- identify statutory and regulatory issues related to listing and buyer representation agreements;
- explain common provisions in listing and buyer representation agreements; and
- define the key terms.

■ KEY TERMS

buyer agency agreement	exclusive-right-to-sell listing	net listing
comparative market analysis (CMA)	multiple-listing service (MLS)	open listing
exclusive agency listing		Real Estate Seller Disclosure Act

■ AGENCY CONTRACTS

The majority of business relationships in real estate are created by written agreement. An agency contract may be used to hire the broker to represent the buyer, the seller, the landlord, or the tenant. (The broker's policies determine which type(s) of agency the company offers.) These are *employment contracts* rather than real estate contracts. That is, they contract for the personal professional services of the broker and are not contracts for the transfer of real estate or a real estate interest. Listing agreements and buyer agency agreements are the fundamental documents of the real estate profession.

Written Agreements

Although it is possible to create an agency relationship orally or by the parties' actions, creating agency relationships with written agreements serves both a legal and practical purpose. The Pennsylvania licensing law requires a written agreement between a broker and a consumer when the consumer is or may be obligated to compensate the broker for services. As a practical matter, a written document provides proof of what the parties are expected to do, which is particularly important if either party takes legal action against the other.

The licensing law (RELRA Section 608.1) requires written agreements to contain

- a statement that the broker's fee and the duration of the contract have been determined as a result of negotiations between the broker and the consumer;
- a statement describing the nature and extent of the broker's services to be provided and the fees that will be charged;
- a statement identifying any possibility that the broker or any licensee employed by the broker may provide services to more than one consumer in a single transaction, along with an explanation of the duties owed to each party;
- statements about the broker's policies regarding cooperation and compensation arrangements with subagents, buyer agents, and listing agents (depending on whether the agreement is with a buyer or a seller), and potential for dual agency;
- a statement describing the purpose of the Real Estate Recovery Fund and the telephone number where a consumer may receive further information; and
- a statement regarding any possible conflicts of interest and ongoing duty to disclose conflicts in a timely manner.

The rules and regulations of the State Real Estate Commission address requirements for written agreements further in Section 35.331.

IN PRACTICE

One of the primary functions of a written agreement between the broker and the consumer is to set forth exactly what professional services the broker will provide to the consumer (buyer or seller). The Consumer Notice (Figure 16.4 in Chapter 16) is just that, a notice about the types of business relationships that are permitted and the duties owed to a consumer who receives real estate services in Pennsylvania. The written agreement forms the actual business relationship that the broker and consumer will have with one another and commits to writing the duties and services associated with that relationship.

The core function of a broker and his or her underlying licensees is to provide professional services, and those services can vary from company to company. While the broker has the right to determine the scope and nature of services his or her firm will provide, some states' regulators and legislators have recently been discussing the prescription of certain minimum service standards for the brokers. These attempts to specify minimum services have attracted the attention of the Department of Justice, the concerns being that minimum standards can thwart brokers' attempts to offer competitive options in the marketplace, hamper price competition, and force consumers to purchase services they neither want nor need.

■ LISTING AGREEMENTS

Brokers obtain listings to acquire inventory. A listing agreement creates a special agency relationship between a broker (agent) and a seller (principal) who authorizes the agent to offer the principal's property for sale and to solicit offers to purchase and submit them to the principal. Although the associate broker or salesperson typically acquires the business and has the most direct contact with the seller, the contract (and the agency relationship) is between the seller and the broker. Several types of listing agreements exist. (See Figure 18.1.) The type of contract determines the specific rights and obligations of the parties.

Exclusive-Right-to-Sell Listing

> **Exclusive-Right-to-Sell Listing**
>
> One authorized agent-broker receives compensation regardless of who sells the property.

In an **exclusive-right-to-sell listing,** one broker is appointed as the sole (exclusive) agent of the seller. The broker has the exclusive right, or authorization, to market the seller's property. If the property is sold while the listing is in effect, the seller must compensate the broker *regardless of who sells the property.* In other words, even if the seller finds a buyer without the broker's assistance, the seller must pay the broker a fee. Sellers benefit from this form of agreement because the broker feels freer to spend time and money to actively market the property, making a timely and profitable sale more likely. From the broker's perspective, an exclusive-right-to-sell listing offers the greatest opportunity to receive compensation. (An example of this form of listing agreement is reproduced later in this chapter.)

According to the Real Estate Commission's Regulations (Section 35.332), an exclusive-right-to-sell or exclusive-right-to-lease agreement must contain a statement in boldface type that *the broker earns a commission on the sale (or lease) of the property, regardless of who, including the owner, makes the sale (or lease) during the listing period.* The agreements also must contain (in addition to the other requirements for written contracts) the:

> **Exclusive Agency Listing**
> - One authorized broker-agent
> - Broker compensated only if the procuring cause
> - Seller retains the right to sell without obligation

- seller's asking price;
- broker's expected commission on the sale price; and
- explanation that payments of money received by the broker shall be held by the broker in an escrow account.

The broker cannot have authority to execute an agreement of sale for the owner or have an option to purchase the listed property. Nor can the broker have authority to confess judgment for the commission in the event of a sale.

Exclusive Agency Listing

In an **exclusive agency listing,** *one* broker is authorized to act as the exclusive agent of the principal. However, the seller *retains the right to sell the property himself or herself* without obligation to the broker. The seller is obligated to

Three Types of Listing Agreements

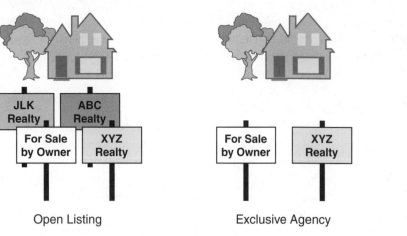

Open Listing   Exclusive Agency   Exclusive-Right-to-Sell

compensate the broker *only* if the broker or an authorized subagent of the broker is the procuring cause of the sale, or produces a ready, willing, and able purchaser for the property according to the terms specified in the contract.

Open Listing

> ### Open Listing
>
> - There are multiple agents.
> - Only the agent who is procuring cause is compensated.
> - Seller retains the right to sell independently without obligation.

In an **open listing** (also known in some areas as a nonexclusive listing or a simple listing), the seller retains the right to contract with any number of brokers as agents. These brokers can act simultaneously, and the seller is obligated to compensate only that broker who successfully produces a ready, willing, and able buyer. If the seller personally sells the property *without the aid of any of the brokers*, the seller is not obligated to pay any of them. The Real Estate Commission's Regulations require any broker taking an *oral* open listing to give the seller a written memorandum stating all the terms of the listing agreement.

Special Listing Provisions

Multiple-listing service.   A multiple-listing service clause authorizes the broker to register the listing with the **multiple-listing service (MLS).** MLSs are marketing organizations whose broker-members share listing information with one another, a benefit to sellers because their properties are exposed to a larger market of prospective buyers through the members of the MLS. MLS rules normally require a broker to register a new listing with the MLS within a specified time period. Because of antitrust concerns, MLS rules cannot interfere with the independent negotiation of the terms of a broker's relationship with a seller, including compensation arrangements and offers of subagency, or the broker's ability to protect fiduciary obligations to the seller. This is especially important when a broker who has an agency relationship with a buyer wants to show or negotiate the purchase of another broker's listing.

IN PRACTICE

MLSs have been essentially internal services to aid the businesses of their member brokers. Today's technology has enhanced those services by providing timely electronic access to properties the member brokers have listed for sale, including changes in price and status of transactions, as well as links to a wide range of information about mortgage loans, real estate taxes and assessments, and municipalities and school districts. Technology has also transformed the way the public accesses information, particularly property listings that have historically been the proprietary domain of MLS members. Today's public Internet sites provide the general population with electronic access to a vast amount of information about properties for sale, communities and school districts, mortgage lending services, and even the ability for home sellers and buyers to do comparison shopping and competitive pricing of properties. The ready access to information has challenged brokers to rethink their roles in delivering information and has challenged MLSs to link their property listings into the public domain or miss an increasingly viable marketing opportunity for their listings.

Net listing.   A **net listing** provision specifies that the seller will receive a net amount of money from a sale, with the excess going to the listing broker as commission. The broker is free to offer the property at any price greater than that net amount. While a net listing may appear to be advantageous for a seller, it can create a conflict of interest between the broker's fiduciary responsibility to the seller and the broker's profit motive. For this reason, the use of net listings is discouraged in the industry. The courts have viewed the absolute prohibition of net listings, however, to be a restraint of trade.

■ TERMINATION OF LISTINGS

A listing agreement is a *personal service contract* between a broker and a seller. Its success depends on the broker's personal, professional efforts. Because the broker's services are unique, he or she cannot turn over the listing to another broker without the principal's written consent. The property owner cannot force the broker to perform, but the broker's failure to work diligently toward fulfilling the contract's terms constitutes abandonment of the listing. In the event the listing is abandoned or revoked by the broker, the owner is entitled to sue for damages.

Of course, the property owner might also fail to fulfill the terms of the agreement. A property owner who refuses to cooperate with the broker's reasonable requests, such as allowing the broker to show the property to prospective buyers, or who refuses to proceed with a complete sales contract, could be liable to the broker for damages. If either party cancels the contract, he or she may be liable for damages to the other.

A listing agreement may be canceled for the following reasons:

- Fulfillment of the agreement's purpose
- Expiration of the time period stated in the agreement
- Breach or cancellation by one of the parties (although that party may be liable to the other for damages)
- Transfer of title to the property by operation of law, as in a bankruptcy
- Mutual consent
- Death or incapacity of either party
- Destruction of the property or a change in property use by outside forces (such as a change in zoning or condemnation by eminent domain)

Expiration of Listing Period   In Your State   **PA** All listings must specify a definite period of time during which the broker is to be employed. The rules and regulations (Section 35.332 c) of the Pennsylvania Real Estate Commission state that the listing period *cannot* exceed 12 months. An automatic renewal provision and the requirement to serve a cancellation notice to terminate an exclusive agreement at the end of the listing period are *prohibited*. An example of an automatic renewal is a listing that provides for a base period of 90 days and "continues thereafter until terminated by either party hereto by 30 days' notice in writing." ■

Some listing contracts contain a "broker protection clause." This clause states that the property owner will compensate the listing broker if, within a specified number of days after the listing expires, the owner sells the property to someone with whom the broker negotiated during the original term of the listing. This protects a broker who was the procuring cause from losing a commission because the transaction was completed after the listing contract expired. The time for such a clause usually parallels the terms of the listing agreement: for example, a six-month listing might carry a broker protection clause of six months after the listing's expiration. To protect the owner from being liable for two separate commissions, the clause may stipulate that it cannot be enforced if the property is re-listed under a new contract with either the original listing broker or with another broker.

■ THE LISTING PROCESS

The listing process is essentially a twofold event. The first step involves a discussion of the Consumer Notice and all of the required disclosures. Secondly, the broker and seller contractually agree to the specific terms of their business relationship, which becomes the listing contract.

Typically, the seller is most concerned about the property's selling price, the net amount of money that can be expected from the sale, and the amount of time needed for the property to sell. Obviously, what the seller wants to know is how the brokerage firm's services will benefit the seller in light of these concerns.

Before discussing these or any other substantive issues, however, the licensee must provide the seller with the Consumer Notice that was discussed in Chapter 16. This is also when the licensee explains the various types of listing agreements, the ramifications of agency relationships, and the broker's policy regarding relationships with other parties who might be involved in the transaction. For instance, does the broker also represent buyer-clients? Does the company customarily offer subagency or practice designated agency? Once the parties agree to the services that are to be provided and the licensee explains the broker's marketing program, the seller should feel comfortable with the decision to list with the broker.

Similarly, before the listing agreement is finalized, the broker should be prepared to fulfill the fiduciary obligations the agreement imposes. The seller should have provided comprehensive information about both the property and his or her personal concerns. Based on this information, the broker can accept the listing with confidence that the seller's goals can be met in a profitable manner for both parties.

Pricing the Property

While the broker or salesperson may advise and assist, ultimately the *seller* must determine a listing price for the property. Because the average seller usually does not have the resources needed to make an informed decision about a reasonable listing price, real estate licensees must be prepared to offer their knowledge, information, and expertise.

> A *comparative market analysis* is an analysis of market activity among comparable properties; it is *not* the same as an appraisal.

A salesperson can help the seller determine a listing price for the property by developing a **comparative market analysis (CMA).** A CMA is a study of the prices of recently sold properties, properties currently on the market for sale, and properties that were listed but did not sell. Comparisons are made with properties similar to the seller's property in location, size, age, style, and amenities. Although a CMA (sometimes known as a *competitive market analysis*) is not a formal appraisal, the salesperson uses many of the same methods and techniques an appraiser uses. The objective is to arrive at a reasonable range of value so that an appropriate listing price can be identified. If no adequate comparisons can be made or if the property is unique in some way, the seller may prefer to have a professional appraiser prepare a formal *appraisal*.

An explanation of appraising and the distinction between an appraisal and a CMA is discussed in Chapter 21. In either case, the figure sought is the property's fair market value: *the most probable price a property would bring in an arm's-length transaction under normal conditions on the open market.* Because a CMA is not an appraisal, the licensing law requires the following statement be printed conspicuously and without change on the first page of the report:

> *"This analysis has not been performed in accordance with the Uniform Standards of Professional Appraisal Practice which require valuers to act as unbiased, disinterested third parties with impartiality, objectivity, and independence and without accommodation of personal interest. It is not to be construed as an appraisal and may not be used as such for any purpose."*

While it is the property owner's privilege to set whatever listing price he or she chooses, the seller should be cautioned about setting a price that is substantially exaggerated or severely out of line with the CMA or appraisal. These tools are the best indicators of what a buyer will likely pay for the property. By accepting an unrealistically priced listing, the licensee does both the seller and the broker a disservice. An overpriced listing gives the seller false hopes about riches to come, which could also result in the seller being uncooperative on other issues later on. The broker will have difficulty marketing the property within the agreed-upon listing period. This also costs the broker time and money, and failure to move an overpriced listing could cost the broker future business opportunities as well. The best advice is to reject such a listing.

Seller's Return

With simple calculations, the licensee can show the seller roughly how much the seller will net from a given sales price or what sales price will produce a certain net amount. The mathematical examples show the net the seller would receive after the sales commission. In addition, there are other expenses that the seller incurs.

MATH CONCEPTS

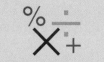

CALCULATING SALES PRICES, COMMISSIONS, AND NETS TO SELLER

When a property sells, the sales price is equal to 100 percent of the money being transferred. Therefore, if a broker is to receive a 6 percent commission, 94 percent will be left for the seller's other expenses and equity. To calculate a commission using a sales price of $80,000 and a commission rate of 6 percent (0.06 as a decimal), multiply the sales price by the commission rate:

$$\$80,000 \times 0.06 = \$4,800 \text{ commission}$$

To calculate a sales price using a commission of $4,550 and a commission rate of 7 percent (0.07 as a decimal), divide the commission by the commission rate:

$$\$4,550 \div 0.07 = \$65,000 \text{ sales price}$$

To calculate a commission rate using a commission of $3,200 and a sales price of $64,000, divide the commission by the sales price:

$$\$3,200 \div \$64,000 = 0.05 \text{ as a decimal} = 5\% \text{ commission rate}$$

To calculate the net to the seller using a sales price of $85,000 and a commission rate of 8 percent (0.08 as a decimal), multiply the sales price by *100 percent minus the commission rate:*

$$\$85,000 \times (100\% - 8\%) = \$85,000 \times 0.92 = \$78,200$$

The same result could be achieved by calculating the commission ($85,000 × 0.08 = $6,800) and deducting it from the sales price ($85,000 − $6,800 = $78,200). However, this involves unnecessary extra calculations.

Sales price × commission rate = commission
Commission ÷ commission rate = sales price
Commission ÷ sales price = commission rate
Sales price (100% − commission rate) = net to seller

IN PRACTICE

Licensees must comply with certain requirements that are detailed in the Real Estate Licensing and Registration Act and rules and regulations when they are listing real estate. Refer to Chapter 13 and Appendix C.

Gathering Information

Once the real estate licensee and the owner agree on a reasonable listing price, the licensee must obtain specific, detailed information about the property. This is particularly important when the listing will be shared with other brokers through an MLS or any others who will rely on the information. Obtaining as many facts as possible ensures that most contingencies can be anticipated. In addition, information is needed to properly complete the listing agreement.

Information generally includes (where appropriate):

■ names and relationships of the owners;
■ street address of the property;
■ asking price;
■ size of lot and number and sizes of rooms and other improvements;
■ age of the improvements and the type of construction;
■ information about the neighborhood (schools, parks, and recreational areas, public transportation, etc.);
■ current (or most recent) taxes and any pending special assessments;
■ financing (interest, payments, other costs, and whether or not the loan is assumable) and the possibility of seller financing;
■ utilities and average payments;
■ any real property to be removed by the seller or personal property to be included in the sale;
■ date of occupancy or possession;
■ any disclosures about property conditions; and
■ zoning classification (especially important for vacant land).

Real Estate Seller Disclosure Act `In Your State`

PA Some of the most important information sellers provide is contained in the seller's property disclosure statement. (An example appears in Figure 18.2.) The disclosure of property conditions as well as agency disclosures have become the focus of consumer safeguards in recent years. As in many states, Pennsylvania has adopted a property disclosure law. The **Real Estate Seller Disclosure Act,** which first became effective in September of 1996 and was most recently updated in June 2004, requires the seller of residential real property (an individual, partnership, corporation, trustee, or combination thereof) who intends to transfer an interest in the property to disclose to the buyer any and all material defects. Although there are some exceptions, the majority of residential transactions will require the seller's completion of such a disclosure document. ■

A wide range of structural, mechanical, and other conditions that a prospective purchaser should know about to make an informed decision must be disclosed. The term *material defect* is defined in the law to mean *a problem with the property or any portion of it that would have a significant adverse impact on the value of the residential real property or that involves an unreasonable risk to people on the land.* The *seller* must complete a disclosure statement; the *licensee* is responsible for advising the seller of this duty and providing an appropriate form for the seller's use. Agents should caution sellers to make truthful disclosures to avoid litigation arising from fraudulent or careless misrepresentations. The signed and dated disclosure statement must be presented to a prospective buyer before he or she signs an agreement of sale.

Example of Seller Property Disclosure Statement

SELLER'S PROPERTY DISCLOSURE STATEMENT
This form recommended and approved for, but not restricted to use by, the members of the Pennsylvania Association of REALTORS® (PAR).   **SPD**

1 **Property Address** _____

2 _____

3 **Seller** _____

4   The Real Estate Seller Disclosure Law (68 P.S. §7301 et. seq.) requires that a seller of a property must disclose to a buyer all known
5 material defects about the property being sold that are not readily observable. **While the Law requires certain disclosures, this disclo-**
6 **sure statement covers common topics beyond the basic requirements of the Law in an effort to assist sellers in complying with dis-**
7 **closure requirements and to assist buyers in evaluating the property being considered. Sellers who wish to see or use the basic dis-**
8 **closure form can find the form on the Web site of the Pennsylvania State Real Estate Commission.**
9   This Statement discloses Seller's knowledge of the condition of the property as of the date signed by Seller and **is not a substitute for**
10 **any inspections or warranties that Buyer may wish to obtain**. This Statement is not a warranty of any kind by Seller or a warranty or
11 representation by any listing real estate broker, any selling real estate broker, or their licensees. Buyer is encouraged to address concerns
12 about the conditions of the property that may not be included in this Statement. This Statement does not relieve Seller of the obligation
13 to disclose a material defect that may not be addressed on this form.
14   A Material Defect is a problem with a residential real property or any portion of it that would have a significant adverse impact on the
15 value of the property or that involves an unreasonable risk to people on the property. The fact that a structural element, system or subsys-
16 tem is at or beyond the end of the normal useful life of such a structural element, system or subsystem is not by itself a material defect.

17 1. **SELLER'S EXPERTISE**   Seller does not possess expertise in contracting, engineering, architecture, environmental assessment or
18   other areas related to the construction and conditions of the property and its improvements, except as follows: _____
19   _____

20 2. **OWNERSHIP/OCCUPANCY**
21   (a) Is the property currently occupied? ____Yes ____ No   If "yes," by whom? ____ Seller ____Other occupants (tenants)
22   If property is not occupied, when was it last occupied? _____
23   (b) How long have you owned the property?_____
24   (c) Are you aware of any pets having lived in the house or other structures during your ownership? ____ Yes ____ No
25   If "yes," describe: _____

26 3. **ROOF**
27   (a) Date roof installed: _____ Documented? ____ Yes ____ No ____ Unknown
28   (b) Has the roof been replaced or repaired during your ownership? ____ Yes ____ No
29   If "yes," was the existing roofing material removed? ____ Yes ____ No ____ Unknown
30   (c) Has the roof ever leaked during your ownership? ____ Yes ____ No
31   (d) Are you aware of any problems with the roof, gutters, flashing or downspouts? ____ Yes ____ No
32 **Explain any "yes" answers in this section, including the location and extent of any problem(s) and any repair or remediation efforts:**
33 _____

34 4. **BASEMENTS AND CRAWL SPACES (Complete only if applicable)**
35   (a) Does the property have a sump pump? ____ Yes ____ No ____ Unknown
36   If "yes," has it ever run? ____ Yes ____ No ____ Unknown   Is it in working order? ____ Yes ____ No ____ Unknown
37   (b) Are you aware of any water leakage, accumulation, or dampness within the basement or crawl space? ____ Yes ____ No
38   (c) Do you know of any repairs or other attempts to control any water or dampness problem in the basement or crawl space? ____ Yes ____ No
39 **Explain any "yes" answers in this section, including the location and extent of any problem(s) and any repair or remediation efforts:**
40 _____

41 5. **TERMITES/WOOD-DESTROYING INSECTS, DRYROT, PESTS**
42   (a) Are you aware of any termites/wood-destroying insects, dryrot, or pests affecting the property? ____ Yes ____ No
43   (b) Are you aware of any damage to the property caused by termites/wood-destroying insects, dryrot, or pests? ____ Yes ____ No
44   (c) Is your property currently under contract by a licensed pest control company? ____ Yes ____ No
45   (d) Are you aware of any termite/pest control reports or treatments for the property? ____ Yes ____ No
46 **Explain any "yes" answers in this section, including the name of any service/treatment provider, if applicable:**
47 _____

48 6. **STRUCTURAL ITEMS**
49   (a) Are you aware of any past or present water leakage in the house or other structures? ____ Yes ____ No
50   (b) Are you aware of any past or present movement, shifting, deterioration, or other problems with walls, foundations, or other
51   structural components? ____ Yes ____ No
52   (c) Are you aware of any past or present problems with driveways, walkways, patios, or retaining walls on the property? ____ Yes ____ No
53   (d) Is your property constructed with an Exterior Insulating Finishing System (EIFS), such as Dryvit or synthetic stucco?
54   ____ Yes ____ No ____ Unknown   If yes, date installed, if known _____
55   (e) Are there any defects (including stains) in flooring or floor coverings? ____ Yes ____ No ____ Unknown
56   (f) Are you aware of any fire, storm, water or ice damage to the property? ____ Yes ____ No
57 **Explain any "yes" answers in this section, including the location and extent of any problem(s) and any repair or remediation efforts:**
58 _____

59 **Buyer Initials:** _____ **Date** _____   SPD **Page 1 of 5**   **Seller Initials:** _____ **Date** _____

F I G U R E   18.2

Example of Seller Property Disclosure Statement (continued)

60   7.   **ADDITIONS/REMODELS**   Have you made any additions, structural changes, or other alterations to the property? ____ Yes ____ No

61   If "yes," describe:_____

62   _____

63   8.   **WATER SUPPLY**

64   (a)   What is the source of your drinking water?   ____ Public Water   ____ Well on Property   ____ Community Water

65   ____ None   ____ Other (explain): _____

66   (b)   When was your water last tested? _____ Test results: _____

67   If your drinking water source is not public, is the pumping system in working order?   ____ Yes   ____ No

68   If "no," explain:_____

69   (c)   Do you have a softener, filter, or other treatment system?   ____ Yes   ____ No

70   If you do not own the system, explain:_____

71   (d)   Have you ever had a problem with your water supply? ____Yes   ____ No

72   (e)   Has your well ever run dry? ____ Yes   ____ No   ____ Not Applicable

73   (f)   Is there a well on the property not used as the primary source of drinking water? ____ Yes   ____ No

74   If yes, is the well capped?   ____ Yes   ____ No

75   (g)   Is the water system shared? ____ Yes   ____ No

76   (h)   Are you aware of any leaks or other problems, past or present, relating to the water supply, pumping system, and related items?

77   ____ Yes   ____ No

78   **Explain any "yes" answers in this section, including the location and extent of any problem(s) and any repair or remediation efforts:**

79   _____

80   9.   **SEWAGE SYSTEM**

81   (a)   What is the type of sewage system?   ____ Public Sewer   ____ Individual On-lot Sewage Disposal System

82   ____Individual On-lot Sewage Disposal System in Proximity to Well   ____ Community Sewage Disposal System

83   ____Ten-acre Permit Exemption   ____ Holding Tank   ____ None   ____ None Available/Permit Limitations in Effect

84   ____Other type of sewage system (explain): _____

85   _____

86   (b)   If Individual On-lot sewage system, what type?   ____ Cesspool   ____ Drainfield   ____ Unknown

87   ____ Other (specify): _____

88   (c)   Are there any septic tanks on the Property?   ____ Yes   ____ No   ____ Unknown

89   If "yes," what type of tank(s)?   ____ Metal/steel   ____ Cement/concrete   ____ Fiberglass   ____ Unknown

90   ____Other (specify): _____

91   (d)   When was the on-site sewage disposal system last serviced? _____

92   (e)   Are there any sewage pumps located on the property?   ____ Yes   ____ No

93   If yes, type(s) of pump(s)_____ Are pump(s) in working order? ____ Yes ____ No

94   Who is responsible for maintenance of sewage pumps? _____

95   (f)   Is the sewage system shared? ____ Yes   ____ No

96   (g)   Are you aware of any past or present leaks, backups, or other problems relating to the sewage system and related items?

97   ____Yes   ____ No

98   **Explain any "yes" answers in this section, including the location and extent of any problem(s) and any repair or remediation efforts:**

99   _____

100   10.   **PLUMBING SYSTEM**

101   (a)   Type of plumbing (check all that apply): ____ Copper ____ Galvanized ____ Lead ____ PVC ____ Polybutylene pipe (PB)

102   ____ Mixed ____ Unknown ____Other (explain): _____

103   (b)   Are you aware of any problems with any of your plumbing fixtures (e.g., including but not limited to: kitchen, laundry, or bath-

104   room fixtures; wet bars; etc.)?   ____ Yes   ____ No

105   If "yes," explain: _____

106   11.   **DOMESTIC WATER HEATING**

107   (a)   Type of water heating: ____ Electric ____Natural Gas ____ Fuel Oil ____Propane ____Solar ____ Summer/Winter Hook-Up

108   Other (explain): _____

109   (b)   Are you aware of any problems with any water heater or related equipment? ____ Yes   ____ No

110   If "yes," explain: _____

111   12.   **AIR CONDITIONING SYSTEM**

112   (a)   Type of air conditioning: ____ Central Air ____ Wall Units ____ Window Units ____ None

113   Other (explain): _____

114   Number of window units included in sale____ Location(s) _____

115   (b)   Age of Central Air Conditioning System: _____ ____ Unknown   Date last serviced, if known _____

116   (c)   List any areas of the house that are not air conditioned: _____

117   _____

118   (d)   Are you aware of any problems with any item in this section? ____ Yes   ____ No

119   If "yes," explain: _____

120   **Buyer Initials:** _____ **Date** _____   **SPD   Page 2 of 5**   **Seller Initials:** _____ **Date** _____

Example of Seller Property Disclosure Statement (continued)

13. **HEATING SYSTEM**
    (a) Type(s) of heating fuel(s) (check all that apply): _____ Electric _____ Fuel Oil _____ Natural Gas _____ Propane
       _____ Coal _____ Wood _____ Other: _____
    (b) Type(s) of heating system(s) (check all that apply): _____ Forced Hot Air _____ Hot Water _____ Heat Pump
       _____ Electric Baseboard _____ Steam _____ Wood Stove (How many? ___) _____ Coal Stove (How many? ___)
       _____ Other: _____
    (c) Age of Heating System: _____ _____ Unknown   Date last serviced, if known _____
    (d) Are there any fireplaces? _____ Yes _____ No   If "yes," how many? _____ Are they working? _____ Yes _____ No
    (e) Are there any chimneys (from a fireplace, water heater or any other heating system)? _____ Yes _____ No
       If "yes," how many? _____ When were they last cleaned? _____ Unknown _____
       Are they working? _____ Yes _____ No   If "no," explain: _____
    (f) List any areas of the house that are not heated: _____
    (g) Are you aware of any heating fuel tanks on the property? _____ Yes _____ No
       Location(s), including underground tank(s): _____
       If you do not own the tanks, explain: _____
    Are you aware of any problems or repairs needed regarding any item in this section? _____ Yes _____ No
    If "yes," explain: _____
    _____

14. **ELECTRICAL SYSTEM**
    (a) Type of Electrical System: _____ Fuses _____ Circuit Breakers   How Many Amps? _____ _____ Unknown
    (b) Are you aware of any knob and tube wiring in the home? _____ Yes _____ No
    Are you aware of any problems or repairs needed in the electrical system? _____ Yes _____ No
    If "yes," explain: _____

15. **OTHER EQUIPMENT AND APPLIANCES**
    This section must be completed for each item that will, or may, be sold with the property. The fact that an item is listed does not mean it is included in the Agreement of Sale. Terms of the Agreement of Sale negotiated between Buyer and Seller will determine which items, if any, are included in the purchase of the Property.
    (a) _____ Electric Garage Door Opener   Number of Transmitters _____ Keyless Entry _____
    (b) _____ Smoke Detectors   How many? _____ Location(s) _____
    (c) _____ Security Alarm System _____ Owned _____ Leased (Lease Information _____)
    (d) _____ Lawn Sprinkler(s)   How many? _____ Automatic Timer _____
    (e) _____ Swimming Pool _____ Hot Tub/Spa _____ Pool/Spa Heater _____ Pool/Spa Cover _____ Whirlpool/Tub
       _____ Pool/Spa Equipment and Accessories (list): _____
    (f) _____ Refrigerator(s) _____ Range/Oven _____ Microwave Oven _____ Dishwasher _____ Trash Compactor
       _____ Garbage Disposal _____ Chest Freezer _____ Washer _____ Dryer _____ Intercom
    (g) _____ Ceiling Fan(s)   How many? _____ Location(s) _____
    (h) _____ Awnings _____ Attic Fan(s) _____ Satellite Dish _____ Storage Shed _____ Deck(s) _____ Electric Animal Fence
    (i) _____ Other: _____
    Are you aware of any problems or repairs needed regarding any item in this section? _____ Yes _____ No
    If "yes," explain: _____

16. **LAND (SOILS, DRAINAGE, FLOODING AND BOUNDARIES)**
    (a) Land/Soils
       1) Are you aware of any fill or expansive soil on the property? _____ Yes _____ No
       2) Are you aware of any sliding, settling, earth movement, upheaval, subsidence, or earth stability problems that have occurred on or affect the property? _____ Yes _____ No
       3) Are you aware of any existing, past or proposed mining, strip-mining, or any other excavations that might affect this property? _____ Yes _____ No
       Note to Buyer: The property may be subject to mine subsidence damage. Maps of the counties and mines where mine subsidence damage may occur and mine subsidence insurance are available through: Department of Environmental Protection, Mine Subsidence Insurance Fund, 25 Technology Drive, California Technology Park, Coal Center, PA 15423 (800) 922-1678 (within Pennsylvania) or (724) 769-1100 (outside Pennsylvania).
       4) Is the property, or a portion of it, preferentially assessed for tax purposes, or subject to limited development rights?
          _____ Yes _____ No   If "yes", check all that apply below:
          _____ **Farmland and Forest Land Assessment Act** - 72 P.S.§5490.1 et seq. (Clean and Green Program)
          _____ **Open Space Act** - 16 P.S. §11941 et seq.
          _____ **Agricultural Area Security Law** - 3 P.S. §901 et seq. (Development Rights)
          _____ Other
       Note to Buyer: Pennsylvania has enacted the Right to Farm Act (3 P.S. § 951-957) in an effort to limit the circumstances under which agricultural operations may be subject to nuisance suits or ordinances. Buyers are encouraged to investigate whether any agricultural operations covered by the Act operate in the vicinity of the property.
    Explain any "yes" answers in this section: _____
    _____

Buyer Initials: _____ Date _____   SPD Page 3 of 5   **Seller Initials:** _____ Date _____

F I G U R E   **18.2**

Example of Seller Property Disclosure Statement (continued)

184   (b) **Flooding/Drainage**

185   1) Is any part of this property located in a wetlands area or a FEMA flood zone?   ____Yes ____ No ____ Unknown

186   2) Do you know of any past or present drainage or flooding problems affecting the property?   ____ Yes   ____ No

187 **Explain any "yes" answers in this section, including dates and extent of flooding:**_____

188 _____

189   (c) **Boundaries**

190   1) Do you know of any encroachments, boundary line disputes, or easements affecting the property?   ____ Yes   ____ No

191 *Note to Buyer: Most properties have easements running across them for utility services and other reasons. In many cases, the*

192 *easements do not restrict the ordinary use of the property, and Seller may not be readily aware of them. Buyers may wish to*

193 *determine the existence of easements and restrictions by examining the property and ordering an Abstract of Title or searching*

194 *the records in the Office of the Recorder of Deeds for the county before entering into an agreement of sale.*

195   2) Do you access the property from a private road or lane? ____ Yes   ____ No

196   If yes, do you have a recorded right of way or maintenance agreement? ____ Yes   ____ No

197   3) Are you aware of any shared or common areas (e.g., driveways, bridges, docks, walls, etc.) or maintenance agreements?

198   ____ Yes   ____ No

199 **Explain any "yes" answers in this section:** _____

200 _____

201 17. **HAZARDOUS SUBSTANCES AND ENVIRONMENTAL ISSUES**

202   (a) Are you aware of any underground tanks (other than home heating fuel or septic tanks disclosed above)?   ____ Yes ____ No

203   (b) Are you aware of any past or present hazardous substances present on the property (structure or soil) such as, but not limited

204   to, asbestos or polychlorinated biphenyls (PCBs), etc.? ____ Yes____ No

205   (c) Are you aware of sewage sludge (other than commercially available fertilizer products) being spread on the property, or have you

206   received written notice of sewage sludge being spread on an adjacent property? ____ Yes ____ No

207   (d) Are you aware of any tests for mold, fungi, or indoor air quality in the property? ____ Yes   ____ No

208   (e) Other than general household cleaning, have you taken any efforts to control or remediate mold or mold-like substances in the

209   property? ____ Yes   ____ No

210 *Note to Buyer: Individuals may be affected differently, or not at all, by mold contamination. If mold contamination or indoor air qual-*

211 *ity is a concern, buyers are encouraged to engage the services of a qualified professional to do testing. Information on this issue is*

212 *available from the United States Environmental Protection Agency and may be obtained by contacting IAQ INFO, P.O. Box 37133,*

213 *Washington, D.C. 20013-7133, 1-800-438-4318.*

214   (f) Are you aware of any dumping on the property? ____ Yes ____ No

215   (g) Have you received written notice regarding the presence of an environmental hazard or biohazard on your property or any

216   adjacent property? ____ Yes   ____ No

217   (h) Are you aware of any tests for radon gas that have been performed in any buildings on the property?   ____ Yes   ____ No

218   If "yes," list date, type, and results of all tests below:

219   DATE   TYPE OF TEST   RESULTS (picocuries/liter or working levels)   NAME OF TESTING SERVICE

220   _____

221   _____

222   (i) Are you aware of any radon removal system on the property?   ____ Yes   ____ No

223   If "yes," list date installed and type of system, and whether it is in working order below:

224   DATE INSTALLED   TYPE OF SYSTEM   PROVIDER   WORKING ORDER?

225   _____ ____ Yes ____ No

226   _____ ____ Yes ____ No

227   (j) If property was constructed, or if construction began, before 1978, you must disclose any knowledge of lead-based paint on the

228   property. Are you aware of any lead-based paint or lead-based paint hazards on the property? ____ Yes   ____ No

229   If "yes," explain how you know of it, where it is, and the condition of those lead-based paint surfaces: _____

230 _____

231   (k) If property was constructed, or if construction began, before 1978, you must disclose any reports or records of lead-based paint

232   or lead-based paint hazards on the property. Are you aware of any reports or records regarding lead-based paint or lead-based

233   paint hazards on the property?   ____ Yes   ____ No

234   If "yes," list all available reports and records: _____

235   (l) Are you aware of testing on the property for any other hazardous substances or environmental concerns ? ____ Yes ____ No

236   (m) Are you aware of of any other hazardous substances or environmental concerns that might impact upon the property?

237   ____ Yes   ____ No

238 **Explain any "yes" answers in this section:** _____

239 _____

240 _____

241 _____

242 **Buyer Initials:** _____ **Date** _____   **SPD Page 4 of 5**   **Seller Initials:** _____ **Date** _____

F I G U R E   18.2

Example of Seller Property Disclosure Statement (continued)

243 18. **CONDOMINIUMS AND OTHER HOMEOWNER ASSOCIATIONS (Complete only if applicable)**
244   Type: _____ Condominium _____ Cooperative _____ Homeowner Association or Planned Community
245   Other: _____
246   *Notice regarding Condominiums, Cooperatives, and Planned Communities: A buyer of a resale unit in a condominium, coopera-*
247   *tive, or planned community must receive a copy of the declaration (other than the plats and plans), the by-laws, the rules or regula-*
248   *tions, and a certificate of resale issued by the association in the condominium, cooperative, or planned com-*
249   *munity. Buyers may be responsible for capital contributions, initiation fees or similar one-time fees in addition to regular monthly*
250   *maintenance fees. The buyer will have the option of canceling the agreement with the return of all deposit monies until the certificate*
251   *has been provided to the buyer and for five days thereafter or until conveyance, whichever occurs first.*
252 19. **MISCELLANEOUS**
253   (a) Are you aware of any historic preservation restriction or ordinance or archeological designation associated with the property?
254   _____ Yes _____ No
255   (b) Are you aware of any existing or threatened legal action affecting the property? _____ Yes _____ No
256   (c) Are you aware of any violations of federal, state, or local laws or regulations relating to this property? _____ Yes _____ No
257   (d) Are you aware of any public improvement, condominium or homeowner association assessments against the property that remain
258   unpaid or of any violations of zoning, housing, building, safety or fire ordinances that remain uncorrected? _____ Yes _____ No
259   (e) Are you aware of any judgment, encumbrance, lien (for example, co-maker or equity loan), overdue payment on a support obli-
260   gation, or other debt against this property that cannot be satisfied by the proceeds of this sale? _____ Yes _____ No
261   (f) Are you aware of any reason, including a defect in title, that would prevent you from giving a warranty deed or conveying title to the
262   property? _____ Yes _____ No
263   (g) Are you aware of any insurance claims filed relating to the property? _____ Yes _____ No
264   (h) Are you aware of any material defects to the property, dwelling, or fixtures which are not disclosed elsewhere on this form?
265   _____ Yes _____ No
266   A material defect is a problem with a residential real property or any portion of it that would have a significant adverse impact
267   on the value of the property or that involves an unreasonable risk to people on the property. The fact that a structural element,
268   system or subsystem is at or beyond the end of the normal useful life of such a structural element, system or subsystem is not by
269   itself a material defect
270 **Explain any "yes" answers in this section:** _____
271 _____

272 **The undersigned Seller represents that the information set forth in this disclosure statement is accurate and complete to the best**
273 **of Seller's knowledge. Seller hereby authorizes the Listing Broker to provide this information to prospective buyers of the prop-**
274 **erty and to other real estate licensees. SELLER ALONE IS RESPONSIBLE FOR THE ACCURACY OF THE INFORMATION**
275 **CONTAINED IN THIS STATEMENT. Seller shall cause Buyer to be notified in writing of any information supplied on this form**
276 **which is rendered inaccurate by a change in the condition of the property following completion of this form.**

277 **WITNESS** _____ **SELLER** _____ **DATE** _____
278 **WITNESS** _____ **SELLER** _____ **DATE** _____
279 **WITNESS** _____ **SELLER** _____ **DATE** _____

280 | **EXECUTOR, ADMINISTRATOR, TRUSTEE SIGNATURE BLOCK** |

281 According to the provisions of the Real Estate Seller Disclosure Law, the undersigned executor, administrator or trustee is not required
282 to fill out a Seller's Property Disclosure Statement. The executor, administrator or trustee, must, however, disclose any known mate-
283 rial defect(s) of the property.
284 _____ **DATE** _____

285 | **RECEIPT AND ACKNOWLEDGEMENT BY BUYER** |

286 **The undersigned Buyer acknowledges receipt of this Disclosure Statement. Buyer acknowledges that this Statement is not a**
287 **warranty and that, unless stated otherwise in the sales contract, Buyer is purchasing this property in its present condition. It**
288 **is Buyer's responsibility to satisfy himself or herself as to the condition of the property. Buyer may request that the property**
289 **be inspected, at Buyer's expense and by qualified professionals, to determine the condition of the structure or its components.**

290 **WITNESS** _____ **BUYER** _____ **DATE** _____
291 **WITNESS** _____ **BUYER** _____ **DATE** _____
292 **WITNESS** _____ **BUYER** _____ **DATE** _____

293

■ THE LISTING CONTRACT FORM

A variety of listing contract forms is available. Some brokers draft their own, some use forms prepared by their MLSs, and others use forms prepared by their professional associations. Some brokers also use a separate information sheet (also known as a profile or data sheet) for recording property features. That sheet is wed to the form that contains the contractual obligations between the seller and the broker.

Although the specifics of contracts vary with the type of listing agreement and other agency issues, all listing agreements tend to require similar information. This is because the same issues commonly arise in most real estate transactions. Licensees should be familiar with the specific forms used in their areas. Figure 18.3 is an example of a typical exclusive-right-to-sell listing agreement. Some of the issues covered in a typical contract include

- type of listing agreement;
- broker's authority and responsibilities;
- name of all parties to the contract (everyone who has an ownership interest);
- name of the broker and the brokerage firm;
- listing price;
- description of the premises;
- description of the real and any personal property to be offered for sale;
- evidence of ownership and any encumbrances that could affect the use or transfer;
- broker's compensation, including a statement that it has been agreed to as a result of negotiation;
- term of the contract and termination provisions, including a statement that the term has been agreed to as a result of negotiations;
- broker protection clause;
- indemnification clause (hold harmless wording);
- nondiscrimination wording;
- antitrust wording;
- Real Estate Recovery Fund information;
- Lead-Based Paint Disclosure, if applicable;
- signatures of all parties;
- date the contract is executed (which may be different than the date that the contract becomes effective); and
- any other disclosures required by law or rule.

■ BUYER REPRESENTATION

As more buyers become better informed, many more seek the level of service that has customarily been available only to sellers in residential transactions, that is, buyers want representation, someone to protect their interests at all points in the transaction. The transformation of the industry in recent years has brought many more brokers into the business of buyer representation. In fact, this practice has become the norm in many markets. While providing client-level services to buyers enhances a broker's business opportunities, the broker's firm also must be prepared to undertake the fiduciary responsibilities it assumes.

F I G U R E   18.3

Exclusive-Right-To-Sell Listing Contract

LISTING CONTRACT   XLS

EXCLUSIVE RIGHT TO SELL REAL ESTATE

This form recommended and approved for, but not restricted to use by, the members of the Pennsylvania Association of REALTORS® (PAR).

1 **BROKER (Company)** _____
2 **LICENSEE(S)** _____
3 **SELLER** _____
4 **Does Seller have a Listing Contract with another Broker?** ☐ Yes   ☐ No
5 **If yes, explain:** _____
6
7 **1. PROPERTY**   **LISTED PRICE $** _____
8   Address _____
9   Municipality (city, borough, township) _____
10   County_____ School District _____
11   Zoning_____ Present Use_____
12   Identification (Tax ID #; Parcel #; Lot, Block; Deed Book, Page, Recording Date)_____
13   _____
14 **2. STARTING & ENDING DATES OF LISTING CONTRACT (ALSO CALLED "TERM")**
15   A. No Association of REALTORS® has set or recommended the term of this contract. By law, the length or term of a listing con-
16   tract may not exceed one year. Broker and Seller have discussed and agreed upon the length or term of this Contract.
17   B. Starting Date: This Contract starts when signed by Broker and Seller, unless otherwise stated here:_____.
18   C. Ending Date: This Contract ends on _____.
19
20 **3. DUAL AGENCY** Seller agrees that Broker may also represent the buyer(s) of the Property. The Broker is a DUAL AGENT when
21   representing both Seller and the buyer in the sale of a property.
22 **4. DESIGNATED AGENCY**
23   ☐ **Not Applicable**
24   ☐ **Applicable.** Broker may designate licensees to represent the separate interests of Seller and the buyer. Licensee (identified
25   above) is the Designated Agent, who will act exclusively as the Seller Agent. If Property is introduced to the buyer by a licensee
26   in the Company who is not representing the buyer, then that licensee is authorized to work on behalf of Seller. If Licensee is also
27   the Buyer's Agent, then Licensee is a DUAL AGENT.
28 **5. BROKER'S FEE** No Association of REALTORS® has set or recommended the Broker's Fee. Broker and Seller have negotiated
29   the fee that Seller will pay Broker. Broker's Fee is _____% of the sales price AND $_____, paid by Seller.
30 **6. COOPERATION WITH OTHER BROKERS**
31   Licensee has explained Broker's company policies about cooperating with other brokers. Broker and Seller agree that Broker will pay
32   from Broker's Fee to another broker who procures the buyer, is a member of a Multiple Listing Service (MLS), and who:
33   A. ☐ **represents Seller (SUBAGENT).** Broker will pay _____ of/from the sale price.
34   B. ☐ **represents the buyer (BUYER'S AGENT).** Broker will pay _____ of/from the sale price.
35   **A Buyer's Agent, even if compensated by Broker for Seller, will represent the interests of the buyer.**
36   C. ☐ **does not represent either Seller or a buyer (TRANSACTION LICENSEE).**
37   Broker will pay _____ of/from the sale price.
38 **7. PAYMENT OF BROKER'S FEE**
39   A. **Seller will pay Broker's Fee if Property, or any ownership interest in it, is sold or exchanged during the term of this**
40   **Contract by Broker, Broker's salespersons, Seller, or by any other person or broker, at the listed price or any price accept-**
41   **able to Seller.**
42   B. Seller will pay Broker's Fee if a ready, willing, and able buyer is found by Broker or by anyone, including Seller. A willing buyer
43   is one who will pay the listed price or more for the Property, or one who has submitted an offer accepted by Seller.
44   C. Seller will pay Broker's Fee if negotiations that are pending at the Ending Date of this Contract result in a sale.
45   D. Seller will pay Broker's Fee for a sale that occurs after the Ending Date of this Contract IF:
46   (1) The sale occurs within _____ of the Ending Date, AND
47   (2) The buyer was shown or negotiated to buy the Property during the term of this contract, AND
48   (3) The Property is not listed under an "exclusive right to sell contract" with another broker at the time of the sale.
49   E. If a buyer signs an agreement of sale then refuses to buy the Property, or if a buyer is unable to buy the Property because of fail-
50   ing to do all the things required of the buyer in the agreement of sale (buyer default), Seller will pay Broker
51   _____ of/from buyer's deposit monies, OR the **Broker's Fee** in Paragraph 5, whichever is less.
52   F. If the Property or any part of it is taken by any government for public use (Eminent Domain), Seller will pay Broker's Fee from
53   any money paid by the government.
54   G. If a sale occurs, Broker's Fee will be paid upon delivery of the deed or other evidence of transfer of title or interest. If the Property
55   is transferred by an installment contract, Broker's Fee will be paid upon the execution of the installment contract.

XLS Page 1 of 4

 Pennsylvania Association of
REALTORS®
REALTOR®   **The Voice for Real Estate® in Pennsylvania**

COPYRIGHT PENNSYLVANIA ASSOCIATION OF REALTORS® 2003
11/03

Exclusive-Right-To-Sell Listing Contract (continued)

8. DUTIES OF BROKER AND SELLER

    A. Broker is acting as a Seller's Agent, as described in the Consumer Notice, to market the Property and to negotiate with potential buyers. Broker will use reasonable efforts to find a buyer for the Property.

    B. Seller will cooperate with Broker and assist in the sale of the Property as asked by Broker.

    C. All showings, negotiations and discussions about the sale of the Property will be done by Broker on Seller's behalf. All written or oral inquiries that Seller receives or learns about regarding the Property, regardless of the source, will be referred to Broker.

    D. If the Property, or any part of it, is rented, Seller will give any leases to Broker before signing this Contract. If any leases are oral, Seller will provide a written summary of the terms, including amount of rent, ending date, and Tenant's responsibilities.

    E. Seller will not enter into or renew any leases during the term of this Contract without first giving notice to Broker.

9. BROKER'S SERVICE TO BUYER

Broker may provide services to a buyer for which Broker may accept a fee. Such services may include, but are not limited to: deed/document preparation; ordering certifications required for closing; financial services; title transfer and preparation services; ordering insurance, construction, repair, or inspection services. Broker will disclose to Seller if any fees are to be paid by Buyer.

10. BROKER NOT RESPONSIBLE FOR DAMAGES

Seller agrees that Broker and Broker's salespersons are not responsible for any damage to the Property or any loss or theft of personal goods from the Property unless such damage, loss or theft is directly caused by Broker or Broker's salespersons.

11. DEPOSIT MONEY

    A. Broker, or any person Seller and the buyer name in the agreement of sale, will keep all deposit monies paid by or for the buyer in an escrow account until the sale is completed or the agreement of sale is terminated. If held by Broker, this escrow account will be held as required by real estate licensing laws and regulations. Seller agrees that the person keeping the deposit monies may wait to deposit any uncashed check that is received as deposit money until Seller has accepted an offer.

    B. If Seller joins Broker or Licensee in a lawsuit for the return of deposit monies, Seller will pay Broker's and Licensee's attorneys' fees and costs.

12. OTHER PROPERTIES

Seller agrees that Broker may list other properties for sale and that Broker may show other properties to prospective buyers.

13. CONFLICT OF INTEREST

A conflict of interest is when Broker or Licensee has a financial or personal interest where Broker or Licensee cannot put Seller's interests before any other. If Broker, Licensee, or any of Broker's salespeople has a conflict of interest, Broker will notify Seller in a timely manner.

14. PUBLICATION OF SALE PRICE

Seller is aware that the Multiple Listing Service (MLS), newspapers, and other media may publish the final sale price of the Property after settlement.

15. SELLER WILL REVEAL DEFECTS & ENVIRONMENTAL HAZARDS

    A. Seller (including Sellers exempt from the Real Estate Seller Disclosure Law) will disclose all known material defects and/or environmental hazards on a separate disclosure statement. A material defect is a problem or condition that:

        (1) is a possible danger to those living on the Property, or

        (2) has a significant, adverse effect on the value of the Property.

        The fact that a structural element, system or subsystem is near, at or beyond the end of the normal useful life of such a structural element, system or subsystem is not by itself a material defect.

    B. If Seller fails to disclose known material defects and/or environmental hazards:

        (1) Seller will not hold Broker or Licensee responsible in any way;

        (2) Seller will protect Broker and Licensee from any claims, lawsuits, and actions that result;

        (3) Seller will pay all of Broker's and Licensee's costs that result. This includes attorneys' fees and court-ordered payments or settlements (money Broker or Licensee pays to end a lawsuit or claim).

Exclusive-Right-To-Sell Listing Contract (continued)

16. IF PROPERTY WAS BUILT BEFORE 1978

The Residential Lead-Based Paint Hazard Reduction Act says that any seller of property built before 1978 must give the buyer an EPA pamphlet titled *Protect Your Family From Lead in Your Home*. The seller also must tell the buyer and the broker what the seller knows about lead-based paint and lead-based paint hazards that are in or on the property being sold. seller must tell the buyer how the seller knows that lead-based paint and lead-based paint hazards are on the property, where the lead-based paint and lead-based paint hazards are, the condition of the painted surfaces, and any other information seller knows about lead-based paint and lead-based paint hazards on the property. Any seller of a pre-1978 structure must also give the buyer any records and reports that the seller has or can get about lead-based paint or lead-based paint hazards in or around the property being sold, the common areas, or other dwellings in multi-family housing. According to the Act, a seller must give a buyer 10 days (unless seller and the buyer agree to a different period of time) from the time an agreement of sale is signed to have a "risk assessment" or inspection for possible lead-based paint hazards done on the property. Buyers may choose not to have the risk assessment or inspection for lead paint hazards done. If the buyer chooses not to have the assessment or inspection, the buyer must inform the seller in writing of the choice. The Act does not require the seller to inspect for lead paint hazards or to correct lead paint hazards on the property. The Act does not apply to housing built in 1978 or later.

17. RECOVERY FUND

Pennsylvania has a Real Estate Recovery Fund (the Fund) to repay any person who has received a final court ruling (civil judgment) against a Pennsylvania real estate licensee because of fraud, misrepresentation, or deceit in a real estate transaction. The Fund repays persons who have not been able to collect the judgment after trying all lawful ways to do so. For complete details about the Fund, call (717) 783-3658, or (800) 822-2113 (within Pennsylvania) and (717) 783-4854 (outside Pennsylvania).

18. NOTICE TO PERSONS OFFERING TO SELL OR RENT HOUSING IN PENNSYLVANIA

Federal and state laws make it illegal for a seller, a broker, or anyone to use RACE, COLOR, RELIGION or RELIGIOUS CREED, SEX, DISABILITY (physical or mental), FAMILIAL STATUS (children under 18 years of age), AGE (40 or older), NATIONAL ORIGIN, USE OR HANDLING/TRAINING OF SUPPORT OR GUIDE ANIMALS, or the FACT OF RELATIONSHIP OR ASSOCIATION TO AN INDIVIDUAL KNOWN TO HAVE A DISABILITY as reasons for refusing to sell, show, or rent properties, loan money, or set deposit amounts, or as reasons for any decision relating to the sale of property.

19. ADDITIONAL OFFERS

If asked by a buyer or cooperating broker, Broker will reveal the existence of offers on the Property, unless prohibited by Seller. ONCE SELLER ENTERS INTO AN AGREEMENT OF SALE, BROKER IS NOT REQUIRED TO PRESENT OTHER OFFERS.

20. TRANSFER OF THIS CONTRACT

A. Broker will notify Seller immediately in writing if Broker transfers this Contract to another broker when:
    (1) Broker stops doing business, OR
    (2) Broker forms a new real estate business, OR
    (3) Broker joins his business with another.
    Seller agrees that Broker may transfer this Contract to another broker. Broker will notify Seller immediately in writing when a transfer occurs or Broker will lose the right to transfer this Contract. Seller will follow all requirements of this Contract with the new broker.

B. Should Seller give or transfer the Property, or an ownership interest in it, to anyone during the term of this Contract, all owners will follow the requirements of this Contract.

21. NO OTHER CONTRACTS

Seller will not enter into another listing contract with another broker that begins before the Ending Date of this Contract.

22. ENTIRE CONTRACT

This Contract is the entire agreement between Broker and Seller. Any verbal or written agreements that were made before are not a part of this Contract.

23. CHANGES TO THIS CONTRACT

All changes to this Contract must be in writing and signed by Broker and Seller.

24. SPECIAL INSTRUCTIONS

The Office of the Attorney General has not pre-approved any special conditions or additional terms added by any parties. Any special conditions or additional terms in this Contract must comply with the Pennsylvania Plain Language Consumer Contract Act.

Exclusive-Right-To-Sell Listing Contract (continued)

163 **25. MARKETING OF PROPERTY**

164   A. Where permitted, Broker, at Broker's option, may use: ☐ For sale sign ☐ Sold sign ☐ Key in office ☐ Lock box

165   ☐ Print /electronic advertising, including photographs ☐ Property address in print/electronic advertising.

166   B. Broker ☐ will /☐ will not use a Multiple Listing Service (MLS) to advertise the Property to other real estate brokers and

167   salespersons.

168   Seller agrees that Broker, Licensee, and the MLS are not responsible for mistakes in the MLS and/or advertising of the Property.

169 **26. ITEMS INCLUDED/NOT INCLUDED IN THE PRICE OF THE PROPERTY**

170   A. Included in the sale and purchase price are all existing items permanently installed in the Property, free of liens, including plumb-

171   ing; heating; lighting fixtures (including chandeliers and ceiling fans); water treatment systems; pool and spa equipment; garage

172   door openers and transmitters; television antennas; shrubbery, plantings, and unpotted trees; any remaining heating and cooking

173   fuels stored on the Property at the time of settlement; wall to wall carpeting; window covering hardware, shades, and blinds; built-

174   in air conditioners; built-in appliances, and the range/oven, unless otherwise stated. Also included: _____

175   _____

176   B. The following items are NOT included in the purchase and price of the Property: _____

177   _____

178   C. Items leased by the Seller: _____

179 | **ADDITIONAL INFORMATION (OPTIONAL)** |

180 **TITLE & POSSESSION**

181   A. Seller will give possession of Property to a buyer at settlement, or on _____

182   B. At settlement, Seller will give full rights of ownership (fee simple) to a buyer except as follows:

183   (1) Mineral Rights Agreements: _____

184   (2) Other: _____

185   C. Seller has:

186   ☐ Mortgage with: _____ Amount of balance $ _____

187   Address: _____ Phone: _____ Acct. #: _____

188   ☐ Equity Loan with: _____ Amount of balance $ _____

189   Address: _____ Phone: _____ Acct. #: _____

190   ☐ Seller authorizes Broker to receive mortgage payoff and/or equity loan payoff information from lender(s).

191   D. Seller has: ☐ Judgments ☐ Municipal Assessment ☐ Past Due Taxes ☐ Other:_____

192         $_____ $_____ $_____ $_____

193   E. If Seller, at any time on or since January 1, 1998, has been obligated to pay support under an order on record in any Pennsylvania

194   county, list the county and the Domestic Relations Number or Docket Number: _____

195 **TAXES, UTILITIES, & ASSOCIATION FEES**

196   A. At settlement, Seller will pay one-half of the total Real Estate Transfer Taxes, unless otherwise stated here: _____

197   _____

198   B. Real Estate Property Tax Assessment $_____ Yearly Taxes $ _____

199   Wage/Income Tax $_____ Per Capita Tax $ _____

200   C. Estimated Utilities (trash, water, sewer, electric, gas, oil, etc.): _____

201   _____

202   D. Association Fees $_____ Include: _____

203 **BUYER FINANCING**   Seller will accept the following arrangements for buyer to pay for the Property:

204   ☐ Cash   ☐ Conventional mortgage   ☐ FHA mortgage   ☐ VA mortgage

205   ☐ Seller's help to buyer (if any): _____

206 **Seller has read the Consumer Notice as adopted by the State Real Estate Commission at 49 Pa. Code §35.336.**

207 **Seller gives permission for Broker to send information about this transaction to the fax number(s) and/or e-mail address(es) listed below.**

208 **Seller has read the entire Contract before signing. All Sellers must sign this Contract.**

209 **Return by facsimile (FAX) constitutes acceptance of this Contract.**

210 **NOTICE BEFORE SIGNING: IF SELLER HAS LEGAL QUESTIONS, SELLER IS ADVISED TO CONSULT AN ATTORNEY.**

211 **SELLER'S MAILING ADDRESS:** _____

212 _____

213 **PHONE:** _____ **FAX:** _____ **E-MAIL:** _____

214 **SELLER** _____ **DATE** _____

215 **SELLER** _____ **DATE** _____

216 **BROKER (Company Name)** _____

217 **ACCEPTED BY** _____ **DATE** _____

XLS Page 4 of 4

Some brokers elect to be *exclusive* buyer-brokers (that is, their firms represent only buyers and refer prospective sellers to other brokers); other brokers offer agency relationships to buyers as well as to sellers. Certain categories of buyers will almost always require client-level service. These include

- relatives and close friends of the licensee;
- former clients or customers;
- buyers requiring anonymity;
- first-time buyers; and
- out-of-town buyers and transferees.

Like a listing agreement, a **buyer agency agreement** is an employment contract. In this case, however, the broker is employed as the buyer's agent. The buyer, rather than the seller, is the principal. The purpose of the agreement is to find a suitable property that meets the buyer's specifications. Just as with listing contracts, buyer agency contracts are between the buyer and broker, even though the salesperson or associate broker typically locates the property and has the most direct contact with the buyer.

Types of Buyer Agency Agreements

Three basic types of buyer agency agreements exist:

1. *Exclusive buyer agency*—This is a completely exclusive agency agreement. The buyer is legally bound to compensate the broker whenever the buyer purchases a property of the type described in the contract. The broker is entitled to compensation regardless of whether the property is located by the broker, the buyer, or another licensee.
2. *Exclusive agency buyer agency*—Like an exclusive buyer agency agreement, this is an exclusive contract between the buyer and one broker. However, this agreement limits the broker's right to compensation. The broker is entitled to payment only if he or she locates the property the buyer ultimately purchases. The buyer is free to locate a suitable property on his or her own without obligation to compensate the broker.
3. *Open buyer agency*—This agreement is a nonexclusive agency contract between a broker and a buyer. It permits the buyer to enter into similar agreements with an unlimited number of brokers. The buyer is obligated to compensate only the broker who locates the property the buyer ultimately purchases.

Contracting with Buyers

The process of contracting with buyers is a twofold event, similar to the steps involved in contracting with sellers, beginning with a discussion of the Consumer Notice and followed by the negotiation of a buyer agency agreement.

Typically, the buyer wants not only the efficiency of someone to scrutinize the marketplace and identify suitable properties but, most important, someone to be the buyer's advocate and achieve the most advantageous terms in negotiations. Obviously, the buyer needs to know what client-level services the brokerage firm provides to accomplish this.

Before these or any other substantive issues can be discussed, however, the licensee must provide the prospective buyer with the Consumer Notice that was discussed in Chapter 16. This is also the licensee's opportunity to explain various types of buyer agency agreements and the ramifications of agency relationships. An important issue in the discussion will be the broker's policy regarding relationships with other parties who might be involved in the transaction. For instance, does the broker also represent seller-clients? Does the company's policy include the appointment of designated agents?

Similarly, before the buyer agency agreement is finalized, the broker should be prepared to fulfill the fiduciary obligations the agreement imposes. The buyer should have provided comprehensive information about the property requirements and his or her personal and financial terms. Based on this information, the broker can accept the agency agreement with confidence that the buyer's goals can be met in a profitable manner for both parties.

Before entering into a buyer agency agreement, compensation also must be discussed. Buyer's agents may be compensated in the form of a flat fee for services, an hourly rate, a percentage of the purchase price, or a specific fee for each service provided. The agent may require a *retainer fee* at the time the agreement is signed to cover initial expenses. The retainer may be applied as a credit toward any fees due at closing. A buyer's agent also may be compensated from the commission paid by the seller. As in any agency agreement, the source of compensation is not the factor that determines the relationship. A buyer's agent may be compensated by either the buyer or the seller (through the listing broker). Issues of compensation are *always* negotiable. Once again, a key point to remember is that representation is an agency issue, while compensation is a contract issue.

Gathering Information

Once the real estate licensee and the buyer have agreed to pursue a buyer-agent relationship, the parties need to discuss specific factual information to enable the licensee to represent the buyer's interests. That information includes

- names of all buyers being represented;
- type of property desired;
- geographic areas covered by the agreement;
- price range of property desired;
- length of time the contract will run;
- scope of work to be performed by the agent;
- exclusive or nonexclusive contract terms;
- terms and source of compensation to the buyer's agent;
- possibility of dual agency;
- financial terms of a purchase; and
- purchase agreement inclusions and contingencies.

■ BUYER REPRESENTATION AGREEMENT

A wide variety of buyer-representation agreement forms are available. Some brokers create their own documents, while others use forms prepared by professional associations. Regardless of the form used, the basic issues listed above are typically addressed in the contracts. Licensees should be familiar with the forms used by their company and be prepared to explain their provisions. As always, licensees must remember that they are not permitted to give legal advice or practice law unless separately licensed as an attorney at law. The buyer representation agreement illustrated in Figure 18.4 contains the following provisions:

- Type of buyer agency relationship
- Time period (the term) of the contract
- Brokerage fee and obligation of buyer to compensate broker (if that's the case)
- Property requirements and terms of purchase
- Broker protection clause
- Provision for licensee to act as designated agent (if applicable)
- Provision for dual agency (if that's the broker's policy)
- Provision for assignment of the contract by the broker
- Signatures of all parties
- Disclosures relating to conflict of interest
- Nondiscrimination wording
- Disclosures regarding zoning issues, the Real Estate Recovery Fund, and any others required by law or rule

■ SUMMARY

To acquire an inventory of property to sell, brokers who have chosen to represent sellers must obtain listings. Types of listing agreements include open listings, exclusive agency listings, and exclusive-right-to-sell listings.

With an exclusive-right-to-sell listing, the seller employs only one broker and must compensate that broker, regardless of whether it is the broker or the seller who finds a buyer, so long as the buyer is found within the listing period.

Under an exclusive agency listing, the broker is given the exclusive right to represent the seller, but the seller can avoid compensating the broker if the owner sells the property without the broker's help.

In an open listing, the seller is permitted to contract with any number of brokers and is obligated to compensate only the broker who procures the buyer.

A multiple-listing provision in a listing contract gives the broker the authority to distribute the listing to other brokers in the multiple-listing service. A net listing is based on the net price the seller will receive if the property is sold.

A listing agreement may be terminated for the same reasons as any other agency relationship.

When listing a property for sale, a comparative market analysis is often prepared to help the seller determine a reasonable listing price. The amount the seller will net from the sale is calculated by subtracting the broker's commission and any other expenses that the seller incurs from the selling price.

A buyer agency agreement is the contract in which a buyer employs the broker to represent the buyer in the purchase of a property. Types of buyer agency agreements include an exclusive buyer agency agreement, an exclusive agency buyer agreement, and an open buyer agency agreement.

Before any agency agreement is signed, the potential client must be given a copy of the Consumer Notice. The law in Pennsylvania also requires sellers to prepare a statement disclosing property conditions.

F I G U R E   **18.4**

Buyer Representation Agreement

BUSINESS RELATIONSHIP   **BR**
BETWEEN BROKER AND BUYER

This form recommended and approved for, but not restricted to use by, the members of the Pennsylvania Association of REALTORS® (PAR).

1 BROKER (Company) _____
2 LICENSEE(S) _____
3 Buyer has read and received the Consumer Notice as adopted by the State Real Estate Commission at 49 Pa. Code §35.336
4 and the Notices to Buyers in this agreement. Pennsylvania law requires that a business relationship between Broker and
5 Buyer be in writing.
6 *Note: The terms "buyer," "seller," and "buy" also will be construed to mean "tenant," "landlord," and "rent," respectively, throughout this agreement.*

7   **BUSINESS RELATIONSHIP AS DESCRIBED IN THE CONSUMER NOTICE**
8 Does Buyer have a business relationship with another broker?   ☐ Yes   ☐ No
9 If yes, explain: _____.
10 Broker and Buyer agree to the following business relationship as allowed by Broker's Company policy:
11 ☐ **SELLER AGENT** (for properties listed with Broker)/**SUBAGENT FOR SELLER** (for properties listed with other companies).
12 ☐ **TRANSACTION LICENSEE** (for properties not listed with Broker; however, if property is listed under an agency
13   contract with Broker, Broker is a Seller's Agent).
14 ☐ **BUYER AGENT** (for properties listed with Broker and other companies, and for properties not listed with any broker)
15   Broker will be Buyer's Agent under the terms agreed to in the Buyer Agency Contract below.

16   **EXCLUSIVE BUYER AGENCY CONTRACT**
17 1. **TERM**
18   **This Contract applies to any property that Buyer chooses to buy during the term of this Contract. Buyer will not**
19   **enter into a Buyer Agency Contract with another broker/licensee that begins before the Ending Date of this Contract.**
20   **Starting Date:** This Contract starts when signed by Buyer and Broker, unless otherwise stated here: _____
21   _____.
22   **Ending Date:** This Contract ends _____.
23   (A) If Buyer is negotiating or has entered into an Agreement of Sale, this Contract ends upon settlement.
24   (B) If Buyer is negotiating or has signed a lease, this Contract ends upon possession.
25 2. **BROKER'S FEE**
26   (A) It is Broker's policy to accept compensation offered by the listing broker and/or the seller. Broker may be paid a fee
27   that is a percentage of the purchase price (or in the case of a lease, a percentage of the total amount of rent due over
28   the term of the lease). Even though Broker's Fee, or a portion of it, may be paid by a seller or listing broker, Broker
29   will continue to represent the interests of Buyer.
30   (B) 1. If the amount received in paragraph 2(A) from a **listing broker** is less than _____,
31   then Buyer will pay Broker the difference or include it as a term in the Agreement of Sale for the seller to pay.
32   2. If the amount received in paragraph 2(A) from a **seller not represented by a broker** is less than
33   _____, then Buyer will pay Broker the difference or include it as a term in the
34   Agreement of Sale for the seller to pay.
35   (C) In addition to any amounts paid to Broker in subparagraphs 2(A) and/or 2(B), Buyer will pay Broker an additional
36   amount of _____ as part of Broker's Fee.
37   (D) 1. **Broker's Fee is earned if Buyer enters into a sale or lease agreement during the term of this Contract,**
38   **whether brought about by Broker, Broker's agents or by any other person, including Buyer.**
39   2. If Buyer enters into a sale/lease agreement for a property after the Ending Date of this Contract, Buyer will pay
40   Broker's Fee:
41   (a) if the sale/lease is a result of Broker's actions during the term of this Contract, OR
42   (b) if the property was seen during the term of this Contract, AND
43   (c) Buyer is not under an exclusive buyer agency contract with another broker at the time Buyer enters into a
44   sale/lease agreement.
45 3. **DUAL AGENCY** Buyer agrees that Broker may also represent the seller of the property that Buyer might buy. The Broker
46   is a DUAL AGENT when representing both the seller and the buyer in the sale of a property.
47 4. **DESIGNATED AGENCY**
48   ☐   **Not Applicable.**
49   ☐   **Applicable.** Broker may designate licensees to represent the separate interests of Buyer and the seller. Licensee
50   (identified above) is the Designated Agent, who will act exclusively as the Buyer Agent. If Licensee is also the Seller
51   Agent, then Licensee is a DUAL AGENT.
52 5. **TRANSFER OF THIS CONTRACT** Buyer agrees that Broker may transfer this Contract to another broker. Broker will
53   notify Buyer immediately in writing if Broker transfers this Contract to another broker.
54 6. **OTHER**
55   _____
56   _____

57 This is the entire agreement between Broker and Buyer. Any verbal or written agreements that were made before are not
58 a part of this agreement. Any changes or additions to this agreement must be in writing and signed by Broker and Buyer.

59 **Return by facsimile (FAX) transmission constitutes acceptance of this agreement.**

60 **NOTICE BEFORE SIGNING: IF BUYER HAS LEGAL QUESTIONS, BUYER IS ADVISED TO CONSULT AN ATTORNEY.**

61 Buyer gives permission for Broker to send information about this transaction to the fax number(s) and/or e-mail address(es)
62 listed below.

63 BUYER'S MAILING ADDRESS: _____
64   _____
65 PHONE: _____ FAX: _____ E-MAIL: _____
66 BUYER _____ DATE_____
67 BUYER _____ DATE_____
68 BROKER (Company Name) _____
69 ACCEPTED BY _____ DATE_____

Pennsylvania Association of
REALTORS®
The Voice for Real Estate® in Pennsylvania

COPYRIGHT PENNSYLVANIA ASSOCIATION OF REALTORS® 2004
7/04

F I G U R E   18.4

Buyer Representation Agreement (continued)

NOTICES TO BUYERS

The following Notices apply to buyers working with Buyer's Agents, Seller's Agents or Subagents for Seller, or Transaction Licensees.

Buyer acknowledges that Buyer has received and understands **the Consumer Notice adopted by the Pennsylvania State Real Estate Commission at 49 Pa. Code §35.336. The Consumer Notice, including the duties, definitions of business relationships, and statements identifying cooperation with other brokers, possibilities of dual agency and designated agency stated therein, and notice of the Real Estate Recovery Fund and zoning classification, are incorporated here as part of this disclosure as though written here in their entirety.**

The terms and length of the business relationship, the fees, and the range of services that Broker will provide have been determined as a result of negotiations between Broker and Buyer and have not been set or recommended by any association of REALTORS®.

SERVICES TO SELLER
Broker may provide services to a seller for which Broker may accept a fee. Such services may include, but are not limited to, listing fees; deed/document preparation; ordering certifications required for closing; financial services; title transfer and preparation services; ordering insurance, construction, repair, or inspection services. Broker will disclose to Buyer if any fees are to be paid by the seller.

OTHER BUYERS
Licensee may show or present the same properties to other buyers.

CONFLICT OF INTEREST
A *conflict of interest* is when Broker or Licensee has financial or personal interest in the property where Broker or Licensee cannot put Buyer's interest before any other. If Broker, or any of Broker's licensees, has a *conflict of interest*, Broker will notify Buyer in a timely manner.

DEPOSIT MONEY
(A) Broker will keep (or will give to the listing broker, who will keep) all deposit monies that Broker/Licensee receives in an escrow account as required by real estate licensing laws and regulations until the sale is completed or the agreement of sale is terminated. Buyer agrees that Broker may wait to deposit any uncashed check that is received as deposit money until Buyer's offer has been accepted.
(B) If Buyer joins Broker/Licensee in a lawsuit for the return of deposit monies, Buyer will pay Licensee's and Broker's attorneys' fees and costs.

CIVIL RIGHTS ACTS
Federal and state laws make it illegal for a seller, broker, or anyone to use RACE, COLOR, RELIGION or RELIGIOUS CREED, SEX, DISABILITY (physical or mental), FAMILIAL STATUS (children under 18 years of age), AGE (40 or older), NATIONAL ORIGIN, USE OR HANDLING/TRAINING OF SUPPORT OR GUIDE ANIMALS, or the FACT OF RELATIONSHIP OR ASSOCIATION TO AN INDIVIDUAL KNOWN TO HAVE A DISABILITY as reasons for refusing to sell, show, or rent properties, loan money, or set deposit amounts, or as reasons for any decision relating to the sale or rental of property.

EXPERTISE OF REAL ESTATE AGENTS
Pennsylvania Real Estate Agents are required to be licensed by the Commonwealth of Pennsylvania and are obligated to disclose adverse factors about a property that are reasonably apparent to someone with expertise in the marketing of real property.
(A) If Buyer wants information regarding specific conditions or components of the property which are outside the Agent's expertise, the advice of the appropriate professional should be sought.
(B) If Buyer wants financial, legal, or any other advice, Buyer is encouraged to seek the services of an accountant, lawyer, or other appropriate professional.

BUYER'S OPTIONS
Unless Buyer and the seller agree otherwise, real estate is sold in its present condition. It is Buyer's responsibility to satisfy himself or herself that the condition of the property is satisfactory. Buyer may request that the property be inspected, at Buyer's expense, by qualified professionals to determine the condition of the structure or its components. Areas of concern may include, but are not limited to, the following: electrical; plumbing, heating, ventilating, air conditioning; appliances and fixtures; water infiltration, basement; roof leakage; boundaries; asbestos, urea formaldehyde foam insulation, carbon monoxide, radon, and environmental hazards or substances; wood-destroying insect infestation; on-site water service and/or sewage system; and lead-based paint. Buyer's request for any inspection should be made to Broker before entering into an Agreement of Sale or lease.

Buyer is advised that information regarding properties considered for purchase by Buyer has been provided by the seller or seller's broker. Such information may include, but is not limited to, the information on the Seller's Property Disclosure Statement, including environmental conditions; MLS information, including information regarding restrictions, taxes, assessments, association fees, zoning restrictions, dimensions, boundaries (if identified); and marketing information. Unless otherwise noted, Broker has not verified the accuracy of this information, and Buyer is advised to investigate its accuracy.

FEES
Buyer understands that, as either a Seller Agent/Subagent for Seller or Transaction Licensee, Broker may receive a fee from the seller. Broker's office policy allows for cooperation with other brokers who may compensate Broker based on a percentage of the purchase price. As a Seller Agent/Subagent for Seller or a Transaction Licensee, Broker may not charge any fee to Buyer without a signed written agreement.

QUESTIONS

1. A listing taken by a real estate salesperson belongs to the
   a. broker.
   b. seller.
   c. salesperson.
   d. salesperson and the broker equally.

2. Which of the following is a similarity between an exclusive agency listing and an exclusive-right-to-sell listing?
   a. Under both types of listings, the seller retains the right to sell the real estate without the broker's help without paying the broker a commission.
   b. Under both, the seller authorizes only one particular salesperson to show the property.
   c. Both give the responsibility of representing the seller to one broker only.
   d. Both are open listings.

3. All of the following may terminate a listing EXCEPT
   a. expiration of the contract.
   b. death or incapacity of the broker.
   c. nonpayment of the commission by the seller.
   d. destruction of the improvements on the property.

4. Seller M has listed his property under an exclusive agency listing with broker K. If M sells his property himself during the term of the listing without using K's services, he will owe K
   a. no commission.
   b. the full commission.
   c. a partial commission.
   d. only reimbursement for broker K's costs.

5. A broker sold a residence for $88,000 and received $6,160 as her commission in accordance with the terms of the listing. What percentage of the sales price was the broker's commission?
   a. 6 percent
   b. 6.5 percent
   c. 7 percent
   d. 7.5 percent

6. A seller's residence is listed with a broker, and the seller stipulates that she wants to receive $85,000 from the sale but the broker can sell the property for as much as possible and keep the difference as the commission. The broker agrees. Which of the following BEST describes this type of listing arrangement?
   a. Exclusive-right-to-sell listing
   b. Exclusive agency listing
   c. Open listing
   d. Net listing

7. All of the following provisions are usually found in a listing agreement EXCEPT the
   a. broker's compensation.
   b. monthly utility bills.
   c. price the seller wants.
   d. contract expiration rights.

8. The listed price for a property should be based on
   a. the net to the seller.
   b. the appraised value.
   c. what the seller chooses.
   d. the maximum of a range of values.

9. Which of the following is true about a listing contract?
   a. It is an employment contract for the professional services of the broker.
   b. It obligates the seller to convey the property if the broker procures a ready, willing, and able buyer.
   c. It obligates the broker to work diligently for both the buyer and the seller.
   d. It automatically requires the payment of a commission while the broker protection clause is in effect.

10. Seller W hired broker N under the terms of an exclusive-right-to-sell listing. While the listing was in effect, W—without informing N—sold the property to his neighbor. Seller W must pay
    a. no commission to broker N.
    b. broker N's marketing expenses.
    c. full commission to broker N.
    d. half commission to broker N.

11. *Seller* G listed her residence with broker D. Broker D brought an offer at full price and terms of the listing from buyers who were willing and able to pay cash for the property. Then seller G rejected the buyers' offer. In this situation seller G
    a. must sell her property.
    b. owes a commission to broker D.
    c. is liable to the buyers for specific performance.
    d. is liable to the buyers for compensatory damages.

12. Which is a similarity between an open listing and exclusive agency listing?
    a. Under both the seller avoids paying the broker a commission if the seller sells the property himself or herself.
    b. Under both the seller is guaranteed to net a certain amount.
    c. Under both the broker earns a commission regardless of who sells the property, as long as it is sold within the listing period.
    d. Both grant an exclusive right to sell to whichever broker procures a buyer for the seller's property.

13. The parties to the listing contract are
    a. the seller and the buyer.
    b. the seller and the broker.
    c. the seller and the salesperson.
    d. the broker and the salesperson.

14. A comparative market analysis
    a. is the same as an appraisal.
    b. can help the seller price the property.
    c. by law must be completed for each listing taken.
    d. should not be retained in the property's listing file.

15. A property was listed with a broker who belonged to a multiple-listing service and was sold by another member broker for $53,500. The total commission was 6 percent of the sale price. The selling broker received 60 percent of the commission, and the listing broker received the balance. What was the listing broker's commission?
    a. $1,284
    b. $1,464
    c. $1,926
    d. $2,142

16. All of the following provisions must, by state regulation, be included in exclusive-listing agreements *EXCEPT* the
    a. amount of commission.
    b. seller's asking price.
    c. date the agreement terminates.
    d. zoning classification.

17. After a buyer signs an agency agreement with a broker, the buyer also signs other agency agreements with other brokers. Despite all of these agency relationships, the buyer finds a house on his own. Under the terms of these agency agreements, the buyer does not owe any broker a commission. What kind of an agency agreements were these?
    a. Exclusive agency agreements
    b. Exclusive agency buyer agency agreements
    c. Exclusive buyer agency agreements
    d. Open buyer agency agreements

18. A written agreement between a broker and a client includes the following language: "In return for the compensation agreed upon, Broker will assist Client in locating and purchasing a suitable property. Broker will receive the agreed compensation regardless of whether Broker, Client, or some other party locates the property ultimately purchased by Client." What kind of agreement is this?
    a. Exclusive agency listing
    b. Exclusive agency buyer agency agreement
    c. Exclusive buyer agency agreement
    d. Open buyer agency agreement

ANSWERS

1. A A licensed real estate salesperson performs services for or on behalf of the employing broker. Listings secured by the salesperson are the property of the employing broker. (p. 319)

2. C Both an exclusive-right-to-sell listing and an exclusive agency listing authorize one broker to represent the seller. However, in an exclusive agency listing, the seller reserves the right to sell the real estate without an obligation to compensate the broker. (p. 319)

3. C Listing agreements may be terminated in a number of ways, including expiration of the contract term, death or incapacity of either party, or destruction of the property. Nonpayment of the commission by a seller does not terminate the agreement and may create legal liability for the seller. (p. 321)

4. A Under an exclusive agency listing agreement, the seller retains the right to sell the property him or herself without obligation to the broker. Broker K would not be entitled to any compensation if seller M sells the property. (p. 319)

5. C The broker's compensation is a percentage of the selling price of the property. Sales price times percent commission equals the commission amount (S.P. × % = $ comm.). Therefore, the amount of commission *divided by* the selling price equals the percent commission, expressed as a decimal ($6,160 divided by $88,000 = 0.07 or 7%). (p. 324)

6. D A listing agreement that specifies that the seller will receive a net amount of money from the sale with the understanding that the broker's compensation is the amount that exceeds that net is called a net listing. (p. 321)

7. B Listing agreements include provisions for the listing price, the compensation due to the broker, and the terms of the contract. Monthly utility bills are not part of the agreement between the broker and the property owner. (p. 325)

8. C The property owner has the right to choose the price at which the property will be offered for sale. The broker has the right to refuse to accept a listing that the broker feels is not being offered at a price that will result in a timely sale. (p. 323)

9. A A listing contract is essentially an employment rather than a real estate contract. The broker agrees to use his or her professional skills to secure a ready, willing, and able buyer according to the terms specified in the contract. In return, the seller agrees to compensate the broker according to the contract terms. (p. 318)

10. C Under the terms of an exclusive-right-to-sell listing, the broker is entitled to compensation if the property is sold by anyone, including the owner, during the term of the contract. (p. 319)

11. B Seller G is not obligated to sell the property. However, the seller is obligated to compensate the broker because Broker D secured a ready, willing, and very able buyer according to the terms of the listing contract. (p. 319)

12. A Both an open listing and an exclusive agency listing provide that the owner will not be liable for compensation to the broker if the property is sold directly by the owner curing the term of the contract. (p. 320)

13. B A listing contract is a contractual agreement between the broker and the owner. Salespersons and associate brokers secure listings on behalf of their employing broker. (p. 318)

14. B One of the best tools available to help the seller establish a realistic listing price is a comparative market analysis (CMA). A CMA, however, is not an appraisal, though there is no requirement that an appraisal be used unless the seller so desires. (p. 323)

15. A Total commission on the transaction is $3,210 ($53,500 × 6% = $3,210). If the selling broker received 60 percent of the $3,210, the listing broker received the balance of $1,284 ($3,210 × 40% = $1,284). (p. 320)

16. D The real estate commission requires that exclusive listing agreements include the seller's asking price, the broker's expected compensation, and a specified termination date. Zoning classification is not a requirement of the Commission's Rules. (p. 319)

17. D A buyer agency agreement is an employment contract between the buyer and the broker. Similar to an open listing, a buyer agency contract is an open agreement under which the buyer could have contracts with several brokers and still retain the right to purchase a property on his or her own without obligation to any of the brokers. (p. 336)

18. C An exclusive buyer agency agreement entitles the broker to compensation regardless of whether the property the buyer purchased was located by the broker, the buyer, or another licensee. (p. 336)

19

SALES CONTRACTS

■ LEARNING OBJECTIVES

When you've finished reading this chapter, you should be able to

- explain statutory and regulatory requirements governing the use of written agreements and disclosure documents;
- summarize rules and regulations governing the handling of earnest money deposits;
- list the key components, elements, and provisions of an agreement of sale;
- describe options and installment contracts and their application in real estate transactions; and
- define the key terms.

■ KEY TERMS

addenda	equitable title	misrepresentation
agreement of sale	fraud	option
contingency	installment contract	stigmatized property
earnest money	latent defect	

■ REACHING AGREEMENT

The culmination of the real estate licensee's efforts to market a seller's property or to help a buyer find a suitable purchase occurs when a buyer and seller form a legally binding sales contract. Most often this contract is an agreement of sale, though option agreements and installment contracts are also used. In any case, the contract states the specific rights and obligations to which the parties mutually agree.

The process of reaching agreement begins with the completion of a document. This document serves as the offer that, if accepted, then "ripens into" a contract that legally binds the parties to their obligations. The terms of an agreement are negotiable. In an agreement of sale, for instance, the parties must agree on terms relating to such issues as the amount of the purchase price and deposit money, the date of settlement, the real and any personal property to be included (or excluded), financing arrangements, property inspections, and the dates of performance for satisfying any contingencies.

Real estate licensees expedite the negotiation of the contract. When acting as an agent for one of the parties, the licensee is the party's advocate and is obligated to negotiate the most favorable terms for that client. While the licensee ultimately wants to bring the parties on both sides of a contract to agreement, the licensee-agent must remember that the priority is to serve the client he or she represents. Mishandling confidential information or any other conduct that harms the principal's bargaining position is a violation of the agent's fiduciary obligations.

Disclosures In Your State

PA Before the buyer and seller begin negotiations to form a contract, Pennsylvania licensees must be sure that all disclosure requirements are satisfied. The Consumer Notice, disclosure of agency relationships, the seller's property disclosure statement, estimated statements of cost and return, and documents relating to condominiums and planned communities (if applicable) must be provided. While all of this information is normally provided well in advance of the buyer beginning the process with an offer, it's possible that the time a buyer decides to make an offer is also the first time the licensee and the buyer work together. However, this situation does not alter the licensee's duty to ensure that the buyer has received all required disclosures before proceeding with an offer. ■

Furthermore, the broker must have evidence that all disclosures and other required documents (which are signed and dated) have been provided to the appropriate parties before entering into an agreement of sale. *Buyers must read and acknowledge receipt of the seller's property disclosure statement before signing an agreement of sale.* Pennsylvania license law requires brokers to retain copies of all documents related to the transaction for three years following consummation or termination of the transaction.

Estimated statements of closing costs.   The financial implications of a contract involve more than simply the sale price. The "bottom line," with all expenses of the transaction accounted for, plays a major role in determining how much a buyer is willing to offer, how much a seller is willing to accept, and ultimately, a price that is mutually agreeable. Consequently, estimates of reasonably foreseeable expenses associated with the sale or purchase of the property are important to their decision making. In addition, real estate licensees are *required* to provide the buyer and seller with written estimated statements of closing costs *before* the parties sign an agreement of sale. The Real Estate Commission's Rules state that the broker's commission, mortgage payments and financing costs, taxes and assessments, and settlement expenses must be included. The estimated cost forms should be as accurate as can be expected of persons having knowledge of and experience in the field.

Uniform Condominium Act and Uniform Planned Community Act. Covenants, conditions, and restrictions on the ownership of a condominium unit or a property in a planned community as well as financial obligations to a homeowner's association are significant issues a buyer must be aware of when purchasing one of these properties. The *Uniform Condominium Act* and the *Uniform Planned Community Act* require a seller to furnish copies of the development's declaration, bylaws, and rules and regulations of the association (and a resale certificate if applicable) for the buyer's review. These laws state that the buyer is entitled to five days to review the documents. Preferably, the buyer has had the documents for the five-day review period before making an offer. If the fifth day extends past the date a binding agreement of sale is formed or even past the closing date, the buyer has the right to void the purchase according to procedures stated in the laws. Obviously, if a buyer elects to exercise this right after reviewing the documents, the seller has no recourse for the buyer's nonperformance on the agreement.

In Your State   **PA**   Amendments to the Uniform Condominium Act, the Uniform Planned Community Act, and the Cooperative Act were signed into law on November 30, 2004, and became effective January 30, 2005. The purpose of the amendments is to improve the operation and governance of the associations in these entities. Prospective purchasers should be aware that, for example, governing documents are easier to amend, powers of the boards of directors are expanded, and lien priorities for unpaid assessments are now clarified. ■

Preparing a Contract

If a contract contains any ambiguity, courts generally interpret the agreement against the person who prepared it.

As discussed in Chapter 11, preprinted contract forms are often used, especially in residential real estate transactions, and real estate licensees are permitted to prepare contracts by filling in the blanks on these forms. However, licensees must complete them properly. Because preprinted language may not satisfactorily express the specific wishes of the parties or may be biased (one party's interests being treated more favorably than the other's), licensees must guard against altering wording or drafting clauses that could injure the parties or create liability for themselves. If a contract contains any ambiguity, the courts generally interpret the agreement against the person who prepared it. *All parties to a transaction must* be *given the opportunity to secure independent legal counsel before signing a contract.* Under no circumstances may a real estate licensee give legal advice or counsel about the provisions in an agreement of sale unless they are also properly licensed attorneys.

IN PRACTICE   It is incumbent on licensees to safeguard the interests of all parties when preparing contracts—regardless of whether the licensee is representing a client or providing customer-level service—and to ensure that the parties get any necessary professional advice from experts.

Preprinted forms designed for residential transactions are rarely suitable for nonresidential transactions. Although preprinted forms for nonresidential transactions are available, contracts are often individually drafted to reflect the specific terms of these complex sales. An attorney, rather than a licensee, should undertake the responsibility of drafting these documents.

Any agreement between two or more parties, whether prepared on a preprinted form or an individually drafted document, must meet certain basic requirements to form a legally binding contract. The essentials of a contract, which were fully discussed in Chapter 11, include

- offer and acceptance,
- consideration,
- legally competent parties,
- legality of object, and
- reality of consent.

Discussions in this chapter demonstrate the process of forming a contract under circumstances that are typical in residential real estate transactions, including requirements imposed by license law and other legislative rules.

Fraud and Misrepresentations

One of the essentials of a valid contract is reality of consent, meaning that people must be able to act prudently, knowledgeably, and without undue influence when they enter into contracts. Reality of consent is most commonly violated because of *fraud* and *misrepresentation*. If a licensee's fraudulent misstatements result in a contract to purchase real estate, not only may the contract be disaffirmed or renounced, but the licensee may lose a commission and be liable for damages as well.

Fraud is the *intentional* misrepresentation of a material fact for the purpose of deceiving and gaining an advantage over another person. The person who relies on this deceptive behavior is then injured. Any statement of fact must be accurate. A fraudulent statement is intentionally false or made without regard to its truthfulness. Fraud also occurs when a person intentionally fails to divulge important facts, or actively attempts to conceal them.

Misrepresentation is an *unintentional* misstatement or omission. Often, this is known as a *negligent misrepresentation* and typically arises from carelessly imparting information or failure to verify a fact. One measure of negligence arises out of how a licensee *should* have acted or what the license *should have known* to prevent a party from being injured. The fact that the licensee may actually be ignorant about the issue is no excuse. The licensee is still liable for any injury caused by his or her negligence.

In Your State   **PA**   In Pennsylvania, licensees also face disciplinary action by the real estate commission if they make representations or give assurances or advice concerning any aspect of a real estate transaction that is known (or should be known) to be incorrect, inaccurate, or improbable. A licensee may not knowingly be a party to a material false or inaccurate representation. ■

When making representations about a property that are based on the seller's representations, the licensee should clearly state that the seller is the source of the information. When acting as a seller's agent, the licensee should caution the seller-client about his or her liability for any misstatement or omission.

Because licensees promote themselves as real estate experts, people tend to assume that statements they make are factual. While licensees may offer opinions as long as they are shared without any intention to deceive, they must clearly differentiate between an *opinion* and *a fact*. A salesperson's opinion such as "I believe the zoning ordinance permits your proposed use" could be misinterpreted as a factual statement about the zoning. If a client or customer who relied on this comment can't obtain a zoning permit, the salesperson could be liable for damages. Exaggerated or superlative comments about a property's benefits are called *puffing.* Unless the general characterizations are factual, the licensee may be liable for damages in this case as well.

Latent Defects

The seller has a duty to disclose any latent defects that threaten structural soundness or personal safety. A **latent defect** is a *hidden structural defect that would not* be *discovered by ordinary inspection.* Buyers have been able to either rescind the sales contract or receive damages when a seller fails to reveal known latent defects. For instance, sellers were found liable where a house was built over a ditch covered with decaying timber, where a buried drain tile caused water to accumulate, and where a driveway was built partly on adjoining property. The courts have also decided in favor of the buyer when the seller neglected to reveal violations of zoning or building codes.

Stigmatized Properties

In recent years, concerns have been raised about **stigmatized properties.** These are properties that society has branded as undesirable because of events that occurred there. Typically, the stigma is a criminal event such as a homicide, illegal drug manufacturing, a gang-related activity, or a tragedy such as a suicide. Some properties have been stigmatized by rumors of paranormal events. Because of liability arising from inadequate research and disclosure of facts about a property's condition, licensees are advised to seek legal counsel when dealing with a stigmatized property. This is especially important when licensees have fiduciary duties to a client under the law of agency. Although laws and court cases in Pennsylvania have not, as yet, specifically addressed socially stigmatized properties, a body of law is developing elsewhere in the country that could be used as the basis in litigation.

■ AGREEMENT OF SALE

The **agreement of sale** sets out in detail the agreement between the buyer and seller and establishes their legal rights and obligations. In effect, the agreement dictates the contents of the deed. Depending on local custom, this agreement may also be known as an *offer to purchase,* a *contract of purchase and sale,* a *purchase agreement,* or an *earnest money agreement.* When the document is prepared and signed by the purchaser, it constitutes the buyer's offer to purchase the property. If the document is accepted and signed by the seller, it then becomes an agreement of sale. The agreement of sale creates the legally enforceable contractual relationship between the seller and buyer. The real estate licensees who represent the parties are not parties to the contract. A sample agreement of sale is shown in Figure 19.1.

Several times in this text the point has been made about the importance of using written agreements from both the real estate license law and statute of frauds perspectives. (See Chapters 11 and 13.) The written agreement of sale establishes the buyer's right to enforce his or her interest in the property by court action as well as obligating the buyer to complete the transaction according to the agreed on terms. The written contract obligates the seller to deliver the property to the buyer.

Offer

A broker lists an owner's real estate for sale at the price and conditions set by the owner. This is considered an invitation for prospective buyers to make offers to purchase. A buyer who wants to purchase the property prepares a proposal (an offer) and signs it. The offer is then presented to the seller. The seller then has three choices: 1) accept the offer exactly as it is presented; 2) reject the offer outright; or 3) reject the offer and propose a counteroffer to the buyer for consideration.

Earnest money.   It is customary for a purchaser to provide a deposit when making an offer. This deposit, usually in the form of a check, is referred to as **earnest money** or *hand money*. The deposit is evidence of the buyer's intention to carry out the terms of the contract in good faith. The earnest money is given to the broker, who then handles the deposit as required by the licensing law and the real estate commission's regulations. (See the discussion of escrow accounts in Chapter 13.)

No mandatory or standard amount of earnest money is required. From the seller's perspective, the amount should be sufficient to discourage the buyer's default, to compensate the seller for taking the property off the market, and to cover any expenses the seller might incur if the buyer does default. On the other hand, the buyer generally prefers to deposit a minimal amount. Hence, the parties must negotiate to arrive at an amount that is mutually agreeable.

The seller's agent must accurately represent the existence and form of earnest money to the seller. The broker incurs considerable risk when representing the existence of a deposit when, in fact, there is none. If the buyer defaults, the broker could be liable to the seller for damages. If the deposit is a promissory note, the seller must be informed of the possible difficulty in collecting the funds. Although the note is payable to the broker (as is a check), it should be a negotiable instrument with a confession of judgment. A defaulted note can then be endorsed to the seller to pursue collection.

The money is, in a sense, the buyer's until the offer is officially accepted. If the offer is not accepted, the earnest money is returned to the would-be buyer. Once the seller accepts the offer, however, the buyer may not secure the return of the money, even though the seller is not entitled to it until the transaction has been completed. Under no circumstances does the money belong to the broker. It is absolutely essential that these funds be properly protected pending a final decision on their disbursement.

IN PRACTICE

It is important to understand the distinction between an earnest money or hand money deposit and the down payment. Earnest money or hand money is given in good faith to demonstrate the seriousness of the buyer's intent to perform on the contract. A down payment relates to the buyer's financing, being the difference between the purchase price and the amount of the mortgage loan the buyer will obtain.

Binder. In some cases, a binder, rather than a complete agreement of sale, is prepared. A binder is a shorter document that states the essential terms of the buyer's offer and, once accepted, is evidence of the parties' agreement until a more formal and detailed contract is prepared. Binders are customary in some parts of the country or in cases where the transaction is more complex than can be addressed in a standardized form.

Counteroffer

Any change the seller makes to the terms proposed by the buyer constitutes a rejection of the offer and creates a *counteroffer*. The buyer may accept or reject the seller's counteroffer. If the buyer wishes, he or she may continue the process by making another counteroffer. Any change in the last offer made results in a counteroffer until either the parties reach agreement or one of them walks away. An offer or counteroffer *may be withdrawn at any time before* it *has been accepted*, even if the person making the offer or counteroffer has agreed to keep the offer open for a set period of time.

As simple as this process sounds, negotiating offers and counteroffers can be complicated. Several buyers could make offers on one property at the same time; a buyer could make an offer while negotiations of another offer or counteroffer on that property is in process; or a buyer might make an offer after another offer or counteroffer has been accepted. The principles guiding the licensee's conduct are that the licensee has no authority to decide the merits of an offer and refuse to present it and that the licensee must present all offers and counteroffers in a timely manner. However, the licensee is not obligated to seek additional offers when his or her client is subject to an existing contract. While the licensee must follow the directives of the principal, the client (buyer or seller) must be cautioned about the liability of entering into multiple agreements. Consistent with fiduciary obligations, licensees must protect the interests of their clients during negotiations.

Acceptance

Once a party agrees to the offer or counteroffer exactly as made and signs the document, the offer is *accepted*. Acceptance of the offer means that a contract is formed. The licensee then must communicate the acceptance. A duplicate of the contract must be provided to each party.

An offer is not considered accepted until the person making the offer receives *notification of the other party's acceptance*. When the parties communicate through agents or at a distance, questions may arise regarding whether an acceptance, a rejection, or a counteroffer has occurred. Current technology makes communication faster; a signed agreement that is faxed, for instance, would constitute adequate communication. The licensee must communicate acceptances or other responses as soon as possible to avoid questions of proper communication. As electronic commerce becomes more common, licensees need to develop systems for documenting agreements negotiated electronically.

Equitable title. A buyer does not receive legal title to a property at the time he or she signs the contract to purchase real estate. The seller has agreed to transfer all of the rights, interests, and claims to the property that he or she holds as of the date of the agreement of sale. In return, the buyer has agreed to pay the seller a certain amount of consideration to acquire what the seller has to convey. Legal title transfers only by delivery and acceptance of a deed, which occurs at closing or settlement. However, after both buyer and seller have executed an agreement of sale, the buyer acquires an *interest* in the property. This interest is known as **equitable title.** A person who holds equitable title has the right to obtain legal title to a property held in another person's name. Equitable title gives the buyer an insurable interest in the property. If the parties decide not to go through with the purchase and sale, the buyer may be required to release the equitable interest in the real estate.

Destruction of premises.   In Pennsylvania, once the parties form the agreement of sale, the buyer bears the risk of any damage to or destruction of the property by fire or other casualty before the deed is delivered. Of course, the contract may provide otherwise. Furthermore, the laws and court decisions in a growing number of states have placed the risk of loss on the seller. The seller may be liable for a loss if the seller was negligent, is unable to deliver good title, or has delayed the closing of the transaction. In practice, the agreement of sale usually explains risk of loss to avoid confusion. In any case, the seller should maintain adequate insurance through the date of closing, and the buyer commonly insures his or her equitable interest.

Parts of an Agreement of Sale

An agreement of sale can be divided into a number of general parts. Although most contract forms contain these divisions, the placement may vary. Study the sample contract in Figure 19.1 (at the end of this chapter) to identify the terms of the agreement. Most sales agreements include the following information:

- Names of the seller and buyer
- Legal or adequate description of the real estate
- Statement of the type of deed the seller will give, including any conditions and provisions (interests of others)
- Statement of consideration (the purchase price) and method of payment, including earnest money deposit and conditions for any mortgage financing
- Provisions for the closing and the purchaser's possession of the property, including dates
- Provisions for title evidence
- Provisions for prorations (adjustments for taxes, insurance, fuel, and the like)
- Provisions in the event of destruction or damage to premises
- Provisions for default
- Provisions for contingencies
- Miscellaneous provisions
- Dates and signatures

Although not essential requirements under basic contract law, the signatures of the seller (including all co-owners or authorized persons on the seller's behalf) and an adequate legal description of the property are required in real estate sales contracts by the statute of frauds. In practice, buyers also sign the agreement.

Addenda and Contingencies

An agreement of sale may include **addenda** (*addendum* is the singular term). An addendum is any provision added to an existing contract *without altering the content of the original* agreement. Essentially, addenda are additional signed agreements that are attached to and made part of an existing contract. An addendum differs from an *amendment*, which *changes* a provision of the original agreement. For example, an addendum might be an agreement to split the cost of repairing certain flaws discovered in a home inspection.

A **contingency** creates an additional condition that must be satisfied before an agreement is fully enforceable. In other words, the agreement is "subject to" the satisfaction of a contingency. A contingency includes three elements:

1. The actions necessary to satisfy the contingency
2. The time frame within which the actions must be performed
3. Who is responsible for paying any costs involved

The most common contingencies include the following:

- *Mortgage contingency*—A mortgage contingency protects the buyer's earnest money until a lender commits the mortgage loan funds. A mortgage contingency in Pennsylvania must state the type and amount of the loan, the maximum interest rate and minimum term, the deadline by which the buyer shall obtain the loan, and the nature and extent of assistance that the broker will provide in helping the buyer obtain the loan.
- *Inspection contingency*—An agreement of sale may be contingent on the buyer's obtaining certain inspections of the property. Inspections may be used to detect wood-boring insects, radon, or other hazardous substances, or to gather impartial information about structural, mechanical, or sewage systems.
- *Property sale contingency*—A purchaser may make the agreement of sale contingent on the sale of his or her current home. This protects the buyer from owning two homes at the same time and also helps ensure the availability of cash for the purchase. Sometimes this is known as a "back-out clause." In such a case, the seller may insist on an escape clause that would allow the seller to continue to solicit additional buyers. If a more favorable offer comes forth, the original buyer retains the right to either eliminate the contingency or to void the contract.

Disclosures in an Agreement of Sale

The licensing law in Pennsylvania requires an agreement of sale to contain

- a statement identifying the capacity in which the broker is engaged in the transaction, and whether the broker or any licensee affiliated with the broker has provided services relating to the subject transaction to any other party in the transaction;
- a statement describing the purpose of the Real Estate Recovery Fund and the telephone number at the Commission where a consumer can receive further information;
- a statement of the zoning classification of the property, except in cases where the property is zoned solely or primarily to permit single-family dwellings; and
- a statement that access to a public road may require issuance of a highway occupancy permit from the Department of Transportation.

In addition, a lead-based paint disclosure for property built prior to 1978 and a sewage facilities disclosure must be included. (See the sample contract form in Figure 19.1.) Finally, if the agreement involves the sale of a time-share, condominium, or planned community, the contract must include disclosures regarding the buyer's right to rescind the purchase.

■ OPTION AGREEMENTS

An **option** is a *contract by which an optionor* (generally an owner) *gives an optionee* (a prospective purchaser or lessee) *the right to buy or lease the owner's property at a fixed price within a stated period of time.* The optionee pays a fee (the agreed-upon consideration) for this option right. The optionee assumes no other obligation until he or she decides to either exercise the option right or allow the option to expire. An option is enforceable by only one party—the optionee.

An option contract is not a sales contract. At the time the option is signed by the parties, the owner does not sell, and the optionee does not buy. The parties merely agree that the optionee is acquiring the right to buy and the owner is obligated to sell *if* the optionee decides to exercise the option right. Options must contain all the terms and provisions required for a valid contract.

The option agreement (which is a unilateral contract) requires that the optionor act only after the optionee gives notice that he or she elects to execute the option. If the option is not exercised within the time specified in the contract, both the optionor's obligation and the optionee's right expire. An option contract may provide for renewal, which often requires additional consideration. The optionee cannot recover the consideration paid for the option right. The contract may state whether the money paid for the option is to be applied to the purchase price of the real estate if the option is exercised.

A common application of an option is a lease that includes an option for the tenant to purchase the property. Options on commercial real estate frequently depend on some specific conditions being fulfilled, such as obtaining a zoning change or a building permit. The optionee may be obligated to exercise the option if the conditions are met. Similar terms could also be included in a sales contract.

■ INSTALLMENT CONTRACTS

A real estate sale can be made under an **installment contract** (sometimes called a *contract for deed, land contract of sale,* or *articles of agreement*). Under a typical installment contract, the seller (also known as the *vendor*) retains legal title. The buyer, known as the *vendee,* takes possession and acquires equitable title to the property. The buyer agrees to give the seller a down payment and pay regular monthly installments of principal and interest over a number of years. The buyer also agrees to pay real estate taxes, insurance premiums, and repairs and upkeep on the property.

Although the buyer obtains possession under the contract, the seller is not obligated to execute and deliver a deed until the terms of the contract have been satisfied. This frequently occurs when the buyer has made enough payments to obtain a mortgage loan and pay off the balance due on the contract. Real estate is occasionally sold with the new buyer assuming an existing installment contract from the original buyer/vendee. Generally, the seller/vendor must approve the new purchaser.

Installment contracts usually include a provision that permits the seller to forfeit the contract, retain all payments already made, and evict the buyer if the buyer defaults on the contract. In some states, however, laws have been enacted that require the seller to refund to the buyer any payments received in excess of a reasonable rental or use value of the property. A defaulted installment contract may have to be foreclosed in the same manner as a mortgage.

IN PRACTICE

Legislatures and courts have not looked favorably on the harsh provisions of some real estate installment contracts. A seller and buyer contemplating such a sale should first consult an attorney to make sure that the agreement meets all legal requirements and addresses the individual concerns of the parties.

■ SUMMARY

Contracts frequently used in the sale of real estate include agreements of sale, options, and installment contracts. To be enforceable, these contracts must be in writing and contain the essential elements for a valid contract.

An agreement of sale binds a buyer and a seller to a definite transaction, as described in detail in the contract. The buyer is bound to purchase the property for the amount stated in the agreement. The seller is bound to deliver a good and marketable title, free from liens and encumbrances (except those allowed by the "subject to" clause of the contract). These contracts frequently include additional provisions and contingencies that must be satisfied.

In Pennsylvania, an agreement of sale must include disclosures of whom the broker represents, the existence of the Real Estate Recovery Fund, zoning classification (unless the property is zoned for single-family dwellings), and a statement regarding highway access. The agreement also must contain a lead-based paint disclosure, the sewage facilities statement and, if the property is a condominium or located in a planned community, notice about rights of rescission. Buyers must be given a copy of the seller's disclosure statement before signing an agreement of sale.

Under an option agreement, the optionee purchases from the optionor, for a limited time period, the exclusive right to purchase or lease the optionor's property. For a potential purchaser or lessee, an option is a means of buying time to consider or complete arrangements for a transaction.

An installment contract, or contract for deed, is a sales/financing arrangement under which a buyer purchases a seller's real estate over time. The buyer may take possession of and responsibility for the property but does not receive the deed until the terms of the contract are complete.

Note: The sample agreement of sale in Figure 19.1 is a reproduction of only the face pages in the contract form. Valuable information is provided on the reverse side of each page in the actual contract. In addition, guidelines for the preparation and use of the contract are available from PAR, the publisher of the form.

F I G U R E   19.1

Sample Agreement of Sale

STANDARD AGREEMENT FOR THE SALE OF REAL ESTATE   A/S-R
This form recommended and approved for, but not restricted to use by, the members of the Pennsylvania Association of REALTORS® (PAR).

SELLER'S BUSINESS RELATIONSHIP WITH PA LICENSED BROKER

BROKER (Company)_____PHONE _____

ADDRESS_____FAX _____

LICENSEE(S) _____Designated Agent? ☐ Yes ☐ No

BROKER IS THE AGENT FOR SELLER.   **OR (if checked below):**

Broker is NOT the Agent for Seller and is a/an: ☐ AGENT FOR BUYER   ☐ TRANSACTION LICENSEE

BUYER'S BUSINESS RELATIONSHIP WITH PA LICENSED BROKER

BROKER (Company)_____PHONE _____

ADDRESS_____FAX _____

LICENSEE(S) _____Designated Agent? ☐ Yes ☐ No

BROKER IS THE AGENT FOR BUYER.   **OR (if checked below):**

Broker is NOT the Agent for Buyer and is a/an: ☐ AGENT FOR SELLER ☐ SUBAGENT FOR SELLER ☐ TRANSACTION LICENSEE

When the same Broker is Agent for Seller and Agent for Buyer, Broker is a Dual Agent. All of Broker's licensees are also Dual Agents UNLESS there are separate Designated Agents for Buyer and Seller. If the same Licensee is designated for Seller and Buyer, the Licensee is a Dual Agent.

1 1. **This Agreement,** dated_____, is between 1

2   SELLER(S): _____ 2

3   _____ 3

4   _____, called "Seller," and 4

5   BUYER(S): _____ 5

6   _____ 6

7   _____, called "Buyer." 7

8 2. **PROPERTY (9-05)** Seller hereby agrees to sell and convey to Buyer, who hereby agrees to purchase: 8

9   **ALL THAT CERTAIN** lot or piece of ground with buildings and improvements thereon erected, if any, known as: 9

10   _____ 10

11   _____ in the _____ of _____ 11

12   **County of** _____ **in the Commonwealth of Pennsylvania. Identification (e.g., Tax ID #; Parcel #;** 12

13   **Lot, Block; Deed Book, Page, Recording Date):** _____ 13

14 3. **TERMS (9-05)** 14

15   (A) **Purchase Price** _____ 15

16   _____ U.S. Dollars, 16

17   **which will be paid to Seller by Buyer as follows:** 17

18   1. Cash or check at signing this Agreement: _____ $ _____ 18

19   2. Cash or check within _____ days of the execution of this Agreement: _____ $ _____ 19

20   3. _____ $ _____ 20

21   4. Cash or cashier's check at time of settlement:_____ $ _____ 21

22   **TOTAL $** _____ 22

23   (B) Deposits paid by Buyer within __30__ DAYS of settlement will be by cash or cashier's check. Deposits, regardless of the form of payment 23

24   and the person designated as payee, will be paid in U.S. Dollars to Broker for Seller (unless otherwise stated here), _____ 24

25   _____, who will retain 25

26   deposits in an escrow account until consummation or termination of this Agreement in conformity with all applicable laws and regulations. Any 26

27   check tendered as deposit monies may be held uncashed pending the acceptance of this Agreement. 27

28   (C) Seller's written approval to be on or before: _____ 28

29   (D) Settlement to be on _____, or before if Buyer and Seller agree. 29

30   (E) Settlement will occur in the county where the Property is located or in an adjacent county, during normal business hours, unless Buyer and 30

31   Seller agree otherwise. 31

32   (F) Conveyance from Seller will be by fee simple deed of special warranty unless otherwise stated here: _____ 32

33   _____ 33

34   (G) Payment of transfer taxes will be divided equally between Buyer and Seller unless otherwise stated here: _____ 34

35   _____ 35

36   (H) At time of settlement, the following will be adjusted pro-rata on a daily basis between Buyer and Seller, reimbursing where applicable: cur- 36

37   rent taxes (see Information Regarding Real Estate Taxes); rents; interest on mortgage assumptions; condominium fees and homeowner asso- 37

38   ciation fees; water and/or sewer fees, together with any other lienable municipal service. All charges will be pro-rated for the period(s) cov- 38

39   ered. Seller will pay up to and including the date of settlement and Buyer will pay for all days following settlement, unless otherwise stated 39

40   here: _____ 40

41   **Buyer Initials:** _____   A/S-R Page 1 of 10   **Seller Initials:** _____ 41

F I G U R E   19.1

Sample Agreement of Sale (continued)

4. **FIXTURES & PERSONAL PROPERTY (9-05)**

   (A) INCLUDED in this sale are all existing items permanently installed in the Property, free of liens, including plumbing; heating; lighting fixtures (including chandeliers and ceiling fans); water treatment systems; pool and spa equipment; garage door openers and transmitters; television antennas; unpotted shrubbery, plantings and trees; any remaining heating and cooking fuels stored on the Property at the time of settlement; sump pumps; storage sheds; mailboxes; wall to wall carpeting; existing window screens, storm windows and screen/storm doors; window covering hardware, shades and blinds; awnings; built-in air conditioners; built-in appliances; and the range/oven unless otherwise stated. Also included: _____

      _____

   (B) LEASED items (not owned by Seller): _____

      _____

   (C) EXCLUDED fixtures and items: _____

      _____

5. **DATES/TIME IS OF THE ESSENCE (9-05)**

   (A) The settlement date and all other dates and times referred to for the performance of any of the obligations of this Agreement are of the essence and are binding.

   (B) For purposes of this Agreement, the number of days will be counted from the date of execution, excluding the day this Agreement was executed and including the last day of the time period. The Execution Date of this Agreement is the date when Buyer and Seller have indicated full acceptance of this Agreement by signing and/or initialing it. All changes to this Agreement should be initialed and dated.

   (C) The settlement date is not extended by any other provision of this Agreement and may only be extended by mutual written agreement of the parties.

   (D) Certain time periods are pre-printed in this Agreement as a convenience to the Buyer and Seller. All pre-printed time periods are negotiable and may be changed by striking out the pre-printed text and inserting a different time period acceptable to all parties.

6. **MORTGAGE CONTINGENCY (9-05)**

   ☐ WAIVED. This sale is NOT contingent on mortgage financing, although Buyer may still obtain mortgage financing.

   ☐ ELECTED.

   (A) This sale is contingent upon Buyer obtaining mortgage financing as follows:

First Mortgage on the Property	**Second Mortgage on the Property**
Loan Amount $_____	Loan Amount $_____
Minimum Term _____ years	Minimum Term _____ years
Type of mortgage _____	Type of mortgage _____
_____	_____
Mortgage lender _____	Mortgage lender _____
_____	_____
Interest rate _____%; however, **Buyer agrees to accept the interest rate as may be committed by the mortgage lender,** not to exceed a maximum interest rate of _____%.	Interest rate _____%; however, **Buyer agrees to accept the interest rate as may be committed by the mortgage lender,** not to exceed a maximum interest rate of _____%.
Discount points, loan origination, loan placement and other fees charged by the lender as a percentage of the mortgage loan (excluding any mortgage insurance premiums or VA funding fee) not to exceed _____% (0% if not specified) of the mortgage loan.	Discount points, loan origination, loan placement and other fees charged by the lender as a percentage of the mortgage loan (excluding any mortgage insurance premiums or VA funding fee) not to exceed _____% (0% if not specified) of the mortgage loan.

      The interest rate(s) and fee(s) provisions in paragraph 6 (A) are satisfied if the mortgage lender(s) gives Buyer the right to guarantee the interest rate(s) and fee(s) at or below the maximum levels stated. Buyer gives Seller the right, at Seller's sole option and as permitted by law and the mortgage lender(s), to contribute financially, without promise of reimbursement, to the Buyer and/or the mortgage lender(s) to make the above mortgage terms available to Buyer.

   (B) Within _____ days (10 if not specified) from the Execution Date of this Agreement, Buyer will make a completed, written mortgage application for the mortgage terms stated above to the mortgage lender(s) identified in paragraph 6 (A), if any, otherwise to a responsible mortgage lender(s) of Buyer's choice. **Broker for Buyer, if any, otherwise Broker for Seller, is authorized to communicate with the mortgage lender(s) to assist in the mortgage loan process.**

   (C) **Should Buyer furnish false or incomplete information to Seller, Broker(s), or the mortgage lender(s) concerning Buyer's legal or financial status, or fail to cooperate in good faith in processing the mortgage loan application, which results in the mortgage lender(s) refusing to approve a mortgage loan commitment, Buyer will be in default of this Agreement.**

   (D) 1. **Mortgage commitment date:** _____. If Seller does not receive a copy of Buyer's mortgage commitment(s) by this date, **Buyer and Seller agree to extend the mortgage commitment date until Seller terminates this Agreement by written notice to Buyer.**

      2. Upon receiving a mortgage commitment, Buyer will promptly deliver a copy of the commitment to Seller.

      3. Seller may terminate this Agreement in writing after the mortgage commitment date, if the mortgage commitment(s):

         a. Is not valid until the date of settlement, OR

         b. Is conditioned upon the **sale and settlement of any other property,** OR

         c. Does not satisfy all the mortgage terms as stated in paragraph 6 (A), OR

         d. Contains any other condition not specified in this Agreement that is not satisfied and/or removed in writing by the mortgage lender(s) within ___7___ DAYS after the **mortgage commitment date in paragraph 6 (D) (1),** other than those conditions that are customarily satisfied at or near settlement, such as obtaining insurance and confirming employment status.

      4. If this Agreement is terminated pursuant to paragraphs 6 (D) (1) or (3), or the mortgage loan(s) is not obtained for settlement, all deposit monies will be returned to Buyer according to the terms of paragraph 30 and this Agreement will be VOID. Buyer will be responsible for any costs incurred by Buyer for any inspections or certifications obtained according to the terms of this Agreement, and any costs incurred by Buyer for: (1) Title search, title insurance and/or mechanics' lien insurance, or any fee for cancellation; (2) Flood insurance and/or fire insurance with extended coverage, mine subsidence insurance, or any fee for cancellation; (3) Appraisal fees and charges paid in advance to mortgage lender(s).

Buyer Initials: _____   **A/S-R Page 2 of 10**   **Seller Initials:** _____

Revised 9/05

FIGURE 19.1

Sample Agreement of Sale (continued)

108   (E)   If the mortgage lender(s), or an insurer providing property and casualty insurance as required by the mortgage lender(s), requires repairs to the
109   Property, Buyer will, upon receiving the requirements, deliver a copy of the requirements to Seller. Within __5__ DAYS of receiving the copy
110   of the requirements, Seller will notify Buyer whether Seller will make the required repairs at Seller's expense.
111   1.   If Seller makes the required repairs to the satisfaction of the mortgage lender(s) or insurer, Buyer accepts the Property and agrees to the
112   RELEASE in paragraph 27 of this Agreement.
113   2.   If Seller will not make the required repairs, **or if Seller fails to respond within the time given,** Buyer will, within __5__ DAYS, notify
114   Seller of Buyer's choice to:
115   a.   Make the required repairs, at Buyer's expense, with permission and access to the Property given by Seller; permission and access may
116   not be unreasonably withheld by Seller, OR
117   b.   Terminate this Agreement by written notice to Seller, with all deposit monies returned to Buyer according to the terms of paragraph
118   30 of this Agreement.
119   (F)   **Seller Assist**
120   ☐   NOT APPLICABLE
121   ☐   APPLICABLE. Seller will pay:
122   ☐ $_____ , or _____ % of Purchase Price, maximum, toward Buyer's costs as acceptable to the mortgage lender(s).
123   ☐   _____

124   **FHA/VA, IF APPLICABLE**
125   (G)   It is expressly agreed that notwithstanding any other provisions of this contract, Buyer will not be obligated to complete the purchase of
126   the Property described herein or to incur any penalty by forfeiture of earnest money deposits or otherwise unless Buyer has been given, in
127   accordance with HUD/FHA or VA requirements, a written statement by the Federal Housing Commissioner, Veterans Administration, or a
128   Direct Endorsement Lender setting forth the appraised value of the Property of not less than $ _____ (the dollar amount
129   to be inserted is the sales price as stated in this Agreement). Buyer will have the privilege and option of proceeding with consummation of
130   the contract without regard to the amount of the appraised valuation. The appraised valuation is arrived at to determine the maximum mort-
131   gage the Department of Housing and Urban Development will insure. HUD does not warrant the value nor the condition of the Property.
132   Buyer should satisfy himself/herself that the price and condition of the Property are acceptable.
133   **Warning:**   Section 1010 of Title 18, U.S.C., Department of Housing and Urban Development and Federal Housing Administration
134   Transactions provides, "Whoever for the purpose of . . . influencing in any way the action of such Department, makes, passes, utters or
135   publishes any statement, knowing the same to be false . . . shall be fined under this title or imprisoned not more than two years, or both."
136   (H)   **U.S. Department of Housing and Urban Development (HUD) NOTICE TO PURCHASERS: Buyer's Acknowledgement**
137   ☐   Buyer has received the HUD Notice "For Your Protection: Get a Home Inspection." Buyer understands the importance of getting
138   an independent home inspection and has thought about this before signing this Agreement. Buyer understands that FHA will not
139   perform a home inspection nor guarantee the price or condition of the Property.
140   (I)   **Certification**   We the undersigned, Seller(s) and Buyer(s) party to this transaction each certify that the terms of this contract for purchase
141   are true to the best of our knowledge and belief, and that any other agreement entered into by any of these parties in connection with this
142   transaction is attached to this Agreement.

143   7.   **WAIVER OF CONTINGENCIES (9-05)**
144   **If this Agreement is contingent on Buyer's right to inspect and/or repair the Property, or to verify insurability, environmental conditions,**
145   **boundaries, certifications, zoning classification or use, or any other information regarding the Property, Buyer's failure to exercise any of**
146   **Buyer's options within the times set forth in this Agreement is a WAIVER of that contingency and Buyer accepts the Property and agrees to**
147   **the RELEASE in paragraph 27 of this Agreement.**
148   8.   **PROPERTY INSURANCE AVAILABILITY (9-05)**
149   ☐   WAIVED. This Agreement is NOT contingent upon Buyer obtaining property and casualty insurance for the Property, although Buyer may
150   still obtain property and casualty insurance.
151   ☐   ELECTED. Contingency Period: _____ DAYS (15 if not specified) from the Execution Date of this Agreement.
152   **Within the Contingency Period,** Buyer will make application for property and casualty insurance for the Property to a responsible insurer. **Broker**
153   **for Buyer, if any, otherwise Broker for Seller, may communicate with the insurer to assist in the insurance process.** If Buyer cannot obtain
154   property and casualty insurance for the Property on terms and conditions reasonably acceptable to Buyer, Buyer will, **within the Contingency**
155   **Period:**
156   (A)   Accept the Property and agree to the RELEASE in paragraph 27 of this Agreement, OR
157   (B)   Terminate this Agreement by written notice to Seller, with all deposit monies returned to Buyer according to the terms of paragraph 30 of this
158   Agreement, OR
159   (C)   Enter into a mutually acceptable written agreement with Seller.
160   **If Buyer and Seller do not reach a written agreement during the Contingency Period, and Buyer does not terminate this Agreement by**
161   **written notice to Seller within that time, Buyer will accept the Property and agree to the RELEASE in paragraph 27 of this Agreement.**
162   9.   **INSPECTIONS (9-05)**
163   (A)   Seller will provide access to insurers' representatives and, as may be required by this Agreement, to surveyors, municipal officials, and inspec-
164   tors. If Buyer is obtaining mortgage financing, Seller will provide access to the Property to appraisers and others reasonably required by mort-
165   gage lender(s). Buyer may attend any inspections.
166   (B)   Buyer may make a pre-settlement walk-through inspection of the Property. Buyer's right to this inspection is not waived by any other provision
167   of this Agreement.
168   (C)   Seller will have heating and all utilities (including fuel(s)) on for all inspections.
169   (D)   All inspectors, including home inspectors, are authorized by Buyer to provide a copy of any inspection report to Broker for Buyer.
170   (E)   Seller has the right, upon request, to receive without charge a copy of any inspection report from the party for whom it was prepared.

171   **Buyer Initials:** _____   A/S-R Page 3 of 10   **Seller Initials:** _____
                                                    Revised 9/05

F I G U R E 19.1

Sample Agreement of Sale (continued)

10. INSPECTION CONTINGENCY OPTIONS (9-05)

The inspection contingencies elected by Buyer in paragraphs 11-15 are controlled by the Options set forth below. The time periods stated in these Options will apply to **all** inspection contingencies in paragraphs 11-15 unless otherwise stated in this Agreement.

Option 1. Within the Contingency Period, as stated in paragraphs 11-15, Buyer will:

    1. **Accept the Property** with the information stated in the report(s) and agree to the RELEASE in paragraph 27 of this Agreement, OR

    2. If Buyer is not satisfied with the information stated in the report(s), **terminate this Agreement** by written notice to Seller, with all deposit monies returned to Buyer according to the terms of paragraph 30 of this Agreement, OR

    3. **Enter into a mutually acceptable written agreement** with Seller providing for any repairs or improvements to the Property and/or any credit to Buyer at settlement, as acceptable to the mortgage lender(s), if any.

    If Buyer and Seller do not reach a written agreement during the specified Contingency Period, and Buyer does not terminate this Agreement by written notice to Seller within that time, Buyer will accept the Property and agree to the RELEASE in paragraph 27 of this Agreement.

Option 2. Within the Contingency Period, as stated in paragraphs 11-15, Buyer will:

    1. **Accept the Property** with the information stated in the report(s) and agree to the RELEASE in paragraph 27 of this Agreement, OR

    2. If Buyer is not satisfied with the information stated in the report(s), **present the report(s) to Seller with a Written Corrective Proposal ("Proposal") listing corrections and/or credits desired by Buyer.** The Proposal may, but is not required to, include the name of a properly licensed or qualified professional to perform the corrections requested in the Proposal, provisions for payment, including retests, and a projected date for completion of the corrections. Buyer agrees that Seller will not be held liable for corrections that do not comply with mortgage lender or governmental requirements if performed in a workmanlike manner according to the terms of Buyer's Proposal, or by a contractor selected by Buyer.

        a. Within _____ days (7 if not specified) of receiving Buyer's Proposal, Seller will inform Buyer in writing of Seller's choice to:

            (1) Satisfy the terms of Buyer's Proposal, OR

            (2) Credit Buyer at settlement for the costs to satisfy the terms of Buyer's Proposal, as acceptable to the mortgage lender(s), if any, OR

            (3) Not satisfy the terms of Buyer's Proposal and not credit Buyer at settlement for the costs to satisfy the terms of Buyer's Proposal.

        b. If Seller agrees to satisfy the terms of Buyer's Proposal or to credit Buyer at settlement as specified above, Buyer accepts the Property and agrees to the RELEASE in paragraph 27 of this Agreement.

        c. If Seller chooses not to satisfy the terms of Buyer's Proposal and not to credit Buyer at settlement as specified above, or **if Seller fails to choose any option within the time given,** Buyer will, within _____ days (5 if not specified):

            (1) Accept the Property with the information stated in the report(s) and agree to the RELEASE in paragraph 27 of this Agreement, OR

            (2) Terminate this Agreement by written notice to Seller, with all deposit monies returned to Buyer according to the terms of paragraph 30 of this Agreement, OR

            (3) Enter into a mutually acceptable written agreement with Seller providing for any repairs or improvements to the Property and/or any credit to Buyer at settlement, as acceptable to the mortgage lender(s), if any.

            If Buyer and Seller do not reach a written agreement during the time specified in Option 2, 2. c., and Buyer does not terminate this Agreement by written notice to Seller within that time, Buyer will accept the Property and agree to the RELEASE in paragraph 27 of this Agreement.

11. PROPERTY INSPECTION CONTINGENCY (9-05) (See Property and Environmental Inspection Notices)

Buyer understands that property inspections, certifications and/or investigations can be performed by professional contractors, home inspectors, engineers, architects and other properly licensed or otherwise qualified professionals, and may include, but are not limited to: structural components; roof; exterior windows and exterior doors; exterior siding, fascia, gutters and downspouts; swimming pools, hot tubs and spas; appliances; electrical, plumbing, heating and cooling systems; water penetration; environmental hazards (e.g., mold, fungi, indoor air quality, asbestos, underground storage tanks, etc.); electromagnetic fields; wetlands inspection; flood plain verification; property boundary/square footage verification; and any other items Buyer may select. Buyer is advised to investigate easements, deed and use restrictions (including any historic preservation restrictions or ordinances) that apply to the Property and to review local zoning ordinances. Other provisions of this Agreement may provide for inspections, certifications and/or investigations that are not waived or altered by Buyer's election here.

    ☐ WAIVED. Buyer has the option to conduct property inspections, certifications and/or investigations. Buyer WAIVES THIS OPTION and agrees to the RELEASE in paragraph 27 of this Agreement.

    ☐ ELECTED. Contingency Period: _____ days (15 if not specified) from the Execution Date of this Agreement.

(A) **Within the Contingency Period,** Buyer, at Buyer's expense, may have inspections, certifications and/or investigations completed by properly licensed or otherwise qualified professionals. If Buyer elects to have a home inspection of the Property, as defined in the Pennsylvania Home Inspection Law (see Information Regarding the Home Inspection Law), the home inspection must be performed by a full member in good standing of a national home inspection association or a person supervised by a full member of a national home inspection association, in accordance with the ethical standards and code of conduct or practice of that association, or by a properly licensed or registered professional engineer, or a properly licensed or registered architect. This contingency does not apply to the following existing conditions and/or items:

_____

_____

(B) If Buyer is not satisfied with the condition of the Property as stated in the written inspection report(s), Buyer will proceed under one of the following Options as listed in paragraph 10 **within the Contingency Period:**

    ☐ **Option 1**

    ☐ **Option 2 For the purposes of Paragraph 11 only,** Buyer agrees to accept the Property with the results of any report(s) and agrees to the RELEASE in paragraph 27 of this Agreement if the total cost to correct the conditions stated in the report(s) is less than $_____ ($0 if not specified) (the "Deductible Amount"). Otherwise, all provisions of paragraph 10, Option 2, shall apply, except that Seller will be deemed to have satisfied the terms of Buyer's Proposal if Seller agrees to perform corrections or offer credits such that the cumulative cost of any uncorrected or uncredited condition(s) is equal to the Deductible Amount.

Sample Agreement of Sale (continued)

237 **12. WOOD INFESTATION INSPECTION CONTINGENCY (9-05)**
238 ☐ WAIVED. Buyer has the option to have the Property inspected for wood infestation by an inspector certified as a wood-destroying pests pesti-
239 cide applicator. BUYER WAIVES THIS OPTION and agrees to the RELEASE in paragraph 27 of this Agreement.
240 ☐ ELECTED. Contingency Period: _____ days (15 if not specified) from the Execution Date of this Agreement.
241 (A) **Within the Contingency Period**, Buyer, at Buyer's expense, may obtain a written "Wood-Destroying Insect Infestation Inspection Report"
242 from an inspector certified as a wood-destroying pests pesticide applicator and will deliver it and all supporting documents and drawings pro-
243 vided by the inspector to Seller. The report is to be made satisfactory to and in compliance with applicable laws, mortgage lender requirements,
244 and/or Federal Insuring and Guaranteeing Agency requirements, if any. The inspection is to be limited to all readily visible and accessible areas
245 of all structures on the Property except fences and the following structures, which will not be inspected: _____
246 _____
247 (B) If the inspection reveals active infestation(s), Buyer, at Buyer's expense, may **within the Contingency Period**, obtain a Proposal from a wood-
248 destroying pests pesticide applicator to treat the Property.
249 (C) If the inspection reveals damage from active or previous infestation(s), Buyer, at Buyer's expense, may **within the Contingency Period,** obtain
250 a written report from a professional contractor, home inspector or structural engineer that is limited to structural damage to the Property caused
251 by wood-destroying organisms and a Proposal to repair and/or treat the Property.
252 (D) If Buyer is not satisfied with the condition of the Property as stated in the written inspection report(s), Buyer will proceed under one of the fol-
253 lowing Options as listed in paragraph 10 **within the Contingency Period:**
254 ☐ **Option 1**
255 ☐ **Option 2**
256 **13. STATUS OF RADON (9-05)** (see Information Regarding Radon)
257 (A) **Seller has no knowledge** concerning the presence or absence of radon unless checked below:
258 ☐ 1. Seller has knowledge that the Property was tested on the dates, by the methods (e.g., charcoal canister, alpha track, etc.), and with the
259 results of all tests indicated below:
260 DATE   TYPE OF TEST   RESULTS (picoCuries/liter or working levels)
261 _____
262
263 ☐ 2. Seller has knowledge that the Property underwent radon reduction measures on the date(s) and by the method(s) indicated below:
264 DATE   RADON REDUCTION METHOD
265 _____
266
267 COPIES OF ALL AVAILABLE TEST REPORTS will be delivered to Buyer with this Agreement. SELLER DOES NOT WARRANT
268 EITHER THE METHODS OR RESULTS OF THE TESTS.
269 (B) **RADON INSPECTION CONTINGENCY**
270 ☐ WAIVED. Buyer has the option to have the Property inspected for radon by a certified inspector. BUYER WAIVES THIS OPTION and
271 agrees to the RELEASE in paragraph 27 of this Agreement.
272 ☐ ELECTED. Contingency Period: _____ days (15 if not specified) from the Execution Date of this Agreement.
273 **Within the Contingency Period,** Buyer, at Buyer's expense, may obtain a radon test of the Property from a certified inspector. If Seller
274 performs any radon remediation, Seller will provide Buyer a certification that the remediation was performed by a properly licensed and
275 certified radon mitigation company.
276 1. If the written test report reveals the presence of radon below 0.02 working levels or 4 picoCuries/liter (4 pCi/L), Buyer accepts the
277 Property and agrees to the RELEASE in paragraph 27 of this Agreement.
278 2. If the written test report reveals the presence of radon at or exceeding 0.02 working levels or 4 picoCuries/liter (4 pCi/L), Buyer will
279 proceed under one of the following Options as listed in paragraph 10 **within the Contingency Period:**
280 ☐ **Option 1**
281 ☐ **Option 2**
282 **14. STATUS OF WATER (9-05)**
283 (A) Seller represents that the Property is served by:
284 ☐ Public Water
285 ☐ On-site Water
286 ☐ Community Water
287 ☐ None
288 ☐ _____
289 (B) **WATER SERVICE INSPECTION CONTINGENCY**
290 ☐ WAIVED. Buyer has the option to have an inspection of the quality and or quantity of the water system for the Property. BUYER WAIVES
291 THIS OPTION and agrees to the RELEASE in paragraph 27 of this Agreement.
292 ☐ ELECTED. Contingency Period: _____ days (15 if not specified) from the Execution Date of this Agreement.
293 1. **Within the Contingency Period,** Buyer, at Buyer's expense, may obtain an inspection of the quality and/or quantity of the water
294 system from a properly licensed or otherwise qualified water/well testing company.
295 2. If required by the inspection company, Seller, at Seller's expense, will locate and provide access to the on-site (or individual) water
296 system. Seller also agrees to restore the Property, at Seller's expense, prior to settlement.
297 3. If Buyer is not satisfied with the condition of the water system as stated in the written inspection report(s), Buyer will proceed under
298 one of the following Options as listed in paragraph 10 **within the Contingency Period:**
299 ☐ **Option 1**
300 ☐ **Option 2**

F I G U R E   **19.1**

Sample Agreement of Sale (continued)

302   **15. STATUS OF SEWER (9-05)**

303   (A) Seller represents that the Property is served by:

304   ☐   Public Sewer

305   ☐   Individual On-lot Sewage Disposal System (see Sewage Notice 1)

306   ☐   Individual On-lot Sewage Disposal System in Proximity to Well (see Sewage Notice 1; see Sewage Notice 4, if applicable)

307   ☐   Community Sewage Disposal System

308   ☐   Ten-Acre Permit Exemption (see Sewage Notice 2)

309   ☐   Holding Tank (see Sewage Notice 3)

310   ☐   None (see Sewage Notice 1)

311   ☐   None Available/Permit Limitations in Effect (see Sewage Notice 5)

312   ☐   _____

313   (B) **INDIVIDUAL ON-LOT SEWAGE DISPOSAL INSPECTION CONTINGENCY**

314   ☐   WAIVED. Buyer has the option to have an inspection of the individual on-lot sewage disposal system for the Property. BUYER

315   WAIVES THIS OPTION and agrees to the RELEASE in paragraph 27 of this Agreement.

316   ☐   ELECTED. Contingency Period: _____ days (15 if not specified) from the Execution Date of this Agreement.

317   1.   **Within the Contingency Period,** Buyer, at Buyer's expense, may obtain an inspection of the individual on-lot sewage disposal sys-

318   tem from a qualified, professional inspector.

319   2.   If and as required by the inspection company, Seller, at Seller's expense, will locate, provide access to and empty the individual on-

320   lot sewage disposal system. Seller will also restore the Property, at Seller's expense, prior to settlement.

321   3.   If the inspection report reveals defects that do not require expansion or replacement of the existing individual on-lot sewage dispos-

322   al system, Buyer will proceed under one of the following Options as listed in paragraph 10 **within the Contingency Period:**

323   ☐ **Option 1**

324   ☐ **Option 2**

325   4.   If the inspection report reveals the need to expand or replace the existing individual on-lot sewage disposal system, Seller may,

326   within ___25___ DAYS of receiving the inspection report, submit a Written Corrective Proposal ("Proposal") to Buyer. The Proposal

327   will include, but not be limited to, the name of the company to perform the expansion or replacement; provisions for payment, includ-

328   ing retests; and a projected completion date for corrective measures. Within ___5___ DAYS of receiving Seller's Proposal, or **if no**

329   **Proposal is provided within the time given,** Buyer will notify Seller in writing of Buyer's choice to:

330   a. Agree to the terms of the Proposal, if any, whereupon Buyer accepts the Property and agrees to the RELEASE in paragraph 27 of

331   this Agreement, OR

332   b. Terminate this Agreement by written notice to Seller, with all deposit monies returned to Buyer according to the terms of para-

333   graph 30 of this Agreement.

334   c. Accept the Property and the existing system and agree to the RELEASE in paragraph 27 of this Agreement, and, if required by

335   any mortgage lender and/or any governmental authority, correct the defects before settlement or within the time required by the

336   mortgage lender and/or governmental authority, at Buyer's sole expense, and with permission and access to the Property given by

337   Seller. Permission and access may not be unreasonably withheld by Seller. If Seller denies Buyer permission and/or access to cor-

338   rect the defects, Buyer may, within ___5___ DAYS of Seller's denial, terminate this Agreement by written notice to Seller, with all

339   deposit monies returned to Buyer according to the terms of paragraph 30 of this Agreement.

340   **16. HOME WARRANTIES (9-05)**

341   At or before settlement, either party may have the opportunity to purchase a home warranty for the Property from a third-party vendor. Buyer and

342   Seller understand that a home warranty for the Property does not alter any disclosure requirements of Seller, will not cover or warrant any pre-

343   existing defects of the Property, and will not alter, waive or extend any provisions of this Agreement regarding inspections or certifications that

344   Buyer has elected or waived as part of this Agreement. Buyer and Seller understand that the licensee, broker or mortgage lender who orders the

345   home warranty may possibly receive a fee paid by the home warranty company.

346   **17. ZONING CLASSIFICATION & VERIFICATION OF USE CONTINGENCY (9-05)**

347   (A) Failure of this Agreement to contain the zoning classification (except in cases where the property {and each parcel thereof, if subdividable} is

348   zoned solely or primarily to permit single-family dwellings) will render this Agreement voidable at Buyer's option, and, if voided, any deposits

349   tendered by the Buyer will be returned to the Buyer without any requirement for court action.

350   **Zoning Classification:**_____.

351   (B) Contingency Period: _____ days (7 if not specified) from the Execution Date of this Agreement.

352   **Within the Contingency Period,** Buyer, at Buyer's expense, may verify that the present use (_____)

353   of the Property is permitted. In the event the present use is not permitted, **Buyer will, within the Contingency Period,** give Seller written

354   notice that the present use of the Property is not permitted and that Buyer will:

355   1.   Accept the Property and agree to the RELEASE in paragraph 27 of this Agreement, OR

356   2.   Terminate this Agreement by written notice to Seller, with all deposit monies returned to Buyer according to the terms of paragraph 30 of

357   this Agreement.

358   **If Buyer fails to respond within the Contingency Period or does not terminate this Agreement by written notice to Seller within that**

359   **time, Buyer will accept the Property and agree to the RELEASE in paragraph 27 of this Agreement.**

360   **18. NOTICES, ASSESSMENTS & CERTIFICATES OF OCCUPANCY (9-05)**

361   (A) Seller represents, as of the date Seller signed this Agreement, that no public improvement, condominium or homeowner association assessments

362   have been made against the Property which remain unpaid, and that no notice by any government or public authority has been served upon Seller

363   or anyone on Seller's behalf, including notices relating to violations of zoning, housing, building, safety or fire ordinances that remain uncor-

364   rected, and that Seller knows of no condition that would constitute a violation of any such ordinances that remain uncorrected, unless otherwise

365   specified here: _____

366   (B) Seller knows of no other potential notices (including violations) and/or assessments except as follows: _____

367   _____

F I G U R E   19.1

Sample Agreement of Sale (continued)

(C) In the event any notices (including violations) and/or assessments are received after Seller has signed this Agreement and before settlement, Seller will provide a copy of the notices and/or assessments to Buyer and will notify Buyer in writing within __5__ DAYS of receiving the notices and/or assessments that Seller will:

    1. Fully comply with the notices and/or assessments at Seller's expense before settlement. If Seller fully complies with the notices and/or assessments, Buyer accepts the Property and agrees to the RELEASE in paragraph 27 of this Agreement. OR

    2. Not comply with the notices and/or assessments. If Seller chooses not to comply with the notices and/or assessments, or **fails within the time given to notify Buyer whether Seller will comply,** Buyer will notify Seller in writing within __5__ DAYS that Buyer will:

        a. Comply with the notices and/or assessments at Buyer's expense, accept the Property, and agree to the RELEASE in paragraph 27 of this Agreement, OR

        b. Terminate this Agreement by written notice to Seller, with all deposit monies returned to Buyer according to the terms of paragraph 30 of this Agreement.

        If Buyer fails to respond within the time stated in paragraph 18 (C) (2) or fails to terminate this Agreement by written notice to Seller within that time, Buyer will accept the Property and agree to the RELEASE in paragraph 27 of this Agreement.

(D) If required by law, within __30__ DAYS from the Execution Date of this Agreement, but in no case later than 15 days prior to settlement, Seller will order at Seller's expense a certification from the appropriate municipal department(s) disclosing notice of any uncorrected violations of zoning, housing, building, safety or fire ordinances and/or a certificate permitting occupancy of the Property. If Buyer receives a notice of any required repairs/improvements, Buyer will promptly deliver a copy of the notice to Seller.

    1. Within __5__ DAYS of receiving notice from the municipality that repairs/improvements are required, Seller will notify Buyer in writing that Seller will:

        a. Make the required repairs/improvements to the satisfaction of the municipality. If Seller makes the required repairs/improvements, Buyer accepts the Property and agrees to the RELEASE in paragraph 27 of this Agreement. OR

        b. Not make the required repairs/improvements. If Seller chooses not to make the required repairs/improvements, Buyer will notify Seller in writing within __5__ DAYS that Buyer will:

            (1) Make the repairs/improvements at Buyer's expense, with permission and access to the Property given by Seller, which will not be unreasonably withheld, OR

            (2) Terminate this Agreement by written notice to Seller, with all deposit monies returned to Buyer according to the terms of paragraph 30 of this Agreement.

        If Buyer fails to respond within the time stated in paragraph 18 (D) (1) (b) or fails to terminate this Agreement by written notice to Seller within that time, Buyer will accept the Property and agree to the RELEASE in paragraph 27 of this Agreement, and Buyer accepts the responsibility to perform the repairs/improvements according to the terms of the notice provided by the municipality.

    2. If Seller denies Buyer permission to make the required repairs/improvements, or does not provide Buyer access before settlement to make the required repairs/improvements, Buyer may, within __5__ DAYS, terminate this Agreement by written notice to Seller, with all deposit monies returned to Buyer according to the terms of paragraph 30 of this Agreement.

    3. If repairs/improvements are required and Seller fails to provide a copy of the notice to Buyer as required in paragraph 18 (D), Seller will perform all repairs/improvements as required by the notice at Seller's expense. **Paragraph 18 (D) (3) will survive settlement.**

(E) Access to a public road may require issuance of a highway occupancy permit from the Department of Transportation.

19. **TITLE, SURVEYS & COSTS (9-05)**

(A) The Property will be conveyed with good and marketable title as is insurable by a reputable title insurance company at the regular rates, free and clear of all liens, encumbrances, and easements, EXCEPTING HOWEVER the following: existing deed restrictions; historic preservation restrictions or ordinances; building restrictions; ordinances; easements of roads; easements visible upon the ground; easements of record; and privileges or rights of public service companies, if any.

(B) Buyer will pay for the following: (1) Title search, title insurance and/or mechanics' lien insurance, or any fee for cancellation; (2) Flood insurance, fire insurance with extended coverage, mine subsidence insurance, or any fee for cancellation; (3) Appraisal fees and charges paid in advance to mortgage lender(s); (4) Buyer's customary settlement costs and accruals.

(C) Any survey or surveys required by the title insurance company or the abstracting attorney for preparing an adequate legal description of the Property (or the correction thereof) will be obtained and paid for by Seller. Any survey or surveys desired by Buyer or required by the mortgage lender will be obtained and paid for by Buyer.

(D) If Seller is unable to give a good and marketable title and such as is insurable by a reputable title insurance company at the regular rates, as specified in paragraph 19 (A), Buyer will:

    1. Accept the Property with such title as Seller can give, with no change to the purchase price, and agree to the RELEASE in paragraph 27 of this Agreement, OR

    2. Terminate this Agreement by written notice to Seller, with all deposit monies returned to Buyer according to the terms of paragraph 30 of this Agreement. Upon termination, Seller will reimburse Buyer for any costs incurred by Buyer for any inspections or certifications obtained according to the terms of this Agreement, and for those items specified in paragraph 19 (B) items (1), (2), (3) and in paragraph 19 (C).

(E) The Property is not a "recreational cabin" as defined in the Pennsylvania Construction Code Act unless otherwise stated here (see Information Regarding Recreational Cabins): _____

20. **CONDOMINIUM/PLANNED COMMUNITY (HOMEOWNER ASSOCIATION) RESALE NOTICE (9-05)**

   ☐ NOT APPLICABLE

   ☐ APPLICABLE: CONDOMINIUM. The Property is a unit of a condominium that is primarily run by a unit owners' association. §3407 of the Uniform Condominium Act of Pennsylvania (see Information Regarding Condominiums and Planned Communities) requires Seller to furnish Buyer with a Certificate of Resale and copies of the condominium declaration (other than plats and plans), the bylaws and the rules and regulations of the association.

   ☐ APPLICABLE: PLANNED COMMUNITY (HOMEOWNER ASSOCIATION). The Property is part of a planned community as defined by the Uniform Planned Community Act (see Information Regarding Condominiums and Planned Communities). §5407(a) of the Act requires Seller to furnish Buyer with a copy of the Declaration (other than plats and plans), the bylaws the rules and regulations of the association, and a Certificate containing the provisions set forth in §5407(a) of the Act.

Buyer Initials: _____ **A/S-R Page 7 of 10** **Seller Initials:** _____

Revised 9/05

F I G U R E   19.1

Sample Agreement of Sale (continued)

436   **THE FOLLOWING APPLIES TO PROPERTIES THAT ARE PART OF A CONDOMINIUM OR A PLANNED COMMUNITY.**

437   (A)   Within ___15___ DAYS from the Execution Date of this Agreement, Seller, at Seller's expense, will request from the association a Certificate of
438   Resale and any other documents necessary to enable Seller to comply with the relevant Act. The Act provides that the association is required to
439   provide these documents within 10 days of Seller's request.

440   (B)   Seller will promptly deliver to Buyer all documents received from the association. Under the Act, Seller is not liable to Buyer for the failure of
441   the association to provide the Certificate in a timely manner, nor is Seller liable to Buyer for any incorrect information provided by the associ-
442   ation in the Certificate.

443   (C)   The Act provides that Buyer may declare this Agreement VOID at any time before Buyer receives the association documents and for 5 days
444   after receipt, OR until settlement, whichever occurs first. Buyer's notice to Seller must be in writing; upon Buyer declaring this Agreement void,
445   all deposit monies will be returned to Buyer according to the terms of paragraph 30 of this Agreement.

446   (D)   If the association has the right to buy the Property (right of first refusal), and the association exercises that right, Seller will reimburse Buyer for
447   any costs incurred by Buyer for any inspections or certifications obtained according to the terms of the Agreement, and any costs incurred by Buyer
448   for: (1) Title search, title insurance and/or mechanics' lien insurance, or any fee for cancellation; (2) Flood insurance and/or fire insurance with
449   extended coverage, mine subsidence insurance, or any fee for cancellation; (3) Appraisal fees and charges paid in advance to mortgage lender(s).

450   **21. MAINTENANCE & RISK OF LOSS (9-05)**

451   (A)   Seller will maintain the Property, grounds, fixtures and personal property specifically listed in this Agreement in its present condition, normal
452   wear and tear excepted.

453   (B)   If any system or appliance included in the sale of the Property fails before settlement, Seller will:

454   1.   Repair or replace the failed system or appliance before settlement, OR

455   2.   Provide prompt written notice to Buyer of Seller's decision to:

456   a.   Credit Buyer at settlement for the fair market value of the failed system or appliance, as acceptable to the mortgage lender(s), if any, OR

457   b.   Not repair or replace the failed system or appliance, and not credit Buyer at settlement for the fair market value of the failed system
458   or appliance.

459   3.   If Seller does not repair or replace the failed system or appliance or agree to credit Buyer for its fair market value, or if Seller fails to noti-
460   fy Buyer of Seller's choice, Buyer will notify Seller in writing within ___5___ DAYS or before settlement, whichever is earlier, that Buyer
461   will:

462   a.   Accept the Property and agree to the RELEASE in paragraph 27 of this Agreement, OR

463   b.   Terminate this Agreement by written notice to Seller, with all deposit monies returned to Buyer according to the terms of paragraph
464   30 of this Agreement.

465   (C)   Seller bears the risk of loss from fire or other casualties until settlement. If any property included in this sale is destroyed and not replaced, Buyer will:

466   1.   Accept the Property in its then current condition together with the proceeds of any insurance recovery obtainable by Seller, OR

467   2.   Terminate this Agreement by written notice to Seller, with all deposit monies returned to Buyer according to the terms of paragraph 30 of
468   this Agreement.

469   **22. COAL NOTICE (Where Applicable)**

470   THIS DOCUMENT MAY NOT SELL, CONVEY, TRANSFER, INCLUDE OR INSURE THE TITLE TO THE COAL AND RIGHTS OF SUPPORT UNDERNEATH THE SURFACE LAND
471   DESCRIBED OR REFERRED TO HEREIN, AND THE OWNER OR OWNERS OF SUCH COAL MAY HAVE THE COMPLETE LEGAL RIGHT TO REMOVE ALL SUCH COAL AND
472   IN THAT CONNECTION, DAMAGE MAY RESULT TO THE SURFACE OF THE LAND AND ANY HOUSE, BUILDING OR OTHER STRUCTURE ON OR IN SUCH LAND. (This
473   notice is set forth in the manner provided in Section 1 of the Act of July 17, 1957, P.L. 984.) "Buyer acknowledges that he may not be obtaining the
474   right of protection against subsidence resulting from coal mining operations, and that the property described herein may be protected from damage
475   due to mine subsidence by a private contract with the owners of the economic interests in the coal. This acknowledgement is made for the purpose
476   of complying with the provisions of Section 14 of the Bituminous Mine Subsidence and the Land Conservation Act of April 27, 1966." Buyer agrees
477   to sign the deed from Seller which deed will contain the aforesaid provision.

478   **23. POSSESSION (9-05)**

479   (A)   Possession is to be delivered by deed, keys and:

480   1.   Physical possession to vacant Property free of debris, with all structures broom-clean, at day and time of settlement, AND/OR

481   2.   Assignment of any existing lease(s), together with any security deposits and interest, at day and time of settlement, if Property is leased at
482   the execution of this Agreement, unless otherwise stated in this Agreement.

483   (B)   Buyer will acknowledge existing lease(s) by initialing the lease(s) at the execution of this Agreement, unless otherwise specified herein.

484   (C)   Seller will not enter into any new leases, extensions of existing leases or additional leases for the Property without the written consent of Buyer.

485   **24. RECORDING (9-05)** This Agreement will not be recorded in the Office of the Recorder of Deeds or in any other office or place of public record.
486   If Buyer causes or permits this Agreement to be recorded, Seller may elect to treat such act as a breach of this Agreement.

487   **25. ASSIGNMENT (9-05)** This Agreement is binding upon the parties, their heirs, personal representatives, guardians and successors, and to the extent
488   assignable, on the assigns of the parties hereto. Buyer will not transfer or assign this Agreement without the written consent of Seller unless other-
489   wise stated in this Agreement.

490   **26. GOVERNING LAW, VENUE & PERSONAL JURISDICTION (9-05)**

491   (A)   The validity and construction of this Agreement, and the rights and duties of the parties, will be governed in accordance with the laws of the
492   Commonwealth of Pennsylvania.

493   (B)   The parties agree that any dispute, controversy or claim arising under or in connection with this Agreement or its performance by either party
494   shall be decided exclusively by and in the state or federal courts sitting in the Commonwealth of Pennsylvania.

495   **27. RELEASE (9-05)**

496   **Buyer releases, quit claims and forever discharges SELLER, ALL BROKERS, their LICENSEES, EMPLOYEES and any OFFICER or**
497   **PARTNER of any one of them and any other PERSON, FIRM or CORPORATION who may be liable by or through them, from any and**
498   **all claims, losses or demands, including, but not limited to, personal injury and property damage and all of the consequences thereof, whether**
499   **known or not, which may arise from the presence of termites or other wood-boring insects, radon, lead-based paint hazards, mold, fungi or**
500   **indoor air quality, environmental hazards, any defects in the individual on-lot sewage disposal system or deficiencies in the on-site water**
501   **service system, or any defects or conditions on the Property. Should Seller be in default under the terms of this Agreement, or in violation of**
502   **any seller disclosure law or regulation, this release does not deprive Buyer of any right to pursue any remedies that may be available under**
503   **law or equity. This release will survive settlement.**

504   Buyer Initials: _____   A/S-R Page 8 of 10   Seller Initials: _____
                                            Revised 9/05

F I G U R E   **19.1**

Sample Agreement of Sale (continued)

505 **28. REPRESENTATIONS (9-05)**
506   (A) All representations, claims, advertising, promotional activities, brochures or plans of any kind made by Seller, Brokers, their licensees, employ-
507   ees, officers or partners are not a part of this Agreement unless expressly incorporated or stated in this Agreement. This Agreement contains the
508   whole agreement between Seller and Buyer, and there are no other terms, obligations, covenants, representations, statements or conditions, oral
509   or otherwise, of any kind whatsoever concerning this sale. This Agreement will not be altered, amended, changed or modified except in writing
510   executed by the parties.
511   (B) **Unless otherwise stated in this Agreement, Buyer has inspected the Property (including fixtures and any personal property specifically**
512   **listed herein) before signing this Agreement or has waived the right to do so, and agrees to purchase the Property IN ITS PRESENT**
513   **CONDITION. Buyer acknowledges that Brokers, their licensees, employees, officers or partners have not made an independent exam-**
514   **ination or determination of the structural soundness of the Property, the age or condition of the components, environmental conditions,**
515   **the permitted uses or of conditions existing in the locale where the Property is situated; nor have they made a mechanical inspection of**
516   **any of the systems contained therein.**
517   (C) Any repairs required by this Agreement will be completed in a workmanlike manner.
518   (D) Broker(s) have provided or may provide services to assist unrepresented parties in complying with this Agreement.
519 **29. DEFAULT (9-05)**
520   (A) Seller has the option of retaining all sums paid by Buyer, including the deposit monies, should Buyer:
521   1. Fail to make any additional payments as specified in paragraph 3, OR
522   2. Furnish false or incomplete information to Seller, Broker(s), or any other party identified in this Agreement concerning Buyer's legal or
523   financial status, OR
524   3. Violate or fail to fulfill and perform any other terms or conditions of this Agreement.
525   (B) **Unless otherwise checked in paragraph 29 (C),** Seller may elect to retain those sums paid by Buyer, including deposit monies:
526   1. On account of purchase price, OR
527   2. As monies to be applied to Seller's damages, OR
528   3. As liquidated damages for such breach.
529   (C) ☐ **SELLER IS LIMITED TO RETAINING SUMS PAID BY BUYER, INCLUDING DEPOSIT MONIES, AS LIQUIDATED DAMAGES.**
530   (D) If Seller retains all sums paid by Buyer, including deposit monies, as liquidated damages pursuant to paragraph 29 (B) or (C), Buyer and Seller
531   are released from further liability or obligation and this Agreement is VOID.
532 **30. TERMINATION & RETURN OF DEPOSITS (9-05)**
533   (A) Where Buyer terminates this Agreement pursuant to any right granted by this Agreement, all deposit monies paid on account of purchase price
534   will be returned to Buyer and this Agreement will be VOID. The broker holding the deposit monies may only release the deposit monies accord-
535   ing to the terms of a fully executed written agreement between Buyer and Seller and as permitted by the Rules and Regulations of the State Real
536   Estate Commission.
537   (B) If there is a dispute over entitlement to deposit monies, a broker is not legally permitted to determine if a breach occurred or which party is enti-
538   tled to deposit monies. A broker holding the deposit monies is required by the Rules and Regulations of the State Real Estate Commission to
539   retain the monies in escrow until the dispute is resolved. In the event of litigation over deposit monies, a broker will distribute the monies accord-
540   ing to the terms of a final order of court or a written agreement of the parties. Buyer and Seller agree that, if any broker or affiliated licensee is
541   joined in litigation regarding deposit monies, the attorneys' fees and costs of the broker(s) and licensee(s) will be paid by the party joining them.
542 **31. REAL ESTATE RECOVERY FUND (9-05)**
543   A Real Estate Recovery Fund exists to reimburse any persons who have obtained a final civil judgment against a Pennsylvania real estate licensee
544   owing to fraud, misrepresentation, or deceit in a real estate transaction and who have been unable to collect the judgment after exhausting all legal
545   and equitable remedies. For complete details about the Fund, call (717) 783-3658 or (800) 822-2113 (within Pennsylvania) and (717) 783-4854 (out-
546   side Pennsylvania).
547 **32. MEDIATION (9-05)**
548   (A) Unless otherwise checked in paragraph 32 (D), Buyer and Seller will submit all disputes or claims that arise from this Agreement to mediation
549   in accordance with the Rules and Procedures of the Home Sellers/Home Buyers Dispute Resolution System. Any agreement reached through
550   mediation and signed by the parties will be binding (see Information Regarding Mediation).
551   (B) Buyer and Seller have received, read, and understand the Rules and Procedures of the Home Sellers/Home Buyers Dispute Resolution System.
552   (C) Any agreement to mediate disputes or claims arising from this Agreement will survive settlement.
553   (D) ☐ **MEDIATION IS WAIVED.** Buyer and Seller understand that they may choose to mediate at a later date should a dispute or claim arise,
554   but that there will be no obligation for any party to do so.
555 **33. RESIDENTIAL LEAD-BASED PAINT HAZARD REDUCTION ACT NOTICE (Required for properties built before 1978) (9-05)**
556   **Lead-Based Paint Hazards Disclosure Requirements:**   The Residential Lead-Based Paint Hazard Reduction Act requires any seller of prop-
557   erty built before 1978 to provide the buyer with an EPA-approved lead hazards information pamphlet titled *Protect Your Family from Lead in*
558   *Your Home* and to disclose to the buyer and the broker(s) the known presence of lead-based paint and/or lead-based paint hazards in or on the
559   property being sold, along with the basis used for determining that the hazards exist, the location of the hazards, and the condition of painted sur-
560   faces. Any seller of a pre-1978 structure must also provide the buyer with any records or reports available to the seller regarding lead-based paint
561   and/or lead-based paint hazards in or about the property being sold, the common areas, or other residential dwellings in multi-family housing.
562   Before a buyer is obligated to purchase any housing constructed prior to 1978, the Act requires the seller to give the buyer 10 days (unless buyer
563   and seller agree in writing to another time period) to conduct a risk assessment or inspection for the presence of lead-based paint and/or lead-
564   based paint hazards. The opportunity to conduct a risk assessment or inspection may be waived by the buyer, in writing. Neither testing nor abate-
565   ment is required of the seller. Housing built in 1978 or later is not subject to the Act.

566   ☐ NOT APPLICABLE. Property was built in 1978 or later.
567   ☐ APPLICABLE. Property was built before 1978. **Broker must attach the Lead-Based Paint Hazards Disclosure and Inspection**
568   **Contingency Addendum (PAR Form LPA) or another acceptable form with the information required by the Act, and provide Buyer**
569   **the pamphlet** *Protect Your Family from Lead in Your Home.* **Buyer(s) must initial below that they have received both documents:**

570   ➜ _____ Lead-Based Paint Hazards Disclosure and Inspection Contingency Addendum (**attached as part of this Agreement**).
571   ➜ _____ *Protect Your Family from Lead in Your Home*

572 **Buyer Initials:**_____   A/S-R Page 9 of 10   **Seller Initials:** _____   572
                                                    Revised 9/05

F I G U R E   **19.1**

Sample Agreement of Sale (continued)

573   **34. SPECIAL CLAUSES (1-02)**   573

574   (A) **The following are part of this Agreement if checked:**   574

575   ☐ Sale & Settlement of Other Property   ☐ Settlement of Other Property Contingency Addendum (PAR Form SOP)   575

576   Contingency Addendum (PAR Form SSP)   ☐ Tenant-Occupied Property Addendum (PAR Form TOP)   576

577   ☐ Sale & Settlement of Other Property Contingency   ☐ _____   577

578   with Right to Continue Marketing   ☐ _____   578

579   Addendum(PAR Form SSP-CM)   ☐ _____   579

580   (B)   580

581   581

582   582

583   583

584   584

585   585

586   586

587   587

588   588

589   589

590   590

591   591

592   592

593   593

594   594

595   595

596   596

597   597

598   Buyer and Seller acknowledge receipt of a copy of this Agreement at the time of signing.   598

599   **NOTICE TO PARTIES: WHEN SIGNED, THIS AGREEMENT IS A BINDING CONTRACT.** Parties to this transaction are advised to consult   599

600   an attorney before signing if they desire legal advice.   600

601   Return by facsimile transmission (FAX) of this Agreement, and any addenda and amendments, bearing the signatures of all parties, constitutes   601

602   acceptance by the parties.   602

603   ☐ Buyer has received the Consumer Notice as adopted by the State Real Estate Commission at 49 Pa. Code §35.336.   603

604   ☐ Buyer has received a statement of Buyer's estimated closing costs before signing this Agreement.   604

605   ☐ Buyer has read and understands the notices and explanatory information in this Agreement.   605

606   ☐ Buyer has received a Seller's Property Disclosure Statement before signing this Agreement, if required by law (see Information Regarding   606

607   the Real Estate Seller Disclosure Law).   607

608   ☐ Buyer has received the Deposit Money Notice (for cooperative sales when Broker for Seller is holding deposit money) before signing this   608

609   Agreement.   609

610   **BUYER'S MAILING ADDRESS:** _____   610

611   _____   611

612   WITNESS_____   BUYER_____   DATE _____   612

613   WITNESS_____   BUYER_____   DATE _____   613

614   WITNESS_____   BUYER_____   DATE _____   614

615   Seller has received the Consumer Notice as adopted by the State Real Estate Commission at 49 Pa. Code §35.336.   615

616   Seller has received a statement of Seller's estimated closing costs before signing this Agreement.   616

617   Seller has read and understands the notices and explanatory information in this Agreement.   617

618   **SELLER'S MAILING ADDRESS:** _____   618

619   _____   619

620   WITNESS_____   SELLER_____   DATE _____   620

621   WITNESS_____   SELLER_____   DATE _____   621

622   WITNESS_____   SELLER_____   DATE _____   622

A/S-R Page 10 of 10
Revised 9/05

QUESTIONS

1. A real estate purchaser is said to have *equitable title* when
   a. the sales contract is signed by both buyer and seller.
   b. the transaction is closed.
   c. escrow is opened.
   d. a contract for deed is paid off.

2. The sales contract says J will purchase only if his wife flies up and approves the sale by the following Saturday. Her approval is a
   a. contingency.
   b. reservation.
   c. warranty.
   d. consideration.

3. When the buyer promises to purchase the seller's property only if he can sell his present home, the buyer's protection from owning two homes is
   a. an escrow.
   b. an option.
   c. an equitable title.
   d. a contingency.

4. An option to purchase binds
   a. the buyer only.
   b. the seller only.
   c. neither buyer nor seller.
   d. both buyer and seller.

5. Which of the following best describes a land contract or installment contract?
   a. A contract to buy land only
   b. A mortgage on land
   c. A means of conveying title immediately whereby the purchaser pays for the property in installments
   d. A method of selling real estate whereby the purchaser pays in regular installments while the seller retains title

6. The purchaser of real estate under an installment contract
   a. generally pays no interest charge.
   b. receives title immediately.
   c. is not required to pay property taxes for the duration of the contract.
   d. is called a vendee.

7. The Fs offer in writing to purchase a house for $120,000, including its draperies, with the offer to expire on Saturday at noon. The Ws reply in writing on Thursday, accepting the $120,000 offer but excluding the draperies. On Friday, while the Fs are considering this counteroffer, the Ws decide to accept the original offer, draperies included, and state that in writing. At this point, the Fs
   a. must buy the house and have the right to insist on the draperies.
   b. are not bound to buy.
   c. must buy the house but are not entitled to the draperies.
   d. must buy the house and can deduct the value of the draperies from the $120,000.

8. Q makes an offer to purchase certain property listed with broker M and leaves a deposit with broker M to show good faith. M should
   a. immediately apply the deposit to the listing expenses.
   b. put the deposit in an account as provided by state law.
   c. give the deposit to the seller when the offer is presented.
   d. put the deposit in her checking account.

9. A buyer wants to make an offer to purchase a house that she suspects has a wet basement. The buyer is afraid that the house may be sold to someone else before she has a chance to get information about the structure. How should she proceed?
   a. Ask the real estate salesperson to guarantee that the basement is dry.
   b. Ask the seller to repair the basement before she makes an offer.
   c. Make an offer to purchase that is contingent on a structural inspection.
   d. Hire a contractor to give an estimate for repair before making an offer.

10. An agreement of sale in Pennsylvania must contain all of the following *EXCEPT* a
    a. disclosure of whom the broker represents.
    b. disclosure that the rate of commission has been negotiated.
    c. statement about the recovery fund.
    d. statement about the zoning classification, except for a house on a lot zoned for single-family dwellings.

11. Estimated statements of closing costs must be provided to buyers and sellers
    a. prior to settlement.
    b. after acceptance of an offer.
    c. within 24 hours of communication of acceptance of an offer.
    d. prior to signature of the agreement of sale.

12. A buyer makes an offer to purchase. The broker cannot locate the seller to present the offer. In the meantime, the broker receives an offer for a higher price from another buyer. How should the broker proceed?
    a. Decide which offer is best to present to the seller.
    b. Present the offer for the higher price.
    c. Call the first buyer and tell the buyer the broker cannot present the offer because it is too low.
    d. Present both offers to the seller.

ANSWERS

1. A Full legal title to property passes to a buyer when the agreement of sale is executed at closing or settlement. However, the buyer obtains an interest in the property, known as equitable title, when both the buyer and seller have signed the agreement of sale. (p. 352)

2. A When a buyer and seller enter into a contract that is subject to a condition, such as the wife's approval of the sale, the condition is referred to as a contingency. (p. 354)

3. D A purchaser can be protected from owning two homes by including a property sale contingency in the offer to purchase. If the seller accepts the offer, the sale is subject to that contingency. To protect the seller's interest, he or she may insist on an escape clause when considering such an offer. (p. 354)

4. B An option is a unilateral contract in which the optionor agrees that the optionee (usually the buyer) has the right to purchase the property at an agreed upon price within an agreed upon period of time. While the optionee is not obligated to purchase the property, the optionor is obligated to sell if the optionee exercises this right. (p. 355)

5. D An installment contract combines elements of both a sale and a finance document into one legal instrument. The seller (vendor) retains legal title, while the purchaser (vendee) takes possession, acquires equitable title, and agrees to make principal and interest payments to the seller for a stated period of time, after which point, the seller will transfer legal title. (p. 355)

6. D The seller is the vendor in an installment contract; the purchaser is known as the vendee. (p. 355)

7. B Any change a seller makes to the terms proposed by a buyer in an offer constitutes a rejection of the buyer's offer and the buyer has no obligation to purchase the property. Those changes, known as a counteroffer, now constitute a new offer being made by the seller to the buyer. The buyer can accept or reject that offer, or make another counteroffer. (p. 352)

8. B Earnest money or hand money is the deposit made by the purchaser when making an offer. In accordance with Pennsylvania law and regulations, money received by the broker on behalf of another must be deposited in the broker's escrow account and held until consummation or termination of the transaction. (p. 351)

9. C A buyer can make an offer that is subject to a structural inspection to address concerns such as a wet basement. The contract would then be subject to an inspection contingency. (p. 354)

10. B According to Pennsylvania law, broker compensation must be addressed in a listing agreement and a buyer agency agreement, not in an agreement of sale between the buyer and seller. (p. 354)

11. D According to the Real Estate Commission's Rules and Regulations (Section 35.334), the seller and buyer must be provided with statements of estimated cost and return before entering into an agreement of sale. (p. 347)

12. D Licensees are required to present all offers in a timely manner. In the case of multiple offers, the broker should present all offers to the seller for his or her consideration. (p. 352)

CHAPTER TWENTY

FINANCING THE REAL ESTATE TRANSACTION

■ LEARNING OBJECTIVES

When you've finished reading this chapter, you should be able to

■ explain the major federal laws that affect residential mortgage lending practices;
■ differentiate between the common loan repayment plans;
■ explain the fundamentals of conventional, FHA-insured, and VA-guaranteed loan programs;
■ describe various alternative financing techniques to address borrowers' different needs; and
■ define the key terms.

■ KEY TERMS

adjustable-rate mortgage (ARM)

balloon payment

blanket loan

buy-down

Community Reinvestment Act (CRA)

computerized loan origination (CLO)

construction loan

conventional loan

discount points

Equal Credit Opportunity Act (ECOA)

FHA loan

Farm Service Agency (FSA)

growing equity mortgage (GEM)

home equity loan

loan-to-value ratio

open-end loan

package loan

private mortgage insurance (PMI)

purchase-money mortgage

Real Estate Settlement Procedure Act (RESPA)

Regulation Z

reverse annuity mortgage (RAM)

sale and leaseback

VA loan

wraparound loan

371

■ COST OF CREDIT

The cost of credit is an important consideration when buyers must rely on other people's money to complete their purchases. From a lender's point of view, a loan is an investment: The interest and finance charges represent income. Because the lender has something the borrower needs (money), the borrower in a sense must pay the lender's price to use that money. Like any prudent investor, the mortgage lender evaluates two aspects of the investment: yield and risk. Yield is the return or income that can be generated. Risk is the likelihood of the investment to lose money.

To enhance the yield of the investment, the lender requires the borrower to pay certain charges when the loan is originated, in addition to the interest paid during the term of a loan. One charge is a loan origination fee. This fee, which is typically 1 percent of the loan amount (but may be higher), covers the lender's expense of generating the loan. Also, a service fee or points may be charged. Points represent prepaid interest and are charged to produce additional income on the loan.

To minimize the risk of the investment if the borrower's down payment is small in relation to the amount of the mortgage loan (the loan-to-value ratio), the lender may also require mortgage insurance to protect the lender's risk. The insurance premium is collected at closing and may also be collected with the monthly payments during a partial term of the loan.

Discount Points

The lender may sell the loan to an investor rather than holding the loan for its full term. By selling loans, lending institutions replenish their supply of funds for additional loans. The interest rate of the loan, however, might be less than the yield (true rate of return) an investor demands. To make up the difference, the lender charges the borrower **discount points.** The number of points varies, depending on the difference between the interest rate and the investor's required yield and on how long the lender expects the loan to be outstanding.

> One *discount point equals* 1 percent of the loan amount, not the purchase price.

For borrowers, one discount point equals 1 percent of the loan amount (not the purchase price) and is charged as prepaid interest at the closing. For instance, a charge of three discount points on a $100,000 loan equals $3,000 ($100,000 × 3%). Depending on the terms of the agreement of sale, the seller may assist the buyer by paying some or all of the points.

■ OBTAINING CREDIT

The process of obtaining a loan begins with the prospective borrower making an application. Then the lender evaluates the application and, if approved, issues a formal loan commitment.

Application for Credit

A prospective borrower must provide certain basic information the lender needs to evaluate in order to determine the acceptability of the proposed loan. Information about the borrower and the collateral is supplied in an application for credit. The application asks about the prospective borrower's employment, earnings, assets, and current financial obligations. To evaluate the collateral, the lender needs the property's legal description, description of the improvements, title and tax information, and a survey. For loans on income property or those made to corporations, additional information such as financial and operating statements, schedules of leases and tenants, and balance sheets will be required.

Typically, the Fannie Mae/Freddie Mac Uniform Loan Application is used. In addition to the borrower's qualifications, the application states the purpose and amount of the loan, the interest rate, and the proposed terms of repayment. This is considered a preliminary offer of a loan agreement; final terms may require further negotiation later.

Historically, buyers applied for credit after they completed negotiation of the agreement of sale. Today, it is more common that prospective buyers are *prequalified* by a lender before they begin searching for a property to purchase. Prequalification tells the prospective buyer how much he or she can borrow and aids in the selection of an affordable property. Sometimes, lenders *preapprove* the buyer based on a preliminary application for credit. This expedites the loan approval process so that the buyer can satisfy a mortgage contingency in the sales contract more quickly. Preapproval can also strengthen a buyer's offer, especially in a highly competitive market, when the seller knows that the buyer is creditworthy.

IN PRACTICE

The information provided in a loan application must be accurate and verifiable. There are serious legal consequences when people obtain loans as a result of false statements made in loan applications. No one, licensees included, should participate in falsifying any information. These are criminal offenses.

What should a person know about making a credit application? Credit reporting agencies hold the key to obtaining credit. Consumer groups have complained that the agencies have been unreasonable and far too slow in fixing mistakes in credit files. To avoid embarrassment and frustration, a potential borrower should order a copy of the credit report and review it before applying for a mortgage loan.

If there are mistakes in a credit report, they can be remedied more easily because of the Credit Reporting Reform Act of 1994. This law makes it cheaper for consumers to look at their own credit files and forces reporting agencies to correct mistakes and remove disputed information from their files unless the creditor verifies it. Credit reporting agencies are also required to set up toll-free phone numbers so that consumers can check the accuracy of their reports and request corrections.

IN PRACTICE

The Fair and Accurate Credit Transactions Act (FACTA) is a recently enacted federal law that gives individuals the right to request a free credit report every 12 months from each of the three major credit reporting bureaus. The implementation of this act began in January 2005 for individuals in the Western states, with the Midwestern states being added in March and the Southern states in June. By September 2005, the act was to be fully implemented with the addition of the Eastern states and U.S. territories. The form to request the free credit reports can be obtained from *www.AnnualCreditReport.com*.

Computerized Loan Origination

A **computerized loan origination (CLO)** system is an electronic network for handling loan applications through remote computer terminals linked to several lenders' computers. With a CLO system, a real estate licensee can call up a menu of mortgage lenders, interest rates, and loan terms, then help a buyer select a lender and apply for a loan right from the brokerage office.

The licensee may assist the applicant in answering the on-screen questions and in understanding the services offered. The broker in whose office the terminal is located may earn fees for providing this service. While an office's CLO computer may represent multiple lenders, consumers must be informed that other lenders are also available. A CLO system may enhance an applicant's ability to comparison shop; the range of options may not be limited.

Scoring and Underwriting the Loan

The lender investigates the information supplied in the loan application and studies the credit report and an appraisal of the property before deciding whether to grant a loan. Lenders have been using credit-scoring systems for years to predict the likelihood of a prospective borrower's default. Credit scoring, when used as part of the traditional evaluation of applicants, provides a useful objective standard against which to balance the more subjective, professional judgment of a loan officer.

Credit scores are based on data about an individual's credit history and payment patterns stored by a credit repository. A score is calculated by statistical models that assign point values to factors characteristic or indicative of repayment. The sum of the values derived from each of the analyzed factors, which is the score, intends to demonstrate credit risk. The five major factors analyzed are past payment performance, credit utilization, credit history, types of credit in use, and credit report inquiries. Scoring models consider not only negative credit information such as late payments and bankruptcies but all information stored about an individual at the time a score report is prepared. Scoring models, however, do not consider race, gender, religion, marital status, income, nationality, neighborhood, employment history and position or title, sexual orientation or preference, or interest rate charged on any particular line of credit.

Today, automated underwriting procedures are often used. Not only does technology shorten the loan approval time from weeks to minutes, it also tends to lower the cost of processing and approving loan applications. Lenders' time spent on the approval process can be reduced by as much as 60 percent. Freddie Mac uses a system called *Loan Prospector*; Fannie Mae has a system called *Desktop Underwriter*. Automated underwriting eliminates one of a borrower's biggest headaches in buying a home—waiting for loan approval. These systems are also used to prequalify prospective borrowers.

As convenient as automated underwriting systems are, they are also somewhat controversial. Critics of automated scoring systems contend that the systems may not be accurate or fair and, in the absence of human discretion, could make it more difficult for worthy low-income and minority borrowers to obtain mortgage loans. The counterbalance to this argument is that even when automated underwriting systems are used, lenders still rely on human judgment when scoring indicates that the loan application is a higher risk.

Loan underwriters, regardless of whether they use traditional methods or automated systems, must consider all three areas of underwriting—collateral, credit reputation, and capacity. When reviewing collateral, underwriters look at property value, down payment, and property type. The track record for paying obligations on time is particularly important when evaluating credit-worthiness. Income, debt, cash reserves, and product type are considered when underwriters look at capacity.

Loan Commitment

A loan commitment is the lender's acceptance of the application. The commitment creates a contract to make a loan and sets forth the details. In some cases, the commitment may be conditional; that is, the lender commits to lending the money subject to the borrower meeting certain conditions. Common conditions include selling a current property or providing a title insurance policy at settlement.

IN PRACTICE

In addition to CLOs, technology links borrowers with money in a variety of other ways. Just as consumers turn to the Internet to search for properties, they can also search for mortgage loan information and even make applications online.

■ FINANCING LEGISLATION

The federal government regulates the lending practices of mortgage lenders through the *Truth-in-Lending Act*, the *Equal Credit Opportunity Act*, the *Real Estate Settlement Procedures Act*, and the *Community Reinvestment Act*.

Truth-in-Lending Act and Regulation Z

Regulation Z, which was promulgated pursuant to the Truth-in-Lending Act by the Federal Trade Commission (FTC), requires that credit institutions inform borrowers of the true cost of obtaining credit. Its purpose is to permit borrowers to compare the costs of various lenders and avoid the uninformed use of credit. Regulation Z applies when credit is extended to individuals for personal, family, or household uses. The amount of credit sought must be $25,000 or less. Regardless of the amount, however, Regulation Z generally applies when a credit transaction is secured by a residence. The regulation does *not* apply to business or commercial loans or to agricultural loans of more than $25,000. (So if an investor purchased a residential property for commercial purposes, Regulation Z would not apply.)

Under Regulation Z, a consumer is entitled to the disclosure of finance charges and the true interest rate before a transaction is completed. The finance charge disclosure must include any loan fees, finders' fees, service charges, and points, as well as interest. Actual costs for title fees, legal fees, appraisal fees, credit reports, survey fees, and closing expenses are not considered part of this disclosure. In the case of a mortgage loan made to finance the purchase of a dwelling, the lender must disclose the *annual percentage rate (APR)* of the loan. However, the lender does not have to indicate the total interest payable during the term of the loan.

Creditor.   A *creditor*, for purposes of Regulation Z, is a person who extends consumer credit more than 25 times a year or more than five times a year if the transactions involve dwellings as security. The credit must be subject to a finance charge or payable in more than four installments by written agreement.

Advertising. Regulation Z strictly regulates real estate advertisements (in all media, including newspapers, flyers, signs, billboards, Web sites, radio or television ads, and direct mailings) that refer to mortgage financing terms. General phrases like "liberal terms available" may be used. Any mention of interest rate must be the annual percentage rate (which includes all charges rather than the interest rate alone). Specific credit terms, such as down payment, monthly payment, dollar amount of the finance charge, or term of the loan are referred to as *trigger terms*. If any of these credit terms are used, the advertisement must include all of the following information:

- Cash price
- Required down payment
- Number, amount, and due dates of all payments
- Annual percentage rate
- Total of all payments to be made over the term of the loan (unless the advertised credit refers to a first mortgage to finance acquisition of a dwelling)

Three-day right of rescission. In the case of most consumer credit transactions covered by Regulation Z, the borrower has three days in which to rescind the transaction by merely notifying the lender. This right of rescission *does not apply* to owner-occupied residential first mortgage loans, but it does apply to refinancing a home mortgage and to a home equity loan.

Penalties. Regulation Z provides penalties for noncompliance. The penalty for violation of an administrative order enforcing Regulation Z is $10,000 for each day the violation continues. A fine of up to $10,000 may be imposed for engaging in an unfair or deceptive practice. In addition, a creditor may be liable to a consumer for twice the amount of the finance charge, for a minimum of $100 and a maximum of $1,000, plus court costs, attorney's fees, and any actual damages. Willful violation is a misdemeanor punishable by a fine of up to $5,000, one year's imprisonment, or both.

Equal Credit Opportunity Act

The federal **Equal Credit Opportunity Act (ECOA)** prohibits lenders and others who grant or arrange credit to consumers from discriminating against credit applicants based on

- race,
- color,
- religion,
- national origin,
- sex,
- marital status,
- age (provided the applicant is of legal age), or
- dependence on public assistance.

In addition, lenders and other creditors must inform all rejected credit applicants of the principal reasons for the denial or termination of credit. The notice must be provided in writing, within 30 days. The ECOA also provides that a borrower is entitled to a copy of the appraisal report if the borrower paid for the appraisal.

Community Reinvestment Act

Community reinvestment refers to the responsibility of financial institutions to help meet their communities' needs for low- and moderate-income housing. Congress passed the **Community Reinvestment Act (CRA)** in 1977. Under CRA, financial institutions are expected to meet the deposit and credit needs of their communities; participate and invest in local community development and rehabilitation projects; and participate in loan programs for housing, small business, and small farms.

The law requires any federally supervised financial institution to prepare a statement containing

- a definition of the geographic boundaries of its community;
- an identification of the types of community reinvestment credit offered (such as residential housing, housing rehabilitation, small business, commercial, and consumer loans), and
- comments from the public about the institution's performance in meeting its community needs.

Financial institutions are periodically reviewed by one of four federal financial supervisory agencies: the Comptroller of the Currency, the Federal Reserve's Board of Governors, the Federal Deposit Insurance Corporation, or the Office of Thrift Supervision. The institutions must post a public notice that their community reinvestment activities are subject to federal review and must also make the results of these reviews public.

Real Estate Settlement Procedures Act

The federal **Real Estate Settlement Procedures Act (RESPA)** was created to encourage homeownership by protecting consumers from unreasonable expenses for settlement. RESPA applies to any residential transaction involving a new first mortgage loan and intends to ensure that the buyer and seller are fully informed of all settlement costs. This law will be discussed in detail in Chapter 22.

■ LOAN PROGRAMS

Mortgage loans are generally classified based on their **loan-to-value ratio**, that is, the ratio of debt to value of the property. For mortgage lending purposes, *value* is the sale price or the appraised value, whichever is *less*. The lower the ratio of debt to value means a higher down payment by the borrower. For the lender, the higher down payment means a more secure loan, minimizing the lender's risk.

Higher LVR = Higher Risk

Lower LVR = Lower Risk

Conventional Loans

Conventional loans are viewed as the most secure loans because the loan-to-value ratio is lowest. Usually the ratio is 80 percent of the value of the property or less; the borrower makes a down payment of 20 percent or more. The security for the loan is provided solely by the mortgage. The payment of the debt rests on the ability of the borrower to pay. In making these loans, the lender relies primarily on its appraisal of the security (the real estate) and information from credit reports that indicate the reliability of the prospective borrower. No additional insurance or guarantee is necessary to protect the lender's interest. These are known as conventional uninsured loans.

Lenders can set criteria by which the borrower and the collateral are evaluated to qualify for the loan. However, many lenders follow the underwriting standards established by Fannie Mae and Freddie Mac so they can sell their loans in the secondary market. Lenders may still fund loans that deviate from these standards, but they would have to retain the loans or find other investors.

Private Mortgage Insurance

One way borrowers can obtain conventional loans with a lower down payment is under a **private mortgage insurance** (PMI) program. These are known as conventional insured loans. Because the loan-to-value ratio is higher than for other conventional loans, the lender requires additional security to minimize its risk. Loans of up to 97 percent of the appraised value of the property (up to 100 percent under certain circumstances) are possible. The lender purchases insurance from a private mortgage insurance company as additional security against the borrower's default. PMI protects a certain percentage of the loan, usually 25 to 35 percent. The borrower normally pays a fee for the insurance at closing plus additional monthly fees while the insurance is in force.

Termination of PMI. Once the loan is repaid to a certain level, the lender terminates the insurance coverage. As of July 1999, a federal law requires that PMI automatically terminate if a borrower has accumulated at least 22 percent equity in the home *and* is current with the loan payments. Under the law, a borrower with a good payment history may request a cancellation of PMI when the borrower's equity equals 20 percent of the purchase price or the appraised value. Lenders are required to inform borrowers of their right to cancel PMI. Before this law was enacted, lenders could (and often did) continue to require monthly PMI payments long after borrowers had built up substantial equity in their homes and the lender no longer risked a loss from a borrower's default.

IN PRACTICE

Recently, some lenders have deviated from the traditional rules and order of mortgage lending and have been offering very creative ways for borrowers to obtain loans. This trend is reflected in many types of loan programs, including PMI loans. To avoid private mortgage insurance, the lender may, for example, write an 80/10/10 loan. The borrower makes a 10-percent down payment, secures a first mortgage loan for 80 percent of the purchase price, and then obtains a second loan for the remaining 10 percent of the purchase price. This eliminates the need for private mortgage insurance, even though the borrower has invested only 10 percent in a down payment, but secures the lender with two mortgage liens against the property. Some lenders may even offer an 80/20 loan in which the borrower makes no down payment, but rather obtains an 80 percent first mortgage loan and a second loan for the remaining 20 percent of the purchase price. Only time will tell the wisdom of these innovations in mortgage lending.

FHA-Insured Loans

The term "FHA loan" properly refers to an FHA-insured loan. A private approved lender provides the loan; the FHA provides the insurance.

Statistically, the majority of home purchases are financed with conventional insured or uninsured loans. However, the federal government still plays a vital role in helping people finance real estate purchases. One way is by providing another alternative for financing real estate with a low down payment, and that is with an FHA-insured loan. The Federal Housing Administration (FHA), which operates under HUD, insures these high loan-to-value ratio loans in an effort to make more affordable loans available. Much like private mortgage insurance, FHA insurance protects the lender against loss from a borrower's default. The common term **FHA loan** refers to a loan that is *insured* by the agency. FHA-approved lending institutions make these loans.

FHA loans are attractive, not just for the low down payment, but because the interest rates are competitive with other types of loans. In addition, the FHA offers a variety of incentives for borrowers to use its programs. Borrowers have the option of fixed-interest-rate loans for 10 to 30 years or one-year adjustable-rate loans. The FHA qualifying ratios (debt to income) are higher than for other types of loans. Although the FHA sets maximum loan amounts, the limits are determined regionally to reflect the housing prices in the area. A local FHA office or mortgage lender can provide current information about prevailing terms and conditions of these loans.

The borrower is charged a percentage of the loan as premium for the FHA insurance. The *upfront* premium is paid at closing by the borrower or some other party. It also may be financed along with the total loan amount. A monthly premium also may be charged. Insurance premiums vary depending on the loan-to-value ratio and the term of the loan.

To be acceptable collateral, the property must meet FHA standards for the type and construction of the properties and the quality of the neighborhoods. FHA-insured loans are available for owner occupancy of one-to-four family residences and condominium units (as long as the condominium complex meets the FHA ratio of owner occupants to renters) and to help residents or investors repair or rehabilitate single-family properties.

Prepayment privileges.   A borrower may prepay an FHA-insured loan on a one-to-four family residence without penalty. For loans made before August 2, 1985, the borrower must give the lender written notice of intention to exercise this privilege at least 30 days before prepayment. If the borrower fails to provide the required notice, then the lender has the option of charging up to 30 days' interest. For loans initiated after August 2, 1985, no written notice of prepayment is required.

Assumption rules.   FHA loans are assumable. However, the assumption rules vary depending on the date the loan was originated, the type of property involved, and the specific FHA loan program under which the original loan was granted. In some cases, there are no restrictions on assumptions. In other cases, assumptions are permitted only when the assuming buyer has been qualified for the loan.

VA-Guaranteed Loans

For eligible veterans and their spouses, VA-guaranteed loans are another alternative for financing the purchase of homes with little or no down payment at competitive interest rates. (The LTV could be 100 percent.) Property purchased with a VA loan must be owner occupied and meet certain requirements.

The Servicemen's Readjustment Act of 1944 and subsequent federal legislation authorizes the Department of Veterans Affairs (usually referred to as the VA) to guarantee loans for the purchase or construction of homes by eligible veterans and their spouses. Eligibility varies depending on the length of service and the years during which the veteran served on active duty. Certain people who serve in the National Guard or in the Reserves are eligible as well. A local VA office or mortgage lender can provide specific details about eligibility and loan procedures.

> The term "VA loan" properly refers to a VA-guaranteed loan. A private approved lender provides the loan; the VA guarantees the loan.

Like the term FHA loan, *VA loan* is something of a misnomer. The term **VA loan** refers to a loan made by a VA-approved lender and *guaranteed* by the agency. The VA does not normally lend the money. Because these are typically high loan-to-value ratio loans, the guarantee provides additional security (instead of insurance) for the loan. The lender would receive the amount of the guarantee from the VA if a foreclosure sale did not bring enough to cover the outstanding loan balance. The benefit to the borrower is that there is no insurance premium required to secure the loan.

Maximum loan terms are 30 years for one-family to four-family dwellings and 40 years for farms. Interest rates are negotiable between the lender and borrower; the VA guarantees fixed-rate and adjustable-rate loans. Lenders may charge VA borrowers reasonable closing costs plus no more than a 1-percent loan origination fee. A VA funding fee, paid either at closing or financed along with the loan, is also charged. The amount of the fee varies depending on the amount of the down payment, the type of property, and the eligibility status of the borrower. Reasonable discount points also may be charged, and either the veteran or the seller may pay them.

To determine eligibility and the amount of loan the VA will guarantee, the veteran must apply for a *certificate of eligibility*. This certificate does not mean that the veteran automatically receives a loan. It merely sets forth the maximum guarantee for which the veteran is eligible. While there is no VA-imposed limit on the amount of loan a veteran can obtain, the VA does limit the amount of loan it will guarantee. For individuals with full eligibility, no down payment would be required for loans up to a certain maximum.

The VA also issues a *certificate of reasonable value* (CRV) for the property being purchased. The CRV states the property's current market value based on a VA-approved appraisal. The CRV places a ceiling on the amount of loan allowed for the property. No down payment is required if the purchase price does not exceed the amount stated in the CRV; if the purchase price is greater, the veteran may pay the difference in cash.

Prepayment privileges.   The borrower under a VA loan can prepay the debt at any time without penalty.

Assumption rules.   VA loans made before March 1, 1988, are freely assumable, although an assumption-processing fee is charged. The fee is ½ percent of the loan balance. For loans made on or after March 1, 1988, the VA must approve the buyer and assumption agreement. The original veteran-borrower remains personally liable for repayment of the loan unless the VA approves a *release of liability*. The release will be issued by the VA only if

- the buyer assumes all of the veteran's liabilities on the loan, and
- the VA and the lender approve both the buyer and the assumption agreement.

A release of liability also would be possible if another veteran used his or her own entitlement in assuming the loan. In any case, the VA's release does not release the veteran's liability to the lender. This must be obtained separately from the lender.

Agricultural Loan Programs

The **Farm Service Agency (FSA),** formerly the Farmers Home Administration, is a federal agency of the Department of Agriculture. The FSA offers programs to help families purchase or operate family farms. Through the Rural Housing and Community Development Service, it also provides loans to help families purchase or improve single-family homes in rural areas (generally with populations of fewer than 10,000). Loans are made to low- and moderate-income families at interest rates as low as 1 percent, depending on the borrower's income. The FSA provides assistance to rural and agricultural businesses and industry through the Rural Business and Cooperative Development Service.

■ LOAN REPAYMENT

Regardless of the loan program used, perhaps the most important issue for both the borrower and the lender is the repayment of the loan. A variety of payment plans are available today. Borrowers can choose a plan that best suits their financial circumstances, and lenders can make good investments, especially as the cost and availability of money fluctuate. Most of the plans have a common characteristic—the principal is amortized. While fixed-interest/fixed-payment amortized loans (discussed in Chapter 12) are popular, other types of payment plans are also very useful.

Adjustable-Rate Mortgage

An **adjustable-rate mortgage (ARM)** is originated at one rate of interest. That rate then fluctuates up or down during the loan term, based on some objective economic indicator. The note describes how and when the interest rate will change during the life of the loan. Common components of an ARM include the following:

- The interest rate is tied to the movement of an objective economic indicator called an *index*. Most indexes are tied to U.S. Treasury securities.

■ Usually, the interest rate is the index rate plus a premium, called the *margin*. The margin represents the lender's cost of doing business. For example, the loan rate may be 2 percent over the U.S. Treasury bill rate.

■ *Rate caps* limit the amount the interest rate may change. Most ARMs have two types of rate caps—periodic and aggregate. A periodic rate cap limits the amount the rate may increase at any one time. An aggregate rate cap limits the amount the rate may increase over the entire life of the loan.

■ The borrower is protected from unaffordable individual payments by a *payment cap*. The payment cap sets a maximum amount for payments. With a payment cap, however, a rate increase could result in negative amortization—that is, an increase in the loan balance.

■ The *adjustment period* establishes how often the rate may be changed. For instance, the adjustment period could be monthly, quarterly, or annually.

■ Lenders may offer a *conversion option*, which permits the borrower to convert from an adjustable to a fixed-rate loan at certain intervals during the loan. The option for conversion is subject to certain terms and conditions.

Interest-Only Loan

Although interest-only or straight loans (discussed in Chapter 12) have generally not been used to finance home purchases since the advent of amortized loans after the Depression, these loans have become quite popular recently. The repayment plan involves only interest, which means that the borrower pays solely for the privilege of borrowing the money and does not repay any principal during the term of the loan. The appeal of interest-only loans is that the monthly payments are lower than for amortized loans. Interest-only loans may be desirable for a borrower who anticipates selling the property in a short period of time and believes that the property's value will appreciate (perhaps significantly) in the meantime. In effect, the borrower anticipates gaining equity in the property from the strength of the marketplace rather than by making periodic payments to principal (as in an amortized loan). The lender also expects the property to gain value, which provides greater security for the loan.

The risk, of course, is that the property may not appreciate as anticipated, thus leaving the borrower with a hefty loan to repay without sufficient proceeds from a sale or adequate value in the collateral to completely refinance the loan. The added risk is that interest rates may increase and/or the borrower's income may fail to increase commensurately to afford a new loan. If property values were overinflated when the buyer purchased the property and then values decline, that could negatively affect the lender's position as well.

The bright side of interest-only loans is that repaying the entire loan amount at the end of the term may not be as unmanageable as first appears. A borrower who owns a property for five years would typically repay little principal on a fully amortized loan during that time (see Chapter 12). Consequently, the difference in the principal remaining after five years on that loan and the principal due on an interest-only loan is relatively small. Over time, however, the difference becomes more significant. Some lenders build into the original note a plan for converting the initial interest-only loan to an amortized loan in later years. This feature is especially desirable if a borrower decides to continue to own the property longer than the interest-only period. However, the monthly payments may be significantly higher depending on the amortization schedule and adjustments in interest rates.

Balloon Payment Loan

When the periodic payments are not large enough to fully amortize the loan by the time the final payment is due, the final payment is larger than the others are. The final payment is called a **balloon payment.** This is a *partially* amortized loan because principal is still owed at the end of the term. Borrowers frequently assume that if payments are made promptly, the lender will extend the balloon payment for another limited term. The lender, however, is not legally obligated to grant this extension and can require payment in full when the note is due.

For example, a loan made for $80,000 at 6 percent interest may be computed on a 30-year amortization schedule but be paid over a 20-year term, with a final balloon payment due at the end of the 20th year. In this case each monthly payment (principal and interest) would be $479.64 (the amount taken from a 30-year amortization schedule), with a final balloon payment of $43,203 (the amount of principal still owing after 20 years).

Growing Equity Mortgage

A **growing equity mortgage (GEM)**, or *rapid-payoff mortgage*, uses a fixed interest rate, but payments of principal increase according to an index or a schedule. Thus, the total payment increases and the loan is paid off more quickly. A GEM is most frequently used when the borrower's income is expected to keep pace with the increasing loan payments.

Reverse Annuity Mortgage

A **reverse annuity mortgage (RAM)** is one in which payments are made *by the lender to the borrower.* The payments, which may be made as regular monthly payments, in one lump sum, or as a line of credit to be drawn against, are based on the equity the homeowner has in the property given as security for the loan. This loan allows senior citizens on fixed incomes to benefit from the equity they have built up in their homes without having to sell. The borrower is charged a fixed rate of interest and the loan is eventually paid from the sale of the property or from the borrower's estate upon his or her death.

■ OTHER FINANCING TECHNIQUES

A variety of other financing techniques have been created to meet specific needs of borrowers and lenders. The following loans, which do not fit strictly into the categories previously described, are among the most common.

Purchase-Money Mortgages

A **purchase-money mortgage** is a note and mortgage created at the time of purchase. Its purpose is to make a sale possible. The term is used in two ways. First, it may refer to any security instrument originating at the time of sale. More often, however, it refers to the instrument given by the purchaser to a seller who takes back a note for all or part of the purchase price. The mortgage may be a first or junior lien, depending on whether prior mortgage liens exist. As with a conventional mortgage, the buyer receives the deed at closing.

Package Loans

In Your State

PA A **package loan** includes not only the real estate, but also *all personal property and appliances installed on the premises.* In recent years, this kind of loan has been used extensively in some parts of the country to finance furnished condominium units. Such loans usually include furniture, drapery, carpeting, kitchen range, refrigerator, dishwasher, garbage disposal unit, washer and dryer, food freezer, and other appliances as part of the real estate in the sales price of the home. However, package mortgages are not permitted in Pennsylvania. State law stipulates that only real estate and fixtures may be subject to a mortgage lien. ■

Blanket Loans

A **blanket loan** covers *more than one parcel or lot.* It is typically used to finance subdivision developments. However, it can be used to finance the purchase of improved properties or to consolidate loans. A blanket loan usually includes a provision known as a *partial release clause.* This clause permits the borrower to obtain the release of any one lot or parcel from the lien by repaying a certain amount of the loan. The lender issues a partial release for each parcel released from the mortgage lien. The release form includes a provision that the lien will continue to cover all other unreleased lots.

Wraparound Loans

A **wraparound loan** enables a borrower with an existing loan to obtain additional financing from a second lender *without paying off the first loan.* The second lender gives the borrower a new, larger loan at a higher interest rate and assumes payment of the existing loan. The total amount of the new loan includes the existing loan as well as the additional funds needed by the borrower. The borrower makes payments to the new lender on the larger loan. The new lender makes the payments on the original loan out of the borrower's payments.

A wraparound mortgage is frequently used to refinance real property or to finance the purchase of a property when an existing mortgage cannot be prepaid or the buyer wishes to make a smaller down payment than an institutional lender requires. The buyer executes a wraparound mortgage to the seller who collects payments on the new loan and continues to make payments on the old loan. To protect themselves against a seller's default on a previous loan, buyers should require protective clauses in wraparound documents to give them the right to make payments directly to the original lender.

IN PRACTICE

A wraparound loan is possible only if the original loan documents permit it. An acceleration and alienation or due-on-sale clause in the original loan documents may prevent a wraparound loan. Real estate licensees could be subject to disciplinary action by licensing authorities if they encourage or assist in any financing that violates loan provisions.

Open-End Loans

An **open-end loan** involves a mortgage that is secured by a note executed by the borrower to the lender, which also secures any *future advances* of funds made by the lender. The interest rate on the initial amount borrowed is fixed, but interest on future advances may be the market rate then in effect. An open-end loan is often a less costly alternative to a home improvement loan. It allows the borrower to "open" the mortgage to increase the debt to its original amount, or the amount stated in the note, after the debt has been reduced by payments over a period of time. The mortgage usually states the maximum amount that can be secured and the terms and conditions under which the loan can be opened as well as the provisions for repayment.

Construction Loans

A **construction loan** is made to *finance the construction of improvements* on real estate such as homes, apartments, and office buildings. The lender commits to the full amount of the loan but disburses the funds periodically during construction. Payments, known as draws, are made to the general contractor or the owner for that part of the construction work that has been completed since the previous payment. Before each payment, the lender inspects the work and typically requires the general contractor (or owner) to submit proof that mechanic's lien rights have been waived for the work covered by the payment.

Interest rates on construction loans are generally higher than market rates because of the risks the lender assumes. These risks include the inadequate protection against mechanics' liens, possible delays in completing construction, and the financial failure of the contractor or subcontractors. The borrower periodically pays interest only on the monies that have actually been disbursed to that payment date. Construction loans are generally short-term or *interim financing*. The borrower is expected to arrange for a permanent loan, also known as an *end loan* or *takeout loan*, which repays or "takes out" the lender on the construction loan when the work is completed. Some lenders now offer construction-to-permanent financing that becomes a fixed mortgage loan upon completion of the construction.

Sale-and-Leaseback

Sale-and-leaseback arrangements are used to finance large commercial or industrial properties. The land and building, usually used by the seller for business purposes, are sold to an investor, such as an insurance company. The real estate is then leased back by the buyer (the investor) to the seller, who continues to conduct business on the property as a tenant. The buyer becomes the lessor, and the original owner becomes the lessee. This arrangement enables a business to free money tied up in real estate to be used as working capital.

Sale-and-leaseback arrangements involve complicated legal procedures, and their success usually relates to the effects the transaction has on the firm's tax situation. Legal and tax experts should be involved in this type of transaction.

Buy-downs

A **buy-down** is a temporary (or permanent) way of lowering the interest rate on a mortgage loan. Perhaps a homebuilder wishes to stimulate sales by offering a lower-than-market rate or a buyer is having trouble qualifying for a loan at the prevailing rates and relatives or the seller want to help the buyer qualify. In any case, a lump sum is paid in cash to the lender at closing. The payment offsets (and so reduces) the interest rate and monthly payments during the loan's first few years. Typical buy-down arrangements reduce the interest rate by 1 to 3 percent over the first one to three years of the loan term. After that, the rate rises. The assumption is that the borrower's income will also increase so the borrower will be more able to absorb the increased monthly payments. In a permanent buy-down, a larger upfront payment reduces the effective interest rate for the life of the loan.

Home Equity Loans

Homeowners can satisfy financial needs by borrowing the equity built up in their homes with **home equity loans.** Often, home equity loans are used to finance the purchase of expensive items, to consolidate existing installment loans or credit card debt, or to pay for medical, education, or home improvement expenses.

A home equity loan is an alternative to refinancing. The original mortgage loan remains in place; the home equity loan is junior to that lien. If the homeowner refinances, the original mortgage loan is paid off and replaced by a new loan. (This is an alternative way to borrow the equity; it's not really a home equity loan.) The homeowner must compare the costs for a new mortgage loan, interest rates, total monthly payments, and income-tax consequences to decide which alternative is best. Interest on a home equity loan secured by a mortgage on the borrower's residence is deductible up to a loan limit of $100,000. (Interest on consumer loans is no longer deductible.)

A home equity loan can be a fixed loan amount or an equity line of credit. If the loan is taken as a line of credit, the lender extends a line of credit that the borrower can use whenever he or she wishes. The borrower may receive the money by check, direct deposit to a checking or savings account, or a book of drafts the borrower can use up to the equity limit.

■ SUMMARY

The cost for credit when financing a real estate purchase includes finance charges such as loan origination fees, points and, in some cases, mortgage insurance premiums that are paid at closing, and the recurring cost of interest and any mortgage insurance premiums.

For the lender to sell a mortgage loan, the loan's income must be competitive in the money market. Discount points may be charged to increase the yield of the loan. Points may be paid by the buyer, the seller, or shared by both.

Regulation Z requires lenders to inform prospective borrowers who use their homes as security for credit of all finance charges involved in such a loan. Severe penalties are provided for noncompliance. The federal Equal Credit Opportunity Act prohibits creditors from discriminating against credit applicants on the basis of race, color, religion, national origin, sex, marital status, age, or dependence on public assistance. The Real Estate Settlement Procedures Act protects the consumer from unreasonable expenses for settlement.

The types of mortgage programs available include conventional loans and those insured by FHA or private mortgage insurance companies or guaranteed by the VA. FHA and VA loans must meet certain requirements for the borrower to obtain the benefits of government backing, which induces the lender to lend its funds.

There are many types of loan repayment plans in addition to fully amortized/ fixed-interest loans. Adjustable-rate mortgages, interest-only loans, growing equity mortgages and reverse-annuity mortgages have been developed.

Other types of real estate financing include purchase-money mortgages, blanket loans, package loans, open-end loans, wraparound loans, construction loans, sale-and-leaseback agreements, installment contracts, and buy-downs.

Note: Chapter 12 is a companion to the discussions in this chapter.

QUESTIONS

1. The Ms are purchasing a lakefront summer home in a new resort development. The house is completely equipped, and the Ms are seeking a loan that covers the purchase price of the residence, including furnishings and appliances. This kind of financing is a(n)
   a. wraparound loan.
   b. package loan.
   c. blanket loan.
   d. unconventional loan.

2. The Ds purchased a residence for $95,000. They made a down payment of $15,000 and agreed to assume the seller's existing mortgage, which had a current balance of $23,000. The Ds financed the remaining $57,000 of the purchase price by executing a mortgage and note to the seller. This type of loan, by which the seller becomes the mortgagee, is called a
   a. wraparound mortgage.
   b. package mortgage.
   c. balloon note.
   d. purchase-money mortgage.

3. Fran purchased her home for cash 30 years ago. Today, Fran receives monthly checks from the bank that supplement her income. Fran most likely has obtained a(n)
   a. shared-appreciation mortgage.
   b. adjustable-rate mortgage.
   c. reverse-annuity mortgage.
   d. overriding deed of trust.

4. Which of the following characteristics is true of a fixed-rate home loan that is amortized according to the original payment schedule?
   a. The amount of interest to be paid is predetermined.
   b. The loan cannot be sold in the secondary market.
   c. The monthly payment amount will fluctuate each month.
   d. The interest rate change may be based on an index.

5. In a loan that requires periodic payments that do not fully amortize the loan balance by the final payment, what term best describes the final payment?
   a. Adjustment payment
   b. Acceleration payment
   c. Balloon payment
   d. Variable payment

6. A developer received a loan that covers five parcels of real estate and provides for the release of the mortgage lien on each parcel when certain payments are made on the loan. This type of loan arrangement is called a
   a. purchase-money mortgage.
   b. blanket loan.
   c. package loan.
   d. wraparound loan.

7. Funds for Federal Housing Administration (FHA) loans are usually provided by
   a. the Federal Housing Administration (FHA).
   b. the Federal Reserve.
   c. qualified lenders.
   d. the seller.

8. Under the provisions of the Truth-in-Lending Act (Regulation Z), the annual percentage rate (APR) of a finance charge includes all of the following components *EXCEPT*
   a. discount points.
   b. the broker's commission.
   c. the loan origination fee.
   d. the loan interest rate.

9. A home is purchased using a fixed-rate, fully amortized mortgage loan. Which of the following is true regarding this mortgage?
   a. A balloon payment will be made at the end of the loan.
   b. Each payment amount is the same.
   c. Each payment reduces the principal by the same amount.
   d. The principal amount in each payment is greater than the interest amount.

10. A borrower obtains a mortgage loan to make repairs on her home. The mortgage document secures the amount of the loan as well as any future funds advanced to the borrower by the lender. This borrower has obtained a(n)
    a. wraparound mortgage.
    b. blanket loan.
    c. open-end loan.
    d. growing equity mortgage.

11. The federal Equal Credit Opportunity Act prohibits lenders from discriminating against potential borrowers on the basis of all of the following *EXCEPT*
    a. race.
    b. sex.
    c. dependence on public assistance.
    d. amount of income.

12. Which of the following is an example of a conventional loan?
    a. A mortgage loan insured by the Federal Housing Administration
    b. A 60-percent loan-to-value ratio first mortgage loan secured through a credit union
    c. A loan obtained through a private lender with a VA guarantee
    d. An installment sale

13. In an adjustable-rate mortgage loan, the interest rate is tied to an objective economic indicator called a(n)
    a. mortgage factor.
    b. discount rate.
    c. index.
    d. reserve requirement.

14. In determining LTV, *value* is
    a. 80 percent of the sale price or less.
    b. 95 percent of the appraised value.
    c. appraisal value or price, whichever is higher.
    d. price or appraised value, whichever is less.

ANSWERS

1. B   A loan that uses personal property and appliances installed on the premises as well as the real estate as security for the debt is a package mortgage. Package mortgages are not permitted in Pennsylvania. (p. 384)

2. D   When the seller finances all or part of the purchase price by accepting a note and mortgage from the buyer, the document that creates the seller's (mortgagee's) interest is a purchase money mortgage. Title passes to the buyer, and the seller essentially becomes the lender. (p. 383)

3. C   The term annuity refers to a stream of payments. Normally, payments flow from a borrower to a lender. In a reverse annuity mortgage the payments flow in reverse, from the lender to the borrower. This arrangement often allows people on fixed incomes to benefit from the equity in their home without having to sell it. (p. 383)

4. A   A fixed-rate, fully amortized loan has a predetermined amount of interest that is due from the point of origination to the time the loan is fully paid. Mortgage loan factors (discussed in Chapter 12, p. 192) are used to make this determination. (p. 381)

5. C   When periodic payments do not fully satisfy the debt by the time the last payment is due, the final payment needed to satisfy the debt is known as a balloon payment. (p. 383)

6. B   When multiple parcels of real estate are financed using one note and mortgage, the loan is known as a blanket loan or blanket mortgage. Generally, the lien can be released on individual parcels as the loan is repaid. (p. 384)

7. C   The FHA is not a direct lender, but rather insures loans made by approved lending institutions. Qualified lenders make the loans; the FHA insures the lender's risk of loss. (p. 379)

8. B   The Truth-in-Lending Act requires certain disclosures so that the consumer knows the true cost of obtaining a loan. Disclosures include loan fees, finance charges, and discount points in addition to the stated interest rate. This information is used to calculate the annual percentage rate (APR). Broker compensation is not a component of APR. (p. 375)

9. B   Each loan payment is the same for a fixed-rate, fully amortized loan (see Chapter 12, p. 192). However, the amount attributed to principal and to interest changes with each payment. This is because the amount of money owed after each payment is less, while the interest rate remains the same. More money is attributed to interest rather than principal in the early stages of the loan. (p. 381)

10. C   An open-end mortgage loan secures not only the original amount borrowed but also future advances made to the borrower. This allows the borrower to "open" the mortgage and increase the amount of debt to the lender. (p. 384)

11. D   The Equal Credit Opportunity Act (ECOA) prohibits lenders from discriminating against a borrower on the basis of race, color, religion, national origin, sex, marital status, age, and dependence on public assistance. The amount of income needed to qualify for a loan is a legitimate business reason for denying a loan. (p. 376)

12. B   A conventional loan relies solely on the ability of the borrower to repay the debt and the security provided by the mortgage. This is generally considered the most secure loan because it has the lowest loan-to-value ratio. A 60-percent LTV would be an example of a conventional loan. (p. 377)

13. C   An adjustable-rate loan (ARM) is originated at one rate of interest, with provisions for the rate to fluctuate in the future based on some identified, objective economic indicator. This indicator is referred to as an index. (p. 381)

14. D   Loan-to-value ratio is the amount of the loan expressed as a percentage of either the sales price or the appraised value of the property, whichever is lower. (p. 377)

CHAPTER TWENTY-ONE

APPRAISING
REAL ESTATE

■ **LEARNING OBJECTIVES**

When you've finished reading this chapter, you should be able to

■ differentiate between an appraisal and a comparative market analysis;
■ describe the concept of value and the basic principles of value;
■ describe the three basic approaches to value;
■ explain the appraisal process; and
■ define the key terms.

■ **KEY TERMS**

anticipation	depreciation	progression
appraisal	economic life	quantity-survey method
appraiser	external depreciation	reconciliation
assemblage	functional obsolescence	regression
broker/appraiser	gross income multiplier (GIM)	replacement cost
capitalization rate		reproduction cost
certified general real estate appraiser	gross rent multiplier (GRM)	sales comparison approach
certified residential real estate appraiser	highest and best use	square-foot method
	income approach	straight-line method
competition	index method	substitution
conformity	market value	supply and demand
contribution	physical deterioration	unit-in-place method
cost approach	plottage	

■ **APPRAISING**

An **appraisal** is an *estimate or opinion of value based on supportable evidence.* Appraisals are usually required when real property is financed. Mortgage lenders want to know that the value of the collateral is sufficient to support the amount of the loan. Appraisals are also common when property is condemned, taxed, and insured, and when estates are probated. Formal appraisals may be used any time an unbiased, professional opinion of value is helpful, including when buyers and sellers make their decisions.

The **appraiser** is the impartial third person who prepares the appraisal. An appraiser does not determine value but rather provides an estimate of value. Professional standards of practice require that the appraisal be based on approved professional methodology and reported in certain forms. The appraiser performs a service for a fee that is determined by the amount of time and effort needed to accomplish the task. To protect impartiality, the appraiser does not have an agency relationship with the party for whom the appraisal is performed, nor is the appraiser's compensation based on the value of the property being appraised.

IN PRACTICE

The importance of an appraiser's objectivity cannot be overemphasized. An appraiser's job is not to tell people what they want to hear about the value of their property or to contrive a value that suits their purposes. Serious business decisions rise and fall based on appraisals, with great risk being associated with decisions that are based on biased or self-serving estimates of value. The financial health of a lending institution, for example, is highly dependent on the estimated statements of value an appraiser prepares. The objectivity of the appraiser is crucial to underwriting solid loans that are secured with adequate collateral (value in the property). The Uniform Standards of Professional Appraisal Practices (USPAP) have become the model for an appraiser's conduct in the preparation of any appraisal.

Regulating Appraisal Activities

In Your State

PA In Pennsylvania, any person who acts as an appraiser and/or prepares an appraisal must be certified to do so by the State Board of Certified Real Estate Appraisers. The purpose is to ensure that competent individuals, whose professional conduct is subject to supervision, perform the appraisals.

Unlike some states, Pennsylvania has regulated appraisers for many years by requiring a real estate broker license to perform appraisals. Since the *Federal Financial Institutions Reform, Recovery, and Enforcement Act* of 1989, all states are required to establish uniform certification procedures for appraisers performing appraisals for federally related transactions. Hence, the Board of Certified Real Estate Appraisers was created and the Real Estate Appraisers Certification Act was adopted in Pennsylvania. Today, this board governs all appraisal activities (not just those for federally related financial transactions), and activities of appraisers and real estate licensees are separate and independently regulated. ■

The rules and regulations of the State Board of Certified Real Estate Appraisers require appraisers to comply with the *Uniform Standards of Professional Appraisal Practice* (adopted by the Appraisal Standards Board of the Appraisal Foundation). The rules also define education, examination, and experience requirements to obtain certification. There are continuing education requirements to renew certificates as well. (The Pennsylvania law and the Appraisal

Board's Rules and Regulations can be obtained online.) The three classes of certification are as follows:

- State **certified general real estate appraiser**—This person is permitted to appraise any residential or nonresidential property. For federally related transactions, only a certified general appraiser may appraise commercial property valued over $1,000,000.
- State **certified residential real estate appraiser**—This person is permitted to appraise only residential property of one to four units. For federally related transactions, a certified residential appraiser may appraise these types of properties valued over $250,000.
- **Broker/appraiser**—This person is permitted to appraise only properties valued under $250,000 that are not involved in federally related transactions. This certification was offered to all licensed real estate brokers who applied by September 3, 1998. After this date, any real estate broker who desires certification must meet the qualifications for a certified general or residential appraiser.

In Your State   **PA**   The appraiser certification act also certifies county assessors who value properties for ad valorem tax purposes in Pennsylvania. *Certified Pennsylvania Evaluator (CPE)* certificates are issued to individuals who meet certain education requirements and pass an exam. ■

Comparative Market Analysis

Not all estimates of value are prepared by professional appraisers, nor are all estimates of value appraisals. A salesperson often helps a seller arrive at a listing price or a buyer determines an offering price for property without the aid of a formal appraisal. In such cases, the salesperson prepares a report compiled from research of the marketplace, primarily similar properties that have been sold, known as a *comparative market analysis (CMA)*. The salesperson must be knowledgeable about the fundamentals of valuation to compile the market data.

A comparative market analysis should never be represented as an appraisal. A CMA is not as comprehensive or technical as an appraisal. In addition, it may be biased by a salesperson's anticipated agency relationship. Furthermore, real estate licensure does not permit appraisal activities. In fact, the real estate licensing law permits a licensee to prepare a CMA *only in conjunction with* a listing or sales transaction.

■ VALUE

Remember the four characteristics of value by the acronym **DUST:**

Demand
Utility
Scarcity
Transferability

To have value in the real estate market, that is, to have monetary worth based on desirability, a property must have the following characteristics:

- *Demand*—the need or desire for possession or ownership backed by the financial means to satisfy that need
- *Utility*—the capacity to satisfy human needs and desires
- *Scarcity*—a finite supply
- *Transferability*—the relative ease with which ownership rights are transferred from one person to another

Market Value

> Market value is the most probable price a property should bring in a fair sale.

Generally, the purpose of an appraisal is to estimate market value. The **market value** of real estate is *the most probable price that a property should bring in a fair sale*. This definition makes three assumptions. First, it presumes a competitive and open market. Second, the buyer and seller are both assumed to be acting prudently and knowledgeably. Finally, market value depends on the price not being affected by unusual circumstances.

The following conditions are essential to market value:

- The most probable price is not the average or highest price.
- The buyer and seller are unrelated and acting without undue pressure.
- Both buyer and seller are well informed about the property's use and potential, including its assets and defects.
- The property is exposed in the marketplace for a reasonable time.
- Payment is made in cash or its equivalent.
- The price represents normal consideration for the property, unaffected by special financing amounts and/or terms, services, fees, costs, or credits associated with the transaction.

> Market price is the actual selling price of a property.
>
> Cost may not equal either market value or market price.

Market value versus market price.   Market value is a professional opinion of value based on an analysis of data. The data may include not only an analysis of comparable sales but also an analysis of potential income and expenses and replacement costs (less depreciation). Market price, on the other hand, is what a property *actually* sells for—its sales price. In theory, the market price should be the same as the market value. However, market price can be taken as accurate evidence of current market value only if the conditions essential to market value exist. A property may sell below market value, such as when the seller is forced to sell quickly or when a sale is arranged between relatives, or above market value when the sale, for example, involves personal property or the seller pays certain of the buyer's purchasing expenses.

Market value versus cost.   There's an important distinction between market value and *cost*. One of the most common misconceptions about valuing property is that cost represents market value. Cost and market value may be the same. In fact, when the improvements on a property are new, cost and value are likely to be equal. But more often, cost does not equal market value. For example, a homeowner may install a swimming pool for $15,000; however, the cost of the improvement may not add $15,000 to the value of the property. (See the principle of contribution later in this chapter.)

Basic Principles of Value

A number of economic principles can affect the value of real estate. The most important are defined in the text that follows.

Anticipation.   The principle of **anticipation** says that value is created by the expectation that certain benefits will be realized in the future. Value can increase or decrease in anticipation of some future benefit or detriment affecting the property. For example, the value of a house may be affected if there are rumors that an adjacent property may be converted to commercial use in the near future.

Change.   The cause and effect of social and economic forces constantly cause property values to be in transition. No physical or economic condition remains constant. Real estate is subject to natural phenomena, such as tornadoes, fires, and routine wear and tear of the elements. The real estate business, like any business, is also subject to the demands of its market. An appraiser must be knowledgeable about the past and, perhaps, the predictable effects of natural phenomena and the behavior of the marketplace.

Competition.   **Competition** is the interaction of supply and demand. Little demand for abundant supply tends to depress value, while great demand for limited supply tends to increase value. A neighborhood or a type of property, for example, in which purchasers see opportunities for profit or high return on an investment, tends to attract other purchasers as well. The greater the competition is, the greater the effect of competitive behavior in driving up value. However, once the focus of competition shifts elsewhere, the values of properties that were highly attractive cease to increase as rapidly and can turn stagnant or decrease.

Conformity.   The principle of **conformity** says that value is created when the components of the property are in harmony with its surroundings. Maximum value is realized if the use of land conforms to existing neighborhood standards. In residential areas of single-family houses, for example, buildings should be similar in design, construction, size, and age.

Contribution.   The principle of **contribution** says that the value of any component of a property is measured by the amount it contributes to the value of the whole or the amount its absence detracts from the value of the whole. For example, the cost of installing an air-conditioning system or remodeling an older office building may be greater than any increase in market value that may result from the improvement.

Highest and best use.   The most profitable single use to which the property may be adapted or the use that is likely to be in demand in the near future is the property's **highest and best use.** The use must be

- legally permitted,
- financially feasible,
- physically possible, and
- maximally productive.

The highest and best use of a site can change with social, political, and economic forces. Highest and best use is noted in every appraisal but may also be the object of a more extensive analysis. For example, a highest-and-best-use study may show that a parking lot in a busy downtown area does not maximize the productivity of the land to the degree that a building would.

Increasing and diminishing returns.   The addition of more improvements to land and structures will increase value only to the asset's maximum value. Beyond that point, additional improvements no longer affect a property's value. As long as money spent on improvements produces an increase in income or value, the law of increasing returns applies. At the point where additional improvements will not produce a proportionate increase in income or value, the law of diminishing returns applies. No matter how much money is spent on the property, the property's value does not keep pace with expenditures.

Plottage. The principle of **plottage** holds that merging or consolidating adjacent lots held by separate landowners into a single larger one produces a greater total land value than the sum of the two sites valued separately. For example, if two adjacent lots are valued at $35,000 each, their total value if consolidated into one larger lot under a single use might be $90,000. The process of merging the two lots under one owner is known as **assemblage.**

Regression and progression. In general, the worth of a better-quality property is adversely affected by the presence of the lesser-quality property. This is known as the principle of **regression.** Thus, in a neighborhood of modest homes, a structure that is larger, better maintained, or more luxurious would tend to be valued in the same range as the less lavish homes. Conversely, under the principle of **progression,** the value of a modest home would be higher if it were located among larger, fancier properties.

Substitution. The principle of **substitution** says that the maximum value of a property tends to be set by how much it would cost to purchase an equally desirable and valuable *substitute* property.

Supply and demand. The principle of **supply and demand** says that the value of a property depends on the number of properties available in the marketplace, that is, the supply of the product. Other factors include the prices of other properties, the number of prospective purchasers, and the price buyers are willing to pay. For example, the last lot to be sold in a residential area where the demand for homes is high would probably be worth more than the first lot sold in that area.

■ THE THREE APPROACHES TO VALUE

To arrive at an accurate estimate of value, appraisers traditionally use three basic valuation techniques: the sales comparison approach, the cost approach, and the income capitalization approach. The three methods serve as checks against each other. Using them narrows the range within which the final estimate of value falls. Each method is generally considered most reliable for specific types of property.

The Sales Comparison Approach

In the **sales comparison approach** an estimate of value is obtained by comparing the subject property (the property being appraised) with recently sold comparable properties (properties similar to the subject). Because no two parcels of real estate are exactly alike, each comparable property must be analyzed for differences and similarities between it and the subject property. This approach is a good example of the principle of substitution. The sales prices of the comparables must be adjusted for any dissimilarities. The principal factors for which adjustments must be made include the following:

- *Property rights*—An adjustment must be made when less than the full fee simple legal bundle of rights is involved. This includes land leases, ground rents, life estates, easements, deed restrictions, and encroachments.
- *Financing concessions*—The financing terms must be considered, including adjustments for differences such as mortgage loan terms and owner financing.
- *Conditions of sale*—Adjustments must be made for motivational factors that would affect the sale, such as foreclosure, a sale between family members, or some nonmonetary incentive.
- *Date of sale*—An adjustment must be made if economic changes occur between the date of sale of the comparable property and the date of the appraisal.
- *Location*—Similar properties might differ in price from neighborhood to neighborhood or even between locations within the same neighborhood.
- *Physical features and amenities*—Physical features that may cause adjustments include the building's age, size of lot, landscaping, construction quality, number of rooms, square feet of living space, interior and exterior condition, presence or absence of a garage, fireplace, or air conditioning, and so forth.

The value of a feature present in the subject, but not in the comparable property, is added to the sale price of the comparable. Likewise, the value of a feature present in the comparable, but not in the subject, is subtracted from the sale price of the comparable. The adjusted sales prices of the comparables represent the probable range of value of the subject property. From this range, a single market value estimate can be selected.

The sales comparison approach is considered the most reliable of the three approaches when appraising single-family homes. Most appraisals include a minimum of three comparable sales reflective of the subject property. Some appraisal forms require the inclusion of currently listed properties that are similar to the subject to indicate the current market competition. An example of the sales comparison approach is shown in Table 21.1.

The Cost Approach

The **cost approach** to value is also based on the principle of substitution. The cost approach consists of five steps:

1. Estimate the value of the land as if it were vacant and available for its highest and best use. (Note that the value of the land is not subject to depreciation.)
2. Estimate the current cost of constructing buildings and site improvements.
3. Estimate the amount of accrued depreciation of the building resulting from physical deterioration, functional obsolescence, and/or external depreciation.
4. Deduct accrued depreciation from the estimated construction cost of new building(s) and site improvements.
5. Add the estimated land value to the depreciated cost of the building(s) and site improvements to arrive at the total property value.

T A B L E 21.1

Sales Comparison Approach to Value

	Subject Property	Comparables			
		A	B	C	D
Sales Price		$118,000	$112,000	$116,500	$110,000
Financing Concessions	none	none	none	none	none
Date of Sale		current	current	current	current
Location	good	same	poorer +6,500	same	same
Age	6 years	same	same	same	same
Size of Lot	60' × 135'	same	same	same	larger −5,000
Landscaping	good	same	same	same	same
Construction	brick	same	same	same	same
Style	ranch	same	same	same	same
No. of Rooms	6	same	same	same	same
No. of Bedrooms	3	same	same	same	same
No. of Baths	1½	same	same	same	same
Sq. Ft. of Living Space	1,500	same	same	same	same
Other Space (basement)	full basement	same	same	same	same
Condition–Exterior	average	better − 1,500	poorer +1,000	same	poorer +2,000
Condition–Exterior	good	same	same	same	same
Garage	2-car attached	same	same	same	none +5,000
Other Improvements	none	none	none	none	none
Net Adjustments		−1,500	+7,500	-0-	+2,000
Adjusted Value		$116,500	$119,500	$116,500	$112,000

Note: Because the value range of the properties in the comparison chart is close, and comparable C required no adjustment, an appraiser would conclude that the indicated market value of the subject is $116,500.

Land value (Step 1) is usually estimated by using the sales comparison approach. The location and site improvements (such as utilities and sewer lines) of the subject property are compared with those of similar nearby sites, and adjustments are made for significant differences.

There are two ways to look at the construction cost of a building for appraisal purposes (Step 2): reproduction cost and replacement cost. **Reproduction cost** is the construction cost at current prices of an exact duplicate of the subject improvement, including both the benefits and the drawbacks of the property. **Replacement cost** is cost at current prices to construct improvements similar to the subject property, but not necessarily an exact duplicate. Replacement cost new is more frequently used in appraising older structures because it eliminates obsolete features and takes advantage of current construction materials and techniques.

An example of the cost approach to value is shown in Table 21.2.

Determining reproduction or replacement cost. An appraiser using the cost approach computes the reproduction or replacement cost of a building using one of the following four methods:

T A B L E   21.2

Cost Approach to Value

Land Valuation: Size 60' × 135' @ $450 per front foot	= $27,000
Plus site improvements: driveway, walks, landscaping, etc:	= 8,000
Total Land Value	$35,000

Building Valuation: Replacement Cost
1,500 sq. ft. @ $65 per sq. ft. = $97,500

Less Depreciation:
Physical depreciation
  curable
    (items of deferred maintenance)
    exterior painting$4,000
  incurable (structural deterioration) 9,750
Functional obsolescence 2,000
External depreciation   -0-
     Total Depreciation   −15,750

Depreciated Value of Building $ 81,750
Indicated Value by Cost Approach $116,750

1. **Square-foot method:** The cost per square foot of a recently built comparable structure is multiplied by the number of square feet (using exterior dimensions) in the subject building. This is the most common and easiest method of cost estimation. The example in Table 21.2 uses the square-foot method, which is also referred to as the *comparison method*. For some properties, the cost per cubic foot of a recently built comparable structure is multiplied by the number of cubic feet in the subject structure.

2. **Unit-in-place method:** In the unit-in-place method, the cost of a structure is estimated based on the construction cost per unit of measure of individual building components, including material, labor, overhead, and builder's profit. Most components are measured in square feet, although items such as plumbing fixtures are estimated by cost. The sum of the components is the cost of the new structure.

3. **Quantity survey method:** The quantity and quality of all materials (such as lumber, brick, and plaster) and the labor are estimated on a unit cost basis. These factors are added to indirect costs (building permit, survey, payroll, taxes, builder's profit, etc.) to arrive at the total cost of the structure. Because it is so detailed and time-consuming, this method is usually used only when appraising historic properties. It is, however, the most accurate method of appraising new construction.

4. **Index method:** A factor representing the percentage increase to the present time of construction costs is applied to the original cost of the subject property. Because this method fails to take into account individual property variables, it is useful only as a check of the estimate reached by one of the other methods.

Depreciation.   In real estate appraising, **depreciation** is a loss in value due to any cause. It refers to a condition that adversely affects the value of an improvement to real property. Land usually does not depreciate—it retains its value indefinitely, except in such rare cases as down-zoned urban parcels, improperly developed land, or misused farmland.

Depreciation is considered to be *curable* or *incurable*, depending on the contribution of the expenditure to the value of the property. For appraisal purposes (as opposed to depreciation for tax purposes), depreciation is divided into three classes, according to its cause:

1. **Physical deterioration**: *Curable*—an item in need of repair, such as painting (deferred maintenance), that is economically feasible and would result in an increase in value equal to or exceeding the cost.

   Incurable—a defect caused by physical wear and tear that its correction would not be economically feasible or contribute a comparable value to the building. A major repair, such as replacement of weatherworn siding, may not warrant the financial investment.

2. **Functional obsolescence.** *Curable*—outmoded or unacceptable physical or design features that are no longer considered desirable by purchasers but could be replaced or redesigned at a cost that would be offset by the anticipated increase in ultimate value. Outmoded fixtures, such as plumbing, are usually easily replaced. Room function may be redefined at no cost if the basic room layout allows for it. A bedroom adjacent to a kitchen may be converted to a family room.

   Incurable—currently undesirable physical or design features that could not be easily remedied because the cost of effecting a cure would be greater than its contribution to the value. An office building that cannot be air-conditioned, for example, suffers from incurable functional obsolescence if the cost outweighs its contribution to the value.

3. **External depreciation**: *Usually incurable*—caused by negative factors not on the subject property, such as environmental, social, or economic forces. This type of depreciation usually cannot be considered curable because the loss in value cannot be affected by expenditures to the property. Proximity to a nuisance, such as a polluting factory or a deteriorating neighborhood, would be unchangeable factors that could not be cured by the owner of the subject property.

Much of the functional obsolescence and all the external depreciation can be evaluated only by considering the actions of buyers in the marketplace.

When determining depreciation, most appraisers use the breakdown method. Depreciation is broken down into all three classes with separate estimates for curable and incurable factors in each class. Depreciation, however, is difficult to measure; and the older the building, the more difficult it is to estimate. The easiest but least precise way to determine depreciation is the **straight-line method,** also called the economic age-life method. This method assumes depreciation occurs at an even rate over a structure's **economic life,** the period during which it is expected to remain useful for its original intended purpose. The property's cost is divided by the number of years of its expected economic life to derive the amount of annual depreciation.

For example, a $120,000 property may have a land value of $30,000 and an improvement value of $90,000. If the improvements are expected to last 60 years, the annual straight-line depreciation would be $1,500 ($90,000 divided by 60 years). Such depreciation can be calculated as an annual dollar amount or as a percentage of the improvement's replacement cost.

The cost approach is most helpful in the appraisal of newer buildings or special-purpose buildings such as schools, churches, and public buildings. Some properties are difficult to appraise using other methods because there are seldom enough local sales to use as comparables and because the properties do not ordinarily generate income.

The Income Approach

The **income approach** to value is based on the present value of the rights to future income. It assumes that the income derived from a property will, to a large extent, control the value of that property. The income approach is used for valuation of income-producing properties such as apartment buildings, office buildings, shopping centers, and the like. In estimating value using the income approach, an appraiser must take the following five steps:

1. Estimate annual *potential gross income*. An estimate of economic rental income must be made based on market studies. Current rental income may not reflect the current market rental rates, especially in the cases of short-term leases or leases about to terminate. Potential income also includes other income to the property from such sources as vending machines, parking fees, and laundry machines.
2. Deduct an appropriate allowance for vacancy and rent loss, based on the appraiser's experience, and arrive at *effective gross income*.
3. Deduct the annual *operating expenses* from the effective gross income to arrive at the annual net operating income. See Table 21.3, Income Capitalization Approach to Value, for expenses. Management costs are always included even if the current owner manages the property. Mortgage payments (principal and interest) are debt service and are not considered operating expenses.
4. Estimate the price a typical investor would pay for the income produced by this particular type and class of property. This is done by estimating the rate of return (or yield) that an investor will demand for the investment of capital in this type of building. This rate of return is called the **capitalization** (or cap) **rate** and is determined by comparing the relationship of net operating income to the sales prices of similar properties that have sold in the current market. For example, a comparable property that is producing an annual net operating income of $15,000 is sold for $187,500. The capitalization rate is $15,000 divided by $187,500 or 8 percent. It may be concluded that 8 percent is the rate that the appraiser should apply to the subject property if other comparable properties sold at prices that yielded substantially the same rate.
5. Apply the capitalization rate to the property's annual net operating income to arrive at the estimate of the property's value.

With the appropriate capitalization rate and the projected annual net operating income, the appraiser can obtain an indication of value by the income approach in the following manner:

$$I = \text{Income} \qquad R = \text{Rate} \qquad V = \text{Value}$$

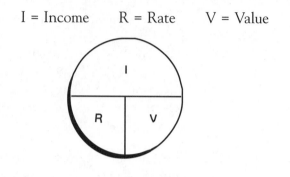

Net Operating Income ÷ Capitalization Rate = Value
Example: $18,000 income ÷ 9% cap rate = $200,000 value or
$18,000 income ÷ 8% cap rate = $225,000 value

Note the inverse relationship between the rate and value. As the rate goes down, the value estimate increases.

This formula and its variations are important in dealing with income property.

Income ÷ Rate = Value
Income ÷ Value = Rate
Value × Rate = Income

A very simplified version of the computations used in applying the income approach is illustrated in Table 21.3.

IN PRACTICE

The most difficult step in the income approach to value is determining the appropriate capitalization rate for the property. This rate must be selected to accurately reflect the recapture of the original investment over the building's economic life, give the owner an acceptable rate of return on investment, and provide for the repayment of borrowed capital. Note that an income property that carries with it a great deal of risk as an investment generally requires a higher rate of return than a property considered a safe investment.

Gross rent or gross income multipliers. Certain properties, such as single-family homes or two-unit buildings, are not purchased primarily for income. As a substitute for a more elaborate income capitalization analysis, the **gross rent multiplier (GRM)** and **gross income multiplier (GIM)** are often used in the appraisal process. Each relates the sales price of a property to its rental income.

Because both single-family and one- to four-unit residences usually produce only a rental income, the gross rent multiplier is used. This relates the sales price to monthly rental income. However, commercial and industrial properties generate income from many other sources (rent, concessions, escalator clause income, and so forth), and they are valued using their annual income from all sources.

TABLE   21.3

Income Capitalization Approach to Value

Potential Gross Annual Income	
Market Rent	$60,000
Income from other sources	
(vending machines and pay phones)	+ 600
	$60,600
Less vacancy and collection losses (estimated) @ 4%	− 2,424
Effective Gross Income	$58,176

Expenses:		
Real estate taxes	$9,000	
Insurance	1,000	
Heat	2,800	
Maintenance	6,400	
Utilities, electricity, water, gas	800	
Repairs	1,200	
Decorating	1,400	
Replacement of equipment	800	
Legal and accounting	600	
Management	3,000	
Total Expenses		$27,000
Annual Net Operating Income		$31,176

Capitalization Rate = 10%

Capitalization of annual net income: $\dfrac{\$31,176}{.10}$

Indicated Value by Income Approach = $311,760

The formulas are as follows:

Sales Price ÷ Gross Income = Gross Income Multiplier (GIM)

or

Sales Price ÷ Gross Rent = Gross Rent Multiplier (GRM)

For example, if a home recently sold for $82,000 and its monthly rental income was $650, the GRM for the property would be computed thus:

$82,000 ÷ $650 = 126.2 GRM

To establish an accurate GRM, an appraiser must have recent sales and rental data from at least four properties that are similar to the subject property. The resulting GRM can then be applied to the estimated fair market rental of the subject property to arrive at its market value. The formula would then be

Rental Income × GRM = Estimated Market Value

Table 21.4 shows some examples of GRM comparisons.

T A B L E   21.4

Gross Rent Multipler

Comparable No.	Sales Price	Monthly Rent	GRM
1	$93,600	$650	144
2	78,500	450	174
3	95,500	675	141
4	82,000	565	145
Subject	?	625	?

Note: Based on an analysis of these comparisons, a GRM of 145 seems reasonable for homes in this area. In the opinion of an appraiser, then, the estimated value of the subject property would be $625 × 145, or $90,625.

IN PRACTICE

Much skill is required to accurately use multipliers. No one multiplier is applicable for all areas or all types of properties, and the data for each comparable must be carefully scrutinized. Consequently, many appraisers view the technique simply as a quick, informal way to check the validity of a value derived by one of the other appraisal methods.

Reconciliation

Reconciliation is the art of analyzing and effectively weighing the findings from the three approaches to value. It is *not* simply a process of averaging.

When the three approaches to value are applied to the same property, they will normally produce three separate indications of value. **Reconciliation** is the art of analyzing and effectively weighing the findings from the three approaches. From this analysis, or reconciliation, a single estimate of market value is produced.

The process of reconciliation is more complicated than simply taking the average of the three value estimates. An average implies that the data and logic applied in each of the approaches are equally valid and reliable for the subject property and should, therefore, be given equal weight. In fact, depending on the type of property, one approach is more valid or reliable than the others.

For instance, when appraising a single-family home, the value derived from the income approach is rarely valid, and the cost approach is of limited use unless the house is relatively new construction. Consequently, the value derived from the sales comparison approach is usually given greatest weight. The value derived from the income approach is normally given the greatest weight for income-producing property. For churches, libraries, museums, schools, and other special-use properties that produce little or no income or sales revenue, the cost approach is generally more reliable.

■ THE APPRAISAL PROCESS

Although appraising is not an exact or precise science, the key to an accurate appraisal lies in the methodical collection and analysis of data. The appraisal process is an orderly set of procedures used to collect and analyze data as prescribed by the *Uniform Standards of Professional Appraisal Practice (USPAP)* to arrive at a conclusion of value. The data are divided into two basic classes:

1. *General data* covering the nation, region, city, and neighborhood, paying particular importance to the neighborhood where physical, economic, social, and political influences directly affect the value and potential of the subject property.
2. *Specific data* covering details of the subject property as well as comparative data relating to costs, sales, income, and expenses of properties similar to and competitive with the subject property.

The steps an appraiser takes in carrying out an appraisal assignment are:

1. State the problem.
2. List the data needed and their sources.
3. Gather, record, and verify the necessary data (general data, specific data, and data for each approach).
4. Determine the highest and best use.
5. Estimate land value.
6. Estimate value by each of the three approaches.
7. Reconcile estimated values for final value estimate.
8. Report final value estimate.

Once the approaches have been reconciled and an opinion of value has been reached, the appraiser prepares a report for the client. Three levels of written reports can be prepared, each differing in the amount of information required to support the appraiser's reasoning and conclusions. However, according to USPAP rules, all written reports should

All appraisals are specific as to:

■ Property
■ Purpose
■ Time

■ identify the real estate and real property interest being appraised;
■ state the purpose and intended use of the appraisal;
■ define the value to be estimated;
■ state the effective date of value and the date of the report;
■ state the extent of the process of collecting, confirming, and reporting data;
■ list all assumptions and limiting conditions that affect analysis, opinion, and conclusion;
■ describe the information considered, the appraisal procedures followed, and the reasoning that supports the analysis, opinion, and the report's conclusions (if an approach was excluded, the report should explain why);
■ describe (if necessary or appropriate) the appraiser's opinion of the highest and best use of the real estate;
■ describe any additional information that may be appropriate to show compliance with or clearly identify and explain permitted departures, from the USPAP guidelines; and
■ include a signed certification, as required by USPAP.

IN PRACTICE

The role of an appraiser is *not* to determine value. Rather, an appraiser develops a supportable and objective report about the value of the subject property. The appraiser relies on experience and expertise in valuation theories to evaluate market data. The appraiser does not establish worth or create numbers; instead he or she verifies what the market indicates. This is important to remember, particularly when dealing with a property owner who may lack objectivity about the realistic value. Lack of objectivity also can complicate the salesperson's ability to list a property within the most probable range of market value.

■ SUMMARY

To appraise real estate means to estimate its value. Although real estate has many types of value, the most common objective of an appraisal is to estimate market value, the most probable sale price of a property. Basic to appraising are certain underlying economic principles, such as highest and best use, substitution, supply and demand, conformity, anticipation, increasing and diminishing returns, regression, progression, plottage, contribution, competition, and change.

Appraisals are concerned with values, prices, and costs; it is vital to understand the distinctions among the terms. Value is an estimate of future benefits, cost represents a measure of past expenditures, and price reflects the actual amount of money paid for a property.

A professional appraiser analyzes a property through three approaches to value. In the sales comparison approach, the value of the subject property is compared with the values of others like it that have sold recently. Because no two properties are exactly alike, adjustments must be made to account for any differences. With the cost approach, an appraiser calculates the cost of building a similar structure on a similar site. The appraiser then subtracts depreciation (losses in value), which reflects the differences between new properties of this type and the present condition of the subject property. The income approach is an analysis based on the relationship between the rate of return that an investor requires and the net income that a property produces.

An informal version of the income approach, called the gross rent multiplier (GRM), may be used to estimate the value of single-family residential properties that are not usually rented but could be. The GRM is computed by dividing the sales price of a property by its gross monthly rent. For commercial or industrial property, a gross income multiplier (GIM), based on annual income from all sources, may be used.

Normally, the application of the three approaches results in three different estimates of value. In the process of reconciliation, the validity and reliability of each approach are weighed objectively to arrive at the single best and most supportable estimate of value.

QUESTIONS

1. Which of the following approaches to value makes use of a rate of investment return?
   a. Sales comparison approach
   b. Cost approach
   c. Income approach
   d. Gross income multiplier

2. The elements of value include which of the following?
   a. Competition
   b. Scarcity
   c. Anticipation
   d. Balance

3. The principle of value that states that two adjacent parcels of land combined into one large parcel would have a greater value than the two parcels valued separately is called
   a. substitution.
   b. plottage.
   c. regression.
   d. progression.

4. The actual amount of money a property commands in the marketplace is its
   a. market price.
   b. market value.
   c. capitalization rate.
   d. index.

5. *H* has his "dream house" constructed for $100,000 in an area where most newly constructed homes are not as well equipped as his and typically sell for only $80,000. The value of *H*'s house is likely to be affected by the principle of
   a. progression.
   b. assemblage.
   c. change.
   d. regression.

6. In question 5, the owners of the lesser-valued homes in *H*'s immediate area may be affected by the principle of
   a. progression.
   b. increasing returns.
   c. competition.
   d. regression.

7. Accrued depreciation for appraisal purposes is *NOT* caused by which of the following?
   a. Functional obsolescence
   b. Physical deterioration
   c. External depreciation
   d. Acceleration depreciation

8. *Reconciliation* refers to which of the following?
   a. Loss of value due to any cause
   b. Separating the value of the land from the total value of the property to compute depreciation
   c. Analyzing the results obtained by the three approaches to value to determine a final estimate of value
   d. The process by which an appraiser determines the highest and best use for a parcel of land

9. One method an appraiser uses to determine a building's cost new involves an estimate of the raw materials needed to build the structure plus the cost of such materials, labor, and other expenses. This is called the
   a. square-foot method.
   b. quantity-survey method.
   c. cubic-foot method.
   d. unit-in-place method.

10. If a property's annual net income is $24,000 and it is valued at $300,000, what is its capitalization rate?
    a. 12.5 percent
    b. 10.5 percent
    c. 15 percent
    d. 8 percent

11. Certain figures must be determined by an appraiser before value can be computed by the income approach. Which one of the following is *NOT* required for this process?
    a. Annual net operating income
    b. Capitalization rate
    c. Accrued depreciation
    d. Annual gross income

12. The income approach would be given the most weight in the valuation of a(n)
    a. single-family residence.
    b. industrial property.
    c. strip shopping center.
    d. school.

13. The market value of a parcel of real estate is
    a. the cost of the land and any improvements.
    b. the amount of money paid for the property.
    c. an estimate of the most probable price it should bring.
    d. its value without improvements.

14. Capitalization is the process by which annual net income is used as the basis to
    a. determine cost.
    b. estimate value.
    c. establish depreciation.
    d. determine potential tax value.

15. From the reproduction or replacement cost of the building, an appraiser deducts depreciation, which represents
    a. the remaining economic life of the building.
    b. remodeling costs to increase rentals.
    c. loss of value due to any cause.
    d. costs to modernize the building.

16. In the sales comparison approach to value, the probable sales price of a building may be estimated by
    a. capitalizing net operating income.
    b. considering recent sales of similar properties.
    c. deducting accrued depreciation.
    d. determining construction costs.

17. Which factor would be least important in comparing properties under the sales comparison approach to value?
    a. Difference in dates of sale
    b. Difference in financing terms
    c. Difference in appearance and condition
    d. Difference in interior decorating

18. In the income approach to value
    a. the reproduction or replacement cost of the building must be computed.
    b. the capitalization rate must be estimated.
    c. depreciation must be determined.
    d. sales of similar properties must be considered.

19. In the cost approach to value, it is necessary to
    a. determine a dollar value for depreciation.
    b. estimate future expenses and operating costs.
    c. check sales prices of recently sold homes in the area.
    d. reconcile differing value estimates.

20. The appraised value of a residence with four bedrooms and one bathroom would probably be reduced because of
    a. external obsolescence.
    b. functional obsolescence.
    c. curable physical deterioration.
    d. incurable physical deterioration.

ANSWERS

1. C The rate of investment return or capitalization rate is used in the income approach to value. (p. 401)

2. B Scarcity is an element of value. Competition, anticipation, and balance are economic principles. (p. 393)

3. B Plottage is the principle that says the value of a large parcel is greater than the sum value of individual smaller parcels. The process of merging parcels is assemblage. (p. 396)

4. A Market price is the actual amount of money a property commands, or its selling price. Market price may or may not be the same as market value, depending on a number of factors that affect the sale. (p. 394)

5. D The principle of regressions says that the value of a better-quality property is adversely affected by the presence of the lesser-quality property. (p. 394)

6. A Conversely, the principle of progression says that the value of a lesser property is enhanced by the presence of better-quality property. (p. 396)

7. D Functional, physical, and external depreciation are considerations when preparing an appraisal. Accelerated depreciation is an accounting function. (p. 400)

8. C Reconciliation is the art of analyzing and effectively weighing the findings from the three approaches to value to derive a single estimate of market value. Reconciliation is not an average of the findings. (p. 404)

9. B The quantity-survey method estimates all costs in quantity and quality of materials and includes indirect costs or expenses (such as labor) as well. (p. 399)

10. D $24,000 divided by $300,000 equals 8 percent. (p. 401)

11. C Accrued depreciation is a function of the cost approach, not the income approach, to value. (p. 401)

12. C The income approach to value is typically most reflective of the value of income-producing properties, such as the shopping center. The cost approach is most reflective of value for special purpose properties, like a school building and an industrial facility, and the sales comparison approach is typically most reflective for a single-family home. (p. 401)

13. C Market value is an estimate of the most probable price a property will bring in a fair sale. Price is the actual money paid. Neither cost nor price necessarily equals value. (p. 394)

14. B Net income divided by the capitalization rate equals value. This formula is the basis for the income approach to value. (p. 401)

15. C The reproduction or replacement cost reflects new construction, but the value has to reflect the actual condition of the property, due to whatever cause, and is captured after deductions for depreciation. (p. 400)

16. B The sales comparison approach relies on comparables or the recent sales of similar properties. The cost approach relies on construction costs and depreciation, and the income approach capitalizes net income. (p. 396)

17. D The sale prices of comparable properties must be adjusted for dissimilarities with the subject property and conditions of sale. Sale dates, financing terms, and the property condition and appearance can significantly affect value. Although a decorating style can certainly affect the appeal of a property, it generally does not have an effect on value that can be measured. (p. 397)

18. B Capitalization rate is the basis for deriving value in the income approach. The estimate of that rate is derived from an analysis of rates of return for similar properties. (p. 401)

19. A In order to properly reflect value using the cost approach, the reproduction or replacement cost must be reduced by stated dollar amounts to derive value. (p. 400)

20. B Deductions for functional obsolescence are intended to adjust for physical or design features that are no longer considered desirable. The proportion of one bathroom to four bedrooms by today's standards would generally be considered obsolete. Only functional obsolescence is considered either curable or incurable. Physical deterioration, by its very nature, is considered curable; external obsolescence is considered incurable because corrective measures are beyond the owner's control. (p. 400)

CHAPTER TWENTY-TWO

CLOSING THE REAL ESTATE TRANSACTION

■ LEARNING OBJECTIVES

When you've finished reading this chapter, you should be able to

■ identify the parties involved in closing a transaction and their interests;
■ list the key requirements of the Real Estate Settlement Procedures Act (RESPA);
■ describe the steps involved in preparing a settlement statement, including proper entry of debits and credits;
■ explain and apply basic rules for prorating items on a settlement statement; and
■ define the key terms.

■ KEY TERMS

accrued items	debit	Real Estate Settlement
affiliated business	escrow	Procedures Act
arrangement (AfBA)	prepaid items	(RESPA)
credit	prorations	

■ CLOSING THE TRANSACTION

Closing or *settlement* is the consummation of the real estate transaction. Closing actually involves two events: first, fulfillment of the promises made in the sales contract; second, closing of the buyer's mortgage loan (if any) and dispersal of the loan funds. An agreement of sale is the blueprint for completing the transaction. Before exchanging documents and funds, the buyer and seller need assurance that the stipulations in the agreement of sale have been met.

Closing is the point at which ownership of a property is transferred in exchange for the selling price.

Closing a transaction is referred to by many names. In some areas, closing is called *settlement and transfer*. In other parts of the country, it is known as *passing papers*. This term comes from the fact that parties sit around a single table and exchange (pass) copies of documents. In still other regions, the buyer and seller may never meet at all; the paperwork is handled by an escrow agent. This process is known as *closing escrow*. Whether the closing occurs face to face or through escrow, the main concerns are that the buyer receives marketable title, the seller receives the purchase price, and certain other financial items are properly adjusted between the two parties.

Closing also marks the end of the real estate transaction for the licensees as well. Generally, the real estate firm's services conclude after closing, and the broker is compensated. While the closing of the transaction is the goal toward which all the licensees' efforts are driven, the period leading up to the actual event can be complicated. New players come on the scene: appraisers, inspectors, loan officers, insurance agents, and lawyers. Negotiations may continue, sometimes right up until the property is finally transferred.

■ PRECLOSING PROCEDURES

Before the property changes hands, a number of important tasks must be performed. Preparation for closing involves ordering and reviewing an array of documents, such as the title insurance or title certificate, surveys, inspection reports, and the property insurance policy. Arrangements must be made with the parties for the time and place of closing. Closing statements and other documents must be prepared.

The buyer will want to be sure that the seller delivers good title. The buyer also should ensure that the property is in the promised condition. This involves inspecting the title evidence, the deed the seller will give, any documents showing that liens have been removed, the survey, the results of any required inspections or repairs, and leases if there are tenants on the premises. Obviously, the seller's main interest is in receiving payment for the property. The seller will want to be sure that the buyer has the necessary funds to complete the sale. Both parties will want to inspect the closing statement to make sure that all monies involved in the transaction have been accounted for properly. The parties may wish to be accompanied by their attorneys at closing.

IN PRACTICE

One of the first efforts to put the NAR/HUD Homebuyer Protection Initiative into action is the Consumer Notice form (a separate Consumer Notice from the one Pennsylvania licensees use) that explains the difference between the appraisal and a home inspection, and that emphasizes the importance of an inspection to protect buyers. This one-page notice must be signed on or before closing transactions in which an FHA-insured mortgage loan is involved.

Checking the Property

The property is checked before closing for several reasons. One is to determine if there are any encroachments. Commonly, a survey is used to spot the location of buildings, driveways, fences, and other improvements located on the property. A survey also indicates any improvements that might be located on adjoining property that are encroaching on the premises. Depending on the nature of the encroachments, they may pose title problems. As a practical matter, it is useful for the new owner to be able to identify the property boundaries and any easements that may be indicated on the survey. Many buyers have the surveyor place stakes to physically identify boundaries.

Another reason for checking the property is to verify its physical condition. Shortly before the closing takes place, the buyer usually makes a *final inspection* (also called a *walk through*) of the property. Through this inspection, the buyer makes sure that the property will be delivered in the condition stated in the agreement of sale. The buyer makes sure that any agreed on repairs have been made, that the property has been well maintained (both inside and out), that all fixtures are in place, and that there has been no unauthorized removal or alteration of any part of the improvements. The buyer also needs to be sure that no unauthorized parties remain in possession of the property. As a practical matter, it is easier to resolve any problems that are discovered before closing rather than having to resort to legal proceedings afterwards.

> Before closing, the buyer should check two things:
>
> 1. The condition of the physical property
> 2. The condition of the title

Title Procedures

In Your State

PA Both the buyer and the buyer's lender will want assurance that the seller's title complies with the requirements of the agreement of sale. In Pennsylvania, the buyer is responsible for determining that he or she is taking good title to the property. This is usually done by obtaining an *abstract of title* from an attorney or a *title commitment* from a title insurance company. Either of these documents will indicate the status of the seller's title and disclose liens, encumbrances, easements, conditions, or restrictions that appear on the record that affect the seller's title. ■

The buyer and seller and their representatives (either agents or attorneys) should review the abstract *before* closing so that any problems that could delay settlement can be resolved. When a buyer is purchasing title insurance, any issues that would make the title uninsurable must be resolved before the title company will issue a policy for settlement.

Unless the buyer has agreed to take title subject to certain liens, the seller will have to satisfy any liens in order to convey clear title. When the purchaser pays cash or obtains a new loan to purchase the property, the seller's existing loan is paid in full and satisfied on the record. The exact amount required to pay the existing loan as of the date of closing is provided in a *payoff statement* from the lender. This payoff statement notes the unpaid amount of principal, the interest due through the date of closing, the fee for issuing the certificate of satisfaction, credits (if any) for tax and insurance reserves, and the amount of any prepayment penalties. The same procedure is followed for any other liens that must be satisfied before the buyer takes title.

In a transaction in which the buyer assumes the seller's existing mortgage loan, the buyer will want to know the exact balance of the loan as of the closing date. In some areas, it is customary for the buyer to obtain a *mortgage reduction certificate* from the lender that certifies the amount owed on the mortgage loan, the interest rate, and the last interest payment made.

■ CONDUCTING CLOSINGS

Closings may be held at a number of locations, including the office of the title company, the lending institution, one of the parties' attorneys, the real estate broker, or the recorder of deeds. Those attending a closing may include

- the buyer;
- the seller;
- the real estate salesperson or broker (from the selling and/or listing office[s]);
- the attorney(s) for the seller and/or buyer;
- the representatives and/or attorneys for lending institutions involved with the buyer's new mortgage loan or the buyer's assumption of the seller's existing loan; and
- the representative of the title insurance company.

Closing agent or closing officer.   This person usually conducts the proceedings at a closing. The closing officer may be the attorney of the buyer or the seller, a real estate broker, or a representative of the lender or the title company. Some title companies and law firms employ paralegal assistants who conduct closings for their firms.

The closing officer is responsible for calculating the official settlement statement (Figure 22.1, discussed later in this chapter) and presenting the array of documents to the parties or their representatives for signature. The settlement statement is the final accounting of the financial arrangements between the parties, including each party's credits and debits.

The Exchange

Once each party is satisfied that all the documents are in order and properly signed, and the deed is delivered by the seller and accepted by the buyer, the purpose of the closing has been accomplished. Following closing, however, several important title procedures remain to be completed.

On the date of closing, the buyer has a title commitment or an abstract that was issued several days or weeks ahead of time. Consequently, the commitment or abstract may not necessarily be accurate as of the date of settlement. For this reason, a second search, known as a *bring down*, is made after the closing and immediately before any documents, including the new deed, are recorded. The purpose of this search is to identify any recordings since the previous search.

As part of this process, the seller may be required to execute an *affidavit of title*. This is a sworn statement in which the seller assures the title insurance company (and the buyer) that there have been no judgments, bankruptcies, or divorces involving the seller since the date of the title examination. The affidavit promises that no unrecorded deeds or contracts have been made, no repair or improvement costs have gone unpaid, and no defects in the title have arisen that the seller knows of. The seller also affirms that he or she is in possession of the premises. In some areas, this form is required before the title insurance company will issue an owner's policy to the buyer. The affidavit gives the title company the right to sue the seller if his or her statements in the affidavit are incorrect.

Once the person conducting the second search (the buyer's attorney or representative of the lender or title company) is satisfied that everything is in order, then the new deed and other documents can be recorded. The documents *must be recorded in the correct order* to avoid creating a defect in the title. For example, if the seller is paying off an existing loan and the buyer is obtaining a new one, the seller's satisfaction of mortgage must be recorded before the deed to the buyer is recorded. The buyer's new mortgage must then be recorded after the deed because the buyer cannot pledge the property as security for the loan until he or she owns it.

IRS Reporting Requirements

Certain real estate closings must be reported to the IRS on Form 1099-S. IRS regulations state the types of property transactions that are affected by this requirement and the information that must be reported. Generally, the information includes the sales price, the amount of property tax reimbursement credited to the seller, and the seller's Social Security number. If the closing agent does not notify the IRS, the responsibility for filing the form then falls on (in the following order) the mortgage lender, *the seller's broker, the buyer's broker,* or other persons as designated in the IRS regulations.

Licensee's Role in Closing the Transaction

Depending on the local custom, the licensee's role can vary from simply attending the closing (to collect the commission check) to the broker actually conducting the closing. The licensee may be authorized to represent one of the parties at closing. In any case, the licensee typically oversees a myriad of details so the transaction can proceed smoothly to closing.

IN PRACTICE

If a real estate licensee is going to represent a party at a closing, the licensee must be authorized to act as the principal's agent under a properly executed power of attorney. The form of this document must meet requirements of Pennsylvania law for a power of attorney, which (among other things) state that a power of attorney must include a specific notice by the principal that clearly describes the scope (or limits) of the authorization. The power of attorney must also include the agent's acknowledgement as agreement to act accordingly. The purpose is to ensure that both the principal and the agent have a clear understanding of the authority that is being delegated and the actions the agent is permitted to take on behalf of the principal.

Although the broker has essentially done what he or she was hired to do once the parties come to terms and sign the sales contract, today's transactions are far too complex to "let the ball drop" at this point. Typically, the licensee or a brokerage firm's staff member oversees the preparation for closing. While the degree of assistance varies, often it involves ordering closing exhibits, coordinating property inspections or repairs, and locating a mortgage lender to satisfy contingencies.

Mortgage lenders, title insurers, settlement companies, home inspectors, and contractors often promote their services to real estate licensees with the hope that licensees will direct business to them. Sometimes, they offer referral fees or a commission as an added incentive. Licensees must be careful *not to recommend* specific providers of services. The licensee could be held liable if the buyer or seller is injured by the service provider. State licensing laws require the licensee to disclose any financial interest he or she has in any services that are provided. Salespersons and associate brokers accepting referral fees or things of value associated with those services may be in violation of both state licensing laws and the Real Estate Settlement Procedures Act (discussed later in this chapter).

Lender's Interest in Closing

Whether a buyer obtains new financing or assumes the seller's existing loan, the lender wants to protect its security interest in the property. The lender has a stake in the condition of both the title and the physical property. The lender wants assurance that the mortgage lien will have priority over other liens and that the property is protected in case it is damaged or destroyed. For this reason, a lender generally requires a title insurance policy and a fire and hazard insurance policy. In addition, a lender may require other information: a survey, a termite or other inspection report, or a certificate of occupancy. A lender also may require that a reserve or escrow account be established for property tax and insurance payments. Lenders sometimes even require representation by their own attorneys at the closing.

■ RESPA REQUIREMENTS

RESPA's Consumer Protections

- CLO regulation
- AfBA disclosure
- Settlement cost booklet
- Good-faith estimate of settlement costs
- Uniform Settlement Statement
- Prohibition of kickbacks and unearned fees

The federal **Real Estate Settlement Procedures Act (RESPA)** aids consumers during the mortgage loan settlement process by ensuring that consumers are provided with important, accurate, and timely information about the actual costs of settling or closing a transaction. RESPA protects consumers from abusive lending practices and eliminates kickbacks and other referral fees that tend to inflate the costs of settlement unnecessarily. RESPA is administered by HUD.

RESPA requirements apply when a purchase is financed by a federally related mortgage loan. *Federally related loans* means loans made by banks, savings and loan associations, or other lenders whose deposits are insured by federal agencies. Loans insured by the FHA or guaranteed by the VA; loans administered by HUD; and loans intended to be sold by the lenders to Fannie Mae, Ginnie Mae, or Freddie Mac are also federally related loans.

RESPA regulations apply to first-lien residential mortgage loans made to finance the purchase of one- to four-unit homes, cooperatives, and condominiums for either investment or occupancy. RESPA also governs second or subordinate liens for home equity loans. A transaction financed solely by a purchase money mortgage taken back by the seller, an installment contract (contract for deed), or the buyer's assumption of the seller's existing loan would not be covered by RESPA. However, if the terms of the assumed loan were modified or the lender charges more than $50 for the assumption, the transaction is subject to RESPA regulations.

Settlement Service Providers

In addition to federally related loan providers, other entities fall under HUD's scrutiny because of the services they provide consumers in the purchase or settlement of a home (not after the settlement). *Settlement service providers* by definition include real estate brokers and agents, title companies and title agents, home warranty companies, hazard insurance companies, appraisers, flood and tax service providers, and home and pest inspectors as well as mortgage bankers and mortgage brokers. HUD's concerns about providers of settlement services are that consumers must be able to choose the service providers with whom they do business and that the consumer not be victimized by undisclosed business (and consequently financial) arrangements those providers may have with one another.

In a sense, the real world of settlement practices is a balancing act. Consumers desire the convenience of "one-stop-shopping," that all of the services they need for settlement can be easily arranged and coordinated through to closing at "one stop." The hub of those arrangements is typically the real estate broker and his or her agents who connect consumers to an array of service providers. The RESPA challenge arises when the consumer's interest is compromised by the arrangement of services or the selection of service providers. RESPA does not intend to prevent settlement service providers from engaging in competitive marketing or business practices, but it does intend to protect against deceptive practices.

Affiliated Business Arrangements

Affiliated business arrangements (AfBAs) are networks of interrelated companies that offer real estate-related services. AfBAs are formal business organizations in which companies are tied to one another by ownership interests. A real estate company, for example, may have an ownership tie with companies that are settlement service providers (as previously defined). AfBAs suit the one-stop-shop service that consumers desire; however, these joint ventures cannot prevent consumers from choosing other service providers. RESPA permits AfBAs *as long as*

■ the joint venture relationship between companies is disclosed when the consumer is referred to a company;
■ the consumer is not required to use an affiliated service provider as a condition for the sale or purchase of a home; and
■ the referring agent does not receive any payments from the joint venture company. The financial benefit of AfBAs is solely a function of enhanced return in the ownership interest of a company and is not based on the volume of referrals to the joint venture company.

In other words, fees may not be exchanged among the affiliated companies simply for referring business to one another.

Disclosure Requirements

Lenders and settlement agents have certain *disclosure* obligations at the time of a loan application and at the closing of a loan.

■ *Special information booklet*— Lenders must provide a copy of a special HUD informational booklet, titled *Settlement Costs and You,* to every person from whom they receive or for whom they prepare a loan application (except for refinancing). The booklet must be given at the time the application is received or within three days afterward. The booklet provides the borrower with general information about settlement (closing) costs. It also explains the various provisions of RESPA, including a line-by-line discussion of the Uniform Settlement Statement.
■ *Good-faith estimate of settlement costs*—No later than three business days after the receipt of the loan application, the lender must provide the

borrower with a good faith estimate of the settlement costs the borrower is likely to incur. This estimate may be a specific figure or a range of costs based on comparable past transactions in the area. In addition, if the lender requires use of a particular attorney or title company to conduct the closing, the lender must state whether it has any business relationship with that firm and must estimate the charges for this service.

■ *Uniform Settlement Statement (HUD-1 Form)*—RESPA requires that a special HUD form be completed to itemize all charges to be paid by the borrower and seller in connection with settlement. The Uniform Settlement Statement includes all charges that will be collected at closing, whether required by the lender or a third party. Items paid by the borrower and seller outside closing and not required by the lender are not included on HUD-1. Charges required by the lender that are paid for before closing are indicated as paid "outside of closing" (POC).

Borrowers have the right to inspect the completed HUD-1, to the extent that the figures are available, *one business day before the closing.* (RESPA does not require that this right be extended to sellers; in practice, however, often they do get to preview the statement.) Lenders must retain these statements for two years after the date of closing, unless the loan (and its servicing) is sold or otherwise disposed of. The Uniform Settlement Statement may be altered to allow for local custom, and certain lines may be deleted if they do not apply in the area.

IN PRACTICE

Real estate licensees in Pennsylvania are required to prepare statements of estimated closing costs for buyers and sellers on appropriate forms prior to their signing the agreement of sale. Therefore, the buyers should already have a general idea of the cash requirements needed for settlement before making the loan application.

Escrow Accounts

Lenders are permitted to set up escrow accounts for property taxes and insurance. (One account per loan is permissible in lieu of separate accounts for tax and insurance.) However, RESPA prohibits lenders from requiring excessive amounts of money be deposited in escrow to protect the borrower from over-billing. Lenders are not permitted to accumulate a cushion of more than two months' payments for taxes and insurance. The two-month calculation is based on the total disbursements for taxes and insurance. RESPA also requires that lenders pay the tax and insurance bills out of the account in a timely manner.

Kickbacks and Referral Fees

RESPA explicitly *prohibits the payment of kickbacks, or unearned fees* associated with a real estate settlement service (such as mortgage loans, title searches, title insurance, services rendered by attorneys, surveys, credit reports, or appraisals). It prohibits both the *payment* and the *receipt of* a fee, kickback, or anything of value for referrals *when no services are actually rendered.* Fee splitting or referral fees between cooperating brokers or members of multiple-listing services, brokerage referral arrangements, or the division of a commission between a broker and the broker's salespeople are not prohibited under RESPA.

In Computerized Loan Origination (CLO) systems, brokers may charge a fair fee for providing the mortgage loan accessing service. However, the *borrower* (not the mortgage broker or lender) *must pay the fee.* According to RESPA, these service and fee arrangements are permissible as long as they are properly disclosed, fees are charged for services actually rendered, and the mortgage broker or lender does not pay a referral fee for the loan. As stated earlier, companies in AfBAs cannot exchange fees simply for referring business.

IN PRACTICE   RESPA rules are detailed and are constantly being clarified. Proposals to reform RESPA are currently being discussed between HUD and industry groups representing settlement service providers. HUD has also been quite vigilant recently in investigating activities of real estate companies, title companies, builders, and others providing services for residential purchases. This introduction to RESPA intends to alert licensees to the major provisions of the rules. Specific questions, including the two-month escrow calculation and interpretation of the rules for AfBAs, CLOs, and kickbacks and referral fees, should be referred to HUD or legal counsel.

■ PREPARATION OF SETTLEMENT STATEMENTS

A typical real estate transaction involves, in addition to the purchase price, expenses for both parties. These include items prepaid by the seller for which he or she must be reimbursed (such as prepaid taxes) and items of expense the seller has incurred, but for which the buyer will be billed (such as mortgage interest paid in arrears when a loan is assumed). The financial responsibility for these items must be *prorated* (or divided) between the buyer and the seller. All expenses and prorated items are accounted for on the settlement statement. This is how the exact amount of cash required from the buyer and the net proceeds to the seller are determined. (See Figure 22.1.)

How the Settlement Statement Works

The completion of a settlement statement involves an accounting of the parties' debits and credits. A **debit** is a charge, that is, an amount that the party being debited owes and must pay at the closing. A **credit** is an amount entered in a person's favor—an amount that has already been paid, an amount being reimbursed, or an amount the buyer promises to pay in the form of a loan.

> A *debt* is an amount *paid by* the buyer or seller.
>
> A *credit* is an amount *payable* to the buyer or seller.

The amount the buyer needs at the closing is determined by totaling the buyer's debits. Any expenses and prorated amount for items prepaid by the seller are added to the purchase price. Then the buyer's credits are totaled. These include the earnest money (already paid), the balance of the loan the buyer obtains or assumes, and the seller's share of any prorated items the buyer will pay in the future. Finally, subtracting the total of the buyer's credits from the total debits equals the actual amount of cash the buyer must bring to closing (usually in the form of a cashier's or certified check).

A similar procedure is followed to determine how much money the seller will actually receive. The seller's debits and credits are each totaled. The credits include the purchase price plus the buyer's share of any prorated items that the seller has prepaid. The seller's debits include expenses, the seller's share of prorated items the buyer will pay later, and the balance of any mortgage loan or other lien that the seller is paying off. Finally, subtracting the total of the seller's charges from the total credits determines the amount the seller will receive.

F I G U R E   22.1

Sample HUD-1 Form

A. **Settlement Statement**   U.S. Department of Housing   OMB Approval No. 2502-0265
                                       and Urban Development

B. Type of Loan

1. ☐ FHA 2. ☐ FmHA 3. ☐ Conv. Unins.	6. File Number:	7. Loan Number:	8. Mortgage Insurance Case Number:
4. ☐ VA 5. ☐ Conv. Ins.			

C. Note: This form is furnished to give you a statement of actual settlement costs. Amounts paid to and by the settlement agent are shown. Items marked "(p.o.c.)" were paid outside the closing; they are shown here for informational purposes and are not included in the totals.

D. Name & Address of Borrower:	E. Name & Address of Seller:	F. Name & Address of Lender:

G. Property Location:	H. Settlement Agent:
	Place of Settlement:	I. Settlement Date:

J. Summary of Borrower's Transaction		K. Summary of Seller's Transaction	
100. Gross Amount Due From Borrower		**400. Gross Amount Due To Seller**	
101. Contract sales price		401. Contract sales price	
102. Personal property		402. Personal property	
103. Settlement charges to borrower (line 1400)		403.	
104.		404.	
105.		405.	
Adjustments for items paid by seller in advance		**Adjustments for items paid by seller in advance**	
106. City/town taxes to		406. City/town taxes to	
107. County taxes to		407. County taxes to	
108. Assessments to		408. Assessments to	
109.		409.	
110.		410.	
111.		411.	
112.		412.	
120. Gross Amount Due From Borrower		**420. Gross Amount Due To Seller**	
200. Amounts Paid By Or In Behalf Of Borrower		**500. Reductions In Amount Due To Seller**	
201. Deposit or earnest money		501. Excess deposit (see instructions)	
202. Principal amount of new loan(s)		502. Settlement charges to seller (line 1400)	
203. Existing loan(s) taken subject to		503. Existing loan(s) taken subject to	
204.		504. Payoff of first mortgage loan	
205.		505. Payoff of second mortgage loan	
206.		506.	
207.		507.	
208.		508.	
209.		509.	
Adjustments for items unpaid by seller		**Adjustments for items unpaid by seller**	
210. City/town taxes to		510. City/town taxes to	
211. County taxes to		511. County taxes to	
212. Assessments to		512. Assessments to	
213.		513.	
214.		514.	
215.		515.	
216.		516.	
217.		517.	
218.		518.	
219.		519.	
220. Total Paid By/For Borrower		**520. Total Reduction Amount Due Seller**	
300. Cash At Settlement From/To Borrower		**600. Cash At Settlement To/From Seller**	
301. Gross Amount due from borrower (line 120)		601. Gross amount due to seller (line 420)	
302. Less amounts paid by/for borrower (line 220) (	)	602. Less reductions in amt. due seller (line 520) (	)
303. Cash ☐ From ☐ To Borrower		**603. Cash** ☐ To ☐ From Seller	

Section 5 of the Real Estate Settlement Procedures Act (RESPA) requires the following: • HUD must develop a Special Information Booklet to help persons borrowing money to finance the purchase of residential real estate to better understand the nature and costs of real estate settlement services; • Each lender must provide the booklet to all applicants from whom it receives or for whom it prepares a written application to borrow money to finance the purchase of residential real estate; • Lenders must prepare and distribute with the Booklet a Good Faith Estimate of the settlement costs that the borrower is likely to incur in connection with the settlement. These disclosures are manadatory.

Section 4(a) of RESPA mandates that HUD develop and prescribe this standard form to be used at the time of loan settlement to provide full disclosure of all charges imposed upon the borrower and seller. These are third party disclosures that are designed to provide the borrower with pertinent information during the settlement process in order to be a better shopper.

The Public Reporting Burden for this collection of information is estimated to average one hour per response, including the time for reviewing instructions, searching existing data sources, gathering and maintaining the data needed, and completing and reviewing the collection of information.

This agency may not collect this information, and you are not required to complete this form, unless it displays a currently valid OMB control number.

The information requested does not lend itself to confidentiality.

F I G U R E 22.1

Sample HUD-1 Form (continued)

L. Settlement Charges				Paid From Borrowers Funds at Settlement	Paid From Seller's Funds at Settlement
700. Total Sales/Broker's Commission based on price $		@	% =		
Division of Commission (line 700) as follows:					
701. $	to				
702. $	to				
703. Commission paid at Settlement					
704.					
800. Items Payable In Connection With Loan					
801. Loan Origination Fee	%				
802. Loan Discount	%				
803. Appraisal Fee	to				
804. Credit Report	to				
805. Lender's Inspection Fee					
806. Mortgage Insurance Application Fee to					
807. Assumption Fee					
808.					
809.					
810.					
811.					
900. Items Required By Lender To Be Paid In Advance					
901. Interest from	to	@$	/day		
902. Mortgage Insurance Premium for		months to			
903. Hazard Insurance Premium for		years to			
904.		years to			
905.					
1000. Reserves Deposited With Lender					
1001. Hazard insurance	months@$	per month			
1002. Mortgage insurance	months@$	per month			
1003. City property taxes	months@$	per month			
1004. County property taxes	months@$	per month			
1005. Annual assessments	months@$	per month			
1006.	months@$	per month			
1007.	months@$	per month			
1008.	months@$	per month			
1100. Title Charges					
1101. Settlement or closing fee	to				
1102. Abstract or title search	to				
1103. Title examination	to				
1104. Title insurance binder	to				
1105. Document preparation	to				
1106. Notary fees	to				
1107. Attorney's fees	to				
(includes above items numbers:			)		
1108. Title insurance	to				
(includes above items numbers:			)		
1109. Lender's coverage	$				
1110. Owner's coverage	$				
1111.					
1112.					
1113.					
1200. Government Recording and Transfer Charges					
1201. Recording fees: Deed $	; Mortgage $	; Releases $			
1202. City/county tax/stamps: Deed $	; Mortgage $				
1203. State tax/stamps: Deed $	; Mortgage $				
1204.					
1205.					
1300. Additional Settlement Charges					
1301. Survey	to				
1302. Pest inspection to					
1303.					
1304.					
1305.					
1400. Total Settlement Charges (enter on lines 103, Section J and 502, Section K)					

Expenses

In addition to the payment of the sales price and the proration of taxes, interest, and the like, a number of other expenses and charges may be involved in a real estate transaction.

Brokerage fees.   The responsibility for paying the broker's fee (or fees) will have been determined by previous agreement. Depending on the provisions of the agency agreement(s), the seller, the buyer, or both may be responsible for paying brokerage fees. These fees may be paid only to the broker, not directly to the salesperson or associate broker involved in the transaction.

Attorney's fees.   If either of the parties' attorneys will be paid from the closing proceeds, that party will be charged with the expense on the closing statement. This expense may include fees for the preparation or review of documents or for representing the parties at settlement.

Recording expenses.   The *seller* usually pays for recording charges (filing fees) necessary to clear all defects and furnish the purchaser with clear title according to the terms of the contract. Items customarily charged to the seller include recording the satisfaction of mortgages, quitclaim deeds, affidavits, and satisfaction of mechanic's lien claims. The *buyer* pays for recording charges that arise from the actual transfer of the title, such as the deed the buyer received and the mortgage the buyer executed. The actual recording charge varies with the page-count of the document and the number of additional registrations involved.

Transfer tax.   State and local transfer taxes on certain real estate transactions are payable at closing. Currently, the amount of the state tax is 1 percent of the consideration or value (if there is no consideration); the amount of local taxes varies. Responsibility for these charges is as stated in the agreement of sale. The buyer and the seller might share this expense equally or they might agree to some other arrangement.

In Your State   **PA**   **Title expenses.**   Responsibility for title expenses varies according to local custom. As discussed earlier, the buyer is normally responsible for charges associated with title evidence (such as the title search and title insurance or certificate of title). When buyers purchase title insurance, they are charged all-inclusive rates that are set by the Pennsylvania Title Insurance Rating Bureau. These rates cover the initial title search, the later search to bring down the title to the closing date and the title insurance policy. (See Figure 22.2.) The Pennsylvania Department of Insurance recently determined that title insurers must disclose that the purchaser of a title policy prior to closing may be entitled to a reduced rate if previous insurance on the same property was issued within ten years. RESPA prohibits sellers from requiring, as a condition of a sale, that a buyer purchase title insurance from a particular company. ■

Letters or certifications from local municipalities, municipal utility authorities (such as water or sewage), or real estate taxing bodies also may be required. Depending on local billing practices and recording procedures, there may be

FIGURE 22.2

Schedule of Title Insurance Rates

ALL INCLUSIVE SCHEDULE OF RATES
Pennsylvania
$0-1,000,000 Effective Jan 1, 2002

SCHEDULE OF RATES UNDER COMPANY OR AGENCY PROCEDURE

The rate of Owners, Leasehold and Mortgage Insurance shall be:

UNIT OF INSURANCE OR FRACTION THEREOF		BASIC	REISSUE
0 -	30,000	420.00	378.00
30,001 -	31,000	427.25	384.53
31,001 -	32,000	434.50	391.05
32,001 -	33,000	441.75	397.58
33,001 -	34,000	449.00	404.10
34,001 -	35,000	456.25	410.63
35,001 -	36,000	463.50	417.15
36,001 -	37,000	470.75	423.68
37,001 -	38,000	478.00	430.20
38,001 -	39,000	485.25	436.73
39,001 -	40,000	492.50	443.25
40,001 -	41,000	499.75	449.78
41,001 -	42,000	507.00	456.30
42,001 -	43,000	514.25	462.83
43,001 -	44,000	521.50	469.35
44,001 -	45,000	528.75	475.88
45,001 -	46,000	534.75	481.28
46,001 -	47,000	540.75	486.68
47,001 -	48,000	546.75	492.08
48,001 -	49,000	552.75	497.48
49,001 -	50,000	558.75	502.88
50,001 -	51,000	564.75	508.28
51,001 -	52,000	570.75	513.68
52,001 -	53,000	576.75	519.08
53,001 -	54,000	582.75	524.48
54,001 -	55,000	588.75	529.88
55,001 -	56,000	594.75	535.28
56,001 -	57,000	600.75	540.68
57,001 -	58,000	606.75	546.08
58,001 -	59,000	612.75	551.48
59,001 -	60,000	618.75	556.
60,001 -	61,000	624.75	
61,001 -	62,000	630.7	
62,001 -	63,000		
63,001 -	64,000		
64,001 -	65,00		
65,001 -			
66,00			

		4,206.38	
	.50	4,209.75	
		4,681.25	4,213.13
01 -	987,000	4,685.00	4,216.50
987,001 -	988,000	4,688.75	4,219.88
988,001 -	989,000	4,692.50	4,223.25
989,001 -	990,000	4,696.25	4,226.63
990,001 -	991,000	4,700.00	4,230.00
991,001 -	992,000	4,703.75	4,233.38
992,001 -	993,000	4,707.50	4,236.75
993,001 -	994,000	4,711.25	4,240.13
994,001 -	995,000	4,715.00	4,243.50
995,001 -	996,000	4,718.75	4,246.88
996,001 -	997,000	4,722.50	4,250.25
997,001 -	998,000	4,726.25	4,253.63
998,001 -	999,000	4,730.00	4,257.00
999,001 -	1,000,000	4,733.75	4,260.38

On The Excess Over $1,000,000:

	BASIC	REISSUE
$1,000,001 - $2,000,000 (add per thousand)	2.75	90% of Basic
$2,000,001 - $7,000,000 (add per thousand)	2.00	2.00
$7,000,001 - $30,000,000 (add per thousand)	1.50	1.50

outstanding obligations that would not be discovered when the title is searched. Lien letters and tax certification letters provide evidence that no charges are pending that could become liens. Fees are often charged for these documents; they are customarily paid by the seller.

Deed preparation fee. This fee is charged by the preparer of the new deed; it is customarily paid by the seller.

Loan fees. The loan origination fee and any discount points the lender charges for the buyer's mortgage loan are due at settlement. If the buyer assumes the seller's existing financing, an assumption fee may be due. The buyer usually pays the fees, though the parties may have stated in the agreement of sale that the seller will bear some or all of this expense. In addition, depending on the terms of the seller's mortgage loan, the seller may be responsible for a prepayment charge or penalty for paying off the loan before its due date.

Tax and insurance reserves (escrow accounts).   Most mortgage lenders require that borrowers provide a reserve fund or **escrow** account to pay future real estate taxes and insurance premiums. The borrower starts the account at closing by depositing funds to cover at least the amount of unpaid real estate taxes from the date of lien to the end of the current month. (The buyer receives a credit from the seller for any taxes due but not yet paid.) Afterward, an amount equal to one month's portion of the estimated taxes is included in the borrower's monthly mortgage payment. For insurance, the first year's premium is generally paid in full at closing. After that, an amount equal to one month's premium is included in the monthly mortgage payment.

Appraisal fees.   Either the seller or the purchaser pays the appraisal fees, depending on who orders the appraisal. When the buyer obtains a mortgage loan, it is customary for the lender to require an appraisal. In this case, the buyer usually bears the cost. If the fee is paid at the time of loan application, it is reflected on the closing statement as having already been paid—that is, paid outside of closing (POC).

Survey fees.   The purchaser who obtains a new mortgage loan customarily pays the survey fees. In some cases the agreement of sale may require the seller to furnish a survey.

Homeowner's insurance.   Typically, the lender requires the buyer to purchase a homeowner's insurance policy and provide evidence that coverage is in effect as of the date of closing. Unless the buyer provides evidence that the annual premium has been paid, this item is charged as a buyer's expense at closing. The seller cancels his or her policy and receives a refund of unused premium directly from the insurance company.

Additional fees.   Depending on the type of mortgage loan, the buyer may have FHA or PMI insurance premiums or VA funding fees to pay at closing. In addition, depending on local custom, fees for preparing and reviewing various closing documents may also be charged.

Accounting for Credits and Debits

The items that must be accounted for in the closing statement fall into two general categories: prorations or other amounts due to either the buyer or seller (credit to) and paid for by the other party (debit to) *and* expenses or items paid by the seller or buyer (debit only).

The *buyer's earnest money*, although credited to the buyer, *is not a debit to the seller*. The buyer receives a credit because that amount has already been paid toward the purchase price. As prescribed by state law, however, the money is held by the broker until settlement and will be included as part of the total amount due the seller. If the seller is paying off an existing loan and the buyer is obtaining a new one, these two items are accounted for with a debit *only to the seller for the amount of the payoff* and a credit *only to the buyer for the amount of the new loan.*

Accounting for expenses. Expenses paid out of the closing proceeds are a debit only to the party making the payment. Occasionally, an expense item (such as the state transfer tax) is shared by the buyer and the seller, and each party is debited for his or her portion of the expense.

The following list shows the items commonly credited to the buyer and the items commonly credited to seller. Other items may be included, depending on local custom.

Items Credited to Buyer (debited to seller)	Items Credited to Seller (debited to buyer)
1. Buyer's earnest money*	1. Sales price*
2. Unpaid principal balance of outstanding mortgage being assumed by buyer*	2. Prorated premium for unearned (prepaid) portion of fire insurance
3. Earned interest on existing assumed mortgage not yet payable (accrued)	3. Coal or fuel oil on hand, usually figured at current market price (prepaid)
4. Earned portion of general real estate tax not yet due (accrued)	4. Insurance and tax reserve (if any) when outstanding mortgage is being assumed by buyer (prepaid)
5. Unearned portion of current rent collected in advance	5. Refund to seller of prepaid water charge and similar expenses
6. Tenants' security deposits*	6. Unearned portion of general real estate tax, if paid in advance
7. Purchase-money mortgage	

* These items are not prorated; they are entered in full as listed.

Prorations

To *prorate* means to divide or distribute proportionately. At settlement, many expenses are prorated between the buyer and the seller.

Proration is the process of distributing financial responsibility between the buyer and the seller at closing for such items as loan interest, real estate taxes, rents, and fuel and utility bills. These allowances are necessary to ensure that the buyer and seller pay their fair share of certain expenses. For example, if the seller owes current taxes that have not yet been billed, the buyer would want an allowance for the portion of the year the seller has owned the property. If taxes have been paid in advance, the seller is entitled to a rebate of the unused amount at the closing. If the buyer assumes the seller's existing mortgage, the seller usually owes the buyer an allowance for accrued interest through the date of closing. Items to be prorated and settlement arrangements should be clearly stated in the agreement of sale.

Accrued items = buyer
credits

Prepaid items = seller
credits

The nature of the item being prorated, whether the item is accrued or prepaid and whether the calculation is based on a 360-day year (commonly called a banking year) or an actual year (365 days or 366 days in a leap year) must be considered when prorating. **Accrued items** are expenses to be prorated that are owed by the seller, but later will be paid by the buyer. The seller, therefore, pays for these items by giving the buyer a credit at closing. **Prepaid items** are expenses to be prorated that have been prepaid by the seller but not fully used up. They are, therefore, credits to the seller.

General rules for prorating.   Because the rules or customs governing computation of prorations vary widely, licensees should be aware of specific local customs and procedures in their area. The most important rule for prorating, however, is to follow the terms stated in the agreement of sale. General rules to keep in mind are as follows:

In Your State   **PA**

- In Pennsylvania, the seller owns the property on the day of closing, and prorations are usually *calculated to include the day of closing*.
- In Pennsylvania, real estate taxes are generally prepaid and may be due in the early part of the year. Depending on the time of year the settlement occurs and the tax payment schedule, proration could be for either accrued or prepaid taxes.
- Special assessments for municipal improvements are usually paid in annual installments over several years. The municipality usually charges the property owner annual interest on the outstanding balance of future installments. In a sales transaction, the seller normally pays the current installment and the buyer assumes all future installments. The special assessment installment generally is not prorated at the closing. Some buyers, however, insist that the seller allow them a credit for the seller's share of the interest to the closing date. The agreement of sale may state the manner in which special assessments are to be handled at settlement.
- Rents are usually prorated on the basis of the actual number of days in the month of closing. Customarily, the seller receives rent for the day of closing and pays all expenses for that day as well. If any rent for the month of settlement is uncollected, the buyer will often agree by a separate letter to collect the rent if possible and remit the prorata share to the seller.
- Security deposits made by tenants to cover the cost of repairing damage caused by the tenant or prepaid rent (rent for the last month of the tenancy) are generally transferred by the seller to the buyer. Because of Pennsylvania's regulations for holding security deposits, it is wise to get the tenant's consent to such a transfer.
- Depending on local custom, evidence of monthly or quarterly municipal utility charges (such as water and sewage charges) may be required at closing. The portion owed by the seller is debited through the date of closing; the prepaid portion is credited to the seller. Private utility companies normally handle their own final billing.

IN PRACTICE

Three taxing bodies levy general real estate taxes in Pennsylvania: county governments, municipal governments, and school districts. County and municipal governments (city, borough, and township) levy and assess taxes on a calendar year (January to December). Most school districts are required to levy and assess taxes on a July 1 to June 30 tax year. Licensees should be aware of the tax year and the due date for payment of each of the taxes.

■ THE ARITHMETIC OF PRORATING

The computation of prorations involves identifying a yearly charge for the item to be prorated, then dividing by 12 to determine a monthly charge for the item. Usually, it is also necessary to establish a daily charge for the item by dividing the monthly charge by the number of days in the month. These smaller portions are then multiplied by the number of months and/or days in the prorated time period to determine the accrued or unearned amount that will be figured in the settlement.

Following this general principle, there are two methods of calculating prorations:

1. Divide the yearly charge by a *360-day year*, or 12 months of 30 days each
2. Divide the yearly charge by 365 (366 in a leap year) to determine the daily charge, then the actual number of days in the proration is determined, and this number is multiplied by the daily charge

The final proration figure varies slightly, depending on which method is used. The final figure also varies according to the number of decimal places to which the division is carried. *All of the computations in this text are computed by carrying the division to three decimal places.* The third decimal place is rounded off to cents only after the final proration figure is determined.

Accrued Items

When the real estate tax is levied for the calendar year but has not yet been paid, the accrued portion is for the period from January 1 to the date of closing. If the current tax bill has not yet been issued, the parties must agree on an estimated amount based on the previous year's bill and any known changes in assessment or tax levy for the current year.

For example, assume a sale is to be closed on April 17, and current real estate taxes of $1,200 are to be prorated accordingly. The accrued period, then, is three months, 17 days. First determine the prorated cost of the real estate tax per month and day:

$$\$1,200 \div 12 = \$100 \text{ per month}$$
$$\$100 \div 30 = \$3.333 \text{ per day}$$

Next, multiply these figures by the accrued period and add the totals to determine the prorated real estate tax:

$$\$100 \times 3 \text{ months} = \$300$$
$$\$3.333 \times 17 \text{ days} = \$56.661$$
$$\$300.000 + 56.661 = \$356.661$$

Thus, the accrued real estate tax for three months, 17 days is $356.66 (rounded off to two decimal places after the final computation). This amount represents the seller's accrued earned tax; it will be *a credit to the buyer and a debit to the seller.*

While these examples prorate the tax as of the date of settlement, the agreement of sale may require otherwise. For instance, a buyer's possession date may not coincide with the settlement date. In this case, the parties could prorate according to the date of possession.

IN PRACTICE

On Pennsylvania licensing examinations, tax prorations are usually based on a 30-day month (360-day year) unless specified otherwise in the problem. In practice, however, it is customary to base prorations on a 365-day year (366 days in leap years) in most areas. This is easily done by using a tax factor chart. The tax proration is determined by simply multiplying the factor given for the closing date by the annual real estate tax.

Prepaid Items

A tax proration could be a prepaid item. Because real estate tax may be paid in the early part of the year, tax prorations calculated for closings taking place later in the year must reflect the fact that the seller has already paid the tax. For example, in the above problem, suppose that the closing did not take place until September 17 and that the taxes had been paid. The buyer, then, must reimburse the seller; the proration is a *credit to the seller and a debit to the buyer.*

In figuring the tax proration, it is necessary to determine the number of future days, months, and years for which the taxes have been paid. The formula commonly used for this purpose is as follows:

	Years	Months	Days
Taxes paid to (Dec. 31, end of tax year)	2006	12	31
Date of closing (Sept. 17, 2006)	2006	9	17
Period for which tax must be paid		3	14

With this formula we can find the amount the buyer will reimburse the seller for the *unearned* portion of the real estate tax. The prepaid period, as determined using the formula for prepaid items, is three months, 14 days. Three months at $100 per month equals $300, and 14 days at $3.333 per day = $46.662. Add this up to determine that the proration is $346.662, or $346.66 *credited to the seller and debited to the buyer.*

Another example of a prepaid item is a water bill. Assume that the water is billed in advance by the city without using a meter. The six months' billing is $8 for the period ending October 31. The sale is to be closed on August 3. Because the water bill is paid to October 31, the prepaid time must be computed. Using a 30-day basis, the time period is the 27 days left in August plus two full months: $8 ÷ 6 = $1.333 per month. For one day, divide $1.333 by 30, which equals $0.044 per day. The prepaid period is two months, 27 days, so:

$$27 \text{ days} \quad \times \$0.044 = \$1.188$$
$$2 \text{ months} \quad \times \$1.333 = \underline{\$2.666}$$
$$\$3.854 \text{ or } \$3.85$$

This is a prepaid item; it is *credited to the seller and debited to the buyer.*

To figure this on the basis of the actual days in the month of closing, use the following process:

$1.333 per month ÷ 31 days in August	=	$.043 per day
August 4 through August 31	=	28 days
28 days × $.043	=	$1.204
2 months × $1.333	=	$2.666
$1.204 + $2.666	=	$3.870 or $3.87

■ SUMMARY

Closing a sale involves both title procedures and financial matters. The broker should be present at the closing to see that the sale is actually concluded and to account for the earnest money deposit.

Most closings must be reported to the IRS on Form 1099-S.

The federal Real Estate Settlement Procedures Act (RESPA) requires disclosure of all settlement costs when a real estate purchase is financed by a federally related mortgage loan. RESPA requires lenders to use a Uniform Settlement Statement (HUD-1) to detail the financial particulars of a transaction.

Usually the buyer orders and pays for the title evidence, such as title insurance, to ensure that the seller's title is acceptable.

The actual amount to be paid by the buyer at the closing is computed by preparation of a closing, or settlement, statement. This lists the sales price, earnest money deposit, and all adjustments and prorations due between buyer and seller. The purpose of this statement is to determine the net amount due to the seller at closing and the cash requirements of the buyer. The form is signed by both parties to evidence their approval.

QUESTIONS

1. Which of the following is true of real estate closings in Pennsylvania?
   a. Closings are generally conducted by real estate salespeople.
   b. The buyer usually receives the rents for the day of closing.
   c. The seller pays the brokers' fees.
   d. The buyer pays for title evidence.

2. All encumbrances and liens shown on the report of title, other than those waived or agreed to by the purchaser and listed in the contract, must be removed so that the title can be delivered free and clear. The removal of such encumbrances is the duty of the
   a. buyer.
   b. seller.
   c. broker
   d. title company.

3. Legal title passes from the seller to the buyer
   a. on the date of execution of the deed.
   b. when the closing statement has been signed by the parties.
   c. when the deed is recorded.
   d. when the deed is delivered and accepted.

4. Which of the following would a lender generally require to be produced at the closing?
   a. Title insurance policy
   b. Market value appraisal
   c. Application
   d. Credit report

5. When an item to be prorated is owed but has not been paid by the seller,
   a. the amount owed is a credit to the buyer.
   b. the amount owed is a debit to the seller.
   c. the amount owed is a debit to the buyer.
   d. Both a and b

6. The RESPA Uniform Settlement Statement must be used to illustrate all settlement charges for
   a. every real estate transaction.
   b. transactions financed by VA and FHA loans only.
   c. residential transactions financed by federally related mortgage loans.
   d. all transactions involving commercial property.

7. A mortgage reduction certificate is executed by a(n)
   a. abstract company.
   b. attorney.
   c. lending institution.
   d. grantor.

8. The principal amount of the purchaser's new mortgage loan is a
   a. credit to the seller.
   b. credit to the buyer.
   c. debit to the seller.
   d. debit to the buyer.

9. The annual real estate taxes amount to $1,800 and have been paid in advance for the calendar year. If closing is set for June 15 with taxes prorated as of the date of settlement, which of the following is true?
   a. Credit seller $825; debit buyer $975
   b. Credit seller $1,800; debit buyer $825
   c. Credit buyer $975; debit seller $975
   d. Credit seller $975; debit buyer $975

10. The seller collected rent of $400, payable in advance, from the tenant on August 1. At the closing on August 15, the
    a. seller owes the buyer $400.
    b. buyer owes the seller $400.
    c. seller owes the buyer $200.
    d. buyer owes the seller $200.

11. Security deposits should be listed on a closing statement as a credit to the
    a. buyer.
    b. seller.
    c. lender
    d. broker.

12. A building was bought for $50,000, with 10 percent down and a loan for the balance. If the lender charged the buyer two discount points, how much cash did the buyer need at closing to pay the fee?
    a. $6,900
    b. $5,900
    c. $5,200
    d. $900

13. A buyer of a $50,000 home has paid $2,000 in earnest money and has a loan commitment for 70 percent of the purchase price. How much more cash does the buyer need to complete the transaction provided there are no other closing costs?
    a. $10,000
    b. $13,000
    c. $15,000
    d. $35,000

14. At the closing, the seller's attorney gave credit to the buyer for certain accrued items. These items were
    a. bills relating to the property that have already been paid by the seller.
    b. bills relating to the property that will have to be paid by the buyer.
    c. all of the seller's real estate bills.
    d. all of the buyer's real estate bills.

15. The Real Estate Settlement Procedures Act (RESPA) applies to the activities of
    a. a broker selling commercial and office buildings.
    b. security salespersons selling limited partnerships.
    c. Ginnie Mae or Fannie Mae when purchasing loans.
    d. lenders financing the purchase of a borrower's residence.

16. The purpose of RESPA is to
    a. make sure buyers do not borrow more than they can repay.
    b. make real estate brokers more responsive to buyer's needs.
    c. prohibit affiliated business arrangements among providers of settlement services.
    d. inform buyers about the costs of settling or closing a transaction.

ANSWERS

1. D Both the buyer and the buyer's lender want assurance that title to the property being conveyed complies with terms of the transfer. The buyer is responsible for determining that he or she is receiving good title to the property. Title evidence, such as an abstract of title or title insurance, is normally a charge paid by the buyer. (p. 421)

2. B Unless the buyer has agreed to take title subject to certain liens or encumbrances, the seller will be expected to satisfy or remove the liens or encumbrances in order to convey clear title to the property. (p. 412)

3. D Transfer of title to real estate occurs when a deed is delivered to and accepted by a grantee. The settlement statement is the final accounting of financial arrangements between the parties. A grantor may execute (sign) the deed prior to settlement, and recording occurs subsequent to the closing to give constructive notice of the grantee's interest. (p. 413)

4. A The application, credit report, and appraisal are required by a lender prior to committing funds for the loan. The lender will require a title insurance policy at closing in order to protect their interest in the property. (p. 415)

5. D A debit is a charge that is owed and will be paid in the future. A credit is an amount entered in a person's favor. An item owed by the seller but not yet paid at the time of closing will be entered as a debt to the seller and as a credit to the buyer. (p. 424)

6. C RESPA requirements apply when a purchase is financed by a federally related mortgage loan. The regulations apply to first lien residential mortgage loans made to finance the purchase of one-to-four family homes, cooperatives, and condominiums for either investment or occupancy. (p. 415)

7. C In a transaction in which a buyer assumes a seller's existing mortgage, it is customary for the buyer to obtain a mortgage reduction certificate executed by the lender that certifies the amount owed on the mortgage loan, the interest rate, and the last interest payment made. (p. 412)

8. B The amount the buyer promises to pay in the form of a loan is entered in the buyer's favor as a credit on the settlement statement. (p. 418)

9. D If real estate taxes amount to $1,800 per year ($150 per month) and have been paid in advance for the year, the seller is entitled to be reimbursed for the period from June 15 to the end of the year. The buyer is responsible for this time period. Therefore, the seller receives a credit for $975 ($150 per month times 6.5 months). This amount is debited to the buyer. (p. 424)

10. C When the August rent of $400 was paid to the seller on August 1 and the property sale closed on August 15, the seller owed the buyer the amount of rent from the closing date to the end of the month, or $200. (p. 424)

11. A A credit is an amount entered in a person's favor on the settlement statement. The amount is due to be paid to the party. Tenant security deposits are entered as a credit to the buyer. (p. 424)

12. D If the purchase price is $50,000 and the buyer has a 10 percent down payment ($5,000), the loan amount is $45,000. Each discount point represents one percent of the loan amount, or $450. If the lender charges two discount points, the buyer will pay $900 at closing. (p. 372)

13. B With a sale price of $50,000 and a loan commitment for 70 percent of the purchase price, the loan amount will be $35,000 ($50,000 × 70%). The loan amount plus the earnest money paid equals $37,000 ($35,000 + 2,000) Therefore, the buyer needs $13,000 to complete the transaction ($50,000 – $37,000). (p. 418)

14. B A credit given by the seller to the buyer for certain accrued items (those items owed but not yet paid) would be entered on the settlement statement to account for bills relating to the property that will be paid by the buyer after closing. (p. 425)

15. D The federal Real Estate Settlement Procedures Act (RESPA) covers federally related loans made by banks, savings and loan associations, or other lenders whose deposits are insured by federal agencies. It also includes lenders who write FHA-insured or VA-guaranteed loans and loans intended to be sold to Fannie Mae, Ginnie Mae, or Freddie Mac. It covers first lien residential mortgage loans on single-family to four-family homes. (p. 415)

16. D The purpose of the Real Estate Settlement Procedures Act (RESPA) is to protect consumers by ensuring that they are provided with important, accurate, and timely information about the actual costs of closing a transaction. (p. 415)

CHAPTER TWENTY-THREE

PROPERTY MANAGEMENT

■ LEARNING OBJECTIVES

When you've finished reading this chapter, you should be able to

■ identify the basic elements of a management agreement;
■ describe a property manager's functions;
■ explain the role of environment regulations and the Americans with Disabilities Act in the property manager's job;
■ distinguish the various ways of managing risk; and
■ define the key terms.

■ KEY TERMS

life-cycle costing	multiperil policies	risk management
management agreement	property manager	tenant improvements

■ THE PROPERTY MANAGER

Property management is a real estate specialization that involves the leasing, management, marketing, and overall maintenance of real estate owned by others. The three principal responsibilities for each property being managed are

1. fiscal management (financial affairs),
2. physical management (structure and grounds), and
3. administrative management (files and records).

The **property manager** is responsible for maintaining the owner's investment and making sure that the property earns income. This can be done in several ways. The physical property must be maintained in good condition. Suitable tenants must be found, rent must be collected, and employees must be hired and supervised. The property manager is responsible for budgeting and controlling expenses, keeping proper accounts, and making periodic reports to

A *property manager*

- maintains the owner's investment and
- ensures that the property produces income.

the owner. In all of these activities, the manager's primary goal is to maximize income and control expenses, and to maintain the physical property in such a way as to preserve and enhance the owner's capital investment.

The services of property managers are valuable to a variety of owners. These services include

- corporations or institutions,
- apartment developers and landlords,
- condominiums,
- homeowners' associations,
- investment syndicates,
- trusts, and
- absentee owners of the real estate.

In Your State

PA In Pennsylvania, a property manager who serves the public for a fee must be a licensed real estate broker. This person may also be a real estate licensee affiliated with a property management company or a brokerage firm that has a property management department. Or a property manager may be an employee of the owner of the real estate. Property managers who are licensed perform under an agency relationship with the owner, which involves greater authority and discretion over management decisions than an employee would typically have. A property manager or an owner may employ building managers to supervise the daily operations of a building. In some cases, these may be residents of the building. Employees of the owners of residential multifamily dwellings performing certain tasks need not be licensed. ■

The Management Agreement

The first step in taking over the management of a property is to enter into a **management agreement** with the owner. This agreement creates an agency relationship between the owner and the property manager. The property manager usually is considered a *general agent* (as opposed to a special agent). As an agent, the property manager is charged with the fiduciary responsibilities of care, obedience, accounting, loyalty, and disclosure. After entering into an agreement with a property owner, a manager handles the property as the owner would. In all activities, the manager's first responsibility is to realize the highest return in a manner consistent with the owner's instructions.

As with any fiduciary relationship, the agent (in this case, the property manager) must be certain that he or she is capable of or willing to assume the responsibilities the relationship imposes. Before agreeing to manage any property, the professional property manager should determine whether the building owner has realistic expectations. Necessary maintenance, unexpected repairs, and effective marketing all take time and money. If the owner has unreasonable expectations, the manager's time will be wasted. Furthermore, the use of dubious methods endangers the manager's professional reputation.

Like any other contract involving real estate, the management agreement should be in writing. It should include the following items:

- Description of the property
- *Time period* of the agreement and specific provisions for termination

- *Definition of management's responsibilities*: The contract should specifically state all of the manager's duties, and the limitations or restrictions should also be included.

- *Statement of owner's purpose*: This statement should clearly state what the owner desires the manager to accomplish with the property. One owner may wish to maximize net income and, therefore, will instruct the manager to cut expenses and minimize reinvestment. Another owner may want to increase the capital value of the investment, in which case the manager should initiate a program for improving the property's physical condition.

- *Extent of manager's authority*: This provision should state what authority the manager is to have in matters such as hiring, firing, and supervising employees; fixing rental rates for space; and making expenditures and authorizing repairs within the limits established previously with the owner. Repairs that exceed a certain expense limit may require the owner's written approval.

- *Reporting*: The frequency and detail of the manager's periodic reports on operations and financial position should be agreed on. These reports serve as a means for the owner to monitor the manager's work. They also form a basis for both the owner and the manager to spot trends that can be used in shaping future management policy.

- *Compensation*: The management fee or other form of compensation may be based on a percentage of gross or net income, a fixed fee, or a combination of other factors. If the property manager also leases the property, commissions may be earned on the rentals as well. Management fees are subject to the same antitrust considerations (price fixing) as sales commissions. Compensation must be determined as a result of negotiations between the agent and the principal.

- *Allocation of costs*: The agreement should state which of the property manager's expenses, such as office rent, office help, telephone, advertising, association fees, and Social Security taxes, will be paid by the manager and which will be paid by the owner.

- *Equal opportunity statement*: The agreement should include a statement that the property will be leased and managed in accordance with all applicable state and federal civil rights laws.

MATH CONCEPTS

RENTAL COMMISSIONS

Residential commissions are usually based on the annualized rent from a property. For example, if an apartment unit rents for $475 per month and the commission payable is 8 percent, the commission will be calculated as follows:

$475 per month × 12 months = $5,700; $5,700 × 0.08 (8%) = $456

■ MANAGEMENT FUNCTIONS

A property manager's specific responsibilities are determined by the management agreement. Certain common duties, however, are found in most agreements. These include budgeting, capital expenditures, setting rental rates, selecting tenants, collecting rent, maintaining the property, and complying with legal requirements. Property managers must live up to both the letter and the spirit of the management agreement.

Budgeting Expenses

Before attempting to rent any property, a property manager should develop an *operating budget*. The budget should be based on anticipated revenues and expenses. In addition, it must reflect the owner's long-term goals. In preparing a budget, the manager should allocate money for continuous, *fixed expenses* such as employees' salaries, real estate taxes, property taxes, and insurance premiums.

Next, the manager should establish a *cash reserve fund* for variable expenses such as repairs, decorating, and supplies. The amount allocated can be computed from the previous yearly costs of the variable expenses.

Capital expenditures.   The owner and a property manager may decide that modernization or renovation of the property will enhance its value. In this case, the manager should budget money to cover the costs of remodeling. The property manager should be thoroughly familiar with the *principle of contribution* (as discussed in Chapter 21) or seek expert advice when estimating any increase in value expected from an improvement. In the case of large-scale construction, the expenditures charged against the property's income should be spread over several years.

The cost of equipment to be installed in a modernization or renovation must be evaluated over its entire useful life. This is called **life-cycle costing.** This term simply means that both the initial and the operating costs of equipment over its expected life must be measured to compare the total cost of one type of equipment with another.

IN PRACTICE

As the use of technology increases, property managers must look at how their properties meet the needs of today's tenants. Provisioning buildings that are *dark wired* (that is, providing internal communication infrastructure) is a capital expenditure that could pay enormous dividends in the long run. The technological capability of a property enhances its market appeal as well as its utility as tenants' needs become more sophisticated.

Renting the Property

Effective rental of the property is essential. However, the role of the manager in managing a property should not be confused with that of a broker acting as a leasing agent. The manager must be concerned with the long-term financial health of the property; the leasing agent is concerned solely with renting space. The property manager may use the services of a leasing agent, but that agent does not undertake the full responsibility of maintenance and management of the property. Leasing agents who are Pennsylvania real estate licensees must adhere to the license law and Real Estate Commission's Regulations, including Section 35.337 concerning the use of the Consumer Notice for the lease of residential or commercial property.

Setting rental rates.   Rental rates are influenced primarily by supply and demand. The property manager should conduct a detailed survey of the competitive space available in the neighborhood, emphasizing similar properties. In establishing rental rates, the property manager has four long-term considerations:

- Rental income must be sufficient to cover the property's fixed charges and operating expenses.
- Rental income must provide a fair return on the owner's investment.
- Rental rates should be in line with the prevailing rates in comparable buildings. These may be slightly higher or slightly lower, depending on the strength of the property.
- Current vacancy rate in the property is a good indicator of how much of a rent increase is advisable. A building with a low vacancy rate, that is, few vacant units, is a better candidate for an increase than one with a high vacancy rate.

Rental rates for residential space are usually stated in monthly amounts per unit. Commercial leases, including office, retail, and industrial space, usually state rental rates as a price per square foot.

If a high level of vacancy exists, the manager should attempt to determine the reason. An elevated level of vacancy does not necessarily indicate that rents are too high. Instead, the problem may be poor management or a defective or undesirable property. The manager should attempt to identify and correct the problems first rather than immediately lowering the rents. On the other hand, although a high percentage of occupancy may appear to indicate an effective rental program, it could also mean that rental rates are too low. Whenever the occupancy level of an apartment house or office building exceeds 95 percent, serious consideration may be given to raising the rents. First, however, the manager should investigate the rental market to determine whether a rent increase is warranted.

Selecting tenants.   A building manager's success depends on establishing and maintaining sound, long-term relationships with the tenants. The first and most important step is selection. The manager should be sure that the premises are suitable for a tenant in size, location, and amenities. If the tenant is likely to expand in the future, ways to accommodate additional space requirements should also be considered. Most important, the manager should be sure that the tenant is able to pay for the space.

A commercial tenant's business should be compatible with the building and the other tenants. The manager must consider the business interests of the current tenants as well as the interests of the potential tenant. The types of businesses or services should be complementary, and the introduction of competitors into the same property should be undertaken with care. This not only pleases existing tenants but also helps diversify the owner's investment and makes profitability more likely. Some commercial leases bar the introduction of similar businesses.

The property manager must comply with all federal, state, and local civil rights laws in the selection of both residential and commercial tenants.

Collecting rents.   The best way to minimize rental collection problems is to accept only those tenants who can be expected to meet their financial obligations. The desire for a high level of occupancy should not override good judgment. The manager should investigate financial references given by the prospect, check with local credit bureaus, and, when possible, interview the prospective tenant's former landlord.

The terms of rental payment should be spelled out in detail in the lease agreement, including

- the time and place of payment,
- provisions and penalties for late payment, and
- provisions for cancellation and damages in case of nonpayment.

The property manager should establish a firm and consistent collection plan. The plan should include a system of notices and records that complies with state and local law. Every attempt must be made to collect rent without resorting to legal action. Legal action is costly and time-consuming and does not contribute to good tenant relations. In some cases, however, legal action is unavoidable. In these instances, a property manager must be prepared to initiate and follow through with the necessary legal steps. Obviously, legal action must be taken in cooperation with the property owner's or management firm's legal counsel.

Maintaining Good Tenant Relations

The ultimate success of a property manager depends greatly on the ability to maintain good relations with tenants. Increased attention being given to landlord-tenant relationships by legal and judicial systems has added to the importance of this part of a manager's job. Dissatisfied tenants eventually vacate the property. A high tenant turnover results in greater expense for advertising and redecorating. It also means less profit for the owner due to uncollected rents.

An effective property manager establishes a good communication system with tenants. Regular newsletters or posted memoranda help keep tenants informed and involved. Maintenance and service requests must be attended to promptly, and all lease terms and building rules must be enforced consistently and fairly. A good manager is tactful and decisive and acts to the benefit of both owner and occupants.

The property manager must be able to handle residents who do not pay their rent on time or who break building regulations. When one tenant fails to follow the rules, the other tenants often become frustrated and dissatisfied. Careful record keeping shows whether rent is being remitted promptly and in the proper amount. Records of all lease renewal dates should be kept so that the manager can anticipate expiration and retain good tenants who might otherwise move when their leases end.

Maintaining the Property

One of the most important functions of a property manager is the supervision of property maintenance. A manager must balance the services provided with their costs. In other words, he or she must satisfy the tenants' needs while minimizing operating expenses.

To maintain the property efficiently, the manager must be able to assess the building's needs and how best to meet them. Staffing and scheduling requirements vary with the type, size, and regional location of the property, so the owner and manager usually agree in advance on maintenance objectives. In some cases, the best plan may be to operate low-rental property with minimal expenditures for services and maintenance. Another property may be more lucrative if kept in top condition and operated with all possible tenant services. A well-maintained, high-service property can command premium rental rates.

A primary maintenance objective is to *protect the physical integrity of the property over the long term.* For example, preserving the property by repainting the exterior or replacing the heating system helps keep the building functional and decreases long-term maintenance costs. Keeping the property in good condition involves four types of maintenance:

1. Preventive maintenance
2. Repair or corrective maintenance
3. Routine maintenance
4. Construction

> **Preventive** maintenance helps prevent problems and expenses.
>
> **Corrective** maintenance corrects problems after they've occurred.

Preventive maintenance includes regularly scheduled activities such as regular painting and seasonal servicing of appliances and systems. Preventive maintenance preserves the long-range value and physical integrity of the building. This is both the most critical and the most neglected maintenance responsibility. Failure to do preventive maintenance invariably leads to greater expense in other areas of maintenance.

Repair or *corrective maintenance* involves the actual repairs that keep the building's equipment, utilities, and amenities functioning. Repairing a boiler, fixing a leaky faucet, and repairing a broken air-conditioning unit are acts of repair maintenance.

A property manager must also supervise the *routine maintenance* of the building. Routine maintenance includes such day-to-day duties as cleaning common areas, performing minor carpentry and plumbing adjustments, and providing regularly scheduled upkeep of heating and air-conditioning systems and landscaping. Good routine maintenance is similar to good preventive maintenance. Both head off problems before they become expensive.

IN PRACTICE

One of the major decisions a property manager faces is whether to contract for maintenance services from an outside firm or to hire on-site employees to perform such tasks. This decision is usually based on factors such as the size of the building, the complexity of the tenants' requirements, and the availability of suitable labor.

Last is new *construction* or *renovation*. Especially when dealing with commercial or industrial space, a property manager may make **tenant improvements.** These are alterations to the interior of the building to meet a tenant's particular needs. Such construction alterations range from simply repainting or recarpeting to completely gutting the interior and redesigning the space. Tenant improvements are especially important when renting new buildings. In new construction, the interiors are usually left incomplete so that they can be adapted to the needs of individual tenants. One matter that must be clarified is which improvements will be considered trade fixtures (personal property belonging to the tenant) and which will belong to the owner of the real estate.

Modernization or renovation of buildings that have become functionally obsolete and thus unsuited to today's building needs is also important. The renovation of a building often enhances the building's marketability and increases its potential income.

Handling Environmental Concerns

With the proliferation of federal and state laws and increasing local regulation, environmental concerns have become a major issue for property managers. A variety of environmental issues, from waste disposal to air quality, must be addressed. Although property managers are not expected to be experts in all the disciplines necessary to operate a modern building, they are expected to be knowledgeable in many diverse subjects, most of which are technical in nature. Environmental concerns are one such subject.

The property manager must be able to respond to a variety of environmental problems. He or she may manage structures containing asbestos or radon or may be called on to arrange an environmental audit of a property. The managers must see that any hazardous wastes produced by their employers or tenants are properly disposed of. Even the normally nonhazardous waste of an office building must be controlled to avoid violating laws requiring segregation of types of wastes. The property manager may have to provide on-site recycling facilities and see that tenants sort their trash properly.

Complying with the ADA

The Americans with Disabilities Act (ADA) has a significant impact on the responsibilities of the property manager, both in building amenities and employment issues.

In Your State **PA** As discussed in Chapter 17, Title I of ADA and the Pennsylvania Human Relations Act (PHRA), obligations of employers to adopt nondiscriminatory employment practices are stipulated. The management of property often requires the employment of a variety of personnel. Property managers must pay particular attention to their recruitment, application, hiring, firing, advancement, compensation, training, and other employment procedures to ensure that the rights of people with disabilities (under ADA) and all persons in the protected classes (PHRA) are protected. ■

Property managers, as agents of the owners, also must comply with Title III of ADA. This addresses requirements for buildings in which business establishments are located and public services are provided. Title III prohibits discrimination against people with disabilities by ensuring access to the facilities and enjoyment of services in a full and equal manner. The property manager is typically responsible for procuring an audit of an existing building to determine whether it meets the accessibility requirements of ADA. The manager also must prepare a plan for retrofitting a building that is not in compliance. There are some income tax advantages available to help offset the cost of complying with ADA. ADA experts may be consulted, as may architectural designers who specialize in accessibility issues.

To protect owners of existing structures from the massive expense of extensive remodeling, the ADA recommends *reasonably achievable accommodations* to provide access to the facilities and services. New construction and remodeling, however, must meet higher standards of accessibility and usability because it costs less to incorporate accessible features in the design than to retrofit. Though the law intends to provide for people with disabilities, many of the accessible design features and accommodations benefit everyone.

Existing barriers must be removed when this can be accomplished in a *readily achievable* manner; that is, it can be done without much difficulty or expense. Typical examples of readily achievable modifications include

- ramping or removing an obstacle from an otherwise accessible entrance,
- lowering wall-mounted public telephones,
- adding raised letters and Braille markings on elevator buttons,
- installing auditory signals in elevators, and
- reversing the direction in which doors open.

Alternative methods can be used to provide reasonable accommodations if extensive restructuring is impractical or if retrofitting is unduly expensive. For instance, installing a cup dispenser at a water fountain that is too high for an individual in a wheelchair may be more practical than installing a lower unit or providing assistance.

Fair Housing Laws

Property managers who are also leasing real estate must be sure to adopt leasing practices that comply with the fair housing laws. Discrimination in rentals is the basis of a majority of the complaints filed with the Pennsylvania Human Relations Commission and HUD. Commercial as well as residential property is covered under the Pennsylvania law. See the chapters on leasing and fair housing for a discussion of the fair housing laws.

■ RISK MANAGEMENT

Remember the four alternative risk management techniques by the acronym **CART:**

Control
Avoid
Retain
Transfer

Enormous monetary losses can result from certain unexpected or catastrophic events. As a result, one of the most critical areas of responsibility for a property manager is risk management. **Risk management** involves answering the question, "What will happen if something goes wrong?" The perils of any risk must be evaluated in terms of options. In considering the possibility of a loss, the property manager must decide whether it is better to:

- *control it* by installing sprinklers, fire doors, and other preventive measures;
- *avoid it* by removing the source of risk, such as a swimming pool;

> - *retain it* to a certain extent, by insuring with a large deductible (loss not covered by the insurer); or
> - *transfer it* by taking out an insurance policy.

Security of Tenants

The physical safety of tenants in the leased premises has become an important issue for property managers and owners. Recent court decisions in several parts of the country have held landlords and their agents responsible for physical harm that was inflicted on tenants by intruders. These decisions have prompted property managers and owners to evaluate measures to protect tenants from unauthorized entry to building complexes and to secure individual apartments from intruders.

Types of Insurance

Insurance is one way to protect against losses. Many types of insurance are available. An insurance audit should be performed by a competent, reliable insurance agent familiar with insurance issues for the type of property involved. The audit will indicate areas in which greater or lesser coverage is recommended and will highlight particular risks. Final decisions, however, must be made by the property owner.

Today, many insurance companies offer **multiperil policies** for apartment and business buildings. These policies offer the property manager an insurance package that includes standard types of commercial coverage such as fire, hazard, public liability, and casualty plus special coverage for natural events such as earthquakes or floods.

IN PRACTICE A property manager's responsibilities often involve contracting for services and improvements on behalf of the owner. The licensing law and Real Estate Commission's Regulations prohibit licensees from personally profiting from expenditures they make on behalf of a principal. They are not permitted to receive any undisclosed commission, rebate, or compensation. Licensees must be careful not to violate the law in the course of their property management activities.

■ SUMMARY

Property management is a specialized service to owners of income-producing properties through which the managerial function is delegated to an individual or a firm with particular expertise in the field. The manager, as agent of the owner, becomes the administrator of the project and assumes the executive functions required for the care and operation of the property.

A management agreement establishing the agency relationship between owner and manager must be prepared carefully to define and authorize the manager's duties and responsibilities.

Projected expenses, combined with the manager's analysis of the condition of the building and the rent patterns in the neighborhood, form the basis on which rental rates for the property are determined. Once a rent schedule is established, the property manager is responsible for soliciting tenants whose needs are suited to the available space and who are financially capable of meeting the proposed rents. The manager is generally obligated to collect rents, maintain the building, hire necessary employees, pay taxes for the building, and deal with tenant problems.

Maintenance includes safeguarding the physical integrity of the property, performing routine cleaning and repair, making tenant improvements, and adapting the interior space and overall design of the property to suit the tenants' needs and to meet the demands of the market.

QUESTIONS

1. Apartment rents are usually expressed
   a. in monthly amounts.
   b. on a per-room basis.
   c. in square feet per month.
   d. in square feet per year.

2. From a management point of view, apartment building occupancy that reaches as high as 98 percent tends to indicate that
   a. the building is poorly managed.
   b. the building has reached its maximum potential.
   c. the building is a desirable place to live.
   d. rents should be raised.

3. Which of the following should *NOT* be a consideration in selecting a tenant?
   a. The size of the space versus the tenant's requirements
   b. The tenant's ability to pay
   c. The race and ethnicity of the tenant
   d. The compatibility of the tenant's business with other tenants' businesses

4. When a property manager chooses an insurance policy with a $250 deductible, the risk management technique being employed is
   a. avoiding risk.
   b. retaining risk.
   c. controlling risk.
   d. transferring risk.

5. Tenant improvements are
   a. fixtures.
   b. adaptations of space to suit tenants' needs.
   c. removable by the tenant.
   d. paid for by the landlord.

6. In preparing a budget, the property manager should set up for variable expenses a(n)
   a. control account.
   b. floating allocation.
   c. cash reserve fund.
   d. asset account.

7. Rents should be determined on the basis of
   a. prevailing rental rates in the area.
   b. the local apartment owners' association.
   c. HUD.
   d. a tenants' union.

8. Which of the following might indicate rents are too low?
   a. A poorly maintained building
   b. Many "For Lease" signs in the area
   c. High building occupancy
   d. High vacancy level

9. Repairing a boiler is classified as which type of maintenance?
   a. Preventive
   b. Corrective
   c. Routine
   d. Construction

ANSWERS

1. A Rental rates for residential properties are usually stated in monthly amounts. Rates for office, retail, and industrial space are based on spatial measure. (p. 437)

2. D Although a high percentage of occupancy may indicate an effective rental program, it could also mean that rental rates are too low and that rates should be raised. (p. 437)

3. C The size, location, and amenities of the premises, and the compatibility of the tenant's business with other tenants are all important considerations in tenant selection. Fair housing laws prohibit considerations based on race or ethnicity. (pp. 437–38)

4. D Risk is transferred when insurance is obtained with a low deductible. Risk is retained when insurance is obtained with a large deductible, with the possible consequence of loss not being covered by insurance. (p. 442)

5. B Tenant improvements are alterations to the interior of the building to meet a tenant's particular needs. Whether these improvements belong to the tenant or the building, or whether the tenant or the landlord incurs the cost of improvements are matters to be negotiated between the parties. (p. 440)

6. C Variable expenses such as repairs, decorating, and supplies are allocated to a cash reserve fund. Because these expenses vary, budget allocations can be derived from previous yearly costs. (p. 436)

7. A Rental rates are derived from the marketplace, based on supply and demand of competitive space in the area. (p. 437)

8. C High occupancy might indicate that rents are too low. Poorly maintained properties, many "For Lease" signs, and high vacancy rates are not typical indicators that rents are too low. (p. 437)

9. B Corrective maintenance involves actual repairs that keep the building's equipment, utilities, and amenities functioning, such as repairing a boiler. (p. 439)

INTERNET RESOURCES

The following is a selection of resources to guide readers to the wealth of information that is available today on the Internet. Readers are encouraged to explore the Internet because other resources are available as well. Often, one Web site provides links to other sites.

American Land Title Association: *www.alta.org*

American Society of Home Inspectors: *www.ashi.com*

Appraisal Foundation: *www.appraisalfoundation.org*

Appraisal Institute: *www.appraisalinstitute.org*

Association of Real Estate License Law Officials: *www.arello.org*

Building Owners and Managers Association International: *www.boma.org*

Building Owners and Managers Institute: *www.bomia-edu.org*

Center for Universal Design: *www.design.ncsu.edu/cud*

Certified International Property Specialist Network: *www.realtor.org/international/index.html*

Counselors of Real Estate: *www.cre.org*

Dearborn™ Real Estate Education: *www.dearbornRE.com*

Fannie Mae (FNMA): *www.fanniemae.com*

Federal Reserve Bank System (the Fed): *www.federalreserve.gov*

Federal Reserve Board: *www.federalreserve.gov/consumers.htm*

Federal Emergency Management Agency (FEMA): *www.fema.gov*

Freddie Mac: *www.freddiemac.com*

Ginnie Mae: *www.ginniemae.gov*

HSH: Fair Housing Act Pamphlet: *www.hsh.com*

Institute of Real Estate Management: *www.irem.org*

International Real Estate Digest: *www.ired.com*

Internal Revenue Service (IRS): *www.irs.gov*

Legal Information Institute: Landlord-Tenant Law: *www.law.cornell.edu/topics/landlord_tenant.html*

Legal Information Institute: Uniform Condominium Act: *www.law.cornell.edu/uniform/vol7%2ehtml*

Land Descriptions in the USA: *www.outfitters.com/genealogy/land*

Manufactured Housing Institute: *www.mfghome.org*

National Association of Exclusive Buyer Agents: *www.naeba.org*

National Association of Home Builders: *www.nahb.com*

National Association of Independent Fee Appraisers: *www.naifa.com*

National Association of Real Estate Brokers, Inc. (NAREB): *www.nareb.com*

National Association of REALTORS® (NAR): *www.realtor.org*

National Association of Residential Property Managers: *www.narpm.org*

National Flood Insurance Program: *www.fema.gov/nfip*

National Safety Council: Radon: *www.nsc.org/ehc/radon.htm*

Office of Federal Housing Enterprise Oversight (OFHEO): *www.ofheo.gov*

Pennsylvania Department of Community and Economic Development: *www.newpa.com/default.aspx?id=15*

Pennsylvania Department of Environmental Protection (mine subsidence. etc.): *www.dep.state.pa.us/dep*

Pennsylvania Housing Finance Agency: *www.phfa.org*

Pennsylvania Office of Vocational Rehabilitation: *www.parac.org*

Pennsylvania Association of REALTORS®: *www.parealtor.org*

Pennsylvania Bulletin: *www.pabulletin.com*

Pennsylvania Code: *www.pacode.com*

Pennsylvania Human Relations Commission: *www.phrc.state.pa.us*

Pennsylvania State Data Center: *www.PASDC.hbg.psu.edu*

Pennsylvania State Real Estate Commission: *www.dos.state.pa.us*

Real Estate Buyer's Agent Council: *www.rebac.net*

Real Estate Educators Association: *www.reea.org*

Rural Housing Services, U.S. Dept. of Agriculture: *www.rur-dev.usda.gov/rhs/index.html*

Small Business Administration: *www.sba.gov*

U.S. Department of Housing and Urban Development: *www.HUD.gov*

RESPA: *www.hud.gov/offices/hsg/sfh/res/respa_hm.cfm*

Fair Housing and Equal Opportunity: *www.hud.gov/offices/fheo/index.cfm-fhe/fheo.html*

FAQs About Escrows (RESPA): *www.hud.gov/offices/hsg/sfh/res/resconsu.cfm*

Healthy Homes for Healthy Children: *www.hud.gov/offices/lead*

Housing Discrimination Complaints: *www.hud.gov/complaints/housediscrim.cfm*

Lead Awareness, Lead-Based Paint and Lead Hazard Control: *www.hud.gov/offices/lead*

Mortgage Loan Programs: *www.hud.gov/mortprog.html*

U.S. Department of Justice: *www.usdoj.gov*

Antitrust Division: *www.usdoj.gov/atr*

ADA Home Page: *www.usdoj.gov/crt/ada/adahom1.htm*

U.S. Department of Veterans Affairs: *www.va.gov*

Mortgage Loan Programs: *www.homeloans.va.gov*

U.S. Environmental Protection Agency (EPA): *www.epa.gov*

Asbestos: *www.epa.gov/oppt/asbestos*

CERCLA/Superfund: *www.epa.gov/superfund/index.htm*

Indoor Air Quality: Carbon Monoxide: *www.epa.gov/iaq/co.html*

Indoor Air Quality: Radon: *www.epa.gov/iaq/radon*

Mold Remediation in Schools and Commercial Buildings: *www.epa.gov/mold/mold-resources.html*

U.S. Farm Service Agency: *www.FSA.usda.gov/pas*

U.S. Geologic Service: *quake.wr.usgs.gov*

U.S. Supreme Court: *www.supremecourtus.gov*

Note: This list is prepared solely as an informational resource for readers. It does not constitute an endorsement of any organization or warranty of the accuracy of the information that appears on any site. Furthermore, Web addresses change and Web sites close from time to time. Although attempts have been made to ensure the accuracy of these addresses, the publisher assumes no responsibility for the representations.

A

PENNSYLVANIA REAL ESTATE LICENSING EXAMINATION

Modern Real Estate Practice in Pennsylvania is designed to introduce the reader to the basic knowledge needed to engage in the real estate business. In addition to satisfying an education requirement, the license law in Pennsylvania requires people seeking certain licenses to pass an examination. Testing is used not to keep people out of the business but to ensure that people are competent to practice real estate.

PSI Examination Services is currently contracted by the Bureau of Professional and Occupational Affairs of the Department of State in Pennsylvania to develop and administer the real estate licensing examinations. Complete information about testing procedures is provided in a comprehensive Candidate Information Bulletin, which is available online at *www.psiexams.com* or by mail from PSI Examination Services at 3210 E. Tropicana, Las Vegas, NV 89121; phone (800) 733-9267. The bulletin is also available from real estate education providers.

■ EXAMINATION ADMINISTRATION PROCEDURES

Before actually taking a licensing examination, brokers, cemetery brokers, associate brokers, real estate salespeople, builder-owner salespeople, and rental listing referral agents must meet eligibility requirements established by the Real Estate Licensing and Registration Act. Candidates for broker, cemetery broker, and associate broker licenses must contact the office of the State Real Estate Commission to secure an examination eligibility application (form SPOA 2103). Salesperson, rental listing referral agent and builder-owner salesperson candidates shall submit a completed *PSI Registration Form* and an examination fee ($56) directly to PSI Examination Services. Certified/original transcripts also must be submitted with the registration form by salesperson and rental listing referral agent candidates as evidence that they have met the education requirements.

Candidates applying for the first time to take an examination must submit the registration by mail. Persons applying to retake an examination may register by mail, phone, fax, or online. The exam fee may be paid by cashier's check, money order, or credit card (MC or VISA). Personal checks and company checks are not acceptable.

Test Reservations

Once a candidate's registration is approved, the candidate will receive a confirmation notice containing instructions for scheduling an appointment to take the exam. Candidates may schedule an appointment any time via the Internet at *www.psiexams.com* or by touch-tone phone by calling (800) 733-9267. To make an appointment directly with a PSI registrar, call Monday through Friday between 8:00 A.M. and 8:00 P.M. Eastern time.

Administration of the Exam

Examinations are offered daily (five to six days per week) at PSI Examination Service locations throughout the state. The Candidate Information Bulletin provides a list of test sites; a complete list of test center locations is also available at PSI's Internet address.

Candidates should arrive 30 minutes prior to their scheduled exam and bring two forms of identification bearing the candidate's signature; one of the forms must have a photograph of the candidate. Candidates are permitted to also bring silent, simple (i.e., four-function) pocket calculators. No reference materials are permitted as all exams are closed-book. Photos of candidates will be taken during check-in at the examination site. If this is an issue for candidates, they are requested to contact PSI two weeks prior to the examination date.

The exam is given on a personal computer. Answers are recorded using a special keyboard. A candidate does not need computer experience or typing skills as all response keys are color-coded and have prominent characters.

■ EXAMINATION CONTENT

The content of licensing examinations, as determined by the State Real Estate Commission, is to reflect information deemed necessary for licensees to practice in Pennsylvania.

The salesperson and broker's exams consist of two portions: the *national* portion, which consists of 80 questions; and the *state-specific* portion, which consists of 30 multiple-choice questions. Candidates will have two hours to complete the national portion and one hour to complete the state portion of the exam.

In addition to the number of examination items specified, a small number of pretest questions (five to ten) may be administered. These questions will not be scored, and the time taken to answer them will not count against the time allotted to complete the exam. This is an essential step in the development of future licensing examinations.

National Examination

The national portion of the examination covers the following information:

I. Property Ownership (Salesperson—7 items; Broker—7 items)

    A. Classes of Property

    B. Land Characteristics

    C. Encumbrances

    D. Types of Ownership

II. Land Use Controls and Regulations (Salesperson—7 items; Broker—7 items)

    A. Government Rights in Land

    B. Public Controls based in Police Powers

    C. Private Controls

III. Valuation and Market Analysis (Salesperson—7 items; Broker—6 items)

    A. Value

    B. Methods of Estimating Value (applicability, key elements)

    C. Competitive Market Analysis

    D. Transactions Requiring Formal Appraisal

IV. Financing (Salesperson—8 items; Broker—7 items)

    A. General Concepts

    B. Types of Loans

    C. Sources of Loans

    D. Government Programs

    E. Mortgages

    F. Financing/Credit Laws

V. Laws of Agency (Salesperson—10 items; Broker—10 items)

    A. Law, Definition, and Nature of Agency Relationships

    B. Common Types of Agency Agreements in Real Estate

    C. Agency Duties

    D. Disclosure of Agency (general; detailed requirements in state portion)

    E. Commission and Fees

VI. Mandated Disclosures (Salesperson—6 items; Broker—7 items)

    A. Property Condition Disclosure Forms

    B. Need for Inspection and Obtaining/Verifying Information

    C. Material Facts

VII.   Contracts (Salesperson—10 items; Broker—10 items)

    A.   General Knowledge of Contract Law

    B.   Offers/Purchase Agreements

    C.   Counteroffers/Multiple Counteroffers

    D.   Leases as Contracts

    E.   Rescission and Cancellation of Agreements/Other Contract Terminations

VIII.   Transfer of Property (Salesperson—7 items; Broker—6 items)

    A.   Title Insurance

    B.   Deeds

    C.   Escrow or Closing

    D.   Tax Aspects

    E.   Special Processes (e.g., probate, foreclosure) [Broker only]

IX.   Practice of Real Estate (Salesperson—10 items; Broker—10 items)

    A.   Fair Housing Laws

    B.   Advertising and Misrepresentation

    C.   Agent Supervision (Broker only)

    D.   Ethical Issues

    E.   Broker/Salesperson Agreements

X.   Real Estate Calculations (Salesperson—5 items; Broker—6 items)

    A.   General Math Concepts

    B.   Property Tax Calculations (not prorations)

    C.   Lending Calculations

    D.   Calculations for Transactions

    E.   Calculations for Valuation

    F.   Mortgage Calculations

XI.   Specialty Areas (Salesperson—3 items; Broker—4 items)

    A.   Property Management and Landlord/Tenant

    B.   Subdivisions

    C.   Commercial Property/Income Property

    D.   Business Opportunities (Broker only)

State-Specific Examination

The state-specific portion of the examination covers the following information:

    I. Real Estate Commission10 percent

      A. Duties and Powers

      B. Complaints and Investigations

      C. Real Estate Recovery Fund

    II. Licensure20 percent

      A. Activities Requiring Licensure

      B. Types of License

      C. Eligibility for License

      D. License Renewal

      E. Change of Employment

      F. Exclusions from Licensure

      G. Suspension and Revocation

    III. Regulation of Conduct of Licensees70 percent

      A. Advertising

      B. Broker/Salesperson Relationship

      C. Compensation

      D. Prohibited Conduct

      E. Disclosures

      F. Conflict of Interest

      G. Documents and Forms

      H. Funds and Accounts

      I. Office Requirements and Inspections

      J. Pennsylvania Human Relations Act

      K. Promotional Land Sales

Score Reports

Candidates receive their scores at the test center immediately after they complete the examination. A score will appear immediately on the computer screen once the candidate indicates that he or she has finished or when the time allotted for the exam has ended. The score report will indicate either "pass" or "do not pass" for each portion of the exam that is completed. A diagnostic report indicating strengths and weaknesses is also provided to guide future study before retaking the exam. Candidates also receive an official paper score report that is printed at the examination site. The photo that is taken at check-in will also appear on the score report.

In order to receive a passing score, candidates must correctly answer a certain minimum number of questions. Note that the minimum passing scores are different for salesperson and broker candidates.

Examination	Portion	# of Items	Minimum Passing Score
Salesperson	National	80	56
	State	30	21
Broker	National	80	60
	State	30	23

If a candidate does not pass one portion of the test, there is no need to retake the entire exam. The candidate simply retakes only the portion of the exam that he or she did not pass. Both portions of the exam must have been passed within three years of the date the person makes application for licensure.

A salesperson or broker license application is printed at the same time as the score report when the candidate successfully completes both portions of the exam. The license application form must be completed and submitted to the Real Estate Commission to obtain a license.

■ EXAMINATION FORMAT

The questions are in the form of four-answer multiple-choice items.

Example: The purpose of requiring a prospective licensee to take an examination is to

1. keep people out of the business.

2. determine the competency of an individual to practice real estate.

3. see if the licensee is good at taking a test.

4. generate revenue from test fees.

The salesperson's exam is less difficult than the broker's exam. The broker's exam is designed to test the applicant in greater detail and includes information indicative of that licensee's practice.

Preparing for the Exam

Courses required for licensure are not designed to "teach the test." The purpose of courses required by the State Real Estate Commission is to develop a fundamental knowledge of real estate. That is the information presented in Modern Real Estate Practice in Pennsylvania. However, the information presented to the reader, enhanced by that presented by the instructor, is the basis of the material that should be studied to pass the license exam. The best way to prepare for the exam is to become thoroughly familiar with the material, particularly what the information means, rather than to memorize. Combining facts and principles and applying that knowledge to real-life situations is needed to pass the exam.

Taking the Exam

For best results, go through the entire examination first and answer those questions about which you are certain, leaving the others for later. After all the questions you know are answered, return to the remaining questions. There is no penalty for guessing; guess if you are unable to arrive at an answer. Remain relaxed. If you are prepared and have an adequate knowledge of the subject, you should be able to complete the exam successfully.

REVIEW
EXAMINATIONS

The following exam questions can be used for review of the national portion of the test material or for license examination preparation. Note that the proration calculations are based on a 30-day month unless otherwise stated.

1. Which of the following is a lien on real estate?
   a. A recorded easement
   b. A recorded mortgage
   c. An encroachment
   d. A deed restriction

2. A contract agreed to under duress is
   a. voidable.
   b. breached.
   c. discharged.
   d. void.

3. A broker receives a check for earnest money from a buyer and deposits the money in an escrow or trust account to protect herself from the charge of
   a. commingling.
   b. novation.
   c. lost or stolen funds.
   d. embezzlement.

4. A mortgage loan that requires monthly payments of $875.70 for 20 years and a final payment of $24,095 is known as a(n)
   a. wraparound loan.
   b. accelerated loan.
   c. balloon loan.
   d. variable loan.

5. The borrower computed the interest she was charged for the previous month on her $60,000 loan balance as $412.50. What is her interest rate?
   a. 7.5%
   b. 7.75%
   c. 8.25%
   d. 8.5%

6. A loan originated by a bank may be sold in which of the following?
   a. Primary market
   b. Secondary market
   c. Mortgage market
   d. Investor market

7. The deed that contains five covenants is the
   a. warranty deed.
   b. quitclaim deed.
   c. grant deed.
   d. deed in trust.

8. Steering is
   a. leading prospective homeowners to or away from certain areas.
   b. refusing to make loans to persons residing in certain areas.
   c. a requirement to join a multiple listing service.
   d. a practice of illegally setting commission rates.

9. *H* grants a life estate to her grandson and stipulates that upon the grandson's death the title to the property will pass to her son-in-law. This second estate is known as an
   a. estate in remainder.
   b. estate in reversion.
   c. estate at sufferance.
   d. estate for years.

10. Under joint tenancy
    a. a maximum of two people can own the real estate.
    b. the fractional interests can be different.
    c. additional owners can be added later.
    d. there is right of survivorship if properly designated.

11. The states in which the lender is the owner of mortgaged real estate are known as
    a. title theory states.
    b. lien theory states.
    c. statutory share states.
    d. strict forfeiture states.

12. What is a tenancy for years?
    a. A tenancy with the consent of the landlord
    b. A tenancy that expires on a specific date
    c. A tenancy created by the death of the owner
    d. A tenancy created by a testator

13. A residence with outmoded plumbing is suffering from
    a. functional obsolescence.
    b. curable physical deterioration.
    c. incurable physical deterioration.
    d. external obsolescence.

14. K built a structure that has six stories. Several years later an ordinance was passed in that area banning any building six stories or higher. This instance represents
    a. a nonconforming use.
    b. a situation in which the structure would have to be demolished.
    c. a conditional use.
    d. a violation of the zoning laws.

15. Assuming that the listing broker and the selling broker in a transaction split their commission equally, what was the sales price of the property if the commission rate was 6.5 percent and the listing broker received $2,593.50?
    a. $39,900
    b. $56,200
    c. $79,800
    d. $88,400

16. According to the statute of frauds in Pennsylvania, an oral lease for five years is
    a. a long-term lease.
    b. renewable.
    c. illegal.
    d. unenforceable.

17. The market value of a parcel of land
    a. is an estimate of the present worth of future benefits.
    b. represents a measure of past expenditures.
    c. is what the seller wants for the property.
    d. is the same as the market price.

18. Police powers include all of the following EXCEPT
    a. zoning.
    b. deed restrictions.
    c. building codes.
    d. subdivision regulations.

19. The seller wants to net $65,000 from the sale of his house after paying the broker's fee of 6 percent. His gross sales price will be
    a. $69,149.
    b. $68,900.
    c. $61,321.
    d. $61,100.

20. An acre contains
    a. 360 degrees.
    b. 36 sections.
    c. 160 square yards.
    d. 43,560 square feet.

21. W is purchasing a condominium unit in a subdivision and obtaining financing from a local savings and loan association. In this situation, which of the following best describes W?
    a. Vendor
    b. Mortgagor
    c. Grantor
    d. Lessor

22. The current value of a property is $40,000. The property is assessed at 40 percent of current value for real estate tax purposes, with an equalization factor of 1.5 applied to the assessed value. If the tax rate is $4 per $100 of assessed valuation, what is the amount of tax due on the property?
    a. $640
    b. $960
    c. $1,600
    d. $2,400

23. A building was sold for $60,000 with the purchaser putting 10 percent down and obtaining a loan for the balance. The lending institution charged a 1 percent loan origination fee. What was the total cash used for the purchase?
    a. $540
    b. $6,000
    c. $6,540
    d. $6,600

24. After a snowstorm, a property owner offers to pay $10 to anyone who will shovel his driveway. This is an example of a(n)
    a. implied contract.
    b. executed contract.
    c. bilateral contract.
    d. unilateral contract.

25. Capitalization rates are
    a. determined by the gross rent multiplier.
    b. the rates of return a property will produce.
    c. a mathematical value determined by the sales price.
    d. determined by the amount of depreciation in the property.

26. An eligible veteran made an offer of $50,000 to purchase a home to be financed with a VA-guaranteed loan. Four weeks after the offer was accepted, a certificate of reasonable value (CRV) for $47,800 was issued for the property. In this case the veteran may
    a. withdraw from the sale with a 1 percent penalty.
    b. purchase the property with a $2,200 down payment.
    c. not withdraw from the sale.
    d. withdraw from the sale upon payment of $2,200.

27. If a house was sold for $40,000 and the buyer obtained an FHA-insured mortgage loan for $38,500, how much money would be paid in discount points if the lender charged 4 points?
    a. $1,600
    b. $1,540
    c. $1,500
    d. $385

28. The commission rate is 7¾ percent on a sale of $50,000. What is the dollar amount of the commission?
    a. .$3,500
    b. $3,875
    c. $4,085
    d. $4,585

29. All of the following will terminate an offer EXCEPT
    a. revocation of the offer before its acceptance.
    b. the death of the offeror before acceptance.
    c. a counteroffer by the offeree.
    d. an offer from a third party.

30. G is purchasing a home under a land contract. Until the contract is paid in full, G has
    a. legal title to the premises.
    b. no interest in the property.
    c. a legal life estate in the premises.
    d. equitable title in the property.

31. F and K enter into an agreement wherein K will mow F's lawn every week during the summer. Shortly thereafter K decides to go into a different business. V would like to assume K's duties mowing F's lawn. F agrees and enters into a new contract with V. F and K tear up their original agreement. This is known as
    a. assignment.
    b. novation.
    c. substitution.
    d. rescission.

32. G borrowed $4,000 from a private lender using the services of a mortgage broker. After deducting the loan costs, G received $3,747. What is the face amount of the note?
    a. $3,747
    b. $4,000
    c. $4,253
    d. $7,747

33. An offer to purchase real estate becomes a contract when it is signed by which of the following?
    a. Buyer
    b. Buyer and seller
    c. Seller
    d. Seller and broker

34. A borrower has just made the final payment on his mortgage loan to his bank. Regardless of this fact, the lender will still hold a lien on the mortgaged property until which of the following is recorded?
    a. A satisfaction of the mortgage document
    b. A reconveyance of the mortgage document
    c. A novation of the mortgage document
    d. An estoppel of the mortgage document

35. If the annual net income from a commercial property is $22,000 and the capitalization rate is 8 percent, what is the value of the property using the income approach?
    a. $275,000
    b. $200,000
    c. $183,000
    d. $176,000

36. A broker enters into a listing agreement with a seller wherein the seller will receive $120,000 from the sale of a vacant lot and the broker will receive any sale proceeds over that amount. This type of agreement is called a(n)
    a. exclusive-agency listing.
    b. net listing.
    c. exclusive-right-to-sell listing.
    d. multiple listing.

37. Angela moved into a cooperative apartment after selling her house. Under the cooperative form of ownership she will
    a. become a stockholder in the corporation.
    b. not lose her apartment if she pays her share of the expenses.
    c. have to take out a new mortgage loan on her unit.
    d. receive a fixed-term lease for her unit.

38. A defect or a cloud on title to property may be cured by
    a. obtaining quitclaim deeds from all interested parties.
    b. bringing an action to register the title.
    c. paying cash for the property at the settlement.
    d. bringing an action to repudiate the title.

39. Discount points on a real estate loan are a potential cost to both the seller and the buyer. The points are
    a. set by the FHA and VA for their loan programs.
    b. charged only on conventional loans.
    c. limited by government regulations.
    d. determined by the market for money.

40. Under the terms of a net lease the tenant would usually be responsible for paying all of the following EXCEPT
    a. maintenance expenses.
    b. mortgage debt service.
    c. fire and extended-coverage insurance.
    d. real estate taxes.

41. The Civil Rights Act of 1866 prohibits in all cases discrimination based on a person's
    a .sex.
    b. religion.
    c. race.
    d. familial status.

42. What would it cost to put new carpeting in a den measuring 15' × 20' if the cost of the carpeting is $6.95 per square yard and installation costs an additional $250?
    a. $232
    b. $482
    c. $610
    d. $2,335

43. What is the difference between a general lien and a specific lien?
    a. A general lien cannot be enforced in court while a specific lien can.
    b. A specific lien is held by only one person while a general lien must be held by two or more.
    c. A general lien is a lien against personal property while a specific lien is a lien against real estate.
    d. A specific lien is a lien against a certain parcel of real estate while a general lien covers all of the debtor's property.

44. In an option to purchase real estate the optionee
    a. must purchase the property but may do so at any time within the option period.
    b. is limited to a refund of the option consideration if the option is exercised.
    c. cannot obtain third-party financing on the property until after the option has expired.
    d. has no obligation to purchase the property during the option period.

45. An individual seeking to be excused from the requirements of a zoning ordinance should request a
    a. building permit.
    b. certificate of alternative usage.
    c. variance.
    d. certificate of nonconforming use.

46. *Acceleration* is a term associated with which of the following documents?
    a. Listings
    b. Mortgages
    c. Leases
    d. Purchase contracts

47. Under the terms in the mortgage the lender must be paid in full if the property is sold. This clause is known as the
    a. acceleration clause.
    b. due-on-sale clause.
    c. subordination clause.
    d. habendum clause.

48. The broker receives a deposit with a written offer that indicates that the offeror will leave the offer open for the seller's acceptance for ten days. On the fifth day, and prior to acceptance by the seller, the offeror notifies the broker that he is withdrawing his offer and demanding the return of his deposit. In this situation
    a. the offeror cannot withdraw the offer—it must be held open for the full ten-day period.
    b. the offeror has the right to withdraw the offer and secure the return of the deposit at any time before he is notified of the seller's acceptance.
    c. the offeror can withdraw the offer, and the seller and the broker will each retain one-half of the forfeited deposit.
    d. the offeror can withdraw the offer, and the broker will declare the deposit forfeited and retain all of it in lieu of a commission.

49. *C* and *L* are joint tenants in a parcel of property. *L* sells her interest to *F*. What is the relationship between *C* and *F* regarding the property?
    a. They are joint tenants.
    b. They are tenants in common.
    c. They are tenants by the entirety.
    d. There is no relationship, because *L* cannot sell her joint tenancy interest.

50. *S* and *W* orally enter into a six-month lease. If *W* defaults, then *S*
    a. may not bring a court action because of the parol evidence rule.
    b. may not bring a court action because of the statute of frauds.
    c. may bring a court action because six-month leases need not be in writing to be enforceable.
    d. may bring a court action because the statute of limitations does not apply to oral leases.

51. On Monday *T* offers to sell his vacant lot to *K* for $12,000. On Tuesday *K* counteroffers to buy the lot for $10,500. On Friday *K* withdraws his counteroffer and accepts *T*'s original price of $12,000. Under these circumstances
    a. there is a valid agreement because *K* accepted *T*'s offer exactly as it was made, even though it was not accepted immediately.
    b. there is a valid agreement because *K* accepted before *T* advised him that the offer was withdrawn.
    c. there is no valid agreement because *T*'s offer was not accepted within 72 hours of its having been made.
    d. there is no valid agreement because *K*'s counteroffer was a rejection of *T*'s offer, and once rejected, it cannot be accepted later.

52. The parcel of property over which an easement runs is known as the
    a. dominant tenement.
    b. servient tenement.
    c. prescriptive tenement.
    d. eminent tenement.

53. If the quarterly interest at 7.5 percent is $562.50, what is the principal amount of the loan?
    a. $7,500
    b. $15,000
    c. $30,000
    d. $75,000

54. Assume a house is sold for $84,500 and the commission rate is 7 percent. If the commission is split 60/40 between the selling broker and the listing broker, and each broker splits his or her share of the commission evenly with the salesperson, how much will the listing salesperson receive from this sale?
   a. $1,183
   b. $1,775
   c. $2,366
   d. $3,549

55. If the mortgage loan is 80 percent of the appraised value of a house and the interest rate of 8 percent amounts to $460 for the first month, what is the appraised value of the house?
   a. $92,875
   b. $86,250
   c. $71,875
   d. $69,000

56. Local zoning ordinances often regulate all of the following EXCEPT
   a. the height of buildings in an area.
   b. the density of population.
   c. the appropriate use of the buildings.
   d. the market value of property.

57. A broker took a listing and later discovered that her client had previously been declared incompetent by the court. The listing is now
   a. unaffected because the broker was acting in good faith as the owner's agent.
   b. of no value to the broker because the contract is void.
   c. the basis for recovery of a commission if the broker produces a buyer.
   d. renegotiable between the broker and her client.

58. A borrower defaulted on his home mortgage loan payments, and the lender obtained a court order to foreclose on the property. At the foreclosure sale, however, the property sold for only $64,000; the unpaid balance of the loan at the time of the foreclosure was $78,000. What must the lender do in an attempt to recover the $14,000 that the borrower still owes?
   a. Sue for specific performance
   b. Sue for damages
   c. Seek a deficiency judgment
   d. Seek a judgment by default

59. All of the following are exemptions to the federal Fair Housing Act of 1968 EXCEPT
   a. the sale of a single-family home where the listing broker does not advertise the property.
   b. the restriction of noncommercial lodgings by a private club to members of the club.
   c. the rental of a unit in an owner-occupied three-family dwelling where an advertisement is placed in the paper.
   d. the restriction of noncommercial housing in a convent where a certified statement has not been filed with the government.

60. G purchases a $37,000 property, depositing $3,000 as earnest money. If G can obtain a 75 percent loan-to-value loan on the property and no additional items are prorated, how much more cash will G need at the settlement?
   a. $3,250
   b. $3,500
   c. $5,250
   d. $6,250

61. In the appraisal of a building constructed in the 1920s, the cost approach would be the least accurate method because of difficulties in
   a. estimating changes in material costs.
   b. obtaining building codes from the 1920s.
   c. estimating changes in labor rates.
   d. estimating depreciation.

62. G sold his property to W. In the deed of conveyance G's only guarantee was that the property was not encumbered during the time G owned it except as noted in the deed. The type of deed used in this transaction was a
   a. general warranty deed.
   b. special warranty deed.
   c. bargain and sale deed.
   d. quitclaim deed.

63. S and T, who are not married, own a parcel of real estate. Each owns an undivided interest, with S owning one-third and T owning two-thirds. The form of ownership under which S and T own their property is
   a. severalty.
   b. joint tenancy.
   c. tenancy at will.
   d. tenancy in common.

64. The buyers agree to purchase a house for $84,500. The buyers pay $2,000 as earnest money and obtain a new mortgage loan for $67,600. The purchase contract provides for a March 15 settlement. The buyers and sellers prorate the previous year's real estate taxes of $1,880.96, which have been prepaid. The buyers have additional closing costs of $1,250, and the sellers have other closing costs of $850. How much cash must the buyers bring to the settlement?
    a. $19,638
    b. $17,638
    c. $17,238
    d. $16,388

65. A broker was advertising a house he had listed for sale at the price of $47,900. J, a Mexican, saw the house and was interested in it. When J asked the broker the price of the house, the broker told J $53,000. Under the federal Fair Housing Act of 1968 such a statement is
    a. legal because all that is important is that J be given the opportunity to buy the house.
    b. legal because the representation was made by the broker and not directly by the owner.
    c. illegal because the difference in the offering price and the quoted price was greater than 10 percent.
    d. illegal because the terms of the potential sale were changed for J.

66. A deed must be signed by which of the following?
    a. The grantor
    b. The grantee
    c. The grantor and the grantee
    d. The grantee and at least two witnesses

67. An appraiser has been hired to prepare an appraisal report of a property for loan purposes. The property is an elegant old mansion that is now used as an insurance company office. To which approach to value should the appraiser give the greatest weight when making this appraisal?
    a. Income approach
    b. Sales comparison approach
    c. Replacement cost approach
    d. Gross rent multiplier

68. Which of the following is true about a term mortgage loan?
    a. All of the interest is paid at the end of the term.
    b. The debt is partially amortized over the life of the loan.
    c. The length of the term is limited by state statutes.
    d. The entire principal amount is due at the end of the term.

69. J recently moved into a condominium. She has the use of many facilities there, including a swimming pool, putting green, and tennis courts. Under the typical condominium arrangement these facilities would be owned by
    a. the association of homeowners in the condominium.
    b. the corporation in which J and the other owners hold stock.
    c. J and the other owners in the condominium in the form of divided interests.
    d. all the condominium owners in the form of percentage undivided interests.

70. Which of the following is NOT usually prorated between the seller and the buyer at the settlement?
    a. Recording charges
    b. Real estate taxes
    c. Prepaid rents
    d. Utility bills

71. T believes that he has been the victim of an unfair discriminatory practice committed by a local real estate broker. In accordance with federal regulations, how long does T have to file his complaint against the broker?
    a. 90 days after the alleged discrimination
    b. 180 days after the alleged discrimination
    c. 9 months after the alleged discrimination
    d. 1 year after the alleged discrimination

72. A real estate loan that uses both real estate and personal property as collateral is known as a
    a. blanket loan.
    b. package loan.
    c. growing-equity loan.
    d. graduated-payment loan.

73. All of the following are true regarding the concept of adverse possession *EXCEPT*
    a. the person taking possession of the property must do so without the consent of the owner of the property.
    b. occupancy of the property by the person taking possession must be continuous over a specified period of time.
    c. the person taking possession of the property must compensate the owner at the end of the adverse possession period.
    d. the person taking possession of the property could ultimately end up owning it.

74. What is the cost of constructing a fence 6½' high around a lot measuring 90' × 175', if the cost of erecting the fence is $1.25 per linear foot and the cost of materials is $0.825 per square foot of fence?
    a. $1,752
    b. $2,054
    c. $2,084
    d. $3,505

75. *K*, who desires to sell his house, enters into a listing agreement with broker *E*. Broker *N* obtains a buyer for the house, and *E* does not receive a commission. The listing agreement between *K* and *E* was probably a(n)
    a. exclusive-right-to-sell listing.
    b. open listing.
    c. exclusive-agency listing.
    d. multiple listing.

76. Antitrust laws prohibit all *EXCEPT*
    a. real estate companies agreeing on fees charged to sellers.
    b. real estate brokers allocating markets based on the value of homes.
    c. real estate companies allocating markets based on the location of commercial buildings.
    d. real estate salespersons allocating markets based on the location of homes.

77. Under the concept of riparian rights, the owners of property adjacent to navigable rivers or streams have the right to use the water and
    a. may erect a dam across the waterway if the owners on each side agree.
    b. are considered to own the submerged land to the center point of the waterway.
    c. are considered owners of the water adjacent to the land.
    d. are considered to own the land to the edge of the water.

78. The landlord of tenant *D* has sold his building to the state so that a freeway can be built. *D*'s lease has expired, but the landlord is letting him remain until the building is torn down. *D* continues to pay the same rent as prescribed in his lease. What kind of tenancy does *D* have?
    a. Holdover tenancy
    b. Month-to-month tenancy
    c. Tenancy at sufferance
    d. Tenancy at will

79. When a form of real estate sales contract has been agreed to and signed by the purchaser and spouse and then given to the seller's broker with an earnest money check,
    a. this transaction constitutes a valid contract.
    b. the purchasers can sue the seller for specific performance.
    c. this transaction is considered to be an offer.
    d. the earnest money will be forfeited if the purchasers default.

80. A seller gives an open listing to several brokers, specifically promising that if one of the brokers finds a buyer for the seller's property, the seller will then be obligated to pay a commission to that broker. Which of the following agreements best describes this offer by the seller?
    a. Executed
    b. Discharged
    c. Unilateral
    d. Bilateral

81. By paying his debt after a foreclosure sale, the borrower has the right to regain his property under which of the following?
    a. Acceleration
    b. Redemption
    c. Reversion
    d. Recovery

82. Which of the following is true of a sale-and-leaseback arrangement?
   a. The seller/vendor retains title to the real estate.
   b. The buyer/vendee gets possession of the property.
   c. The buyer/vendee is the lessor.
   d. This arrangement is prohibited in most states.

83. Fannie Mae and Ginnie Mae
   a. work together as primary market lenders.
   b. are both federal agencies.
   c. are both privately owned entities.
   d. are involved in the secondary market.

84. Q decided she could make more money from her tree farm by dividing it into small parcels and selling them to numerous buyers. Subsequently, Q entered into a series of purchase agreements in which she agreed to operate the property and distribute proceeds from its income to the buyers of the parcels. Under these circumstances Q has sold
   a. real estate because the object of the sale was the land.
   b. securities because the object of the purchase was the trees and the underlying land was merely incidental to the sale.
   c. real estate because the property was subdivided before the sales ever took place.
   d. securities because the buyers were investors relying on Q's activities to generate a profit from the premises purchased.

85. All of the following situations are in violation of the federal Fair Housing Act of 1968 EXCEPT
   a. the refusal of a property manager to rent an apartment to a Catholic couple who are otherwise qualified.
   b. the general policy of a loan company to avoid granting home improvement loans to individuals living in transitional neighborhoods.
   c. the intentional neglect of a broker to show an Asian family any property listings of homes in all-white neighborhoods.
   d. the insistence of a widowed woman on renting her spare bedroom only to another widowed woman.

86. If a storage tank that measures 12' × 9' × 8' was designed to store natural gas and the cost of the gas is $1.82 per cubic foot, what does it cost to fill the tank to one-half its capacity?
   a. $685
   b. $786
   c. $864
   d. $1,572

87. When a buyer signs a purchase contract and the seller accepts, the buyer acquires an immediate interest in the property known as
   a. legal title.
   b. equitable title.
   c. statutory title.
   d. defeasible title.

88. Which of the following requires that finance charges be stated as an annual percentage rate?
   a. Truth-in-Lending Act (Regulation Z)
   b. Real Estate Settlement Procedures Act
   c. Equal Credit Opportunity Act
   d. Federal Fair Housing Act

89. J owns an apartment building in a large city. After discussing the matter with his advisers, J decided to alter the type of occupancy in the building from rental to condominium status. This procedure is known as
   a. amendment.
   b. partition.
   c. deportment.
   d. conversion.

90. In question 89, after checking the applicable laws, J discovered that in connection with the change to condominium status he must initially offer to sell each unit to the tenant who currently occupies the unit. If the tenant rejects the offer, J may then offer the unit for sale to the general public. The requirement that J offer the property to the tenant in this situation is known as a
   a. contingent restriction.
   b. conditional sales option.
   c. right of first refusal.
   d. covenant of prior acceptance.

91. Which of the following real estate documents is least likely to be recorded?
   a. A standard form deed
   b. A long-term lease
   c. An option agreement
   d. A purchase agreement

92. Broker *U* represented the seller in a transaction. Her client told her that he did not want to recite the actual consideration that was paid for the house. In this situation Broker *U*
    a. must inform her client that only the actual price of the real estate may appear on the deed.
    b. may show the nominal consideration of only $10 on the deed.
    c. should inform the seller that either the full price should be stated in the deed or all references to consideration should be removed from it.
    d. may show a price on the deed other than the actual price, provided that the variance is not greater than 10 percent of the purchase price.

93. A broker obtained a listing agreement to act as the agent in the sale of a seller's house. A buyer has been found for the property, and all of the agreements have been signed. As an agent for the seller, the broker is responsible for the buyer's
    a. completion of the loan application.
    b. receipt of copies of all documents.
    c. qualification for the new mortgage loan.
    d. inspection of the property.

94. G and M, co-owners of a parcel of vacant commercial property, have executed three open listing agreements with three brokers around town. All three brokers would like to place "For Sale" signs on the sellers' property. Under these circumstances
    a. a broker does not have to obtain the sellers' permission before placing a sign on the property.
    b. only one "For Sale" sign may be placed on the property at one time.
    c. upon obtaining the sellers' written consent, all brokers can place their "For Sale" signs on the property.
    d. the broker who obtained the first open listing must consent to all signs being placed on the property.

95. In estimating the value of real estate using the cost approach, the appraiser should
    a. estimate the replacement cost of the improvements.
    b. deduct for the depreciation of the land and buildings.
    c. determine the original cost and adjust for inflation.
    d. review the sales prices of comparable properties.

ANSWERS
APPENDIX B: REVIEW EXAMINATION

1. b	37. a	73. c
2. a	38. a	74. d
3. a	39. d	75. b
4. c	40. b	76. d
5. c	41. c	77. d
6. b	42. b	78. d
7. a	43. d	79. c
8. a	44. d	80. c
9. a	45. c	81. b
10. d	46. b	82. c
11. a	47. b	83. d
12. b	48. b	84. d
13. a	49. b	85. d
14. a	50. c	86. b
15. c	51. d	87. b
16. d	52. b	88. a
17. a	53. c	89. d
18. b	54. a	90. c
19. a	55. b	91. d
20. d	56. d	92. b
21. b	57. b	93. b
22. b	58. c	94. c
23. c	59. a	95. a
24. d	60. d	
25. b	61. d	
26. b	62. b	
27. b	63. d	
28. b	64. b	
29. d	65. d	
30. d	66. a	
31. b	67. a	
32. b	68. d	
33. b	69. d	
34. a	70. a	
35. a	71. d	
36. b	72. b	

REVIEW QUESTIONS
PENNSYLVANIA STATE-SPECIFIC EXAM

1. The Real Estate Commission conducts its activities to
   a. safeguard all real estate licensees.
   b .protect the public interest.
   c. satisfy the legislature.
   d. assist the Commissioner of Professional and Occupational Affairs.

2. The Commission has the authority to
   a. issue licenses.
   b. conduct licensing examinations.
   c. appoint Commissioners.
   d. promulgate rules and regulations.

3. The Commission has authority to take disciplinary action against
   a. landlords.
   b. campground membership salespeople.
   c. attorneys-in-fact.
   d. licensed auctioneers.

4. The Commission can take which of the following actions if a salesperson advertises a property for sale without the owner's permission?
   a. Assess the salesperson a criminal penalty of $500
   b. Award the owner damages from the Recovery Fund
   c. Suspend the salesperson's license
   d. Tell the owner to file a complaint with a local real estate board

5. An individual has applied for a salesperson license. This person can do which of the following?
   a. Solicit listings
   b. Advertise a house for sale
   c. Negotiate an agreement of sale
   d. Attend the broker's sales training program

6. Applicants for licensure must satisfy an education requirement in all of the following cases EXCEPT
   a. a builder-owner salesperson license.
   b.a campground membership salesperson license.
   c. a time-share salesperson license.
   d. a rental listing referral agent license.

7. A broker is responsible for which of the following activities?
   a. Conducting title searches
   b. Attending closings
   c. Training builder-owner salespersons
   d. Business that is conducted in branch offices

8. To be eligible for a broker license, an individual must do all of the following EXCEPT
   a. obtain 240 hours of education.
   b. be at least 21 years of age.
   c. be a citizen of the United States.
   d. pass an examination.

9. When a salesperson owns the house that the salesperson is selling, which of the following is true?
   a. The salesperson must list the property with another broker.
   b. The salesperson must disclose to a prospective purchaser that the salesperson is licensed.
   c. The act does not apply to a licensee who is selling his or her own property.
   d. A salesperson cannot collect a commission on the sale of his or her own property.

10. If a salesperson is unable to collect from the employing broker a commission that the salesperson has earned, what recourse does the salesperson have to collect his money?
    a. File a complaint with the Commission.
    b. Sue the broker.
    c. Make application to the Recovery Fund.
    d. Change employing brokers.

11. A broker decides to open a branch office. Which of the following is true?
    a. The broker is not responsible for the branch office if an associate broker is the manager.
    b. A branch office license will be issued if the broker's license is suspended at the main office.
    c. The number of branch offices that a broker can open is limited by the Commission.
    d. The broker could open the branch office in his or her home if there is a separate entrance to the office.

12. A seller offers a $500 bonus to a salesperson who sells the house within 30 days. Which of the following is true?
    a. The seller may pay the bonus to the salesperson who produces a buyer.
    b. Bonuses of this nature are strictly prohibited.
    c. The salesperson who produces a buyer cannot accept this bonus directly from the seller.
    d. The bonus could be paid by the seller to a salesperson if it is a lesser amount.

13. Which of the following is true about a salesperson's license?
    a. The broker must display the license in the office where the salesperson works.
    b. The broker must display the license in the broker's main office.
    c. The license is issued to the salesperson and can be taken to any broker of the salesperson's choice.
    d. The salesperson cannot use the license until completion of the broker's training program.

14. Estimated statements of closing costs must meet which of the following requirements?
    a. They must be signed by the seller.
    b. They must be an exact representation of the costs incurred by a buyer and seller at settlement.
    c. They must be presented to a buyer and seller prior to their signing an agreement of sale.
    d. They must disclose whom the broker represents.

15. A broker can be subject to disciplinary action if a salesperson is found guilty of misconduct
    a. any time the salesperson's license is suspended.
    b. when the Commission files a complaint against the broker.
    c. if the broker directed the illegal course of action.
    d. only if the salesperson is licensed.

16. When a buyer gives the salesperson a check for escrow money, which of the following is true?
    a. The salesperson must deposit it immediately in the broker's escrow account.
    b. The salesperson must give the check to the seller.
    c. The check must be deposited in an interest-bearing account.
    d. The check must be deposited in the broker's escrow account by the end of the next business day after receipt.

17. When a property is advertised for sale by a salesperson, what information must be included in the ad?
    a. The address of the broker
    b. The business name of the broker
    c. The name of the salesperson
    d. The phone number of the salesperson

18. When a buyer and seller enter into an agreement of sale, the broker is responsible for all of the following EXCEPT
    a. giving a copy of the agreement to the buyer and seller.
    b. keeping a copy for three years after the consummation of the sale.
    c. giving a copy to the mortgage lender.
    d. using a written contract.

19. A mortgage contingency must include all of the following information EXCEPT the
    a. amount of the mortgage payment.
    b. amount of the loan.
    c. maximum interest rate for the loan.
    d. minimum number of years for the loan.

20. A salesperson is discussing the possibility of listing a seller's home. What information should the salesperson give to the seller before the listing agreement is signed?
    a. The common rate of commission charged in the area
    b. The approximate number of times the house will be advertised
    c. That a listing must last for at least one year
    d. Existence of the Real Estate Recovery Fund

21. A listing in which the seller owes a commission even if the seller finds the buyer is a(n)
    a. open listing.
    b. exclusive agency.
    c. multiple listing.
    d. exclusive-right-to-sell.

22. K signed an agreement of sale to purchase a time-share property. Three days later K decided that she didn't really want the property. Which of the following is true?
    a. K must return the cookware she received at the time of the purchase.
    b. K can recover her hand money from the Recovery Fund.
    c. K can cancel the contract.
    d. The broker is due a commission on the sale.

23. Under what circumstances can a broker deposit his or her own money in the escrow account?
    a. Never
    b. Only with the seller's permission
    c. To cover any fees for the account charged by the bank
    d. With permission from the Commission

24. The owner tells the salesperson not to rent an apartment to a family with children. What should the salesperson do?
    a. Follow the instructions because the owner is the client
    b. Tell the owner to rent the property himself
    c. Rent the apartment to anyone who is financially qualified
    d. Both the owner and the salesperson have the right to deny the apartment to a family with children

25. An agreement of sale must include certain information. Which of the following is NOT a requirement?
    a. Disclosure of whom the broker represents
    b. Disclosure that the amount of commission has been determined by negotiations
    c. Disclosure of the zoning classification unless the property is zoned for single family
    d. Disclosure of the existence of the Recovery Fund

26. The owner of a house does not want it to be rented to anyone who has a pet. The salesperson has a prospect with a visual disability who uses a guide dog. What should the salesperson do?
    a. Find the prospect a house to rent where pets are allowed
    b. Charge a higher security deposit and rent the house to the prospect
    c. Have the tenant sign a commitment to be responsible for any damage done by the guide dog
    d. Rent the house to the prospect without further concern for the pet restriction

27. A buyer was concerned about a clause in the agreement of sale. The salesperson, who represents the seller, told the buyer that it was not something for the buyer to worry about. In this situation
    a. the salesperson should have referred the buyer to a lawyer.
    b. the salesperson did the right thing.
    c. the salesperson should not have said anything because the salesperson doesn't represent the buyer.
    d. the license law does not apply.

28. A brokerage firm advertises that it is the best to do business with because it sells more property than any other firm in the area. This kind of advertising is
    a. good business.
    b. not addressed by the Commission.
    c. allowed if the claim is based on closed transactions.
    d. illegal under the act.

29. An exclusive-right-to-lease agreement must include certain information. Which of the following is NOT a requirement?
    a. An automatic renewal clause
    b. Lease price
    c. Duration of the agreement
    d. Commission expected on the lease

30. A buyer is concerned about how much a property will appreciate over the next five years. The salesperson assures the buyer that its value will double in eight years. Which of the following is true?
    a. This sounds like a good investment.
    b. The salesperson should not have made such a comment.
    c. The comment is good salesmanship.
    d. The buyer should rely on the comment because of the salesperson's knowledge and experience.

31. The purpose of the real estate license law is to
    a. keep criminals from practicing real estate.
    b. control the number of people who get a real estate license.
    c. ensure that the public interest is protected.
    d. create the State Real Estate Commission.

32. You have passed the salesperson's exam and selected a broker with whom you are going to work but your license hasn't been issued yet. Now your neighbor tells you he needs to list his home and get it sold quickly. How can you help him?
    a. Suggest your neighbor contact the broker you've selected to work for to list his property.
    b. Tell your neighbor to run an ad for an open house and that you will conduct the open house for him.
    c. Tell your neighbor that you can list the property but can't show it until your license comes.
    d. Do a competitive market analysis of the neighbor's property and negotiate a listing contract but don't date the contract yet.

33. A salesperson had an offer from a buyer-customer to purchase a property that was listed exclusively with another real estate company. The salesperson asked the seller to cancel the listing and sign a new listing with the salesperson's company before presenting the offer. This way, the salesperson would earn more money by selling the company's own listing. Which of the following is true?
    a. The buyer should have made the offer through the company that listed the property rather than with this salesperson.
    b. The salesperson should not attempt to disrupt the exclusive relationship the seller has with the listing broker.
    c. The salesperson is permitted to do whatever is necessary to personally gain from a transaction and earn a living.
    d. The salesperson's broker rather than the salesperson should have approached the seller with the request to break the listing contract with the other company.

34. When a salesperson changes employing brokers, the salesperson should
    a. notify the local real estate association.
    b. notify a member of the Real Estate Commission.
    c. rely on the employing broker to notify the Real Estate Commission.
    d. notify the Real Estate Commission in writing.

35. The broker's license will expire at the end of May. Which of the following is true as of June 1?
    a. The broker can renew the license as of June 1 and complete the continuing education courses within the following two years.
    b. The license will be inactive and the broker must cease practice on June 1 if the broker fails to renew it.
    c. The broker can continue to practice for 60 days after June 1 before renewing the license.
    d. If the broker has been in business for more than 25 years, he or she can renew the license as of June 1 without taking continuing education courses.

36. The broker wants to hire someone to handle the daily management of the sales office so that the broker can concentrate on other activities. A licensed salesperson, who currently works for the broker and is extremely competent, has been selling for 15 years. The broker wants to hire this person to manage the office. Which of the following is true?
    a. The broker can hire this licensed salesperson to manage the office as long as the person is not given the title of manager.
    b. Because the salesperson has 15 years experience, this salesperson can manage the office.
    c. The broker is the manager of the office unless someone else with a broker license is hired as the manager.
    d. This salesperson can become the manager as long as the person is in the process of qualifying for a broker license.

37. To obtain a salesperson license, a person must
    a. be at least 21 years of age.
    b. complete 30 hours of instruction.
    c. complete not less than 30 days of on-site training.
    d. pass an examination.

38. The purpose of the Recovery Fund is to
    a. enable people to get payment of uncollected judgments against licensees.
    b. enable sellers to recover money when buyers default on sales agreements.
    c. enable licensees to recover commissions that their brokers have failed to pay.
    d. enable sellers to recover escrow money that brokers have handled improperly.

39. On Thursday evening, a buyer makes an offer to purchase a property and gives the salesperson a check for $3,000 hand money. The offer is presented to the seller, then the seller makes a counteroffer. The buyer finally accepts the counteroffer and the acceptance is communicated to the seller on Monday evening. How is the check to be handled between Thursday and Monday evenings?
   a. The check should be held by the salesperson and given to the broker on Tuesday morning.
   b. The check should be given to the broker to hold until Tuesday.
   c. The broker is responsible for depositing the check by the end of business on Friday.
   d. The check should be given to the seller when the acceptance is communicated on Monday evening.

40. A buyer makes an offer on a house that is listed by another brokerage company. With the offer the buyer gives a hand-money check that is made payable to the selling company. What should be done with the hand money check according to the Rules and Regulations?
   a. The salesperson should refuse to accept the check until the seller accepts the offer.
   b. The real estate company to whom the check is made payable is responsible for depositing it in its escrow account.
   c. The broker of the company to whom the check is made payable must endorse it over to the listing broker.
   d. The listing broker should ask the buyer for another hand-money check.

ANSWERS AND RATIONALES
APPENDIX B: REVIEW QUESTIONS

1. B. The Real Estate Licensing and Registration Act was passed to protect the public interest. The duties and powers of the Commission are to administer the act, including promulgating its Rules and Regulations.

2. D. The Department of State issues licenses and contracts with a testing agency. The Commission has the authority to prescribe the subjects to be tested (not conduct the tests) and promulgate Rules and Regulations. The Governor appoints commissioners.

3. B. By Section 604 of the Act, owners, attorneys-in-fact, and licensed auctioneers are exempt from licensure. The Commission has authority to take disciplinary actions against licensees, including campground membership salespersons.

4. C. Criminal penalties apply to unlicensed practice. Awards from the Recovery Fund apply to individuals who have an uncollectable judgment from a civil action against a licensee for fraud, deceit, and misrepresentation. The Commission is not connected with any real estate organization. The Commission has the authority to fine a licensee and to suspend or revoke a license for violations under Section 604 of the Act.

5. D. An individual cannot perform any activity for which licensure is required until the license is issued. Attending a training program is not a licensed activity.

6. A. All of the named licenses have an education requirement except a builder-owner salesperson.

7. D. The broker is responsible for all activities conducted by licensees employed by the broker in all of the broker's offices.

8. C. There is no citizenship requirement for any real estate licenses.

9. B. The act applies to licensees when dealing with their own properties. The licensee is responsible for disclosing that she or he is licensed. The act does not prohibit an individual from dealing with self-owned property or from collecting a commission in those transactions.

10. B. The Commission has no jurisdiction over a situation involving broker/salesperson commission disputes. The salesperson should seek recovery of the money due through civil court action.

11. D. The broker is always responsible for the activities, even if a branch office is managed by an associate broker. A branch office license can only be issued if the broker's license is currently renewed and not subject to disciplinary action; there is nothing in the Regulations that limits the number of branch offices.

12. C. The bonus can be accepted only by the salesperson's broker; the salesperson can receive compensation only from the employing broker.

13. A. The license must be displayed at the office in which the licensee works. The broker keeps records at the main office indicating the office in which each licensee works.

14. C. Estimated statements of closing costs are estimates. There is no requirement that they be signed. The disclosure of whom the broker represents is made in agreements of sale.

15. C. The employment of a salesperson by a broker does not automatically implicate the broker in the case of a violation. For the broker to be in violation, the broker must have had actual knowledge of the event, directed a course of action, or allowed a course of action to continue.

16. D. The broker is responsible for depositing the check. Interest is suggested to be paid if the money is to be held for more than six months. The broker's duty to escrow is nonwaivable.

17. B. The Commission requires that ads include the broker's business name. If a salesperson's name or phone number is included in the ad, the broker's name and phone number must appear in at least the same size print.

18. C. All of the other statements are requirements by the Commission's Regulations.

19. A. All of the other statements are requirements by the Commission's Regulations.

20. D. Necessary disclosures prior to the seller's signing a listing contract include whether the broker is an agent for the seller or for the buyer; that the commission and term of listing are negotiable; the existence of the Recovery Fund; and the requirement that an agreement of sale contain the zoning classification of the property, unless zoned primarily for single-family use.

21. D. In the other cases, the seller may sell his or her own property without being liable for a commission. A multiple listing is not a kind of listing, but a multiple-listing clause could exist in a listing agreement.

22. C. The agreement of sale for a time-share must disclose the purchaser's right to cancel the contract by midnight of the fifth day after the signing of the contract. The purchaser may keep any gifts awarded prior to purchase and is entitled to recovery of any hand money without further action. The Recovery Fund serves a different purpose.

23. C. This is the only situation in which broker and client funds can be mixed.

24. C. Families with children are protected by the fair housing laws. These laws apply to both owners and licensees. The licensee is obligated to follow only lawful instructions of the principal.

25. B. The disclosure that commissions have been determined as a result of negotiations appears in a listing contract.

26. D. Individuals who have a disability are protected under the fair housing laws. A guide animal is not a pet. Individuals in the protected classes cannot be charged different amounts or be subjected to different conditions than are others.

27. A. Licensees are not to practice law. Any concern about the provisions in a contract should be referred to legal counsel.

28. C. The Commission's Regulations specify that such claims must be based on closed transactions.

29. A. An automatic renewal clause is prohibited in exclusive listing contracts.

30. B. The Commission's Regulations prohibit giving assurances that the licensee knows or should be expected to know are inaccurate or improbable. There is no way a licensee could assure such a claim; only historical information is verifiable.

31. C. Protecting the public is the law's primary purpose. It does not intend to restrict people from getting into the business but rather to ensure that people who are licensed meet certain standards. The Real Estate Commission exists to administer and enforce the law.

32. A. Holding an open house, listing properties, and negotiating listings are all activities for which a license is required. The only way you can help the neighbor is to suggest he contact someone, your prospective broker is fine, to get the property marketed quickly.

33. B. Section 604 (11) of the Act prohibits a licensee from inducing any party to a contract to substitute a new contract where the substitution is motivated by personal gain. Neither the salesperson nor the salesperson's broker can do this. The buyer and seller are innocent victims of the salesperson's behavior.

34. D. The salesperson, not the broker, is responsible for notifying the Commission within ten days of the change of employment.

35. B. Any license that is not renewed is considered inactive and the person is not permitted to practice until it is properly renewed. Licensed brokers and salespeople must satisfy the continuing education requirement during the two years prior to the renewal date, regardless of their length of practice.

36. C. Only a licensed broker can manage a real estate office. Working to qualify for a broker license, lengthy sales experience, and titles do not alter this requirement.

37. D. To qualify for a salesperson license the individual must be at least 18 years of age (21 for a broker) and satisfy a 60-hour education requirement (30 hours for time-share salespeople). Time-share and campground membership salespeople are required to complete on-site training.

38. A. According to Section 803 of the Act, any aggrieved person who obtains a final judgment against a licensee for fraud, misrepresentation, or deceit and is unsuccessful collecting it from the licensee can recover the money from the Recovery Fund. The fund does not exist for any other purpose.

39. C. The Act and the Regulations require the hand money to be deposited by the end of business following the day of receipt. The only way it can be held until there is a contract is if both the buyer and seller agree in writing. The duty of the broker to escrow is nonwaivable, which means that once money is tendered to the licensee it must be escrowed.

40. B. The broker to whom the check is made payable has the responsibility for escrowing. Only when the buyer has been informed in accordance with the Regulations is the broker permitted to endorse the check over to the other broker. The same rules apply as cited in the previous question regarding the timing of the deposit.

REAL ESTATE
LICENSING AND
REGISTRATION ACT
AND
RULES AND
REGULATIONS

REAL ESTATE LICENSING AND REGISTRATION ACT (RELRA)

Act of 1980, P.L. 15, No. 9 (Current through 1/1/2004)

63 P.S. §§455.101 – 455.902

(When referring to section numbers, use the number after the decimal point. For example, §455.603 can be referred to as Section 603.)

TABLE OF CONTENTS

Chapter 8. Real Estate Recovery Fund.

Section 801. Establishment of the fund.
Section 802. Funding of the fund.
Section 803. Application for recovery from fund.

Chapter 9. Repealer and effective Date.

Section 901. Repealer.
Section 902. Effective date.

Chapter 1
General Provisions

§ 455.101. Short title

This act shall be known and may be cited as the "Real Estate Licensing and Registration Act."

Chapter 2
Definitions

§ 455.201. Definitions

The following words and phrases when used in this act shall have, unless the context clearly indicates otherwise, the meanings given to them in this section:

"AGENCY RELATIONSHIP." A relationship whereby the broker or licensees in the employ of the broker act as fiduciaries for a consumer of real estate services by the express authority of the consumer of real estate services.

"ASSOCIATE BROKER." A broker employed by another broker.

"BROKER." Any person who, for another and for a fee, commission or other valuable consideration:

(1) negotiates with or aids any person in locating or obtaining for purchase, lease or an acquisition of interest in any real estate;

(2) negotiates the listing, sale, purchase, exchange, lease, time share and similarly designated interests, financing or option for any real estate;

(3) manages any real estate;

(4) represents himself to be a real estate consultant, counselor, agent or finder;

(5) undertakes to promote the sale, exchange, purchase or rental of real estate: Provided, however, That this provision shall not include any person whose main business is that of advertising, promotion or public relations;

(5.1) undertakes to perform a comparative market analysis; or

(6) attempts to perform any of the above acts.

"BUILDER-OWNER SALESPERSON." Any person who is a full-time employee of a builder-owner of single and multifamily dwellings located within the Commonwealth and as such employee shall be authorized and empowered to list for sale, sell or offer for sale, or to negotiate the sale or exchange of real estate, or to lease or rent, or offer to lease, rent or place for rent, any real estate owned by his builder-owner employer, or collect or offer, or attempt to collect, rent for the use of real estate owned by his builder-owner employer, for and on behalf of such builder-owner employer.

"BUYER AGENT." Any licensee who has entered into an agency relationship with a consumer buyer of real estate.

"CAMPGROUND MEMBERSHIP." An interest, other than in fee simple or by lease, which gives the purchaser the right to use a unit of real property for the purpose of locating a recreational vehicle, trailer, tent, tent trailer, pickup camper or other similar device on a periodic basis pursuant to a membership contract allocating use and occupancy rights between other similar users.

"CAMPGROUND MEMBERSHIP SALESPERSON." A person who either as an employee or an independent contractor sells or offers to sell campground memberships. Such person shall sell campground memberships under the active supervision of a broker. A person licensed as a broker, as a salesperson or as a time-share salesperson shall not be required to be licensed as a campground membership salesperson as a condition for selling or offering to sell campground memberships.

"CEMETERY." A place for the disposal or burial of deceased human beings, by cremation or in a grave, mausoleum, vault, columbarium or other receptacle, but the term does not include a private family cemetery.

"CEMETERY BROKER." Any person engaging in or carrying on the business or acting in the capacity of a broker within this Commonwealth exclusively within the limited field or branch of business which applies to cemetery lots, plots and mausoleum spaces or openings.

"CEMETERY COMPANY." Any person who offers or sells to the public the ownership, or the right to use, any cemetery lot.

"CEMETERY SALESPERSON." Any person employed by a broker or cemetery broker to perform duties as defined herein under "cemetery broker."

"COMMISSION." The State Real Estate Commission.

"COMMISSIONER." Commissioner of Professional and Occupational Affairs.

"COMPARATIVE MARKET ANALYSIS." A written analysis, opinion or conclusion by a contracted buyer's agent, transactional licensee, or an actual or potential seller's agent relating to the probable sale price of a specified piece of real estate in an identified real estate market at a specified time, offered either for the purpose of determining the asking/offering price for the property by a specific actual or potential consumer or for the purpose of securing a listing agreement with a seller.

"CONSUMER." A person who is the recipient of any real estate service.

"DEPARTMENT." The Department of State acting through the Commissioner of Professional and Occupational Affairs.

"DESIGNATED AGENT." One or more licensees designated by the employing broker, with the consent of the principal, to act exclusively as an agent or as agents on behalf of the principal to the exclusion of all other licensees within the broker's employ.

"DISCLOSURE." Provision of all relevant facts, without reservation, ambiguity or distortion so as to enable a consumer to understand the options and weigh the risks and benefits in order to make a decision in his or her own best interest.

"DUAL AGENT." A licensee who acts as an agent for the buyer and seller, or lessee and landlord, in the same transaction.

"EMPLOY, EMPLOYED, EMPLOYEE, EMPLOYMENT." The use of the words employ, employed, employee or employment in this act shall apply to the relationship of independent contractor as well as to the relationship of employment, except as applied to builder-owner salespersons.

"LICENSE." The term includes both a standard license and a reciprocal license.

"LICENSEE." A person who holds a standard license or a reciprocal license.

"LISTING BROKER." A broker engaged as a seller's agent, dual agent or transaction licensee to market the property of a seller/landlord for sale or lease pursuant to a written agreement with the seller/landlord.

"PERSON." Any individual, corporation, corporate fiduciary, partnership, association or other entity, foreign or domestic.

"PRINCIPAL." A consumer of real estate services who has entered into an agency relationship with a broker.

"REAL ESTATE." Any interest or estate in land, whether corporeal, incorporeal, freehold or nonfreehold, whether the land is situated in this Commonwealth or elsewhere including leasehold interests and time share and similarly designated interests. A sale of a mobile home shall be deemed to be a transfer of an interest in real estate if accompanied by the assignment of the lease or sale of the land on which the mobile home is situated.

"REAL ESTATE SERVICE." An act or acts requiring a real estate license.

"RECIPROCAL LICENSE." A license issued under section 602 (a) through (e).

"RENTAL LISTING REFERRAL AGENT." Any person who owns or manages a business which collects rental information for the purpose of referring prospective tenants to rental units or locations of such units. The term "rental listing referral agent" shall not include any employee or official of any public housing authority created pursuant to State or Federal law.

"SALESPERSON." Any person employed by a licensed real estate broker to perform comparative market analyses or to list for sale, sell or offer for sale, to buy or offer to buy or to negotiate the purchase or sale or exchange of real estate or to negotiate a loan on real estate or to lease or rent or offer to lease, rent or place for rent any real estate or collect or offer or attempt to collect rent for the use of real estate for or in behalf of such real estate broker. No person employed by a broker to perform duties other than those activities as defined herein under "broker" shall be required to be licensed as a salesperson.

"SCHOOL." Any person who conducts classes in real estate subjects but is not a college, university or institute of higher learning duly accredited by the Middle States Association of Colleges and Secondary Schools or equivalent accreditation.

"SELLER AGENT." Any licensee who has entered into an agency relationship with a seller of real estate.

"STANDARD LICENSE." Any license issued under this act that is not a reciprocal license.

"SUBAGENT." A broker, not in the employ of the listing broker, who is engaged to act for, or cooperate with, the listing broker in selling property as an agent of the seller. A subagent is deemed to have an agency relationship with the seller.

"TIME SHARE." The right, however evidenced or documented, to use or occupy any one or more units on a periodic basis according to an arrangement allocating use and occupancy rights of that unit or those units between other similar users. As used in this definition, the term "unit" is a building or portion thereof permanently affixed to real property and designated for separate occupancy or a campground or portion thereof designated for separate occupancy. The phrase "time share" does not include campground membership.

"TIME-SHARE SALESPERSON." A person who either as an employee or independent contractor sells or offers to sell time shares. Such person shall sell time shares under the active supervision of a broker. A person licensed as a broker or as a salesperson shall not be required to be licensed as a time-share salesperson as a condition for selling or offering to sell time shares.

"TRANSACTION LICENSEE." A licensed broker or salesperson who provides communication or document preparation services or performs acts described under the definition of "broker" or "salesperson" for which a license is required, without being an agent or advocate of the consumer.

§ 455.202. State Real Estate Commission

(a) The State Real Estate Commission is hereby created and shall consist of the Commissioner of Professional and Occupational Affairs; the Director of the Bureau of Consumer Protection, or his designee; three members who shall be persons representing the public at large; five other persons, each of whom shall at the time of his appointment be a licensed

and qualified real estate broker under the existing law of this Commonwealth, and shall have been engaged in the real estate business in this Commonwealth for a period of not less than ten years immediately prior to his appointment; and one other person who shall have been licensed as a real estate broker, or cemetery broker, for a period of at least five years and shall have been engaged in selling cemetery lots for at least ten years immediately prior to his appointment. Each of said members of the commission shall be appointed by the Governor.

(b) The term of office of each of said members shall be five years from his appointment, or until his successor has been appointed and qualified but not longer than six months beyond the five-year period. In the event that any of said members shall die or resign during his term of office, his successor shall be appointed in the same way and with the same qualifications as above set forth and shall hold office for the unexpired term.

(c) A majority of the members currently serving on the commission shall constitute a quorum. The commission shall elect a chairman, vice-chairman and secretary from among its members. A commission member who fails to attend three consecutive meetings shall forfeit his seat unless the Commissioner of Professional and Occupational Affairs, upon written request from the member, finds that the member should be excused from a meeting because of illness or the death of a family member.

(d) Each member of the commission other than the Commissioner of Professional and Occupational Affairs shall receive reimbursement for reasonable expenses in accordance with Commonwealth regulations and per diem compensation at the rate of $ 60 per day for the time actually devoted to the business of the commission.

(e) In addition to regularly scheduled meetings of the commission, there shall be at least one public meeting each year in Pittsburgh, one public meeting each year in Philadelphia and one public meeting each year in Harrisburg. At least 15 days prior to the holding of any public meeting pursuant to this subsection, the commission shall give public notice of the meeting in a newspaper of general circulation in each of the areas where the public meeting is to be held. The purpose of these special meetings shall be to solicit from members of the public, suggestions, comments and objections about real estate practice in this Commonwealth.

Chapter 3
Application of the Act and Penalties

§ 455.301. Unlawful to conduct business without license or registration certificate

It shall be unlawful for any person, directly or indirectly, to engage in or conduct, or to advertise or hold himself out as engaging in or conducting the business, or acting in the capacity of a broker or salesperson, cemetery broker, cemetery salesperson, campground membership salesperson, time-share salesperson, builder-owner salesperson, rental listing referral agent or cemetery company within this Commonwealth without first being licensed or registered as provided in this act, unless he is exempted from obtaining a license or registration certificate under the provisions of section 304.

§ 455.302. Civil suits

No action or suit shall be instituted, nor recovery be had, in any court of this Commonwealth by any person for compensation for any act done or service rendered, the doing or rendering of which is prohibited under the provisions of this act by a person other than a licensed broker, salesperson, cemetery broker, cemetery salesperson, campground membership salesperson, time-share salesperson, builder-owner salesperson or rental listing referral agent, unless such person was duly licensed and registered hereunder as broker or salesperson at the time of offering to perform any such act or service or procuring any promise or contract for the payment of compensation for any such contemplated act or service.

§ 455.303. Criminal penalties

Any person who shall engage in or carry on the business, or act in the capacity of a broker, salesperson, cemetery broker, cemetery salesperson, campground membership salesperson, time-share salesperson, builder-owner salesperson, rental listing referral agent or cemetery company, within this Commonwealth, without a license or registration certificate, or shall carry on or continue business after the suspension or revocation of any such license or registration certificate issued to him, or shall employ any person as a salesperson or cemetery salesperson to whom a license has not been issued, or whose license or registration certificate as such shall have been revoked or suspended, shall be guilty of a summary offense and upon conviction thereof for a first offense shall be sentenced to pay a fine not exceeding $ 500 or suffer imprisonment, not exceeding three months, or both and for a second or subsequent offense shall be guilty of a felony of the third degree and upon conviction thereof, shall be sentenced to pay a fine of not less than $ 2,000 but not more than $ 5,000 or to imprisonment for not less than one year but not more than two years, or both.

§ 455.304. Exclusions

Except as otherwise provided in this act, the provisions of this act shall not apply to the following:

(1) An owner of real estate with respect to property owned or leased by such owner. In the case of a partnership or corporation, this exclusion shall not extend to more than five of its partners or officers, respectively, nor to other partnership or corporation personnel or employees.

(2) The employees of a public utility acting in the ordinary course of utility-related business under the provisions of Title 66 of the Pennsylvania Consolidated Statutes (relating to public utilities), with respect to negotiating the purchase, sale or lease of property.

(3) The officers or employees of a partnership or corporation whose principal business is the discovery, extraction, distribution or transmission of energy or mineral resources, provided that the purchase, sale or lease of real estate is a common and necessary transaction in the conduct of such principal business.

(4) The services rendered by an attorney-in-fact under an executed and recorded power of attorney from the owner or lessor (provided such power of attorney is not utilized to circumvent the intent of this act) or by an attorney at law.

(5) A person acting as trustee in bankruptcy, administrator, executor, trustee or guardian while acting under a court order or under the authority of a will or of a trust instrument.

(6) The elected officer or director of any banking institution, savings institution, savings bank, credit union or trust company operating under applicable Federal or State laws where only the real estate of the banking institution, savings institution, savings bank, credit union or trust company is involved.

(7) Any officer or employee of a cemetery company who, as incidental to his principal duties and without remuneration therefor, shows lots in such company's cemetery to persons for their use as a family burial lot and who accepts deposits on such lots for the representatives of the cemetery company legally authorized to sell the same.

(8) Cemetery companies and cemeteries owned or controlled by a bona fide church or religious congregation or fraternal organization or by any association created by a bona fide church or religious organization or by a fraternal organization.

(9) An auctioneer licensed under the act of September 29, 1961 (P.L. 1745, No. 708), known as "The Auctioneers' License Act," while performing authorized duties at any bona fide auction.

(10) Any person employed by an owner of real estate for the purpose of managing or maintaining multifamily residential property: Provided, however, That such person is not authorized or empowered by such owner to enter into leases on behalf of the owner, to negotiate terms or conditions of occupancy with current or prospective tenants or to hold money belonging to tenants other than on behalf of the owner. So long as the owner retains the authority to make all such decisions, the employees may show apartments and provide information on rental amounts, building rules and regulations and leasing determinations.

(11) The elected officer, director or employee of any banking institution, savings institution, savings bank, credit union or trust company operating under applicable Federal or State laws when acting on behalf of the institution in performing appraisals or other evaluations of real estate in connection with a loan transaction.

§ 455.305. Civil penalty

In addition to any other civil remedy or criminal penalty provided for in this act, the commission, by a vote of the majority of the maximum number of the authorized membership of the commission as provided by law, or by a vote of the majority of the duly qualified and confirmed membership or a minimum of five members, whichever is greater, may levy a

civil penalty of up to $ 1,000 on any current licensee who violates any provision of this act or on any person who practices real estate without being properly licensed to do so under this act. The commission shall levy this penalty only after affording the accused party the opportunity for a hearing, as provided in Title 2 of the Pennsylvania Consolidated Statutes (relating to administrative law and procedure).

Chapter 4
Powers and Duties of the
State Real Estate Commission—General

§ 455.401. Duty to issue licenses and registration certificates

It shall be the duty of the department to issue licenses and registration certificates to any person who shall comply with the provisions of this act.

§ 455.402. Approval of schools

Any school which shall offer or conduct any course or courses of study in real estate shall first obtain approval from, and thereafter abide by the rules and regulations of the commission covering such schools.

§ 455.403. Authority to examine applicants

The commission is empowered to prescribe the subjects to be tested. The department shall arrange for the services of professional testing services to write and administer examinations on behalf of the commission in accordance with commission guidance and approval.

§ 455.404. Power to promulgate regulations

The commission shall have the power to promulgate rules or regulations in order to administer and effectuate the purposes of this act. All existing rules or regulations shall remain in full force and effect until modified by the commission.

§ 455.404a. Continuing education

(a) The commission shall adopt, promulgate and enforce rules and regulations consistent with the provisions of this act establishing requirements of continuing education to be met by individuals licensed as real estate brokers and real estate salespersons under this act as a condition for renewal of their licenses. The commission may waive all or part of the continuing education requirement for a salesperson or broker who shows evidence, to the commission's satisfaction, that he was unable to complete the requirement due to illness, emergency or hardship. Such regulations shall include any fees necessary for the commission to carry out its responsibilities under this section.

(b) Beginning with the license period designated by regulation, each person licensed pursuant to this act shall be required to obtain 14 hours of mandatory continuing education during each two-year license period. A licensed broker or salesperson who wishes to activate a license which has been placed on inactive status shall be required to document 14 hours of continuing education.

(c) All courses, materials, locations and instructors shall be approved by the commission. No credit shall be given for any course in office management, except for courses offered to brokers that are intended to promote knowledge of the supervisory duties imposed upon brokers by this act and by the rules and regulations promulgated by the commission having to do with document preparation and retention, recordkeeping, deposit and maintenance of escrow accounts, advertising and solicitation limitations and requirements, conflicts of interest, disclosures to prospective sellers and buyers and the general ethical responsibilities of licensees.

(d) The commission shall initiate the promulgation of regulations to carry out the provisions of this section within six months of the effective date of this section.

(e) The commission shall inform licensees of the continuing education requirement prior to the renewal period when continuing education is required. Each renewal notice thereafter shall include the following additional information:

(1) That licenses may be placed on inactive status for no more than five years.

(2) That individuals must show evidence of 14 hours of continuing education in order to reactivate a license which has been placed on inactive status.

(3) The procedure and fee required for activating an inactive license.

(4) That a licensee who fails to activate his license after five years must retake the appropriate examination.

§ 455.405. Repealed. 1984, March 29, P.L. 162, No. 32, § 7, effective in 90 days

§ 455.406. Administration and enforcement

The commission shall have the power and its duty shall be to administer and enforce the laws of the Commonwealth relating to:

(1) Those activities involving real estate for which licensing is required under this act and to instruct and require its agents to bring prosecutions for unauthorized and unlawful practice.

(2) Those activities involving cemeteries and cemetery companies for which registration is required under this act and to instruct and require its agents to bring prosecutions for unauthorized or unlawful activities.

(3) Those activities involving campground memberships for which licensing is required under this act and to instruct and require its agents to bring prosecutions for unauthorized or unlawful activities.

§ 455.407. Fees

(a) All fees required under this act shall be fixed by the commission, by regulation and shall be subject to review in accordance with the act of June 25, 1982 (P.L. 633, No. 181), known as the "Regulatory Review Act." If the projected revenues to be generated by fees, fines and civil penalties imposed in accordance with the provisions of this act are not sufficient to match expenditures over a two-year period, the commission shall increase those fees by regulation, subject to review in accordance with the "Regulatory Review Act," such that the projected revenues will meet or exceed projected expenditures.

(b) If the Bureau of Professional and Occupational Affairs determines that the fees established by the commission are inadequate to meet the minimum enforcement efforts required, then the bureau, after consultation with the commission, shall increase the fees by regulation, subject to review in accordance with the "Regulatory Review Act," so that adequate revenue is raised to meet the required enforcement effort.

§ 455.408. Reports to legislative committees

(a) The commission shall submit annually a report to the Professional Licensure Committee of the House of Representatives and to the Consumer Protection and Professional Licensure Committee of the Senate a description of the types of complaints received, status of cases, board action which has been taken and the length of time from the initial complaint to final board resolution.

(b) The commission shall also submit annually to the House of Representatives and the Senate Appropriations Committees, 15 days after the Governor has submitted his budget to the General Assembly, a copy of the budget request for the upcoming fiscal year which the commission previously submitted to the department.

Chapter 5
Qualifications and Applications for Licenses and Registration Certificates

Subchapter A
General

§ 455.501. Reputation; inactive licensee; revoked license

(a) Licenses shall be granted only to and renewed only for persons who bear a good reputation for honesty, trustworthiness, integrity and competence to transact the business of broker, salesperson, cemetery broker, cemetery salesperson, campground membership salesperson, time-share salesperson, builder-owner salesperson or rental listing referral agent, in such manner as to safeguard the interest of the public, and only after satisfactory proof of such qualifications has been presented to the commission as it shall by regulation require. An applicant for renewal of a reciprocal license shall provide evidence that the applicant continues to hold a current license in the state where the applicant's principal place of business is located.

(b) Any person who remains inactive for a period of five years without renewing his license shall, prior to having a license reissued to him, submit to and pass the examination pertinent to the license for which the person is reapplying.

(c) Unless ordered to do so by Commonwealth Court, the commission shall not reinstate the license, within five years of the date of revocation, of any person whose license has been revoked under this act. Any person whose license has been revoked may reapply for a license at the end of the five-year period but must meet all of the licensing qualifications of this act for the license applied for, to include the examination requirement.

Subchapter B
Broker's License

§ 455.511. Qualifications for license

The applicant for a broker's license, shall as a condition precedent to obtaining a license, take the broker's license examination and score a passing grade. Prior to taking the examination:

(1) The applicant shall be at least 21 years of age.

(2) The applicant shall be a high school graduate or shall produce proof satisfactory to the commission of an education equivalent thereto.

(3) The applicant shall have completed 240 hours in real estate instruction in areas of study prescribed by the rules of the commission, which rules shall require instruction in the areas of fair housing and professional ethics.

(4) The applicant shall have been engaged as a licensed real estate salesperson for at least three years or possess educational or experience qualifications which the commission deems to be the equivalent thereof.

§ 455.512. Application for license

(a) An application for a license as real estate broker shall be made in writing, to the department, upon a form provided for the purpose by the department and shall contain such information as to the applicant as the commission shall require.

(b) The application shall state the place of business for which such license is desired.

(c) The application shall be received by the commission within three years of the date upon which the applicant passed the examination.

§ 455.513. Corporations, partnerships and associations

If the applicant for a broker's license is a corporation, partnership or association, then the provisions of sections 511 and 512 shall apply to the individual designated as broker of record. The employees of said corporation, partnership or association actually engaging in or intending to engage in the real estate business shall meet the provisions of sections 521 and 522.

Subchapter C
Salesperson's License

§ 455.521. Qualifications for license

Each applicant shall as a condition precedent to obtaining a license, take the salesperson license examination and score a passing grade. Prior to taking the examination:

(1) The applicant shall be at least 18 years of age.

(2) The applicant shall have completed 60 hours in real estate instruction in areas of study prescribed by the rules of the commission, which rules shall require instruction in the areas of fair housing and professional ethics.

§ 455.522. Application for license

(a) An application for a license as salesperson shall be made, in writing, to the department, upon a form provided for the purpose by the department, and shall contain such information as to the applicant, as the commission shall require.

(b) The applicant shall submit a sworn statement by the broker with whom he desires to be affiliated certifying that the broker will actively supervise and train the applicant.

(c) The application shall be received by the commission within three years of the date upon which the applicant passed the examination.

Subchapter D
Cemetery Broker's License

§ 455.531. Qualifications for license

Each applicant for a cemetery broker's license shall as a condition to obtaining a license take the cemetery broker's license examination and score a passing grade. Prior to taking the examination:

(1) The applicant shall be at least 21 years of age.

(2) The applicant shall have been engaged full time as a sales person or cemetery salesperson for at least three years or possess educational or experience qualifications which the commission deems to be the equivalent thereof.

§ 455.532. Application for license

(a) An application for a license as a cemetery broker shall be made, in writing, to the department, upon a form provided for the purpose by the department and shall contain such information as to the applicant, as the commission shall require.

(b) The applicant shall have completed 60 hours in real estate instruction in areas of study prescribed by the rules of the commission, which rules shall require instruction in the area of professional ethics.

(c) The application shall be received by the commission within three years of the date upon which the applicant passed the examination.

§ 455.533. Corporations, partnerships, associations or other entities

If the applicant for a cemetery broker's license is a corporation, partnership, association, or other entity, foreign or domestic, then the provisions of sections 531 and 532 shall apply to the individual designated as Broker of Record, as well as those members actually engaging in or intending to engage in the real estate business.

11

Subchapter E
Cemetery Salesperson's License

§ 455.541. Qualifications for license

The applicant for a cemetery salesperson's license shall be at least 18 years of age.

§ 455.542. Application for license

(a) An application for a license as a cemetery salesperson shall be made, in writing, to the department, upon a form provided for the purpose by the department, and shall contain such information as to the applicant, as the commission shall require.

(b) The applicant for a license shall submit a sworn affidavit by the broker or cemetery broker with whom he desires to be affiliated certifying that the broker will actively supervise and train the applicant and certifying the truth and accuracy of the certification of the applicant.

Subchapter F
Builder-Owner Salesperson's License

§ 455.551. Qualifications for license

Each applicant for a builder-owner salesperson's license, shall as a condition precedent to obtaining a license, take the standard real estate salesperson's license examination and score a passing grade. Prior to taking the examination:

(1) The applicant shall be 18 years of age.

(2) The applicant shall be employed by a builder-owner possessing those qualifications as contained in section 501.

§ 455.552. Application for license

(a) An application for a license as a builder-owner salesperson shall be made, in writing to the department, upon a form provided for the purpose by the department, and shall contain such information as to the applicant as the commission shall require.

(b) The applicant shall submit a sworn statement by the builder-owner by whom he is employed certifying to such employment.

(c) The application shall be received by the commission within three years of the date upon which the applicant passed the examination.

Subchapter G
Rental Listing Referral Agent's License

§ 455.561. Qualifications for license

The qualification for licensure as a rental listing referral agent shall be the same as those set forth in sections 521 and 522 except that the applicant need not be affiliated with a broker.

Subchapter H
Cemetery Company Registration Certificate

§ 455.571. Application and fee for registration certificate

An application for a registration certificate for a cemetery company to operate a cemetery shall be made, in writing to the department, upon a form provided for the purpose by the department, and shall contain such information as to the applicant as the commission shall require.

12

Subchapter I
Campground Membership Salesperson's License

§ 455.581. Qualifications for license

(a) The applicant for a campground salesperson's license shall be at least 18 years of age.

(b) The applicant shall have successfully completed 15 hours in the following areas of study:

(1) Basic contract law.

(2) Sales practices and procedures.

(3) Sales ethics.

(4) Basic theory of campground memberships.

(c) The applicant shall undergo not less than 30 days of onsite training at a campground membership facility.

§ 455.582. Application for license

(a) An application for a license as a campground membership salesperson shall be made in writing to the department upon a form provided for the purpose by the department and shall contain such information as to the applicant as the commission shall require.

(b) The applicant for a license shall submit a sworn affidavit by a broker certifying that the broker will actively supervise and train the applicant and certifying the truth and accuracy of the certification of the applicant.

(c) A license shall be renewed biennially.

(d) The commission shall establish an application fee and a biennial renewal fee by regulation.

Subchapter J
Time-Share Salesperson's License

§ 455.591. Qualifications for license

(a) The applicant for a time-share salesperson's license shall be at least 18 years of age.

(b) The applicant shall have successfully completed 30 hours of instruction in the following areas of study:

(1) Basic contract law.

(2) Sales practices and procedures.

(3) Sales ethics.

(4) Basic theory of resort time sharing.

(c) The applicant shall undergo not less than 30 days of onsite training at a time-share facility.

§ 455.592. Application for license

(a) An application for a license as a time-share salesperson shall be made in writing to the department upon a form provided for the purpose by the department and shall contain such information as to the applicant as the commission shall require.

(b) The applicant shall submit a sworn statement by a broker certifying that the broker will actively supervise and train the applicant and certifying the truth and accuracy of the certification of the applicant.

(c) A license shall be renewed biennially.

(d) The commission shall establish an application fee and a biennial renewal fee by regulation.

Chapter 6
Duties of Licensees

§ 455.601. Duty of brokers, cemetery brokers and rental listing referral agents to maintain office

(a) Each broker (which term in this section shall include cemetery broker) and rental listing referral agent who holds a standard license shall maintain a fixed office within this Commonwealth. The current license of such a rental listing referral agent or broker and of each licensee employed by such broker or rental listing referral agent shall be prominently displayed in an office of the broker or rental listing referral agent. The address of the office shall be designated on the current license. In case of removal of a broker's office from the designated location, all licensees registered at that location shall make application to the commission before such removal or within ten days thereafter, designating the new location of the office, and shall pay the required fees, whereupon the commission shall issue a current license at the new location for the unexpired period, if the new location complies with the terms of this act. Each broker who holds a standard license shall maintain a sign on the outside of his office indicating the proper licensed brokerage name.

(b) If the applicant for a standard broker's license intends to maintain more than one place of business within the Commonwealth, he shall apply for and obtain an additional license in his name at each office. Every such application shall state the location of such office. Each office shall be under the direction and supervision of a manager who is either the broker or an associate broker: Provided, however, That such broker or an associate broker may direct and supervise more than one office.

§ 455.602. Reciprocal licenses

(a) Any person who holds a current license to provide real estate services issued by another state and whose principal place of business for the provision of those services is outside of this Commonwealth may be issued a reciprocal license under this act in accordance with this section. The reciprocal license shall be the type of license that the commission determines is most similar to the type of license issued by the other state.

(b) Obtaining a reciprocal license shall constitute sufficient contact with this Commonwealth for the exercise of personal jurisdiction by the commission and the courts of this Commonwealth over the licensee in any action or proceeding arising out of acts or omissions by the licensee:

(1) in this Commonwealth; or

(2) relating to an actual or proposed transaction involving real property located in this Commonwealth.

(c) The commission shall issue a reciprocal license upon the filling with the commission of an application and the receipt of:

(1) a duly certified copy of a current license issued to the applicant by the state in which the principal place of business of the applicant is located, or a certified statement that the applicant holds a current license in that state, in either case sent to the commission by the appropriate licensing body in that state;

(2) a certified statement sent to the commission by that licensing body as to whether the applicant has been the subject of any disciplinary proceeding and the details of those proceedings; and

(3) a verified statement from the applicant that:

(i) to the knowledge of the applicant, the applicant is not the subject of discipline or a current investigation or proceeding alleging misconduct under a licensing law or criminal law of either this Commonwealth or another jurisdiction;

(ii) the applicant has reviewed and is familiar with this act and the rules and regulations of the commission and that the applicant agrees to be bound by this act and those rules and regulations; and

(iii) the applicant agrees to permit the disclosure to the commission of the record in any disciplinary proceeding involving alleged misconduct by the applicant from any jurisdiction in which the applicant is or has been licensed.

(4) payment of a fee in the same amount as the fee required to be paid in connection with the issuance of a standard license of the same type; and

(5) a consent to service of process in a form prescribed by the rules and regulation of the commission.

(d) This section may be implemented by written reciprocal licensing agreements with the real estate licensing authorities of other states as follows:

(1) The Commission may enter into such an agreement whenever the commission in its discretion determines that such an agreement is necessary or desirable to provide residents of the Commonwealth with the opportunity to secure a license in the other state substantially comparable to the opportunity afforded to residents of the other state by this section.

(2) It shall not be necessary for the commission to have entered into an agreement with a particular state in order for the commission to issue a reciprocal license under this section to an applicant from that state, subject to the restrictions in subsection (e).

(e) Whenever the commission determines that another state does not offer reciprocal licensure opportunities to residents of this Commonwealth that are substantially comparable to those afforded to residents of that state by this section, the commission shall require applicants from that state who apply for a reciprocal license to meet education, experience and examination requirements substantially comparable to those required by that state with respect to residents of this Commonwealth who seek reciprocal licensure in that state, except that any requirements imposed under this subsection shall not exceed the requirements for obtaining a license under this act imposed on residents of this Commonwealth.

(f) The commission shall publish annually in the Pennsylvania Bulletin and make available both on request and via the Internet:

(1) a list of those states with which the commission has signed agreements under subsection (d), and a summary of the terms of each agreement; and

(2) a list of those states that the commission has identified under subsection (e) as not offering substantially comparable reciprocal licensure opportunities, and a description of the additional requirements the commission has determined are necessary to comply with that subsection.

(g) A person who holds a reciprocal license shall promptly notify the commission if the person's principal place of business for the provision of real estate services becomes located in this Commonwealth. Upon receipt of the notice by the commission, the person's reciprocal license shall not be renewed and the person shall be required to obtain a standard license.

(h) A reciprocal licensee shall have the same rights and responsibilities as if the person held a standard license, except that a person holding a reciprocal license:

(1) shall not be eligible to be a member of the commission;

(2) shall be exempt from the requirements of sections 404.1, 501(b), 513 and 533; and

(3) shall be exempt from taking and passing the examination required for standard licenses.

(i) An associate broker, salesperson, campground membership salesperson or time-share salesperson holding a reciprocal license shall not conduct business in this Commonwealth except in affiliation with a broker holding either a standard or a reciprocal license.

(j) If the applicant for a reciprocal broker's license is a corporation, partnership or association, the applicant must designate in its application a broker of record who is an individual holding a current reciprocal or standard broker's license.

§ 455.603. Employment of associate brokers, salespersons

(a) No associate broker or salesperson (which term in this section shall include cemetery salespersons) shall be employed by any other broker than is designated upon the current license issued to said associate broker or said salesperson. Whenever a licensed salesperson or associate broker desires to change his employment from one licensed broker to another, he shall notify the commission in writing no later than ten days after the intended date of change, pay the required fee, and return his current license. The commission, shall, upon receipt of acknowledgment from the new broker of the change of employment issue a new license. In the interim at such time as the change in affiliation of the salesperson or associate broker occurs, he shall maintain a copy of the notification sent to the commission as his temporary license pending receipt of his new current license. It shall be the duty of the applicant to notify the commission if a new license or other pertinent communication is not received from the commission within 30 days.

(b) No campground membership salesperson or time-share salesperson shall be supervised by any other broker than is designated upon the current license issued to such salesperson. Whenever a campground membership salesperson or a time-share salesperson desires to be supervised by a different broker, such licensee and the commission shall follow the procedure specified in subsection (a) for real estate salespersons.

§ 455.604. Prohibited acts

(a) The commission may upon its own motion, and shall promptly upon the verified complaint in writing of any person setting forth a complaint under this section, ascertain the facts and, if warranted, hold a hearing for the suspension or revocation of a license or registration certificate or for the imposition of fines not exceeding $1,000, or both. The commission shall have power to refuse a license or registration certificate for cause or to suspend or revoke a license or registration certificate or to levy fines up to $1,000, or both, where the said license has been obtained by false representation, or by fraudulent act or conduct, or where a licensee or registrant, in performing or attempting to perform any of the acts mentioned herein, is found guilty of:

(1) Making any substantial misrepresentation.

(2) Making any false promise of a character likely to influence, persuade or induce any person to enter into any contract or agreement when he could not or did not intend to keep such promise.

(3) Pursuing a continued and flagrant course of misrepresentation or making of false promises through salesperson, associate broker, other persons, or any medium of advertising, or otherwise.

(4) Any misleading or untruthful advertising, or using any other trade name or insignia or membership in any real estate association or organization, of which the licensee is not a member.

(5) Failure to comply with the following requirements:

(i) all deposits or other moneys accepted by every person, holding a real estate broker license under the provisions of this act, shall be retained by such real estate broker pending consummation or termination of the transaction involved, and shall be accounted for in the full amount thereof at the time of the consummation or termination;

(ii) every salesperson and associate broker promptly on receipt by him of a deposit or other moneys on any transaction in which he is engaged on behalf of his broker-employer, shall pay over the deposit to the broker;

(iii) a broker shall not commingle the money or other property of his principal with his own;

(iv) every broker shall immediately deposit such moneys, of whatever kind or nature, belonging to others, in a separate custodial or trust fund account maintained by the broker with some bank or recognized depository until the transaction involved is consummated or terminated, at which time the broker shall account for the full amount received. Under no circumstances shall a broker permit any advance payment of funds belonging to others to be deposited in the broker's business or personal account, or to be commingled with any funds he may have on deposit;

(v) every broker shall keep records of all funds deposited therein, which records shall indicate clearly the date and from whom he received money, the dates deposited, the dates of withdrawals, and other pertinent information concerning the transaction, and shall show clearly for whose account the money is deposited and to whom the money belongs. All such records and funds shall be subject to inspection by the commission. Such separate custodial or trust fund account shall designate the broker, as trustee, and such account must provide for withdrawal of funds without previous notice. All such records shall be available to the commission, or its representatives, immediately after proper demand or after written notice given, or upon written notice given to the depository;

(vi) a broker is not required to hold in escrow rents that he receives for property management for a lessor. A broker shall deposit rents received into a rental management account that is separate from the broker's escrow account and general business accounts; or

(vii) a broker shall be permitted to deposit moneys into his escrow account to cover service charges to this account assessed by the banking institution.

(6) Failing to preserve for three years following its consummation records relating to any real estate transaction.

(7) Acting for more than one party in a transaction without the knowledge and consent in writing of all parties for whom he acts.

(8) Placing a "for sale" or "for rent" sign on or advertising any property without the written consent of the owner, or his authorized agent.

(9) Failing to voluntarily furnish a copy of any listing, sale, lease, or other contract relevant to a real estate transaction to all signatories thereof at the time of execution.

(10) Failing to specify a definite termination date that is not subject to prior notice, in any listing contract.

(11) Inducing any party to a contract, sale or lease to break such contract for the purpose of substitution in lieu thereof of a new contract, where such substitution is motivated by the personal gain of the licensee.

(12) Accepting a commission or any valuable consideration by a salesperson or associate broker for the performance of any acts specified in this act, from any person, except the licensed real estate broker with whom he is affiliated.

(12.1) Paying of a commission or any valuable consideration by a broker to anyone other than his licensed employees or another real estate broker for the performance of any acts specified in this act.

(13) Failing to disclose to an owner in writing his intention or true position if he directly or indirectly through a third party, purchased for himself or acquires or intends to acquire any interest in or any option to purchase property which has been listed with his office to sell or lease.

(14) Being convicted in a court of competent jurisdiction in this or any other state, or Federal court, of forgery, embezzlement, obtaining money under false pretenses, bribery, larceny, extortion, conspiracy to defraud, or any similar offense or offenses, or any felony or pleading guilty or nolo contendere to any such offense or offenses.

(15) Violating any rule or regulation promulgated by the commission in the interest of the public and consistent with the provisions of this act.

(15.1) Failing to provide a disclosure required by this act or any other Federal or State law imposing a disclosure obligation on licensees in connection with real estate transactions.

(16) In the case of a broker licensee, failing to exercise adequate supervision over the activities of his licensed salespersons or associate brokers within the scope of this act.

(17) Failing, within a reasonable time as defined by the commission, to provide information requested by the commission as the result of a formal or informal complaint to the commission, which would indicate a violation of this act.

(18) Soliciting, selling or offering for sale real property by offering free lots, or conducting lotteries or contests or offering prizes for the purpose of influencing by deceptive conduct any purchaser or prospective purchaser of real property. The commission shall promulgate necessary rules and regulations to provide standards for nondeception conduct under this paragraph.

(i) Any offering by mail or by telephone of any prize, gift, award or bonus in relation to the offering of sale of real property, shall be accompanied by a statement of the fair market value, not suggested retail price, of all prizes offered, plus a statement of the odds of receiving any such prize. If the offering is by mail the statement of value and odds shall be printed in a clear and conspicuous manner.

(ii) If a prize is to be awarded as a rebate, coupon or discount certificate, a statement of that fact shall be included. An offering by mail shall include a statement of any fees and the maximum amount of each which the prizewinner must pay in order to receive the prize. Such fees shall include, but not be limited to, dealer preparation, shipping, handling, redemption and shipping insurance. Each fee associated with a prize and the odds of receiving the prize shall appear in a clear and conspicuous manner on any offering by mail.

(iii) An offering by mail shall be written in a clear and coherent manner, using common usages of words and terms. A concise description of the real property or interest being promoted shall appear in any offering and shall include a statement that the interest is a time share, where applicable. If the prospective prizewinner must personally visit and inspect the real property or interest being promoted and listen to a sales presentation in order to win a prize, the offering shall include a statement of that fact. An offering may include instructions for a recipient to contact a certain telephone number within a specified time period or by a specified date, if the offeror identifies the business entity and its relationship to the offeror and complies with this paragraph.

(iv) Substitutions of prizes having equal or greater fair market value may be made if the offeror complies with this paragraph.

(v) As used in this paragraph, the term "prize" includes, but is not limited to, money, personal property, vacations, travel certificates, motor vehicles and appliances.

(19) Paying or accepting, giving or charging any undisclosed commission, rebate, compensation or profit or expenditures for a principal, or in violation of this act.

(20) Any conduct in a real estate transaction which demonstrates bad faith, dishonesty, untrustworthiness, or incompetency.

(21) Performing any act for which an appropriate real estate license is required and is not currently in effect.

(22) Violating any provision of the act of October 27, 1955 (P.L. 744, No. 222), known as the "Pennsylvania Human Relations Act," or any order or consent decree of the Pennsylvania Human Relations Commission issued pursuant to such act if such order or consent decree resulted from a complaint of discrimination in the area of activities authorized by virtue of this act.

(i) Such activities include but are not limited to:

(A) Accepting listings on the understanding that illegal discrimination in the sale or rental of housing is to be practiced due to race, color, religious creed, sex, ancestry, national origin, privately; except that the commission shall not have the authority to levy a fine solely on the basis of this paragraph.

(b) All fines and civil penalties imposed in accordance with section 305 and this section shall be paid into the Professional Licensure Augmentation Account.

§ 455.605. Promotional land sales; approval

(a) Any person who proposes to engage in real estate transactions of a promotional nature in this Commonwealth for a property located inside or outside of this Commonwealth, shall first register with the commission for its approval before so doing, and shall comply with such restrictions and conditions pertaining thereto as the commission may impose by rule or regulation. Registration shall not be required for property located within or outside of this Commonwealth which is subject to a statutory exemption under the Federal Interstate Land Sales Full Disclosure Act (Public Law 90-448, 82 Stat. 590, *15 U.S.C. § 1702).*

(b) As used in this section the term "promotional real estate" means an interest in property as defined in this act which is a part of a common promotional plan undertaken by a single developer or group of developers acting together to offer interests in real estate for sale or lease through advertising by mail, newspaper or periodical, by radio, television, telephone or other electronic means which is contiguous, known, designated or advertised as a common unit or by a common name: Provided, however, That the term shall not mean real estate interest involving less than 50 lots or shares, cemetery lots and land involving less than 25 acres.

(c) A person may apply to the commission for registration of promotional land sales by filing a statement of record and meeting the requirements of this section. Each registration shall be renewed annually. In lieu of registration or renewal, the commission shall accept registrations, property reports or similar disclosure documents filed in other states or with the Federal Government: Provided, That the commission may suspend or revoke the registration when the Federal Government or a registering state suspends or revokes a regulation. The commission shall, by rule and regulation, cooperate with similar jurisdictions in other states to establish uniform filing procedures and forms, public offering statements and similar forms. The commission shall charge an application fee as determined by regulation to cover costs associated with processing applications for registrations and renewals.

(d) Unless prior approval has been granted by the commission or the promotional plan is currently registered with the Department of Housing and Urban Development pursuant to the Federal Interstate Land Sales Full Disclosure Act or pursuant to State law, the statement of record shall contain the information and be accompanied by documents specified as follows:

(1) The name and address of each person having an interest in the property to be covered by the statement of record and the extent of such interest, except that in the case of a corporation the statement shall list all officers and all holders of 10% or more of the subscribed or issued stock of the corporations.

(2) A legal description of, and a statement of the total area included in the property and a statement of the topography thereof, together with a map showing the division proposed and the dimensions of the property to be covered by the statement of record and their relation to existing streets and roads.

(3) A statement of the condition of the title to the land comprising the property including all encumbrances, mortgages, judgments, liens or unpaid taxes and deed restrictions and covenants applicable thereto.

(4) A statement of the general terms and conditions, including the range of selling prices or rents at which it is proposed to dispense of the property.

(5) A statement of the present condition of access to the property, the existence of any unusual conditions relating to safety which are known to the developer, completed improvements including, but not limited to, streets, sidewalks, sewage disposal facilities and other public utilities, the proximity in miles of the subdivision to nearby municipalities and the nature of any improvements to be installed by the developer and his estimated schedule for completion.

---

physical handicap, disability or use of a guide dog because of blindness of user of a prospective lessee or purchaser.

(B) Giving false information for purposes of discrimination in the rental or sale of housing due to race, color, religious creed, sex, ancestry, national origin, physical handicap, disability or use of a guide dog because of blindness of user of a prospective lessee or purchaser.

(C) Making distinctions in locations of housing or dates of availability of housing for purposes of discrimination in the rental or sale of such housing due to race, color, religious creed, sex, ancestry, national origin, physical handicap, disability or use of a guide dog because of blindness of user of the prospective lessee or purchaser.

(ii) Nothing contained in this paragraph is intended to preclude the State Real Estate Commission from conducting its own investigation and maintaining its own file on any complaint of discrimination. The intent hereunder is to allow the Pennsylvania Human Relations Commission a reasonable period of time to conduct its own investigations, hold hearings, render its decisions and inform the State Real Estate Commission of its findings prior to the State Real Estate Commission taking action against any broker, salesperson or sales associate charged with a violation of this paragraph.

(iii) If in the event the Pennsylvania Human Relations Commission does not act on a discrimination complaint within 90 days after it is filed with the Pennsylvania Human Relations Commission then the State Real Estate Commission may proceed with action against such licensee.

(iv) The 90-day waiting period delaying State Real Estate Commission action against licensee accused of discrimination applies only in initial complaints against such licensee, second or subsequent complaints may be brought by individuals or the Pennsylvania Human Relations Commission directly to the State Real Estate Commission.

(v) The Pennsylvania Human Relations Commission shall notify the State Real Estate Commission of findings of violations by the Human Relations Commission against licensees under this act concerning the sale, purchase or lease of real estate in violation of the "Pennsylvania Human Relations Act."

(23) In the case of a cemetery company registrant, violating any provisions of Title 9 of the Pennsylvania Consolidated Statutes (relating to burial grounds).

(24) In the case of a cemetery company registrant, violating any provisions of the act of August 14, 1963 (P.L.1059, No.459), entitled "An act prohibiting future need sales of cemetery merchandise and services, funeral merchandise and services, except under certain conditions; requiring the establishment of and deposit into a merchandise trust fund of certain amount of the proceeds of any such sale; providing for the administration of such trust funds and the payment of money therefrom; conferring powers and imposing duties on orphans' courts, and prescribing penalties."

(25) Violating section 606 or 607.

(26) Violating section 609.

(27) In the case of a broker licensee, failing to exercise adequate supervision over the activities of a campground membership salesperson or a time-share salesperson within the scope of this act.

(28) Failure of a broker, campground membership salesperson or time-share salesperson to comply with the requirements of paragraph (5), or such alternative requirements established by the rules of the commission, in connection with deposits or other moneys received by the broker, campground membership salesperson or time-share salesperson in conjunction with the sale of a campground membership or a time share.

(29) Violating section 602.

(30) Having been disciplined under a real estate licensing law of another jurisdiction, including, but not limited to, having a license suspended or revoked, a fine or penalty imposed, or being censured or reprimanded publicly or

(6) A statement of any encumbrance, a statement of the consequences for the purchaser of a failure by the person or persons bound to fulfill obligations under any instrument or instruments creating such encumbrance and the steps, if any, taken to protect the purchaser in such eventuality.

(7) A copy of the articles of incorporation with all amendments thereto, if the developer is a corporation, copies of all instruments by which a deed of trust is created or declared, if the developer is a trust, copies of articles of partnership or association and all other papers pertaining to its organization if the developer is a partnership, unincorporated association, joint stock company or other form of organization and if the purported holder of legal title is a person other than the developer, copies of the above documents for such person.

(8) Copies of the deed or other instrument establishing title to the property in the developer or other person and copies of any instrument creating a lien or encumbrance upon the title of the developer or other person or copies of the opinion or opinions of counsel in respect to the title to the subdivision in the developer or other person or copies of the title insurance policy guaranteeing such title.

(9) Copies of all forms of conveyance to be used in selling or leasing lots to purchasers.

(10) Copies of instruments creating easements or other restrictions.

(11) Certified financial statements of the developer or an uncertified financial statement if a certified statement is not available as may be required by the commission.

(12) Such other information and such other documents and certifications as the commission may require as being reasonably necessary or appropriate to assure that prospective purchasers have access to truthful and accurate information concerning the offering.

(13) Consent to submit to the jurisdiction of the Commonwealth Court with respect to any action arising under this section.

(e) If at any time subsequent to the date of filing of a statement of record with the commission, a change shall occur affecting any material facts required to be contained in the statement, the developer shall promptly file an amendment thereto.

(f) If it appears to the commission that the statement of record or any amendment thereto, is on its face incomplete or inaccurate in any material respect, the commission shall so advise the developer within a reasonable time after the filing of the statement or amendment. Failure of the developer to provide the information requested by the commission within 90 days shall result in an automatic denial of an application or a suspension of registration.

(g) If it appears to the commission that a statement of record includes any untrue statement of material facts or omits to state any material fact required to be stated therein or necessary to make the statements therein not misleading, the commission may reject such application. The commission shall make an investigation of all consumer complaints concerning real estate promotions in the absence of a reciprocal agreement to handle on-site inspections. Under no circumstances shall a member or an employee of the commission perform an on-site inspection. If the commission determines that a violation of this section has occurred, the commission may:

(1) suspend or revoke any registration;

(2) refer the complaint to the Consumer Protection Bureau of the Office of Attorney General; or

(3) seek an injunction or temporary restraining order to prohibit the complained of activity in the Commonwealth Court.

(h) Upon rejection of an application or amendment, the applicant may within 20 days after such notice request a hearing before the commission. Prior to, and in conjunction with such hearing, the commission, or its designee, shall have access to and may demand the production of any books and papers of, and may examine, the developer, any agents or any other person in respect of any matter relevant to the application. If the developer or any agents fail to cooperate or obstruct or refuse to permit the making of an investigation, such conduct shall be grounds for the denial of the application.

§ 455.606. Relationships between brokers and consumers of real estate services

A broker may act in a real estate transaction, subject to the provisions of this act, as a seller/landlord agent, buyer/tenant agent, as a dual agent for seller/landlord and buyer/tenant or as a transaction licensee. Licensees employed by a broker shall bear the same relationship to the consumer as the broker, except that a broker, including one serving as a dual agent, may designate a licensee to act exclusively as agent of a particular seller/landlord and may designate another licensee to act exclusively as agent of a particular buyer/tenant.

§ 455.606a. Duties of licensee generally

(a) Regardless of whether a licensee is acting within the scope of an agency relationship with a consumer, a licensee owes to all consumers to whom the licensee renders real estate services the following duties, which may not be waived:

(1) to exercise reasonable professional skill and care which meets the practice standards required by this act;

(2) to deal honestly and in good faith;

(3) to present all written offers, written notices and other written communications to and from parties to a real estate transaction in a timely manner, except that the duty of a licensee under this paragraph to present written offers may be waived by a seller of a property that is subject to an existing contract for sale if:

(i) the waiver is in writing; and

(ii) the waiver is in the manner prescribed by the commission by regulation;

(4) to comply with those obligations imposed upon a licensee by the act of July 2, 1996 (P.L. 500, No. 84), known as the "Real Estate Seller Disclosure Act";

(5) to account in a timely manner for all money and property received from or on behalf of any consumer to a transaction consistent with the provisions of section 604(a)(5);

(6) to provide the consumer with information at the initial interview pursuant to section 608;

(7) to timely disclose to the consumer any conflicts of interest;

(8) to advise the consumer to seek expert advice on matters relating to the transaction that are beyond the licensee's expertise;

(9) to ensure that all services that are to be provided to the consumer are provided in a reasonable, professional and competent manner in accordance with the practice standards of this act;

(10) to advise the consumer regarding the status of the transaction;

(11) to advise the consumer of tasks that must be completed to satisfy an agreement or condition for settlement, provide assistance with document preparation and advise the consumer regarding compliance with laws pertaining to real estate transactions;

(12) to present all offers and counter offers in a timely manner, unless a party has directed the licensee otherwise in writing; and

(13) to provide disclosure to the consumer regarding any financial interest, including, but not limited to, a referral fee or commission, which a licensee has in any services to be provided to the consumer by any other person, including, but not limited to, financial services, title transfer and preparation services, insurance, construction, repair or inspection services. The licensee shall also provide disclosure regarding any financial interest which an affiliated licensee may have in any services to be provided to the consumer by any other person. The disclosures required by this paragraph shall be made at the time the licensee first recommends that the consumer purchase a service in which the licensee or an affiliated licensee has a financial interest or when the licensee first learns that the consumer will be purchasing a service in which the licensee or an affiliated licensee has a financial interest.

(b)   (1) A licensee may not perform a service for a consumer of real estate services for a fee, commission or other valuable consideration paid by or on behalf of the consumer unless the nature of the service and the fee to be charged are set forth in a written agreement between the broker and the consumer that is signed by the consumer. This paragraph shall not prohibit a licensee from performing services before such an agreement is signed, but the licensee is not entitled to recover a fee, commission or other valuable consideration in the absence of such a signed agreement.

(2) Notwithstanding paragraph (1), an open listing agreement or a nonexclusive agreement for a licensee to act as a buyer/tenant agent may be oral if the seller or buyer is provided with a written memorandum stating the terms of the agreement.

(3) Nothing in this subsection shall require a transaction licensee or subagent who is cooperating with the listing broker to obtain a written agreement from the seller.

(4) A subagent or transaction licensee who is cooperating with the listing broker for a fee paid by the listing broker or seller shall provide the buyer, prior to performing any services, with a written disclosure statement signed by the buyer, describing the nature of the services to be performed by the subagent or transaction licensee and containing the information required by section 608. If the buyer refuses to sign the statement, the licensee shall note the refusal on the statement and retain it for six months.

(c) A broker may not extend or delegate the broker's agency relationship with a principal to another broker without the written consent of the principal.

(d) A broker may compensate another broker who assists in the marketing and sale/lease of a consumer's property. Payment of compensation alone does not create an agency relationship between the consumer and the other broker.

(e) The fact that a licensee representing a seller/landlord also presents alternative properties to prospective buyer/tenants does not in itself constitute a breach of a duty or obligation owed by the licensee to the seller/landlord.

(f) The fact that a licensee representing a buyer/tenant also presents alternative properties in which that buyer/tenant is interested to other prospective buyer/tenants does not in itself constitute a breach of a duty or obligation owed by the licensee to that buyer/tenant.

(g) A licensee may not knowingly, during or following the termination of an agency relationship reveal confidential information of the principal, or use confidential information of the principal to the advantage of the licensee or a third party, except when:

(1) disclosure is made with the consent of the principal;

(2) the information is disclosed to another licensee or third party acting solely on the principal's behalf and not for any other party;

(3) the information is required to be disclosed under subpoena or court order;

(4) it is the intention of the principal to commit a crime and the disclosure of information is believed necessary to prevent the crime; or

(5) the information is used to defend the licensee in a legal proceeding against an accusation of wrongful conduct.

(h) A consumer of real estate services shall not be liable for the acts of a licensee unless the licensee is acting pursuant to the express direction of the consumer or the licensee is acting based upon a representation of the consumer reasonably relied upon by the licensee. A licensee shall not be liable for acts of a consumer of real estate services unless the consumer is acting at the express direction of the licensee or the consumer is acting as a result of a representation by a licensee reasonably relied on by the consumer.

(i) Unless otherwise agreed, a licensee owes no duty to conduct an independent inspection of the property and owes no duty to independently verify the accuracy or completeness of any representation made by a consumer to a transaction reasonably believed by the licensee to be accurate and reliable.

(j) Nothing in this section shall be construed to relieve a licensee of any duty imposed by another provision of this act.

§ 455.606b. Duties of seller's agent

In addition to the duties generally required of a licensee as set forth in section 606.1, the duties of the broker acting as an agent for the seller include the following:

(1) to be loyal to the seller by taking action that is consistent with the seller's interest in a transaction; and

(2) to make a continuous and good faith effort to find a buyer for the property, except that a seller's broker is not obligated to seek additional offers to purchase the property while the property is subject to an existing agreement for sale.

§ 455.606c. Duties of buyer's broker

In addition to the duties generally required of a licensee as set forth in section 606.1, the duties of the broker acting as an agent of the buyer include the following:

(1) to be loyal to the buyer by taking action that is consistent with the buyer's interest in a transaction;

(2) to make a continuous and good faith effort to find a property for the buyer, except that a buyer's broker is not obligated to seek additional properties for purchase while the buyer is subject to an existing contract for sale; and

(3) to disclose to the listing broker, at first contact, that the broker has been engaged as a buyer's agent. In the absence of a listing broker, this disclosure shall be made to the seller.

§ 455.606d. Duties of dual agent

(a) A licensee may act as a dual agent only with the written consent of both parties to the transaction following the disclosures given at the initial interview required by section 608. The consent must include a statement of the terms of compensation.

(b) In addition to the duties generally required of a licensee as set forth in section 606.1, the duties of a dual agent include the following:

(1) to take no action that is adverse or detrimental to either party's interest in a transaction;

(2) unless otherwise agreed to in writing, to make a continuous and good faith effort to find a buyer for the property, except that a dual agent is not obligated to seek additional offers to purchase the property while it is subject to an existing contract for sale; and

(3) unless otherwise agreed to in writing, to make a continuous and good faith effort to find a property for the buyer, except that a dual agent is not obligated to seek additional properties to purchase while the buyer is a party to an existing contract to purchase.

(c) A dual agent may show alternative properties not owned by the seller to prospective buyers and may list competing properties for sale without breaching any duty to the seller. A dual agent may show properties in which the buyer is interested to other prospective buyers without breaching any duty to the buyer.

§ 455.606e. Duties of designated agent

(a)   (1) In an agency relationship with a principal, the broker may, with the written consent of the principal, designate one or more licensees employed by the broker to serve as the designated agent of the principal to the exclusion of all other licensees employed by the same broker. A broker who represents both the seller/landlord and the buyer/tenant in the same transaction is a dual agent. Dual agency is permitted only as provided in section 606.4.

(2) A broker designating licensees to act as designated agents shall take reasonable care to protect any confidential information disclosed by a principal to his or her designated agent.

(3) A broker has the responsibility to direct and supervise the business activities of designated agents and thereby owes duties to both the seller/landlord and the buyer/tenant as a dual agent.

(b) In addition to the duties generally required of a licensee as set forth in section 606.1, where principals to a transaction are represented by designated agents employed by the same broker, the duties of a designated agent include the following:

(1) to be loyal to the principal with whom the agent is working by taking action that is consistent with that principal's interest in the transaction;

(2) to make a continuous and good faith effort to find a buyer for a principal who is a seller, or to find a property for a principal who is a buyer. A designated agent is not, however, obligated to seek additional offers for a seller principal while the property is subject to an existing contract for sale or, with regard to a principal buyer, to seek additional properties while the buyer is a party to an existing contract for purchase; and

(3) to disclose to the principal, prior to writing or presenting an offer to purchase, that the other party to the transaction is also represented by a licensee employed with the same broker. The disclosure shall confirm that the broker is a dual agent in the transaction.

§ 455.606f. Duties of transaction licensee

In addition to the duties generally required of a licensee as set forth in section 606.1, the duties of a transaction licensee include the following:

(1) to advise the consumer to be assisted that the licensee is not acting as an agent or advocate of the consumer and should not be provided with confidential information; and

(2) to provide limited confidentiality. A licensee shall not disclose information that the seller will accept a price less than the asking price or listed price, that the buyer will pay a price greater than the price submitted in a written offer or that a seller or buyer will agree to financing terms other than those offered.

§ 455.607. Deleted. 1998, Nov. 25, P.L. 908, No. 112, § 6, effective in one year

§ 455.608. Information to be given at initial interview

(a) Except as set forth in subsections (b), (c), (d) and (e), the commission shall establish rules or regulations which shall set forth the manner and method of disclosure of information to the prospective buyer/tenant or seller/landlord during the initial interview. For the purposes of this section, the initial interview is the first contact between a licensee and a consumer of real estate-related services where a substantive discussion about real estate needs occurs. Such disclosure shall be provided on a form adopted by the commission by regulation and shall include, but shall not be limited to:

(1) A disclosure of the relationships in which the broker may engage with the consumer. The disclosure shall describe the duties that the broker owes in each relationship provided for in this act.

(2) A statement informing sellers and buyers of their option to have an agency relationship with a broker, that an agency relationship is not to be presumed and that it will exist only as set forth in a written agreement between the broker and consumer of real estate service acknowledged by the consumer.

(3) A statement that a real estate consumer has the right to enter into a negotiated agreement with the broker limiting the activities or practices that the broker will provide for on behalf of the consumer and that the fee and services to be provided are to be determined by negotiations between the consumer and the broker.

(4) A statement identifying any possibility that the broker may provide services to another consumer who may be party to the transaction and, if so, an explanation of the duties the broker may owe the other party and whether the broker may accept a fee for those services.

(5) A statement identifying any possibility that the broker may designate one or more licensees affiliated with the broker to represent the separate interest of the parties to the transaction.

(6) A statement of the broker's policies regarding cooperation with other brokers, including the sharing of fees.

(7) A statement that a buyer's broker may be paid a fee that is a percentage of the purchase price and the buyer's broker, even if compensated by the listing broker, will represent the interests of the buyer.

(8) A statement that the duration of the broker's employment and the broker's fees are negotiable.

(9) The purpose of the Real Estate Recovery Fund and the telephone number of the commission at which further information about the fund may be obtained.

(10) A statement that the duration of the listing agreement or contract and the broker's commission are negotiable.

(11) A statement that any sales agreement must contain the zoning classification of a property except in cases where the property (or each parcel thereof, if subdividable) is zoned solely or primarily to permit single-family dwellings.

(b) The following apply to leases:

(1) Subsection (a) shall not apply and disclosure shall be in accordance with paragraph (2) if the licensee is providing information on a property or otherwise dealing with a prospective tenant for the purpose of rental only and if the licensee is:

(i) the actual owner/landlord of the real property, including the owner of an equity interest in an actual owner/landlord of the real property;

(ii) the direct employee of the owner/landlord of the real property; or

(iii) leasing the real property pursuant to a property management agreement or an exclusive leasing agreement with the owner/landlord of the real property.

(2) In cases under paragraph (1), the licensee shall provide to the prospective tenant a written statement indicating the capacity in which the licensee is acting. The written statement shall be provided at the time of the initial interview unless a rental application is required by the licensee, in which case the written statement shall be provided at the time the rental application is taken. The written statement shall be provided at the beginning of the rental application and shall be in the following form:

CONSUMER NOTICE

THIS IS NOT A CONTRACT

(licensee) _____ hereby states that with respect to this property, _____ (describe property), I am acting in the following capacity: (check one)

(i) owner/landlord of the property;

(ii) a direct employee of the owner/landlord; or

(iii) an agent of the owner/landlord pursuant to a property management or exclusive leasing agreement.

I acknowledge that I have received this notice:

(consumer)   (date)

I certify that I have provided this notice:

(licensee)   (date)

(3) The licensee shall provide a copy of the statement under paragraph (2) to the consumer and shall retain a copy signed by the consumer and the licensee for six months. If the prospective tenant refuses to sign the statement, the licensee shall note the refusal on the form and retain it for six months.

§ 455.608a. Written agreement with broker

An agreement between a broker and a principal, or any agreement between a broker and a consumer whereby the consumer is or may be committed to pay a fee, commission or other valuable consideration, that is required to be in writing by section 606.1, shall be signed by the consumer and shall identify the services to be provided and the fee to be paid, if any. The agreement shall also contain the following information which shall be disclosed in the manner and method the commission shall establish by regulation:

(1) A statement that the broker's fee and the duration of the contract have been determined as a result of negotiations between the broker and the seller/landlord or buyer/tenant.

(2) A statement describing the nature and extent of the broker's services to be provided to the seller/landlord or buyer/tenant and the fees that will be charged.

(3) A statement identifying any possibility that the broker, or any licensee employed by the broker, may provide services to more than one consumer in a single transaction and if so, an explanation of the duties that may be owed the other party and whether the broker may accept a fee for those services.

(4) In an agreement between a broker and seller, a statement of the broker's policies regarding cooperation with subagents and buyer agents, a disclosure that a buyer agent, even if compensated by the broker or seller will represent the interests of the buyer and a disclosure of any potential for the broker to act as a disclosed dual agent.

(5) In an agreement between a broker and a buyer, a statement identifying any possibility that the broker's compensation may be based upon a percentage of the purchase price, a disclosure of the broker's policies regarding cooperation with listing brokers willing to pay buyer's brokers, a disclosure that the broker, even if compensated by the listing broker or seller, will represent the interests of the buyer and disclosure of any potential for the buyer broker to act as a disclosed dual agent.

(6) A statement describing the purpose of the Real Estate Recovery Fund established under section 801 and the telephone number of the commission at which the seller can receive further information about the fund.

(7) A statement regarding any possible conflicts of interest and informing the consumer of the licensee's continuing duty to timely disclose any conflicts of interest.

§ 455.608b. Mandatory provisions of sales contract

In a sales agreement or sales contract, a broker shall disclose the following information which shall be disclosed in the manner and method the commission shall establish by regulation:

(1) A statement identifying the capacity in which the broker is engaged in the transaction and whether the broker, or any licensee affiliated with the broker, has provided services relating to the subject transaction to any other party to the transaction.

(2) A statement describing the purpose of the Real Estate Recovery Fund established under section 801 and the telephone number of the commission at which the parties to the transaction can receive further information about the fund.

(3) A statement of the zoning classification of the property, except in cases where the property or each parcel of the property, if subdividable, is zoned solely or primarily to permit single-family dwellings. Failure to comply with this requirement shall render the sales agreement or sales contract voidable at the option of the buyer, and if voided, any deposits tendered by the buyer shall be returned to the buyer without a requirement for court action.

(4) A statement that access to a public road may require issuance of a highway occupancy permit from the Department of Transportation.

28

---

(3) The licensee shall provide a copy of the written statement under paragraph (2) to the prospective tenant and shall retain a copy signed by the prospective tenant and the licensee for six months. If the prospective tenant refuses to sign the statement, the licensee shall note the refusal on the form and retain it for six months.

(c) If an initial interview with a consumer in a situation which is not covered by subsection (b) or (e) does not occur in person, the licensee shall orally advise the consumer of the various business relationships that the licensee may have with the consumer and provide an oral disclosure to the consumer as follows:

The Real Estate Law requires that I provide you with a written consumer notice that describes the various business relationship choices that you may have with a real estate licensee. Since we are discussing real estate without you having the benefit of the consumer notice, I have the duty to advise you that any information you give me at this time is not considered to be confidential, and any information you give me will not be considered confidential unless and until you and I enter into a business relationship. At our first meeting I will provide you with a written consumer notice which explains those business relationships and my corresponding duties to you.

(d) If an oral disclosure is given in subsection (c), the written disclosure form required by subsection (a) shall be provided to the consumer not later than the earlier of:

(1) the first meeting that the licensee has in person with the consumer after the initial interview; or

(2) the time a property is first shown to the consumer by the licensee or any person working with the licensee.

(e) The following apply to time-share estates:

(1) Subsection (a) shall not apply and disclosure shall be in accordance with paragraph (2) if the licensee is showing a time-share estate as defined in 68 Pa.C.S. § 3403(a) (relating to public offering statement; time-share estates).

(2) In cases under paragraph (1), the licensee shall provide the consumer with a written statement indicating the capacity in which the licensee is acting. The statement shall be provided at the time of the initial interview and shall be in the following form:

CONSUMER NOTICE

THIS IS NOT A CONTRACT

(licensee)   hereby states that with respect to this property, (describe property)   , I am acting in the following capacity: (check one)(i) owner of the property; (ii) a direct employee of the owner; or (iii) an agent of the owner pursuant to a property management or exclusive leasing or selling agreement.

I acknowledge that I have received this notice:

(consumer)   (date)

I certify that I have provided this notice:

(licensee)   (date)

27

§ 455.608c. Comparative market analysis disclosure

A comparative market analysis must contain the following statement printed conspicuously and without change on the first page:

> This analysis has not been performed in accordance with the Uniform Standards of Professional Appraisal Practice which require valuers to act as unbiased, disinterested third parties with impartiality, objectivity and independence and without accommodation of personal interest. It is not to be construed as an appraisal and may not be used as such for any purpose.

A comparative market analysis prepared in accordance with this act shall not be deemed to be an appraisal within the scope of the act of July 10, 1990 (P.L. 404, No. 98), known as the Real Estate Appraisers Certification Act.

§ 455.608d. Cemetery broker's disclosure

In any sales agreement or sales contract, a cemetery broker shall be subject to the requirements of section 608.2(2) as it relates to the Real Estate Recovery Fund and the disclosure of information.

§ 455.609. Right to cancel purchase of time share and campground membership

(a) A purchaser shall have the right to cancel the purchase of a time share or a campground membership until midnight of the fifth day following the date on which the purchaser executed the purchase contract.

(b) The right of cancellation shall be set forth conspicuously in boldface type of at least ten point in size immediately above the signature of the purchaser on the purchase contract in substantially the following form:

> "You, the purchaser, may cancel this purchase at any time prior to midnight of the fifth day following the date of this transaction. If you desire to cancel, you are required to notify the seller, in writing, at (address). Such notice shall be given by certified return receipt mail or by any other bona fide means of delivery which provides you with a receipt. Such notice shall be effective upon being postmarked by the United States Postal Service or upon deposit of the notice with any bona fide means of delivery which provides you with a receipt."

This clause is to be separately initialed by the purchaser. Copies of all documents which place an obligation upon a purchaser shall be given to the purchaser upon execution by the purchaser.

(c) Notice of cancellation shall be given by certified return receipt mail or by any other bona fide means of delivery, provided that the purchaser obtains a receipt. A notice of cancellation given by a bona fide means of delivery shall be effective on the date postmarked or on the date of deposit of the notice with any bona fide means of delivery.

(d) Within ten business days after the receipt of a notice of cancellation, all payments made under the purchase contract shall be refunded to the purchaser and an acknowledgment that the contract is void shall be sent to the purchaser. In the event of a cancellation pursuant to this section, any promotional prizes, gifts and premiums issued to the purchaser by the seller shall remain the property of the purchaser.

(e) The right of cancellation shall not be waivable by any purchaser.

(f) A purchaser who exercises the right of cancellation shall not be liable for any damages as a result of the exercise of that right.

(g) In addition to constituting a violation of this act, a violation of this section by any individual, corporation, partnership, association or other entity shall also be deemed a violation of the act of December 17, 1968 (P.L. 1224, No. 387), known as the "Unfair Trade Practices and Consumer Protection Law." The Attorney General is authorized to enforce this section. Any actions brought by the Attorney General to enforce this section shall be in addition to any actions which the commission may bring under this act.

(h) The right of the purchaser to bring an action to enforce this section shall be independent of any rights of action which this section confers on the Attorney General and the commission.

(i) Nothing in this act shall affect any rights conferred upon the purchaser by 68 Pa.C.S. Pt. II Subpt. B (relating to condominiums).

(j) This act shall be applicable to time shares and campground memberships which are located within this Commonwealth and to time shares and campground memberships which are located outside this Commonwealth but for which the purchase contract was executed by the purchaser within this Commonwealth.

Chapter 7
Proceedings Before The Commission

§ 455.701. Hearings held by commission

(a) The said hearings may be held by the commission or any members thereof, or by any of its duly authorized representatives, or by any other person duly authorized by the commission for such purpose in any particular case.

(b) The commission may adopt the findings in the report or may, with or without additional testimony, either return the matter to the representative for such further consideration as the commission deems necessary or make additional or other findings of fact on the basis of all the legally probative evidence of the record and enter its conclusions of law and order in accordance with the requirements for the issuance of an adjudication under Title 2 of the Pennsylvania Consolidated Statutes (relating to administrative law and procedure).

(c) Proceedings before the commission shall be conducted in accordance with Title 1, Part 2 of the Pennsylvania Code.

§ 455.702. Imputed knowledge, limitations

(a) No violation of any of the provisions of this act on the part of any salesperson, associate broker, or other employee of any licensed broker, shall be grounds for the revocation or suspension of the license of the employer of such salesperson, associate broker, or employee, unless it shall appear upon the hearings held, that such employer had actual knowledge of such violation.

(b) No violation of any of the provisions of this act on the part of any cemetery broker or cemetery salesperson or other employee of any registered cemetery company, shall be grounds for the revocation or suspension of the registration certificate of the cemetery company, unless it shall appear that such cemetery company had actual knowledge of such violation.

(c) A course of dealing shown to have been followed by such employee shall constitute prima facie evidence of such knowledge upon the part of his employer.

(d) No violation of any of the provisions of this act on the part of any campground membership salesperson or time-share salesperson shall be grounds for the revocation or suspension of the license of the broker responsible for supervising such salesperson unless it shall appear upon the hearings held that such broker had actual knowledge of such violation. A course of dealing shown to have been followed by such salesperson shall constitute prima facie evidence of such knowledge upon the part of such broker.

Chapter 8
Real Estate Recovery Fund

§ 455.801. Establishment of the fund

(a) There is hereby established the Real Estate Recovery Fund for the purposes hereinafter set forth in this act.

(b) The Real Estate Recovery Fund shall not apply to the sale of, or the offer to sell, a campground membership or to a campground membership salesperson.

§ 455.802. Funding of the fund

Each licensee entitled to renew his license on or after February 28, 1980, shall, when so renewing his license pay in addition to the applicable license fee a further fee of $ 10, which shall be paid and credited to the Real Estate Recovery Fund, thereafter any person upon receiving his initial real estate license or cemetery company registration certificate, shall, in addition to all fees, pay into the Real Estate Recovery Fund a sum of $ 10. If at the commencement of any biennial renewal period beginning in 1982 and thereafter, the balance of the fund is less than $ 300,000, the commission may assess an additional fee, in addition to the renewal fee, against each licensee and registrant in an amount not to exceed $ 10 which will yield revenues sufficient to bring the balance of the fund to $ 500,000. All said fees shall be paid into the State Treasury and credited to the Real Estate Recovery Fund, and said deposits shall be allocated solely for the purposes of the fund as provided in this act. The fund shall be invested and interest/dividends shall accrue to the fund.

§ 455.803. Application for recovery from fund

(a) When any aggrieved person obtains a final judgment in any court of competent jurisdiction against any person licensed under this act, upon grounds of fraud, misrepresentation or deceit with reference to any transaction for which a license or registration certificate is required under this act (including with respect to cemetery companies any violation of 9 Pa.C.S. § 308(b) (relating to accounts of qualified trustee)) and which cause of action occurred on or after the effective date of this act, the aggrieved person may, upon termination of all proceedings, including reviews and appeals, file an application in the court in which the judgment was entered for an order directing payment out of the Real Estate Recovery Fund of the amount unpaid upon the judgment.

(b) The aggrieved person shall be required to show:

(1) That he is not a spouse of the debtor, or the personal representative of said spouse.

(2) That he has obtained a final judgment as set out in this section.

(3) That all reasonable personal acts, rights of discovery and such other remedies at law and in equity as exist have been exhausted in the collection thereof.

(4) That he is making said application no more than one year after the termination of the proceedings, including reviews and appeals in connection with the judgment.

(c) The commission shall have the right to answer actions provided for under this section, and subject to court approval, it may compromise a claim based upon the application of the aggrieved party.

(d) When there is an order of the court to make payment or a claim is otherwise to be levied against the fund, such amount shall be paid to the claimant in accordance with the limitations contained in this section. Notwithstanding any other provisions of this section, the liability of that portion of the fund allocated for the purpose of this act shall not exceed $ 20,000 for any one claim and shall not exceed $ 100,000 per licensee. If the $ 100,000 liability of the Real Estate Recovery Fund as provided herein is insufficient to pay in full claims adjudicated valid of all aggrieved persons against any one licensee or registrant, such $ 100,000 shall be distributed among them in such ratio that the respective claims of the aggrieved applicants bear to the aggregate of such claims held valid. If, at any time, the money deposited in the Real Estate Recovery Fund is insufficient to satisfy any duly authorized claim or portion thereof, the commission shall, when sufficient money has been deposited in the fund, satisfy such unpaid claims or portions thereof, in the order that such claims or portions thereof were originally filed, plus accumulated interest at the rate of 6% a year.

31

(e) Upon petition of the commission the court may require all claimants and prospective claimants against one licensee or registrant to be joined in one action, to the end that the respective rights of all such claimants to the Real Estate Recovery Fund may be equitably adjudicated and settled.

(f) Should the commission pay from the Real Estate Recovery Fund any amount in settlement of a claim as provided for in this act against a licensee:

(1) The license of that person shall automatically suspend upon the effective date of the payment thereof by the commission.

(2) No such licensee shall be granted reinstatement until he has repaid in full plus interest at the rate of 10% a year, the amount paid from the Real Estate Recovery Fund.

(3) The commission shall have the right to petition the court that entered the judgment against the licensee to enter a judgment under this subsection, and, upon proof of the amount paid by the fund, the court shall enter a judgment against the licensee for that amount in favor of the commission.

(g) Should the commission pay from the Real Estate Recovery Fund any amount in settlement of a claim as provided for in this act against a registrant the registrant shall automatically be denied the right to sell cemetery lots upon the effective date of the payment thereof by the commission. No such registrant shall be granted the right to sell cemetery lots until he has repaid in full plus interest at the rate of 10% a year, the amount paid from the Real Estate Recovery Fund.

Chapter 9
Repealer and Effective Date

§ 455.901. Repealer

The act of May 1, 1929 (P.L. 1216, No. 427), known as the "Real Estate Brokers License Act of one thousand nine hundred and twenty-nine," is repealed to the following conditions:

(1) All valid licenses issued prior to the effective date of this act under the provisions of said 1929 act shall continue with full force and validity during the period for which issued. For the subsequent license period, and each license period thereafter, the commission shall renew such licenses without requiring any license examination to be taken: Provided, however, That applicants for renewal or holders of such licenses shall be subject to all other provisions of this act.

(2) All proceedings in progress on the effective date shall continue to proceed under the terms of the act under which they were brought.

(3) All offenses alleged to have occurred prior to the effective date of this act shall be processed under the act of May 1, 1929 (P.L. 1216, No. 427).

§ 455.902. Effective date

Section 561 shall take effect September 1, 1980 and the remaining provisions of this act shall take effect immediately.

32

§ 35.171. [Reserved].

Source

The provisions of this § 35.171 adopted August 5, 1983, effective August 6, 1983, 13 Pa.B. 2400; reserved February 24, 1989, effective February 25, 1989, 19 Pa.B. 781. Immediately preceding text appears at serial pages (88264) and (130235).

§ 35.172. [Reserved].

Source

The provisions of this § 35.172 adopted August 5, 1983, effective August 6, 1983, 13 Pa.B. 2400; reserved February 24, 1989, effective February 25, 1989, 19 Pa.B. 781. Immediately preceding text appears at serial page (130235).

§ 35.173. [Reserved].

Source

The provisions of this § 35.173 adopted August 5, 1983, effective August 6, 1983, 13 Pa.B. 2400; reserved February 24, 1989, effective February 25, 1989, 19 Pa.B. 781. Immediately preceding text appears at serial page (130235).

§ 35.174. [Reserved].

Source

The provisions of this § 35.174 adopted August 5, 1983, effective August 6, 1983, 13 Pa.B. 2400; reserved February 24, 1989, effective February 25, 1989, 19 Pa.B. 781. Immediately preceding text appears at serial page (130235).

§ 35.175. [Reserved].

Source

The provisions of this § 35.175 adopted August 5, 1983, effective August 6, 1983, 13 Pa.B. 2400; reserved February 24, 1989, effective February 25, 1989, 19 Pa.B. 781. Immediately preceding text appears at serial pages (130235) to (130236).

§ 35.176. [Reserved].

Source

The provisions of this § 35.176 adopted August 5, 1983, effective August 6, 1983, 13 Pa.B. 2400; reserved February 24, 1989, effective February 25, 1989, 19 Pa.B. 781. Immediately preceding text appears at serial page (130236).

Subchapter B. GENERAL PROVISIONS

35-15

§ 35.201. Definitions.

The following words and terms, when used in this chapter, have the following meanings, unless the context clearly indicates otherwise:

Act—The Real Estate Licensing and Registration Act (63 P.S. §§ 455.101—455.902).

Agency relationship—A fiduciary relationship between a broker or licensees employed by a broker and a consumer who becomes a principal.

Associate broker—An individual broker who is employed by another broker.

Branch office—Any fixed location in this Commonwealth, other than the main office, maintained by a broker or cemetery broker, devoted to the transaction of real estate business.

Broker—An individual or entity holding either a standard or reciprocal license, that, for another and for a fee, commission or other valuable consideration, does one or more of the following:

(i) Negotiates with or aids a person in locating or obtaining for purchase, lease or acquisition of interest in real estate.

(ii) Negotiates the listing, sale, purchase, exchange, lease, time share and similarly designated interests, financing or option for real estate.

(iii) Manages real estate.

(iv) Represents himself or itself as a real estate consultant, counsellor or house finder.

(v) Undertakes to promote the sale, exchange, purchase or rental of real estate. This subparagraph does not apply to an individual or entity whose main business is that of advertising, promotion or public relations.

(vi) Undertakes to perform a comparative market analysis.

(vii) Attempts to perform one of the actions listed in subparagraphs (i)—(vi).

Broker of record—The individual broker responsible for the real estate transactions of a partnership, association or corporation that holds a broker's license.

Builder-owner salesperson—An individual holding either a standard or reciprocal license, who is a full-time employee of a builder-owner of single- and multi-family dwellings located in this Commonwealth and who is authorized, for and on behalf of, the builder-owner, to do one or more of the following:

(i) List for sale, sell or offer for sale real estate of the builder-owner.

(ii) Negotiate the sale or exchange of real estate of the builder-owner.

(iii) Lease or rent, or offer to lease, rent or place for rent, real estate of the builder-owner.

(iv) Collect or offer, or attempt to collect, rent for real estate of the builder-owner.

35-16

Bureau—The Bureau of Professional and Occupational Affairs of the Department.

Buyer agent—A licensee who enters into an agency relationship with a buyer/tenant.

Campground membership—An interest, other than in fee simple or by lease, which gives the purchaser the right to use a unit of real property for the purpose of locating a recreational vehicle, trailer, tent, tent trailer, pickup camper or other similar device on a periodic basis under a membership contract allocating use and occupancy rights between other similar users.

Campground membership salesperson—An individual holding either a standard or reciprocal license, who, either as an employee or an independent contractor, sells or offers to sell campground memberships under the active supervision of a broker. A licensed broker, salesperson or time-share salesperson does not need to possess a campground membership salesperson's license to sell campground memberships.

Cemetery—

(i) A place for the disposal or burial of deceased human beings, by cremation or in a grave, mausoleum, vault, columbarium or other receptacle.

(ii) The term does not include a private family cemetery.

Cemetery associate broker—An individual cemetery broker employed by another cemetery broker or by a broker.

Cemetery broker—An individual or entity holding either a standard or reciprocal license, that is engaged as, or carrying on the business or acting in the capacity of, a broker exclusively within the limited field or branch of business that applies to cemetery lots, plots and mausoleum spaces or openings.

Cemetery company—An individual or entity that offers or sells to the public the ownership, or the right to use, a cemetery lot.

Cemetery salesperson—An individual holding either a standard or reciprocal license, employed by a broker or cemetery broker exclusively to perform the duties of a cemetery broker.

Commission—The State Real Estate Commission.

Comparative market analysis—A written analysis, opinion or conclusion by a contracted buyer's agent, transactional licensee or an actual or potential seller's agent relating to the probable sale price of a specified piece of real estate in an identified real estate market at a specified time, offered either for the purpose of determining the asking/offering price for the property by a specific actual or potential consumer or for the purpose of securing a listing agreement with a seller.

Consumer—An individual or entity who is the recipient of any real estate service.

Credit—A period of 15 hours of instruction.

Department—The Department of State of the Commonwealth.

35-17

Designated agent—One or more licensees designated by the employing broker, with the consent of the principal, to act exclusively as the agent or agents for the principal to the exclusion of all other licensees within the broker's employ.

Distance education—Real estate instruction delivered in an independent or instructor-led format during which the student and the instruction are separated by distance and sometimes time.

Dual agent—A licensee who acts as an agent for the buyer/tenant and seller/landlord in the same transaction.

Hour of instruction—A period of at least 50 minutes.

Independent learning—An interactive educational program, including computer-based technology courses, that provides no contact with an instructor.

Initial interview—The first communication between a broker or salesperson and a consumer involving the personal/business or financial needs and motivations of the consumer. A discussion of the objective facts about the property, including dimensions, zoning classification, age, description or list price/lease amount, is not by itself a substantive discussion.

Instructor-led learning—An interactive educational program, including a classroom or simulated classroom, that provides significant ongoing contact from the instructor to the participant during the learning process.

Licensee—An individual or entity holding either a standard or reciprocal license, under the act. For purposes of the consumer notice in § 35.336(a)(relating to disclosure summary for the purchase or sale of residential or commercial real estate or for the lease of residential or commercial real estate when the licensee is working on behalf of the tenant), the term means a broker or salesperson.

Listing broker—A broker who has entered into a written agreement with a seller/landlord to market property as a seller's agent, dual agent or transaction licensee.

Main office—The fixed location other than a branch office of the broker or cemetery broker in this Commonwealth or another state devoted to the transaction of real estate business.

Manager of record—The individual rental listing referral agent responsible for the rental listing transactions of a partnership, association or corporation that holds a rental listing referral agent's license.

Nonexclusive buyer agency agreement—A nonexclusive agreement governed by a memorandum or contract wherein the buyer retains the right to employ multiple brokers to purchase or lease a property.

Open listing agreement—A nonexclusive listing agreement governed by a memorandum or contract wherein the seller retains the right to employ multiple brokers to sell or lease a property.

35-18

Ch. 35   STATE REAL ESTATE COMMISSION   49 § 35.201

Principal—A consumer who has entered into an agency relationship with a broker or another licensee employed by the broker.

Principal place of business—The fixed location of the broker or cemetery broker in the state where the licensee holds the equivalent of a standard license.

Real estate—An interest or estate in land—whether corporeal or incorporeal, whether freehold or nonfreehold, whether the land is situated in this Commonwealth or elsewhere—including leasehold interests and time share and similarly designated interests.

Real estate education provider—A person or institution who offers real estate education regardless of whether the learning is instructor-led or independent, excluding colleges, universities or institutes of higher learning accredited by the Middle States Association of Colleges and Secondary Schools or equivalent accreditation.

Reciprocal license—A license issued to an individual or entity whose principal place of business for the provision of real estate services is outside of this Commonwealth and who holds a current license to provide real estate services from a state that either has executed a reciprocal agreement with the Commission or has qualifications for licensure which are substantially comparable to those required by the Commission.

Rental listing referral agent—
(i) An individual or entity that owns or manages a business which collects rental information for the purpose of referring prospective tenants to rental units or locations of rental units.
(ii) The term does not include an official or employee of a public housing authority that is created under State or Federal law.

Salesperson—An individual holding either a standard or reciprocal license, who is employed by a broker to do one or more of the following:
(i) Sell or offer to sell real estate, or list real estate for sale.
(ii) Buy or offer to buy real estate.
(iii) Negotiate the purchase, sale or exchange of real estate.
(iv) Negotiate a loan on real estate.
(v) Lease or rent real estate, or offer to lease or rent real estate or to place real estate for rent.
(vi) Collect rent for the use of real estate, or offer or attempt to collect rent for the use of real estate.
(vii) Assist a broker in managing property.
(viii) Perform a comparative market analysis.

Seller agent—A licensee who enters into an agency relationship with a seller/landlord.

Standard license—A license, other than a reciprocal license, issued to an individual or entity who has fulfilled the education/experience and examination requirements of the act.

49 § 35.202   DEPARTMENT OF STATE   Pt. I

Subagent—A licensee, not in the employ of the listing broker, who acts or cooperates with the listing broker in selling property as a seller's/landlord's agent and is deemed to have an agency relationship with the seller.

Time share—
(i) The right, however evidenced or documented, to use or occupy one or more units on a periodic basis according to an arrangement allocating use and occupancy rights of that unit or those units between other similar users. As used in this definition, the term "unit" is a building or portion thereof permanently affixed to real property and designed for separate occupancy or a campground membership or portion thereof designed for separate occupancy.
(ii) The term does not include a campground membership.

Time-share salesperson—An individual who, either as an employee or an independent contractor, sells or offers to sell time shares.

Transaction licensee—A licensee who, without entering into an agency relationship with the consumer, provides communication or document preparation services or performs other acts listed in the definition of "broker" or "salesperson."

Authority

The provisions of this § 35.201 issued under the Real Estate Licensing and Registration Act (63 P.S. §§ 455.101—455.902); amended under sections 402, 404, 404.1, 513, 602, 606—606.6 and 608—608.3 of the Real Estate Licensing and Registration Act (63 P.S. §§ 455.402, 455.404, 455.404a, 455.513, 455.602, 455.606—455.606f and 455.608—455.608c); amended under sections 201, 501, 601, 602 and 604 of the Real Estate Licensing and Registration Act (63 P.S. §§ 455.201, 455.501, 455.601, 455.602 and 455.604).

Source

The provisions of this § 35.201 adopted February 24, 1989, effective February 25, 1989, 19 Pa.B. 781; amended June 10, 1994, effective June 11, 1994, 24 Pa.B. 2904; amended January 7, 2000, effective January 8, 2000, 30 Pa.B. 228; amended November 17, 2000, effective November 18, 2000, 30 Pa.B. 5954; amended March 29, 2002, effective March 30, 2002, 32 Pa.B. 1644; amended December 10, 2004, effective December 11, 2004, 34 Pa.B. 6530; corrected April 29, 2005, effective December 11, 2004, 35 Pa.B. 2630; amended August 19, 2005, effective August 20, 2005, 35 Pa.B. 4711. Immediately preceding text appears at serial pages (287878), (308315) to (308316) and (311095) to (311096).

§ 35.202. Exclusions from the act.

The following categories of individuals and entities are excluded from the act and this chapter:
(1) An owner of real estate with respect to property owned or leased by the owner. In the case of a corporation or partnership, this exclusion does not extend to more than five of the partnership's partners or the corporation's officers, nor to the other employes of the partnership or corporation.
(2) An employe of a public utility acting in the ordinary course of utility-related business under 66 Pa.C.S. §§ 101—3315 (relating to the Public Utility Code), with respect to negotiating the purchase, sale or lease of real estate.

Ch. 35   STATE REAL ESTATE COMMISSION   49 § 35.202

(3) An officer or employe of a partnership or corporation whose principal business is the discovery, extraction, distribution or transmission of energy or mineral resources, if the purchase, sale or lease of real estate is a common and necessary transaction in the conduct of the principal business.

(4) An attorney in fact who renders services under an executed and recorded power of attorney from an owner or lessor of real estate, if the power of attorney is not used to circumvent the intent of the act. The Commission will consider it a circumvention of the intent of the act for an owner or lessor of real estate to grant a power of attorney to a property manager for the sole purpose of avoiding the necessity of having the property managed by a real estate broker licensed under the act.

(5) An attorney-at-law who receives a fee from his client for rendering services within the scope of the attorney-client relationship and does not hold himself out as a real estate broker.

(6) A trustee in bankruptcy, administrator, executor, trustee or guardian who is acting under authority of a court order, will or trust instrument.

(7) An elected officer or director of a banking institution, savings institution, savings bank, credit union or trust company operating under applicable Federal or State statutes when only the real estate of the banking institution, savings institution, savings bank, credit union or trust company is involved.

(8) An officer or employe of a cemetery company who, as an incidental part of his principal duties and without remuneration therefore, shows lots in the company's cemetery to persons for use as family burial lots and who accepts deposits on the lots for a representative of the cemetery company legally authorized to sell them.

(9) A cemetery company or cemetery owned or controlled by a bona fide church or religious congregation or fraternal organization or by an association created by a bona fide church or religious organization or fraternal organization.

(10) An auctioneer licensed under The Auctioneers' License Act (63 P.S. §§ 701—732) (Repealed) or The Auctioneer and Auction Licensing Act (63 P.S. §§ 734.1—734.34) while performing authorized duties at a bona fide auction.

(11) An individual who is employed by the owner of multifamily residential dwellings to manage or maintain the dwellings and who is not authorized by the owner to enter into leases on the owner's behalf, to negotiate terms and conditions of occupancy with current or prospective tenants, or to hold money belonging to the tenants other than on the owner's behalf. So long as the owner retains authority to make decisions, the individual may show apartments and provide information on rental amounts, building rules and regulations and leasing determinations.

49 § 35.203   DEPARTMENT OF STATE   Pt. I

(12) An elected officer, director or employe of a banking institution, savings institution, savings bank, credit union or trust company operating under applicable Federal or State statutes when acting on behalf of the banking institution, savings institution, savings bank, credit union or trust company in performing appraisals or other evaluations of real estate in connection with a loan transaction.

Authority

The provisions of this § 35.202 issued under the Real Estate Licensing and Registration Act (63 P.S. §§ 455.101—455.902).

Source

The provisions of this § 35.202 adopted February 24, 1989, effective February 25, 1989, 19 Pa.B. 781; amended June 10, 1994, effective June 11, 1994, 24 Pa.B. 2904. Immediately preceding text appears at serial pages (185623) to (185624).

§ 35.203. Fees.

The following fees are charged by the Commission:

Review of qualifications of candidate for broker or cemetery broker licensing examination $40

Application for standard or reciprocal licensure of:
(i) Broker, cemetery broker or rental listing referral agent ... $75
(ii) Branch office $65
(iii) Associate broker, salesperson, cemetery associate broker, builder-owner salesperson, time-share salesperson, campground membership salesperson, or broker of record, partner or officer for a partnership, association or corporation $25
(iv) Cemetery salesperson $20

Application for registration of cemetery company $25

Initial standard or reciprocal licensure for broker, cemetery broker, branch office, rental listing referral agent, or broker of record, partner or officer for a partnership, association or corporation:
(i) If issued in first half of biennial period .... 100% of biennial renewal fee
(ii) If issued in second half of biennial period .... 50% of biennial renewal fee

Initial standard or reciprocal registration for cemetery company or initial standard or reciprocal licensure for associate broker, salesperson, cemetery associate broker, cemetery salesperson, builder-owner salesperson, time-share salesperson or campground membership salesperson:
(i) If issued in first half of biennial period .... 100% of biennial renewal fee
(ii) If issued in second half of biennial period .... 50% of biennial renewal fee

Ch. 35 STATE REAL ESTATE COMMISSION 49 § 35.203

Biennial renewal of standard or reciprocal license of broker, cemetery broker, branch office, rental listing referral agent, or broker of record, partner or officer for a partnership, association or corporation $84

Biennial renewal of cemetery company registration or standard or reciprocal license of associate broker, salesperson, cemetery associate broker, cemetery salesperson or campground membership salesperson $64

Registration of promotional real estate $120

Annual renewal of registration of promotional real estate $75

Approval of real estate education provider $120

Reinspection of real estate education provider after first failure .. $65

Annual renewal of approval of real estate education provider . $250 plus $10 for each satellite location, course and instructor

Change of name or office location of broker, cemetery broker or rental listing referral agent $75

Change of name or address for cemetery company or change of employer, change of employer's name or change of employer's address for associate broker, cemetery associate broker, salesperson, cemetery salesperson, builder-owner salesperson, time-share salesperson, campground membership salesperson, or broker of record, partner or officer for a partnership, association or corporation $20

Reinspection after failure for change of name or office location of broker, cemetery broker or rental listing referral agent $55

Change of ownership or directorship of real estate education provider $75

Change of name of real estate education provider $45

Change of location of real estate education provider $70

Addition of satellite location or instructor for real estate education provider $20

Addition of course for real estate education provider $25

Certification of current status of standard or reciprocal licensure, registration or approval $15

Certification of history of standard or reciprocal licensure, registration or approval $40

Duplicate standard or reciprocal license $5

Late renewal of standard or reciprocal license .... In addition to the prescribed renewal fee, $5 for each month or part of the month beyond the renewal date

---

49 § 35.204 DEPARTMENT OF STATE Pt. I

Authority

The provisions of this § 35.203 issued under the Real Estate Licensing and Registration Act (63 P. S. §§ 455.101—455.902); amended under sections 402, 403, 404, 404.1, 407(a) and 513 of the Real Estate Licensing and Registration Act (63 P. S. §§ 455.402, 455.403 404.1, 455.407(a) and 455.513); sections 201, 501, 601, 602 and 604 of the Real Estate Licensing and Registration Act (63 P. S. §§455.201, 455.501, 455.601, 455.602 and 455.604); and section 812.1 of The Administrative Code of 1929 (71 P.S. § 279.3a).

Source

The provisions of this § 35.203 adopted February 24, 1989, effective February 25, 1989, 19 Pa.B. 781; amended July 31, 1992, effective August 1, 1992, except for the amendment relating to the biennial renewal fees for real estate licensees, which takes effect on, and be retroactive to, May 1, 1992, 22 Pa.B. 3984; amended November 5, 1993, effective upon publication and apply retroactively for July 1, 1993, 23 Pa.B. 5304; amended May 20, 1994, effective June 1, 1994, 24 Pa.B. 2613; amended August 14, 1998, effective July 1, 1998, 28 Pa.B. 3938; amended May 26, 2000, effective May 27, 2000, 30 Pa.B. 2586; amended September 3, 2004, effective September 4, 2004, 34 Pa.B. 4883; amended December 10, 2004, effective December 11, 2004, 34 Pa.B. 6530; amended August 19, 2005, effective August 20, 2005, 35 Pa.B. 4711. Immediately preceding text appears at serial pages (308320) and (308321).

Cross References

This section cited in 49 Pa. Code § 35.221 (relating to general requirements); 49 Pa. Code § 35.243 (relating to licensure of branch office); 49 Pa. Code § 35.271 (relating to examination for broker's license); 49 Pa. Code § 35.273 (relating to examination for limited broker's license); 49 Pa. Code § 35.341 (relating to approval of real estate education provider); and 49 Pa. Code § 35.343 (relating to renewal of real estate education provider approval).

§ 35.204. Accuracy and veracity of papers filed with the Commission.

(a) An application, statement, character reference or other paper that is required to be filed by, or on behalf of, an applicant for examination, licensure, registration or approval under the act or this chapter will be subject to investigation by the Commission to confirm its accuracy and truthfulness.

(b) An applicant's knowing failure to provide accurate and truthful information in the application, or in the statements and papers that accompany the application, will be grounds for the Commission's denial of the application.

(c) A licensee's knowing failure to provide accurate and truthful information in connection with an application for examination, licensure, registration or approval under the act or this chapter will be grounds for disciplinary action against the licensee.

Authority

The provisions of this § 35.204 issued under the Real Estate Licensing and Registration Act (63 P. S. §§ 455.101—455.902).

Source

The provisions of this § 35.204 adopted February 24, 1989, effective February 25, 1989, 19 Pa.B. 781.

Ch. 35   STATE REAL ESTATE COMMISSION   49 § 35.221

Subchapter C. LICENSURE

LICENSURE REQUIREMENTS

Sec.
35.221. General requirements.
35.222. Licensure as broker.
35.223. Licensure as salesperson.
35.224. Licensure as cemetery broker.
35.225. Licensure as cemetery salesperson.
35.226. Licensure as builder-owner salesperson.
35.227. Licensure as rental listing referral agent.
35.228. Licensure as campground membership salesperson.
35.229. Licensure as time-share salesperson.

OFFICES

35.241. General office requirement.
35.242. Office of broker or cemetery broker.
35.243. Licensure of branch office.
35.244. Supervision and operation of office.
35.245. Display of licenses in office.
35.246. Inspection of office.

STATUS OF LICENSURE

35.251. Relicensure following revocation.
35.252. Termination of business of deceased broker with sole proprietorship.
35.253. Replacement of broker kof record due to death.
35.254. Substitution of broker or broker of record due to illness or injury.
35.255. Reciprocal licenses.

LICENSURE REQUIREMENTS

§ 35.221. General requirements.

In addition to meeting the other requirements of this subchapter pertaining to the specific license sought, an applicant for a standard or reciprocal real estate license shall submit the following to the Commission with the license application:

(1) The license fee prescribed in § 35.203 (relating to fees).

(2) Complete details of a conviction of, or plea of guilty or nolo contendere to, a felony or misdemeanor and the sentence imposed. In the case of an applicant that is a corporation, partnership or association, this requirement applies to each member of the partnership or association and to each officer of the corporation.

(3) Written consent that valid and binding service of process may be made on the applicant by serving the Chairperson of the Commission and the Secretary of the Commonwealth if the service of process cannot be made on the

---

49 § 35.222   DEPARTMENT OF STATE   Pt. I

applicant under 231 Pa. Code (relating to rules of civil procedure) for actions at law or in equity arising out of the applicant's real estate activities in this Commonwealth.

Authority

The provisions of this § 35.221 issued under the Real Estate Licensing and Registration Act (63 P. S. §§ 455.101—455.902); amended under sections 201, 501, 601, 602 and 604 of the Real Estate Licensing and Registration Act (63 P. S. §§ 455.201, 455.501, 455.601, 455.602 and 455.604).

Source

The provisions of this § 35.221 adopted February 24, 1989, effective February 25, 1989, 19 Pa.B. 781; amended August 19, 2005, effective August 20, 2005, 35 Pa.B. 4711. Immediately preceding text appears at serial page (308323).

Cross References

This section cited in 49 Pa. Code § 35.222 (relating to licensure as a broker); 49 Pa. Code § 35.223 (relating to licensure as salesperson); 49 Pa. Code § 35.224 (relating to licensure as cemetery broker); 49 Pa. Code § 35.225 (relating to licensure as cemetery salesperson); 49 Pa. Code § 35.226 (relating to licensure as builder-owner salesperson); 49 Pa. Code § 35.227 (relating to licensure as campground membership salesperson); 49 Pa. Coce § 35.228 (relating to licensure as campground membership salesperson); and 49 Pa. Code § 35.229 (relating to licensure as time-share salesperson).

§ 35.222. Licensure as a broker.

(a) An individual who wants to obtain a standard broker's license shall comply with § 35.221 (relating to general requirements) and:

(1) Have scored a passing grade on each part of the broker's licensing examination within 3 years prior to submission of a properly completed license application except that an applicant who has been actively licensed as a broker by another state within the last 5 years shall take and pass only the Pennsylvania portion of the examination. See § 35.271 (relating to examination for broker's license).

(2) Comply with §§ 35.241 and 35.242 (relating to general office requirement; and office of broker or cemetery broker).

(3) Submit a completed application to the Commission with recommendations attesting to the applicant's good reputation for honesty, trustworthiness, integrity and competence from:

(i) One real estate broker holding either a current standard or reciprocal license issued by the Commission.

(ii) Two persons unrelated to the applicant who own property in the county where the applicant resides or has a place of business.

(iii) Two persons unrelated to the applicant who own property in the county where the applicant previously resided, if the applicant changed his county of residence within 1 year prior to the submission of the application.

(b) An individual who wants to obtain a reciprocal broker's license shall comply with § 35.221 and:

(1) Possess a current broker's license issued by another state that agrees to issue a license to a standard Pennsylvania licensee without further requirement, or has qualifications for licensure substantially comparable to those required by the Commission. When a reciprocal applicant applies from a state which would require a Pennsylvania licensee to complete additional education, experience or

examination requirements, the reciprocal applicant shall complete equivalent requirements for licensure in this Commonwealth.

(2) Comply with § 35.241 and § 35.242.

(3) Submit a completed license application to the Commission with a verified statement that:

(i) To the applicant's knowledge, the applicant is not the subject of discipline or a current investigation or proceeding alleging misconduct under a licensing law or criminal law of either the Commonwealth or another state.

(ii) The applicant has reviewed, is familiar with and agrees to be bound by the act and this chapter.

(iii) The applicant agrees to permit the disclosure of the record in any disciplinary proceeding involving alleged misconduct by the applicant from any state in which the applicant is or has been licensed.

(4) If the applicant will be acting as an associate broker, submit a sworn statement from the broker with whom the applicant desires to be affiliated:

(i) Attesting to the applicant's good reputation for honesty, trustworthiness, integrity and competence.

(ii) Certifying that the applicant will be actively supervised and trained by the broker.

(5) Submit a certification from the real estate licensing authority of the other state:

(i) Confirming that the applicant's license is active and in good standing.

(ii) Describing any past disciplinary action taken by the licensing authority against the applicant.

(iii) Listing the applicant's office address and the name of the applicant's employing broker.

(c) A partnership, association or corporation that wants to obtain a standard or reciprocal broker's license shall:

(1) Ensure that each member of the partnership or association, or each officer of the corporation, who intends to engage in the real estate business holds either a current standard or reciprocal license issued by the Commission as a salesperson or broker.

(2) Designate an individual who is licensed by the Commission as a broker to serve as broker of record.

(3) Comply with §§ 35.241 and 35.242.

(4) Submit a completed license application to the Commission.

Authority

The provisions of this § 35.222 issued under the Real Estate Licensing and Registration Act (63 P.S. §§ 455.101—455.902); amended under sections 201, 501, 601, 602 and 604 of the Real Estate Licensing and Registration Act (63 P.S. §§ 455.201, 455.501, 455.501, 455.601, 455.602 and 455.604).

Source

The provisions of this § 35.222 adopted February 24, 1989, effective February 25, 1989, 19 Pa.B. 781; amended June 10, 1994, effective June 11, 1994, 24 Pa.B. 2904; amended August 19, 2005, effective August 20, 2005, 35 Pa.B. 4711. Immediately preceding text appears at serial pages (308324) to (308325).

§ 35.223. Licensure as salesperson.

(a) An individual who wants to obtain a standard salesperson's license shall comply with § 35.221 (relating to general requirements) and:

(1) Have scored a passing grade on each part of the salesperson's licensing examination within 3 years prior to the submission of a properly completed license application except that an applicant who has been actively licensed as a broker or a salesperson by another state within the last 5 years shall take and pass only the Pennsylvania portion of the examination. See § 35.272 (relating to examination for salesperson's license).

(2) Submit a completed license application to the Commission with:

(i) A sworn statement from the broker with whom the applicant desires to be affiliated:

(A) Attesting to the applicant's good reputation for honesty, trustworthiness, integrity and competence.

(B) Certifying that he will actively supervise and train the applicant.

(ii) Official transcripts evidencing the acquisition of degrees or course credits required by § 35.272(a)(2).

(b) An individual who wants to obtain a reciprocal salesperson's license shall comply with § 35.221 and:

(1) Possess a current broker's or salesperson's license issued by another state that agrees to issue a license to a standard Pennsylvania licensee without further requirement or has qualifications for licensure which are substantially comparable to those required by the Commission. When a reciprocal applicant applies from a state which would require a Pennsylvania licensee to complete additional education, experience or examination requirements, the reciprocal applicant shall complete equivalent requirements for licensure in this Commonwealth.

(2) Submit a completed license application to the Commission with a verified statement that:

(i) To the applicant's knowledge, the applicant is not the subject of discipline or a current investigation or proceeding alleging misconduct under a licensing law or criminal law of either the Commonwealth or another state.

(ii) The applicant has reviewed, is familiar with and agrees to be bound by the act and this chapter.

(iii) The applicant agrees to permit the disclosure of the record in any disciplinary proceeding involving alleged misconduct by the applicant from any state in which the applicant is or has been licensed.

(3) Submit a certification from the real estate licensing authority of the other state:

Ch. 35   STATE REAL ESTATE COMMISSION   49 § 35.224

(i) Confirming that the applicant's license is active and in good standing.

(ii) Describing any past disciplinary action taken by the licensing authority against the applicant.

(iii) Listing the applicant's office address and the name of the applicant's employing broker.

(4) Submit a sworn statement from a standard or reciprocal broker with whom the applicant will be affiliated:

(i) Attesting to the applicant's good reputation for honesty, trustworthiness, integrity and competence.

(ii) Certifying that the applicant will be actively supervised and trained by the broker.

Authority

The provisions of this § 35.223 issued under the Real Estate Licensing and Registration Act (63 P. S. §§ 455.101—455.902); amended under sections 201, 501, 601, 602 and 604 of the Real Estate Licensing and Registration Act (63 P. S. §§ 455.201, 455.501, 455.601, 455.602 and 455.604).

Source

The provisions of this § 35.223 adopted February 24, 1989, effective February 25, 1989, 19 Pa.B. 781; amended June 10, 1994, effective June 11, 1994, 24 Pa.B. 2904; amended August 19, 2005, effective August 20, 2005, 35 Pa.B. 4711. Immediately preceding text appears at serial pages (308325) to (308326).

§ 35.224. **Licensure as cemetery broker.**

(a) An individual who wants to obtain a standard cemetery broker's license shall comply with § 35.221 (relating to general requirements) and:

(1) Have scored a passing grade on each part of the salesperson's licensing examination within 3 years prior to submission of a properly completed license application except that an applicant who has been actively licensed as a cemetery broker by another state within the last 5 years shall take and pass only the Pennsylvania portion of the examination. See § 35.273 (relating to examination for cemetery broker's license).

(2) Comply with §§ 35.241 and 35.242 (relating to general office requirement; and office of broker or cemetery broker).

(3) Submit a completed application to the Commission with recommendations attesting to the applicant's good reputation for honesty, trustworthiness, integrity and competence from:

(i) One real estate broker holding either a current standard or reciprocal license issued by the Commission.

(ii) Two persons unrelated to the applicant who own property in the county where the applicant resides or has a place of business.

(iii) Two persons unrelated to the applicant who own property in the county where the applicant previously resided, if the applicant changed his county of residence within 1 year prior to the submission of the application.

(b) An individual who wants to obtain a reciprocal cemetery broker's license shall comply with § 35.221 and:

(312823) No. 371 Oct. 05

35-29

---

49 § 35.224   DEPARTMENT OF STATE   Pt. I

(1) Possess a current cemetery broker's license issued by a state that agrees to issue a license to a standard Pennsylvania licensee without further requirement or has qualifications for licensure which are substantially comparable to those required by the Commission. When a reciprocal applicant applies from a state that would require a Pennsylvania licensee to complete additional education, experience or examination requirements, the reciprocal applicant shall complete equivalent requirements for licensure in this Commonwealth.

(2) Comply with § 35.241 and § 35.242.

(3) Submit a completed license application to the Commission with a verified statement that:

(i) To the applicant's knowledge, the applicant is not the subject of discipline or a current investigation or proceeding alleging misconduct under a licensing law or criminal law of either this Commonwealth or another state.

(ii) The applicant has reviewed, is familiar with and agrees to be bound by the act and this chapter.

(iii) The applicant agrees to permit the disclosure of the record in any disciplinary proceeding involving alleged misconduct by the applicant from any state in which the applicant is or has been licensed.

(4) If the applicant will be acting as an associate cemetery broker, submit a sworn statement from the broker with whom the applicant will be affiliated:

(i) Attesting to the applicant's good reputation for honesty, trustworthiness, integrity and competence.

(ii) Certifying that the applicant will be actively supervised and trained by the broker.

(5) Submit a certification from the real estate licensing authority of the other state:

(i) Confirming that the applicant's license is active and in good standing.

(ii) Describing any past disciplinary action taken by the licensing authority against the applicant.

(iii) Listing the applicant's office address and the name of the applicant's employing broker.

(c) A partnership, association or corporation that wants to obtain a standard cemetery broker's license shall:

(1) Ensure that each member of the partnership, association or each officer of the corporation, who intends to engage in the real estate business possesses a standard license as a broker or cemetery broker issued by the Commission.

(2) Designate an individual who is licensed by the Commission as a broker or cemetery broker to serve as broker of record.

(3) Comply with §§ 35.241 and 35.242.

(4) Submit a complete license application to the Commission.

(d) A partnership, association or corporation that wants to obtain a reciprocal cemetery broker's license shall:

(312824) No. 371 Oct. 05

35-30

(1) Ensure that each member of the partnership, association or each officer of the corporation, who intends to engage in the real estate business possesses a standard or reciprocal license as a broker or cemetery broker issued by the Commission.

(2) Designate a broker or cemetery broker holding a standard or reciprocal license to serve as broker of record.

(3) Comply with §§ 35.241 and 35.242.

(4) Submit a complete license application to the Commission.

Authority

The provisions of this § 35.224 issued under the Real Estate Licensing and Registration Act (63 P. S. §§ 455.101—455.902); amended under sections 201, 501, 601, 602 and 604 of the Real Estate Licensing and Registration Act (63 P. S. §§ 455.201, 455.501, 455.601, 455.602 and 455.604).

Source

The provisions of this § 35.224 adopted February 24, 1989, effective February 25, 1989, 19 Pa.B. 781; amended June 10, 1994, effective June 11, 1994, 24 Pa.B. 2904; amended August 19, 2005, effective August 20, 2005, 35 Pa.B. 4711. Immediately preceding text appears at serial pages (308326) to (308327).

§ 35.225. Licensure as cemetery salesperson.

(a) An individual who wants to obtain a standard cemetery salespersons license shall comply with § 35.221 (relating to general requirements) and:

(1) Be 18 years of age or older.

(2) Submit a completed license application to the Commission with a sworn affidavit from the broker or cemetery broker with whom the applicant will be affiliated:

(i) Attesting to the applicant's good reputation for honesty, integrity, trustworthiness and competence.

(ii) Certifying that he will actively supervise and train the applicant.

(b) An individual who wants to obtain a reciprocal cemetery salesperson's license shall comply with § 35.221 and:

(1) Possess a current cemetery salesperson's license issued by a state that agrees to issue a license to a standard Pennsylvania licensee without further requirement or has qualifications for licensure which are substantially comparable to those required by the Commission. When a reciprocal applicant applies from a state that would require a Pennsylvania licensee to complete additional education, experience or examination requirements, the reciprocal applicant shall complete equivalent requirements for licensure in this Commonwealth.

(2) Submit a certification from the real estate licensing authority of the other state:

(i) Confirming that the applicant's license is active and in good standing.

(ii) Describing any past disciplinary action taken by the licensing authority against the applicant.

(iii) Listing the applicant's office address and the name of the applicant's employing broker.

35-31

(3) Submit a completed license application to the Commission with a verified statement that:

(i) To the applicant's knowledge, the applicant is not the subject of discipline or a current investigation or proceeding alleging misconduct under a licensing law or criminal law of either this Commonwealth or another state.

(ii) The applicant has reviewed, is familiar with and agrees to be bound by the act and this chapter.

(iii) The applicant agrees to permit the disclosure of the record in any disciplinary proceeding involving alleged misconduct by the applicant from any state in which the applicant is or has been licensed.

(4) Submit a sworn statement from the broker with whom the applicant will be affiliated:

(i) Attesting to the applicant's good reputation for honesty, trustworthiness, integrity and competence.

(ii) Certifying that the applicant will be actively supervised and trained by the broker.

Authority

The provisions of this § 35.225 issued under the Real Estate Licensing and Registration Act (63 P. S. §§ 455.101—455.902); amended under sections 201, 501, 601, 602 and 604 of the Real Estate Licensing and Registration Act (63 P. S. §§ 455.201, 455.501, 455.601, 455.602 and 455.604).

Source

The provisions of this § 35.225 adopted February 24, 1989, effective February 25, 1989, 19 Pa.B. 781; amended June 10, 1994, effective June 11, 1994, 24 Pa.B. 2904; amended August 19, 2005, effective August 20, 2005, 35 Pa.B. 4711. Immediately preceding text appears at serial page (308327).

§ 35.226. Licensure as builder-owner salesperson.

(a) An individual who wants to obtain a standard builder-owner salesperson's license shall comply with § 35.221 (relating to general requirements) and:

(1) Have scored a passing grade on each part of the salesperson's licensing examination within 3 years prior to submission of a properly completed license application except that an applicant who has been actively licensed as a broker, salesperson or builder-owner salesperson by another state within the last 5 years shall take and pass only the Pennsylvania portion of the examination. See § 35.274 (relating to examination for builder-owner salesperson's license).

(2) Submit a completed license application to the Commission with a sworn statement from a builder-owner:

(i) Attesting to the applicant's good reputation for honesty, trustworthiness, integrity and competence.

(ii) Certifying that he:

(A) Is a builder-owner of single or multifamily dwellings.

(B) Employs the applicant.

(b) An individual who wants to obtain a reciprocal license as a builder-owner salesperson shall comply with § 35.221 and:

(1) Possess a current builder-owner salesperson license issued by a state that agrees to issue a license to a standard Pennsylvania licensee without fur-

35-32

ther requirement or has qualifications for licensure which are substantially comparable to those required by the Commission. When a reciprocal applicant applies from a state that would require a Pennsylvania licensee to complete additional education, experience or examination requirements, the reciprocal applicant shall complete equivalent requirements for licensure in this Commonwealth.

(2) Submit a certification from the real estate licensing authority of the other state:

(i) Confirming that the applicant's license is active and in good standing.

(ii) Describing any past disciplinary action taken by the licensing authority against the applicant.

(iii) Listing the applicant's office address and the name of the applicant's employing broker.

(3) Submit a completed license application to the Commission with a verified statement that:

(i) To the applicant's knowledge, the applicant is not the subject of discipline or a current investigation or proceeding alleging misconduct under a licensing law or criminal law of either this Commonwealth or another state.

(ii) The applicant has reviewed, is familiar with and agrees to be bound by the act and this chapter.

(iii) The applicant agrees to permit the disclosure of the record in any disciplinary proceeding involving alleged misconduct by the applicant from any state in which the applicant is or has been licensed.

(4) Submit a sworn statement from the builder-owner with whom the applicant will be affiliated:

(i) Attesting to the applicant's good reputation for honesty, trustworthiness, integrity and competence.

(ii) Certifying that the builder-owner is a builder-owner of single or multifamily dwellings and employs the applicant.

Authority

The provisions of this § 35.226 issued under the Real Estate Licensing and Registration Act (63 P.S. §§ 455.101—455.902); amended under sections 201, 501, 601, 602 and 604 of the Real Estate Licensing and Registration Act (63 P.S. §§ 455.201, 455.501, 455.601, 455.602 and 455.604).

Source

The provisions of this § 35.226 adopted February 24, 1989, effective February 25, 1989, 19 Pa.B. 781; amended June 10, 1994, effective June 11, 1994, 24 Pa.B. 2904; amended August 19, 2005, effective August 20, 2005, 35 Pa.B. 4711. Immediately preceding text appears at serial pages (308327) to (308328).

§ **35.227. Licensure as rental listing referral agent.**

(a) An individual who wants to obtain a standard rental listing referral agent's license shall comply with § 35.221 (relating to general requirements) and:

35-33

(1) Have scored a passing grade on each part of the salesperson's examination within 3 years prior to submis-sion of a properly completed license application except that an applicant who has been actively licensed as a broker, salesperson or rental listing referral agent by another state within the last 5 years shall take and pass only the Pennsylvania portion of the examination. See § 35.275 (relating to examination for rental listing referral agent's license).

(2) Comply with § 35.241 (relating to general office requirement).

(3) Submit a completed license application to the Commission.

(b) An individual who wants to obtain a reciprocal rental listing referral agent's license shall comply with § 35.221 and:

(1) Possess a current rental listing referral agent's license issued by a state that agrees to issue a license to a standard Pennsylvania licensee without further requirement or has qualifications for licensure which are substantially comparable to those required by the Commission. When a reciprocal applicant applies from a state that would require a Pennsylvania licensee to complete additional education, experience or examination requirements, the reciprocal applicant shall complete equivalent requirements for licensure in this Commonwealth.

(2) Submit a certification from the real estate licensing authority of the other state:

(i) Confirming that the license is active and in good standing.

(ii) Describing any past disciplinary action taken by the licensing authority against the applicant.

(iii) Listing the applicant's office address and the name of the applicant's employing broker.

(3) Submit a completed license application to the Commission with a verified statement that:

(i) To the applicant's knowledge, the applicant is not the subject of discipline or a current investigation or proceeding alleging misconduct under a licensing law or criminal law of either this Commonwealth or another state.

(ii) The applicant has reviewed, is familiar with and agrees to be bound by the act and this chapter.

(iii) The applicant agrees to permit the disclosure of the record in any disciplinary proceeding involving alleged misconduct by the applicant from any state in which the applicant is or has been licensed.

(4) Comply with § 35.241 (relating to general office requirement).

(c) A partnership, association or corporation that wants to obtain a standard or reciprocal rental listing referral agent's license shall:

(1) Designate an individual who holds either a current standard or reciprocal license as a rental listing referral agent issued by the Commission to serve as manager of record.

(2) Comply with § 35.241.

(3) Submit a completed license application to the Commission.

35-34

Ch. 35   STATE REAL ESTATE COMMISSION   49 § 35.228

Authority

The provisions of this § 35.227 issued under the Real Estate Licensing and Registration Act (63 P.S. §§ 455.101—455.902); amended under sections 201, 501, 601, 602 and 604 of the Real Estate Licensing and Registration Act (63 P.S. §§ 455.201, 455.501, 455.601, 455.602 and 455.604).

Source

The provisions of this § 35.227 adopted February 24, 1989, effective February 25, 1989, 19 Pa.B. 781; amended June 10, 1994, effective June 11, 1994, 24 Pa.B. 2904; amended August 19, 2005, effective August 20, 2005, 35 Pa.B. 4711. Immediately preceding text appears at serial page (308328).

§ 35.228. Licensure as campground membership salesperson.

(a) An individual who wants to obtain a standard campground membership salesperson's license shall comply with § 35.221 (relating to general requirements) and:

(1) Be 18 years of age or older.

(2) Have successfully completed the one-credit (15 hours), Commission-developed course titled Campground Membership Sales, provided the following conditions are met:

(i) The course was taken prior to onsite training.

(ii) The course was taught at an accredited college, university or institute of higher learning in this Commonwealth or a real estate education provider in this Commonwealth approved by the Commission.

(3) Have successfully completed 30 days of onsite training at a campground membership facility subject to the following conditions:

(i) The 30 days of onsite training shall be completed during a 90-day period within 3 years prior to the submission of a license application.

(ii) The trainee shall be actively supervised and trained by a broker.

(4) Submit a completed license application to the Commission with:

(i) An official transcript evidencing acquisition of the qualifying coursework or degree.

(ii) A sworn statement from the broker under whom the applicant received his onsite training certifying that he actively trained and supervised the applicant and providing other information regarding the onsite training as the Commission may require.

(b) An individual who wants to obtain a reciprocal campground membership salesperson's license shall comply with § 35.221 and:

(1) Possess a current campground membership salesperson's license issued by a state that agrees to issue a license to a standard Pennsylvania licensee without further requirement or has qualifications for licensure which are substantially comparable to those required by the Commission. When a reciprocal applicant applies from a state that would require a Pennsylvania licensee to complete additional education, experience or examination requirements, the reciprocal applicant shall complete equivalent requirements for licensure in this Commonwealth.

(2) Submit a certification from the real estate licensing authority of the other state:

49 § 35.229   DEPARTMENT OF STATE   Pt. I

(i) Confirming that the applicant's license is active and in good standing.

(ii) Describing any past disciplinary action taken by the licensing authority against the applicant.

(iii) Listing the applicant's office address and the name of the applicant's employing broker.

(3) Submit a completed license application to the Commission with a verified statement that:

(i) To the applicant's knowledge, the applicant is not the subject of discipline or a current investigation or proceeding alleging misconduct under a licensing law or criminal law of either the Commonwealth or another state.

(ii) The applicant has reviewed, is familiar with and agrees to be bound by the act and this chapter.

(iii) The applicant agrees to permit the disclosure of the record in any disciplinary proceeding involving alleged misconduct by the applicant from any state in which the applicant is or has been licensed.

(4) Submit a sworn statement from the broker from whom the applicant received his onsite training certifying that the broker actively trained and supervised the applicant and providing other information regarding the onsite training the Commission may require.

Authority

The provisions of this § 35.228 issued under the Real Estate Licensing and Registration Act (63 P.S. §§ 455.101—455.902); amended under sections 201, 501, 601, 602 and 604 of the Real Estate Licensing and Registration Act (63 P.S. §§ 455.201, 455.501, 455.601, 455.602 and 455.604).

Source

The provisions of this § 35.228 adopted June 10, 1994, effective June 11, 1994, 24 Pa.B. 2904; amended December 10, 2004, effective December 11, 2004, 34 Pa.B. 6530; amended August 19, 2005, effective August 20, 2005, 35 Pa.B. 4711. Immediately preceding text appears at serial pages (308328) to (308329).

§ 35.229. Licensure as time-share salesperson.

(a) An individual who wants to obtain a standard time-share salesperson's license shall comply with § 35.221 (relating to general requirements) and:

(1) Be at least 18 years of age.

(2) Have successfully completed the two-credit (30 hours), Commission-developed course titled Time Share Sales, provided the following conditions are met:

(i) The course was taken prior to onsite training.

(ii) The course was taught at an accredited college, university or institute of higher learning in this Commonwealth or a real estate education provider in this Commonwealth approved by the Commission.

(3) Have successfully completed 30 days of onsite training at a time share facility subject to the following conditions:

(i) The 30 days of onsite training shall be completed during a 90-day period within 3 years prior to the submission of a license application.

(ii) The trainee shall be actively supervised and trained by a broker.

(4) Submit a completed license application to the Commission with:

(i) An official transcript evidencing acquisition of the qualifying coursework or degree.

(ii) A sworn statement from the broker under whom the applicant received his onsite training certifying that he actively trained and supervised the applicant and providing other information regarding the onsite training the Commission may require.

(b) An individual who wants to obtain a reciprocal time-share salesperson's license shall comply with § 35.221 and:

(1) Possess a current time-share salesperson's license issued by a state that agrees to issue a license to a standard Pennsylvania licensee without further requirement or has qualifications for licensure which are substantially comparable to those required by the Commission. When a reciprocal applicant applies from a state that would require a Pennsylvania licensee to complete additional education, experience or examination requirements, the reciprocal applicant shall complete equivalent requirements for licensure in this Commonwealth.

(2) Submit a certification from the real estate licensing authority of the other state:

(i) Confirming that the applicant's license is active and in good standing.

(ii) Describing any past disciplinary action taken by the licensing authority against the applicant.

(iii) Listing the applicant's office address and the name of the applicant's employing broker.

(3) Submit a completed license application to the Commission with a verified statement that:

(i) To the applicant's knowledge, the applicant is not the subject of discipline or a current investigation or proceeding alleging misconduct under a licensing law or criminal law of either this Commonwealth or another state.

(ii) The applicant has reviewed and is familiar with the act and the regulations and agrees to be bound by the act and regulations.

(iii) The applicant agrees to permit the disclosure of the record in any disciplinary proceeding involving alleged misconduct by the applicant from any state in which the applicant is or has been licensed.

(4) Submit a sworn statement from the broker from whom the applicant received his onsite training certifying that he actively trained and supervised the applicant and providing other information regarding the onsite training the Commission may require.

Authority

The provisions of this § 35.229 issued under the Real Estate Licensing and Registration Act (63 P. S. §§ 455.101—455.902); amended under sections 201, 501, 601, 602 and 604 of the Real Estate Licensing and Registration Act (63 P. S. §§ 455.201, 455.501, 455.601, 455.602 and 455.604).

Source

The provisions of this § 35.229 adopted June 10, 1994, effective June 11, 1994, 24 Pa.B. 2904; amended December 10, 2004, effective December 11, 2004, 34 Pa.B. 6530; amended August 19, 2005, effective August 20, 2005, 35 Pa.B. 4711. Immediately preceding text appears at serial pages (308329) to (308330).

OFFICES

§ 35.241. General office requirement.

(a) A broker, cemetery broker, or rental listing referral agent shall maintain a main office in this Commonwealth unless he maintains a main office in another state where he holds the equivalent of a standard license.

(b) A broker, cemetery broker or rental listing referral agent may maintain more than one office in this Commonwealth. A branch office license is required for each additional office maintained by a broker or cemetery broker. See § 35.243 (relating to licensure of branch office).

Authority

The provisions of this § 35.241 issued under the Real Estate Licensing and Registration Act (63 P. S. §§ 455.101—455.902); amended under sections 201, 501, 601, 602 and 604 of the Real Estate Licensing and Registration Act (63 P. S. §§ 455.201, 455.501, 455.601, 455.602 and 455.604).

Source

The provisions of this § 35.241 adopted February 24, 1989, effective February 25, 1989, 19 Pa.B. 781; amended June 10, 1994, effective June 11, 1994, 24 Pa.B. 2904; amended August 19, 2005, effective August 20, 2005, 35 Pa.B. 4711. Immediately preceding text appears at serial pages (308330).

Cross References

This section cited in 49 Pa. Code § 35.222 (relating to licensure as cemetery broker); 49 Pa. Code § 35.224 (relating to licensure as cemetery broker); and 49 Pa. Code § 35.227 (relating to licensure as rental listing referral agent).

§ 35.242. Office of broker or cemetery broker.

(a) The office of a broker or cemetery broker in this Commonwealth shall be devoted to the transaction of real estate business and be arranged to permit business to be conducted in privacy.

(b) If the office of a broker or cemetery broker in this Commonwealth is located in a private residence, the entrance to the office shall be separate from the entrance to the residence.

(c) The business name of the broker or cemetery broker, as designated on the license, shall be displayed prominently and in permanent fashion outside the office in this Commonwealth.

(d) A branch office operated by a broker or cemetery broker in this Commonwealth shall be in compliance with this section.

Authority

The provisions of this § 35.242 issued under the Real Estate Licensing and Registration Act (63 P. S. §§ 455.101—455.902); amended under sections 201, 501, 601, 602 and 604 of the Real Estate Licensing and Registration Act (63 P. S. §§ 455.201, 455.501, 455.601, 455.602 and 455.604).

35-39

Copyright © 2005 Commonwealth of Pennsylvania

35-40

Source

The provisions of this § 35.242 adopted February 24, 1989, effective February 25, 1989, 19 Pa.B. 781; amended June 10, 1994, effective June 11, 1994, 24 Pa.B. 2904; amended August 19, 2005, effective August 20, 2005, 35 Pa.B. 4711. Immediately preceding text appears at serial page (308331).

Cross References

This section cited in 49 Pa. Code § 35.222 (relating to licensure as broker); 49 Pa. Code § 35.224 (relating to licensure as cemetery broker); and 49 Pa. Code § 43a.10 (relating to schedule of civil penalties—real estate and cemetery brokers, real estate schools).

§ 35.243. Licensure of branch office.

(a) A broker or cemetery broker may not open a branch office in this Commonwealth without first obtaining a branch office license for that location from the Commission. A broker or cemetery broker who wants to obtain a Pennsylvania branch office license shall submit a completed license application to the Commission with the license fee prescribed in § 35.203 (relating to fees).

(b) A branch office license will be issued in the name under which the broker or cemetery broker is licensed to conduct business at the main office.

(c) A branch office license terminates automatically with the suspension, revocation or discontinuance, for whatever reason, of the license of the broker or cemetery broker to whom the branch office license was issued.

Authority

The provisions of this § 35.243 issued under the Real Estate Licensing and Registration Act (63 P. S. §§ 455.101—455.902).

Source

The provisions of this § 35.243 adopted February 24, 1989, effective February 25, 1989, 19 Pa.B. 781; amended June 10, 1994, effective June 11, 1994, 24 Pa.B. 2904. Immediately preceding text appears at serial pages (135743) to (135744).

Cross References

This section cited in 49 Pa. Code § 35.241 (relating to general office requirement); and 49 Pa. Code § 43a.10 (relating to schedule of civil penalties—real estate and cemetery brokers, real estate schools).

§ 35.244. Supervision and operation of office.

(a) The main or branch office in this Commonwealth of a broker shall be under the direction and supervision of a broker or associate broker holding either a standard or reciprocal license.

(b) The main or branch office in this Commonwealth of a cemetery broker shall be under the direction and supervision of a broker, cemetery broker, associate broker or associate cemetery broker holding either a standard or reciprocal license.

(c) An associate broker, salesperson, cemetery salesperson, campground membership salesperson or time-share salesperson shall practice in affiliation with a broker holding either a reciprocal or standard license issued by the Commission.

(d) A branch office in this Commonwealth may not be operated in a manner that permits, or is intended to permit, an employee to carry on the business of the office for the employee's sole benefit.

(e) The office in this Commonwealth of a rental listing referral agent shall be under the direction and supervision of a rental listing referral agent holding either a standard or reciprocal license issued by the Commission. A rental listing referral agent may not supervise more than one office.

Authority

The provisions of this § 35.244 issued under the Real Estate Licensing and Registration Act (63 P. S. §§ 455.101—455.902); amended under sections 201, 501, 601, 602 and 604 of the Real Estate Licensing and Registration Act (63 P. S. §§ 455.201, 455.501, 455.601, 455.602 and 455.604).

Source

The provisions of this § 35.244 adopted February 24, 1989, effective February 25, 1989, 19 Pa.B. 781; amended June 10, 1994, effective June 11, 1994, 24 Pa.B. 2904; amended August 19, 2005, effective August 20, 2005, 35 Pa.B. 4711. Immediately preceding text appears at serial page (308332).

§ 35.245. Display of licenses in office.

(a) Commencing with the 2006-2008 renewal period the current license of a broker, cemetery broker or rental listing referral agent and those licensees employed by or affiliated with that broker, cemetery broker or rental listing referral agent shall be maintained at the main office.

(b) A broker or cemetery broker shall maintain a list of licensees employed or affiliated with the broker or cemetery broker at the branch office out of which each licensee works.

Authority

The provisions of this § 35.245 issued under the Real Estate Licensing and Registration Act (63 P. S. §§ 455.101—455.902); amended under sections 201, 501, 601, 602 and 604 of the Real Estate Licensing and Registration Act (63 P. S. §§ 455.201, 455.501, 455.601, 455.602 and 455.604).

Source

The provisions of this § 35.245 adopted February 24, 1989, effective February 25, 1989, 19 Pa.B. 781; amended June 10, 1994, effective June 11, 1994, 24 Pa.B. 2904; amended August 19, 2005, effective August 20, 2005, 35 Pa.B. 4711. Immediately preceding text appears at serial pages (308332) to (308333).

Cross References

This section cited in 49 Pa. Code § 43a.10 (relating to schedule of civil penalties—real estate and cemetery brokers, real estate schools).

§ 35.246. Inspection of office.

(a) *Routine inspections.* No more than four times a year during regular business hours, the Commission or its authorized representatives may conduct a routine inspection of the main office or branch office of a broker, cemetery broker or rental listing referral agent for the purpose of determining whether the office is being operated in compliance with the act and this chapter.

(b) *Special inspections.* In addition to the routine inspections authorized by subsection (a), the Commission or its authorized representatives may conduct a special inspection of a main or branch office:

(1) Upon a complaint or reasonable belief that the broker, cemetery broker or rental listing referral agent, or a licensed employe of a broker, cemetery broker or rental listing referral agent, has violated the act or this chapter.

(2) As a follow-up to a previous inspection that revealed the office's non-compliance with the act or this chapter.

(c) *Commission notice.* Prior to the start of a routine or special inspection, the Commission or its authorized representatives will advise the broker, cemetery broker, rental listing referral agent or other licensee who may be in charge of the office at the time of the inspection that the inspection is being made under this section and is limited in scope by this section.

(d) *Permissible Commission actions.* During the course of a routine or special inspection, the Commission or its authorized representatives will be permitted to:

(1) Examine the records of the office pertaining to:
(i) Real estate transactions or rental listing referrals.
(ii) The corporation, partnership or association that holds a broker's or cemetery broker's license.

(2) Inspect all areas of the office.

(3) Interview the broker, cemetery broker, rental listing referral agent and other licensed or unlicensed employes who work in the office.

(4) Obtain the broker's or cemetery broker's written authorization to the bank or depository where the broker or cemetery broker maintains his escrow account that it may release copies of the records of the account to the Commission or its authorized representatives.

Authority

The provisions of this § 35.246 issued under the Real Estate Licensing and Registration Act (63 P. S. §§ 455.101—455.902).

Source

The provisions of this § 35.246 adopted February 24, 1989, effective February 25, 1989, 19 Pa.B. 781; amended June 10, 1994, effective June 11, 1994, 24 Pa.B. 2904. Immediately preceding text appears at serial pages (135745) to (135746).

Cross References

This section cited in 49 Pa. Code § 35.286 (relating to retention and production of records); 49 Pa. Code § 35.325 (relating to escrow account); and 49 Pa. Code § 35.328 (relating to escrow records).

STATUS OF LICENSURE

§ 35.251. Relicensure following revocation.

The Commission will not authorize relicensure of an individual whose license has been revoked for at least 5 years following the date revocation begins. After the 5-year period, the individual may petition the Commission for relicensure.

The decision to permit relicensure is within the Commission's discretion. If relicensure is permitted, the individual shall comply with current requirements for licensure before the license is issued.

Authority

The provisions of this § 35.251 issued under the Real Estate Licensing and Registration Act (63 P. S. §§ 455.101—455.902).

Source

The provisions of this § 35.251 adopted February 24, 1989, effective February 25, 1989, 19 Pa.B. 781.

§ 35.252. Termination of business of deceased broker with sole proprietorship.

(a) Within 15 days following the death of a broker with a sole proprietorship, the deceased broker's estate shall notify the Commission that the estate has appointed another licensed broker to supervise the termination of the deceased broker's business. The appointment is subject to verification that the appointed broker has a current license.

(b) The appointed broker shall observe the following rules during the termination period:
(1) New listing agreements may not be entered into.
(2) Unexpired listing agreements may be promoted unless the seller or lessor elects to cancel the agreement. Unexpired listings will expire automatically 90 days after the broker dies and may not be renewed.
(3) Pending agreements of sale or lease may proceed to consummation.
(4) New licensees may not be hired.

Authority

The provisions of this § 35.252 issued under the Real Estate Licensing and Registration Act (63 P. S. §§ 455.101—455.902).

Source

The provisions of this § 35.252 adopted February 24, 1989, effective February 25, 1989, 19 Pa.B. 781; amended December 10, 2004, effective December 11, 2004, 34 Pa.B. 6530. Immediately preceding text appears at serial pages (287884) and (305557).

§ 35.253. Replacement of broker of record due to death.

Within 15 days following the death of a broker of record, a partner or corporate officer shall file an application with the Commission designating another individual to serve as broker of record.

Authority

The provisions of this § 35.253 issued under sections 402, 404, 404.1 and 513 of the Real Estate Licensing and Registration Act (63 P. S. §§ 455.402, 455.404, 455.404a and 455.513).

Source

The provisions of this § 35.253 adopted December 10, 2004, effective December 11, 2004, 34 Pa.B. 6530.

§ 35.254. Substitution of broker or broker of record due to illness or injury.

If a broker with a sole proprietorship or broker of record is unable to act as a broker/broker of record due to illness or injury, the broker's attorney or another with power of attorney for the broker in a sole proprietorship, a corporate officer or partner shall notify the Commission within 15 days that it has appointed another licensed broker to act as the interim broker/broker of record for the corporation, partnership or sole proprietorship until the broker/broker of record is able to resume his responsibilities.

Authority

The provisions of this § 35.254 issued under sections 402, 404, 404.1, and 513 of the Real Estate Licensing and Registration Act (63 P.S. §§ 455.402, 455.404, 455.404a and 455.513).

Source

The provisions of this § 35.254 adopted December 10, 2004, effective December 11, 2004, 34 Pa.B. 6530.

§ 35.255. Reciprocal licenses.

(a) *Renewal.* In addition to completing the application and paying the fee, a licensee applying for renewal of a reciprocal license shall provide the Commission with a certification that the license is current and in good standing from the state where the licensee has his principal place of business.

(b) *Reactivation.* A licensee who fails to renew a reciprocal license may reactivate the license without being reexamined provided that he holds the equivalent of a current standard license in the state where the licensee has his principal place of business.

(c) *Conversion to standard license.* A reciprocal licensee who designates his principal place of business as in this Commonwealth or who fails to maintain a current standard license in the state of his principal place of business shall notify the Commission within 30 days of the change. To continue to practice in this Commonwealth at the end of the renewal period, the reciprocal licensee shall obtain a standard license in accordance with the applicable requirements of this chapter. Thereafter, the standard licensee shall comply with the requirements for a standard license, including completion of the continuing education requirement.

Authority

The provisions of this § 35.255 issued under sections 201, 501, 601, 602 and 604 of the Real Estate Licensing and Registration Act (63 P.S. §§ 455.201, 455.501, 455.601, 455.602 and 455.604).

Source

The provisions of this § 35.255 adopted August 19, 2005, effective August 20, 2005, 35 Pa.B. 4711.

Subchapter D. LICENSING EXAMINATIONS

---

§ 35.271. Examination for broker's license.

(a) An individual who wants to take the broker's examination for a standard broker's license shall:

(1) Be 21 years of age or older.

(2) Be a high school graduate or have passed a high school general education equivalency examination.

(3) Have worked at least 3 years as a licensed salesperson, with experience qualifications that the Commission considers adequate for practice as a broker, or possess at least 3 years of other experience, education, or both, that the Commission considers the equivalent of 3 years' experience as a licensed salesperson.

(4) Have acquired 16 credits, or 240 hours of instruction, in professional real estate education as determined by the Commission under subsection (b).

(5) Submit a completed examination application to the Commission or its designee with:

(i) Official transcripts evidencing the acquisition of course credits.

(ii) A detailed resume of real estate activities performed by the candidate while working as a salesperson and a sworn statement from the candidate's employing broker confirming that these activities were performed if the candidate is a licensed salesperson.

(iii) A complete description of work experience and education that the candidate considers relevant to the requirements of paragraph (3) if the candidate is not a licensed salesperson.

(iv) A certification from the real estate licensing authority of the jurisdiction in which the candidate is licensed stating that the candidate had an active license for each year that credits are claimed if the candidate is applying brokerage experience to satisfy the professional education requirement.

(v) The fee for review of the candidate's qualifications to take the examination prescribed in § 35.203 (relating to fees) and the fees for administration of the examination.

(b) The Commission will apply the following standards in determining whether an examination candidate has met the education requirement of subsection (a)(4):

(1) A candidate who has obtained one of the following degrees will be deemed to have met the education requirement and will not be required to show completion of coursework in specific areas of study:

(i) A bachelor's degree with a major in real estate from an accredited college, university or institute of higher learning.

(ii) A bachelor's degree from an accredited college, university or institute of higher learning, having completed coursework equivalent to a major in real estate.

(iii) A juris doctor degree from an accredited law school.

(2) Two of the required 16 credits shall be in a Commission-developed or approved real estate office management course and 2 of the required 16 credits shall be in Commission-developed or approved law course. At least 6 of the remaining 12 credits shall be in 3 or more of the Commission-developed courses listed in this paragraph. The remaining 6 credits shall be in real estate courses but not necessarily those listed in this paragraph. A candidate may not apply credits used to qualify for the salesperson's examination toward fulfillment of the broker education requirement.

(3) To be counted toward the education requirement, a real estate course shall have been offered by:

(i) An accredited college, university or institute of higher learning, whether in this Commonwealth or outside this Commonwealth.

(ii) A real estate education provider in this Commonwealth approved by the Commission.

(iii) A real estate education provider outside this Commonwealth, that has been approved by the real estate licensing authority of the jurisdiction where the real estate education provider is located. The course transcript or certificate of completion shall state that the course is approved by the licensing authority of the jurisdiction where the real estate education provider is located.

(iv) A real estate industry organization outside this Commonwealth, if the course is approved by the licensing jurisdiction of another state. The course transcript or certificate of completion shall state that the course is approved by the licensing jurisdiction which has approved it.

(4) A maximum of four credits will be allowed for each real estate course. A maximum of four credits will be allowed for each area of real estate study listed in paragraph (2).

(5) Courses shall have been completed within 10 years prior to the date of successful completion of the licensing examination.

(6) Two credits will be allowed for each year of active practice the candidate has had a licensed broker in another state during the 10-year period immediately preceding the submission of the examination application.

(c) A reciprocal licensee who is converting that license to a standard broker's license is exempt from subsection (a) and is only required to pass the state portion of the examination.

35-44.1

Authority

The provisions of this § 35.271 issued under the Real Estate Licensing and Registration Act (63 P.S. §§ 455.101—455.902); amended under sections 201, 404, 501, 601, 602 and 604 of the Real Estate Licensing Registration Act (63 P.S. §§ 455.201, 455.404, 455.501, 455.601, 455.602 and 455.604); and section 812.1 of The Administrative Code of 1929 (71 P.S. 279.3a).

Source

The provisions of this § 35.271 adopted February 24, 1989, effective February 25, 1989, 19 Pa.B. 781; corrected July 14, 1989, effective February 25, 1989, 19 Pa.B. 3036; amended June 10, 1994, effective June 11, 1994, 24 Pa.B. 2904; amended November 17, 2000, effective November 18, 2000, 30 Pa.B. 5954; corrected December 15, 2000, effective December 16, 2000, 30 Pa.B. 6429; amended September 3, 2004, effective September 4, 2004, 34 Pa.B. 4883; amended December 10, 2004, effective December 11, 2004, 34 Pa.B. 6530; amended August 19, 2005, effective August 20, 2005, 35 Pa.B. 4711; corrected September 16, 2005, effective August 20, 2005, 35 Pa.B. 5119. Immediately preceding text appears at serial pages (312838) to (312840).

Notes of Decisions

The possession of a salesperson's license for 3 or more years does not allow a person to sit for a broker's examination. *Bhala v. State Real Estate Commission*, 617 A.2d 841 (Pa. Cmwlth. 1992).

Cross References

This section cited in 49 Pa. Code § 35.222 (relating to licensure as broker).

§ 35.272. Examination for salesperson's license.

(a) An individual who wants to take the salesperson's examination for the purpose of obtaining a standard salesperson's license shall:

(1) Be 18 years of age or older.

(2) Have successfully completed four credits, or 60 hours of instruction, in basic real estate courses as determined by the Commission under subsection (b).

(3) Submit a completed examination application to the Commission or its designee with the examination fee.

(b) The Commission will apply the following standards in determining whether an examination candidate has met the education requirement of subsection (a)(2):

(1) A candidate who has obtained one of the following degrees will be deemed to have met the education requirement and will not be required to show completion of coursework in specific areas of study:

(i) A bachelor's degree with a major in real estate from an accredited college, university or institute of higher learning.

(ii) A bachelor's degree from an accredited college, university or institute of higher learning, having completed coursework equivalent to a major in real estate.

(iii) A juris doctor degree from an accredited law school.

35-44.2

(2) Credits will be allowed for each of the Commission-developed real estate courses—Real Estate Fundamentals and Real Estate Practice—when offered by:

(i) An accredited college, university or institution of higher learning located outside this Commonwealth.

(ii) A real estate education provider in this Commonwealth approved by the Commission.

(3) Credits will be allowed for acceptable basic real estate courses when offered by:

(i) An accredited college, university or institution of higher learning located outside this Commonwealth.

(ii) A real estate education provider outside this Commonwealth that has been approved by the real estate licensing authority of the jurisdiction where the real estate education provider is located.

(4) Courses shall have been completed within 10 years prior to the date of successful completion of the licensing examination.

(c) A licensee who is converting a reciprocal license to a standard salesperson's license is exempt from the requirements in subsections (a) and (b) and is only required to pass the state portion of the examination.

Authority

The provisions of this § 35.272 issued under the Real Estate Licensing and Registration Act (63 P. S. §§ 455.101—455.902); amended under section 812.1 of The Administrative Code of 1929 (71 P. S. § 279.3a); amended under sections 201, 501, 601, 602 and 604 of the Real Estate Licensing and Registration Act (63 P. S. §§ 455.201, 455.501, 455.601, 455.602 and 455.604).

Source

The provisions of this § 35.272 adopted February 24, 1989, effective February 25, 1989, 19 Pa.B. 781; amended September 3, 2004, effective September 4, 2004, 34 Pa.B. 4883; amended December 10, 2004, effective December 11, 2004, 34 Pa.B. 6530; amended August 19, 2005, effective August 20, 2005, 35 Pa.B. 4711. Immediately preceding text appears at serial pages (308338) to (308339).

Cross References

This section cited in 49 Pa. Code § 35.223 (relating to licensure as salesperson).

§ 35.273. Examination for cemetery broker's license.

(a) An individual who wants to take the salesperson's examination for the purpose of obtaining a standard cemetery broker's license shall:

(1) Be 21 years of age or older.

(2) Have worked at least 3 years as a licensed salesperson or cemetery salesperson, with experience qualifications that the Commission considers adequate for practice as a cemetery broker, or possess at least 3 years of other experience, education, or both, that the Commission considers the equivalent of 3 years' experience as a licensed salesperson or cemetery salesperson.

(3) Have successfully completed four credits, or 60 hours of instruction, in basic real estate courses as determined by the Commission under subsection (b).

(4) Submit a completed examination application to the Commission or its designee with:

(i) Official transcripts evidencing the acquisition of degrees or course credits.

(ii) A detailed resume of real estate activities performed by the candidate while working as a salesperson or cemetery salesperson, and a sworn statement from the candidate's employing broker confirming that these activities were performed if the candidate is a licensed salesperson or cemetery salesperson.

(iii) A complete description of work experience and education that the candidate considers relevant to the requirements of paragraph (2) if the candidate is not a licensed salesperson or cemetery salesperson.

(iv) The fee for review of the candidate's qualifications to take the examination prescribed in § 35.203 (relating to fees) and the fee for administration of the examination.

(b) The Commission will apply the following standards in determining whether an examination candidate has met the education requirements of subsection (a)(3):

(1) A candidate who has obtained one of the following degrees will be deemed to have met the education requirement and will not be required to show completion of course work in specific areas of study:

(i) A bachelor's degree with a major in real estate from an accredited college, university or institute of higher learning.

(ii) A bachelor's degree from an accredited college, university or institute of higher learning, having completed course work equivalent to a major in real estate.

(iii) A juris doctor degree from an accredited law school.

(2) Credits will be allowed for each of the Commission-developed real estate courses—Real Estate Fundamentals and Real Estate Practice—when offered by:

(i) An accredited college, university or institute of higher learning in this Commonwealth.

(ii) A real estate education provider approved by the Commission in this Commonwealth.

(3) Credits will be allowed for cemetery courses when offered by:

(i) An accredited college, university or institute of higher learning in this Commonwealth.

(ii) A real estate education provider in this Commonwealth approved by the Commission.

(4) Credits will be allowed for acceptable basic real estate courses when offered by:

(i) An accredited college, university or institute of higher learning located outside this Commonwealth.

(ii) A real estate education provider outside this Commonwealth that has been approved by the real estate licensing authority of the jurisdiction where the real estate education provider is located.

(iii) A cemetery association outside this Commonwealth, if the course taught by the cemetery association is equivalent to a course taught by a real estate school in this Commonwealth approved by the Commission.

(5) Courses shall have been completed within 10 years prior to the date of successful completion of the licensing examination.

(c) A reciprocal licensee who is converting a reciprocal license to a standard cemetery broker's license is exempt from subsection (a) and is only required to pass the state portion of the examination.

Authority

The provisions of this § 35.273 issued under the Real Estate Licensing and Registration Act (63 P. S. §§ 455.101—455.902); amended under section 812.1 of The Administrative Code of 1929 (71 P. S. § 279.3a); amended under sections 201, 501, 601, 602 and 604 of the Real Estate Licensing and Registration Act (63 P. S. §§ 455.201, 455.501, 455.601, 455.602 and 455.604).

Source

The provisions of this § 35.273 adopted February 24, 1989, effective February 25, 1989, 19 Pa.B. 781; amended June 10, 1994, effective June 11, 1994, 24 Pa.B. 2904; amended September 3, 2004, effective September 4, 2004, 34 Pa.B. 4883; amended December 10, 2004, effective December 11, 2004, 34 Pa.B. 6530; amended August 19, 2005, effective August 20, 2005, 35 Pa.B. 4711. Immediately preceding text appears at serial pages (308339) to (308341).

Cross References

This section cited in 49 Pa. Code § 35.224 (relating to licensure as cemetery broker).

§ 35.274. Examination for builder-owner salesperson's license.

(a) An individual who wants to take the salesperson's examination for the purpose of obtaining a standard builder-owner salesperson's license shall:

(1) Be 18 years of age or older.

(2) Be employed by a builder-owner who has a good reputation for honesty, trustworthiness, integrity and competence.

(3) Submit a completed examination application to the Commission or its designee with the examination fee.

(b) A reciprocal licensee who is converting a reciprocal license to a standard builder-owner salesperson's license is only required to pass the state portion of the examination.

35-44.5

(312843) No. 371 Oct. 05

Authority

The provisions of this § 35.274 issued under the Real Estate Licensing and Registration Act (63 P. S. §§ 455.101—455.902); amended under section 812.1 of The Administrative Code of 1929 (71 P. S. § 279.3a); amended under sections 201, 501, 601, 602 and 604 of the Real Estate Licensing and Registration Act (63 P. S. §§ 455.201, 455.501, 455.601, 455.602 and 455.604).

Source

The provisions of this § 35.274 adopted February 24, 1989, effective February 25, 1989, 19 Pa.B. 781; amended September 3, 2004, effective September 4, 2004, 34 Pa.B. 4883; amended August 19, 2005, effective August 20, 2005, 35 Pa.B. 4711. Immediately preceding text appears at serial pages (308341) to (308342).

Cross References

This section cited in 49 Pa. Code § 35.226 (relating to licensure as builder-owner salesperson).

§ 35.275. Examination for rental listing referral agent's license.

(a) An individual who wants to take the salesperson's examination for the purpose of obtaining a standard rental listing referral agent's license shall:

(1) Be 18 years of age or older.

(2) Have successfully completed four credits, or 60 hours of instruction, in basic real estate courses as determined by the Commission under subsection (b).

(3) Submit a completed examination application to the Commission or its designee with the examination fee.

(b) The Commission will apply the following standards in determining whether an examination candidate has met the requirements of subsection (a)(2):

(1) A candidate who has obtained one of the following degrees will be deemed to have met the education requirement and will not be required to show completion of coursework in specific areas of study:

(i) A bachelor's degree with a major in real estate from an accredited college, university or institute of higher learning.

(ii) A bachelor's degree from an accredited college, university or institute of higher learning, having completed coursework equivalent to a major in real estate.

(iii) A juris doctor degree from an accredited law school.

(2) Credits will be allowed for each of the Commission-developed real estate courses—Real Estate Fundamentals and Real Estate Practice—when offered by:

(i) An accredited college, university or institute of higher learning in this Commonwealth.

(ii) A real estate education provider in this Commonwealth approved by the Commission.

(3) Credits will be allowed for acceptable basic real estate courses when offered by:

35-44.6

(312844) No. 371 Oct. 05

(i) An accredited college, university or institute of higher learning in this Commonwealth.

(ii) A real estate education provider outside this Commonwealth that has been approved by the real estate licensing authority of the jurisdiction where the real estate education provider is located.

(4) Courses shall have been completed within 10 years prior to the date of successful completion of the licensing examination.

(c) A reciprocal licensee who is converting a reciprocal license to a standard rental listing referral agent's license is exempt from the requirements in subsections (a) and (b) and is only required to pass the state portion of the examination.

Authority

The provisions of this § 35.275 issued under the Real Estate Licensing and Registration Act (63 P. S. §§ 455.101—455.902); amended under section 812.1 of The Administrative Code of 1929 (71 P. S. § 279.3a); amended under sections 201, 501, 601, 602 and 604 of the Real Estate Licensing and Registration Act (63 P. S. §§ 455.201, 455.501, 455.601, 455.602 and 455.604).

Source

The provisions of this § 35.275 adopted February 24, 1989, effective February 25, 1989, 19 Pa.B. 781; amended September 3, 2004, effective September 4, 2004, 34 Pa.B. 4883; amended December 10, 2004, effective December 11, 2004, 34 Pa.B. 6530; amended August 19, 2005, effective August 20, 2005, 35 Pa.B. 4711. Immediately preceding text appears at serial pages (308342) and (309621).

Cross References

This section cited in 49 Pa. Code § 35.227 (relating to licensure as rental listing referral agent).

Subchapter E. STANDARDS OF CONDUCT AND PRACTICE

GENERAL ETHICAL RESPONSIBILITIES

35-44.7

ADVERTISING AND SOLICITATION

PERMITTED RELATIONSHIPS

ESCROW REQUIREMENTS

REAL ESTATE DOCUMENTS

35-44.8

Ch. 35   STATE REAL ESTATE COMMISSION   49 § 35.281

Cross References

This subchapter cited in 49 Pa. Code § 35.384 (relating to qualifying courses).

GENERAL ETHICAL RESPONSIBILITIES

§ 35.281. Putting contracts, commitments and agreements in writing.

(a) All contracts, commitments and agreements between a broker, or a licensee employed by the broker, and a principal or a consumer who is required to pay a fee, commission or other valuable consideration shall be in writing and contain the information specified in § 35.331 (relating to written agreements generally).

(b) The following are exceptions to subsection (a):

(1) Open listing agreements or nonexclusive buyer agency agreements may be oral if the seller/buyer or landlord/tenant is provided with a written memorandum stating the terms of the agreement.

(2) Transaction licensees or subagents cooperating with listing brokers are not required to obtain a written agreement from the seller/landlord.

(3) Transaction licensees or subagents who provide services to the buyer/tenant but are paid by the seller/landlord or listing broker shall provide, and have signed, a written disclosure statement describing the nature of the services to be performed and containing the information required by section 608 of the act (63 P. S. § 455.608).

(c) A licensee may perform services before an agreement is signed, but the licensee is not entitled to recover a fee, commission or other valuable consideration in the absence of a signed agreement.

Authority

The provisions of this § 35.281 issued under the Real Estate Licensing and Registration Act (63 P. S. §§ 455.101—455.902); amended under sections 404, 602, 606—606.6 and 608—608.3 of the Real Estate Licensing and Registration Act (63 P. S. §§ 455.404, 455.602, 455.606—455.606f and 455.608—455.608c).

Source

The provisions of this § 35.281 adopted February 24, 1989, effective February 25, 1989, 19 Pa.B. 781; amended November 17, 2000, effective November 18, 2000, 30 Pa.B. 5954; amended March 29, 2002, effective March 30, 2002, 32 Pa.B. 1644. Immediately preceding text appears at serial page (271735).

Cross References

This section cited in 49 Pa. Code § 35.286 (relating to retention and production of records).

§ 35.282. Misleading advice, assurances and representations.

(a) A licensee may not give assurances or advice concerning an aspect of a real estate transaction that he knows, or reasonably should be expected to know, is incorrect, inaccurate or improbable.

(b) A licensee may not knowingly be a party to a material false or inaccurate representation in a writing regarding a real estate transaction in which he is acting in a representative capacity.

49 § 35.283   DEPARTMENT OF STATE   Pt. I

Authority

The provisions of this § 35.282 issued under the Real Estate Licensing and Registration Act (63 P. S. §§ 455.101—455.902).

Source

The provisions of this § 35.282 adopted February 24, 1989, effective February 25, 1989, 19 Pa.B. 781.

§ 35.283. Disclosure of interest.

(a) A licensee may not participate in a real estate transaction involving property in which he has an ownership interest unless he first discloses his interest in writing to all parties concerned.

(b) A licensee may not represent, or purport to represent, more than one party to a real estate transaction without the written consent of all parties concerned.

(c) A broker who manages rental property may not accept a commission, rebate or profit on expenditures made for the lessor without the lessor's written consent.

(d) A licensee who provides financial services, title transfer and preparation, insurance, construction, repair or inspection services, may not require a consumer to use any of these services.

(e) If the consumer chooses to use any of the services in subsection (d), the licensee shall provide the consumer with a written disclosure of any financial interest, including, a referral fee or commission, that the licensee has in the service. This disclosure shall be made at the time the licensee first advises the consumer that an ancillary service is available or when the licensee first learns that the consumer will be using the service.

(f) A licensee has a continuing obligation to disclose to a principal any conflict of interest in a reasonably practicable period of time after the licensee learns or should have learned of the conflict of interest.

Authority

The provisions of this § 35.283 issued under the Real Estate Licensing and Registration Act (63 P. S. §§ 455.101—455.902); amended under sections 404, 606—606.6 and 608—608.3 of the Real Estate Licensing and Registration Act (63 P. S. §§ 455.404, 455.606—455.606f and 455.608—455.608c).

Source

The provisions of this § 35.283 adopted February 24, 1989, effective February 25, 1989, 19 Pa.B. 781; amended March 29, 2002, effective March 30, 2002, 32 Pa.B. 1644. Immediately preceding text appears at serial page (271736).

Cross References

This section cited in 49 Pa. Code § 35.292 (relating to duties of licensees generally).

§ 35.284. Disclosures of business relationships.

(a) *Disclosure to consumers seeking to sell or purchase residential or commercial real estate.*

(1) A licensee shall provide the disclosure summary in § 35.336 (relating to disclosure summary for the purchase or sale of residential or commercial real estate or for the lease of residential or commercial real estate when the licensee is working on behalf of the tenant) to consumers seeking to purchase or sell real estate at the initial interview if the interview occurs in person.

(2) If the initial interview does not occur in person, the licensee shall provide the oral disclosure in § 35.339 (relating to the oral disclosure) at the initial interview and the written disclosure statement in § 35.336 no later than the earlier of:

(i) The first meeting that the licensee has in person with the consumer after the initial interview.

(ii) The time the licensee or any person working with the licensee first shows a property to the consumer.

(b) *Disclosure to tenants seeking to lease residential or commercial real estate.*

(1) A licensee who is working on behalf of the tenant shall provide the disclosure summary in § 35.336 as required in subsection (a).

(2) A licensee who is working on behalf of the owner shall provide the disclosure summary in § 35.337 (relating to disclosure summary for the lease

of residential or commercial real estate when the licensee is working on behalf of the owner) to tenants seeking to lease residential or commercial property at the initial interview.

(c) *Disclosure to consumers seeking to sell time shares.* A licensee shall provide the disclosure summary in § 35.338 (relating to disclosure summary for time-share estates) to consumers seeking to purchase time-share estates at the initial interview.

(d) *Signed disclosure.* A licensee shall provide a copy of the signed disclosure to the consumers referenced in subsections (a)—(c) and shall retain the signed acknowledgment under § 35.286 (relating to retention and production of records). If a consumer refuses to sign the acknowledgment, the refusal shall be noted on the acknowledgment.

Authority

The provisions of this § 35.284 issued under the Real Estate Licensing and Registration Act (63 P. S. §§ 455.101—455.902); amended under sections 404, 606—606.6 and 608—608.3 of the Real Estate Licensing and Registration Act (63 P. S. §§ 455.404, 455.606—455.606f and 455.608—455.608c).

Source

The provisions of this § 35.284 adopted February 24, 1989, effective February 25, 1989, 19 Pa.B. 781; amended June 10, 1994, effective June 11, 1994, 24 Pa.B. 2904; amended March 29, 2002, effective March 30, 2002, 32 Pa.B. 1644. Immediately preceding text appears at serial pages (271736) to (271737).

§ 35.285. Disclosure of real estate affiliations.

A licensee shall provide to the Commission or its representatives upon proper demand information regarding a franchisor, network or other parent real estate company with which the licensee is, or may become, affiliated.

Authority

The provisions of this § 35.285 issued under the Real Estate Licensing and Registration Act (63 P. S. §§ 455.101—455.902).

Source

The provisions of this § 35.285 adopted February 24, 1989, effective February 25, 1989, 19 Pa.B. 781.

§ 35.286. Retention and production of records.

(a) *Retention.* A broker or cemetery broker shall retain records pertaining to a real estate transaction for at least 3 years following consummation except for the following which shall be retained for 6 months:

(1) The acknowledgement portion of the consumer notice applicable to the sale or purchase of real estate in § 35.336 (relating to disclosure summary for the purchase or sale of residential or commercial real estate or the lease of

Ch. 35   STATE REAL ESTATE COMMISSION   49 § 35.287

residential or commercial real estate or lease of residential or commercial real estate when the licensee is working on behalf of the tenant) when there is not a real estate transaction.

(2) The acknowledgement portion of the consumer notice applicable to time shares in § 35.338 (relating to disclosure summary for time-share estates).

(3) The acknowledgement portion of the consumer notice applicable to leases in § 35.336 and § 35.337 (relating to disclosure summary for the lease of residential or commercial real estate when the licensee is working on behalf of the owner).

(4) The written disclosure statement establishing a subagent or transaction licensee relationship required by § 35.281(b)(3) (relating to putting contracts, commitments and agreements in writing).

(b) *Production of documents.*

(1) A broker or cemetery broker shall produce the records required in subsection (a) for examination by the Commission or its authorized representatives upon written request or pursuant to an office inspection under § 35.246 (relating to inspection of office).

(2) A corporation, partnership or association that holds a broker's or cemetery broker's license shall produce its corporate, partnership or association records for examination by the Commission or its authorized representatives upon written request or pursuant to an office inspection under § 35.246.

Authority

The provisions of this § 35.286 issued under the Real Estate Licensing and Registration Act (63 P. S. §§ 455.101—455.902); amended under sections 404, 606—606.6 and 608—608.3 of the Real Estate Licensing and Registration Act (63 P. S. §§ 455.404, 455.606—455.606f and 455.608c).

Source

The provisions of this § 35.286 adopted February 24, 1989, effective February 25, 1989, 19 Pa.B. 781; amended June 10, 1994, effective June 11, 1994, 24 Pa.B. 2904; amended March 29, 2002, effective March 30, 2002, 32 Pa.B. 1644. Immediately preceding text appears at serial pages (271737) to (271738).

Cross References

This section cited in 49 Pa. Code § 35.284 (relating to disclosures of business relationships).

§ 35.287. Supervised property management assistance by salespersons.

A salesperson may assist in property management if the salesperson's work is supervised and controlled by the employing broker. The salesperson may not independently negotiate the terms of a lease nor execute a lease on behalf of the lessor.

---

49 § 35.288   DEPARTMENT OF STATE   Pt. I

Authority

The provisions of this § 35.287 issued under the Real Estate Licensing and Registration Act (63 P. S. §§ 455.101—455.902); amended under sections 404, 606—606.6 and 608—608.3 of the Real Estate Licensing and Registration Act (63 P. S. §§ 455.404, 455.606—455.606f and 455.608c).

Source

The provisions of this § 35.287 adopted February 24, 1989, effective February 25, 1989, 19 Pa.B. 781; amended November 17, 2000, effective November 18, 2000, 30 Pa.B. 5954; amended March 29, 2002, effective March 30, 2002, 32 Pa.B. 1644. Immediately preceding text appears at serial page (271738).

§ 35.288. Duties when selling or leasing own real estate.

(a) A broker or salesperson who sells or leases his own real estate shall comply with the requirements of the act and this chapter.

(b) A broker or salesperson who is selling or leasing his own real estate shall disclose his licensed status to a prospective buyer or lessee before the buyer or lessee enters into an agreement of sale or lease. See § 35.304 (relating to disclosure of licensure when advertising own real estate).

Authority

The provisions of this § 35.288 issued under the Real Estate Licensing and Registration Act (63 P. S. §§ 455.101—455.902).

Source

The provisions of this § 35.288 adopted February 24, 1989, effective February 25, 1989, 19 Pa.B. 781.

§ 35.289. Valid list of rentals.

The list of rental units that a rental listing referral agent gives to a prospective tenant shall meet the desired specifications sought by the prospective tenant as set forth in the rental listing agreement. The rental listing referral agent shall verify the availability of the rental units no more than 4 days prior to the date the agent collects a fee from the prospective tenant.

Authority

The provisions of this § 35.289 issued under the Real Estate Licensing and Registration Act (63 P. S. §§ 455.101—455.902).

Source

The provisions of this § 35.289 adopted February 24, 1989, effective February 25, 1989, 19 Pa.B. 781.

§ 35.290. Reporting of crimes and disciplinary actions.

(a) A licensee shall notify the Commission of being convicted of, or pleading guilty or nolo contendere to, a felony or misdemeanor, within 30 days of the verdict or plea.

(b) A licensee shall notify the Commission of disciplinary action taken against him by the real estate licensing authority of another jurisdiction within 30 days of receiving notice of the disciplinary action.

Authority

The provisions of this § 35.290 issued under the Real Estate Licensing and Registration Act (63 P.S. §§ 455.101—455.902).

Source

The provisions of this § 35.290 adopted February 24, 1989, effective February 25, 1989, 19 Pa.B. 781.

§ 35.291. Posting of suspension notice.

A broker or cemetery broker whose license is suspended by the Commission shall return his license to the Commission and shall post a notice of the Commission's action at the main office and at branch offices. The notice, which will be provided by the Commission, shall be posted prominently on or near the public entrance to each office. Failure to post the notice constitutes grounds for further disciplinary action by the Commission.

Authority

The provisions of this § 35.291 issued under the Real Estate Licensing and Registration Act (63 P.S. §§ 455.101—455.902).

Source

The provisions of this § 35.291 adopted February 24, 1989, effective February 25, 1989, 19 Pa.B. 781; amended June 10, 1994, effective June 11, 1994, 24 Pa.B. 2904. Immediately preceding text appears at serial pages (135759) to (135760).

§ 35.292. Duties of licensees generally.

(a) The following duties are owed to all consumers of real estate services and may not be waived:

(1) Exercise reasonable professional skill and care.

(2) Deal honestly and in good faith.

(3) Present, in a reasonably practicable period of time, all offers, counter-offers, notices and communications to and from the parties in writing, unless the property is subject to an existing contract and the seller/landlord has agreed in a written waiver.

(4) Comply with the Real Estate Seller Disclosure Act (68 P.S. §§ 1021—1036).

35-49

(5) Account for escrow and deposits funds as required by section 604(a)(5) of the act (63 P.S. § 455.604(a)(5)) and §§ 35.321—35.328 (relating to escrow requirements).

(6) Provide consumers with the information in section 608 of the act (63 P.S. § 455.608) at the initial interview.

(7) Disclose, in a reasonably practicable period of time, all conflicts of interest and financial interests as required in § 35.283 (relating to disclosure of interest).

(8) Advise the consumer to seek expert advice on matters about the transaction that are beyond the licensee's expertise.

(9) Ensure that all services are provided in a reasonable, professional and competent manner.

(10) Keep the consumer informed about the transaction and the tasks to be completed.

(11) Provide assistance with document preparation.

(12) Advise the consumer about compliance with laws pertaining to real estate transactions without rendering legal advice.

(b) A licensee is not required to conduct an independent inspection of the property.

(c) A licensee is not required to independently verify the accuracy or completeness of any representation made by the consumer to a transaction which the licensee reasonably believes to be accurate and reliable.

(d) A licensee is not liable for the acts of a consumer unless the consumer is acting at the express direction of the licensee or as a result of a representation by a licensee reasonably relied on by the consumer.

Authority

The provisions of this § 35.292 issued under sections 404, 606—606.6 and 608—608.3 of the Real Estate Licensing and Registration Act (63 P.S. §§ 455.404, 455.606—455.606f and 455.608—455.608c).

Source

The provisions of this § 35.292 adopted March 29, 2002, effective March 30, 2002, 32 Pa.B. 1644.

Cross References

This section cited in 49 Pa. Code § 35.311 (relating to generally); 49 Pa. Code § 35.313 (relating to duties of buyer's agent); 49 Pa. Code § 35.315 (relating to duties of designated agent); and 49 Pa. Code § 35.316 (relating to duties of transaction licensee).

35-50

ADVERTISING AND SOLICITATION

§ 35.301. Unauthorized advertising and solicitation.

(a) A licensee may not advertise the sale or lease of real estate, or otherwise solicit prospective buyers or tenants for the real estate, without the authority of the seller or lessor or of the agent of the seller or lessor.

(b) A rental listing referral agent may not publish information about a rental property if the lessor or property manager expressly states that the property is not to be included in lists prepared by rental listing referral agents.

Authority

The provisions of this § 35.301 issued under the Real Estate Licensing and Registration Act (63 P. S. §§ 455.101—455.902).

Source

The provisions of this § 35.301 adopted February 24, 1989, effective February 25, 1989, 19 Pa.B. 781.

§ 35.302. Harassment.

A licensee, whether acting on behalf of a prospective buyer or not, may not solicit—by personal contact, telephone, mail or advertising—the sale or other disposition of real estate with such frequency as to amount to clear harassment of the owner or other person who controls the sale or disposition of the real estate.

Authority

The provisions of this § 35.302 issued under the Real Estate Licensing and Registration Act (63 P. S. §§ 455.101—455.902).

Source

The provisions of this § 35.302 adopted February 24, 1989, effective February 25, 1989, 19 Pa.B. 781.

§ 35.303. Panic selling.

(a) The Commission will regard an attempt by a licensee to bring about panic selling in order to profit from it as bad faith under section 604(a)(20) of the act (63 P. S. § 455.604(a)(20)). For purposes of this section, "panic selling" is frequent efforts to sell residential real estate in a particular neighborhood because of fear of declining real estate values when the fear is not based on facts relating to the intrinsic value of the real estate itself.

(b) Proof of systematic solicitation of sales listings may be considered sufficient, but not conclusive, evidence of an attempt to bring about panic selling.

Authority

The provisions of this § 35.303 issued under the Real Estate Licensing and Registration Act (63 P. S. §§ 455.101—455.902).

Source

The provisions of this § 35.303 adopted February 24, 1989, effective February 25, 1989, 19 Pa.B. 781.

§ 35.304. Disclosure of licensure when advertising own real estate.

A licensee who sells or leases his own real estate shall disclose that he is a real estate licensee in advertisements for the property. This requirement does not apply if the property is listed with a real estate company.

Authority

The provisions of this § 35.304 issued under the Real Estate Licensing and Registration Act (63 P. S. §§ 455.101—455.902); amended under sections 404 and 602 of the Real Estate Licensing Registration Act (63 P. S. §§ 455.404 and 455.602).

Source

The provisions of this § 35.304 adopted February 24, 1989, effective February 25, 1989, 19 Pa.B. 781; amended November 17, 2000, effective November 18, 2000, 30 Pa.B. 5954. Immediately preceding text appears at serial page (256781).

Cross References

This section cited in 49 Pa. Code § 35.288 (relating to duties when selling or leasing own real estate).

§ 35.305. Business name on advertisements.

(a) Brokerage companies, including sole proprietorships, cemetery companies and rental listing referral agencies shall advertise or otherwise hold *themselves* out to the public only under the business name designated on *their* license.

(b) Licensees who wish to use and advertise a nickname for their first names shall include the nickname on their licensure applications or biennial renewal applications.

(c) An advertisement by an associate broker, salesperson, cemetery associate broker or cemetery salesperson shall contain the business name and telephone number of the employing broker. The names and telephone numbers shall be of equal size.

Authority

The provisions of this § 35.305 issued under the Real Estate Licensing and Registration Act (63 P. S. §§ 455.101—455.902); amended under sections 201, 404, 501, 601, 602 and 604 of the Real Estate Licensing Registration Act (63 P. S. §§ 455.201, 455.404, 455.501, 455.601, 455.602 and 455.604).

Source

The provisions of this § 35.305 adopted February 24, 1989, effective February 25, 1989, 19 Pa.B. 781; amended June 10, 1994, effective June 11, 1994, 24 Pa.B. 2904; amended November 17, 2000, effective November 18, 2000, 30 Pa.B. 5954; amended August 19, 2005, effective August 20, 2005, 35 Pa.B. 4711. Immediately preceding text appears at serial pages (287896) to (287897).

Notes of Decisions

Employing Broker Information

Several real estate salespersons and associate brokers violated the regulation requiring them to list the business name and telephone number of their employing broker in advertisements, where the advertisements each contained the name of the employing broker and one telephone number, which, although purchased by the employing broker, provides a direct connection to the salesperson or associate broker featured in the advertisement, and where directory assistance provides a different number appearing in none of the advertisements for the employing broker. *Campo v. State Real Estate Commission*, 723 A.2d 260 (Pa. Cmwlth. 1998).

An advertisement failed to meet the requirements of subsection (b) where telephone numbers, owned and maintained by the employing broker but assigned to various salespeople to answer, were displayed in the advertisement, and the numbers provided in the advertisements did not match the telephone numbers given by directory assistance for the employing broker. *D'Alonzo v. State Real Estate Commission*, 702 A.2d 1102 (Pa. Cmwlth. 1997).

Validity

The court found ample authority in the Real Estate Licensing and Regulation Act for the State Real Estate Commission's promulgation of a regulation requiring the employing broker's telephone number in advertisements, where employing brokers are required to supervise employed salespersons and associate brokers, and misleading advertisements are forbidden; the regulation advances the twin aims of employe supervision and prevention of public misconception by providing the public with unfettered access to the employe's supervisor, and it also prevents the public from mistakenly believing that the salesperson or associate broker is self-employed. *Campo v. State Real Estate Commission*, 723 A.2d 260 (Pa. Cmwlth. 1998).

Cross References

This section cited in 49 Pa. Code § 43a.10 (relating to schedule of civil penalties—real estate and cemetery brokers, real estate schools).

§ 35.306. Advertisements of lotteries, contests, prizes, certificates, gifts and lots.

(a) An advertisement by a licensee for the solicitation, sale or offering for sale of real estate that employs lotteries or contests or that offers prizes, certificates, gifts or free lots shall contain:

(1) A description of each prize, certificate, gift or lot offered.

(2) The prerequisites for receiving each prize, certificate, gift or lot offered.

(3) Limitation on the number of prizes, certificates, gifts or lots offered.

(4) The fair market value of each prize, certificate, gift or lot offered. If the advertisement is in a print medium, the statement of fair market value shall be in the same size type as the description of the prize, certificate, gift or lot

offered. For purposes of this paragraph, "fair market value" is the price or value that a prospective buyer would expect to pay, or be charged for, if he were to acquire a similar item of like quality and quantity in a retail outlet that offers the item for sale to the general public.

(5) The odds of winning or receiving each prize, certificate, gift or lot offered. If the advertisement is in a print medium, the statement of odds shall be the same size type as the description of the prize, certificate, gift or lot, and shall appear immediately adjacent to the description.

(b) A licensee who solicits, sells or offers for sale real estate by using the mails or by offering prizes, certificates, gifts or lots shall maintain records that contain:

(1) The number and description of each prize, certificate, gift or lot distributed or awarded.

(2) The name and address of each person who received a prize, certificate, gift or lot.

(3) The name and address of each person who responded to the advertisement or solicitation but did not receive a prize, certificate, gift or lot.

(c) The Commission will regard the following as deceptive conduct within the meaning of section 604(a)(18) of the act (63 P. S. § 455.604(a)(18)):

(1) Failure to comply with subsection (a) or (b).

(2) Failure to disclose the possibility that a particular prize, certificate, gift or lot may not be distributed or awarded.

(3) Advertising the availability of a prize, certificate, gift or lot when it is not available for distribution or awarding.

(4) Giving a misleading description of a prize, certificate, gift or lot.

Authority

The provisions of this § 35.306 issued under the Real Estate Licensing and Registration Act (63 P. S. §§ 455.101—455.902).

Source

The provisions of this § 35.306 adopted February 24, 1989, effective February 25, 1989, 19 Pa.B. 781.

§ 35.307. Advertisements of sales volume, market position and numbers of offices.

(a) An advertisement by a broker about "sales volume" or "production" shall refer only to closed transactions. For purpose of this subsection, a "closed transaction" is either a listing sold or a sale made after a fully executed deed is delivered.

(b) An advertisement by a broker about his production or position in the "market" shall identify the municipality that the market comprises.

(c) An advertisement by a broker about the number of offices that he operates shall refer only to those offices that have been issued branch office licenses by the Commission.

Authority

The provisions of this § 35.307 issued under the Real Estate Licensing and Registration Act (63 P. S. §§ 455.101—455.902).

Source

The provisions of this § 35.307 adopted February 24, 1989, effective February 25, 1989, 19 Pa.B. 781.

§ 35.308. Relationship with educational institution.

A real estate company, franchise or network may promote, endorse, or advertise its association, affiliation or connection with a real estate school or with a college, university or institute of higher learning regarding its offering of real estate instruction. An association, affiliation or connection which includes an ownership interest shall be disclosed in all promotions, endorsements or advertisements. For purposes of this section, an ownership interest will be considered by the Commission to include proprietary or beneficial interests through which the real estate company, franchise or network earns or has the potential to earn income, or which produces a direct or indirect economic benefit.

Authority

The provisions of this § 35.308 issued under the Real Estate Licensing and Registration Act (63 P. S. §§ 455.101—455.902); amended under sections 404 and 602 of the Real Estate Licensing Registration Act (63 P. S. §§ 455.404 and 455.602).

Source

The provisions of this § 35.308 adopted June 10, 1994, effective June 11, 1994, 24 Pa.B. 2904; amended November 17, 2000, effective November 18, 2000, 30 Pa.B. 5954. Immediately preceding text appears at serial page (201871).

PERMITTED RELATIONSHIPS

§ 35.311. Generally.

(a) A licensee and a consumer may enter into the relationship specified in sections 606.2—606.6 and 606.4 of the act (63 P.S. §§ 455.606—455.606d and 455.606f).

(b) A broker may not extend or delegate the broker's agency relationship without the written consent of the principal.

(c) Compensation paid by a broker to another broker who assists in the marketing and sale/lease of a consumer's property does not create an agency relationship between the consumer and that other broker.

35-52.3

(d) A licensee in an agency relationship may not knowingly, during or following the termination of an agency relationship, reveal or use confidential information of the principal, except when one or more of the following apply:

(1) The principal consented to the disclosure.

(2) The information is disclosed to another licensee or third party acting solely on behalf of the principal.

(3) The information is required to be disclosed under subpoena or court order.

(4) The disclosure is necessary to prevent the principal from committing a crime.

(5) The information is used by the licensee to defend in a legal proceeding against an accusation of wrongdoing.

Authority

The provisions of this § 35.311 issued under sections 404, 606—606.6 and 608—608.3 of the Real Estate Licensing and Registration Act (63 P. S. §§ 455.404, 455.606—455.606f and 455.608—455.608c).

Source

The provisions of this § 35.311 adopted March 29, 2002, effective March 30, 2002, 32 Pa.B. 1644.

§ 35.312. Duties of seller's agent.

(a) In addition to the duties required in § 35.292 (relating to duties of licensees generally), a seller's agent owes the additional duties of:

(1) Loyalty to the seller/landlord by acting in the seller's/landlord's best interest.

(2) Confidentiality, except that a licensee has a duty to reveal known material defects about the property.

(3) Making a continuous and good faith effort to find a buyer/tenant for the property except when the property is subject to an existing agreement of sale/lease.

(4) Disclosure to other parties in the transaction that the licensee has been engaged as a seller's agent.

(b) A licensee does not breach a duty to a seller/landlord by showing alternative properties to a prospective buyer/tenant or listing competing properties.

(c) A seller's agent may compensate other brokers as subagents if the seller/landlord agrees in writing. Subagents have the same duties and obligations to the seller/landlord as the seller's agent.

(d) A seller's agent may also compensate a buyer's agent and a transaction licensee who do not have the same duties and obligations to the seller/landlord as the seller's agent.

35-52.4

(e) Upon entering into a written agreement with the seller/landlord, each licensee employed by the broker will act as a seller's agent unless a licensee has been named, or is thereafter named, a designated agent under § 35.315 (relating to designated agency).

Authority

The provisions of this § 35.312 issued under sections 404, 606—606.6 and 608—608.3 of the Real Estate Licensing and Registration Act (63 P. S. §§ 455.404, 455.606—455.606f and 455.608—455.608c).

Source

The provisions of this § 35.312 adopted March 29, 2002, effective March 30, 2002, 32 Pa.B. 1644.

§ 35.313. Duties of buyer's agent.

(a) In addition to the duties required in § 35.292 (relating to duties of licensees generally), a buyer's agent owes the additional duties of:
(1) Loyalty to the buyer/tenant by acting in the buyer's/tenant's best interest.
(2) Confidentiality.
(3) Making a continuous and good faith effort to find a property for the buyer/tenant except when the buyer/tenant is subject to an existing contract for sale/lease.
(4) Disclosure to other parties in the transaction that the licensee has been engaged as a buyer's agent.

(b) A licensee does not breach a duty to a buyer/tenant by showing a property the buyer/tenant is interested in to other buyer/tenants.

(c) A buyer's agent represents the interests of the buyer/tenant even if paid by the seller/landlord.

(d) Upon entering into a written agreement with the buyer/tenant, each licensee employed by the broker will act as a buyer's agent unless a licensee has been named, or is thereafter named, a designated agent under § 35.315 (relating to duties of designated agency).

Authority

The provisions of this § 35.313 issued under sections 404, 606—606.6 and 608—608.3 of the Real Estate Licensing and Registration Act (63 P. S. §§ 455.404, 455.606—455.606f and 455.608—455.608c).

Source

The provisions of this § 35.313 adopted March 29, 2002, effective March 30, 2002, 32 Pa.B. 1644.

§ 35.314. Duties of dual agent.

(a) A licensee may act as a dual agent if both parties consent in writing.
(b) In addition to the duties required in § 35.292 (relating to duties of licensees generally), a dual agent owes the additional duties of:

(1) Taking no action that is adverse or detrimental to either party's interest in the transaction.
(2) Unless otherwise agreed in writing, making a continuous and good faith effort to find a buyer/tenant for the property and a property for the buyer/tenant except when the buyer/tenant or seller/landlord is subject to an existing contract.
(3) Confidentiality, except that a licensee is required to disclose known material defects about the property.

(c) A dual agent does not breach a duty to the seller/landlord by showing properties not owned by the seller/landlord to a prospective buyer/tenant or listing competing properties for sale/lease.

(d) A dual agent does not breach a duty to a buyer/tenant by showing a property the buyer/tenant is interested in to other prospective buyer/tenants.

Authority

The provisions of this § 35.314 issued under sections 404, 606—606.6 and 608—608.3 of the Real Estate Licensing and Registration Act (63 P. S. §§ 455.404, 455.606—455.606f and 455.608—455.608c).

Source

The provisions of this § 35.314 adopted March 29, 2002, effective March 30, 2002, 32 Pa.B. 1644.

Cross References

This section cited in 49 Pa. Code § 35.315 (relating to duties of designated agent).

§ 35.315. Duties of designated agent.

(a) A broker, with the written consent of the principal, may designate one or more licensees to act exclusively as the agent of the seller/landlord, and designate one or more licensees to act exclusively as the agent of the buyer/tenant in the same transaction.

(b) Designation may take place at any time. If designation takes place after the initial designation or after a written agreement has been entered into, the broker shall:
(1) Obtain the principal's consent, in writing, to the newly designated licensee.
(2) Obtain, when applicable, the principal's agreement to renounce any previous agency relationship with the other licensees employed by the broker.

(c) Regardless of when the designation takes place, the broker and the designated agents shall use reasonable care to ensure that confidential information is not disclosed or used.

(d) The licensees employed by the broker who are not designated have no agency relationship with either party in the transaction.

(e) Each licensee employed by the same broker who is a designated agent in the same transaction, owes the following additional duties, in addition to those required in § 35.292 (relating to duties of licensees generally):

(1) Loyalty to the principal with whom the designated agent is acting by working in that principal's best interest.

(2) Make a continuous and good faith effort to find a buyer/tenant for a principal who is a seller/landlord or to find a property for a principal who is the buyer/tenant except where the seller/landlord is subject to an existing contract for sale or lease or the buyer/tenant is subject to an existing contract to purchase or lease.

(3) Disclose to the principal prior to writing or presenting an offer to purchase that the other party to the transaction is represented by a designated agent also employed by the broker.

(4) Confirm that the broker is a dual agent in the transaction.

(f) In the transaction specified in subsection (e), the employing broker, as a dual agent, has the additional duties, in addition to those specified in § 35.292 and § 35.314 (relating to duties of dual agents), of:

(1) Taking reasonable care to protect any confidential information that has been disclosed to the designated licensees.

(2) Taking responsibility to direct and supervise the business activities of the designated licensees while taking no action that is adverse or detrimental to either party's interest in the transaction.

Authority

The provisions of this § 35.315 issued under sections 404, 606—606.6 and 608—608.3 of the Real Estate Licensing and Registration Act (63 P. S. §§ 455.404, 455.606—455.606f and 455.608—455.608c).

Source

The provisions of this § 35.315 adopted March 29, 2002, effective March 30, 2002, 32 Pa.B. 1644.

Cross References

This section cited in 49 Pa. Code § 35.312 (relating to duties of sellers agent); and 49 Pa. Code § 35.313 (relating to duties of buyer's agent).

§ 35.316. Duties of transaction licensee.

In addition to the duties required in § 35.292 (relating to duties of licensees generally), a transaction licensee shall advise the consumer that the licensee:

(1) Is not acting as an agent or advocate for the consumer and should not be provided with confidential information.

(2) Owes the additional duty of limited confidentiality in that the following information may not be disclosed:

(i) The seller/landlord will accept a price less than the asking/listing price.

35-52.7

(ii) The buyer/tenant will pay a price greater than the price submitted in a written offer.

(iii) The seller/landlord or buyer/tenant will agree to financing terms other than those offered.

Authority

The provisions of this § 35.316 issued under sections 404, 606—606.6 and 608—608.3 of the Real Estate Licensing and Registration Act (63 P. S. §§ 455.404, 455.606—455.606f and 455.608—455.608c).

Source

The provisions of this § 35.316 adopted March 29, 2002, effective March 30, 2002, 32 Pa.B. 1644.

ESCROW REQUIREMENTS

§ 35.321. Duty to deposit money belonging to another into escrow account.

(a) Except as provided in subsection (b), a broker shall deposit money that the broker receives belonging to another into an escrow account in a Federally or State-insured bank or depository to be held pending consummation of the transaction or a prior termination thereof that does not involve a dispute between the parties to the transaction, at which time the broker shall pay over the full amount to the party entitled to receive it. If a broker is a partnership, association or corporation, its broker of record shall be responsible for ensuring that the escrow duty is performed.

(b) A broker is not required to hold in escrow rents that he receives as a property manager for a lessor. A broker shall deposit rents received into a rental management account that is separate from the broker's escrow and general business accounts.

(c) If a broker receives money belonging to another under an installment land purchase agreement, the transaction shall be considered consummated, for purposes of subsection (a), when the buyer has been afforded the opportunity, by means of the seller's written acknowledgement on or affixed to the agreement, to record the agreement, unless the agreement specifies otherwise.

(d) If a broker receives money belonging to another under an agreement of sale involving cemetery property, the transaction shall be considered consummated, for purposes of subsection (a), when the buyer receives a copy of the agreement of sale.

(e) If a broker receives a security deposit belonging to another under a lease agreement, the broker's duty to pay over the deposit for purposes of subsection (a), shall arise when the tenancy ends. If a sale of the leased premises or a change in a property management contract occurs during the term of the tenancy, the broker may transfer the security deposit from the broker's escrow account to the escrow account of the lessor or the lessor's broker upon notification in writing to

35-52.8

Ch. 35   STATE REAL ESTATE COMMISSION   49 § 35.322

each tenant from whom the broker received a deposit of the name and address of the banking institution in which the deposits will be held, and the amount of the deposits.

Authority

The provisions of this § 35.321 issued under the Real Estate Licensing and Registration Act (63 P. S. §§ 455.101—455.902); amended under sections 404 and 602 of the Real Estate Licensing Registration Act (63 P. S. §§ 455.404 and 455.602).

Source

The provisions of this § 35.321 adopted February 24, 1989, effective February 25, 1989, 19 Pa.B. 781; amended November 17, 2000, effective November 18, 2000, 30 Pa.B. 5954. Immediately preceding text appears at serial pages (201871) to (201872).

§ 35.322. Nonwaiver of escrow duty.

A broker's escrow duty may not be waived or altered by an agreement between the parties to the transaction, between the broker and the parties, or between the broker and other brokers who may be involved in the transaction.

Authority

The provisions of this § 35.322 issued under the Real Estate Licensing and Registration Act (63 P. S. §§ 455.101—455.902).

Source

The provisions of this § 35.322 adopted February 24, 1989, effective February 25, 1989, 19 Pa.B. 781.

§ 35.323. Responsibility for escrow in cobrokerage transactions.

(a) If a sales deposit is tendered by a buyer to the listing broker rather than to the selling broker, the listing broker shall assume the escrow duty.

Ch. 35   STATE REAL ESTATE COMMISSION   49 § 35.324

(b) If a sales deposit is tendered by a buyer to the selling broker with the buyer having prior notice that the selling broker intends to deliver the deposit to the listing broker, the listing broker shall assume the escrow duty. The selling broker shall require the buyer to acknowledge in writing, prior to his signing the agreement of sale, that the prior notice contained the following information:

(1) The name of the listing broker.

(2) That the selling broker's acceptance of the buyer's deposit is on behalf of the listing broker as subagent for the listing broker.

(3) That the listing broker is a licensed real estate broker who is required to hold the deposit in escrow.

(4) That the listing broker be designated as payee, if the buyer's deposit is in the form of a check.

(c) If a sales deposit is tendered by a buyer to the selling broker without the buyer having the prior notice in subsection (b), the selling broker shall assume the escrow duty.

Authority

The provisions of this § 35.323 issued under the Real Estate Licensing and Registration Act (63 P. S. §§ 455.101—455.902).

Source

The provisions of this § 35.323 adopted February 24, 1989, effective February 25, 1989, 19 Pa.B. 781.

§ 35.324. Deadline for depositing money into escrow account.

(a) Except as provided in subsection (b), a broker shall deposit money belonging to another into an escrow account by the end of the next business day following its receipt in the real estate office where the escrow records are maintained.

(b) If the money of another has been tendered to the broker in the form of a check under an offer to purchase or lease real estate, the broker may, with the written permission of both the buyer and the seller or the lessee and the lessor, refrain from depositing the money into an escrow account by the deadline in subsection (a) pending the seller's or lessor's acceptance of the offer. The broker shall deposit the check into an escrow account within 1 business day of the seller's or lessor's acceptance of the offer.

Authority

The provisions of this § 35.324 issued under the Real Estate Licensing and Registration Act (63 P. S. §§ 455.101—455.902).

Source

The provisions of this § 35.324 adopted February 24, 1989, effective February 25, 1989, 19 Pa.B. 781.

35-53

49 § 35.325   DEPARTMENT OF STATE   Pt. I

§ 35.325. Escrow account.

(a) An escrow account shall:

(1) Be maintained in a Federally- or State-insured bank or recognized depository.

(2) Designate the broker as trustee.

(3) Provide for the withdrawal of funds without prior notice.

(4) Be used exclusively for escrow purposes.

(b) A broker who is a sole proprietor or broker of record may give an employee written authority to deposit money into an escrow account and may give a licensed employee written authority to withdraw funds from the escrow account for payments that are properly chargeable to the account.

(c) If money is expected to be held in escrow for more than 6 months, the broker is encouraged to deposit the money into an interest-bearing escrow account. Interest earned on an escrow account shall be held and disbursed, pro rata, in the same manner as the principal amount, unless the parties to the transaction direct otherwise by agreement. A broker may not claim the interest earned on an escrow account, unless the broker is a lessor as provided in section 511.2 of the Landlord and Tenant Act (68 P. S. § 250.511b).

(d) A broker shall provide the Commission or its authorized representatives, upon written request or under an office inspection under § 35.246 (relating to inspection of office), a letter addressed to the bank or depository where the escrow account is maintained authorizing the release of records pertaining to the account.

Authority

The provisions of this § 35.325 issued under the Real Estate Licensing and Registration Act (63 P. S. §§ 455.101—455.902); amended under sections 201, 501, 601, 602 and 604 of the Real Estate Licensing and Registration Act (63 P. S. §§ 455.201, 455.501, 455.601, 455.602 and 455.604).

Source

The provisions of this § 35.325 adopted February 24, 1989, effective February 25, 1989, 19 Pa.B. 781; amended August 19, 2005, effective August 20, 2005, 35 Pa.B. 4711. Immediately preceding text appears at serial page (201874).

§ 35.326. Prohibition against commingling or misappropriation.

(a) Except as provided in subsection (b), a broker may not commingle money that is required to be held in escrow—or interest earned on an escrow account—with business, personal or other funds.

(b) A broker may deposit business or personal funds into an escrow account to cover service charges assessed to the account by the bank or depository where the account is located or to maintain a minimum balance in the account as required by the regulations of the bank or depository.

35-54

(c) A broker may not misappropriate money that is required to be held in escrow—or interest earned on an escrow account—for business, personal or other purposes.

Authority

The provisions of this § 35.326 issued under the Real Estate Licensing and Registration Act (63 P.S. §§ 455.101—455.902).

Source

The provisions of this § 35.326 adopted February 24, 1989, effective February 25, 1989, 19 Pa.B. 781; amended June 10, 1994, effective June 11, 1994, 24 Pa.B. 2904. Immediately preceding text appears at serial page (135767).

§ 35.327. Procedure when entitlement to money held in escrow is disputed.

If a dispute arises between the parties to a real estate transaction over entitlement to money that is being held in escrow by a broker, the broker shall retain the money in escrow until the dispute is resolved. If resolution of the dispute appears remote without legal action, the broker may, following 30 days' notice to the parties, petition the county court having jurisdiction in the matter to interplead the rival claimants.

Authority

The provisions of this § 35.327 issued under the Real Estate Licensing and Registration Act (63 P.S. §§ 455.101—455.902).

Source

The provisions of this § 35.327 adopted February 24, 1989, effective February 25, 1989, 19 Pa.B. 781.

§ 35.328. Escrow records.

A broker shall keep records of monies received by him that are required to be held in escrow and shall produce the records for examination by the Commission or its authorized representatives upon written request or pursuant to an office inspection under § 35.246 (relating to inspection of office). The records shall contain:

(1) The name of the party from whom the broker received the money.
(2) The name of the party to whom the money belongs.
(3) The name of the party for whose account the money is deposited.
(4) The date the broker received the money.
(5) The date the broker deposited the money into the escrow account.
(6) The date the broker withdrew the money from the escrow account.

Authority

The provisions of this § 35.328 issued under the Real Estate Licensing and Registration Act (63 P.S. §§ 455.101—455.902).

Source

The provisions of this § 35.328 adopted February 24, 1989, effective February 25, 1989, 19 Pa.B. 781.

REAL ESTATE DOCUMENTS

§ 35.331. Written agreements generally.

(a) A written agreement between a broker and a principal or between a broker and a consumer whereby the consumer is or may be committed to pay a fee, commission or other valuable consideration shall contain the following:

(1) Notification that a Real Estate Recovery Fund exists to reimburse a person who has obtained a final civil judgment against a Commonwealth real estate licensee owing to fraud, misrepresentation or deceit in a real estate transaction and who has been unable to collect the judgment after exhausting legal and equitable remedies. Details about the Fund may be obtained by calling the Commission at (717) 783-3658.

(2) Notification that payments of money received by the broker on account of a sale—regardless of the form of payment and the person designated as payee (if payment is made by an instrument)—shall be held by the broker in an escrow account pending consummation of the sale or a prior termination thereof.

(3) Notification that the broker's commission and the duration of the agreement have been determined as a result of negotiations between the broker, or a licensee employed by the broker, and the seller/landlord or buyer/tenant.

(4) A description of the services to be provided and the fees to be charged.

(5) Notification about the possibility that the broker or any licensee employed by the broker may provide services to more than one party in a single transaction, and an explanation of the duties owed to the other party and the fees which the broker may receive for those services.

(6) Notification of the licensee's continuing duty to disclose in a reasonably practicable period of time any conflict of interest.

(7) In an agreement between a broker and a seller/landlord, a statement regarding cooperation with subagents and buyers agents, a disclosure that a buyer agent, even if compensated by the listing broker or seller/landlord will represent the interests of the buyer/tenant and a disclosure of any potential for the broker to act as a dual agent.

(8) In an agreement between a broker and a buyer/tenant, an explanation that the broker may be compensated based upon a percentage of the purchase price, the broker's policies regarding cooperation with listing brokers willing to pay buyer's brokers, a disclosure that the broker, even if compensated by the listing broker or seller/landlord will represent the interests of the buyer/tenant and a disclosure of any potential for the broker to act as a dual agent.

(b) To the extent that any of the information required in subsection (a) is set forth in the disclosure summaries in §§ 35.336—35.338 (relating to disclosure summary for the purchase or sale of residential or commercial real estate or for the lease of residential or commercial real estate when the licensee is working on behalf of the tenant; disclosure summary for the lease of residential or commercial real estate when the licensee is working on behalf of the owner; and disclosure summary for time-share estates), those provisions need not be repeated, but may be incorporated by reference.

Authority

The provisions of this § 35.331 issued under the Real Estate Licensing and Registration Act (63 P.S. §§ 455.101—455.902); amended under sections 404, 606—606.6 and 608—608.3 of the Real Estate Licensing and Registration Act (63 P.S. §§ 455.404, 455.606—455.606f and 455.608—455.608c).

Source

The provisions of this § 35.331 adopted February 24, 1989, effective February 25, 1989, 19 Pa.B. 781; amended June 10, 1994, effective June 11, 1994, 24 Pa.B. 2904; corrected October 14, 1994, effective June 11, 1994, 24 Pa.B. 5229; amended March 29, 2002, effective March 30, 2002, 32 Pa.B. 1644. Immediately preceding text appears at serial page (201876).

Cross References

This section cited in 49 Pa. Code § 35.281 (relating to putting contracts, commitments and agreements in writing); and 49 Pa. Code § 35.332 (relating to exclusive listing agreements).

§ 35.332. Exclusive listing agreements.

(a) An exclusive listing agreement may comprise one of the following:
(1) The exclusive agency of the broker.
(2) The exclusive right-to-sell or exclusive right-to-lease.
(b) An exclusive listing agreement shall contain, in addition to the requirements in § 35.331 (relating to written agreements generally), the following:
(1) The sale or lease price.
(2) The commission, fees or other compensation expected on the sale or lease price.
(3) The duration of the agreement.
(4) In the case of an exclusive right-to-sell agreement, a statement in bold face type that the broker earns a commission on the sale of the property during the listing period by whomever made, including the owner.
(5) In the case of an exclusive right-to-lease agreement, a statement in bold print that the broker earns a commission on the lease of the property during the listing period by whomever made, including the lessor.
(c) An exclusive listing agreement may not contain:
(1) A listing period exceeding 1 year.
(2) An automatic renewal clause.

35-57

(3) A cancellation notice to terminate the agreement at the end of the listing period set forth in the agreement.
(4) Authority of the broker to execute a signed agreement of sale or lease for the owner or lessor.
(5) An option by the broker to purchase the listed property.
(6) Authority of the broker to confess judgment against the owner or lessor for the Commission in the event of a sale or lease.

Authority

The provisions of this § 35.332 issued under the Real Estate Licensing and Registration Act (63 P.S. §§ 455.101—455.902); amended under sections 404, 606—606.6 and 608—608.3 of the Real Estate Licensing and Registration Act (63 P.S. §§ 455.404, 455.606—455.606f and 455.608—455.608c).

Source

The provisions of this § 35.332 adopted February 24, 1989, effective February 25, 1989, 19 Pa.B. 781; amended March 29, 2002, effective March 30, 2002, 32 Pa.B. 1644. Immediately preceding text appears at serial pages (201876) to (201878).

§ 35.333. Agreements of sale.

(a) An agreement of sale, other than for a cemetery lot, mausoleum or cremation space or opening, shall contain:
(1) The date of the agreement.
(2) The names of the buyer and seller.
(3) A description of the property and the interest to be conveyed.
(4) The sale price.
(5) The dates for payment and conveyance.
(6) The zoning classification of the property, except if the property (or each parcel thereof, if subdividable) is zoned solely or primarily to permit single-family dwellings, together with a statement that the failure of the agreement of sale to contain the zoning classification of the property shall render the agreement voidable at the option of the buyer and, if voided, deposits tendered by the buyer shall be returned to the buyer without a requirement of court action.
(7) A statement identifying the capacity in which the broker, or a licensee employed by the broker is involved in the transaction and whether services have been provided to another party in the transaction.
(8) A provision that payments of money received by the broker on account of the sale—regardless of the form of payment and the person designated as payee (if payment is made by an instrument)—shall be held by the broker in an escrow account pending consummation of the sale or a prior termination thereof.
(9) The following statement:
"A Real Estate Recovery Fund exists to reimburse any person who has

35-58

obtained a final civil judgment against a Pennsylvania real estate licensee owing to fraud, misrepresentation, or deceit in a real estate transaction and who has been unable to collect the judgment after exhausting all legal and equitable remedies. For complete details about the Fund, call (717) 783-3658."

(10) A statement that access to a public road may require issuance of a highway occupancy permit from the Department of Transportation.

(11) In the case of an agreement of sale for the purchase of a time share or campground membership, a statement regarding the purchaser's right of cancellation that is set forth conspicuously in bold face type of at least 10 point size immediately above the signature line for the purchaser and that is in substantially the following form:

"You, the purchaser, may cancel this purchase at any time prior to midnight of the fifth day following the date of this transaction. If you desire to cancel, you are required to notify the seller, in writing, at (insert address). Such notice shall be given by certified return receipt mail or by any other bona fide means of delivery which provides you with a receipt. Such notice shall be effective upon being postmarked by the United States Postal Service or upon deposit of the notice with any bona fide means of delivery which provides you with a receipt."

(b) An agreement of sale that is conditioned upon the ability of the buyer to obtain a mortgage shall contain:

(1) The type of mortgage.

(2) The mortgage principal.

(3) The maximum interest rate of the mortgage.

(4) The minimum term of the mortgage.

(5) The deadline for the buyer to obtain the mortgage.

(6) The nature and extent of assistance that the broker will render to the buyer in obtaining the mortgage.

(c) The following terms shall be printed in bold face if made part of an agreement of sale:

(1) A provision relieving the seller from responsibility for defects involving the sale property, or a provision requiring the buyer to execute a release to that effect at the time of settlement, or a provision of similar import.

(2) A provision reserving to the builder-seller the right to change, or depart from, the building specifications for the sale property.

(d) An agreement of sale for a cemetery lot or plot or a mausoleum space or opening shall contain the requirements in subsection (a)(1)—(5) and (9).

Authority

The provisions of this § 35.333 issued under the Real Estate Licensing and Registration Act (63 P. S. §§ 455.101—455.902); amended under sections 404, 606—606.6 and 608—608.3 of the Real Estate Licensing and Registration Act (63 P. S. §§ 455.404, 455.606—455.606f and 455.608—455.608c).

Source

The provisions of this § 35.333 adopted February 24, 1989, effective February 25, 1989, 19 Pa.B. 781; amended June 10, 1994, effective June 11, 1994, 24 Pa.B. 2904; amended March 29, 2002, effective March 30, 2002, 32 Pa.B. 1644. Immediately preceding text appears at serial pages (201878) to (201879).

§ 35.334. Statements of estimated cost and return.

(a) Before an agreement of sale is executed, the brokers involved in the transaction shall provide each party with a written estimate of reasonably foreseeable expenses associated with the sale that the party may be expected to pay, including, but not limited to:

(1) The broker's commission.

(2) The mortgage payments and financing costs.

(3) Taxes and assessments.

(4) Settlement expenses.

(b) The estimates of costs required under subsection (a) shall be as accurate as may be reasonably expected of a person having knowledge of, and experience in, real estate sales.

(c) The following statement of estimated costs to the buyer at settlement is exemplary of the requirements of subsection (a):

STATEMENT OF ESTIMATED COSTS TO BUYER AT SETTLEMENT

Estimated Settlement Date _____

Property _____

Broker _____

Purchase Price _____

Payment on Account _____

Balance at Settlement _____

Estimated Closing Expenses

Title Search and Insurance _____

Conveyancing or Preparation of Papers Charge _____

Recording Fees

Deed _____

Mortgage _____

Mortgagee's Charges

Appraisal Fee _____

Credit Report _____

Origination and Placement Fees _____

Mortgage Service Charge _____

Fire Insurance ($ _____ for _____ years) _____

Miscellaneous Charges _____

Local Realty Transfer Tax (_____ %) _____

Ch. 35   STATE REAL ESTATE COMMISSION   49 § 35.334

Pennsylvania Realty Transfer
Tax   (_____ %)   _____
Notary Fees   _____
Other Charges   _____
Total Closing Expenses   _____
Costs for Rebates and Advances
Rebates to Seller
Insurance   _____
Annual Taxes and Water-
Sewer Rents   _____
Advances by Buyer
Insurance   _____
Taxes (Escrow)   _____
Total Costs for Rebates and
Advances   _____
Total Estimated Costs at Settlement   _____
Estimated Monthly Payments
First Lien $ _____ years at _____ %.
Interest and Principal $ _____
Monthly FHA Mortgage
Insurance Premium $ _____
Real Estate Taxes $ _____
Fire Insurance $ _____
Water-Sewer Rents $ _____
Total Estimated Monthly Payments $ _____

I/we have read and received a copy of the estimated settlement costs and estimated monthly carrying charges prior to the signing of an agreement of sale to purchase the property noted above.

I/we understand that the above costs are estimated and based on the best information available at this date and that they are subject to change, particularly in the case of the escrow charges such as taxes, water and sewage, rent and insurance.

WITNESS:

_____   _____ (SEAL)
                          Buyer

_____   _____ (SEAL)
                          Buyer

(d) The following statement of estimated costs to the seller at settlement is exemplary of the requirements of subsection (a):

STATEMENT OF ESTIMATED COSTS TO SELLER AT SETTLEMENT

Estimated Settlement Date _____

35-61

(287913) No. 331 Jun. 02

49 § 35.335   DEPARTMENT OF STATE   Pt. I

Property _____
Broker _____

Purchase Price   _____
Payment on Account   _____
Balance   _____
Estimated Closing Expenses
Penna. Realty Transfer Tax
(_____ %)   _____
Local Realty Transfer Tax
(_____ %)   _____
Federal Documentary
Stamps   _____
Notary Fee   _____
Mortgage Discount   _____
Unpaid Annual Taxes   _____
Broker's Commission   _____
Total Expenses   _____
Estimated Closing Credits Tax
Refund   _____
Estimated Net Charges   _____
Estimated Net Proceeds   _____

WITNESS:

_____   _____
                          Seller

_____   _____
                          Seller

Authority

The provisions of this § 35.334 issued under the Real Estate Licensing and Registration Act (63 P. S. §§ 455.101—455.902).

Source

The provisions of this § 35.334 adopted February 24, 1989, effective February 25, 1989, 19 Pa.B. 781.

§ 35.335. **Rental listing referral agreements.**

The agreement between a rental listing referral agent and a prospective tenant shall contain:

(1) The rental specifications desired by the prospective tenant, such as location and rent.

(2) The following statement in bold print:

"We are a referral service only. We are not acting as real estate salespersons or brokers. We do not guarantee that the purchaser will find a satisfac-

35-62

(287914) No. 331 Jun. 02

Ch. 35   STATE REAL ESTATE COMMISSION   49 § 35.336

tory rental unit through our service. Our only purpose is to furnish the purchaser with lists of available rental units."

Authority

The provisions of this § 35.335 issued under the Real Estate Licensing and Registration Act (63 P.S. §§ 455.101—455.902).

Source

The provisions of this § 35.335 adopted February 24, 1989, effective February 25, 1989, 19 Pa.B. 781.

§ 35.336. Disclosure summary for the purchase or sale of residential or commercial real estate or for the lease of residential or commercial real estate when the licensee is working on behalf of the tenant.

The Disclosure Summary shall be entitled "Consumer Notice" and shall be in the following format available from the Commission office upon request by phone, fax or internet:

CONSUMER NOTICE
THIS IS NOT A CONTRACT

Pennsylvania law requires real estate brokers and salespersons (licensees) to advise consumers who are seeking to sell or purchase residential or commercial real estate or tenants who are seeking to lease residential or commercial real estate where the licensee is working on behalf of the tenant of the business relationships permitted by the Real Estate Licensing and Registration Act. This notice must be provided to the consumer at the first contact where a substantive discussion about real estate occurs unless an oral disclosure has been previously provided. If the oral disclosure was provided, this notice must be provided at the first meeting or the first time a property is shown to the consumer by the broker or salesperson.

Before you disclose any information to a licensee, be advised that unless you select an agency relationship the licensee is not representing you. A business relationship of any kind will not be presumed but must be established between the consumer and the licensee.

Any licensee who provides you with real estate services owes you the following duties:

• Exercise reasonable professional skill and care which meets the practice standards required by the act.
• Deal honestly and in good faith.
• Present, in a reasonably practicable period of time, all offers, counteroffers, notices, and communications to and from the parties in writing. The duty to present written offers and counteroffers may be waived if the waiver is in writing.

---

49 § 35.336   DEPARTMENT OF STATE   Pt. I

• Comply with Real Estate Seller Disclosure Act.
• Account for escrow and deposit funds.
• Disclose all conflicts of interest in a reasonably practicable period of time.
• Provide assistance with document preparation and advise the consumer regarding compliance with laws pertaining to real estate transactions.
• Advise the consumer to seek expert advice on matters about the transaction that are beyond the licensee's expertise.
• Keep the consumer informed about the transaction and the tasks to be completed.
• Disclose financial interest in a service, such as financial, title transfer and preparation services, insurance, construction, repair or inspection, at the time service is recommended or the first time the licensee learns that the service will be used.

A licensee may have the following business relationships with the consumer:

Seller Agency:

Seller agency is a relationship where the licensee, upon entering into a written agreement, works only for a seller/ landlord. Seller's agents owe the additional duties of:

• Loyalty to the seller/landlord by acting in the seller's/landlord's best interest.
• Confidentiality, except that a licensee has a duty to reveal known material defects about the property.
• Making a continuous and good faith effort to find a buyer for the property, except while the property is subject to an existing agreement.
• Disclosure to other parties in the transaction that the licensee has been engaged as a seller's agent.

A seller's agent may compensate other brokers as subagents if the seller/landlord agrees in writing. Subagents have the same duties and obligations as the seller's agent. Seller's agents may also compensate buyer's agents and transaction licensees who do not have the same duties and obligations as seller's agents.

If you enter into a written agreement, the licensees in the real estate company owe you the additional duties identified above under seller agency. The exception is designated agency. See the designated agency section in this notice for more information.

Buyer Agency:

Buyer agency is a relationship where the licensee, upon entering into a written agreement, works only for the buyer/tenant. Buyer's agents owe the additional duties of:

• Loyalty to the buyer/tenant by acting in the buyer's/tenant's best interest.
• Confidentiality, except that a licensee is required to disclose known material defects about the property.
• Making a continuous and good faith effort to find a property for the buyer/tenant, except while the buyer is subject to an existing contract.

Ch. 35   STATE REAL ESTATE COMMISSION   49 § 35.336

• Disclosure to other parties in the transaction that the licensee has been engaged as a buyer's agent.

A buyer's agent may be paid fees, which may include a percentage of the purchase price, and, even if paid by the seller/landlord, will represent the interests of the buyer/tenant.

If you enter into a written agreement, the licensees in the real estate company owe you the additional duties identified above under buyer agency. The exception is designated agency. See the designated agency section in this notice for more information.

Dual Agency:

Dual agency is a relationship where the licensee acts as the agent for both the seller/landlord and the buyer/tenant in the same transaction with the written consent of all parties. dual agents owe the additional duties of:

• Taking no action that is adverse or detrimental to either party's interest in the transaction.

• Unless otherwise agreed to in writing, making a continuous and good faith effort to find a buyer for the property and a property for the buyer, unless either are subject to an existing contract.

• Confidentiality, except that a licensee is required to disclose known material defects about the property.

Designated Agency:

In designated agency, the employing broker may, with your consent, designate one or more licensees from the real estate company to represent you. Other licensees in the company may represent another party and shall not be provided with any confidential information. The designated agent(s) shall have the duties as listed above under seller agency and buyer agency.

In designated agency, the employing broker will be a dual agent and have the additional duties of:

• Taking reasonable care to protect any confidential information disclosed to the licensee.

• Taking responsibility to direct and supervise the business activities of the licensees who represent the seller and buyer while taking no action that is adverse or detrimental to either party's interest in the transaction.

The designation may take place at the time that the parties enter into a written agreement, but may occur at a later time. Regardless of when the designation takes place, the employing broker is responsible for ensuring that confidential information is not disclosed.

Transaction Licensee:

A transaction licensee is a broker or salesperson who provides communication or document preparation services or performs other acts for which a license is required without being the agent or advocate for either the seller/landlord or the buyer/tenant. Upon signing a written agreement or disclosure statement, a trans-

35-62.3

---

49 § 35.336   DEPARTMENT OF STATE   Pt. I

action licensee has the additional duty of limited confidentiality in that the following information may not be disclosed:

• The seller/landlord will accept a price less than the asking/listing price.

• The buyer/tenant will pay a price greater than the price submitted in a written offer.

• The seller/landlord or buyer/tenant will agree to financing terms other than those offered.

Other information deemed confidential by the consumer shall not be provided to the transaction licensee.

OTHER INFORMATION ABOUT REAL ESTATE TRANSACTIONS

The following are negotiable and shall be addressed in an agreement/disclosure statement with the licensee:

• The duration of the employment, listing agreement or contract.

• The fees or commissions.

• The scope of the activities or practices.

• The broker's cooperation with other brokers, including the sharing of fees.

Any sales agreement must contain the zoning classification of a property except in cases where the property is zoned solely or primarily to permit single family dwellings.

The Real Estate Recovery Fund exists to reimburse any person who has obtained a final civil judgment against a Pennsylvania real estate licensee owing to fraud, misrepresentation, or deceit in a real estate transaction and who has been unable to collect the judgment after exhausting all legal and equitable remedies. For complete details about the Fund, call (717) 783-3658.

ACKNOWLEDGMENT

I ACKNOWLEDGE THAT I HAVE RECEIVED THIS DISCLOSURE.
DATE:

PRINT (CONSUMER)   PRINT (CONSUMER)

SIGNED (CONSUMER)   SIGNED (CONSUMER)

ADDRESS (OPTIONAL):   ADDRESS (OPTIONAL):

PHONE NUMBER   PHONE NUMBER
(OPTIONAL):   (OPTIONAL):

I CERTIFY THAT I HAVE PROVIDED THIS DOCUMENT TO THE ABOVE CONSUMER.

DATE: PRINT   LICENSEE

SIGNED   LICENSEE
ADOPTED BY THE STATE REAL ESTATE COMMISSION AT 49 PA. CODE § 35.336.

35-62.4

Ch. 35   STATE REAL ESTATE COMMISSION   49 § 35.337

Authority

The provisions of this § 35.336 issued under section 608 of the Real Estate Licensing and Registration Act (63 P. S. § 455.608); amended under sections 404, 606—606.6 and 608—608.3 of the Real Estate Licensing and Registration Act (63 P. S. §§ 455.404, 455.606—455.606f and 455.608—455.608c).

Source

The provisions of this § 35.336 adopted January 7, 2000, effective January 8, 2000, 30 Pa.B. 228; amended March 29, 2002, effective March 30, 2002, 32 Pa.B. 1644. Immediately preceding text appears at serial pages (262281) to (262284).

Cross References

This section cited in 49 Pa. Code § 35.201 (relating to definitions); 49 Pa. Code § 35.284 (relating to disclosures of business relationships); 49 Pa. Code § 35.286 (relating to retention and production of records); and 49 Pa. Code § 35.331 (relating to written agreements generally).

§ 35.337. Disclosure summary for the lease of residential or commercial real estate when the licensee is working on behalf of the owner.

The disclosure summary for the lease of residential or commercial property shall be in the following format:

CONSUMER NOTICE
THIS IS NOT A CONTRACT

(LICENSEE)   HEREBY STATES THAT WITH RESPECT TO THIS PROPERTY, (DESCRIBE PROPERTY) I AM ACTING IN THE FOLLOWING CAPACITY: (CHECK ONE)

(I)   OWNER/LANDLORD OF THE PROPERTY;
(II) A DIRECT EMPLOYEE OF THE OWNER/LANDLORD; OR
(III) AN AGENT OF THE OWNER/LANDLORD PURSUANT TO A PROPERTY MANAGEMENT OR EXCLUSIVE LEASING AGREEMENT.

I ACKNOWLEDGE THAT I HAVE RECEIVED THIS NOTICE:

DATE: _____

PRINT (CONSUMER)   PRINT (CONSUMER)

SIGNED (CONSUMER)   SIGNED (CONSUMER)

ADDRESS (OPTIONAL):   ADDRESS (OPTIONAL):

PHONE NUMBER (OPTIONAL):   PHONE NUMBER (OPTIONAL):

I CERTIFY THAT I HAVE PROVIDED THIS NOTICE:

_____   _____
(LICENSEE)   (DATE)

35-62.5

---

49 § 35.338   DEPARTMENT OF STATE   Pt. I

Authority

The provisions of this § 35.337 issued under sections 404, 606—606.6 and 608—608.3 of the Real Estate Licensing and Registration Act (63 P. S. §§ 455.404, 455.606—455.606f and 455.608—455.608c).

Source

The provisions of this § 35.337 adopted March 29, 2002, effective March 30, 2002, 32 Pa.B. 1644.

Cross References

This section cited in 49 Pa. Code § 35.284 (relating to disclosures of business relationships); 49 Pa. Code § 35.286 (relating to retention and production of records); and 49 Pa. Code § 35.331 (relating to written agreements generally).

§ 35.338. Disclosure summary for time-share estates.

The disclosure summary for time-share estates shall be in the following format:

CONSUMER NOTICE
THIS IS NOT A CONTRACT

(LICENSEE)   HEREBY STATES THAT WITH RESPECT TO THIS PROPERTY, (DESCRIBE PROPERTY) I AM ACTING IN THE FOLLOWING CAPACITY: (CHECK ONE)

(I)   OWNER OF THE PROPERTY;
(II) A DIRECT EMPLOYEE OF THE OWNER; OR
(III) AN AGENT OF THE OWNER PURSUANT TO A PROPERTY MANAGEMENT OR EXCLUSIVE LEASING OR SELLING AGREEMENT.

I ACKNOWLEDGE THAT I HAVE RECEIVED THIS NOTICE:

_____   _____
(CONSUMER)   (DATE)

I CERTIFY THAT I HAVE PROVIDED THIS NOTICE:

_____   _____
(LICENSEE)   (DATE)

35-62.6

Ch. 35   STATE REAL ESTATE COMMISSION   49 § 35.339

§ 35.339. Oral disclosure.

The disclosure shall be read verbatim:

"THE REAL ESTATE LAW REQUIRES THAT I PROVIDE YOU WITH A WRITTEN CONSUMER NOTICE THAT DESCRIBES THE VARIOUS BUSINESS RELATIONSHIP CHOICES THAT YOU MAY HAVE WITH A REAL ESTATE LICENSEE. SINCE WE ARE DISCUSSING REAL ESTATE WITHOUT YOU HAVING THE BENEFIT OF THE CONSUMER NOTICE, I HAVE THE DUTY TO ADVISE YOU THAT ANY INFORMATION YOU GIVE ME AT THIS TIME IS NOT CONSIDERED TO BE CONFIDENTIAL, AND ANY INFORMATION YOU GIVE ME WILL NOT BE CONSIDERED CONFIDENTIAL UNLESS AND UNTIL YOU AND I ENTER INTO A BUSINESS RELATIONSHIP. AT OUR FIRST MEETING I WILL PROVIDE YOU WITH A WRITTEN CONSUMER NOTICE WHICH EXPLAINS THOSE BUSINESS RELATIONSHIPS AND MY CORRESPONDING DUTIES TO YOU."

Authority

The provisions of this § 35.339 issued under sections 404, 606—606.6 and 608—608.3 of the Real Estate Licensing and Registration Act (63 P.S. §§ 455.404, 455.606—455.606f and 455.608—455.608c).

Source

The provisions of this § 35.339 adopted March 29, 2002, effective March 30, 2002, 32 Pa.B. 1644.

Cross References

This section cited in 49 Pa. Code § 35.284 (relating to disclosures of business relationships).

§ 35.340. Comparative market analysis.

A comparative market analysis shall contain the following statement printed conspicuously and without change on the first page:

This analysis has not been performed in accordance with the Uniform Standards of Professional Appraisal Practice which requires valuers to act as unbiased, disinterested third parties with impartiality, objectivity and independence and without accommodation of personal interest. It is not to be construed as an appraisal and may not be used as such for any purpose.

Authority

The provisions of this § 35.340 issued under sections 404, 606—606.6 and 608—608.3 of the Real Estate Licensing and Registration Act (63 P.S. §§ 455.404, 455.606—455.606f and 455.608—455.608c).

49 § 35.340   DEPARTMENT OF STATE   Pt. I

Source

The provisions of this § 35.340 adopted March 29, 2002, effective March 30, 2002, 32 Pa.B. 1644.

Ch. 35   STATE REAL ESTATE COMMISSION   49 § 35.341

Subchapter F. REAL ESTATE SCHOOLS

APPROVAL OF REAL ESTATE EDUCATION PROVIDERS

ADMINISTRATION OF REAL ESTATE EDUCATION PROVIDERS

APPROVAL OF SCHOOLS AND SCHOOL DIRECTORS

§ 35.341. Approval of real estate education provider.

A real estate education provider shall obtain the Commission's approval before commencing operations in this Commonwealth. To obtain approval from the Commission, the real estate education provider shall:

(1) Be owned by persons who possess good moral character, or, if the owner is a corporation, have officers and directors who meet this requirement.

(2) Have a name that is acceptable to the Commission.

(3) Have a director of operations who meets the requirements of § 35.342 (relating to approval of director).

(4) Designate a person or entity to serve as custodian of records if the real estate education provider were to terminate operations.

(5) Post a surety bond of $10,000 to the Commonwealth for the protection of the contractual rights of the real estate education provider's students.

(6) Submit a completed real estate education provider approval application to the Commission with:

---

49 § 35.341   DEPARTMENT OF STATE   Pt. I

(i) A completed real estate education provider owner application with:

(A) A resume of the applicant's experience in owning, administering or teaching in, a college or university or as a real estate education provider.

(B) Two letters of reference from responsible persons relating to the applicant's integrity and to the applicant's previous experience, if any, in the administration of an educational program.

(C) Certified copies of court documents related to a conviction of, or plea of guilty or nolo contendere to, a felony or misdemeanor and the sentence imposed.

(ii) A completed real estate education provider director application with:

(A) Credentials evidencing the qualifications required of the applicant under § 35.342.

(B) Certified copies of court documents related to conviction of, or plea of guilty or nolo contendere to, a felony or misdemeanor and the sentence imposed.

(iii) A fictitious name registration, if the real estate education provider has a fictitious name.

(iv) A certificate of incorporation, if the real estate education provider is a corporation.

(v) A copy of the surety bond required under paragraph (5).

(vi) A copy of the student enrollment agreement.

(vii) A copy of the school transcript.

(viii) A statement of the prerequisites for admission.

(ix) A statement of policy regarding refund of tuition and other fees.

(x) The approval fee prescribed in § 35.203 (relating to fees).

(xi) For the main school location and each proposed satellite location, a sketch or photograph of the real estate education provider's sign.

Authority

The provisions of this § 35.341 issued under the Real Estate Licensing and Registration Act (63 P.S. §§ 455.101—455.902).

Source

The provisions of this § 35.341 adopted February 24, 1989, effective February 25, 1989, 19 Pa.B. 781; amended June 10, 1994, effective June 11, 1994, 24 Pa.B. 2904; amended December 10, 2004, effective December 11, 2004, 34 Pa.B. 6530; corrected March 4, 2005, effective December 11, 2004, 35 Pa.B. 1567. Immediately preceding text appears at serial pages (308347) to (308348).

Cross References

This section cited in 49 Pa. Code § 35.342 (relating to approval of educational director); 49 Pa. Code § 35.344 (relating to withdrawal of real estate education provider or director approval); and 49 Pa. Code § 35.354 (relating to prohibited forms of advertising and solicitation).

Ch. 35   STATE REAL ESTATE COMMISSION   49 § 35.342

§ 35.342. Approval of real estate educational director.

(a) A real estate education provider shall obtain the Commission's approval of its director before commencing operations in this Commonwealth. The applicant for director shall have a combination of experience in teaching, supervision and educational administration which, in the opinion of the Commission, will enable the applicant to competently administer a real estate education program in areas that include, but are not limited to, the following: evaluation of instructor performance; evaluation of curriculum and specific course content; analysis of course examinations; and management of records and facilities.

(b) The Commission may provisionally approve an otherwise qualified applicant for director who lacks sufficient background in teaching, supervision or educational administration. A provisionally approved director shall obtain the requisite qualifications in the time and manner prescribed by the Commission.

(c) An approved real estate education provider shall obtain the Commission's approval before changing directors. The prospective director shall submit to the Commission the information required by § 35.341(6)(ii) (relating to approval of real estate education provider).

(d) If the director dies, withdraws or is terminated, an approved real estate education provider will not lose its approved status, nor will it be required to terminate operations within the Commonwealth provided that:

(1) The real estate education provider shall submit the name of an interim director to the Commission within 15 days of the death, withdrawal or termination of the director.

(2) The interim director is authorized to operate for up to 90 days following the death, withdrawal or termination of the director. Thereafter, continued operation is contingent upon approval of a director under subsection (a) or (b).

(3) No changes may be made to the curriculum, testing or facilities until the new director is approved by the Commission.

Authority

The provisions of this § 35.342 issued under the Real Estate Licensing and Registration Act (63 P.S. §§ 455.101—455.902).

Source

The provisions of this § 35.342 adopted February 24, 1989, effective February 25, 1989, 19 Pa.B. 781; amended December 10, 2004, effective December 11, 2004, 34 Pa.B. 6530. Immediately preceding text appears at serial page (263899).

Notes of Decisions

Experience

The Commission's conclusion that applicant's term as a school board director did not provide applicant with sufficient experience in educational supervision and administration to run a real estate school was not arbitrary and capricious. *Black v. Barnes*, 776 F. Supp. 1000 (3rd Cir. 1991).

Cross References

This section cited in 49 Pa. Code § 35.341 (relating to approval of real estate education provider); and 49 Pa. Code § 35.351a (relating to assistant school director).

49 § 35.343   DEPARTMENT OF STATE   Pt. I

§ 35.343. Renewal of real estate education provider approval.

An approved real estate education provider shall renew its approval annually. To obtain renewal of approval, a real estate education provider shall submit a completed renewal of approval application to the Commission with:

(1) A notarized certification of compliance with this chapter signed by the director.

(2) A copy of the $10,000 surety bond showing coverage for the upcoming renewal period.

(3) The fee for renewal of approval prescribed in § 35.203 (relating to fees).

Authority

The provisions of this § 35.343 issued under the Real Estate Licensing and Registration Act (63 P.S. §§ 455.101—455.902).

Source

The provisions of this § 35.343 adopted February 24, 1989, effective February 25, 1989, 19 Pa.B. 781; amended June 10, 1994, effective June 11, 1994, 24 Pa.B. 2904; amended December 10, 2004, effective December 11, 2004, 34 Pa.B. 6530. Immediately preceding text appears at serial pages (263899) to (263900).

§ 35.344. Withdrawal of real estate education provider or director approval.

(a) The Commission may, following notice and hearing under 2 Pa.C.S. §§ 501—508 (relating to practice and procedure of Commonwealth agencies), withdraw the approval of a real estate education provider that it finds guilty of:

(1) Having acquired the Commission's approval by misrepresentation.

(2) Failing to maintain compliance with § 35.341 (relating to approval of real estate education provider).

(3) Violating a requirement of §§ 35.351—35.363 (relating to administration of real estate education providers).

(b) The Commission may, following notice and hearing under 2 Pa.C.S. §§ 501—508, withdraw the approval of a director that it finds guilty of:

(1) Any conduct in connection with the administration of a real estate education provider which demonstrates bad faith, dishonesty, untrustworthiness or incompetency.

(2) Failing to comply with § 35.341 (relating to approval of real estate education provider).

(3) Having had a real estate license revoked or suspended by the Commission or by a real estate licensing authority of another jurisdiction.

(4) Having been convicted of, or having pled guilty or nolo contendere to a felony.

(5) Having been convicted of, or having pled guilty or nolo contendere to a misdemeanor related to the practice of real estate, forgery, embezzlement, obtaining money under false pretenses, bribery, larceny, extortion, conspiracy to defraud, or any similar offense.

Authority

The provisions of this § 35.344 issued under the Real Estate Licensing and Registration Act (63 P. S. §§ 455.101—455.902).

Source

The provisions of this § 35.344 adopted February 24, 1989, effective February 25, 1989, 19 Pa.B. 781; amended December 10, 2004, effective December 11, 2004, 34 Pa.B. 6530. Immediately preceding text appears at serial page (263900).

ADMINISTRATION OF REAL ESTATE EDUCATION PROVIDERS

§ 35.351. Duty of director.

The director for a real estate education provider is responsible for day-to-day administration, including evaluation of instructor performance, evaluation of curriculum and specific course content, analysis of course examinations, management of records and facilities and otherwise assuring compliance with §§ 35.352—35.363.

Authority

The provisions of this § 35.351 issued under the Real Estate Licensing and Registration Act (63 P. S. §§ 455.101—455.902).

Source

The provisions of this § 35.351 adopted February 24, 1989, effective February 25, 1989, 19 Pa.B. 781; amended December 10, 2004, effective December 11, 2004, 34 Pa.B. 6530. Immediately preceding text appears at serial pages (263900) and (201887).

Cross References

This section cited in 49 Pa. Code § 35.344 (relating to withdrawal of real estate education provider or director approval); and 49 Pa. Code § 35.362 (relating to inspection of school).

§ 35.351a. [Reserved].

Source

The provisions of this § 35.351a adopted June 10, 1994, effective June 11, 1994, 24 Pa.B. 2904; reserved December 10, 2004, effective December 11, 2004, 34 Pa.B. 6530. Immediately preceding text appears at serial page (201887).

§ 35.352. Location and facilities.

(a) A real estate education provider shall have a main location that contains its administrative offices, its records, and a telephone with a listed number for the real estate education provider's exclusive use.

(b) The location where classes are taught must:

(1) Be suitable for classroom space.

(2) Not share office space, instruction space or a common space with a real estate franchise, network or organization. This paragraph does not apply to a real estate trade association or to a contractual arrangement between a real estate licensee and a real estate education provider to provide continuing education courses.

(3) Be in conformance with applicable building, fire safety and sanitary requirements imposed by State, county and municipal governments.

Authority

The provisions of this § 35.352 issued under the Real Estate Licensing and Registration Act (63 P. S. §§ 455.101—455.902).

Source

The provisions of this § 35.352 adopted February 24, 1989, effective February 25, 1989, 19 Pa.B. 781; amended June 11, 1994, effective June 11, 1994, 24 Pa.B. 2904; amended December 10, 2004, effective December 11, 2004, 34 Pa.B. 6530. Immediately preceding text appears at serial pages (201887) to (201888).

Cross References

This section cited in 49 Pa. Code § 35.344 (relating to withdrawal of real estate education provider or director); 49 Pa. Code § 35.351 (relating to duty of director); and 49 Pa. Code § 35.362 (relating to inspection of school).

§ 35.353. Selection of instructors.

(a) *Qualified instructors.* A real estate education provider shall employ instructors who are qualified to teach the courses for which the instructors have been hired. The real estate education provider may consider an individual qualified to teach a course if the individual satisfies one of the following criteria:

(1) Possesses an undergraduate, graduate or postgraduate degree in the subject matter of the course to be taught.

(2) Has 3 years of practical or teaching experience in a profession, trade or occupation directly related to the subject matter of the course to be taught.

(b) *Proof of qualifications.* A real estate education provider shall maintain documentation substantiating the instructor's education and experience.

Authority

The provisions of this § 35.353 issued under the Real Estate Licensing and Registration Act (63 P. S. §§ 455.101—455.902).

Source

The provisions of this § 35.353 adopted February 24, 1989, effective February 25, 1989, 19 Pa.B. 781; amended June 11, 1994, effective June 11, 1994, 24 Pa.B. 2904; amended December 10, 2004, effective December 11, 2004, 34 Pa.B. 6530. Immediately preceding text appears at serial pages (201888) to (201890).

Cross References

This section cited in 49 Pa. Code § 35.344 (relating to withdrawal of real estate education provider or director approval); 49 Pa. Code § 35.351 (relating to duty of director); 49 Pa. Code § 35.351a (relating to assistant school director); 49 Pa. Code § 35.360 (relating to records); and 49 Pa. Code § 35.362 (relating to inspection of school).

§ 35.354. Prohibited forms of advertising and solicitation.

(a) A real estate education provider may not:

(1) Hold itself out under a name other than the name approved for it by the Commission under § 35.341 (relating to approval of real estate education provider).

(2) Hold itself out as being recommended or endorsed by the Commission, the Department of Education or other agency of the Commonwealth, except that the real estate education provider may advertise that it has been approved by the Commission to provide instruction in real estate courses and that credits earned in certain named courses will be accepted by the Commission toward

fulfillment of the professional education prerequisite for taking the Pennsylvania real estate licensing examinations.

(3) Hold itself out to be an educational institution that conforms to the standards and requirements prescribed for colleges and universities by the Department of Education, unless the real estate education provider meets those standards and requirements.

(4) Make a guarantee of employment, conditional or unconditional, to a student or prospective student.

(5) Guarantee that successful completion of its curriculum will result in the student's passing a real estate licensing examination.

(6) Promote the business of a real estate licensee or a real estate organization, franchise or network.

(7) Recruit students for employment or affiliation with a real estate licensee or a real estate organization, franchise or network.

(8) Solicit students for membership in a real estate organization, franchise or network.

(9) Permit an instructor or guest lecturer while on the real estate education provider's premises to wear any identification relating to the name of the real estate licensee or a real estate organization, franchise or network.

(10) Solicit enrollments by means of advertisements in the employment columns of newspapers and other publications.

(11) Engage in advertising that is false, misleading, deceptive or degrading to the dignity of the real estate profession.

(b) A real estate education provider may not allow its main or satellite locations to be used by others for the solicitation or recruitment of students for employment or affiliation with a real estate licensee or a real estate organization, franchise or network. Students shall be informed of this prohibition through a written statement which shall contain the following:

"No recruiting for employment opportunities for any real estate brokerage firm is allowed in this class. Any recruiting should be promptly reported to the State Real Estate Commission by calling this number: 1-800-822-2113."

Authority

The provisions of this § 35.354 issued under the Real Estate Licensing and Registration Act (63 P. S. §§ 455.101—455.902).

Source

The provisions of this § 35.354 adopted February 24, 1989, effective February 25, 1989, 19 Pa.B. 781; amended June 10, 1994, effective June 11, 1994, 24 Pa.B. 2904; amended December 10, 2004, effective December 11, 2004, 34 Pa.B. 6530. Immediately preceding text appears at serial pages (201890) to (201891).

Cross References

This section cited in 49 Pa. Code § 35.344 (relating to withdrawal of real estate education provider or director approval); 49 Pa. Code § 35.351 (relating to duty of director); and 49 Pa. Code § 35.362 (relating to inspection of school).

35-69

§ 35.355. Prospectus materials.

(a) A real estate education provider shall provide copies of catalogs, bulletins, pamphlets and other prospectus materials to the Commission upon request. Prospectus materials shall state the following in clear and unambiguous terms:

(1) Admission requirements.

(2) Curriculum, including a specification of courses that meet the Commission's requirements for prelicensure education or continuing education.

(3) Tuition and other fees, and the refund policy in the event of cancellation.

(4) Completion requirements.

(b) Prospectus materials for courses shall be directed towards the general licensee population without regard to the licensees' affiliation with a particular educational institution or a particular real estate organization, franchise or network.

Authority

The provisions of this § 35.355 issued under the Real Estate Licensing and Registration Act (63 P. S. §§ 455.101—455.902).

Source

The provisions of this § 35.355 adopted February 24, 1989, effective February 25, 1989, 19 Pa.B. 781; amended June 10, 1994, effective June 11, 1994, 24 Pa.B. 2904; amended December 10, 2004, effective December 11, 2004, 34 Pa.B. 6530. Immediately preceding text appears at serial page (201891).

Cross References

This section cited in 49 Pa. Code § 35.344 (relating to withdrawal of real estate education provider or director approval); 49 Pa. Code § 35.351 (relating to duty of director); and 49 Pa. Code § 35.362 (relating to inspection of school).

§ 35.356. Tuition and other fees.

A real estate education provider shall charge tuition that bears a reasonable relationship to the quality and quantity of instructional services rendered. If additional fees are charged for books, supplies and other materials needed for coursework, the real estate education provider shall itemize the fees and the books, supplies and materials, upon payment therefor, shall become the property of the student.

Authority

The provisions of this § 35.356 issued under the Real Estate Licensing and Registration Act (63 P. S. §§ 455.101—455.902).

Source

The provisions of this § 35.356 adopted February 24, 1989, effective February 25, 1989, 19 Pa.B. 781; amended December 10, 2004, effective December 11, 2004, 34 Pa.B. 6530. Immediately preceding text appears at serial page (201892).

Cross References

This section cited in 49 Pa. Code § 35.344 (relating to withdrawal of real estate education provider or director approval); 49 Pa. Code § 35.351 (relating to duty of director); and 49 Pa. Code § 35.362 (relating to inspection of school).

35-70

§ 35.357. Student enrollment agreements.

A real estate education provider shall require each of its students to enter into a student enrollment agreement. The agreement must:

(1) Itemize the tuition and other fees and the services and materials to be received from them.

(2) State the real estate education provider's policy regarding the refund of tuition and fees if the student were to withdraw or be dismissed or if the school were to terminate operations before the end of the academic year.

(3) Contain the Bureau's toll-free telephone number, (800) 822-2113, that the student may call to obtain information about filing a complaint against the real estate education provider.

Authority

The provisions of this § 35.357 issued under the Real Estate Licensing and Registration Act (63 P. S. §§ 455.101—455.902).

Source

The provisions of this § 35.357 adopted February 24, 1989, effective February 25, 1989, 19 Pa.B. 781; amended June 10, 1994, effective June 11, 1994, 24 Pa.B. 2904; amended December 10, 2004, effective December 11, 2004, 34 Pa.B. 6530. Immediately preceding text appears at serial pages (201892) to (201894).

Cross References

This section cited in 49 Pa. Code § 35.344 (relating to withdrawal of real estate education or director approval); 49 Pa. Code § 35.351 (relating to duty of director); and 49 Pa. Code § 35.362 (relating to inspection of school).

§ 35.358. Administration of curriculum.

(a) Real estate education providers shall observe the following standards in the administration of prelicensure and continuing education curriculum:

(1) Instructor-led learning may not exceed 7 1/2 clock hours of instruction per day. For purposes of this section, a clock hour is defined as a 60-minute period comprising 50 minutes of instruction and a 10-minute break. A student may not be required to attend class for more than 90 consecutive minutes without a break.

(2) The substantive content of the course, as evidenced by the course outline, text and other instructional materials, shall adequately reflect the stated purpose of the course, as evidenced by the course title and course description. Instruction in a Commission required course shall conform to the content or the outline developed by the Commission for the course.

(3) Unless the course is taught by means of distance education, a student shall be physically present during at least 80% of the classroom instruction for a prelicensure course and during at least 90% of the classroom instruction for a continuing education course, to receive credit. The real estate education provider shall be responsible for verifying student attendance.

(4) Courses delivered by distance education, in addition to meeting the content requirements in § 35.384 (relating to qualifying courses), must have the delivery method approved by the Association of Real Estate License Law Officials or another certifying body with similar approval standards approved by the Commission.

(b) In addition to the requirements in subsection (a), a real estate education provider shall observe the following standards in the administration of its prelicensure curriculum:

(1) A prelicensure course must be assigned one credit for every 15 clock hours of instruction.

(2) A prelicensure course must be graded by proctored examination, except when a student's handicap or disability would make grading by examination impractical.

Authority

The provisions of this § 35.358 issued under the Real Estate Licensing and Registration Act (63 P. S. §§ 455.101—455.902).

Source

The provisions of this § 35.358 adopted February 24, 1989, effective February 25, 1989, 19 Pa.B. 781; amended June 10, 1994, effective June 11, 1994, 24 Pa.B. 2904; amended December 10, 2004, effective December 11, 2004, 34 Pa.B. 6530. Immediately preceding text appears at serial pages (201894) to (201895).

Cross References

This section cited in 49 Pa. Code § 35.344 (relating to withdrawal of real estate education provider or director approval); 49 Pa. Code § 35.351 (relating to duty of director); 49 Pa. Code § 35.362 (relating to inspection of school).

§ 35.359. Course transcripts.

(a) *Prelicensure.* Within 30 days after a course has been taught, a real estate education provider shall provide each student in the course with an official course transcript that contains the information in § 35.360(a)(5) (relating to records) and is signed by the director.

(b) *Continuing education.* Effective with the renewal period commencing June 1, 2004, within 30 days after a continuing education course has ended, the continuing education provider shall provide the Commission with a roster in a format approved by the Commission, listing each licensee who satisfactorily completed/taught the course. Continuing education providers shall be required to issue course transcripts/certificates of instruction to students only upon request.

Authority

The provisions of this § 35.359 issued under the Real Estate Licensing and Registration Act (63 P. S. §§ 455.101—455.902).

Source

The provisions of this § 35.359 adopted February 24, 1989, effective February 25, 1989, 19 Pa.B. 781; amended December 10, 2004, effective December 11, 2004, 34 Pa.B. 6530. Immediately preceding text appears at serial page (201895).

Cross References

This section cited in 49 Pa. Code § 35.344 (relating to withdrawal of real estate education provider or director approval); 49 Pa. Code § 35.351 (relating to duty of director); and 49 Pa. Code § 35.362 (relating to inspection of school).

§ 35.360. Records.

(a) A real estate education provider shall maintain complete and accurate records in the following areas:

Ch. 35   STATE REAL ESTATE COMMISSION   49 § 35.360

(1) *Financial.* The real estate education provider's assets and liabilities and the sources and amounts of its income.

(2) *Physical plant.* For the main location and for each satellite location, the following:

(i) Copies of documentation showing compliance with applicable building, fire safety and sanitary requirements imposed by state, county or municipal governments.

(ii) A copy of the lease or rental agreement, if the real estate education provider does not own the building being used.

(3) *Personnel.* The qualifications of each instructor and the documentary evidence of those qualifications. See § 35.353 (relating to selection of instructors).

(4) *Curriculum.* For each course the real estate education provider has offered, the following:

(i) The course title.

(ii) The course prerequisites.

(iii) The course objectives.

(iv) The course outline.

(v) The requirements for successful completion of the course.

(vi) Copies of texts and other instructional materials used in teaching the course.

(vii) The supplies required of students for the course.

(viii) The course schedule.

(ix) Copies of published descriptions of the course.

(x) The course instructor.

(5) *Scholastic.* An academic transcript for each student which must contain the following:

(i) The real estate education provider's name and Commission approval number.

(ii) The location at which the course was taught.

(iii) The name of the student.

(iv) The course title.

(v) The date that the student completed the course.

(vi) The number of hours of the course.

(vii) The student's final grade in the course, if an examination is required for the course.

(viii) The date that the transcript was issued.

(ix) The fact that the course will be accepted by the Commission towards fulfillment of the education requirement for either the real estate broker's examination or real estate salesperson's examination, as the care may be.

(6) *Attendance.*

(b) A real estate education provider shall store its records at its main location. Upon termination of operations, a real estate education provider shall transfer its records to the designated custodian of records. The real estate education provider shall notify the Commission whenever it changes the custodian of records.

---

49 § 35.361   DEPARTMENT OF STATE   Pt. I

(c) A real estate education provider shall produce its records for examination by the Commission or its representatives upon written request or pursuant to an inspection under § 35.362 (relating to inspection of real estate education providers).

(d) A real estate education provider shall make copies of a student's scholastic and attendance records available to the student upon request.

(e) A real estate education provider must retain attendance and scholastic records as follows:

(1) Continuing education records must be maintained for 4 years.

(2) All other records must be retained for 10 years.

Authority

The provisions of this § 35.360 issued under the Real Estate Licensing and Registration Act (63 P. S. §§ 455.101—455.902).

Source

The provisions of this § 35.360 adopted February 24, 1989, effective February 25, 1989, 19 Pa.B. 781; amended June 10, 1994, effective June 11, 1994, 24 Pa.B. 2904; amended December 10, 2004, effective December 11, 2004, 34 Pa.B. 6530. Immediately preceding text appears at serial pages (201895) to (201897).

Cross References

This section cited in 49 Pa. Code § 35.344 (relating to withdrawal of real estate education provider or director approval); 49 Pa. Code § 35.351 (relating to duty of director); 49 Pa. Code § 35.359 (relating to course transcripts); and 49 Pa. Code § 35.362 (relating to inspection of school).

§ 35.361. Display of documents and approved name.

(a) A real estate education provider's certificate of approval shall be displayed prominently at the real estate education provider's main location.

(b) A real estate education provider's approved name must be displayed prominently at each location where courses are taught.

(c) An alphabetical list of the real estate education provider's satellite locations shall be displayed prominently at the real estate education provider's main location.

Authority

The provisions of this § 35.361 issued under the Real Estate Licensing and Registration Act (63 P. S. §§ 455.101—455.902).

Source

The provisions of this § 35.361 adopted February 24, 1989, effective February 25, 1989, 19 Pa.B. 781; amended June 10, 1994, effective June 11, 1994, 24 Pa.B. 2904; amended December 10, 2004, effective December 11, 2004, 34 Pa.B. 6530. Immediately preceding text appears at serial pages (201897) to (201898).

Cross References

This section cited in 49 Pa. Code § 35.344 (relating to withdrawal of real estate education provider or director approval); 49 Pa. Code § 35.351 (relating to duty of director); 49 Pa. Code § 35.362 (relating to inspection of school); and 49 Pa. Code § 43a.10 (relating to schedule of civil penalties—real estate and cemetery brokers, real estate schools).

§ 35.362. Inspection of real estate education providers.

(a) *Routine inspections.* No more than four times a year while classes are in session, the Commission or those authorized representatives may conduct a routine inspection of the main location or satellite location of a real estate education provider for the purpose of determining whether the real estate education provider is in compliance with §§ 35.351—35.363 (relating to administration of real estate education providers).

(b) *Special inspections.* In addition to the routine inspections authorized by subsection (a), the Commission or its authorized representatives may conduct a special inspection of a real estate education provider's main location or satellite location:

(1) Upon a complaint or reasonable belief that the real estate education provider is not in compliance with §§ 35.351—35.363.

(2) As a follow-up to a previous inspection that revealed the real estate education provider's noncompliance with §§ 35.351—35.363.

(c) *Scope of inspection.* Prior to the start of a routine or special inspection, the Commission or its authorized representatives will advise the real estate education provider, director or other person in charge at the time of the inspection that the inspection is being made under this section and is limited in scope by this section.

(d) During the course of a routine or special inspection or investigation, the Commission or its authorized representatives will be permitted to:

(1) Examine real estate education provider records.

(2) Inspect all areas of the real estate education provider's premises.

(3) Monitor the performance of instructors in classrooms.

(4) Interview the real estate education provider, director and other administrative personnel, instructors and students.

Authority

The provisions of this § 35.362 issued under the Real Estate Licensing and Registration Act (63 P. S. §§ 455.101—455.902).

Source

The provisions of this § 35.362 adopted February 24, 1989, effective February 25, 1989, 19 Pa.B. 781; amended December 10, 2004, effective December 11, 2004, 34 Pa.B.6530. Immediately preceding text appears at serial page (201898).

Cross References

This section cited in 49 Pa. Code § 35.344 (relating to withdrawal of real estate provider or director approval); 49 Pa. Code § 35.351 (relating to duty of director); and 49 Pa. Code § 35.360 (relating to records).

§ 35.363. Termination of operations.

A real estate education provider that desires to terminate operations shall submit to the Commission, within 60 days of the planned termination, a termination plan that includes the following:

(1) The date of termination.

(2) The date that real estate education provider records will be transferred to the designated records custodian.

(3) The procedure for refunding tuition and allocating credits to currently enrolled students.

Authority

The provisions of this § 35.363 issued under the Real Estate Licensing and Registration Act (63 P. S. §§ 455.101—455.902).

Source

The provisions of this § 35.363 adopted February 24, 1989, effective February 25, 1989, 19 Pa.B. 781; amended June 10, 1994, effective June 11, 1994, 24 Pa.B. 2904; amended December 10, 2004, effective December 11, 2004, 34 Pa.B. 6530. Immediately preceding text appears at serial page (201899).

Cross References

This section cited in 49 Pa. Code § 35.344 (relating to withdrawal of school or director approval); and 49 Pa. Code § 35.362 (relating to inspection of school).

Subchapter G. PROMOTIONAL LAND SALES

Sec.
35.371. General requirements.
35.372. Nonresident requirements.
35.373. Offering statements.
35.374. Review and approval of documents.
35.375. Affidavit of consent to service of jurisdiction.

§ 35.371. General requirements.

(a) A broker, developer or subdivider referred to in this subchapter as "applicant," who proposes to engage in sales of a promotional nature in this Commonwealth of property located outside of this Commonwealth shall submit to the Commission, for its approval before doing so, full particulars regarding the property and proposed terms of sale, and they and their salesmen shall comply with all rules and regulations, restrictions and conditions pertaining thereto as the Commission may impose. Expenses reasonably incurred by the Commission in investigating and inspecting the property and proposed sale thereof in this Commonwealth shall be borne by the applicant. No broker, developer or salesman may refer to the Commission or to an official or employe of the Commission in selling, offering for sale or advertising, or otherwise promoting the sale, mortgage or lease of the property, nor make representation that the property has been inspected or approved or otherwise passed upon by the Commission, or by a State official, department or employe.

(b) An applicant approved to engage in sales set forth in this chapter shall notify the Commission at least 10 days in advance of the date, time and place of efforts to sell or advertise through parties or reception or other group media.

Authority

The provisions of this § 35.371 issued under the Real Estate Licensing and Registration Act (63 P. S. §§ 455.101—455.902).

Source

The provisions of this § 35.371 adopted February 24, 1989, effective February 25, 1989, 19 Pa.B. 781.

Notes of Decisions

The possession of a salesperson's license for 3 or more years does not automatically qualify a person to sit for a broker's examination. *Bhala v. State Real Estate Commission,* 617 A.2d 841 (Pa. Cmwlth. 1992).

§ 35.372. Nonresident requirements.

(a) A nonresident applicant shall also file an irrevocable consent that suits and actions may be commenced against the applicant in the proper court of a county of this Commonwealth in which a cause of action may arise, or in which plaintiff may reside, by the service of a process or pleadings authorized by the laws of the Commonwealth on the Commission in Harrisburg, Pennsylvania. The consent shall stipulate and agree that the service of process or pleadings on the Commission shall be taken and held in all courts to be as valid and binding as if service had been made upon the applicant personally within this Commonwealth.

(b) If process or pleadings are served upon the Commission, they shall be by duplicate copy, one of which shall be filed in the office of the Commission and the other immediately forwarded by certified mail to the main office of the applicant against which the process or pleadings are directed.

Authority

The provisions of this § 35.372 issued under the Real Estate Licensing and Registration Act (63 P.S. §§ 455.101—455.902).

Source

The provisions of this § 35.372 adopted February 24, 1989, effective February 25, 1989, 19 Pa.B. 781.

Cross References

This section cited in 49 Pa. Code § 35.375 (relating to affidavit of consent to service of jurisdiction).

§ 35.373. Offering statements.

(a) The Commission also requires the applicant to prepare and deliver at its own expense, to each prospective purchaser in this Commonwealth an offering statement which shall be revised annually. The offering statement shall be approved by the Commission and shall contain a detailed description, price and terms of the offer as well as financial information disclosing assets and liabilities of the applicant. The offering statement shall also inform prospective purchasers of the following:

(1) Tax liabilities.
(2) Basis for guarantees.
(3) Public transportation facilities.
(4) Terrain details.
(5) Climate.
(6) Proposed and existing improvements.
(7) Roads.
(8) Water supply.
(9) Public utilities.
(10) An objectionable condition of air, sight or terrain.
(11) Sewage disposal facilities.

35-77

(12) Recreational and community facilities.
(13) The distances to a nearby populated area.

(b) The offering statement shall also set forth on the front page in large bold face type or italics, the following statement:

"The State Real Estate Commission's requirements of this broker, developer or subdivider does not constitute approval of the land being offered for sale or lease. The State Real Estate Commission has not in any way passed upon the merits of such offer."

Authority

The provisions of this § 35.373 issued under the Real Estate Licensing and Registration Act (63 P.S. §§ 455.101—455.902).

Source

The provisions of this § 35.373 adopted February 24, 1989, effective February 25, 1989, 19 Pa.B. 781.

§ 35.374. Review and approval of documents.

The following information and documents shall be furnished annually to the Commission in report form for its review and approval:

(1) Name of owner, including the following:
 (i) Names and addresses of the owners or partners.
 (ii) Lists of the officers and holders of 10% or more of total subscribed or issued stock of the corporation.
 (iii) Copy of most recent certified audit of records including financial statements.
(2) Names of subsidiary organizations or companies.
(3) Name of development.
(4) Address of development.
(5) Addresses of administrative offices.
(6) Representative of the Commonwealth, including a list of the sales offices and personnel in this Commonwealth.
(7) Status of property, including the following:
 (i) Owner of the land.
 (ii) Whether land is free and clear.
 (iii) If land is mortgaged, whether the mortgage is assignable, including the following:
  (A) Whether individual lots can be released.
  (B) Cost per lot.
 (iv) Whether there are judgments against or unpaid taxes due on the land.
 (v) Whether abstracts or title policies will be furnished.
 (vi) Copy of type of deed used.
 (vii) Whether deeds are issued in fee simple.
 (viii) Whether there is additional charge for issuing a deed.
(8) Improvements completed, including the following:
 (i) Paved streets.
 (ii) Sidewalks.

35-78

Ch. 35 STATE REAL ESTATE COMMISSION 49 § 35.374

   (iii) Street lights.
   (iv) Public utilities.
   (v) Whether improvements are paid for.
   (vi) Tax rates.
   (vii) If no improvements, plans for completion.
   (viii) If FHA approved, copy of approval.
  (9) Whether bond has been posted with a governmental authority to guarantee completion of promised improvements, including the following:
   (i) Specification for what purpose.
   (ii) Amount.
   (iii) Name of bonding company.
   (iv) How this bond will protect the purchasers from the Commonwealth.
   (v) Certified copy of the bonds used.
  (10) Sewage, including the following:
   (i) Sanitary sewers.
   (ii) Storm sewers.
   (iii) Whether water mains or individual wells are necessary.
   (iv) Whether septic tanks are necessary.
   (v) If septic tanks are necessary, whether they are authorized by appropriate government authorities.
   (vi) Whether level of land and type of soil is suitable for septic tanks.
  (11) Drainage, including the following:
   (i) Whether land is dry.
   (ii) Copy of the drainage plan of the engineer.
   (iii) Depth of water table.
   (iv) Depth of average well.
  (12) Zoning restrictions, including the following:
   (i) Copy of topographical map.
   (ii) Copy of State Board of Health Percolation Test one hole per 5 acres where septic tanks are used.
  (13) Advertising, including the following:
   (i) Size of lots offered.
   (ii) Price and terms of sale.
   (iii) Whether these lots are large enough for building purposes that would comply with zoning requirements.
  (14) Location, including the following:
   (i) Aerial photo showing exact area with at least 1 mile of bordering properties.
   (ii) How far property is presently from the following:
   (A) Highway.
   (B) Incorporated town.
   (C) Major shopping center.
   (D) Industrial area including type and size.
   (E) Transportation including bus and train.
   (F) Schools—public, trade, parochial or private.

49 § 35.375 DEPARTMENT OF STATE Pt. I

   (G) Lighted streets.
   (H) Type of pavement and curbs.
   (I) Fire protection.
   (J) Garbage and trash removal.
   (K) Police protection.
   (L) Airport and airlines operated therefrom.
  (15) Current selling price of lots in adjoining area and owners of these lots.
  (16) Financial arrangements, including the following:
   (i) Whether the down payment will be placed in escrow and terms of release of the down payment.
   (ii) Type of financing obtainable and percent of interest charged.
   (iii) Closing costs, specifying for what.
   (iv) Specific listing of carrying charges.
   (v) Types of contracts used.

Authority

The provisions of this § 35.374 issued under the Real Estate Licensing and Registration Act (63 P. S. §§ 455.101—455.902).

Source

The provisions of this § 35.374 adopted February 24, 1989, effective February 25, 1989, 19 Pa.B. 781.

§ 35.375. Affidavit of consent to service of jurisdiction.

The following affidavit of consent to service of jurisdiction is exemplary of the requirements of § 35.372 (relating to nonresident requirements):

AFFIDAVIT OF CONSENT TO SERVICE OF
JURISDICTION

That the undersigned _____ (give legal designation of applicant, individual, partnership, corporation) does hereby irrevocably consent that any action brought against the above named applicant in the proper court of any county of the State of Pennsylvania or in which the plaintiff in such action may reside and that in the event proper service of process cannot be had upon such applicant in any such proceeding in such county, service of any process may be made therein by the sheriff of such county by the service of any process or pleadings authorized by the Laws of Pennsylvania on the Real Estate Commission, hereby stipulating and agreeing that such service of such process or pleadings on said Chairman shall be taken and held in all courts to be valid and binding as if due process had been made upon said applicant in the State of Pennsylvania.

                    _____ President

                    _____ Secretary

Corporate Seal

Witness _____

Personally appeared _____ before me the undersigned notary public in and for the above named county and state, the day and date above named, and acknowledged the execution of the foregoing instrument to be the voluntary act and deed of such applicant for the purpose therein set forth (if applicant is an individual, strike out the following) and that they are the President and Secretary, respectively, of such corporation and are duly authorized to execute the foregoing instrument.

(Seal)

State of _____ SS

COUNTY OF _____

Authority

The provisions of this § 35.375 issued under the Real Estate Licensing and Registration Act (63 P. S. §§ 455.101—455.902).

Source

The provisions of this § 35.375 adopted February 24, 1989, effective February 25, 1989, 19 Pa.B. 781.

Subchapter H. CONTINUING EDUCATION

Sec.
35.381.   [Reserved].
35.382.   Requirement.
35.383.   Waiver of continuing education requirement.
35.384.   Qualifying courses.
35.385.   Continuing education providers.
35.386.—35.392.   [Reserved].

§ 35.381. [Reserved].

Source

The provisions of this § 35.381 adopted July 31, 1992, effective August 1, 1992, 22 Pa.B. 3980; reserved December 10, 2004, effective December 11, 2004, 34 Pa.B. 6530. Immediately preceding text appears at serial page (201905).

§ 35.382. Requirement.

(a) *Condition precedent to renewal of current standard license.* A broker or salesperson holding a standard license who desires to renew a current license shall, as a condition precedent to renewal, complete 14 hours of Commission-approved continuing education during the preceding license period. The continuing education shall be completed by the May 31 renewal deadline.

(b) *Condition precedent to reactivation and renewal of noncurrent standard license.* A broker or salesperson holding a standard license who desires to reactivate and renew a noncurrent license shall, as a condition precedent to reactivation and renewal, complete 14 hours of Commission-approved continuing education during the 2-year period preceding the date of submission of the reactivation

35-81

application. A broker or salesperson holding a standard license may not use the same continuing education coursework to satisfy the requirements of this subsection and subsection (a).

(c) *Exception.* The continuing education requirement does not apply to reciprocal license holders or cemetery brokers, cemetery salespersons, builder-owner salespersons, timeshare salespersons, campground membership salespersons and rental listing referral agents who hold standard licenses.

(d) *Documentation.* A licensee shall provide the Commission with information necessary to establish the licensee's compliance with this subchapter.

Authority

The provisions of this § 35.382 issued under sections 402, 404, 404.1 and 513 of the Real Estate Licensing and Registration Act (63 P. S. §§ 455.402, 455.404, 455.404a and 455.513); amended under sections 201, 501, 601, 602 and 604 of the Real Estate Licensing and Registration Act (63 P. S. §§ 455.201, 455.501, 455.601, 455.602 and 455.604).

Source

The provisions of this § 35.382 adopted July 31, 1992, effective August 1, 1992, 22 Pa.B. 3980; amended December 10, 2004, 34 Pa.B. 6530; amended August 19, 2005, effective August 20, 2005, 35 Pa.B. 4711. Immediately preceding text appears at serial pages (308365) to (308366).

Cross References

This section cited in 49 Pa. Code § 35.383 (relating to waiver of continuing education requirement).

§ 35.383. Waiver of continuing education requirement.

(a) The Commission may waive all or part of the continuing education requirement of § 35.382 (relating to requirement) upon proof that the standard license holder seeking the waiver is unable to fulfill the requirement because of illness, emergency or hardship. The following are examples of situations in which hardship waivers will be granted.

(1) A standard license holder who seeks to renew a current license that was initially issued within 6 months of the biennial license period for which renewal is sought will be deemed eligible, on the basis of hardship, for a full waiver of the continuing education requirement.

(2) A standard license holder who seeks to renew a current license that was reactivated from noncurrent status within 6 months of the biennial license period for which renewal is sought will be deemed eligible, on the basis of hardship, for a full waiver of the continuing education requirement.

(3) A standard license holder who is a qualified continuing education instructor will be deemed eligible, for the waiver of 1 hour of continuing education for each hour of actual classroom instruction in an approved continuing education topic that the instructor is qualified to teach. Duplicate hours of instruction in the same topic during the same biennial license period will not be considered for waiver purposes.

(b) Requests to waive the continuing education requirement must be filed with the Commission on or before March 31 of the renewal year unless the applicant proves to the satisfaction of the Commission that it was impracticable to do so.

35-82

Authority

The provisions of this § 35.383 issued under sections 402, 404, 404.1 and 513 of the Real Estate Licensing and Registration Act (63 P.S. §§ 455.402, 455.404, 455.404a and 455.513); amended under sections 201, 501, 601, 602 and 604 of the Real Estate Licensing and Registration Act (63 P. S. §§ 455.201, 455.501, 455.601, 455.602 and 455.604).

Source

The provisions of this § 35.383 adopted July 31, 1992, effective August 1, 1992, 22 Pa.B. 3980; amended December 10, 2004, effective December 11, 2004, 34 Pa.B. 6530; amended August 19, 2005, effective August 20, 2005, 35 Pa.B. 4711. Immediately preceding text appears at serial pages (308367).

§ 35.384. Qualifying courses.

(a) Except as provided in subsection (b), a licensee shall complete 14 hours of continuing education in acceptable courses in a minimum of 2-hour increments. A standard license holder shall satisfy the continuing education requirement by doing one of the following:

(b) The Commission may, for a given biennial license period and with adequate notice to standard license holders, require that all or part of the 14 hours be completed in required topics.

(c) Acceptable courses include the following:

(1) Real estate ethics.
(2) Laws affecting real estate.
(3) Real estate financing and mathematics.
(4) Real estate valuation and evaluation.
(5) Property management.
(6) Land use and zoning.
(7) Income taxation as applied to real property.
(8) Ad valorem tax assessment and special assessments.
(9) Consumer protection and disclosures.
(10) Agency relationships.
(11) Landlord-tenant laws.
(12) Environmental issues in real estate.
(13) Antitrust issues in real estate.
(14) Current litigation related to real estate.
(15) Legal instruments related to real estate transactions.
(16) Legalities of real estate advertising.
(17) Developments in building construction techniques, materials and mechanical systems.
(18) Real estate investment analysis.
(19) Management of real estate brokerage operations.
(20) Property development.
(21) Real estate securities and syndication.
(22) Real property exchange.
(23) Broker courses encompassing supervisory duties and standards of conduct and practice contained in Subchapter E (relating to standards of conduct and practice).
(24) Marketing promotion and advertising of real estate inventory.
(25) Use of technology in delivering real estate services.

(d) Unacceptable courses include: mechanical office and business skills; for example, typing, speed writing, preparation of advertising copy, development of sales promotional devices, word processing, calculator and computer operation and office management and related internal operations procedures that do not have a bearing on the public interest.

Authority

The provisions of this § 35.384 issued under sections 402, 404, 404.1 and 513 of the Real Estate Licensing and Registration Act (63 P.S. §§ 455.402, 455.404, 455.404a and 455.513); amended under sections 201, 501, 601, 602 and 604 of the Real Estate Licensing and Registration Act (63 P. S. §§ 455.201, 455.501, 455.601, 455.602 and 455.604).

Source

The provisions of this § 35.384 adopted July 31, 1992, effective August 1, 1992, 22 Pa.B. 3980; amended December 10, 2004, effective December 11, 2004, 34 Pa.B. 6530; amended August 19, 2005, effective August 20, 2005, 35 Pa.B. 4711. Immediately preceding text appears at serial pages (308367) to (308368).

§ 35.385. Continuing education providers.

The following providers may offer instruction for continuing education:

(1) An accredited college, university or institute of higher learning, whether in this Commonwealth or outside this Commonwealth.

(2) A real estate education provider in this Commonwealth approved by the Commission.

(3) A real estate education provider outside this Commonwealth that has been approved by the real estate licensing authority of the jurisdiction where the real estate education provider is located.

Authority

The provisions of this § 35.385 issued under sections 402, 404, 404.1 and 513 of the Real Estate Licensing and Registration Act (63 P. S. §§ 455.402, 455.404, 455.404a and 455.513).

Source

The provisions of this § 35.385 adopted July 31, 1992, effective August 1, 1992, 22 Pa.B. 3980; amended December 10, 2004, effective December 11, 2004, 34 Pa.B. 6530. Immediately preceding text appears at serial pages (201908) to (201909).

§§ 35.386—35.392. [Reserved].

Source

The provisions of these §§ 35.386—35.392 adopted July 31, 1992, effective August 1, 1992, 22 Pa.B. 3980; amended December 10, 2004, effective December 11, 2004, 34 Pa.B. 6530. Immediately preceding text appears at serial pages (201909) to (201911).

[Next page is 36-1.]

APPENDIX D

CODE OF ETHICS AND STANDARDS OF PRACTICE OF THE NATIONAL ASSOCIATION OF REALTORS®

Code of Ethics and Standards of Practice
of the NATIONAL ASSOCIATION OF REALTORS®
Effective January 1, 2006

Where the word REALTORS® is used in this Code and Preamble, it shall be deemed to include REALTOR-ASSOCIATE®s.

While the Code of Ethics establishes obligations that may be higher than those mandated by law, in any instance where the Code of Ethics and the law conflict, the obligations of the law must take precedence.

Preamble

Under all is the land. Upon its wise utilization and widely allocated ownership depend the survival and growth of free institutions and of our civilization. REALTORS® should recognize that the interests of the nation and its citizens require the highest and best use of the land and the widest distribution of land ownership. They require the creation of adequate housing, the building of functioning cities, the development of productive industries and farms, and the preservation of a healthful environment.

Such interests impose obligations beyond those of ordinary commerce. They impose grave social responsibility and a patriotic duty to which REALTORS® should dedicate themselves, and for which they should be diligent in preparing themselves. REALTORS®, therefore, are zealous to maintain and improve the standards of their calling and share with their fellow REALTORS® a common responsibility for its integrity and honor.

In recognition and appreciation of their obligations to clients, customers, the public, and each other, REALTORS® continuously strive to become and remain informed on issues affecting real estate and, as knowledgeable professionals, they willingly share the fruit of their experience and study with others. They identify and take steps, through enforcement of this Code of Ethics and by assisting appropriate regulatory bodies, to eliminate practices which may damage the public or which might discredit or bring dishonor to the real estate profession. REALTORS® having direct personal knowledge of conduct that may violate the Code of Ethics involving misappropriation of client or customer funds or property, willful discrimination, or fraud resulting in substantial economic harm, bring such matters to the attention of the appropriate Board or Association of REALTORS®. *(Amended 1/00)*

Realizing that cooperation with other real estate professionals promotes the best interests of those who utilize their services, REALTORS® urge exclusive representation of clients; do not attempt to gain any unfair advantage over their competitors; and they refrain from making unsolicited comments about other practitioners. In instances where their opinion is sought, or where REALTORS® believe that comment is necessary, their opinion is offered in an objective, professional manner, uninfluenced by any personal motivation or potential advantage or gain.

The term REALTOR® has come to connote competency, fairness, and high integrity resulting from adherence to a lofty ideal of moral conduct in business relations. No inducement of profit and no instruction from clients ever can justify departure from this ideal.

In the interpretation of this obligation, REALTORS® can take no safer guide than that which has been handed down through the centuries, embodied in the Golden Rule, "Whatsoever ye would that others should do to you, do ye even so to them."

Accepting this standard as their own, REALTORS® pledge to observe its spirit in all of their activities and to conduct their business in accordance with the tenets set forth below.

Duties to Clients and Customers

Article 1

When representing a buyer, seller, landlord, tenant, or other client as an agent, REALTORS® pledge themselves to protect and promote the interests of their client. This obligation to the client is primary, but it does not relieve REALTORS® of their obligation to treat all parties honestly. When serving a buyer, seller, landlord, tenant or other party in a non-agency capacity, REALTORS® remain obligated to treat all parties honestly. *(Amended 1/01)*

- **Standard of Practice 1-1**
  REALTORS®, when acting as principals in a real estate transaction, remain obligated by the duties imposed by the Code of Ethics. *(Amended 1/93)*

- **Standard of Practice 1-2**
  The duties the Code of Ethics imposes are applicable whether REALTORS® are acting as agents or in legally recognized non-agency capacities except that any duty imposed exclusively on agents by law or regulation shall not be imposed by this Code of Ethics on REALTORS® acting in non-agency capacities.

  As used in this Code of Ethics, "client" means the person(s) or entity(ies) with whom a REALTOR® or a REALTOR®'s firm has an agency or legally recognized non-agency relationship; "customer" means a party to a real estate transaction who receives information, services, or benefits but has no contractual relationship with the REALTOR® or the REALTOR®'s firm; "prospect" means a purchaser, seller, tenant, or landlord who is not subject to a representation relationship with the REALTOR® or REALTOR®'s firm; "agent" means a real estate licensee (including brokers and sales associates) acting in an agency relationship as defined by state law or regulation; and "broker" means a real estate licensee (including brokers and sales associates) acting as an agent or in a legally recognized non-agency capacity. *(Adopted 1/95, Amended 1/04)*

- **Standard of Practice 1-3**
  REALTORS®, in attempting to secure a listing, shall not deliberately mislead the owner as to market value.

- **Standard of Practice 1-4**

  REALTORS®, when seeking to become a buyer/tenant representative, shall not mislead buyers or tenants as to savings or other benefits that might be realized through use of the REALTOR®'s services. *(Amended 1/93)*

- **Standard of Practice 1-5**

  REALTORS® may represent the seller/landlord and buyer/tenant in the same transaction only after full disclosure to and with informed consent of both parties. *(Adopted 1/93)*

- **Standard of Practice 1-6**

  REALTORS® shall submit offers and counter-offers objectively and as quickly as possible. *(Adopted 1/93, Amended 1/95)*

- **Standard of Practice 1-7**

  When acting as listing brokers, REALTORS® shall continue to submit to the seller/landlord all offers and counter-offers until closing or execution of a lease unless the seller/landlord has waived this obligation in writing. REALTORS® shall not be obligated to continue to market the property after an offer has been accepted by the seller/landlord. REALTORS® shall recommend that sellers/landlords obtain the advice of legal counsel prior to acceptance of a subsequent offer except where the acceptance is contingent on the termination of the pre-existing purchase contract or lease. *(Amended 1/93)*

- **Standard of Practice 1-8**

  REALTORS®, acting as agents or brokers of buyers/tenants, shall submit to buyers/tenants all offers and counter-offers until acceptance but have no obligation to continue to show properties to their clients after an offer has been accepted unless otherwise agreed in writing. REALTORS®, acting as agents or brokers of buyers/tenants, shall recommend that buyers/tenants obtain the advice of legal counsel if there is a question as to whether a pre-existing contract has been terminated. *(Adopted 1/93, Amended 1/99)*

- **Standard of Practice 1-9**

  The obligation of REALTORS® to preserve confidential information (as defined by state law) provided by their clients in the course of any agency relationship or non-agency relationship recognized by law continues after termination of agency relationships or any non-agency relationships recognized by law. REALTORS® shall not knowingly, during or following the termination of professional relationships with their clients:

  1) reveal confidential information of clients; or
  2) use confidential information of clients to the disadvantage of clients; or
  3) use confidential information of clients for the REALTOR®'s advantage or the advantage of third parties unless:
     a) clients consent after full disclosure; or
     b) REALTORS® are required by court order; or
     c) it is the intention of a client to commit a crime and the information is necessary to prevent the crime; or
     d) it is necessary to defend a REALTOR® or the REALTOR®'s employees or associates against an accusation of wrongful conduct.

  Information concerning latent material defects is not considered confidential information under this Code of Ethics. *(Adopted 1/93, Amended 1/01)*

- **Standard of Practice 1-10**

  REALTORS® shall, consistent with the terms and conditions of their real estate licensure and their property management agreement, competently manage the property of clients with due regard for the rights, safety and health of tenants and others lawfully on the premises. *(Adopted 1/95, Amended 1/00)*

- **Standard of Practice 1-11**

  REALTORS® who are employed to maintain or manage a client's property shall exercise due diligence and make reasonable efforts to protect it against reasonably foreseeable contingencies and losses. *(Adopted 1/95)*

- **Standard of Practice 1-12**

  When entering into listing contracts, REALTORS® must advise sellers/landlords of:

  1) the REALTOR®'s company policies regarding cooperation and the amount(s) of any compensation that will be offered to subagents, buyer/tenant agents, and/or brokers acting in legally recognized non-agency capacities;
  2) the fact that buyer/tenant agents or brokers, even if compensated by listing brokers, or by sellers/landlords may represent the interests of buyers/tenants; and
  3) any potential for listing brokers to act as disclosed dual agents, e.g. buyer/tenant agents. *(Adopted 1/93, Renumbered 1/98, Amended 1/03)*

- **Standard of Practice 1-13**

  When entering into buyer/tenant agreements, REALTORS® must advise potential clients of:

  1) the REALTOR®'s company policies regarding cooperation;
  2) the amount of compensation to be paid by the client;
  3) the potential for additional or offsetting compensation from other brokers, from the seller or landlord, or from other parties;
  4) any potential for the buyer/tenant representative to act as a disclosed dual agent, e.g. listing broker, subagent, landlord's agent, etc., and
  5) the possibility that sellers or sellers' representatives may not treat the existence, terms, or conditions of offers as confidential unless confidentiality is required by law, regulation, or by any confidentiality agreement between the parties. *(Adopted 1/93, Renumbered 1/98, Amended 1/06)*

- **Standard of Practice 1-14**

  Fees for preparing appraisals or other valuations shall not be contingent upon the amount of the appraisal or valuation. *(Adopted 1/02)*

- **Standard of Practice 1-15**

  REALTORS®, in response to inquiries from buyers or cooperating brokers shall, with the sellers' approval, disclose the existence of offers on the property. Where disclosure is authorized, REALTORS® shall also disclose whether offers were obtained by the listing licensee, another licensee in the listing firm, or by a cooperating broker. *(Adopted 1/03, Amended 1/06)*

Article 2

REALTORS® shall avoid exaggeration, misrepresentation, or concealment of pertinent facts relating to the property or the transaction. REALTORS® shall not, however, be obligated to discover latent defects in the property, to advise on matters outside the scope of their real estate license, or to disclose facts which are confidential under the scope of agency or non-agency relationships as defined by state law. *(Amended 1/00)*

- **Standard of Practice 2-1**

  REALTORS® shall only be obligated to discover and disclose adverse factors reasonably apparent to someone with expertise in those areas required by their real estate licensing authority. Article 2 does not impose upon the REALTOR® the obligation of expertise in other professional or technical disciplines. *(Amended 1/96)*

- **Standard of Practice 2-2**

  (Renumbered as Standard of Practice 1-12 1/98)

- **Standard of Practice 2-3**

  (Renumbered as Standard of Practice 1-13 1/98)

- **Standard of Practice 2-4**

  REALTORS® shall not be parties to the naming of a false consideration in any document, unless it be the naming of an obviously nominal consideration.

- **Standard of Practice 2-5**

  Factors defined as "non-material" by law or regulation or which are expressly referenced in law or regulation as not being subject to disclosure are considered not "pertinent" for purposes of Article 2. *(Adopted 1/93)*

Article 3

REALTORS® shall cooperate with other brokers except when cooperation is not in the client's best interest. The obligation to cooperate does not include the obligation to share commissions, fees, or to otherwise compensate another broker. *(Amended 1/95)*

- **Standard of Practice 3-1**

  REALTORS®, acting as exclusive agents or brokers of sellers/landlords, establish the terms and conditions of offers to cooperate. Unless expressly indicated in offers to cooperate, cooperating brokers may not assume that the offer of cooperation includes an offer of compensation. Terms of compensation, if any, shall be ascertained by cooperating brokers before beginning efforts to accept the offer of cooperation. *(Amended 1/99)*

- **Standard of Practice 3-2**

  REALTORS® shall, with respect to offers of compensation to another REALTOR®, timely communicate any change of compensation for cooperative services to the other REALTOR® prior to the time such REALTOR® produces an offer to purchase/lease the property. *(Amended 1/94)*

- **Standard of Practice 3-3**

  Standard of Practice 3-2 does not preclude the listing broker and cooperating broker from entering into an agreement to change cooperative compensation. *(Adopted 1/94)*

- **Standard of Practice 3-4**

  REALTORS®, acting as listing brokers, have an affirmative obligation to disclose the existence of dual or variable rate commission arrangements (i.e., listings where one amount of commission is payable if the listing broker's firm is the procuring cause of sale/lease and a different amount of commission is payable if the sale/lease results through the efforts of the seller/landlord or a cooperating broker). The listing broker shall, as soon as practical, disclose the existence of such arrangements to potential cooperating brokers and shall, in response to inquiries from cooperating brokers, disclose the differential that would result in a cooperative transaction or in a sale/lease that results through the efforts of the seller/landlord. If the cooperating broker is a buyer/tenant representative, the buyer/tenant representative must disclose such information to their client before the client makes an offer to purchase or lease. *(Amended 1/02)*

- **Standard of Practice 3-5**

  It is the obligation of subagents to promptly disclose all pertinent facts to the principal's agent prior to as well as after a purchase or lease agreement is executed. *(Amended 1/93)*

- **Standard of Practice 3-6**

  REALTORS® shall disclose the existence of accepted offers, including offers with unresolved contingencies, to any broker seeking cooperation. *(Adopted 5/86, Amended 1/04)*

- **Standard of Practice 3-7**

  When seeking information from another REALTOR® concerning property under a management or listing agreement, REALTORS® shall disclose their REALTOR® status and whether their interest is personal or on behalf of a client and, if on behalf of a client, their representational status. *(Amended 1/95)*

- **Standard of Practice 3-8**

  REALTORS® shall not misrepresent the availability of access to show or inspect a listed property. *(Amended 11/87)*

Article 4

REALTORS® shall not acquire an interest in or buy or present offers from themselves, any member of their immediate families, their firms or any member thereof, or any entities in which they have any ownership interest, any real property without making their true position known to the owner or the owner's agent or broker. In selling property they own, or in which they have any interest, REALTORS® shall reveal their ownership or interest in writing to the purchaser or the purchaser's representative. *(Amended 1/00)*

- **Standard of Practice 4-1**

  For the protection of all parties, the disclosures required by Article 4 shall be in writing and provided by REALTORS® prior to the signing of any contract. *(Adopted 2/86)*

Article 5

REALTORS® shall not undertake to provide professional services concerning a property or its value where they have a present or contemplated interest unless such interest is specifically disclosed to all affected parties.

Article 6

REALTORS® shall not accept any commission, rebate, or profit on expenditures made for their client, without the client's knowledge and consent.

When recommending real estate products or services (e.g., homeowner's insurance, warranty programs, mortgage financing, title insurance, etc.), REALTORS® shall disclose to the client or customer to whom the recommendation is made any financial benefits or fees, other than real estate referral fees, the REALTOR® or REALTOR®'s firm may receive as a direct result of such recommendation. *(Amended 1/99)*

- **Standard of Practice 6-1**

  REALTORS® shall not recommend or suggest to a client or a customer the use of services of another organization or business entity in which they have a direct interest without disclosing such interest at the time of the recommendation or suggestion. *(Amended 5/88)*

Article 7

In a transaction, REALTORS® shall not accept compensation from more than one party, even if permitted by law, without disclosure to all parties and the informed consent of the REALTOR®'s client or clients. *(Amended 1/93)*

Article 8

REALTORS® shall keep in a special account in an appropriate financial institution, separated from their own funds, monies coming into their possession in trust for other persons, such as escrows, trust funds, clients' monies, and other like items.

Article 9

REALTORS®, for the protection of all parties, shall assure whenever possible that all agreements related to real estate transactions including, but not limited to, listing and representation agreements, purchase contracts, and leases are in writing in clear and understandable language expressing the specific terms, conditions, obligations and commitments of the parties. A copy of each agreement shall be furnished to each party to such agreements upon their signing or initialing. *(Amended 1/04)*

- **Standard of Practice 9-1**

  For the protection of all parties, REALTORS® shall use reasonable care to ensure that documents pertaining to the purchase, sale, or lease of real estate are kept current through the use of written extensions or amendments. *(Amended 1/93)*

Duties to the Public

Article 10

REALTORS® shall not deny equal professional services to any person for reasons of race, color, religion, sex, handicap, familial status, or national origin. REALTORS® shall not be parties to any plan or agreement to discriminate against a person or persons on the basis of race, color, religion, sex, handicap, familial status, or national origin. *(Amended 1/90)*

REALTORS®, in their real estate employment practices, shall not discriminate against any person or persons on the basis of race, color, religion, sex, handicap, familial status, or national origin. *(Amended 1/00)*

- **Standard of Practice 10-1**

  When involved in the sale or lease of a residence, REALTORS® shall not volunteer information regarding the racial, religious or ethnic composition of any neighborhood nor shall they engage in any activity which may result in panic selling, however, REALTORS® may provide other demographic information. *(Adopted 1/94, Amended 1/06)*

- **Standard of Practice 10-2**

  When not involved in the sale or lease of a residence, REALTORS® may provide demographic information related to a property, transaction or professional assignment to a party if such demographic information is (a) deemed by the REALTOR® to be needed to assist with or complete, in a manner consistent with Article 10, a real estate transaction or professional assignment and (b) is obtained or derived from a recognized, reliable, independent, and impartial source. The source of such information and any additions, deletions, modifications, interpretations, or other changes shall be disclosed in reasonable detail. *(Adopted 1/05, Renumbered 1/06)*

- **Standard of Practice 10-3**

  REALTORS® shall not print, display or circulate any statement or advertisement with respect to selling or renting of a property that indicates any preference, limitations or discrimination based on race, color, religion, sex, handicap, familial status, or national origin. *(Adopted 1/94, Renumbered 1/05 and 1/06)*

- **Standard of Practice 10-4**

  As used in Article 10 "real estate employment practices" relates to employees and independent contractors providing real estate-related services and the administrative and clerical staff directly supporting those individuals. *(Adopted 1/00, Renumbered 1/05 and 1/06)*

Article 11

The services which REALTORS® provide to their clients and customers shall conform to the standards of practice and competence which are reasonably expected in the specific real estate disciplines in which they engage; specifically, residential real estate brokerage, real property management, commercial and industrial real estate brokerage, real estate appraisal, real estate counseling, real estate syndication, real estate auction, and international real estate.

REALTORS® shall not undertake to provide specialized professional services concerning a type of property or service that is outside their field of competence unless they engage the assistance of one who is competent on such types of property or service, or unless the facts are fully disclosed to the client. Any persons engaged to provide such assistance shall be so identified to the client and their contribution to the assignment should be set forth. *(Amended 1/95)*

- **Standard of Practice 11-1**

  When REALTORS® prepare opinions of real property value or price, other than in pursuit of a listing or to assist a potential purchaser in formulating a purchase offer, such opinions shall include the following:
  1) identification of the subject property
  2) date prepared
  3) defined value or price
  4) limiting conditions, including statements of purpose(s) and intended user(s)
  5) any present or contemplated interest, including the possibility of representing the seller/landlord or buyers/tenants
  6) basis for the opinion, including applicable market data
  7) if the opinion is not an appraisal, a statement to that effect *(Amended 1/01)*

- **Standard of Practice 11-2**

  The obligations of the Code of Ethics in respect of real estate disciplines other than appraisal shall be interpreted and applied in accordance with the standards of competence and practice which clients and the public reasonably require to protect their rights and interests considering the complexity of the transaction, the availability of expert assistance, and, where the REALTOR® is an agent or subagent, the obligations of a fiduciary. *(Adopted 1/95)*

- **Standard of Practice 11-3**

  When REALTORS® provide consultive services to clients which involve advice or counsel for a fee (not a commission), such advice shall be rendered in an objective manner and the fee shall not be contingent on the substance of the advice or counsel given. If brokerage or transaction services are to be provided in addition to consultive services, a separate compensation may be paid with prior agreement between the client and REALTOR®. *(Adopted 1/96)*

- **Standard of Practice 11-4**

  The competency required by Article 11 relates to services contracted for between REALTORS® and their clients or customers; the duties expressly imposed by the Code of Ethics; and the duties imposed by law or regulation. *(Adopted 1/02)*

Article 12

REALTORS® shall be careful at all times to present a true picture in their advertising and representations to the public. REALTORS® shall also ensure that their professional status (e.g., broker, appraiser, property manager, etc.) or status as REALTORS® is clearly identifiable in any such advertising. *(Amended 1/93)*

- **Standard of Practice 12-1**

  REALTORS® may use the term "free" and similar terms in their advertising and in other representations provided that all terms governing availability of the offered product or service are clearly disclosed at the same time. *(Amended 1/97)*

- **Standard of Practice 12-2**

  REALTORS® may represent their services as "free" or without cost even if they expect to receive compensation from a source other than their client provided that the potential for the REALTOR® to obtain a benefit from a third party is clearly disclosed at the same time. *(Amended 1/97)*

- **Standard of Practice 12-3**

  The offering of premiums, prizes, merchandise discounts or other inducements to list, sell, purchase, or lease is not, in itself, unethical even if receipt of the benefit is contingent on listing, selling, purchasing, or leasing through the REALTOR® making the offer. However, REALTORS® must exercise care and candor in any such advertising or other public or private representations so that any party interested in receiving or otherwise benefiting from the REALTOR®'s offer will have clear, thorough, advance understanding of all the terms and conditions of the offer. The offering of any inducements to do business is subject to the limitations and restrictions of state law and the ethical obligations established by any applicable Standard of Practice. *(Amended 1/95)*

- **Standard of Practice 12-4**

  REALTORS® shall not offer for sale/lease or advertise property without authority. When acting as listing brokers or as subagents, REALTORS®

shall not quote a price different from that agreed upon with the seller/landlord. *(Amended 1/93)*

- **Standard of Practice 12-5**

  REALTORS® shall not advertise nor permit any person employed by or affiliated with them to advertise listed property without disclosing the name of the firm. *(Adopted 11/86)*

- **Standard of Practice 12-6**

  REALTORS®, when advertising unlisted real property for sale/lease in which they have an ownership interest, shall disclose their status as both owners/landlords and as REALTORS® or real estate licensees. *(Amended 1/93)*

- **Standard of Practice 12-7**

  Only REALTORS® who participated in the transaction as the listing broker or cooperating broker (selling broker) may claim to have "sold" the property. Prior to closing, a cooperating broker may post a "sold" sign only with the consent of the listing broker. *(Amended 1/96)*

Article 13

REALTORS® shall not engage in activities that constitute the unauthorized practice of law and shall recommend that legal counsel be obtained when the interest of any party to the transaction requires it.

Article 14

If charged with unethical practice or asked to present evidence or to cooperate in any other way, in any professional standards proceeding or investigation, REALTORS® shall place all pertinent facts before the proper tribunals of the Member Board or affiliated institute, society, or council in which membership is held and shall take no action to disrupt or obstruct such processes. *(Amended 1/99)*

- **Standard of Practice 14-1**

  REALTORS® shall not be subject to disciplinary proceedings in more than one Board of REALTORS® or affiliated institute, society or council in which they hold membership with respect to alleged violations of the Code of Ethics relating to the same transaction or event. *(Amended 1/95)*

- **Standard of Practice 14-2**

  REALTORS® shall not make any unauthorized disclosure or dissemination of the allegations, findings, or decision developed in connection with an ethics hearing or appeal or in connection with an arbitration hearing or procedural review. *(Amended 1/92)*

- **Standard of Practice 14-3**

  REALTORS® shall not obstruct the Board's investigative or professional standards proceedings by instituting or threatening to institute actions for libel, slander or defamation against any party to a professional standards proceeding or their witnesses based on the filing of an arbitration request, an ethics complaint, or testimony given before any tribunal. *(Adopted 11/87, Amended 1/99)*

- **Standard of Practice 14-4**

  REALTORS® shall not intentionally impede the Board's investigative or disciplinary proceedings by filing multiple ethics complaints based on the same event or transaction. *(Adopted 11/88)*

Duties to REALTORS®

Article 15

REALTORS® shall not knowingly or recklessly make false or misleading statements about competitors, their businesses, or their business practices. *(Amended 1/92)*

- **Standard of Practice 15-1**

  REALTORS® shall not knowingly or recklessly file false or unfounded ethics complaints. *(Adopted 1/00)*

Article 16

REALTORS® shall not engage in any practice or take any action inconsistent with exclusive representation or exclusive brokerage relationship agreements that other REALTORS® have with clients. *(Amended 1/04)*

- **Standard of Practice 16-1**

  Article 16 is not intended to prohibit aggressive or innovative business practices which are otherwise ethical and does not prohibit disagreements with other REALTORS® involving commission, fees, compensation or other forms of payment or expenses. *(Adopted 1/93, Amended 1/95)*

- **Standard of Practice 16-2**

  Article 16 does not preclude REALTORS® from making general announcements to prospects describing their services and the terms of their availability even though some recipients may have entered into agency agreements or other exclusive relationships with another REALTOR®. A general telephone canvass, general mailing or distribution addressed to all prospects in a given geographical area or in a given profession, business, club, or organization, or other classification or group is deemed "general" for purposes of this standard. *(Amended 1/04)*

  Article 16 is intended to recognize as unethical two basic types of solicitations:

  First, telephone or personal solicitations of property owners who have been identified by a real estate sign, multiple listing compilation, or other information service as having exclusively listed their property with another REALTOR®; and

  Second, mail or other forms of written solicitations of prospects whose properties are exclusively listed with another REALTOR® when such solicitations are not part of a general mailing but are directed specifically to property owners identified through compilations of current listings, "for sale" or "for rent" signs, or other sources of information required by Article 3 and Multiple Listing Service rules to be made available to other REALTORS® under offers of subagency or cooperation. *(Amended 1/04)*

- **Standard of Practice 16-3**

  Article 16 does not preclude REALTORS® from contacting the client of another broker for the purpose of offering to provide, or entering into a contract to provide, a different type of real estate service unrelated to the type of service currently being provided (e.g., property management as opposed to brokerage) or from offering the same type of service for property not subject to other brokers' exclusive agreements. However, information received through a Multiple Listing Service or any other offer of cooperation may not be used to target clients of other REALTORS® to whom such offers to provide services may be made. *(Amended 1/04)*

- **Standard of Practice 16-4**

  REALTORS® shall not solicit a listing which is currently listed exclusively with another broker. However, if the listing broker, when asked by the REALTOR®, refuses to disclose the expiration date and nature of such listing; i.e., an exclusive right to sell, an exclusive agency, open listing, or other form of contractual agreement between the listing broker and the client, the REALTOR® may contact the owner to secure such information and may discuss the terms upon which the REALTOR® might take a future listing or, alternatively, may take a listing to become effective upon expiration of any existing exclusive listing. *(Amended 1/94)*

- **Standard of Practice 16-5**

  REALTORS® shall not solicit buyer/tenant agreements from buyers/tenants who are subject to exclusive buyer/tenant agreements. However, if asked by a REALTOR®, the broker refuses to disclose the expiration date of the exclusive buyer/tenant agreement, the REALTOR® may contact the buyer/tenant to secure such information and may discuss the terms upon which the REALTOR® might enter into a future buyer/tenant agreement or, alternatively, may enter into a buyer/tenant agreement to become effective upon the expiration of any existing exclusive buyer/tenant agreement. *(Adopted 1/94, Amended 1/98)*

- **Standard of Practice 16-6**

  When REALTORS® are contacted by the client of another REALTOR® regarding the creation of an exclusive relationship to provide the same type of service, and REALTORS® have not directly or indirectly initiated such discussions, they may discuss the terms upon which they might enter into a future agreement or, alternatively, may enter into an agreement which becomes effective upon expiration of any existing exclusive agreement. *(Amended 1/98)*

- **Standard of Practice 16-7**

  The fact that a prospect has retained a REALTOR® as an exclusive representative or exclusive broker in one or more past transactions does not preclude other REALTORS® from seeking such prospect's future business. *(Amended 1/04)*

- **Standard of Practice 16-8**

  The fact that an exclusive agreement has been entered into with a REALTOR® shall not preclude or inhibit any other REALTOR® from entering into a similar agreement after the expiration of the prior agreement. *(Amended 1/98)*

- **Standard of Practice 16-9**

  REALTORS®, prior to entering into a representation agreement, have an affirmative obligation to make reasonable efforts to determine whether the prospect is subject to a current, valid exclusive agreement to provide the same type of real estate service. *(Amended 1/04)*

- **Standard of Practice 16-10**

  REALTORS®, acting as buyer or tenant representatives or brokers, shall disclose that relationship to the seller/landlord's representative or broker at first contact and shall provide written confirmation of that disclosure to the seller/landlord's representative or broker not later than execution of a purchase agreement or lease. *(Amended 1/04)*

- **Standard of Practice 16-11**

  On unlisted property, REALTORS® acting as buyer/tenant representatives or brokers shall disclose that relationship to the seller/landlord at first contact for that buyer/tenant and shall provide written confirmation of such disclosure to the seller/landlord not later than execution of any purchase or lease agreement. *(Amended 1/04)*

  REALTORS® shall make any request for anticipated compensation from the seller/landlord at first contact. *(Amended 1/98)*

- **Standard of Practice 16-12**

  REALTORS®, acting as representatives or brokers of sellers/landlords or as subagents of listing brokers, shall disclose that relationship to buyers/tenants as soon as practicable and shall provide written confirmation of such disclosure to buyers/tenants not later than execution of any purchase or lease agreement. *(Amended 1/04)*

- **Standard of Practice 16-13**

  All dealings concerning property exclusively listed, or with buyer/tenants who are subject to an exclusive agreement shall be carried on with the client's representative or broker, and not with the client, except with the consent of the client's representative or broker or except where such dealings are initiated by the client.

  Before providing substantive services (such as writing a purchase offer or presenting a CMA) to prospects, REALTORS® shall ask prospects whether they are a party to any exclusive representation agreement. REALTORS® shall not knowingly provide substantive services concerning a prospective transaction to prospects who are parties to exclusive representation agreements, except with the consent of the prospects' exclusive representatives or at the direction of prospects. *(Adopted 1/93, Amended 1/04)*

- **Standard of Practice 16-14**

  REALTORS® are free to enter into contractual relationships or to negotiate with sellers/landlords, buyers/tenants or others who are not subject to an exclusive agreement but shall not knowingly obligate them to pay more than one commission except with their informed consent. *(Amended 1/98)*

- **Standard of Practice 16-15**

  In cooperative transactions REALTORS® shall compensate cooperating REALTORS® (principal brokers) and shall not compensate nor offer to compensate, directly or indirectly, any of the sales licensees employed by or affiliated with other REALTORS® without the prior express knowledge and consent of the cooperating broker.

- **Standard of Practice 16-16**

  REALTORS®, acting as subagents or buyer/tenant representatives or brokers, shall not use the terms of an offer to purchase/lease to attempt to modify the listing broker's offer of compensation to subagents or buyer/tenant representatives or brokers nor make the submission of an executed offer to purchase/lease contingent on the listing broker's agreement to modify the offer of compensation. *(Amended 1/04)*

- **Standard of Practice 16-17**

  REALTORS®, acting as subagents or as buyer/tenant representatives or brokers, shall not attempt to extend a listing broker's offer of cooperation and/or compensation to other brokers without the consent of the listing broker. *(Amended 1/04)*

- **Standard of Practice 16-18**

  REALTORS® shall not use information obtained from listing brokers through offers to cooperate made through multiple listing services or through other offers of cooperation to refer listing brokers' clients to other brokers or to create buyer/tenant relationships with listing brokers' clients, unless such use is authorized by listing brokers. *(Amended 1/02)*

- **Standard of Practice 16-19**

  Signs giving notice of property for sale, rent, lease, or exchange shall not be placed on property without consent of the seller/landlord. *(Amended 1/93)*

- **Standard of Practice 16-20**

  REALTORS®, prior to or after terminating their relationship with their current firm, shall not induce clients of their current firm to cancel exclusive contractual agreements between the client and that firm. This does not preclude REALTORS® (principals) from establishing agreements with their associated licensees governing assignability of exclusive agreements. *(Adopted 1/98)*

Article 17

In the event of contractual disputes or specific non-contractual disputes as defined in Standard of Practice 17-4 between REALTORS® (principals) associated with different firms, arising out of their relationship as REALTORS®, the REALTORS® shall submit the dispute to arbitration in accordance with the regulations of their Board or Boards rather than litigate the matter.

In the event clients of REALTORS® wish to arbitrate contractual disputes arising out of real estate transactions, REALTORS® shall arbitrate those disputes in accordance with the regulations of their Board, provided the clients agree to be bound by the decision.

The obligation to participate in arbitration contemplated by this Article includes the obligation of REALTORS® (principals) to cause their firms to arbitrate and be bound by any award. *(Amended 1/01)*

- **Standard of Practice 17-1**

  The filing of litigation and refusal to withdraw from it by REALTORS® in an arbitrable matter constitutes a refusal to arbitrate. *(Adopted 2/86)*

- **Standard of Practice 17-2**

  Article 17 does not require REALTORS® to arbitrate in those circumstances when all parties to the dispute advise the Board in writing that they choose not to arbitrate before the Board. *(Amended 1/93)*

- **Standard of Practice 17-3**

  REALTORS®, when acting solely as principals in a real estate transaction, are not obligated to arbitrate disputes with other REALTORS® absent a specific written agreement to the contrary. *(Adopted 1/96)*

- **Standard of Practice 17-4**

  Specific non-contractual disputes that are subject to arbitration pursuant to Article 17 are:

  1) Where a listing broker has compensated a cooperating broker and another cooperating broker subsequently claims to be the procuring cause of the sale or lease. In such cases the

complainant may name the first cooperating broker as respondent and arbitration may proceed without the listing broker being named as a respondent. Alternatively, if the complaint is brought against the listing broker, the listing broker may name the first cooperating broker as a third-party respondent. In either instance the decision of the hearing panel as to procuring cause shall be conclusive with respect to all current or subsequent claims of the parties for compensation arising out of the underlying cooperative transaction. *(Adopted 1/97)*

2) Where a buyer or tenant representative is compensated by the seller or landlord, and not by the listing broker, and the listing broker, as a result, reduces the commission owed by the seller or landlord and, subsequent to such actions, another cooperating broker claims to be the procuring cause of sale or lease. In such cases the complainant may name the first cooperating broker as respondent and arbitration may proceed without the listing broker being named as a respondent. Alternatively, if the complaint is brought against the listing broker, the listing broker may name the first cooperating broker as a third-party respondent. In either instance the decision of the hearing panel as to procuring cause shall be conclusive with respect to all current or subsequent claims of the parties for compensation arising out of the underlying cooperative transaction. *(Adopted 1/97)*

3) Where a buyer or tenant representative is compensated by the buyer or tenant and, as a result, the listing broker reduces the commission owed by the seller or landlord and, subsequent to such actions, another cooperating broker claims to be the procuring cause of sale or lease. In such cases the complainant may name the first cooperating broker as respondent and arbitration may proceed without the listing broker being named as a respondent. Alternatively, if the complaint is brought against the listing broker, the listing broker may name the first cooperating broker as a third-party respondent. In either instance the decision of the hearing panel as to procuring cause shall be conclusive with respect to all current or subsequent claims of the parties for compensation arising out of the underlying cooperative transaction. *(Adopted 1/97)*

4) Where two or more listing brokers claim entitlement to compensation pursuant to open listings with a seller or landlord who agrees to participate in arbitration (or who requests arbitration) and who agrees to be bound by the decision. In cases where one of the listing brokers has been compensated by the seller or landlord, the other listing broker, as complainant, may name the first listing broker as respondent and arbitration may proceed between the brokers. *(Adopted 1/97)*

5) Where a buyer or tenant representative is compensated by the seller or landlord, and not by the listing broker, and the listing broker, as a result, reduces the commission owed by the seller or landlord and, subsequent to such actions, claims to be the procuring cause of sale or lease. In such cases arbitration shall be between the listing broker and the buyer or tenant representative and the amount in dispute is limited to the amount of the reduction of commission to which the listing broker agreed. *(Adopted 1/05)*

The Code of Ethics was adopted in 1913. Amended at the Annual Convention in 1924, 1928, 1950, 1951, 1952, 1955, 1956, 1961, 1962, 1974, 1982, 1986, 1987, 1989, 1990, 1991, 1992, 1993, 1994, 1995, 1996, 1997, 1998, 1999, 2000, 2001, 2002, 2003, 2004 and 2005.

Explanatory Notes

The reader should be aware of the following policies which have been approved by the Board of Directors of the National Association:

In filing a charge of an alleged violation of the Code of Ethics by a REALTOR®, the charge must read as an alleged violation of one or more Articles of the Code. Standards of Practice may be cited in support of the charge.

The Standards of Practice serve to clarify the ethical obligations imposed by the various Articles and supplement, and do not substitute for, the Case Interpretations in *Interpretations of the Code of Ethics*.

Modifications to existing Standards of Practice and additional new Standards of Practice are approved from time to time. Readers are cautioned to ensure that the most recent publications are utilized.

MATH FAQS

Answers to Your Most Frequently
Asked Real Estate Math Questions

SECTION

FRACTIONS, DECIMALS, AND PERCENTAGES

■ WHAT ARE THE PARTS OF A FRACTION?

The **denominator** shows the number of equal parts in the whole or total. The **numerator** shows the number of those parts with which you are working. In the example below, the whole or total has been divided into eight equal parts, and you have seven of those equal parts.

$\dfrac{7}{8}$ $\dfrac{\text{Numerator}}{\text{Denominator}}$ $\dfrac{\text{(Top Number)}}{\text{(Bottom Number)}}$

■ WHAT IS MEANT BY A "PROPER FRACTION"?

⅞ is an example of a **proper fraction.** In a proper fraction the numerator is less than the whole or less than 1.

■ WHAT IS AN "IMPROPER FRACTION"?

$\dfrac{11}{8}$ $\dfrac{\text{Numerator}}{\text{Denominator}}$

This is an example of an **improper fraction.** In an improper fraction, the numerator is greater than the whole or greater than 1.

■ WHAT IS A MIXED NUMBER?

11½ is a **mixed number.** You have a whole number plus a fraction. A mixed number is greater than the whole or greater than 1.

■ HOW DO I MULTIPLY FRACTIONS?

When multiplying fractions, the numerator is multiplied by the numerator, and the denominator by the denominator. Let's start with an easy question. What is ½ × ¾?

First multiply the numerators (top numbers) 1 × 3 = 3; then the denominators (bottom numbers) 2 × 4 = 8. Thus, ½ × ¾ = ⅜.

What is 4⅔ × 10⅝? The first step is to convert the whole number 4 into thirds. This is done by multiplying 4 × 3 = 12. (Multiply the whole number, 4, by the denominator of the fraction, 3.) Thus, the whole number 4 is equal to ¹²⁄₃.

4⅔ is equal to ¹²⁄₃ + ⅔ = ¹⁴⁄₃.

The next step is to convert the whole number 10 into eighths. This is done by multiplying 10 × 8 = 80. (Multiply the whole number, 10, by the denominator of the fraction, 8.) Thus, the whole number 10 is equal to ⁸⁰⁄₈. ⁸⁰⁄₈ + ⅝ = ⁸⁵⁄₈.

So, what is ¹⁴⁄₃ × ⁸⁵⁄₈? First multiply 14 × 85 = 1,190. Then, 3 × 8 = 24. ¹,¹⁹⁰⁄₂₄ = 49.58. (That is, 1,190 ÷ 24 = 49.58.)

An easier way to work the question is to convert the fractions to decimals.

⅔ is equal to 2 ÷ 3 or .67.

⅝ is equal to 5 ÷ 8 or .625.

4.67 × 10.625 = 49.62.

Whenever working with fractions or decimals equivalents, the answers will be close but not exact.

■ HOW DO I DIVIDE BY FRACTIONS?

Dividing by fractions is a two-step process. What is ¾ ÷ ¼?

First, invert the ¼ to ⁴⁄₁. Then, multiply ¾ × ⁴⁄₁ = ¹²⁄₄. Finally, 12 ÷ 4 = 3.

You may also convert ¾ to the decimal .75 and ¼ to the decimal .25.

.75 ÷ .25 = 3. (There are three .25 in .75.)

What is 100 ⅞ ÷ ¾?

100 × 8 = 800.

800 + 7 = ⁸⁰⁷⁄₈.

¾ is inverted to ⁴⁄₃.

⁸⁰⁷⁄₈ × ⁴⁄₃ = 807 × 4 = 3,228; 8 × 3 = 24. ³,²²⁸⁄₂₄ = 3,228 ÷ 24 = 134.5

Or 7 ÷ 8 = .875 and 3 ÷ 4 = .75.

100.875 ÷ .75 = 134.50.

■ HOW DO I CONVERT FRACTIONS TO DECIMALS?

Fractions will sometimes be used in real estate math problems. Since calculators may be used on most licensing examinations, it is best to convert fractions to decimals.

MATH TIP

To convert a fraction to a decimal, the top number, called the numerator, is divided by the bottom number, the denominator.

For example:

⅞ = 7 ÷ 8 = **0.875**
11⅛ = 11 ÷ 8 = **1.375**
11½ = 1 ÷ 2 = 0.5 + 11 = **11.5**

Once fractions have been converted to decimals, other calculations can be easily completed using the calculator. Note that many calculators automatically add the zero before the decimal point as in the first two examples above.

■ HOW DO I ADD OR SUBTRACT DECIMALS?

Line up the decimals, add or subtract, and bring the decimal down in the answer. You may add zeros if necessary as place holders. For example, 0.5 is the same as 0.50, or .5.

$$
\begin{array}{r}
0.50 \\
+\ 3.25 \\
\hline
=\ 3.75
\end{array}
\qquad
\begin{array}{r}
8.20 \\
-\ 0.75 \\
\hline
=\ 7.45
\end{array}
$$

MATH TIP

When you use a calculator, the decimal will be in the correct place in the answer.
0.5 + 3.25 = 3.75, and 8.2 − 0.75 = 7.45

■ HOW DO I MULTIPLY DECIMALS?

Multiply the numbers, then count the number of decimal places in each number. Next, start with the last number on the right and move the decimal the total number of decimal places to the left in the answer.

Multiply as you normally would to get the 1,500, then count the four decimal places in the numbers (.20 and .75). In the 1,500, start at the last zero on the right, and count four decimal places to the left. The decimal is placed to the left of the **1.**

$$
\begin{array}{r}
0.20 \\
\times\ 0.75 \\
\hline
100 \\
140\ \ \\
\hline
.1500 \text{ or } .15
\end{array}
$$

Note: When you use a calculator, the decimal will be in the correct place in the answer (0.2 × 0.75 = **0.15**).

■ HOW DO I DIVIDE DECIMALS?

Divide the **dividend** (the number being divided) by the **divisor** (the number you are dividing by) and bring the decimal in the dividend straight up in the **quotient** (answer). If the divisor has a decimal, move the decimal to the right of the divisor and move the decimal the same number of places to the right in the dividend. Now divide as stated above.

$$
\begin{array}{r}
= 0.75 \\
2\overline{)1.5} \\
\underline{1.4} \\
10 \\
\underline{10} \\
0
\end{array}
\qquad
0.5\overline{)15.5} =
\begin{array}{r}
= 31. \\
5\overline{)155.} \\
\underline{15} \\
05 \\
\underline{5} \\
0
\end{array}
$$

M A T H ✓ T I P

When you use a calculator, you can have a decimal in the divisor and the decimal will be in the correct place in the answer.

1.5 ÷ 2 = 0.75, and 15.5 ÷ 0.5 = 31

■ WHAT IS A PERCENTAGE?

Percent (%) means *per hundred* or *per hundred parts*. The whole or total always represents 100 percent.

$$5\% = 5 \text{ parts of } 100 \text{ parts, or } 5 \div 100 = 0.05 \text{ or } \tfrac{1}{20}$$
$$75\% = 75 \text{ parts of } 100 \text{ parts, or } 75 \div 100 = 0.75 \text{ or } \tfrac{3}{4}$$
$$120\% = 120 \text{ parts of } 100 \text{ parts, or } 120 \div 100 = 1.2 \text{ or } 1\tfrac{1}{5}$$

■ HOW CAN I CONVERT A PERCENTAGE TO A DECIMAL?

Move the decimal *two places* to the *left* and *drop* the % sign.

$$20\% = 2 \div 100 = 0.20 \text{ or } \mathbf{0.2}$$
$$1\% = 1 \div 100 = \mathbf{0.01}$$
$$12\tfrac{1}{4}\% = 12.25\%, \ 12.25 \div 100 = \mathbf{0.1225}$$

See Figure 1.1.

■ HOW CAN I CONVERT A DECIMAL TO A PERCENTAGE?

Move the decimal *two places* to the *right* and *add* the % sign.

$$0.25 = \mathbf{25\%}$$
$$0.9 = \mathbf{90\%}$$
$$0.0875 = \mathbf{8.75\%} \text{ or } 8\tfrac{3}{4}\%$$

See Figure 1.1.

FIGURE 1.1

Converting Percentage to Decimal

Decimal to Percentage

.10 ⟹ 10%

Move decimal two places to the right

Percentage to Decimal

.10 ⟸ 10%

Move decimal two places to the left

■ HOW DO I MULTIPLY BY PERCENTAGES?

$$500 \times 25\% = 500 \times \frac{25}{100} = \frac{12{,}500}{100} = 125$$

or

$$500 \times 25\% = 125, \text{ or } 500 \times .25 = 125$$

■ HOW DO I DIVIDE BY PERCENTAGES?

$$100 \div 5\% = 100 \div \frac{5}{100} = 100 \times \frac{100}{5} = \frac{10{,}000}{5} = 2{,}000$$

or

$$100 \div 5\% = 2{,}000, \text{ or } 100 \div .05 = 2{,}000$$

■ IS THERE ANY EASY WAY TO REMEMBER HOW TO SOLVE PERCENTAGE PROBLEMS?

The following three formulas are important for solving all percentage problems:

$$
\begin{array}{rcl}
\text{TOTAL} \times \text{RATE} &=& \text{PART} \\
\text{PART} \div \text{RATE} &=& \text{TOTAL} \\
\text{PART} \div \text{TOTAL} &=& \text{RATE}
\end{array}
$$

There is a simple way to remember how to use these formulas:

■ *MULTIPLY* when PART is UNKNOWN.

■ *DIVIDE* when PART is KNOWN.

■ When you divide, always enter PART into the calculator first.

■ WHAT IS THE "T-BAR" METHOD?

The T-Bar is another tool to use to solve percentage problems. For some people, the "three-formula method" is more difficult to remember than the visual image of a *T*.

■ HOW DO I USE THE T-BAR?

The procedure for using the T-Bar is as follows:

1. Enter the two *known* items in the correct places.
2. If the line between the two items is *vertical*, you *multiply* to equal the missing item.

FIGURE 1.2

FIGURE 1.2

Using the T-Bar

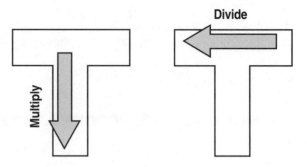

3. If the line between the two items is *horizontal,* you *divide* to equal the missing item. When you divide, the top (**Part**) always goes into the calculator first and is divided by the bottom (**Total** or **Rate**).

See Figure 1.2.

The following examples show how the T-Bar can be used to solve percentage problems. These examples deal with discounts because everyone can relate to buying an item that is on sale. Later we will see how the T-Bar can be used for many types of real estate problems.

■ **FOR EXAMPLE** John purchased a new suit that was marked $500. How much did John save if it was on sale for 20 percent off?

	= ? ($100)		**$100 Saved**
$500		20%	
Total Price		0.2	

×

$500 × 20% (.20) = $100

How much did John pay for the suit?

$500 Total Price – $100 Discount   **$400 Paid**
or
100% Total Price – 20% Discount = 80% Paid

	= ? ($400)		**$400 Paid**
$500		80%	
Total Price		0.8	

×

$500 × 80% (.80) = $400

■ **FOR EXAMPLE** Susie paid $112.50 for a dress that was reduced 25 percent. How much was it originally marked?

100% Original Price – 25% Discount = 75% Paid

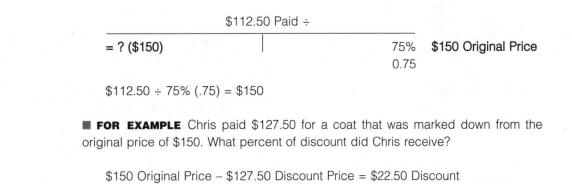

$112.50 ÷ 75% (.75) = $150

■ **FOR EXAMPLE** Chris paid $127.50 for a coat that was marked down from the original price of $150. What percent of discount did Chris receive?

$150 Original Price – $127.50 Discount Price = $22.50 Discount

	÷ 22.50 Discount		
$150 Original Price		= ? (0.15 = 15%)	15% Discount

$22.50 ÷ $150 = .15 or 15%

or

	÷ $127.50 Paid		
$150		= ? (0.85 = 85%)	85% of Original Price Paid

$127.50 ÷ $150 = .85 or 85%

85% was the percent paid; therefore

100% Original Price – 85% Paid = **15% Discount**

■ WORD PROBLEMS CAN BE TRICKY. HOW SHOULD I DEAL WITH THEM?

There are five important steps that must be taken to solve word problems.

1. **Read** the problem carefully and completely. Never touch the calculator until you have read the entire problem.
2. **Analyze** the problem to determine what is being asked, what facts are given that *will* be needed to solve for the answer, and what facts are given that *will not* be needed to solve for the answer. Eliminate any information and/or numbers given that are not needed to solve the problem. Take the remaining information and/or numbers and determine which will be needed first, second, etc., depending on the number of steps it will take to solve the problem.
3. **Choose** the proper formula(s) and steps it will take to solve the problem.
4. **Insert** the known elements and calculate the answer.
5. **Check** your answer to be sure you keyed in the numbers and functions properly on your calculator. Be sure you finished the problem. For example, when the problem asks for the salesperson's share of the commission, do not stop at the broker's share of the commission and mark that answer just because it is one of the choices.

PERCENTAGE PROBLEMS

■ HOW DO I WORK COMMISSION PROBLEMS?

The full **commission** is a percentage of the sales price unless stated differently in the problem. Remember that full commission rates, commission splits between brokers, and commission splits between the broker and salespersons are always negotiable. Always read a problem carefully to determine the correct rate(s).

÷ Full Commission ÷	
Sales Price	Full Commission Rate
×	

Sales Price × Full Commission Rate = **Full Commission**
Full Commission ÷ Full Commission Rate = **Sales Price**
Full Commission ÷ Sales Price = **Full Commission Rate**

÷ Broker's Share of the Commission ÷	
Full Commission	% of Full Commission to the Broker
×	

Full Commission	×	% of Full Commission to the Broker	=	**Broker's Share of the Commission**

Broker's Share of the Commission	÷	% of Full Commission to the Broker	=	**Full Commission**

Broker's Share of the Commission	÷	Full Commission	=	**% of Full Commission to the Broker**

÷ Salesperson's Share of the Commission ÷	
Broker's Share of the Commission	Salesperson's % of the Broker's Share
×	

Broker's Share of the Commission	×	Salesperson's % of the Broker's Share	=	**Salesperson's Share of the Commission**

Salesperson's Share of the Commission	÷	Salesperson's % of the Broker's Share	=	**Broker's Share of the Commission**

Salesperson's Share of the Commission	÷	Broker's Share of the Commission	=	**Salesperson's % of the Broker's Share**

■ **FOR EXAMPLE** A seller listed a home for $200,000 and agreed to pay a full commission rate of 5 percent. The home sold four weeks later for 90 percent of the list price. The listing broker agreed to give the selling broker 50 percent of the commission. The listing broker paid the listing salesperson 50 percent of her share of the commission, and the selling broker paid the selling salesperson 60 percent of his share of the commission. How much commission did the selling salesperson receive?

= $180,000 Sales Price

$200,000 List Price		90% or 0.9
	×	

$200,000 × 90% (.90) = $180,000

= $9,000 Full Commission

$180,000 Sales Price		5% or 0.05
	×	

$180,000 × 5% (.05) = $9,000

= $4,500 Broker's Share of the Commission

$9,000 Full Commission		50% or 0.5
	×	

$9,000 × 50% (.50) = $4,500

= $2,700 Selling Salesperson's Commission

$4,500 Broker's Share of Comm.		60% or 0.6
	×	

$4,500 × 60% (.60) = $2,700

$2,700 Selling Salesperson's Commission is the answer.

■ WHAT IS MEANT BY "SELLER'S DOLLARS AFTER COMMISSION"?

The first deduction from the sales price is the real estate commission. For example, if a house sold for $100,000 and a 7% commission was paid, that means $7,000 was paid in commissions. The seller still has 93% or $93,000. The seller's dollars after commission will be used to pay the seller's other expenses and hopefully will leave some money for the seller.

$$\frac{\div \text{ Seller's Dollars after Commission} \div}{\text{Sales Price} \quad | \quad \text{Percent after Commission}}$$
$$\times$$

Remember, the sales price is 100%. Thus 100% − Commission % = Percent after Commission.

$$\text{Sales Price} \quad \times \quad \text{Percent after Commission} \quad = \quad \text{Seller's Dollars after Commission}$$

$$\text{Seller's Dollars after Commission} \quad \div \quad \text{Percent after Commission} \quad = \quad \text{Sales Price}$$

$$\text{Seller's Dollars after Commission} \quad \div \quad \text{Sales Price} \quad = \quad \text{Percent after Commission}$$

■ **FOR EXAMPLE** After deducting $5,850 in closing costs and a 5 percent broker's commission, the sellers received their original cost of $175,000 plus a $4,400 profit. What was the sales price of the property?

$5,850 Closing Costs + $175,000 Original Cost + $4,400 Profit = $185,250 Seller's Dollars after Commission

100% Sales Price − 5% Commission = 95% Percent after Commission

$$\frac{\$185,250 \text{ Seller's Dollars after Commission} \div}{}$$

= $195,000	95%
Sales Price	or 0.95

$185,250 ÷ 95% (.95) = $195,000

$195,000 Sales Price is the answer.

■ HOW DO I DETERMINE INTEREST?

Interest is the cost of using money. The amount of interest paid is determined by the agreed-on annual interest rate, the amount of money borrowed (loan amount) or amount of money still owed (loan balance), and the period of time the money is held. When a lender grants a loan for real estate, the loan-to-value (LTV) ratio is the percentage of the sales price or appraised value, whichever is less, that the lender is willing to lend.

÷ Loan Amount ÷

Sales Price or Appraised Value (whichever is less)	Loan-to-Value Ratio (LTV)

×

Sales Price or Appraised Value (whichever is less)	×	Loan-to-Value Ratio (LTV)	=	**Loan Amount**

Loan Amount	÷	Loan-to-Value Ratio (LTV)	=	**Sales Price** or **Appraised Value** (whichever is less)

Loan Amount	÷	Sales Price or Appraised Value (whichever is less)	=	**Loan-to-Value Ratio** (LTV)

÷ Annual Interest ÷

Loan Amount (Principal)	Annual Interest Rate

×

Loan Amount	×	Annual Interest Rate	=	**Annual Interest**

Annual Interest	÷	Annual Interest Rate	=	**Loan Amount**

Annual Interest	÷	Loan Amount	=	**Annual Interest Rate**

■ **FOR EXAMPLE** A parcel of real estate sold for $335,200. The lender granted a 90 percent loan at 7.5 percent for 30 years. The appraised value on this parcel was $335,500. How much interest is paid to the lender in the first monthly payment?

= $301,680 Loan Amount

$335,200 Sales Price	90% or 0.9

×

$335,200 × 90% (.90) = $301,680 Loan

= $22,626 Annual Interest

$301,680 Loan Amount	7.5% or .075

×

$301,680 × 7.5% (.075) = $22,626

$22,626 Annual Interest ÷ 12 Months = $1,885.50 Monthly Interest

$1,885.50 Interest in the First Monthly Payment is the answer.

■ HOW DO I DETERMINE MONTHLY PRINCIPAL AND INTEREST PAYMENTS?

A **loan payment factor** can be used to calculate the monthly principal and interest (PI) payment on a loan. The factor represents the monthly principal and interest payment to amortize a $1,000 loan and is based on the annual interest rate and the term of the loan.

See Table 16.2 for a loan factor chart found on page 321.

Loan Amount ÷ $1,000 × Loan Payment Factor = **Monthly PI Payment**
Monthly PI Payment ÷ Loan Payment Factor = **Loan Amount**

■ **FOR EXAMPLE** If the lender in the previous example uses a loan payment factor of $6.99 per $1,000 of loan amount, what will be the monthly PI (principal and interest) payment?

$301,680 Loan Amount ÷ $1,000 × $6.99 = $2,108.74 Monthly PI Payment

$2,108.74 Monthly PI Payment is the answer.

■ HOW DO I WORK PROBLEMS ABOUT POINTS?

One **point** equals 1 percent of the loan amount.

÷ Amount for Points ÷	
Loan Amount	Points Converted to a Percent
×	

Loan Amount	×	Points Converted to a Percent	= **Amount for Points**
Amount of Points	÷	Points Converted to a Percent	= **Loan Amount**
Amount of Points	÷	Loan Amount	= **Points Converted to a Percent**

■ **FOR EXAMPLE** The lender will charge 3½ loan discount points on an $80,000 loan. What will be the total amount due?

= $2,800 for Points	
$80,000 Loan Amount	3.5% or 0.035
×	

$80,000 × 3.5% (.035) = $2,800

$2,800 for Points is the answer.

■ HOW DO I DETERMINE PROFIT?

A **profit** is made when we sell something for more than we paid for it. If we sell something for less than we paid, we have suffered a **loss.**

Sales Price – Cost = Profit

	÷ Profit ÷	
Cost		Percent of Profit
	×	

Cost	×	Percent of Profit	=	**Profit**
Profit	÷	Percent of Profit	=	**Cost**
Profit	÷	Cost	=	**Percent of Profit**
Cost	+	Profit	=	**Sales Price**

	÷ Sales Price ÷	
Cost		Percent Sold of Cost
	×	

(100% Cost + % Profit = % Sales Price)

Cost	×	Percent Sold of Cost	=	**Sales Price**
Sales Price	÷	Percent Sold of Cost	=	**Cost**
Sales Price	÷	Cost	=	**Percent Sold of Cost**

■ **FOR EXAMPLE** Your home listed for $125,000 and sold for $123,200, which gave you a 10 percent profit over the original cost. What was the original cost?

100% Original Cost + 10% Profit = 110% Sales Price

$123,200 Sales Price		
= $112,000 Original Cost		110% or 1.1
	×	

$123,200 ÷ 110% (1.1) = $112,000

$112,000 Original Cost is the answer.

■ WHAT IS THE DIFFERENCE BETWEEN APPRECIATION AND DEPRECIATION?

Appreciation is increase in value. **Depreciation** is decrease in value. Both are based on the original cost. We only will cover the **straight-line method,** which is what should be used in math problems unless you are told differently. The straight-line method means that the value is increasing (appreciating) or decreasing (depreciating) the same amount each year. The amount of appreciation or depreciation is based on the original cost.

■ HOW DO I SOLVE APPRECIATION PROBLEMS?

$$\div \text{ Annual Appreciation } \div$$

Cost | Annual Appreciation Rate
×

Cost × Annual Appreciation Rate = **Annual Appreciation**

Annual Appreciation ÷ Annual Appreciation Rate = **Cost**

Annual Appreciation ÷ Cost = **Annual Appreciation Rate**

Annual Appreciation Rate × Number of Years = **Total Appreciation Rate**
100% Cost + Total Appreciation Rate = **Today's Value as a Percent**

$$\div \text{ Today's Value (Appreciated Value) } \div$$

Cost | Today's Value as a Percent
×

Cost × Today's Value as a Percent = **Today's Value (Appreciated Value)**

Today's Value (Appreciated Value) ÷ Today's Value as a Percent = **Cost**

Today's Value (Appreciated Value) ÷ Cost = **Today's Value as a Percent**

■ HOW DO I SOLVE DEPRECIATION PROBLEMS?

$$\div \text{ Annual Depreciation } \div$$

Cost	Annual Depreciation Rate

×

Cost	×	Annual Depreciation Rate	=	**Annual Depreciation**
Annual Depreciation	÷	Annual Depreciation Rate	=	**Cost**
Annual Depreciation	÷	Cost	=	**Annual Depreciation Rate**

Annual Depreciation Rate × Number of Years = **Total Depreciation Rate**

100% Cost ÷ Total Depreciation Rate = **Today's Value as a Percent**

$$\div \text{ Today's Value (Depreciated Value) } \div$$

Cost	Today's Value as a Percent

×

Cost	×	Today's Value as a Percent	=	**Today's Value (Depreciated Value)**
Today's Value (Depreciated Value)	÷	Today's Value as a Percent	=	**Cost**
Today's Value (Depreciated Value)	÷	Cost	=	**Today's Value as a Percent**

■ **FOR EXAMPLE** Seven years ago you purchased a piece of real estate for $93,700, including the original cost of the land, which was $6,700. What is the total value of the land today using an appreciation rate of 8 percent per year?

8% Appreciation per Year × 7 Years = 56% Total Appreciation Rate

100% Cost + 56% Appreciation = 156% Today's Value

= **$10,452 Today's Value**

$6,700 Original Cost	156% or 1.56

×

$6,700 × 156% (1.56) = $10,452

$10,452 Today's Value is the answer.

■ **FOR EXAMPLE** The value of a house without the lot at the end of four years is $132,300. What was the original cost of the house if the yearly rate of depreciation was 2.5 percent?

2.5% depreciation per year × 4 years = 10% total depreciation rate

100% cost – 10% depreciation = 90% today's value

$$\frac{\$132,300 \text{ Today's Value} \div}{\begin{array}{c|c} = \$147,000 & 90\% \\ \text{Original Cost} & \text{or } 0.9 \end{array}}$$

$132,300 ÷ 90% (.90) = $147,000

$147,000 Original Cost is the answer.

■ HOW DO I DETERMINE VALUE FOR INCOME-PRODUCING PROPERTIES?

When appraising income-producing property, the value is determined by using the annual net operating income (NOI) and the current market rate of return or capitalization rate. Annual scheduled gross income is adjusted for vacancies and credit losses to arrive at the annual effective gross income. The annual operating expenses are deducted from the annual effective gross income to arrive at the annual NOI.

$$\begin{array}{ccccc} \text{Annual} & & \text{Vacancies} & & \textbf{Annual} \\ \text{Scheduled} & - & \text{and Credit} & = & \textbf{Effective} \\ \text{Gross Income} & & \text{Losses} & & \textbf{Gross Income} \end{array}$$

$$\begin{array}{ccccc} \text{Annual} & & \text{Annual} & & \\ \text{Effective Gross} & - & \text{Operating} & = & \textbf{Annual NOI} \\ \text{Income} & & \text{Expenses} & & \end{array}$$

$$\frac{\div \text{ Annual NOI} \div}{\begin{array}{c|c} \text{Value} & \text{Annual Rate of Return} \\ & \text{or Annual} \\ & \text{Capitalization Rate} \end{array}}$$

×

$$\text{Annual NOI} \div \frac{\text{Annual Rate}}{\text{of Return}} = \textbf{Value}$$

$$\text{Value} \times \frac{\text{Annual Rate}}{\text{of Return}} = \textbf{Annual NOI}$$

$$\text{Annual NOI} \div \text{Value} = \frac{\textbf{Annual Rate}}{\textbf{of Return}}$$

■ **FOR EXAMPLE** An office building produces $132,600 annual gross income. If the annual expenses are $30,600 and the appraiser estimates the value using an 8.5 percent rate of return, what is the estimated value?

$132,600 Annual Gross Income – $30,600 Annual Expenses = $102,000 Annual NOI

$102,000 Annual NOI ÷

= $1,200,000 Value		8.5% or 0.085

$102,000 ÷ 8.5% = $1,200,000

$1,200,000 Value is the answer.

The above formulas also can be used for investment problems. The total becomes *original cost* or *investment* instead of value.

■ **FOR EXAMPLE** You invest $335,000 in a property that should produce a 9 percent rate of return. What monthly NOI will you receive?

= $30,150 Annual NOI

$335,000 Investment		9% or 0.09
	×	

$335,000 × 9% (.09) = $30,150
$30,150 Annual NOI ÷ 12 Months = $2,512.50

$2,512.50 Monthly NOI is the answer.

■ HOW DO I SOLVE PROBLEMS INVOLVING PERCENTAGE LEASES?

When establishing the rent to be charged in a lease for retail space, the lease may be a **percentage lease** instead of a lease based on dollars per square foot. In the percentage lease, there is normally a base or minimum monthly rent plus a percentage of the gross sales in excess of an amount set in the lease. The percentage lease also can be set up as a percentage of the total gross sales or of the base/minimum rent, whichever is larger. We shall look at the minimum plus percentage lease only.

$$\text{Gross Sales} - \begin{array}{c}\text{Gross Sales Not} \\ \text{Subject to the} \\ \text{Percentage}\end{array} = \textbf{Gross Sales Subject} \atop \textbf{to the Percentage}$$

$$\frac{\div \text{ Percentage Rent } \div}{\begin{array}{c|c} \text{Gross Sales Subject} & \text{\% in the Lease} \\ \text{to the Percentage} & \\ & \times \end{array}}$$

Gross Sales Subject to the Percentage	×	% in the Lease	=	**Percentage Rent**
Percentage Rent	÷	% in the Lease	=	**Gross Sales Subject to the Percentage**
Percentage Rent	÷	Gross Sales Subject to the Percentage	=	**% in the Lease**
Percentage Rent	+	Base/ Minimum Rent	=	**Total Rent**

■ **FOR EXAMPLE** A lease calls for monthly minimum rent of $900 plus 3 percent of annual gross sales in excess of $270,000. What was the annual rent in a year when the annual gross sales were $350,600?

$900 Monthly Minimum Rent × 12 Months = $10,800 Annual Minimum Rent

$350,600 Annual Gross Sales – $270,000 Annual Gross Sales Not Subject to the Percentage = $80,600 Annual Gross Sales Subject to the Percentage

$$\frac{= \$2,418 \text{ Annual Percentage Rent}}{\begin{array}{c|c} \$80,600 \text{ Annual Gross} & 3\% \\ \text{Subject to the Percentage} & \text{or } 0.03 \\ & \times \end{array}}$$

$10,800 Annual Minimum Rent + $2,418 Annual Percentage Rent = $13,218

$13,218 Total Annual Rent is the answer.

SECTION 3

MEASUREMENT PROBLEMS

■ WHAT ARE LINEAR MEASUREMENTS?

Linear measurement is line measurement. When the terms

- *per foot,*
- *per linear foot,*
- *per running foot,* or
- *per front foot*

are used, you are being asked to determine the *total length* of the object whether measured in a straight line, crooked line, or curved line. The abbreviation for feet is '. Thus, 12 feet could be written as 12'. The abbreviation for inches is ". Thus, 12 inches could be written as 12".

■ WHAT DOES THE PHRASE "FRONT FOOT" REFER TO?

When the term *per front foot* is used, you are dealing with the number of units on the **frontage** of a lot. The frontage is normally the street frontage, but it could be the water frontage if the lot is on a river, lake, or ocean. If two dimensions are given for a tract of land, the first dimension given is the frontage if the dimensions are not labeled.

■ HOW DO I CONVERT ONE KIND OF LINEAR MEASUREMENT TO ANOTHER?

12 inches = 1 foot

Inches ÷ 12 = Feet (144 inches ÷ 12 = 12 feet)
Feet × 12 = Inches (12 feet × 12 = 144 inches)

36 inches = 1 yard

Inches ÷ 36 = Yards (144 inches ÷ 36 = 4 yards)
Yards × 36 = Inches (4 yards × 36 = 144 inches)

3 feet = 1 yard

Feet ÷ 3 = Yards (12 feet ÷ 3 = 4 yards)
Yards × 3 = Feet (4 yards × 3 = 12 feet)

5,280 feet = 1 mile

Feet ÷ 5,280 = Miles (10,560 feet ÷ 5,280 = 2 miles)
Miles × 5,280 = Feet (2 miles × 5,280 = 10,560 feet)

16½ feet = 1 rod

> Feet ÷ 16.5 = Rods (82.5 feet ÷ 16.5 = 5 rods)
> Rods × 16.5 = Feet (5 rods × 16.5 = 82.5 feet)

320 rods = 1 mile

> Rods ÷ 320 = Miles (640 rods ÷ 320 = 2 miles)
> Miles × 320 = Rods (2 miles × 320 = 640 rods)

■ **FOR EXAMPLE** A rectangular lot is 50 feet × 150 feet. The cost to fence this lot is priced per linear/running foot. How many linear/running feet will be used to calculate the price of the fence?

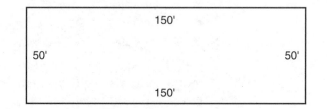

50 Feet + 150 Feet + 50 Feet + 150 Feet = 400 Linear/Running Feet

400 Linear/Running Feet is the answer.

■ **FOR EXAMPLE** A parcel of land that fronts on Interstate 90 in Elgin, Illinois, is for sale at $5,000 per front foot. What will it cost to purchase this parcel of land if the dimensions are 150' by 100'?

> 150 is the frontage because it is the first dimension given.
> 150 Front Feet × $5,000 = $750,000 Cost

$750,000 Cost is the answer.

■ HOW DO I SOLVE FOR AREA MEASUREMENT?

Area is the two-dimensional surface of an object. Area is quoted in *square units* or in *acres*. We will look at calculating the area of squares, rectangles, and triangles. Squares and rectangles are four-sided objects. All four sides of a square are the same. Opposite sides of a rectangle are the same. A triangle is a three-sided object. The three sides of a triangle can be the same dimension or three different dimensions.

When two dimensions are given, we assume it to be a rectangle unless told otherwise.

■ HOW DO I CONVERT ONE KIND OF AREA MEASUREMENT TO ANOTHER?

144 square inches = 1 square foot

> Square Inches ÷ 144 = Square Feet (14,400 square inches ÷ 144 = 100 square feet)
> Square Feet × 144 = Square Inches ÷ (100 square feet × 144 = 14,400 square inches)

1,296 square inches = 1 square yard

> Square Inches ÷ 1,296 = Square Yards (12,960 ÷ 1,296 = 10 square yards)
> Square Yards × 1,296 = Square Inches (10 square yards × 1,296 = 12,960 square yards)

9 square feet = 1 square yard

> Square Feet ÷ 9 = Square Yards (90 square feet ÷ 9 = 10 square yards)
> Square Yards × 9 = Square Feet (10 square yards × 9 = 90 square feet)

43,560 square feet = 1 acre

> Square Feet ÷ 43,560 = Acres (87,120 ÷ 43,560 = 2 acres)
> Acres × 43,560 = Square Feet (2 acres × 43,560 = 87,120 square feet)

640 acres = 1 section = 1 square mile

> Acres ÷ 640 = Sections (Square Miles) (1,280 acres ÷ 640 = 2 sections)
> Sections (Square Miles) × 640 = Acres (2 sections × 640 = 1,280 acres)

■ HOW DO I DETERMINE THE AREA OF A SQUARE OR RECTANGLE?

Length × Width = **Area of a Square or Rectangle**

■ **FOR EXAMPLE** How many square feet are in a room 15'6" × 30'9"?

Remember, we must use like dimensions, so the inches must be converted to feet.

6" ÷ 12 = 0.5' + 15' = 15.5' wide
9" ÷ 12 = 0.75' + 30' = 30.75' long
30.75' × 15.5' = 476.625 Square Feet

476.625 Square Feet is the answer.

■ **FOR EXAMPLE** If carpet costs $63 per square yard to install, what would it cost to carpet the room in the previous example?

476.625 Square Feet ÷ 9 = 52.958333 Square Yards × $63 per Square Yard = $3,336.375 or $3,336.38 rounded

$3,336.38 Carpet Cost is the answer.

■ **FOR EXAMPLE** How many acres are there in a parcel of land that measures 450' × 484'?

484' × 450' = 217,800 Square Feet ÷ 43,560 = 5 Acres

5 Acres of Land is the answer.

■ HOW DO I DETERMINE THE AREA OF A TRIANGLE?

½ Base × Height = Area of a Triangle

or

Base × Height ÷ 2 = Area of a Triangle

■ **FOR EXAMPLE** How many square feet are contained in a triangular parcel of land that is 400 feet on the base and 200 feet high?

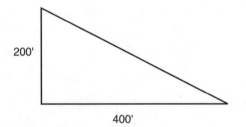

200'

400'

400' × 200' ÷ 2 = 40,000 Square Feet

40,000 Square Feet is the answer.

■ **FOR EXAMPLE** How many acres are in a three-sided tract of land that is 300' on the base and 400' high?

300' × 400' ÷ 2 = 60,000 Square Feet ÷ 43,560 = 1.377 Acres

1.377 Acres is the answer.

■ HOW DO I SOLVE FOR VOLUME?

Volume is the space inside a three-dimensional object. Volume is quoted in *cubic units*. We will look at calculating the volume of boxes and triangular prisms.

■ HOW DO I CONVERT FROM ONE KIND OF VOLUME MEASUREMENT TO ANOTHER?

1,728 cubic inches = 1 cubic foot

Cubic Inches ÷ 1,728 = Cubic Feet
(17,280 cubic inches ÷ 1,728 = 10 cubic feet)

Cubic Feet × 1,728 = Cubic Inches
(10 cubic feet × 1,728 = 17,280 cubic inches)

46,656 cubic inches = 1 cubic yard

> Cubic Inches ÷ 46,656 = Cubic Yards
> (93,312 cubic inches ÷ 46,656 = 2 cubic yards)
>
> Cubic Yards × 46,656 = Cubic Inches
> (2 cubic yards × 46,656 = 93,312 cubic inches)

27 cubic feet = 1 cubic yard

> Cubic Feet ÷ 27 = Cubic Yards (270 cubic feet ÷ 27 = 10 cubic yards)
> Cubic Yards × 27 = Cubic Feet (10 cubic yards × 27 = 270 cubic feet)

■ HOW DO I DETERMINE THE VOLUME OF A ROOM?

For purposes of determining volume, think of a room as if it were a box.

$$\text{Length} \times \text{Width} \times \text{Height} = \textbf{Volume of a Box}$$

■ **FOR EXAMPLE** A building is 500 feet long, 400 feet wide, and 25 feet high. How many cubic feet of space are in this building?

500' × 400' × 25' = 5,000,000 Cubic Feet

5,000,000 Cubic Feet is the answer.

■ **FOR EXAMPLE** How many cubic yards of concrete would it take to build a sidewalk measuring 120 feet long; 2 feet, 6 inches wide; and 3 inches thick?

6" ÷ 12' = .5' + 2' = 2.5' Wide
3" ÷ 12' = .25' Thick
120' × 2.5' × .25' = 75 Cubic Feet ÷ 27 = 2.778 Cubic Yards (rounded)

2.778 Cubic Yards is the answer.

■ HOW DO I DETERMINE THE VOLUME OF A TRIANGULAR PRISM?

The terms *A-frame*, *A-shaped*, or *gable roof* on an exam describe a triangular prism.

$$\tfrac{1}{2}\text{ Base} \times \text{Height} \times \text{Width} = \textbf{Volume of a Triangular Prism}$$

or

$$\text{Base} \times \text{Height} \times \text{Width} \div 2 = \textbf{Volume of a Triangular Prism}$$

■ **FOR EXAMPLE** An A-frame cabin in the mountains is 50 feet long and 30 feet wide. The cabin is 25 feet high from the base to the highest point. How many cubic feet of space does this A-frame cabin contain?

50' × 30' × 25' ÷ 2 = 18,750 Cubic Feet

18,750 Cubic Feet is the answer.

■ **FOR EXAMPLE** A building is 40 feet by 25 feet with a 10-foot-high ceiling. The building has a gable roof that is 8 feet high at the tallest point. How many cubic feet are in this structure, including the roof?

40' × 25' × 10' = 10,000 Cubic Feet in the Building
40' × 25' × 8' ÷ 2 = 4,000 Cubic Feet in the Gable Roof
10,000 Cubic Feet + 4,000 Cubic Feet = 14,000 Total Cubic Feet

14,000 Cubic Feet is the answer.

REAL ESTATE MATH PRACTICE PROBLEMS

1. The value of your house, not including the lot, is $91,000 today. What was the original cost if it has depreciated 5 percent per year for the past seven years?
   a. $67,407.41   c. $122,850.00
   b. $95,789.47   d. $140,000.00

2. What did the owners originally pay for their home if they sold it for $98,672, which gave them a 12 percent profit over their original cost?
   a. $86,830   c. $89,700
   b. $88,100   d. $110,510

3. What would you pay for a building producing $11,250 annual net income and showing a minimum rate of return of 9 percent?
   a. $125,000   c. $101,250
   b. $123,626   d. $122,625

4. An owner agrees to list his property on the condition that he will receive at least $47,300 after paying a 5 percent broker's commission and paying $1,150 in closing costs. At what price must it sell?
   a. $48,450   c. $50,875
   b. $50,815   d. $51,000

5. The Loving Gift Shop pays rent of $600 per month plus 2.5 percent of gross annual sales in excess of $50,000. What was the average monthly rent last year if gross annual sales were $75,000?
   a. $1,125.00   c. $600.00
   b. $756.25   d. $652.08

6. If your monthly rent is $525, what percent would this be of an annual income of $21,000?
   a. 25 percent   c. 33 percent
   b. 30 percent   d. 40 percent

7. Two brokers split the 6 percent commission on a $73,000 home. The selling salesperson, Joe, was paid 70 percent of his broker's share. The listing salesperson, Janice, was paid 30 percent of her broker's share. How much did Janice receive?
   a. $657   c. $1,533
   b. $4,380   d. $1,314

8. The buyer has agreed to pay $175,000 in sales price, 2.5 loan discount points, and a 1 percent origination fee. If the buyer receives a 90 percent loan-to-value ratio, how much will the buyer owe at closing for points and the origination fee?
   a. $1,575.00   c. $5,512.50
   b. $3,937.50   d. $6,125.00

9. Calculate eight months' interest on a $5,000 interest-only loan at 9.5 percent.
   a. $475.00   c. $237.50
   b. $316.67   d. $39.58

10. A 100-acre farm is divided into lots for homes. The streets require ⅛ of the whole farm, and there are 140 lots. How many square feet are in each lot?
    a. 43,560   c. 31,114
    b. 35,004   d. 27,225

11. What is the monthly net income on an investment of $115,000 if the rate of return is 12.5 percent?
    a. $1,150.00   c. $7,666.67
    b. $1,197.92   d. $14,375.00

12. A salesperson sells a property for $58,500. The contract he has with his broker is 40 percent of the full commission earned. The commission due the broker is 6 percent. What is the salesperson's share of the commission?
    a. $2,106   c. $3,510
    b. $1,404   d. $2,340

13. What is the interest rate on a $10,000 loan with semiannual interest of $450?

    a. 7%   c. 11%
    b. 9%   d. 13.5%

14. A warehouse is 80' wide and 120' long with ceilings 14' high. If 1,200 square feet of floor surface has been partitioned off, floor to ceiling, for an office, how many cubic feet of space will be left in the warehouse?

    a. 151,200   c. 133,200
    b. 134,400   d. 117,600

15. The lot you purchased five years ago for $15,000 has appreciated 3.5 percent per year. What is it worth today?

    a. $12,375   c. $17,250
    b. $15,525   d. $17,625

16. A lease calls for $1,000 per month minimum plus 2 percent of annual sales in excess of $100,000. What is the annual rent if the annual sales were $150,000?

    a. $12,000   c. $14,000
    b. $13,000   d. $15,000

17. There is a tract of land that is 1.25 acres. The lot is 150 feet deep. How much will the lot sell for at $65 per front foot?

    a. $9,750   c. $23,595
    b. $8,125   d. $8,725

18. Sue earns $20,000 per year and can qualify for a monthly PITI payment equal to 25 percent of her monthly salary. If the annual tax and insurance is $678.24, what is the loan amount she will qualify for if the monthly PI payment factor is $10.29 per $1,000 of loan amount?

    a. $66,000   c. $40,500
    b. $43,000   d. $35,000

19. You pay $65.53 monthly interest on a loan bearing 9.25 percent annual interest. What is the loan amount rounded to the nearest hundred dollars?

    a. $1,400   c. $6,300
    b. $2,800   d. $8,500

20. What percentage of profit would you make if you paid $10,500 for a lot, built a home on the lot that cost $93,000, and then sold the lot and house together for $134,550?

    a. 13 percent   c. 30 percent
    b. 23 percent   d. 45 percent

21. An income-producing property has $62,500 annual gross income and monthly expenses of $1,530. What is the appraised value if the appraiser uses a 10 percent capitalization rate?

    a. $441,400   c. $183,600
    b. $625,000   d. $609,700

22. Alfred pays $2,500 each for four parcels of land. He subdivides them into six parcels and sells each of the six parcels for $1,950. What was Alfred's percentage of profit?

    a. 14.5 percent   c. 52 percent
    b. 17 percent   d. 78 percent

23. A property sells for $96,000. If it has appreciated 4 percent per year straight line for the past five years, what did the owner pay for the property five years ago?

    a. $76,800   c. $92,300
    b. $80,000   d. $115,200

24. If you purchase a lot that is 125' ×150' for $6,468.75, what price did you pay per front foot?

    a. $23.52   c. $51.75
    b. $43.13   d. $64.69

25. Calculate the amount of commission earned by a broker on a property selling for $61,000 if 6 percent is paid on the first $50,000 and 3 percent on the remaining balance.

    a. $3,330   c. $3,600
    b. $3,830   d. $3,930

ANSWER KEY FOR REAL ESTATE MATH PRACTICE PROBLEMS

1. d $140,000.00 Original Cost

5% Depreciation per Year × 7 Years = 35% Total Depreciation
100% Original Cost − 35% Total Depreciation = 65% Today's Value

$$\frac{\$91,000 \text{ Today's Value} \div}{= \$140,000 \qquad\qquad | \qquad\qquad 65\%}$$

Original Cost   or 0.65

$91,000 ÷ 65% (.65) = **$140,000 Original Cost**

2. b $88,100 Original Cost

100% Original Cost + 12% Profit = 112% Sales Price

$$\frac{\$98,672 \text{ Sales Price} \div}{= \$88,100 \qquad\qquad | \qquad\qquad 112\%}$$

Original Cost   or 1.12

$98,672 ÷ 112% (1.12) = **$88,100 Original Cost**

3. a $125,000 Price

$$\frac{\$11,250 \text{ Annual Net Income} \div}{= \$125,000 \qquad\qquad | \qquad\qquad 9\%}$$

Price   or 0.09

$11,250 ÷ 9% (.09) = **$125,000 Price**

4. d $51,000 Sales Price

$47,300 Net to Seller + $1,150 Closing Costs =
$48,450 Seller's Dollars after Commission
100% Sales Price − 5% Commission = 95% Seller's Percent after
Commission

$$\frac{\$48,450 \text{ Seller's Dollars after Commission} \div}{= \$51,000 \qquad\qquad | \qquad\qquad 95\%}$$

Sales Price   or 0.95

$48,450 ÷ 95% (.95) = **$51,000 Sales Price**

5. d $652.08 Average Monthly Rent

$75,000 Gross Annual Sales − $50,000 =
$25,000 Gross Annual Sales Subject to 2.5%

= $625 Annual Percentage Rent		
$25,000		2.5%
Gross Annual Sales	×	or .025

$25,000 × 2.5% (.025) = $625

$625 Annual Percentage Rent ÷ 12 Months =
$52.08 Monthly Percentage Rent
$600 Monthly Minimum Rent + $52.08 Monthly Percentage Rent =
$652.08 Average Monthly Rent

6. b   30%

$525 Monthly Rent × 12 Months = $6,300 Annual Rent

÷ $6,300 Annual Rent		
$21,000 Annual Income		**= 0.3 or 30%**

$6,300 ÷ $21,000 = .30 or **30%**

7. a $657 Commission to Janice

= $4,380 Full Commission		
$73,000		6%
Sales Price	×	.06

$73,000 × 6% (.06) = $4,380
$4,380 Full Commission ÷ 2 Brokers =
$2,190 Broker's Share of the Commission

= $657 Janice's Commission		
$2,190 Broker's Share		30%
of the Commission	×	.3

$2,190 × 30% (.30) = **$657 Commission**

8. c $5,512.50 for Points and the Origination Fee

2.5 Points Loan Discount + 1 Point Origination Fee = 3.5 Points

= $157,500 Loan		
$175,000 Sales Price		90%
	×	or 0.9

$175,000 × 90% or (.90) = $157,500

= \$5,512.50 for Points and Origination Fees

$157,500 Loan		3.5%
	$\times$	or 0.035

$157,500 × 3.5% (.035) = **\$5,512.50 for Points and Origination Fees**

9. b   \$316.67 Interest

= \$475 Annual Interest

$5,000 Loan		9.5%
	$\times$	or 0.095

$5,000 × 9.5% (.095) = $475
$475 Annual Interest ÷ 12 Months × 8 Months = **\$316.67 Interest**

10. d   27,225 Square Feet per Lot

⅛ = 1 ÷ 8 = 0.125 for Streets
100 Acres × 0.125 = 12.5 Acres for Streets
100 Acres − 12.5 Acres for Streets = 87.5 Acres for Lots × 43,560 =
3,811,500 Square Feet ÷ 140 Lots = **27,225 Square Feet per Lot**

11. b   \$1,197.92 Monthly Net Operating Income

= \$14,375 Annual Net Operating Income

$115,000 Investment		12.5%
	$\times$	or 0.125

$115,000 × 12.5% (.125) = $14,375
$14,375 Annual Net Operating Income ÷ 12 Months =
\$1,197.92 Monthly Net Operating Income

12. b   \$1,404 Salesperson's Commission

= \$3,510 Full Commission

$58,500 Sales Price		6%
	$\times$	or 0.06

$58,500 × 6% (.06) = $3,510

= \$1,404 Salesperson's Commission

$3,510 Full Commission		40%
	$\times$	or 0.4

$3,510 × 40% (.40) = **\$1,404 Salesperson's Commission**

13. b   9% Annual Interest Rate

$450 × 2 = $900 Annual Interest

÷ \$900 Annual Interest

$10,000 Loan		= 0.9 or 9%

$900 ÷ $10,000 = **0.9 or 9% Interest Rate**

14. d   117,600 Cubic Feet

120' × 80' = 9,600 Square Feet in Building − 1,200 Square Feet for Office
= 8,400 Square Feet Left in Warehouse × 14' Ceiling =
117,600 Cubic Feet Left in Warehouse

15. d $17,625 Today's Value

3.5% Appreciation per Year × 5 Years = 17.5% Total Appreciation
100% Cost + 17.5% Total Appreciation = 117.5% Today's Value

= $17,625 Today's Value		
$15,000 Original Cost		117.5%
	×	or 1.175

$15,000 × 117.5% (1.175) = **$17,625 Today's Value**

16. b $13,000 Annual Rent

$1,000 Monthly Minimum Rent × 12 Months =
$12,000 Annual Minimum Rent
$150,000 Annual Sales − $100,000 = $50,000 Annual Sales Subject to 2%

= $1,000 Annual Percentage Rent		
$50,000 Annual Sales		2%
Subject to 2%	×	or 0.02

$50,000 × 2% (.02) = $1,000

$12,000 Annual Minimum Rent + $1,000 Annual Percentage Rent =
$13,000 Annual Rent

17. c $23,595 Sales Price

1.25 Acres × 43,560 = 54,450 Square Feet ÷ 150' Deep = 363' Frontage ×
$65 per Front Foot = **$23,595 Sales Price**

18. d $35,000 Loan

$20,000 Annual Salary ÷ 12 Months = $1,666.67 Monthly Salary

= $416.67 Monthly PITI Payment		
$1,666.67 Monthly Salary		25%
	×	or 0.25

$1,666.67 × 25% = $416.67

$678.24 Annual Tax and Insurance ÷ 12 Months =
$56.52 Monthly Tax and Insurance
$416.67 Monthly PITI Payment − $56.52 Monthly TI =
$360.15 Monthly PI Payment
$360.15 Monthly PI Payment ÷ $10.29 × $1,000 = **$35,000 Loan**

19. d $8,500 Loan

$65.53 Monthly Interest × 12 Months = $786.36 Annual Interest

$$\frac{\$786.36 \text{ Annual Interest} \div}{}$$

| = $8,501.19 | 9.25% |
| or **$8,500 Loan** | or 0.0925 |

$786.36 ÷ 9.25% (.0925) = **$8501.19 Loan**

20. c   30%

$10,500 Cost of Lot + $93,000 Cost of Home = $103,500 Total Cost
$134,550 Sales Price − $103,500 Total Cost = $31,050 Profit

$$\frac{\div \ \$31,050 \text{ Profit}}{}$$

| $103,500 Total Cost | = **0.3 or 30%** |

$31,050 ÷ $103,500 = **0.3 or 30%**

21. a $441,400 Value

$1,530 Monthly Expenses × 12 Months = $18,360 Annual Expenses
$62,500 Annual Gross Income − $18,360 Annual Expenses =
$44,140 Annual Net Operating Income

$$\frac{\$44,140 \text{ Annual Net Operating Income} \div}{}$$

| = **$441,400 Value** | 10% |
| | or 0.1 |

$44,140 ÷ 10% (.10) = **$441,400 Value**

22. b   17% Profit

$2,500 Cost × 4 Parcels = $10,000 Total Cost
$1,950 Sales Price × 6 Parcels = $11,700 Sales Price
$11,700 Sales Price − $10,000 Cost = $1,700 Profit

$$\frac{\div \ \$1,700 \text{ Profit}}{}$$

| $10,000 Cost | = **0.17 or 17% Profit** |

$1,700 ÷ $10,000 Cost = 0.17 or **17% Profit**

23. b $80,000 Original Cost

4% Annual Appreciation × 5 Years = 20% Total Appreciation
100% Cost + 20% Total Appreciation = 120% Today's Value

$$\frac{\$96,000 \text{ Today's Value} \div}{}$$

| = **$80,000 Original Cost** | 120% |
| | 1.2 |

$96,000 ÷ 120% (1.20) = **$80,000 Original Cost**

24. c $51.75 per Front Foot

$6,468.75 Price ÷ 125 Front Feet = **$51.75 per Front Foot**

25. a $3,330 Total Commission

= $3,000 Commission	
$50,000 Sales Price	6%
×	or 0.06

$50,000 × 6% (.06) = $3,000

$61,000 Total Sales Price – $50,000 Sales Price at 6% =
$11,000 Sales Price at 3%

= $330 Commission	
$11,000 Sales Price	3%
×	or 0.03

$11,000 × 3% (.03) = $330
$3,000 Commission + $330 Commission = **$3,330 Total Commission**

GLOSSARY

abstract of title The condensed history of a title to a particular parcel of real estate, consisting of a summary of the original grant and all subsequent conveyances and encumbrances affecting the property and a certification by the abstractor that the history is complete and accurate.

acceleration clause The clause in a mortgage or trust deed that can be enforced to make the entire debt due immediately if the mortgagor defaults on an installment payment or other covenant.

accession Acquiring title to additions or improvements to real property resulting from the annexation of fixtures or the accretion of alluvial deposits along the banks of streams.

accretion The increase or addition of land by the deposit of sand or soil washed up naturally from a river, lake, or sea.

accrued interest The amount of interest that is due for the period of time since interest was last paid.

accrued items On a closing statement, expense items that are incurred but not yet payable, such as interest on a mortgage loan or taxes on real property.

acknowledgment A formal declaration made before a duly authorized officer, usually a notary public, by a person who has signed a document.

acre A measure of land equal to 43,560 square feet, 4,840 square yards, 4,047 square meters, 160 square rods, or 0.4047 hectares.

actual eviction The result of legal action, originated by a lessor, whereby a defaulted tenant is physically ousted from the rented property pursuant to a court order. *See also* eviction.

actual notice Express information or fact; that which is known; direct knowledge.

addenda Additional material attached to and made part of a document, as in a supplement that is added to an agreement of sale.

adjustable-rate mortgage (ARM) A loan characterized by a fluctuating interest rate, usually one tied to a bank or savings and loan association cost-of-funds index.

adjusted basis *See* basis.

ad valorem tax A tax levied according to value; generally used to refer to real estate tax. Also called the *general tax.*

adverse possession The actual, visible, hostile, notorious, exclusive, and continuous possession of another's land under a claim of title. Possession for a statutory period may be a means of acquiring title.

agency The relationship between a principal and an agent, wherein the agent is authorized to represent the principal in certain transactions.

agency coupled with an interest An agency relationship in which the agent is given an estate or interest in the subject of the agency (the property).

agent One who acts or has the power to act for another. A fiduciary relationship is created under the *law of agency* when a principal authorizes a licensed real estate broker to be his or her agent.

agreement of sale An offer to purchase that has been accepted by the seller and has become a binding contract.

air lot A designated airspace over a piece of land. An air lot, like surface property, may be transferred.

air rights The right to use the open space above a property, generally allowing the surface to be used for another purpose.

alienation The act of transferring property to another. Alienation may be voluntary, such as by gift or sale, or involuntary, such as through eminent domain or adverse possession.

alienation clause The clause in a mortgage that states that the balance of the secured debt becomes immediately due and payable at the mortgagee's option if the mortgagor sells the property. In effect, this clause prevents the mortgagor from assigning the debt without the mortgagee's approval.

allodial system A system of land ownership in which land is held free and clear of any rent or service due to the government; commonly contrasted to the feudal system. Land is held under the allodial system in the United States.

amenities Features, tangible and intangible, that enhance the value or desirability of real estate.

Americans with Disabilities Act (ADA) A federal law passed in 1990 to open doors, both figuratively and literally, for people with disabilities to become part of the economic and social mainstream of society. The law mandates equal access to employment and goods and services. Title I prohibits discriminatory employment practices. Title III requires anyone providing goods and services to the public to make them accessible by removing architectural and communications barriers and, if that is not readily achievable, to provide reasonable accommodations to people with disabilities.

amortized loan A loan in which the principal as well as the interest is payable in monthly or other periodic installments over the term of the loan.

annual percentage rate (APR)   The relationship of the total finance charges associated with a loan. This must be disclosed to borrowers by lenders under the Truth-in-Lending Act.

anticipation   The appraisal principle that holds that value can increase or decrease based on the expectation of some future benefit or detriment produced by the property.

antitrust laws   Laws designed to preserve the free enterprise of the open marketplace by making illegal certain private conspiracies and combinations formed to minimize competition. Violations of antitrust laws in the real estate business generally involve either *price-fixing* (brokers conspiring to set fixed compensation rates) or *allocation of customers or markets* (brokers agreeing to limit their areas of trade or dealing to certain areas or properties).

appraisal   An estimate of the quantity, quality, or value of something. The process through which conclusions of property value are obtained; also refers to the report that sets forth the process of estimation and conclusion of value.

appraiser   A person who prepares a professional opinion of estimated value. By state licensing law, only persons who are properly qualified and certified are permitted to engage in appraisal activities of real estate and prepare appraisal reports.

appreciation   An increase in the worth or value of a property due to economic or related causes, which may prove to be either temporary or permanent; opposite of depreciation.

appurtenance   A right, privilege, or improvement belonging to, and passing with, the land.

appurtenant easement   An easement that is annexed to the ownership of one parcel and allows the owner the use of the neighbor's land.

APR   *See* annual percentage rate.

ARM   *See* adjustable-rate mortgage.

asbestos   A mineral once used in insulation and other materials that can cause respiratory diseases.

assemblage   The combining of two or more adjoining lots into one larger tract to increase their total value.

assessment   The imposition of a tax, charge, or levy, usually according to established rates.

assignment   The transfer in writing of interest in a bond, mortgage, lease, or other instrument.

associate broker   A person licensed as a real estate broker who chooses to work under the supervision of another broker.

assumption of mortgage   Acquiring title to property on which there is an existing mortgage and agreeing to be personally liable for the terms and conditions of the mortgage, including payments.

attachment   The act of taking a person's property into legal custody by writ or other judicial order to hold it available for application to that person's debt to a creditor.

attorney's opinion of title   An abstract of title that an attorney has examined and has certified to be, in his or her opinion, an accurate statement of the facts concerning the property ownership.

automatic renewal   A clause in a listing agreement stating that the agreement will continue automatically for a certain period of time after its expiration date. In many states, use of this clause is discouraged; in Pennsylvania it is prohibited.

automated underwriting   Computer systems that permit lenders to expedite the loan approval process and reduce lending costs.

avulsion   The sudden tearing away of land, as by earthquake, flood, volcanic action, or the sudden change in the course of a stream.

balance   The appraisal principle that states that the greatest value in a property will occur when the type and size of the improvements are proportional to each other as well as the land.

balloon payment   A final payment of a mortgage loan that is considerably larger than the required periodic payments because the loan amount was not fully amortized.

bargain and sale deed   A deed that carries with it no warranties against liens or other encumbrances but that does imply that the grantor has the right to convey title. The grantor may add warranties to the deed at his or her discretion.

base line   The main imaginary line running east and west and crossing a principal meridian at a definite point, used by surveyors for reference in locating and describing land under the rectangular (government) survey system of legal description.

basis   The financial interest that the Internal Revenue Service attributes to an owner of an investment property for the purpose of determining annual depreciation and gain or loss on the sale of the asset. If a property was acquired by purchase, the owner's basis is the cost of the property plus the value of any capital expenditures for improvements to the property, minus any depreciation allowable or actually taken. This new basis is called the *adjusted basis*.

bench mark   A permanent reference mark or point established for use by surveyors in measuring differences in elevation.

beneficiary (1) The person for whom a trust operates or in whose behalf the income from a trust estate is drawn. (2) A lender in a deed of trust loan transaction.

bilateral contract *See* contract.

binder An agreement that may accompany an earnest money deposit for the purchase of real property as evidence of the purchaser's good faith and intent to complete the transaction.

blanket loan A mortgage covering more than one parcel of real estate, providing for each parcel's partial release from the mortgage lien upon repayment of a definite portion of the debt.

blockbusting The illegal practice of attempting, for profit, to induce homeowners to sell their properties by making representations about the entry or prospective entry of persons in the protected classes into the neighborhood. Also known as *panic selling*.

blue-sky laws Common name for those state and federal laws that regulate the registration and sale of investment securities.

boot Money or property given to make up any difference in value or equity between two properties in an *exchange*.

branch office A secondary place of business apart from the broker's principal or main office from which real estate business is conducted. If the broker delegates the responsibility for managing a branch office, the manager must be an associate broker. The broker remains ultimately responsible for the conduct of activities in the branch office.

breach of contract Violation of any terms or conditions in a contract without legal excuse; for example, failure to make a payment when it is due.

broker One who buys and sells for another for a commission. In real estate, a broker must be properly licensed to perform certain activities specified in the real estate license laws and collect compensation.

brokerage The bringing together of parties interested in making a real estate transaction.

broker/appraiser A real estate broker who is licensed by the Certified Appraisers Act in Pennsylvania to perform appraisals on properties for nonfederally related transactions under $250,000.

broker of record The individual broker responsible for the real estate transactions and activities of licensees in a partnership or corporation.

buffer zone A strip of land, usually designated as a park or for a similar use, separating land dedicated to one use from land dedicated to another use (e.g., residential from commercial).

builder-owner salesperson An individual who is a full-time employee of the owner or builder of single-family or multifamily residences who is licensed to perform certain acts on behalf of the builder-owner.

building code An ordinance that specifies minimum standards of construction for buildings to protect public safety and health.

building permit Written governmental permission for the construction, alteration, or demolition of an improvement, showing compliance with building codes and zoning ordinances.

bulk transfer *See* Uniform Commercial Code.

bundle of legal rights The concept of land ownership that includes *ownership of all legal rights to the land*—for example, possession, control within the law, and enjoyment.

business name The name in which the broker's license is issued. Any time the name of the business appears, it must be represented exactly as it appears on the broker's license.

buydown A financing technique used to reduce the monthly payments for the first few years of a loan. Funds in the form of discount points are given to the lender by the builder or seller to buy down or lower the effective interest rate paid by the buyer, thus reducing the monthly payments for a set time.

buyer agent A licensee who has entered into an agency relationship with a consumer buyer of real estate, as defined in Pennsylvania license law. This relationship is normally established by a buyer agency agreement. *See* buyer agency representation.

buyer agency representation (agency) A principal/agent relationship in which the broker is the agent for the buyer, with fiduciary responsibilities to the buyer. The broker represents the buyer under the law of agency.

campground membership An interest, other than in fee simple or by lease, that gives the purchaser the right to use a unit of real property for the purpose of locating a recreational vehicle, trailer, tent, camper, or other similar device on a periodic basis pursuant to a membership contract.

campground membership salesperson A licensee who, either as an employee or independent contractor, sells campground memberships under the supervision of a broker.

capital gain Profit earned from the sale of an asset.

capitalization A mathematical process for estimating the value of a property using a proper rate of return on the investment and the annual net income expected to be produced by the property. The formula is expressed as Income ÷ Rate = Value.

capitalization rate The rate of return a property will produce on the owner's investment.

carbon monoxide (CO)   A colorless, odorless gas that occurs as a natural by-product of combustion that in high concentrations can cause serious health problems and even death. Malfunctioning or improperly ventilated fuel-burning equipment (furnaces, stoves, and fireplaces) are often the culprits.

cash flow   The net spendable income from an investment determined by deducting all operating and fixed expenses from the gross income. When expenses exceed income, a *negative cash flow* results.

caveat emptor   A Latin phrase meaning "Let the buyer beware."

cemetery associate broker   A licensed cemetery broker employed by another cemetery broker or broker.

cemetery broker   An individual or entity licensed to engage exclusively in the sale of cemetery lots, plots, and mausoleum spaces or openings.

cemetery salesperson   A licensee employed by a broker or cemetery broker to sell cemetery lots exclusively.

certificate of reasonable value (CRV)   A form indicating the appraised value of a property being financed with a VA loan.

certificate of sale   The document generally given to the purchaser at a tax foreclosure sale. A certificate of sale does not convey title; generally, it is an instrument certifying that the holder received title to the property after the redemption period had passed and that the holder paid the property taxes for that interim period.

certificate of title   A statement of opinion on the status of the title to a parcel of real property based on an examination of specified public records.

certified general real estate appraiser   An individual who is certified under the state Certified Appraisers Act to perform appraisals of any type or value of property for federally related real estate transactions.

certified residential real estate appraiser   An individual who is certified under the state Certified Appraisers Act to perform residential (one- to four-unit dwellings) appraisals for federally related real estate transactions.

chain of title   The succession of conveyances, from some accepted starting point, whereby the present holder of real property derives title.

change   The appraisal principle that holds that no physical or economic condition remains constant.

chattel   *See* personal property.

Civil Rights Act of 1866   An act that prohibits racial discrimination in the sale and rental of housing.

client   The person who is the principal who hires the agent and delegates to the agent the responsibility of representing the principal's interests. In a real estate transaction, the client may be the seller/property owner or buyer/tenant who has an agency relationship with the broker.

CLO   *See* computerized loan origination system.

closing statement   A detailed cash accounting of a real estate transaction showing all cash received, all charges and credits made and all cash paid out in the transaction.

cloud on title   Any document, claim, unreleased lien, or encumbrance that may impair the title to real property or make the title doubtful; usually revealed by a title search and removed by either a quitclaim deed or suit to quiet title.

CMA   *See* comparative market analysis.

CO   *See* carbon monoxide.

code of ethics   A written system of standards for ethical conduct.

codicil   A supplement or an addition to a will, executed with the same formalities as a will, which normally does not revoke the entire will.

coinsurance clause   A clause in insurance policies covering real property that requires the policyholder to maintain fire insurance coverage generally equal to at least 80 percent of the property's actual replacement cost.

commingling   The illegal act by a real estate broker of placing client or customer funds with personal funds. By law brokers are required to maintain a separate *escrow account* for other parties' funds held temporarily by the broker.

commission   Payment to a broker for services rendered, such as in the sale or purchase of real property; usually a percentage of the selling price of the property.

common elements   Parts of a property that are necessary or convenient to the existence, maintenance, and safety of a condominium or are normally in common use by all of the condominium residents. Each condominium owner has an undivided ownership interest in the common elements.

common law   The body of law based on custom, usage, and court decisions.

community property   A system of property ownership based on the theory that each spouse has an equal interest in the property acquired by the efforts of either spouse during marriage. A holdover of Spanish law, found predominantly in western states, the system was unknown under English common law.

Community Reinvestment Act (CRA)   A federal law established in 1977 that prescribes certain activities for financial institutions to help meet the needs in their communities for low- and moderate-income housing.

comparables   Properties used in an appraisal report that are substantially equivalent to the subject property.

comparative market analysis (CMA)   A written analysis, opinion, or conclusion by a contracted buyer's agent, transaction licensee, or an actual or potential seller's agent relating to the probable price of a specified piece of real estate. A CMA is a comparison of the prices of recently sold homes that are similar to a listing seller's home in terms of location, style, and amenities. Also sometimes called a *competitive market analysis*, it is not an appraisal.

competition   The appraisal principle that states that excess profits generate competition.

Comprehensive Environmental Response, Compensation and Liability Act (CERCLA)   A law administered by the Environmental Protection Agency that established a process for identifying waste sites, forcing liable parties to clean up toxic sites, bringing legal action against responsible parties, and funding the abatement of toxic sites. *See* Superfund.

comprehensive plan   *See* master plan.

computerized loan origination (CLO)   An electronic network system for handling loan applications through remote computer terminals linked to various lenders' computers.

condemnation   A judicial or administrative proceeding to exercise the power of eminent domain, through which a government agency takes private property for public use and compensates the owner. *See* eminent domain.

conditional-use permit   Written governmental permission allowing a use inconsistent with zoning but necessary for the common good, such as locating an emergency medical facility in a predominantly residential area.

condominium   The absolute ownership of a unit in a multiunit building based on a legal description of the airspace the unit actually occupies, plus an undivided interest in the ownership of the common elements, which are owned jointly with the other condominium unit owners.

confession of judgment clause   Permits judgment to be entered against a debtor without the creditor's having to institute legal proceedings.

conformity   The appraisal principle that holds that the greater the similarity among properties in an area, the better they will hold their value.

consideration   (1) That received by the grantor in exchange for his or her deed. (2) Something of value that induces a person to enter into a contract.

construction loan   *See* interim financing.

constructive eviction   Actions of a landlord that so materially disturb or impair a tenant's enjoyment of the leased premises that the tenant is effectively forced to move out and terminate the lease without liability for any further rent.

constructive notice   Notice given to the world by recorded documents. All people are charged with knowledge of such documents and their contents, whether or not they have actually examined them. Possession of property is also considered constructive notice that the person in possession has an interest in the property.

consumer   A person who is the recipient of any real estate service, as defined by Pennsylvania's licensing law. This person may receive client or customer services, depending on the nature of the relationship established with the real estate broker.

Consumer Notice   A specific form adopted by the Real Estate Commission in Pennsylvania to disclose information about permitted business relationships and specific agency procedures in real estate transactions. This notice must be presented at an initial interview to any consumer of real estate services.

contingency   Provisions in a contract that require a certain act to be done or a certain event to occur before the contract becomes binding.

contract   A legally enforceable promise or set of promises that must be performed and for which, if a breach of the promise occurs, the law provides a remedy. A contract may be either *unilateral*, by which only one party is bound to act, or *bilateral*, by which all parties to the instrument are legally bound to act as prescribed.

contract for deed   *See* installment contract.

contribution   The appraisal principle that states that the value of any component of a property is what it gives to the value of the whole or what its absence detracts from that value.

controlled business arrangement   The bundling of related services among service providers to offer consumers "one stop shop" convenience. The Real Estate Settlement Procedures Act (RESPA) requires certain disclosures to consumers about these arrangements and prohibits fees being exchanged among affiliated companies simply for referring business to one another.

conventional loan   A loan that is not insured or guaranteed by a government or private source.

conveyance   A term used to refer to any document that transfers title to real property. The term is also used in describing the act of transferring.

cooperating broker   Normally referred to as the selling broker, who may be *either* a subagent acting on behalf of a seller or a buyer's agent who cooperates with the listing broker, to effect the sale of a property.

cooperative   A residential multiunit building whose title is held by a trust or corporation that is owned by and operated for the benefit of persons living within the building, who are the beneficial owners of the trust or stockholders of the corporation, each possessing a proprietary lease.

co-ownership Title ownership held by two or more persons.

corporation An entity or organization, created by operation of law, whose rights of doing business are essentially the same as those of an individual. The entity has continuous existence until it is dissolved according to legal procedures.

cost approach The process of estimating the value of a property by adding to the estimated land value the appraiser's estimate of the reproduction or replacement cost of the building, less depreciation.

cost recovery An Internal Revenue Service term for *depreciation.*

counteroffer A new offer made as a reply to an offer received. It has the effect of rejecting the original offer, which cannot be accepted thereafter unless revived by the offeror.

covenant A written agreement between two or more parties in which a party or parties pledge to perform or not perform specified acts with regard to property; usually found in such real estate documents as deeds, mortgages, leases, and contracts for deed.

covenant of quiet enjoyment The covenant implied by law by which a landlord guarantees that a tenant may take possession of leased premises and that the landlord will not interfere in the tenant's possession or use of the property.

CRA *See* Community Reinvestment Act.

credit On a closing statement, an amount entered in a person's favor—an amount the party has paid or an amount for which the party must be reimbursed.

CRV *See* certificate of reasonable value.

curtesy A life estate, usually a fractional interest, given by some states to the surviving husband in real estate owned by his deceased wife. Most states have abolished curtesy.

customer A person who is a consumer of real estate services, who is not a client of the real estate licensee. A customer receives customer-level services rather than client-level services, which means the customer is *not* being represented by the licensee as the principal in an agency relationship.

datum A horizontal plane from which heights and depths are measured.

debit On a closing statement, an amount charged, that is, an amount that the debited party must pay.

decedent A person who has died.

dedication The voluntary transfer of private property by its owner to the public for some public use, such as for streets or schools.

deed A written instrument that, when executed and delivered, conveys title to or an interest in real estate.

deed in lieu of foreclosure A deed given by the mortgagor to the mortgagee when the mortgagor is in default under the terms of the mortgage. This is a way for the mortgagor to avoid foreclosure.

deed in trust An instrument that grants a trustee full power to sell, mortgage, and subdivide a parcel of real estate. The beneficiary controls the trustee's use of these powers under the provisions of the trust agreement.

deed of trust *See* trust deed.

deed restriction A clause in a deed limiting the future use of the property. Deed restrictions may impose a vast variety of limitations and conditions—for example, they may limit the density of buildings, dictate the types of structures that can be erected, or prevent buildings from being used for specific purposes or even from being used at all.

default The nonperformance of a duty, whether arising under a contract or otherwise; failure to meet an obligation when due.

defeasance clause A clause used in leases and mortgages that cancels a specified right upon the occurrence of a certain condition, such as cancellation of a mortgage upon repayment of the mortgage loan.

defeasible fee estate An estate in which the holder has a fee simple title that may be divested upon the occurrence or nonoccurrence of a specified event. There are two categories of defeasible fee estates: fee simple on condition precedent (fee simple determinable) and fee simple on condition subsequent.

deficiency judgment A personal judgment levied against the borrower when a foreclosure sale does not produce sufficient funds to pay the mortgage debt in full.

demand The amount of goods people are willing and able to buy at a given price; often coupled with supply.

density zoning Zoning ordinances that restrict the average maximum number of houses per acre that may be built within a particular area, generally a subdivision.

depreciation (1) In appraisal, a loss of value in property due to any cause, including *physical deterioration, functional obsolescence,* and *external obsolescence.* (2) In real estate investment, an expense deduction for tax purposes taken over the period of ownership of income property.

descent Acquisition of an estate by inheritance in which an heir succeeds to the property by operation of law.

designated agent One or more licensees designated by the employing broker to act exclusively as agent(s) on behalf of the principal to the exclusion of all other licensees within the broker's employ.

developer One who attempts to put land to its most profitable use through the construction of improvements.

devise A gift of real property by will. The donor is the devisor, and the recipient is the devisee.

discount point A unit of measurement used for various loan charges; one point equals 1 percent of the amount of the loan.

disparate impact The effect of an action that results in people in the protected classes being treated differently than others.

doctrine of prior appropriation *See* prior appropriation.

dominant tenement A property that includes in its ownership the appurtenant right to use an easement over another person's property for a specific purpose.

dower The legal right or interest, recognized in some states, that a wife acquires in the property her husband held or acquired during their marriage. During the husband's lifetime, the right is only a possibility of an interest; upon his death, it can become an interest in land.

dual agency Representing both parties to a transaction. This is unethical unless both parties agree to it, and it is illegal in many states.

dual agent A licensee who acts as an agent for the buyer and seller or lessee and landlord in the same transaction. Because of the potential for conflicts arising from the licensee attempting to serve two masters, the dual agent can only lawfully act in this capacity according to the provisions of the licensing law.

due-on-sale clause A provision in the mortgage that states that the entire balance of the note is immediately due and payable if the mortgagor transfers (sells) the property.

duress Unlawful constraint or action exercised upon a person whereby the person is forced to perform an act against his or her will. A contract entered into under duress is voidable.

earnest money Money deposited by a buyer under the terms of a contract, to be forfeited if the buyer defaults but applied to the purchase price if the sale is closed. Also known as *hand money*.

easement A right to use the land of another for a specific purpose, such as for a right-of-way or utilities; an incorporeal interest in land.

easement by condemnation An easement created by the government or government agency that has exercised its right under eminent domain.

easement by necessity An easement allowed by law as necessary for the full enjoyment of a parcel of real estate; for example, a right of ingress and egress over a grantor's land.

easement by prescription An easement acquired by continuous, open, and hostile use of the property for the period of time prescribed by state law.

easement in gross An easement that is not created for the benefit of any *land* owned by the owner of the easement but that attaches *personally to the easement owner*. For example, a right granted by Eleanor Franks to Joe Fish to use a portion of her property for the rest of his life would be an easement in gross.

ECOA *See* Equal Credit Opportunity Act.

economic life The number of years during which an improvement will add value to the land.

electromagnetic fields (EMFs) The movement of electrical currents, especially noticeable around high-voltage lines, secondary transmission lines, and transformers, that some people assert are health hazards.

emblements Growing crops, such as grapes and corn, which are produced annually through labor and industry; also called *fructus industriales*.

eminent domain The right of a government or municipal quasi-public body to acquire property for public use through the legal process called *condemnation*.

employee Someone who works as a direct employee of an employer and has employee status. The employer is obligated to withhold income taxes and Social Security taxes from the compensation of employees. *See also* independent contractor.

employment contract A document evidencing formal employment between employer and employee or between principal and agent. In the real estate business, this may take on the form of a listing agreement, a buyer agency agreement, or management agreement.

enabling acts State legislation that confers zoning powers on municipal governments.

encapsulation A method of controlling environmental contamination by sealing off a dangerous substance.

encroachment A building or some portion of it—a wall or fence, for instance—that extends beyond the land of the owner and illegally intrudes on some land of an adjoining owner or a street or alley.

encumbrance Anything—such as a mortgage, tax, or judgment lien, an easement, a restriction on the use of the land, or an outstanding dower right—that may diminish the value of a property.

Equal Credit Opportunity Act (ECOA) The federal law that prohibits discrimination in the extension of credit because of race, color, religion, national origin, sex, age, or marital status.

equalization The raising or lowering of assessed values for tax purposes in a particular county or taxing district to make them equal to assessments in other counties or districts.

equalization factor A factor (number) by which the assessed value of a property is multiplied to arrive at a value for the property that is in line with statewide tax assessments. The *ad valorem tax* would be based on this adjusted value.

equitable lien *See* statutory lien.

equitable right of redemption The right of a defaulted property owner to recover the property prior to its sale by paying the appropriate fees and charges.

equitable title The interest held by a vendee under an installment contract or agreement of sale; the equitable right to obtain absolute ownership to property when legal title is held in another's name.

equity The interest or value that an owner has in property over and above any indebtedness.

erosion The gradual wearing away of land by water, wind, and general weather conditions; the diminishing of property caused by the elements.

escheat The reversion of property to the state or county, as provided by state law, in cases where a decedent dies intestate without heirs capable of inheriting, or when the property is abandoned.

escrow The closing of a transaction through a third party called an *escrow agent*, or *escrowee*, who receives certain funds and documents to be delivered upon the performance of certain conditions outlined in the escrow instructions.

escrow account The trust account established by a broker under the provisions of the license law for the purpose of holding funds on behalf of the broker's principal or some other person until the consummation or termination of a transaction.

estate (tenancy) at sufferance The tenancy of a lessee who lawfully comes into possession of a landlord's real estate but who continues to occupy the premises improperly after his or her lease rights have expired.

estate (tenancy) at will An estate that gives the lessee the right to possession until the estate is terminated by either party; the term of this estate is indefinite.

estate (tenancy) for years An interest for a specified time in property leased for a specified consideration.

estate (tenancy) from period to period An interest in leased property that continues from period to period—week to week, month to month, or year to year.

estate in land The degree, quantity, nature, and extent of interest that a person has in real property.

estate taxes Federal taxes on a decedent's real and personal property.

estoppel Method of creating an agency relationship in which someone states incorrectly that another person is his or her agent, and a third person relies on that representation.

estoppel certificate A document in which a borrower certifies the amount owed on a mortgage loan and the rate of interest.

ethics The system of moral principles and rules that becomes the standards for professional conduct.

eviction A legal process to oust a person from possession of real estate.

evidence of title Proof of ownership of property; commonly a certificate of title, or title insurance.

exchange A transaction in which all or part of the consideration is the transfer of *like-kind* property (such as real estate for real estate).

exclusive-agency listing A listing contract under which the owner appoints a real estate broker as his or her exclusive agent for a designated period of time to sell the property, on the owner's stated terms, for a commission. The owner reserves the right to sell without paying anyone a commission if he or she sells to a prospect that has not been introduced or claimed by the broker.

exclusive-right-to-sell listing A listing contract under which the owner appoints a real estate broker as his or her exclusive agent for a designated period of time, to sell the property on the owner's stated terms, and agrees to pay the broker a commission when the property is sold, whether by the broker, the owner, or another broker.

executed contract A contract in which all parties have fulfilled their promises and thus performed the contract.

execution The signing and delivery of an instrument. Also, a legal order directing an official to enforce a judgment against the property of a debtor.

executory contract A contract under which something remains to be done by one or more of the parties.

express agreement An oral or written contract in which the parties state the contract's terms and express their intentions in words.

express contract *See* express agreement.

external depreciation Reduction in a property's value caused by outside factors (those that are off the property).

Fair Housing Act The federal law that prohibits discrimination in housing based on race, color, religion, sex, handicap, familial status, and national origin.

Fannie Mae A quasi-government agency established to purchase any kind of mortgage loans in the secondary mortgage market from the primary lenders. Formerly known as the Federal National Mortgage Association (FNMA).

Farm Service Agency (FSA)   An agency of the federal government that provides credit assistance to farmers and other individuals who live in rural areas. Formerly known as the Farmers Home Administration.

Federal Deposit Insurance Corporation (FDIC)   An independent federal agency that insures the deposits in commercial banks.

Federal Reserve System (the Fed)   The country's central banking system, which is responsible for the nation's monetary policy by regulating the supply of money and interest rates.

fee simple   The maximum possible estate or right of ownership of real property, continuing forever. Also known as *fee simple absolute*.

fee simple defeasible   *See* defeasible fee estate.

feudal system   A system of ownership usually associated with precolonial England, in which the king or other sovereign is the source of all rights. The right to possess real property was granted by the sovereign to an individual as a life estate only. Upon the death of the individual, title passed back to the sovereign, not to the decedent's heirs.

FHA loan   A loan insured by the Federal Housing Administration and made by an approved lender in accordance with the FHA's regulations.

fiduciary   One in whom trust and confidence is placed under the common-law of agency; usually a reference to a broker employed under the terms of a listing contract or buyer agency agreement.

fiduciary relationship   A relationship between trustee and beneficiary, attorney and client, or principal and agent.

Financial Institutions Reform, Recovery and Enforcement Act (FIRREA)   This act restructured the savings and loan association regulatory system; enacted in response to the savings and loan crisis of the 1980s.

financing statement   *See* Uniform Commercial Code.

first mortgage   The mortgage lien that takes first lien position, or priority, by being recorded first.

fiscal policy   The government's policy in regard to taxation and spending programs. The balance between these two areas determines the amount of money the government will withdraw from or feed into the economy, which can counter economic peaks and slumps.

fixture   An item of personal property that has been converted to real property by being permanently affixed to the realty.

foreclosure   A legal procedure whereby property used as security for a debt is sold to satisfy the debt in the event of default in payment of the mortgage note or default of other terms in the mortgage document. The foreclosure procedure brings the rights of all parties to a conclusion and passes the title in the mortgaged property to either the holder of the mortgage or a third party who may purchase the realty at the foreclosure sale, free of all encumbrances affecting the property subsequent to the mortgage.

fraud   Deception intended to cause a person to give up property or a lawful right.

Freddie Mac   A corporation established to purchase primarily conventional mortgage loans in the secondary mortgage market.

freehold estate   An estate in land in which ownership is for an indeterminate length of time, in contrast to a *leasehold estate*.

front footage   The measurement of a parcel of land by the number of feet of street or road frontage.

functional obsolescence   A loss of value to an improvement to real estate arising from functional problems, often caused by age or poor design.

future interest   A person's present right to an interest in real property that will not result in possession or enjoyment until some time in the future, such as a reversion or right of reentry.

gap   A defect in the chain of title of a particular parcel of real estate; a missing document or conveyance that raises doubt as to the present ownership of the land.

GEM   *See* growing equity mortgage.

general agent   One who is authorized by a principal to represent the principal in a range of matters.

general contractor   A construction specialist who enters into a formal construction contract with a landowner or master lessee to construct a real estate building or project. The general contractor often contracts with several *subcontractors* specializing in various aspects of the building process to perform individual jobs.

general lien   The right of a creditor to have all of a debtor's property—both real and personal—sold to satisfy a debt.

general partnership   *See* partnership.

general warranty deed   A deed to the premises. Used in most real estate deed transfers, a general warranty deed offers the greatest protection of any deed.

GIM   *See* gross income multiplier.

Ginnie Mae   A government agency that plays an important role in the secondary mortgage market. It sells mortgage-backed securities that are backed by pools of FHA and VA loans. Formerly known as the Government National Mortgage Association (GNMA).

government lot   Fractional sections in the rectangular (government) survey system that are less than one quarter-section in area.

government survey system   *See* rectangular (government) survey system.

graduated-payment mortgage (GPM)   A loan in which the monthly principal and interest payments increase by a certain percentage each year for a certain number of years and then level off for the remaining loan term.

grantee   A person who receives a conveyance of real property from a grantor.

granting clause   Words in a deed of conveyance that state the grantor's intention to convey the property at the present time. This clause is generally worded as "convey and warrant," "grant," "grant, bargain, and sell," or the like.

grantor   The person transferring title to or an interest in real property to a grantee.

GRM   *See* gross rent multiplier.

gross income multiplier (GIM)   A figure used as a multiplier of the gross annual income of a property to produce an estimate of the property's value.

gross lease   A lease of property according to which a landlord pays all property charges regularly incurred through ownership, such as repairs, taxes, insurance premiums, and operating expenses. Most residential leases are gross leases.

gross rent multiplier (GRM)   The figure used as a multiplier of the gross monthly income of a property to produce an estimate of the property's value.

ground lease   A lease of land only, on which the tenant usually owns a building or is required to build as specified in the lease. Such leases are usually long-term net leases; the tenant's rights and obligations continue until the lease expires or terminates through default.

growing equity mortgage (GEM)   A loan in which the monthly payments increase annually, with the increased amount being used to reduce directly the principal balance outstanding and thus shorten the overall term of the loan.

habendum clause   That part of a deed beginning with the words "to have and to hold," following the granting clause, and defining the extent of ownership the grantor is conveying.

hand money   *See* earnest money.

heir   One who might inherit or succeed to an interest in land under the state law of descent when the owner dies without leaving a valid will.

highest and best use   The possible use of a property that would produce the greatest net income and thereby develop the highest value.

holdover tenancy   A tenancy whereby a lessee retains possession of leased property after the lease has expired and the landlord, by continuing to accept rent, agrees to the tenant's continued occupancy as defined by state law.

holographic will   A will that is written, dated, and signed in the testator's handwriting.

home equity loan   A loan (sometimes called a *line of credit*) under which a property owner uses his or her residence as collateral and can then draw funds up to a prearranged amount against the property.

homeowner's insurance policy   A standardized package insurance policy that covers a residential real estate owner against financial loss from fire, theft, public liability, and other common risks.

homestead   Land owned and occupied as the family home. In many states a portion of the area or value of this land is protected or exempt from judgments for debts.

hypothecation   The pledge of property as security for a loan.

impact fees   Charges assessed developers by a municipality that relate to expenses incurred by the municipality for additional improvements necessitated by increased development.

implied agency   An agency that arises by conduct or inference from other acts or circumstances, often creating an agency relationship when none was intended.

implied agreement   A contract under which the agreement of the parties is demonstrated by their acts and conduct.

implied contract   *See* implied agreement.

implied warranty of habitability   A theory in landlord/tenant law in which the landlord renting residential property implies that the property is habitable and fit for its intended use.

improvement   (1) Any structure, usually privately owned, erected on a site to enhance the value of the property—for example, building a fence or a driveway. (2) A publicly owned structure added to or benefiting land, such as a curb, sidewalk, street, or sewer.

income approach   The process of estimating the value of an income-producing property through capitalization of the annual net income expected to be produced by the property during its remaining useful life.

incorporeal right   A nonpossessory right in real estate; for example, an easement or a right-of-way.

independent contractor   Someone who is retained to perform a certain act but who is subject to the control and direction of another only as to the end result and not as to the way in which the act is performed. Unlike an employee, an independent contractor pays for all expenses and Social Security, and income taxes, and receives no employee benefits. Many real estate salespeople are independent contractors.

index method The appraisal method of estimating building costs by multiplying the original cost of the property by a percentage factor to adjust for current construction costs.

inflation The gradual reduction of the purchasing power of the dollar, usually related directly to the increases in the money supply by the federal government.

inheritance taxes State-imposed taxes on a decedent's real and personal property.

initial interview The first contact between a licensee and a consumer of real estate-related services where a substantive discussion about real estate occurs. Pennsylvania law contemplates that this will be the first face-to-face meeting. However, because in today's practice, substantive conversations could evolve by telephone or e-mail, licensees are required to provide a disclosure statement to ensure that a consumer is aware that personal information should not be divulged to a licensee who is not, and may not become, the consumer's agent.

installment contract A contract for the sale of real estate whereby the purchase price is paid in periodic installments by the purchaser, who is in possession of the property even though title is retained by the seller until a future date, which may not be until final payment. Also called a *contract for deed* or *articles of agreement for warranty deed*.

installment sale A transaction in which the sales price is paid in two or more installments over two or more years. If the sale meets certain requirements, a taxpayer can postpone reporting such income until future years by paying tax each year only on the proceeds received that year.

interest A charge made by a lender for the use of money.

interim financing A short-term loan usually made during the construction phase of a building project (in this case often referred to as a *construction loan*).

Interstate Land Sales Full Disclosure Act A federal law that regulates the sale of certain real estate in interstate commerce.

intestate The condition of a property owner who dies without leaving a valid will. Title to the property will pass to the decedent's heirs as provided in the state law of descent.

intrinsic value An appraisal term referring to the value created by a person's personal preferences for a particular type of property.

investment Money directed toward the purchase, improvement, and development of an asset in expectation of income or profits.

involuntary alienation *See* alienation.

involuntary lien A lien placed on property without the consent of the property owner.

joint tenancy Ownership of real estate between two or more parties who have been named in one conveyance as joint tenants. Upon the death of a joint tenant, the decedent's interest passes to the surviving joint tenant or tenants by the *right of survivorship*.

joint venture The joining of two or more people to conduct a specific business enterprise. A joint venture is similar to a partnership in that it must be created by agreement between the parties to share in the losses and profits of the venture. It is unlike a partnership in that the venture is for one specific project only, rather than for a continuing business relationship.

judgment The formal decision of a court upon the respective rights and claims of the parties to an action or suit. After a judgment has been entered and recorded with the county recorder, it usually becomes a general lien on the property of the defendant.

judicial deed A deed that is delivered pursuant to court order.

judicial precedent In law, the requirements established by prior court decisions.

junior lien An obligation, such as a second mortgage, that is subordinate in right or lien priority to an existing lien on the same realty.

laches An equitable doctrine used by courts to bar a legal claim or prevent the assertion of a right because of undue delay or failure to assert the claim or right.

land The earth's surface, extending downward to the center of the earth and upward infinitely into space, including things permanently attached by nature, such as trees and water.

land contract *See* installment contract.

latent defect A hidden structural defect that is not discovered by ordinary inspection and that threatens the property's soundness or the safety of its inhabitants. Sellers and licensees have a duty to inspect for and disclose latent defects.

law of agency *See* agency.

lead An element found in oil-based paint and plumbing systems that when ingested in sufficient quantities over time can pose significant health problems. Real estate licensees and certain others are required to comply with the federal Residential Lead-Based Paint Hazard Reduction Act when dealing with housing constructed before 1978.

lease A written or oral contract between a landlord (the lessor) and a tenant (the lessee) that transfers the right to exclusive possession and use of the landlord's real property to the lessee for a specified period of time and for a stated consideration (rent). By state law, leases for longer than a certain period of time (generally one year) must be in writing to be enforceable.

leasehold estate A tenant's right to occupy real estate during the term of a lease, generally considered to be a personal property interest.

lease option A lease under which the tenant has the right to purchase the property either during the lease term or at its end.

lease purchase The purchase of real property, the consummation of which is preceded by a lease, usually long-term. Typically done for tax or financing purposes.

legacy A disposition of money or personal property by will.

legal description A description of a specific parcel of real estate complete enough for an independent surveyor to locate and identify it.

legally competent parties People who are recognized by law as being able to contract with others; those of legal age and sound mind.

lessee *See* lease.

lessor *See* lease.

leverage The use of borrowed money to finance the bulk of an investment.

levy To assess; to seize or collect. To levy a tax is to assess a property and set the rate of taxation. To levy an execution is to officially seize the property of a person in order to satisfy an obligation.

liability coverage Insurance that indemnifies a property owner who is found liable for damage in the event of an individual's being injured on the insured's property.

license (1) A privilege or right granted to a person by a state to operate as a real estate broker or salesperson. (2) The revocable permission for a temporary use of land—a personal right that cannot be sold.

lien A right given by law to certain creditors to have their debts paid out of the property of a defaulting debtor, usually by means of a court sale.

lien theory Some states interpret a mortgage as being purely a lien on real property. The mortgagee thus has no right of possession but must foreclose the lien and sell the property if the mortgagor defaults.

life-cycle costing In property management, comparing one type of equipment with another based on both purchase cost and operating cost over its expected useful lifetime.

life estate An interest in real or personal property that is limited in duration to the lifetime of its owner or some other designated person or persons.

life tenant A person in possession of a life estate.

limited liability company (LLC) An alternative, hybrid business entity with the combined characteristics and benefits of a limited partnership and an S corporation that is established according to the laws of the state in which the LLC is chartered.

limited partnership *See* partnership.

liquidated damages An amount predetermined by the parties to a contract as the total compensation to an injured party should the other party breach the contract.

liquidity The ability to sell an asset and convert it into cash, at a price close to its true value, in a short time.

lis pendens A recorded legal document giving constructive notice that an action affecting a particular property has been filed in either a state or federal court.

listing agreement A contract between an owner (as principal) and a real estate broker (as agent) by which the broker is employed as agent to find a buyer for the owner's real estate on the owner's terms, for which service the owner agrees to pay a commission.

listing broker The broker in a multiple-listing situation from whose office a listing agreement is initiated.

littoral rights (1) A landowner's claim to use water in large navigable lakes and oceans adjacent to his or her property. (2) The ownership rights to land bordering these bodies of water up to the high-water mark.

loan origination fee A fee charged to the borrower by the lender for making a mortgage loan. The fee is usually computed as a percentage of the loan amount.

loan-to-value ratio The relationship between the amount of the mortgage loan and the value of the real estate being pledged as collateral.

lot-and-block (recorded plat) description A method of describing real property that identifies a parcel of land by reference to lot and block numbers within a subdivision, as specified on a recorded subdivision plat.

management agreement A contract between the owner of income property and a management firm or individual property manager that outlines the scope of the manager's authority.

market A place where goods can be bought and sold and a price established.

marketable title Good or clear title, reasonably free from the risk of litigation over possible defects.

market value The most probable price property would bring in an arm's-length transaction under normal conditions on the open market.

master plan   A comprehensive plan to guide the long-term physical development of a particular area.

mechanic's lien   A statutory lien created in favor of contractors, laborers, and materialmen who have performed work or furnished materials in the erection or repair of a building.

metes-and-bounds description   A legal description of a parcel of land that begins at a well-marked point and follows the boundaries, using directions and distances around the tract, back to the place of beginning.

mill   One-tenth of one cent. Some states use a mill rate to compute real estate taxes; for example, a rate of 52 mills would be $0.052 tax for each dollar of assessed valuation of a property.

minor   Someone who has not reached the age of majority and therefore does not have legal capacity to transfer title to real property.

MLS   *See* multiple listing service.

monetary policy   Governmental regulation of the amount of money in circulation through such institutions as the Federal Reserve Board.

monetary judgment   A court judgment ordering payment of money rather than specific performance of a certain action. *See also* judgment.

month-to-month tenancy   A periodic tenancy under which the tenant rents for one month at a time. In the absence of a rental agreement (oral or written) a tenancy is generally considered to be month to month.

monument   A fixed natural or artificial object used to establish real estate boundaries for a metes-and-bounds description.

mortgage   A conditional transfer or pledge of real estate as security for the payment of a debt. Also, the document creating a mortgage lien.

mortgage banker   Mortgage loan companies that originate, service, and sell loans to investors.

mortgage broker   An agent of a lender who brings the lender and borrower together. The broker receives a fee for this service.

mortgagee   A lender in a mortgage loan transaction.

mortgage lien   A lien or charge on the property of a mortgagor that secures the underlying debt obligations.

mortgagor   A borrower in a mortgage loan transaction.

multiperil policies   Insurance policies that offer protection from a range of potential perils, such as those of a fire, hazard, public liability, and casualty.

multiple-listing clause   A provision in an exclusive listing for the authority and obligation on the part of the listing broker to distribute the listing to other brokers in the multiple-listing organization.

multiple listing service (MLS)   A marketing organization composed of member brokers who agree to share their listing agreements with one another in the hope of procuring ready, willing, and able buyers for their properties more quickly than they could on their own.

negotiable instrument   A written promise or order to pay a specific sum of money that may be transferred by endorsement or delivery. The transferee then has the original payee's right to payment.

net lease   A lease requiring the tenant to pay not only rent but also costs incurred in maintaining the property, including taxes, insurance, utilities, and repairs.

net listing   A listing based on the net price the seller will receive if the property is sold. Under a net listing the broker can offer the property for sale at the highest price obtainable to increase the commission. This type of listing is illegal in many states.

net operating income (NOI)   The income projected for an income-producing property after deducting losses for vacancy and collection and operating expenses.

nonconforming use   A use of property that is permitted to continue after a zoning ordinance prohibiting it has been established for the area.

nonhomogeneity   A lack of uniformity; dissimilarity. Because no two parcels of land are exactly alike, real estate is said to be nonhomogeneous.

note   *See* promissory note.

novation   Substituting a new obligation for an old one or substituting new parties to an existing obligation.

nuncupative will   An oral will declared by the testator in his or her final illness, made before witnesses and afterward reduced to writing.

obsolescence   The loss of value due to factors that are outmoded or less useful. Obsolescence may be functional or economic.

occupancy permit   A permit issued by the appropriate local governing body to establish that the property is suitable for habitation by meeting certain safety and health standards.

offer and acceptance   Two essential components of a valid contract; a "meeting of the minds."

offeror/offeree   The person who makes the offer is the offeror. The person to whom the offer is made is the offeree.

open-end loan   A mortgage loan that is expandable by increments up to a maximum dollar amount, the full loan being secured by the same original mortgage.

open listing   A listing contract under which the broker's commission is contingent on the broker's producing a ready, willing, and able buyer before the property is sold by the seller or another broker.

option An agreement to keep open for a set period an offer to sell or purchase property.

ostensible agency A form of implied agency relationship created by the actions of the parties involved rather than by written agreement or document.

package loan A real estate loan used to finance the purchase of both real property and personal property, such as in the purchase of a new home that includes carpeting, window coverings, and major appliances.

parol evidence rule A rule of evidence providing that a written agreement is the final expression of the agreement of the parties, not to be varied or contradicted by prior or contemporaneous oral or written negotiations.

participation mortgage A mortgage loan wherein the lender has a partial equity interest in the property or receives a portion of the income from the property.

partition The division of cotenants' interests in real property when the parties do not all voluntarily agree to terminate the co-ownership; takes place through court procedures.

partnership An association of two or more individuals who carry on a continuing business for profit as co-owners. Under the law a partnership is regarded as a group of individuals rather than as a single entity. A *general partnership* is a typical form of joint venture in which each general partner shares in the administration, profits, and losses of the operation. A *limited partnership* is a business arrangement whereby the operation is administered by one or more general partners and funded, by and large, by limited or silent partners, who are by law responsible for losses only to the extent of their investments.

party wall A wall that is located on or at a boundary line between two adjoining parcels of land and is used or is intended to be used by the owners of both properties.

payment cap The limit on the amount the monthly payment can be increased on an adjustable-rate mortgage when the interest rate is adjusted.

payoff statement *See* reduction certificate.

Pennsylvania Human Relations Act (PHRA) The state law that prohibits discrimination in the sale or rental of real estate, both housing and commercial properties, on the basis of race, color, religion, ancestry, national origin, sex, familial status, handicap or disability, or use of guide or support animal due to a handicap or disability.

Pennsylvania Municipalities Planning Code The state law that governs the procedures municipalities must follow when enacting comprehensive plans, zoning, and subdivision ordinances.

Pennsylvania Planned Community Act The state law adopted to govern the development of planned communities. The law also provides for certain disclosures to purchasers of property located in these developments.

Pennsylvania Uniform Condominium Act The state law adopted from the national model act that governs the development and operation of condominiums. The law also provides for certain disclosures to purchasers of condominium units.

percentage lease A lease, commonly used for commercial property, whose rental is based on the tenant's gross sales at the premises; it usually stipulates a base monthly rental plus a percentage of any gross sales above a certain amount.

percolation test A test of the soil to determine if it will absorb and drain water adequately to use a septic system for sewage disposal.

periodic tenancy *See* estate from period to period.

personal assistant An individual who is employed to perform certain activities to assist a real estate licensee in the course of his or her business. A personal assistant may be licensed or unlicensed; this status determines the scope of the activities that are permitted and whether the broker or an associate broker or salesperson is the assistant's employer.

personal property Items, called *chattels*, which do not fit into the definition of real property; movable objects.

physical deterioration A reduction in a property's value resulting from a decline in physical condition; can be caused by action of the elements or by ordinary wear and tear.

planned unit development (PUD) A planned combination of diverse land uses, such as housing, recreation, and shopping, in one contained development or subdivision.

plat map A map of a town, section, or subdivision indicating the location and boundaries of individual properties.

plottage The increase in value or utility resulting from the consolidation (*assemblage*) of two or more adjacent lots into one larger lot.

PMI *See* private mortgage insurance.

point of beginning (POB) In a metes-and-bounds legal description, the starting point of the survey, situated in one corner of the parcel; all metes-and-bounds descriptions must follow the boundaries of the parcel back to the point of beginning.

police power The government's right to impose laws, statutes, and ordinances, including zoning ordinances and building codes, to protect the public health, safety, and welfare.

power of attorney A written instrument authorizing a person, the *attorney-in-fact*, to act as agent for another person to the extent indicated in the instrument.

prepaid items On a closing statement, items that have been paid in advance by the seller, such as insurance premiums and some real estate taxes, for which he or she must be reimbursed by the buyer.

prepayment penalty A charge imposed on a borrower who pays off the loan principal early. This penalty compensates the lender for interest and other charges that would otherwise be lost.

price-fixing *See* antitrust laws.

primary mortgage market The mortgage market in which loans are originated and consisting of lenders such as commercial banks, savings and loan associations, and mutual savings banks.

principal (1) A sum loaned or employed as a fund or an investment, as distinguished from its income or profits. (2) The original amount (as in a loan) of the total due and payable at a certain date. (3) A main party to a transaction—the person for whom the agent works.

principal meridian The main imaginary line running north and south and crossing a base line at a definite point, used by surveyors for reference in locating and describing land under the rectangular (government) survey system of legal description.

prior appropriation A concept of water ownership in which the landowner's right to use available water is based on a government-administered permit system.

priority The order of position or time. The priority of liens is generally determined by the chronological order in which the lien documents are recorded; tax liens, however, have priority even over previously recorded liens.

private mortgage insurance (PMI) Insurance provided by a private carrier protecting a lender against a loss in the event of a foreclosure and deficiency.

probate A legal process by which a court determines who will inherit a decedent's property and what the estate's assets are.

procuring cause The effort that brings about the desired result. Under an open listing the broker who is the procuring cause of the sale receives the commission.

progression An appraisal principle that states that, between dissimilar properties, the value of the lesser-quality property is favorably affected by the presence of the better-quality property.

promissory note A financing instrument that states the terms of the underlying obligation, is signed by its maker, and is negotiable (transferable to a third party).

property manager Someone who manages real estate for another person for compensation. Duties include collecting rents, maintaining the property, and keeping up all accounting.

property reports The mandatory federal and state documents compiled by subdividers and developers to provide potential purchasers with facts about a property prior to their purchase.

proprietary lease A lease given by the corporation that owns a cooperative apartment building to the shareholder for the shareholder's right as a tenant to an individual apartment.

proration Expenses, either prepaid or paid in arrears, that are divided or distributed between buyer and seller at the closing.

protected class Any group of people designated as such by the Department of Housing and Urban Development (HUD) in consideration of federal and state civil rights legislation. Currently includes ethnic minorities, women, religious groups, the handicapped, and others.

public offering statement A disclosure document given to a prospective purchaser under applicable federal and state laws. It contains the material facts about the property to allow the consumer to make an informed decision.

PUD *See* planned unit development.

puffing Exaggerated or superlative comments or opinions.

pur autre vie "For the life of another." A life estate pur autre vie is a life estate that is measured by the life of a person other than the grantee.

purchase-money mortgage (PMM) A note secured by a mortgage or deed of trust given by a buyer, as borrower, to a seller, as lender, as part of the purchase price of the real estate.

quantity-survey method The appraisal method of estimating building costs by calculating the cost of all of the physical components in the improvements, adding the cost to assemble them, and then including the indirect costs associated with such construction.

quiet title A court action to remove a cloud on the title.

quitclaim deed A conveyance by which the grantor transfers whatever interest he or she has in the real estate, without warranties or obligations.

radon A naturally occurring gas that is suspected of posing a health hazard, especially causing lung cancer.

RAM *See* reverse annuity mortgage.

rate cap The limit on the amount the interest rate can be increased at each adjustment period in an adjustable-rate loan. The cap may also set the maximum interest rate that can be charged during the life of the loan.

ready, willing, and able buyer One who is prepared to buy property on the seller's terms and is ready to take positive steps to consummate the transaction.

real estate Land; a portion of the earth's surface extending downward to the center of the earth and upward infinitely into space, including all things permanently attached to it, whether naturally or artificially.

Real Estate Commission *See* State Real Estate Commission.

real estate investment syndicate *See* syndicate.

real estate investment trust (REIT) Trust ownership of real estate by a group of individuals who purchase certificates of ownership in the trust, which in turn invests the money in real property and distributes the profits back to the investors free of corporate income tax.

Real Estate Licensing and Registration Act The Pennsylvania law that protects the public interest by governing real estate practices and the activities of licensees.

real estate mortgage investment conduit (REMIC) A tax entity that issues multiple classes of investor interests (securities) backed by a pool of mortgages.

real estate recovery fund A fund established for aggrieved parties who have obtained uncollectible judgments against real estate licensees for fraud, deceit, or misrepresentation.

Real Estate Settlement Procedures Act (RESPA) The federal law that requires certain disclosures to consumers about mortgage loan settlements. The law also prohibits the payment or receipt of kickbacks and certain kinds of referral fees.

real estate tax *See* taxation.

real property The interests, benefits, and rights inherent in real estate ownership.

REALTOR® A registered trademark term reserved for the sole use of active members of local REALTOR® boards affiliated with the National Association of REALTORS®.

reconciliation The final step in the appraisal process, in which the appraiser combines the estimates of value received from the sales comparison, cost, and income approaches to arrive at a final estimate of market value for the subject property.

recorder of deeds The county office in which matters relating to the real estate located within that county are filed.

recording The act of entering or recording documents affecting or conveying interests in real estate in the recorder's office established in each county. Until it is recorded, a deed or mortgage ordinarily is not effective against subsequent purchasers or mortgagees.

rectangular (government) survey system A system established in 1785 by the federal government, providing for surveying and describing land by reference to principal meridians and base lines.

redemption The right of a defaulted property owner to recover his or her property by curing the default.

redemption period A period of time established by state law during which a property owner has the right to redeem his or her real estate from a foreclosure or tax sale by paying the sales price, interest, and costs. Many states do not have mortgage redemption laws.

redlining The illegal practice of a lending institution denying loans or restricting their numbers for certain areas of a community.

reduction certificate (payoff statement) The document signed by a lender indicating the amount required to pay a loan balance in full and satisfy the debt; used in the settlement process to protect both the seller's and the buyer's interests.

regression An appraisal principle that states that, between dissimilar properties, the value of the better-quality property is affected adversely by the presence of the lesser-quality property.

Regulation Z Implements the Truth-in-Lending Act requiring credit institutions to inform borrowers of the true cost of obtaining credit.

REIT *See* real estate investment trust.

remainder interest The remnant of an estate that is conveyed to take effect and be enjoyed after the termination of a prior estate, such as when an owner conveys a life estate to one party and the remainder to another.

rent A fixed, periodic payment made by a tenant of a property to the owner for possession and use, usually by prior agreement of the parties.

rent schedule A statement of proposed rental rates, determined by the owner or the property manager or both, based on a building's estimated expenses, market supply and demand, and the owner's long-range goals for the property.

rental listing referral agent A licensee who owns or manages a business that collects rental information for the purpose of referring tenants to rental units or locations.

replacement cost The construction cost at current prices of a property that is not necessarily an exact duplicate of the subject property but serves the same purpose or function as the original.

reproduction cost The construction cost at current prices of an exact duplicate of the subject property.

RESPA *See* Real Estate Settlement Procedures Act.

restrictive covenants A clause in a deed that limits the way the real estate ownership may be used.

reverse-annuity mortgage (RAM) A loan under which the homeowner receives monthly payments based on his or her accumulated equity rather than a lump sum.

The loan must be repaid at a prearranged date or upon the death of the owner or the sale of the property.

reversionary interest The remnant of an estate that the grantor holds after granting a life estate to another person.

reversionary right The return of the rights of possession and quiet enjoyment to the lessor at the expiration of a lease or life estate.

right of survivorship *See* joint tenancy.

right-of-way The right given by one landowner to another to pass over the land, construct a roadway, or use as a pathway, without actually transferring ownership.

riparian rights An owner's rights in land that borders on or includes a stream, river, or lake. These rights include access to and use of the water.

risk management Evaluation and selection of appropriate courses of action to minimize legal liability; also the selection of appropriate insurance coverage.

Rules and Regulations Real estate licensing authority orders that govern licensees' activities; they usually have the same force and effect as statutory law.

sale and leaseback A transaction in which an owner sells his or her improved property and, as part of the same transaction, signs a long-term lease to remain in possession of the premises.

sales comparison approach The process of estimating the value of a property by examining and comparing actual sales of comparable properties.

salesperson A person who performs real estate activities while employed by or associated with a licensed real estate broker.

SAM *See* share-appreciation mortgage.

satisfaction of mortgage A document acknowledging the payment of a mortgage debt.

secondary mortgage market A market for the purchase and sale of existing mortgages, designed to provide greater liquidity for mortgages; also called the *secondary money market*. Mortgages are first originated in the *primary mortgage market*.

section A portion of township under the rectangular (government) survey system. A township is divided into 36 sections, numbered one through 36. A section is a square with mile-long sides and an area of one square mile, or 640 acres.

security agreement *See* Uniform Commercial Code.

security deposit A payment by a tenant, held by the landlord during the lease term, and kept (wholly or partially) on default or destruction of the premises by the tenant.

seller agent Any licensee who has entered into an agency relationship with a seller of real estate.

separate property Under community property law, property owned solely by either spouse before the marriage, acquired by gift or inheritance after the marriage, or purchased with separate funds after the marriage.

servient tenement Land on which an easement exists in favor of an adjacent property (called a *dominant estate*); also called a *servient estate*.

setback The amount of space local zoning regulations require between a lot line and a building line.

severalty Ownership of real property by one person only, also called *sole ownership*.

severance Changing an item of real estate to personal property by detaching it from the land; for example, cutting down a tree.

sharecropping In an agricultural lease, the agreement between the landowner and the tenant farmer to split the crop or the profit from its sale, actually sharing the crop.

shared-appreciation mortgage (SAM) A mortgage loan in which the lender, in exchange for a loan with a favorable interest rate, participates in the profits (if any) the borrower receives when the property is eventually sold.

single agency The broker acts as the agent of one principal, either the seller/landlord *or* the buyer/tenant, in a transaction. The broker may practice exclusive single agency or may represent sellers and buyers, but never both in a transaction.

situs The personal preference of people for one area over another, not necessarily based on objective facts and knowledge.

special agent One who is authorized by a principal to perform a specified single act on behalf of a principal.

special assessment A tax or levy customarily imposed against only those specific parcels of real estate that will benefit from a proposed public improvement like a street or sewer.

special warranty deed A deed in which the grantor warrants, or guarantees, the title only against defects arising during the period of his or her tenure and ownership of the property and not against defects existing before that time, generally using the language, "by, through or under the grantor but not otherwise."

specific lien A lien affecting or attaching only to a certain, specific parcel of land or piece of property.

specific performance A legal action to compel a party to carry out the terms of a contract.

square-foot method The appraisal method of estimating building costs by multiplying the number of square feet in the improvements being appraised by the cost per square foot for recently constructed similar improvements.

State Real Estate Commission The agency established by the Pennsylvania Real Estate Licensing and Registration Act to administer this law and supervise the activities of licensees.

statute of frauds That part of a state law that requires certain instruments, such as deeds, real estate sales contracts, and certain leases to be in writing to be legally enforceable.

statute of limitations That law pertaining to the period of time within which certain actions must be brought to court.

statutory lien A lien imposed on property by statute—a tax lien, for example—in contrast to an *equitable lien*, which arises out of common law.

statutory redemption The right of a defaulted property owner to recover the property after its sale by paying the appropriate fees and charges.

steering The illegal practice of channeling home seekers to particular areas to maintain the homogeneity of an area or to change the character of an area in order to create a speculative situation.

stigmatized property A property that has acquired an undesirable reputation due to an event that occurred on or near it, such as violent crime, gang-related activity, illness, or personal tragedy.

straight-line method A method of calculating depreciation for tax purposes, computed by dividing the adjusted basis of a property by the estimated number of years of remaining useful life.

straight loan (or term loan) A loan in which only interest is paid during the term of the loan, with the entire principal amount due with the final interest payment.

subagency An agency relationship in which the broker-agent appoints other brokers as *subagents* to help perform client-based functions on behalf of the principal. The subagent assumes the same fiduciary responsibilities as the agent. In Pennsylvania, the principal must authorize the broker to engage subagents.

subagent One who is employed by a person already acting as an agent. Typically a reference to a salesperson licensed under a broker (agent) who is employed under the terms of a listing agreement.

subdivider One who buys undeveloped land, divides it into smaller, usable lots, and sells the lots to potential users.

subdivision A tract of land divided by the owner, known as the *subdivider*, into blocks, building lots, and streets according to a recorded subdivision plat, which must comply with local ordinances and regulations.

subdivision and land development ordinances Municipal ordinances that establish requirements for subdivisions and development.

subdivision plat *See* plat map.

sublease *See* subletting.

subletting The leasing of premises by a lessee to a third party for part of the lessee's remaining term. *See also* assignment.

subordination Relegation to a lesser position, usually in respect to a right or security.

subordination agreement A written agreement between holders of liens on a property that changes the priority of mortgage, judgment, and other liens under certain circumstances.

subrogation The substitution of one creditor for another, with the substituted person succeeding to the legal rights and claims of the original claimant. Subrogation is used by title insurers to acquire from the injured party rights to sue in order to recover any claims they have paid.

substitution An appraisal principle that states that the maximum value of a property tends to be set by the cost of purchasing an equally desirable and valuable substitute property, assuming that no costly delay is encountered in making the substitution.

subsurface rights Ownership rights in a parcel of real estate to the water, minerals, gas, oil, and so forth that lie beneath the surface of the property.

suit for possession A court suit initiated by a landlord to evict a tenant from leased premises after the tenant has breached one of the terms of the lease or has held possession of the property after the lease's expiration.

suit for specific performance *See* specific performance.

suit to quiet title A court action intended to establish or settle the title to a particular property, especially when there is a cloud on the title.

Superfund Popular name of the hazardous-waste cleanup fund established by the Comprehensive Environmental Response, Compensation, and Liability Act (CERCLA).

Superfund Amendments and Reauthorization Act (SARA) An amendatory statute that contains stronger cleanup standards for contaminated sites, increased funding for the Superfund, and clarifications of lender liability and innocent landowner immunity. *See* Comprehensive Environmental Response, Compensation and Liability Act (CERCLA).

supply The amount of goods available in the market to be sold at a given price. The term is often coupled with *demand*.

supply and demand The appraisal principle that follows the interrelationship of the supply of and demand for real estate. As appraising is based on economic concepts, this principle recognizes that real property is subject to the influences of the marketplace just as is any other commodity.

surface rights Ownership rights in a parcel of real estate that are limited to the surface of the property and do not include the air above it (*air rights*) or the minerals below the surface (*subsurface rights*).

survey The process by which boundaries are measured and land areas are determined; the on-site measurement of lot lines, dimensions, and position of a house on a lot, including the determination of any existing encroachments or easements.

syndicate A combination of people or firms formed to accomplish a business venture of mutual interest by pooling resources. In a *real estate investment syndicate* the parties own and/or develop property, with the main profit generally arising from the sale of the property.

tacking Adding or combining successive periods of continuous occupation of real property by adverse possessors. This concept enables someone who has not been in possession for the entire statutory period to establish a claim of adverse possession.

taxation The process by which a government or municipal quasi-public body raises monies to fund its operation.

tax credit An amount by which tax owed is reduced directly.

tax deed An instrument, similar to a certificate of sale, given to a purchaser at a tax sale. *See also* certificate of sale.

tax lien A charge against property, created by operation of law. Tax liens and assessments take priority over all other liens.

tax sale A court-ordered sale of real property to raise money to cover delinquent taxes.

tenancy by the entirety The joint ownership, recognized in some states, of property acquired by husband and wife during marriage. Upon the death of one spouse the survivor becomes the owner of the property.

tenancy in common A form of co-ownership by which each owner holds an undivided interest in real property as if he or she were sole owner. Each individual owner has the right to partition. Unlike joint tenants, tenants in common have right of inheritance.

tenant One who holds or possesses lands or tenements by any kind of right or title.

tenant improvements Alterations to the interior of a building to meet the functional demands of the tenant.

testate Having made and left a valid will.

testator A person who has made a valid will. A woman often is referred to as a *testatrix*, although testator can be used for either gender.

time is of the essence A phrase in a contract that requires the performance of a certain act within a stated period of time.

time-share A form of ownership interest that may include an estate interest in property or a contract for use, which allows use of the property for a fixed or variable time period.

time-share salesperson A licensee who, either as an employee or independent contractor, sells time-shares under the supervision of a broker.

title (1) The right to or ownership of land. (2) The evidence of ownership of land.

title insurance A policy insuring the owner or mortgagee against loss by reason of defects in the title to a parcel of real estate, other than encumbrances, defects, and matters specifically excluded by the policy.

title search The examination of public records relating to real estate to determine the current state of the ownership.

title theory Some states interpret a mortgage to mean that the lender is the owner of mortgaged land. Upon full payment of the mortgage debt the borrower becomes the landowner.

Torrens system A method of evidencing title by registration with the proper public authority, generally called the *registrar*, named for its founder, Sir Robert Torrens.

township The principal unit of the rectangular (government) survey system. A township is a square with six-mile sides and an area of 36 square miles.

trade fixture An article installed by a tenant under the terms of a lease and removable by the tenant before the lease expires.

transaction licensee A licensee who provides services to a consumer without an agency relationship.

transfer tax Tax stamps required to be affixed to a deed by state and/or local law.

trust A fiduciary arrangement whereby property is conveyed to a person or institution, called a *trustee*, to be held and administered on behalf of another person, called a *beneficiary*. The one who conveys the trust is called the *trustor*.

trust deed An instrument used to create a mortgage lien by which the borrower conveys title to a trustee, who holds it as security for the benefit of the note holder (the lender); also called a *deed of trust*.

trustee The holder of bare legal title in a deed of trust loan transaction.

trustee's deed   A deed executed by a trustee conveying land held in a trust.

trustor   A borrower in a deed of trust loan transaction.

undivided interest   *See* tenancy in common.

unenforceable contract   A contract that has all the elements of a valid contract, yet neither party can sue the other to force performance of it. For example, an unsigned contract is generally unenforceable.

Uniform Commercial Code (UCC)   A codification of commercial law, adopted in most states, that attempts to make uniform all laws relating to commercial transactions, including chattel mortgages and bulk transfers. Security interests in chattels are created by an instrument known as a *security agreement*. To give notice of the security interest, a *financing statement* must be recorded. Article 6 of the code regulates *bulk transfers*—the sale of a business as a whole, including all fixtures, chattels, and merchandise.

unilateral contract   A one-sided contract wherein one party makes a promise to induce a second party to do something. The second party is not legally bound to perform; however, if the second party does comply, the first party is obligated to keep the promise.

unit-in-place method   The appraisal method of estimating building costs by calculating the costs of all of the physical components in the structure, with the cost of each item including its proper installation, connection, and so on; also called the *segregated cost method*.

unit of ownership   The four unities that are traditionally needed to create a joint tenancy—unity of title, time, interest, and possession.

usury   Charging interest at a higher rate than the maximum rate established by state law.

valid contract   A contract that complies with all the essentials of a contract and is binding and enforceable on all parties to it.

VA loan   A mortgage loan on approved property made to a qualified veteran by an authorized lender and guaranteed by the Department of Veterans Affairs in order to limit the lender's possible loss.

value   The power of a good or service to command other goods in exchange for the present worth of future rights to its income or amenities.

variance   Permission obtained from zoning authorities to build a structure or conduct a use that is expressly prohibited by the current zoning laws; an exception from the zoning ordinances.

vendee   A buyer, usually under the terms of a land contract.

vendor   A seller, usually under the terms of a land contract.

void contract   A contract that has no legal force or effect because it does not meet the essential elements of a contract.

voidable contract   A contract that seems to be valid on the surface but may be rejected or disaffirmed by one or both of the parties.

voluntary alienation   *See* alienation.

voluntary lien   A lien placed on property with the knowledge and consent of the property owner.

warranty of habitability   *See* implied warranty of habitability.

waste   An improper use or an abuse of a property by a possessor who holds less than fee ownership, such as a tenant, life tenant, mortgagor, or vendee. Such waste ordinarily impairs the value of the land or the interest of the person holding the title or the reversionary rights.

will   A written document, properly witnessed, providing for the transfer of title to property owned by the deceased, called the *testator*.

wraparound loan   A method of refinancing in which the new mortgage is placed in a secondary, or subordinate, position; the new mortgage includes both the unpaid principal balance of the first mortgage and whatever additional sums are advanced by the lender. In essence it is an additional mortgage in which another lender refinances a borrower by lending an amount over the existing first mortgage amount without disturbing the existence of the first mortgage.

zoning ordinance   An exercise of police power by a municipality to regulate and control the character and use of property.

INDEX